Take the Next Step in Your IT Career

Save 10% on Exam Vouchers*

(up to a $35 value)

*Some restrictions apply. See web page for details.

CompTIA

Use coupon code WILEY10 during checkout. Redeeming the coupon code is easy:

1. Go to www.comptiastore.com.
2. Browse Certification Vouchers and select the exam voucher you want.
3. Add the voucher to the cart (note that for A+ you will need a separate voucher for each exam).
4. Enter the code WILEY10 on the purchase screen, click Apply and then click Proceed to Checkout to continue and complete the payment process.

CompTIA® A+®
Complete Review Guide

Sixth Edition

CompTIA A+
Complete Review Guide

Core 1 Exam 220-1201 and
Core 2 Exam 220-1202

Sixth Edition

Troy McMillan

Copyright © 2025 by John Wiley & Sons, Inc.

Published by John Wiley & Sons, Inc., Hoboken, New Jersey.
Published simultaneously in Canada.

No part of this publication may be reproduced, stored in a retrieval system, or transmitted in any form or by any means, electronic, mechanical, photocopying, recording, scanning, or otherwise, except as permitted under Section 107 or 108 of the 1976 United States Copyright Act, without either the prior written permission of the Publisher, or authorization through payment of the appropriate per-copy fee to the Copyright Clearance Center, Inc., 222 Rosewood Drive, Danvers, MA 01923, (978) 750–8400, fax (978) 750–4470, or on the web at www.copyright.com. Requests to the Publisher for permission should be addressed to the Permissions Department, John Wiley & Sons, Inc., 111 River Street, Hoboken, NJ 07030, (201) 748–6011, fax (201) 748–6008, or online at http://www.wiley.com/go/permission.

The manufacturer's authorized representative according to the EU General Product Safety Regulation is Wiley-VCH GmbH, Boschstr. 12, 69469 Weinheim, Germany, e-mail: Product_Safety@wiley.com.

Trademarks: Wiley, Wiley logo, and the Sybex logo are trademarks or registered trademarks of John Wiley & Sons, Inc. and/or its affiliates in the United States and other countries and may not be used without written permission. CompTIA and A+ are registered trademarks or registered service marks of CompTIA, Inc. All other trademarks are the property of their respective owners. John Wiley & Sons, Inc. is not associated with any product or vendor mentioned in this book.

Limit of Liability/Disclaimer of Warranty: While the publisher and author have used their best efforts in preparing this book, they make no representations or warranties with respect to the accuracy or completeness of the contents of this book and specifically disclaim any implied warranties of merchantability or fitness for a particular purpose. No warranty may be created or extended by sales representatives or written sales materials. The advice and strategies contained herein may not be suitable for your situation. You should consult with a professional where appropriate. Further, readers should be aware that websites listed in this work may have changed or disappeared between when this work was written and when it is read. Neither the publisher nor authors shall be liable for any loss of profit or any other commercial damages, including but not limited to special, incidental, consequential, or other damages.

For general information on our other products and services or for technical support, please contact our Customer Care Department within the United States at (800) 762–2974, outside the United States at (317) 572–3993 or fax (317) 572–4002. For product technical support, you can find answers to frequently asked questions or reach us via live chat at https://sybexsupport.wiley.com

Wiley also publishes its books in a variety of electronic formats. Some content that appears in print may not be available in electronic formats. For more information about Wiley products, visit our website at www.wiley.com

Library of Congress Control Number: 2025911953

Paperback ISBN: 978-1-394-33078-2
ePDF ISBN: 978-1-394-33080-5
ePub ISBN: 978-1-394-33079-9

Cover Image: Lighthouse in Maine. © Jeremy Woodhouse/Getty Images
Cover Design: Wiley

Set in 9.5/12 Sabon LT Std by Lumina Datamatics

SKY10119669_062725

This book is dedicated to my sweet wife, Heike.

Acknowledgments

I would like to thank Jan Lynn Neal and Cathleen Small for keeping me on track, Ken Brown for continuing to publish my work, and Dan Neville for his work in making sure I'm technically correct.

About the Author

Troy McMillan writes practice tests, study guides, and online course materials for N2K while also running his own consulting and training business. He holds more than 30 industry certifications and also appears in training videos for OnCourse Learning and Pearson Press. Troy can be reached at mcmillantroy@hotmail.com.

About the Technical Editor

Dan Neville, BS and MS in Computer Information Systems, ITF+, A+, Network+, Security+, has more than 20 years of experience in IT education. His career in education was a result of almost two decades of training IT newcomers and breaking down highly technical material into concepts and terms that the layman would understand. He has always been in educational environments where students sought career-based training and education. In 2009, Dan was recruited to build one of the first associate-degree cybersecurity programs in the United States, creating partnerships with CompTIA and Linux Professional Institutes. He has been instrumental in creating CompTIA Academic Partner academies at several colleges.

As a result of his work to help people change careers to IT during the COVID-19 pandemic, he received the Academic Innovation Award for North America from CompTIA. He also served on the executive committee of the National Career and Technical Education Advisory Council. He has been a member of many program advisory boards, helping colleges, universities, and workforce development centers develop certification-based IT curriculum programs.

Dan writes practice tests and other course material for CompTIA certifications for N2K.

Contents at a Glance

Introduction — *xxxi*

Part I	**CompTIA A+ Core 1 Exam 220-1201**	**1**
Chapter 1	Mobile Devices	3
Chapter 2	Networking	45
Chapter 3	Hardware	95
Chapter 4	Virtualization and Cloud Computing	183
Chapter 5	Hardware and Network Troubleshooting	197
Part II	**CompTIA A+ Core 2 Exam 220-1202**	**241**
Chapter 6	Operating Systems	243
Chapter 7	Security	417
Chapter 8	Software Troubleshooting	515
Chapter 9	Operational Procedures	545
Appendix	Answers to the Review Questions	607

Index — *627*

Contents

Introduction   *xxxi*

Part	I		**CompTIA A+ Core 1 Exam 220-1201**	**1**
Chapter	1		**Mobile Devices**	**3**

    1.1 Given a scenario, monitor mobile device hardware and use
        appropriate replacement techniques   5
        Battery   5
        Keyboard/keys   7
        Random-access memory (RAM)   7
        Hard disk drive (HDD)/solid-state drive (SSD)   8
        Wireless cards   12
        Physical privacy and security components   14
        Wi-Fi antenna connector/placement   16
        Camera/webcam   16
        Microphone   16
    Exam essentials   18
    1.2 Compare and contrast accessories and connectivity options   18
        Connection methods   18
        Accessories   23
        Docking station   27
        Port replicator   28
        Trackpad/drawing pad/track points   28
    Exam essentials   28
    1.3 Given a scenario, configure basic mobile device network
        connectivity and provide application support   29
        Wireless/cellular data network (enable/disable)   29
        Bluetooth   31
        Location services   32
        Mobile device management (MDM)   33
        Mobile device synchronization   34
    Exam essentials   40
    Review Questions   41

Chapter	2		**Networking**	**45**

    2.1 Compare and contrast Transmission Control Protocol (TCP)
        and User Datagram Protocol (UDP) ports, protocols,
        and their purposes   50
        Ports and protocols   50
        TCP vs. UDP   53
    Exam essentials   54

2.2 Explain wireless networking technologies	55
Frequencies	55
Channels	56
Bluetooth	57
802.11 standards	58
Exam essentials	60
2.3 Summarize services provided by networked hosts	60
Server roles	60
Internet appliances	63
Legacy/embedded systems	64
Internet of Things (IoT) devices	64
Exam essentials	65
2.4 Explain common network configuration concepts	66
DNS	66
DHCP	68
Virtual LAN (VLAN)	69
Virtual private network (VPN)	69
Exam essentials	71
2.5 Compare and contrast common networking hardware devices	71
Routers	71
Switches	71
Access points	72
Patch panel	72
Firewall	72
Power over Ethernet (POE)	73
Cable modem	74
Digital subscriber line (DSL)	75
Optical network terminal (ONT)	75
Network interface card	75
Exam essentials	76
2.6 Given a scenario, configure basic wired/wireless small office/home office (SOHO) networks	76
Internet Protocol (IP) addressing	77
Automatic Private IP Addressing (APIPA)	82
Static vs. dynamic	83
Subnet mask	83
Gateway	84
Exam essentials	84
2.7 Compare and contrast internet connection types, network types, and their characteristics	85
Internet connection types	85
Network types	86
Exam essentials	88

	2.8 Explain networking tools and their purposes	88
	Crimper	88
	Cable stripper	88
	Wi-Fi analyzer	89
	Toner probe	89
	Punchdown tool	90
	Cable tester	90
	Loopback plug	90
	Network tap	90
	Exam essentials	90
	Review Questions	91
Chapter 3	**Hardware**	**95**
	3.1 Compare and contrast display components and attributes	103
	Types	103
	Touch screen/digitizer	105
	Inverter	105
	Attributes	105
	Exam essentials	106
	3.2 Summarize basic cable types and their connectors, features, and purposes	106
	Network cables	106
	Peripheral cables	111
	Thunderbolt	112
	Video cables	113
	DisplayPort	113
	Hard drive cables	116
	Adapters	117
	Connector types	119
	Exam essentials	124
	3.3 Compare and contrast RAM characteristics	125
	Form factors	125
	Double data rate (DDR) iterations	126
	Error correcting code (ECC) vs. non-ECC RAM	127
	Channel configurations	128
	Exam essentials	129
	3.4 Compare and contrast storage devices	130
	Hard drives	130
	Solid-state drives (SSD)	132
	Communications interfaces	132
	Drive configurations	134
	Removable storage	136
	Optical drives	139
	Exam essentials	141

3.5 Given a scenario, install and configure motherboards, central processing units (CPUs), and add-on cards	141
Motherboard form factors	141
Motherboard connector types	143
Motherboard compatibility	147
Basic Input/Output System/Unified Extensible Firmware Interface (BIOS/UEFI) settings	152
Boot options	152
Virtualization support	154
Encryption	154
CPU architecture	155
Expansion cards	156
Cooling	158
Exam essentials	159
3.6 Given a scenario, install the appropriate power supply	160
Input 110–120VAC vs. 220–240 VAC	160
Output 3.3Vvs. 5V vs. 12V	160
20+4 pin motherboard connector	160
Redundant power supply	160
Modular power supply	161
Wattage rating	161
Energy efficiency	162
Exam essentials	162
3.7 Given a scenario, deploy and configure multifunction devices/printers and settings	162
Properly unbox device and consider setup location	163
Use appropriate drivers for a given operating system	163
Firmware	163
Device connectivity	164
Public/shared devices	165
Configuration settings	166
Security	167
Network scan services	167
Automatic document feeder (ADF)/flatbed scanner	168
Exam essentials	168
3.8 Given a scenario, perform appropriate printer maintenance	169
Laser	169
Inkjet	170
Thermal	173
Impact	174
Exam essentials	176
Review Questions	177

Chapter	**4**	**Virtualization and Cloud Computing**	**183**
		4.1 Explain virtualization concepts	185
		Purpose of virtual machines	185
		Requirements	187
		Desktop virtualization	189
		Containers	189
		Hypervisors	189
		Exam essentials	191
		4.2 Summarize cloud computing concepts	191
		Common cloud models	191
		Cloud characteristics	192
		Exam essentials	193
		Review Questions	194
Chapter	**5**	**Hardware and Network Troubleshooting**	**197**
		5.1 Given a scenario, troubleshoot motherboards, RAM, CPUs, and power	201
		Common symptoms	201
		Exam essentials	210
		5.2 Given a scenario, troubleshoot drive and RAID issues	210
		Common symptoms	210
		Exam essentials	215
		5.3 Given a scenario, troubleshoot video, projector, and display issues	215
		Common symptoms	215
		Exam essentials	219
		5.4 Given a scenario, troubleshoot common mobile device issues	219
		Common symptoms	220
		Exam essentials	226
		5.5 Given a scenario, troubleshoot network issues	227
		Common symptoms	227
		Exam essentials	230
		5.6 Given a scenario, troubleshoot printer issues	230
		Lines down the printed pages	230
		Garbled print	231
		Paper jams	232
		Faded prints	233
		Paper not feeding	233
		Multipage misfeed	233
		Multiple prints pending in queue	233
		Speckling on printed pages	234
		Double/echo images on the print	234

	Grinding noise	234
	Finishing issues	235
	Incorrect page orientation	235
	Tray not recognized	235
	Connectivity issues	236
	Frozen print queue	236
Exam essentials		236
Review Questions		237

Part II CompTIA A+ Core 2 Exam 220-1202 241

Chapter 6 Operating Systems 243

1.1 Explain common operating system (OS) types and their purpose	255
Workstation systems (OSes)	255
Mobile OSes	256
Various file system types	257
Vendor life-cycle limitations	258
Compatibility concerns between operating systems	259
Exam essentials	259
1.2 Given a scenario, perform OS installations and upgrades in a diverse environment	259
Boot methods	260
Types of installations	261
Partitioning	266
Drive format	268
Upgrade considerations	268
Feature updates	269
Exam essentials	269
1.3 Compare and contrast basic features of Microsoft Windows editions	269
Windows 10 editions	269
Windows 11 editions	270
N versions	271
Feature differences	271
Upgrade paths	273
Hardware requirements	275
Exam essentials	275
1.4 Given a scenario, use Microsoft Windows operating system features and tools	276
Task Manager	276
Microsoft Management Console (MMC) snap-in	282
Additional tools	297
Exam essentials	304

1.5 Given a scenario, use the appropriate Microsoft command-line tools	305
Navigation	305
Network	306
Disk management	315
File management	318
Informational	319
OS management	323
Exam essentials	327
1.6 Given a scenario, configure Microsoft Windows settings	327
Internet options	327
Devices and Printers	334
Programs and Features	334
Network and Sharing Center	336
System	336
Windows Defender Firewall	338
Mail	340
Sound	340
User Accounts	342
Device Manager	342
Indexing Options	342
Administrative Tools	342
File Explorer Options	346
Power Options	349
Time and Language	352
Update and Security	354
Personalization	356
Apps	356
Privacy	359
System	360
Devices	361
Network and Internet	361
Gaming	363
Accounts	364
Exam essentials	365
1.7 Given a scenario, configure Microsoft Windows networking features on a client/desktop	365
Domain joined vs. workgroup	366
Local OS firewall settings	369
Client network configuration	371
Establish network connections	371
Proxy settings	372
Public network vs. private network	373

File Explorer navigation—network paths	373
Metered connections and limitations	375
Exam essentials	375
1.8 Explain common features and tools of the macOS/desktop operating system	375
Installation and uninstallation of applications	375
System folders	377
Apple ID and corporate restrictions	378
Best practices	378
System Preferences	379
Features	384
Disk Utility	387
Exam essentials	389
1.9 Identify common features and tools of the Linux client/desktop operating system	390
Common commands	390
File management	390
Filesystem management	394
Administrative	395
Package management	396
Network	397
Informational	399
Text editors	401
Common configuration files	402
OS components	402
Root account	403
Exam essentials	403
1.10 Given a scenario, install applications according to requirements	404
System requirements for applications	404
Distribution methods	406
Impact considerations for new applications	407
Exam essentials	408
1.11 Given a scenario, install and configure cloud-based productivity tools	409
Email systems	409
Storage	409
Collaboration tools	411
Identity synchronization	412
Licensing assignment	412
Exam essentials	413
Review Questions	414

Chapter	**7**	**Security**	**417**
		2.1 Summarize various security measures and their purposes	427
		Physical security	427
		Physical access security	432
		Logical security	435
		Exam essentials	439
		2.2 Given a scenario, configure and apply basic Microsoft Windows OS security settings	440
		Defender Antivirus	440
		Firewall	441
		Users and Groups	442
		Login OS options	444
		NTFS vs. share permissions	445
		Run as administrator vs. standard user	450
		User Account Control (UAC)	450
		BitLocker	450
		BitLocker to Go	451
		Encrypting File System (EFS)	451
		Active Directory	452
		Exam essentials	455
		2.3 Compare and contrast wireless security protocols and authentication methods	455
		Protocols and encryption	456
		Authentication	457
		Exam essentials	459
		2.4 Summarize types of malware and tools/methods for detection, removal, and prevention	459
		Malware	459
		Adware	466
		Potentially unwanted program (PUP)	466
		Tools and methods	466
		Exam essentials	470
		2.5 Compare and contrast common social engineering attacks, threats, and vulnerabilities	470
		Social engineering	471
		Threats	473
		Vulnerabilities	477
		Exam essentials	478
		2.6 Given a scenario, implement procedures for basic small office/home office (SOHO) malware removal	479
		Investigate and verify malware symptoms	479
		Quarantine infected systems	479

Disable System Restore in Windows	479
Remediate infected systems	479
Schedule scans and run updates	480
Enable System Restore and create a restore point in Windows	480
Educate the end user	480
Exam essentials	481
2.7 Given a scenario, apply workstation security options and hardening techniques	481
Data-at-rest encryption	481
Password considerations	482
Basic Input/Output System (BIOS)/Unified Extensible Firmware Interface (UEFI) passwords	483
End-user best practices	483
Account management	484
Change default administrator's user account/password	485
Disable AutoRun	485
Disable unused services	486
Exam essentials	486
2.8 Given a scenario, apply common methods for securing mobile devices	486
Hardening techniques	486
Patch management	488
Endpoint security software	489
Locator applications	489
Remote wipes	490
Remote backup applications	490
Failed login attempts restrictions	490
Policies and procedures	490
Exam essentials	491
2.9 Compare and contrast common data destruction and disposal methods	491
Physical destruction of hard drives	492
Recycling or repurposing best practices	493
Outsourcing concepts	494
Regulatory and environmental requirements	495
Exam essentials	495
2.10 Given a scenario, apply security settings on SOHO wireless and wired networks	495
Router settings	496
Wireless specific	500
Firewall settings	500
Port forwarding/mapping	502
Exam essentials	502

	2.11 Given a scenario, configure relevant security settings in a browser	502
	Browser download/installation	502
	Browser patching	503
	Extensions and plug-ins	503
	Password managers	503
	Secure connections/sites—valid certificates	504
	Settings	504
	Browser feature management	507
	Exam essentials	509
	Review Questions	510
Chapter 8	**Software Troubleshooting**	**515**
	3.1 Given a scenario, troubleshoot common Windows OS issues	518
	Blue screen of death (BSOD)	518
	Degraded performance	519
	Boot issues	519
	Frequent shutdowns	520
	Services not starting	520
	Applications crashing	520
	Low memory warnings	521
	USB controller resource warnings	521
	System instability	522
	No OS found	522
	Slow profile load	523
	Time drift	523
	Common troubleshooting steps	524
	Exam essentials	527
	3.2 Given a scenario, troubleshoot common mobile OS and application issues	527
	Application fails to launch	528
	Application fails to close/crashes	528
	Application fails to update	528
	Application fails to install	529
	Slow to respond	530
	OS fails to update	530
	Battery life issues	530
	Random reboots	530
	Connectivity issues	531
	Screen does not autorotate	532
	Exam essentials	532
	3.3 Given a scenario, troubleshoot common mobile OS and application security issues	533

	Security concerns	533
	Common symptoms	535
Exam essentials		536
3.4 Given a scenario, troubleshoot common personal computer (PC) security issues		537
	Common symptoms	537
	Browser-related symptoms	539
Exam essentials		541
Review Questions		542

Chapter 9   Operational Procedures   545

4.1 Given a scenario, implement best practices associated with documentation and support systems information management		553
	Ticketing systems	553
	Asset management	555
	Types of documents	557
Exam essentials		559
4.2 Given a scenario, apply change management procedures		559
	Documented business processes	559
	Change management	560
Exam essentials		563
4.3 Given a scenario, implement workstation backup and recovery methods		563
	Backup	564
	Recovery	565
	Backup testing	565
	Backup rotation schemes	565
Exam essentials		568
4.4 Given a scenario, use common safety procedures		568
	Electrostatic discharge (ESD) straps	569
	ESD mats	569
	Electrical safety	570
	Equipment grounding	570
	Proper power handling	571
	Proper component handling and storage	571
	Cable management	571
	Antistatic bags	572
	Compliance with government regulations	572
	Personal safety	572
Exam essentials		573
4.5 Summarize environmental impacts and local environment controls		574

Material Safety Data Sheet (MSDS) documentation for handling and disposal	574
Temperature, humidity-level awareness, and proper ventilation	575
Power surges, brownouts, and blackouts	578
Exam essentials	580
4.6 Explain the importance of prohibited content/activity and privacy, licensing, and policy concepts	580
Incident response	580
Licensing/digital rights management (DRM)/end-user license agreement (EULA)	583
Nondisclosure agreement (NDA)/mutual nondisclosure agreement (MNDA)	584
Regulated data	584
Acceptable use policy (AUP)	585
Regulatory and business compliance requirements	586
Exam essentials	586
4.7 Given a scenario, use proper communication techniques and professionalism	587
Professional appearance and attire	587
Use proper language and avoid jargon, acronyms, and slang, when applicable	588
Maintain a positive attitude/project confidence	588
Actively listen, take notes, and avoid interrupting the customer	588
Be culturally sensitive	589
Be on time (if late, contact the customer)	589
Avoid distractions	590
Appropriately deal with difficult customers or situations	590
Set and meet expectations/timeline and communicate status with the customer	592
Appropriately handle customers' confidential and private materials	593
Exam essentials	593
4.8 Explain the basics of scripting	594
Script file types	594
Use cases for scripting	594
Other considerations when using scripts	596
Exam essentials	596
4.9 Given a scenario, use remote access technologies	596
Methods/tools	597

	Security considerations of each access method	599
	Exam essentials	599
	4.10 Explain basic concepts related to artificial intelligence (AI)	600
	Application integration	600
	Policy	600
	Limitations	601
	Private vs. public	602
	Exam essentials	603
	Review Questions	604

Appendix   Answers to the Review Questions   607

Chapter 1: Mobile Devices	608
Chapter 2: Networking	609
Chapter 3: Hardware	611
Chapter 4: Virtualization and Cloud Computing	615
Chapter 5: Hardware and Network Troubleshooting	616
Chapter 6: Operating Systems	618
Chapter 7: Security	619
Chapter 8: Software Troubleshooting	622
Chapter 9: Operational Procedures	623

Index   627

Introduction

The A+ certification program was developed by the Computing Technology Industry Association (CompTIA) to provide an industry-wide means of certifying the competency of computer service technicians. The A+ certification is granted to those who have proven, through rigorous testing, the level of knowledge and troubleshooting skills that are needed to provide capable support in the field of personal computers. CompTIA is a widely respected industry leader in this area.

CompTIA's A+ exam objectives are periodically updated to keep the certification applicable to the most recent hardware and software. This is necessary because a technician must be able to work on the latest equipment. The most recent revisions to the objectives—and to the whole program—were introduced in 2025 and are reflected in this book.

This book and the Sybex *CompTIA A+ Complete Study Guide* (both the Standard and Deluxe Editions) are tools to help you prepare for this certification—and for the new areas of focus of a modern computer technician's job.

What Is A+ Certification?

The A+ certification program was created to offer a wide-ranging certification, in the sense that it's intended to certify competence with personal computers from many different makers/vendors. Everyone must take and pass two exams: 220-1201 and 220-1202.

You don't have to take the 220-1201 exam and the 220-1202 exam at the same time. The A+ certification isn't awarded until you've passed both tests. For the latest pricing on the exams and updates to the registration procedures, call Pearson VUE at (877) 551-7587. You can also go to Pearson VUE for additional information or to register online at www.pearsonvue.com/comptia. If you have further questions about the scope of the exams or related CompTIA programs, refer to the CompTIA website at www.comptia.org.

Who Should Buy This Book?

If you want to acquire a solid foundation in personal computer basics and your goal is to prepare for the exams by filling in any gaps in your knowledge, this book is for you. You'll find clear explanations of the concepts you need to grasp and plenty of help to achieve the high level of professional competency you need to succeed in your chosen field.

If you want to become certified as an A+ holder, this book is definitely what you need. However, if you just want to attempt to pass the exam without really understanding the basics of personal computers, this guide isn't for you. It's written for people who want to acquire skills and knowledge of personal computer basics.

How to Use This Book

We've included several learning tools in the book. These tools will help you retain vital exam content as well as prepare to sit for the actual exams.

Exam Essentials Each chapter includes a number of exam essentials. These are the key topics that you should take from the chapter in terms of areas on which you should focus when preparing for the exam.

Chapter Review Questions To test your knowledge as you progress through the book, there are review questions at the end of each chapter. As you finish each chapter, answer the review questions and then check your answers—the correct answers are in the appendix. You can go back to reread the section that deals with each question you got wrong to ensure that you answer correctly the next time you're tested on the material.

One important thing to remember is that the key to passing the exam is not through memorizing review questions, but rather through understanding the concepts and material covered in the questions.

Interactive Online Learning Environment and Test Bank

The interactive online learning environment that accompanies *CompTIA® A+® Complete Review Guide: Core 1 Exam 220-1201 and Core 2 Exam 220-1202, Sixth Edition*, provides a test bank with study tools to help you prepare for the certification exam—and increase your chances of passing it the first time! The test bank includes the following:

Sample Tests All the questions in this book are provided, including the review questions at the end of each chapter. In addition, there are four practice exams. Use these questions to test your knowledge of the study guide material. The online test bank runs on multiple devices.

Flashcards Two sets of questions are provided in digital flashcard format (i.e. a question followed by a single correct answer). You can use these flashcards to reinforce your learning and provide last-minute test prep before the exam.

Other Study Tools A glossary of key terms from this book and their definitions is available as a fully searchable PDF.

 You can access all these resources at www.wiley.com/go/sybextestprep.

Tips for Taking the A+ Exams

Here are some general tips for taking your exams successfully:

- Bring two forms of ID with you. One must be a photo ID, such as a driver's license. The other can be a major credit card or a passport. Both forms must include a signature.
- Arrive early at the exam center so that you can relax and review your study materials, particularly tables and lists of exam-related information.
- It is also possible to take the exam online. For more information on this process, see CompTIA Online Exam | CompTIA IT Certifications.
- Read the questions carefully. Don't be tempted to jump to an early conclusion. Make sure you know exactly what the question is asking.
- Don't leave any unanswered questions. Unanswered questions are scored against you.
- There will be questions with multiple correct responses. When there is more than one correct answer, a message at the bottom of the screen will prompt you to either "Choose two" or "Choose all that apply." Be sure to read the messages displayed to know how many correct answers you must choose.
- When answering multiple-choice questions that you're not sure about, use a process of elimination to get rid of the obviously incorrect answers first. Doing so will improve your odds if you need to make an educated guess.
- Because the hard questions (on form-based tests [i.e. nonadaptive]) will eat up the most time, save them for last. You can move forward and backward through the exam.
- For the latest pricing on the exams and updates to the registration procedures, visit CompTIA's website at www.comptia.org.

CompTIA A+ 1200 Series Exam Objectives

CompTIA goes to great lengths to ensure that its certification programs accurately reflect the IT industry's best practices. The company does this by establishing Cornerstone Committees for each of its exam programs. Each committee consists of a small group of IT professionals, training providers, and publishers who are responsible for establishing the exam's baseline competency level and who determine the appropriate target audience level.

Once these factors are determined, CompTIA shares this information with a group of hand-selected subject-matter experts (SMEs). These folks are the true brainpower behind the certification program. They review the committee's findings, refine them, and shape them into the objectives you see before you. CompTIA calls this process a *job task analysis* (JTA).

Finally, CompTIA conducts a survey to ensure that the objectives and weightings truly reflect the job requirements. Only then can the SMEs go to work writing the hundreds of questions needed for the exam. In many cases, they have to go back to the drawing board for further refinements before the exam is ready to go live in its final state. So, rest assured, the content you're about to learn will serve you long after you take the exam.

Exam objectives are subject to change at any time without prior notice and at CompTIA's sole discretion. Please visit the certification page of CompTIA's website at `www.comptia.org` for the most current listing of exam objectives.

CompTIA also publishes relative weightings for each of the exam's objectives. The following tables list the objective domains and the extent to which they're represented on each exam:

220–1201 Exam Domains	Percent of Exam
1.0 Mobile Devices	13%
2.0 Networking	23%
3.0 Hardware	25%
4.0 Virtualization and Cloud Computing	11%
5.0 Hardware and Network Troubleshooting	28%
Total	100%

220–1202 Exam Domains	Percent of Exam
1.0 Operating Systems	28%
2.0 Security	28%
3.0 Software Troubleshooting	23%
4.0 Operational Procedures	21%
Total	100%

CompTIA A+ Core 1 Exam 220-1201

PART I

Chapter 1   Mobile Devices
Chapter 2   Networking
Chapter 3   Hardware
Chapter 4   Virtualization and Cloud Computing
Chapter 5   Hardware and Network Troubleshooting

Chapter 1

Mobile Devices

COMPTIA A+ 220-1201 EXAM OBJECTIVES COVERED IN THIS CHAPTER:

✓ **1.1 Given a scenario, monitor mobile device hardware and use appropriate replacement techniques**

- Battery
- Keyboard/keys
- Random-access memory (RAM)
- Hard disk drive (HDD)/solid-state drive (SSD)
- Wireless cards
- Physical privacy and security components
- Wi-Fi antenna connector/placement
- Camera/webcam
- Microphone
- Exam essentials

✓ **1.2 Compare and contrast accessories and connectivity options for mobile devices**

- Connection methods
- Accessories
- Docking station
- Port replicator
- Trackpad/drawing pad/track points
- Exam essentials

✓ **1.3 Given a scenario, configure basic mobile device network connectivity and provide application support**

- Wireless/cellular data network (enable/disable)
- Bluetooth
- Location services
- Mobile device management (MDM)
- Mobile device synchronization
- Exam essentials

This chapter will focus on the exam topics related to mobile devices. It will follow the structure of the CompTIA A+ 220-1201 exam blueprint, Objective 1, and cover the three subobjectives that you will need to master before taking the exam. The mobile devices domain represents 13% of the total exam.

1.1 Given a scenario, monitor mobile device hardware and use appropriate replacement techniques

In today's environment, laptops and tablets (those names will be used interchangeably) share many of the same types of components. In this section, I'll discuss how to monitor the performance of some of the basic components and how to replace them when appropriate.

The following topics are addressed in Exam Objective 1.1:

- Battery
- Keyboard/keys
- Random-access memory (RAM)
- Hard disk drive (HDD)/solid-state drive (SSD)
- Wireless cards
- Physical privacy and security components
- Wi-Fi antenna connector/placement
- Camera/webcam
- Microphone

Battery

Monitoring and maintaining the battery in a mobile device is very important. After all, you don't want your notebook to die just as you are about to advance to the next level of your favorite video game! In addition to watching the battery-power level, you can manage several items that control how your battery consumes power. In a Windows machine, type **Power & Battery** in the search bar, which will bring you to the corresponding systems control screen, as shown in Figure 1.1. Here you can adjust the power and battery settings to get the most usefulness when you're running on battery power.

If you find yourself needing to replace your laptop battery, check out the following steps.

Replacing a laptop battery is simply a matter of removing the battery storage bay, removing the old battery from the bay, inserting the new battery into the bay, and replacing the bay. Determining the battery type for the replacement will probably take longer than the replacement procedure. In fact, many users carry extra batteries for situations where they know they will need to use the laptop for longer than the battery life (such as a long plane trip) and change the battery as needed.

FIGURE 1.1   Power and battery settings

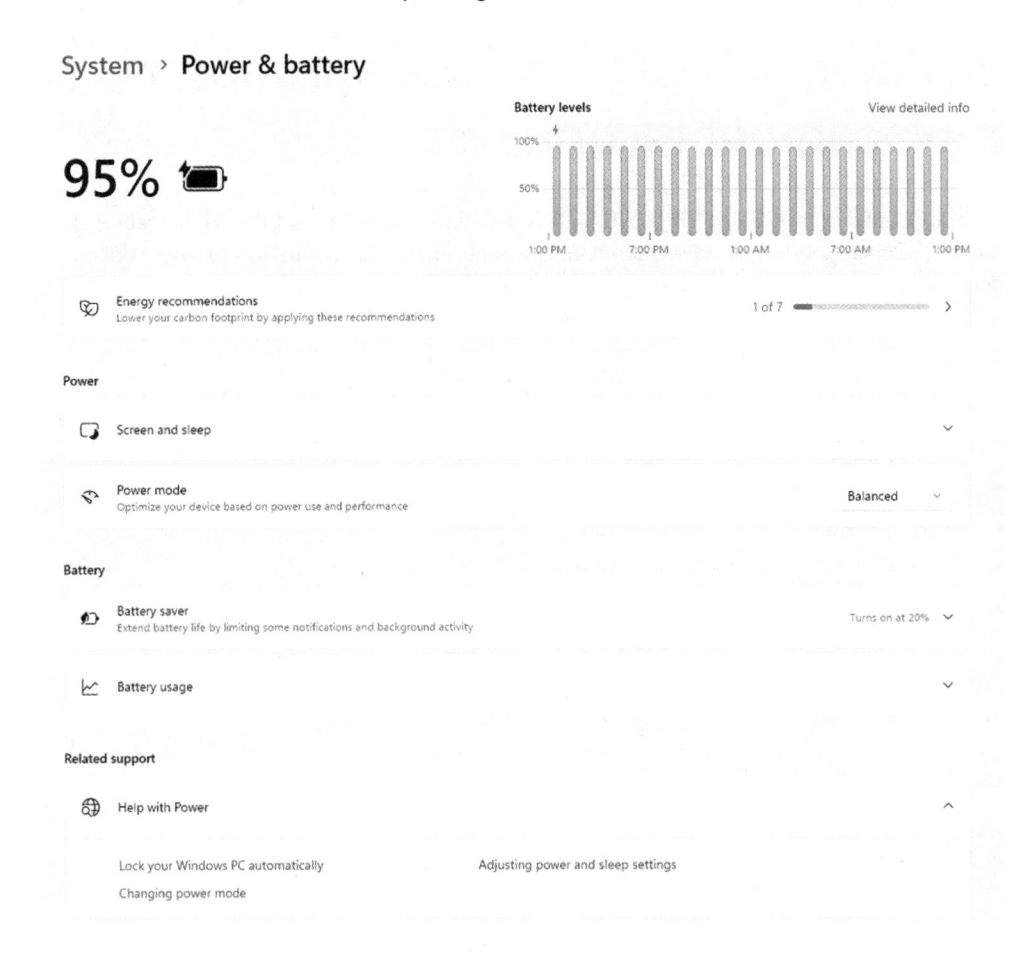

With all of this said, if the laptop or mobile device does not have an externally accessible battery, opening the case to replace the battery will void the warranty.

Keyboard/keys

Keyboards on laptops are not replaced very often, considering that it is often easier to use an external keyboard. However, if you spill something on your keyboard or the keys break or wear down, you might find yourself in need of a replacement keyboard. While these steps work on most laptops, it's always a good idea to refer to the manufacturer's website for model-specific instructions.

When replacing the keyboard, one of the main things you want to keep in mind is not to damage the data cable connector to the system board. Follow these steps for a smooth replacement:

1. With the laptop fully powered off and unplugged from the electricity source, remove the battery. Examine the screws on the back of the laptop. Ideally, icons indicating which screws are attached to the keyboard will be available on the back of the laptop. If not, look up the model online and determine which of the screws are attached to the keyboard.
2. Remove the screws with a T8 or Phillips-head screwdriver. With the laptop turned back over, open it. If the keyboard is tucked under any plastic pieces, determine whether those pieces must have screws removed to get them out of the way; if so, remove the screws and those plastic pieces. In some cases, there may simply be clamps that can easily be removed.
3. With any plastic covers out of the way, remove any screws at the top and then remove the keyboard itself from top to bottom. There should be a thin but wide data cable to the system board at the bottom. This is the piece to be careful with because it can be easily damaged!
4. Take a pick and lift the plastic connectors holding this data cable in place. Remove the data cable. Take the new keyboard and slip the data cable back in between the plastic connectors on the system board. Ensure it's all the way in.
5. Put the plastic connector back into place and ensure it's holding the data cable in. Position the keyboard into place and refasten the keyboard in place at the top, replacing any screws that were there previously.
6. Replace any plastic pieces that were covering the keyboard, turn the laptop over, and replace all of the keyboard screws. When you replace the battery and turn the laptop back on, check functionality. If the keyboard doesn't work, the main component to check is the data connector.

Random-access memory (RAM)

You can monitor your RAM usage a couple of different ways. In Windows, the Task Manager is a great place to start. Hit Ctrl-Alt-Del simultaneously, and in the menu screen, select Task Manager. What you should see is the Task Manager, as shown in Figure 1.2.

FIGURE 1.2 Task Manager

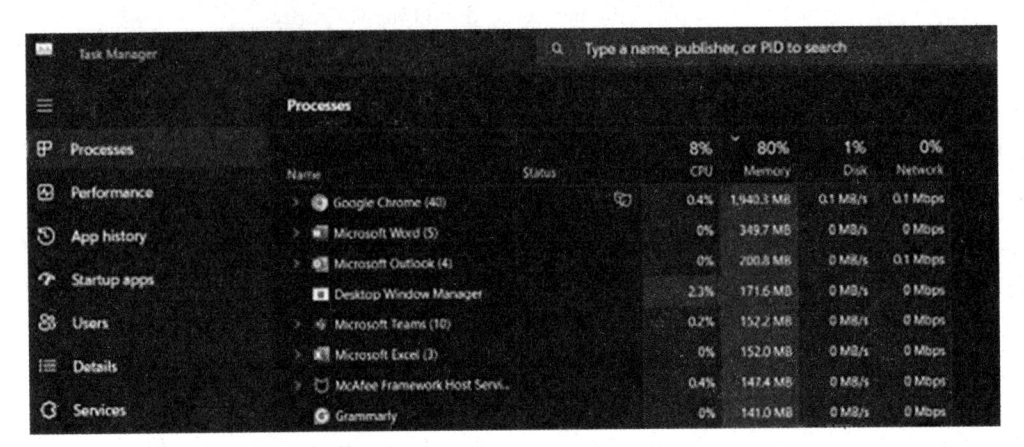

			8%	80%	1%	0%
Name		Status	CPU	Memory	Disk	Network
> Google Chrome (40)			0.4%	1,940.3 MB	0.1 MB/s	0.1 Mbps
> Microsoft Word (5)			0%	349.7 MB	0 MB/s	0 Mbps
> Microsoft Outlook (4)			0%	200.8 MB	0 MB/s	0.1 Mbps
Desktop Window Manager			2.3%	171.6 MB	0 MB/s	0 Mbps
> Microsoft Teams (10)			0.2%	152.2 MB	0 MB/s	0 Mbps
> Microsoft Excel (3)			0%	152.0 MB	0 MB/s	0 Mbps
> McAfee Framework Host Servi...			0.4%	147.4 MB	0 MB/s	0 Mbps
Grammarly			0%	141.0 MB	0 MB/s	0 Mbps

The Processes tab will show you some key metrics, including Memory (RAM) usage by application. As shown in Figure 1.2, Google Chrome is consuming a considerable amount of RAM. Time to shut down some browser tabs!

With that said, installing more RAM in your computer is usually one of the best upgrades to perform.

There should be a panel used for access to the memory modules. If the panels are not marked (as many are not), refer to your laptop instruction manual to locate the bottom panel. Follow these steps to perform a memory upgrade:

1. Remove any screws holding the panel in place, then remove the panel from the laptop and set it aside. If you're removing an existing memory module, remove it by undoing the module clamps, gently lift the edge of the module to a 45-degree angle, and then pull the module out of the slot.

2. Align the notch of the new module with that of the memory slot and gently insert the module into the slot at a 45-degree angle. With all pins in the slot, gently rotate the module down flat until the clamps lock the module into place.

3. Replace the memory access panel, replace any screws, and power up the system. When the computer is powered back up, it may be necessary to go into the computer BIOS to let the system properly detect the new RAM that has been installed in the computer. Please refer to the computer system's user manual for any additional information.

Hard disk drive (HDD)/solid-state drive (SSD)

The Task Manager also allows you to monitor your disk performance, whether it is an HDD or SSD. Figure 1.3 shows the Performance tab, indicating disk usage.

FIGURE 1.3 The Performance tab

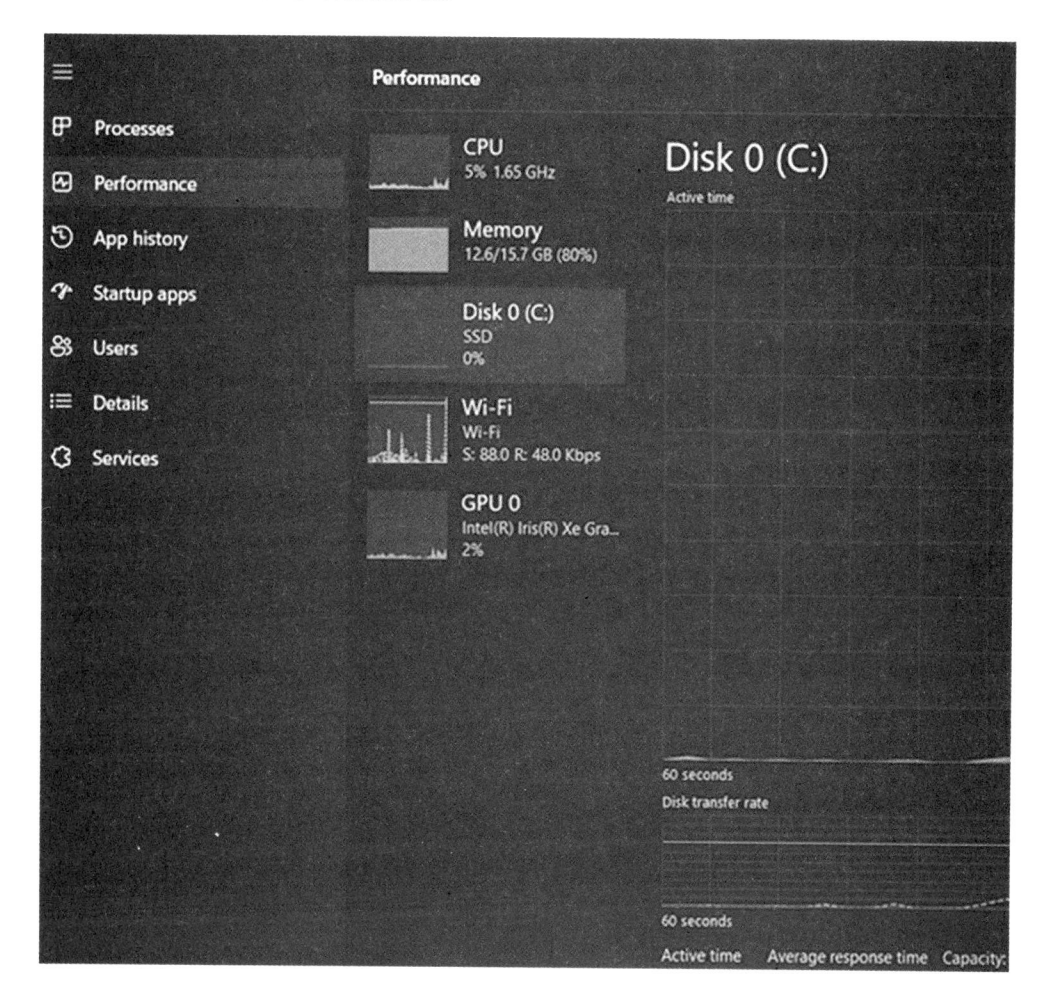

![Performance tab screenshot showing CPU 5% 1.65 GHz, Memory 12.6/15.7 GB (80%), Disk 0 (C:) SSD 0%, Wi-Fi S: 88.0 R: 48.0 Kbps, GPU 0 Intel(R) Iris(R) Xe Gra... 2%, with Disk 0 (C:) Active time graph displayed]

You can also right-click on the Windows logo and select Disk Management from the menu, as shown in Figure 1.4, which will show you the drive status.

HDD/SSD replacement

Before changing a hard drive, you should back up the old hard drive if the data is needed. Then to change the hard drive, follow these steps:

1. Turn the laptop upside down and look for a removable panel or a hard drive release mechanism. Laptop drives are usually accessible from the bottom or side of the chassis. Release the drive by flicking a lock/unlock button and/or removing a screw that holds the drive in its place.

FIGURE 1.4 Disk Management

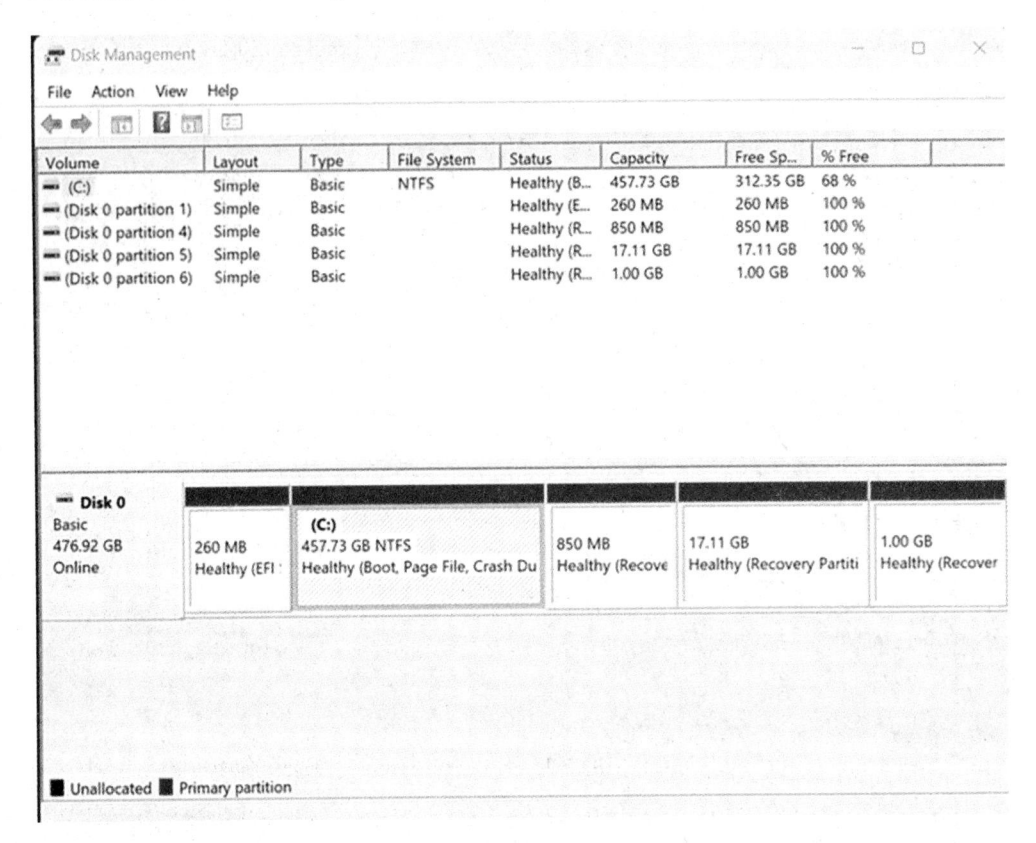

Volume	Layout	Type	File System	Status	Capacity	Free Sp...	% Free
(C:)	Simple	Basic	NTFS	Healthy (B...	457.73 GB	312.35 GB	68 %
(Disk 0 partition 1)	Simple	Basic		Healthy (E...	260 MB	260 MB	100 %
(Disk 0 partition 4)	Simple	Basic		Healthy (R...	850 MB	850 MB	100 %
(Disk 0 partition 5)	Simple	Basic		Healthy (R...	17.11 GB	17.11 GB	100 %
(Disk 0 partition 6)	Simple	Basic		Healthy (R...	1.00 GB	1.00 GB	100 %

Disk 0
Basic
476.92 GB
Online

| 260 MB Healthy (EFI | (C:) 457.73 GB NTFS Healthy (Boot, Page File, Crash Du | 850 MB Healthy (Recove | 17.11 GB Healthy (Recovery Partiti | 1.00 GB Healthy (Recover |

■ Unallocated ■ Primary partition

2. You might be required to remove the drive from a caddy or detach mounting rails from its sides. Attach the rails or caddy to the new drive using the same screws and washers. If required, remove the connector attached to the old drive's signal pins and attach it to the new drive, ensuring it is right side up. Do not force it into place. Damaging the signal pins may render the drive useless.

3. Reverse your steps to place the drive (and caddy if present) into the case. Replace the screws and start the laptop. The system should recognize the drive. If you or the user created a bootable backup disk or a complete image disk (before the drive failed, by the way), place it in the optical drive and follow the instructions for restoring the data.

SSDs

Although many devices still use a magnetic disk hard drive, most laptop vendors are moving to using either solid-state drives or hybrid drives. Hybrids are a combination of magnetic disk and solid-state technology.

The advantage of solid-state drives is that they are not as susceptible to damage if the device is dropped, and they are generally faster because no moving parts are involved. They are, however, more expensive, and when they fail, they don't typically display any advanced warning symptoms like a magnetic drive will do.

Hybrid storage products have a magnetic disk and some solid-state memory. These drives monitor the data being read from the hard drive, and they cache the most frequently accessed bits to the high-speed flash memory. These drives tend to cost slightly more than traditional hard drives (but far less than solid-state drives), but the addition of the SSD memory for cached bits creates a surprising improvement in performance. This improvement will not appear initially because the drive must "learn" the most frequently accessed data on the drive.

1.8 inch vs. 2.5 inch

The 2.5 inch hard drives are small (which makes them attractive for a laptop where space is minimal), but in comparison to 3.5 inch hard drives, they have less capacity and cache and operate at a lower speed.

Moreover, whereas 2.5 inch drives operate from 5,400 to 7,200 rpm, 3.5 inch drives can operate from 7,200 to 10,000 rpm. However, 2.5 inch drives use about half the power (again, good for a laptop) of a 3.5 inch drive (2.5 W rather than 5 W).

The 1.8 inch drive is the smallest of the three I'm discussing here. It was originally used in subnotebooks and audio players. It has the least capacity of the three, with the largest up to 320 GB.

Hard disk drive (HDD)/solid-state drive (SSD) migration

When you have made the decision to migrate data from HDDs to SSDs, the process may be easier than you think.

1. First, ensure both drives are connected to the motherboard. Make sure both the power cable and the data cable are set in place.
2. In Windows, go to Disk Management, select the SSD and Initialize Disk, as shown in Figure 1.5. (This assumes the HDD has already been initialized to the local system.)
3. Open the Control Panel and go to Control Panel > System, Security > Backup, and then Restore (Windows 7).
4. Click Create a System Image in the left pane. On the Do You Want to Save Backup page under the On a Hard Disk drop box, choose the SSD. After selecting the destination disk or volume, click Next.
5. Make sure both the System Reserved (System) and (C:) (System) drives (assuming C is where the operating system is located) are selected. Also, select any other drives that may hold data as well. Click Next. Confirm the backup settings and then click Start Backup.

FIGURE 1.5 Initialize Disk

Wireless cards

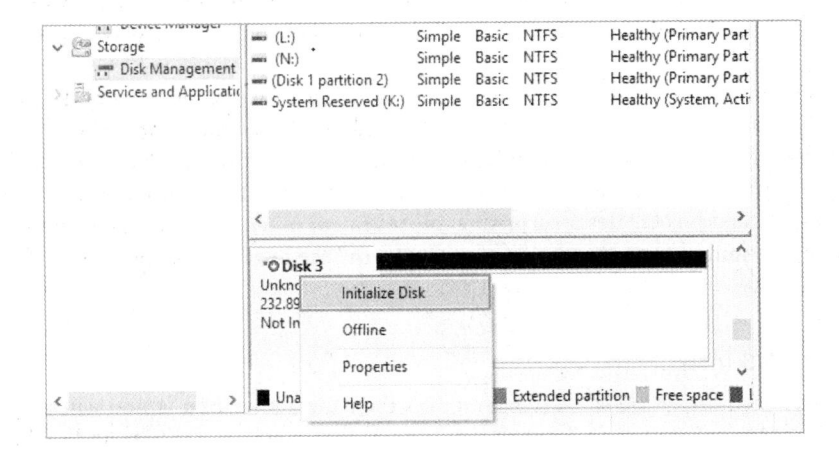

Wireless cards in notebooks are usually accessed through a panel on the case, but this may vary. In any event, the wireless card is often replaceable in case you want to upgrade to the latest and greatest Wi-Fi version. With that said, there are many settings for performance and access, which are generally described here.

The Task Manager can help you monitor your Wi-Fi performance. Figure 1.6 shows the Wi-Fi tab.

You can also see your wireless card performance by right-clicking on the Wi-Fi symbol in the system tray, then selecting Network and Internet Settings. In the window that pops up, select Advanced Network Settings, then select your wireless adapter. Figure 1.7 shows the Advanced Network Settings tab.

Finally, click on Edit next to More Adapter Options to show the Wi-Fi Properties screen. Here you will find the details on how the wireless card is configured. Figure 1.8 shows the Wi-Fi Properties screen.

Wireless cards

Both 802.11 and Bluetooth wireless cards that are built in can be replaced if they go bad. Sometimes they reside near the memory, so you would open the same panel that holds the memory. In other cases (such as for Dell Inspiron), you have to remove the memory, keyboard, optical drive, and hand rest to get to the card. The Bluetooth card may be located in the same place, or it may be located at the edge of the laptop with its own small panel to remove. Consult your laptop's documentation.

Once you've found either type of wireless card, disconnect the two antenna contacts from the card. Do not pull by the wire; pull by the connector itself. Remove any screws from the

FIGURE 1.6 The Wi-Fi tab

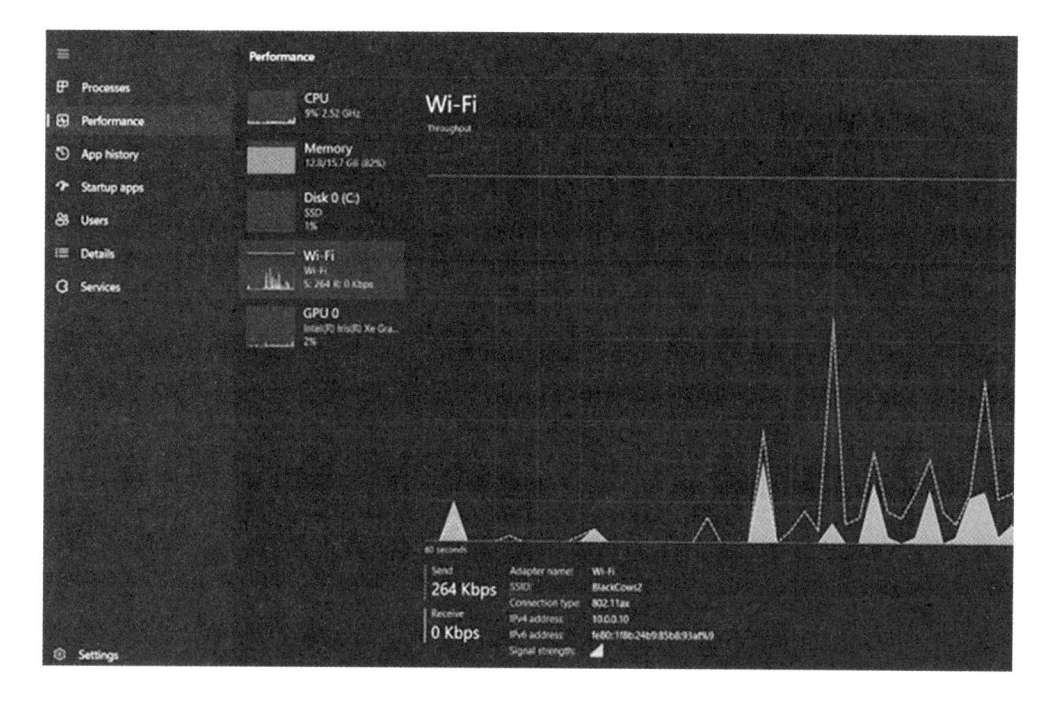

wireless card and gently pull out the card from the slot. Insert the replacement card into the slot at a 45-degree angle, replace the screws, and reconnect the antenna to the adapter. Replace the parts you were required to remove to get to the card, reversing your steps carefully.

Cellular card

Changing an external mobile broadband card is as simple as pulling out the old USB stick and plugging in the new one. Because the USB is plug and play, you shouldn't have to do anything. But even in the case of an issue, the manufacturer usually provides a link to their website where the drivers may be downloaded. Changing an internal card is much like changing an internal 802.11 card; follow the instructions indicated in the previous section.

Mini PCIe

Since many of the wireless cards are mini PCIe, replacing any other card in this format will follow the same procedure, with the exception of removing and reconnecting the antenna cables (present only on the wireless cards). You can find the card's location in the laptop's documentation. Make sure that the new card is firmly inserted into the slot after removing the old card.

FIGURE 1.7 The Advanced Network Settings tab

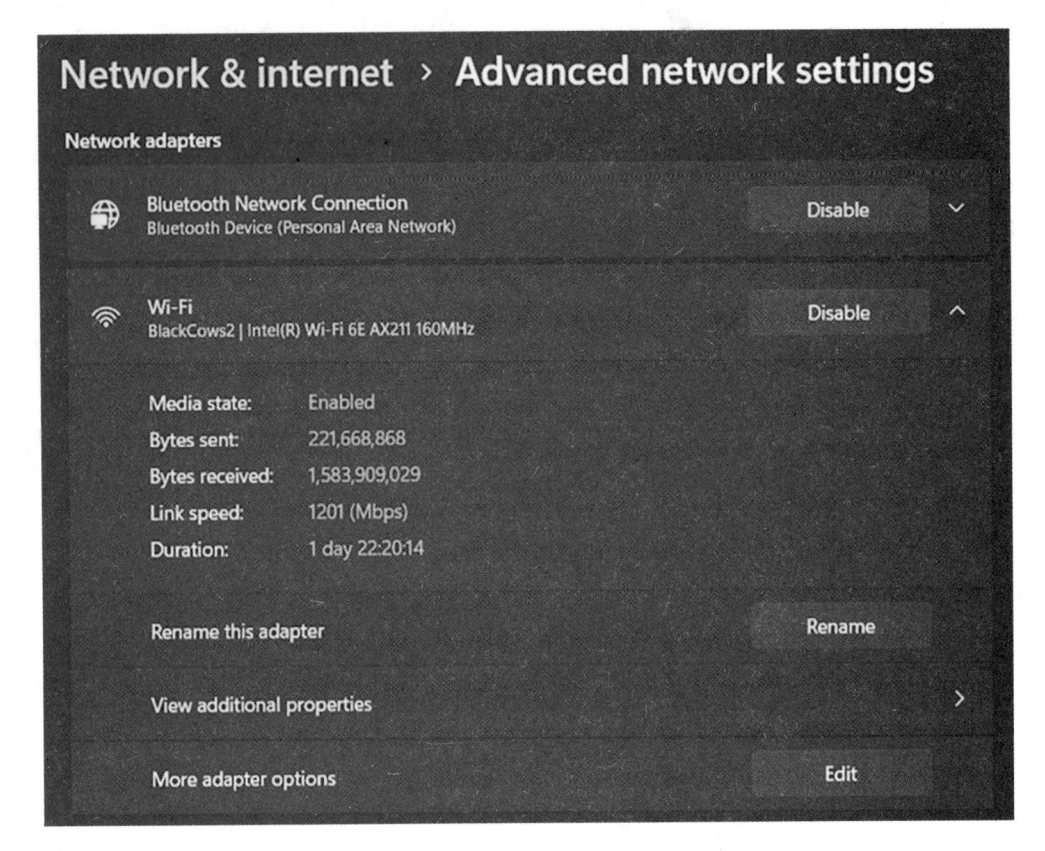

Physical privacy and security components

In Windows 11, one of the most common ways to secure your mobile device is through Windows Hello, commonly known as a personal identification number (PIN). This feature allows you to store log-on credentials securely. When you open an application or a website, Windows Hello will retrieve your credentials and apply them once you supply your PIN.

Some features are designed to enhance the privacy of data on a device and the transmission of said data by enhancing physical security. In the following section, you'll learn about two concepts that help to provide additional security in this regard.

Biometrics

Most mobile devices now offer the option to incorporate biometrics as an authentication mechanism. The two most common implementations use fingerprint or facial recognition technology. While there can be issues with both false negatives (i.e. the denial of a legitimate user)

FIGURE 1.8 Wi-Fi Properties

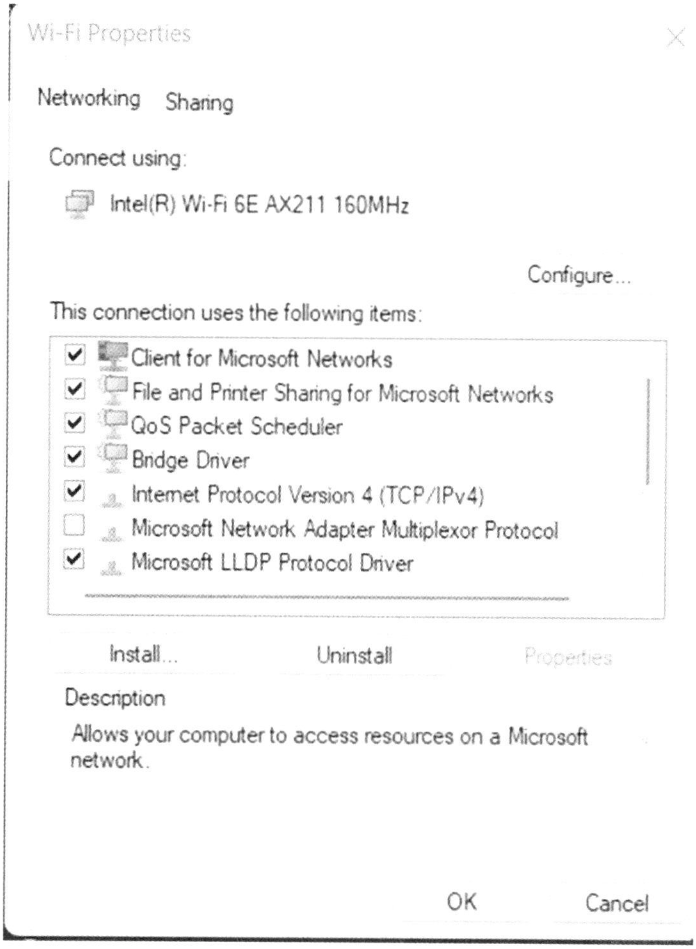

and false positives (i.e. the admission of an illegitimate user), biometric implementations offer much better security than other authentication mechanisms.

A good example is a fingerprint lock, which uses the user's fingerprint as a credential to authenticate the user and, when authentication successfully completes, unlocks the screen. Because it relies on biometrics, it is, for the most part, more secure than using a passcode or a swipe.

To set up fingerprint authentication in Windows 11, follow these steps:

1. Search for Settings in the Start menu and click on it. This action will open the Settings app.
2. Select Accounts > Sign-in Options. On the right panel, find the Fingerprint section under Windows Hello and click on the Set Up button.

3. On the Welcome screen, click the Get Started button to continue.

4. Authenticate yourself with a PIN or password to continue.

5. Scan your finger on the fingerprint sensor multiple times. As you scan your finger, you will see a fingerprint animation filling. When you see the All Set screen, you are finished.

Near-field scanner features

Near-field scanners allow you to use the chip feature on credit and debit cards. When the chip end of the card is inserted into the payment device, the near-field scanner reads the information off the chip and processes the transaction.

A near-field scanner allows you to measure and map the electromagnetic interference (EMI) that may be leaking from a system or its cables, creating a physical security issue. While these devices are used for much more than detecting EMI, they can be used for that purpose. They can also be used to analyze potential circuit designs for flaws. These devices are typically handheld.

Wi-Fi antenna connector/placement

The wireless antenna is located in the display. You may recall that when replacing a laptop screen, you encountered a number of wires coming from the screen to the laptop's body. One of these is the cable that connects the wireless antenna (located in the display) with the wireless card located in the body of the laptop.

The antennas built into the display usually work quite well. In any specific situation, you might improve your signal by moving your laptop around. This movement changes the antenna's polarization and may cause it to align better with the incoming signal.

Camera/webcam

Many displays today, especially laptop displays, have a webcam built in. They come ready to go with all drivers preinstalled and nothing to configure or set up. If you need to replace your webcam, you will have to disconnect the laptop lid (which holds the display) from the base, remove the screw covers and screws holding the display bezel in place, and remove the bezel. After removing the screws holding the mounting rails to the hinges, remove the LED screen from the lid assembly. Now you can get at the camera, but first you must carefully remove the tape that holds the camera cable in place and remove it and the camera. Attach the replacement cable to the new camera, install the new camera, and reverse these steps.

Webcams are widely available as a USB peripheral. You might find that purchasing an external camera is a much easier option than replacing the built-in camera.

Microphone

In Windows, controls for the microphone and speakers are located under System > Sound. You can troubleshoot issues with your microphone and speakers in this panel, as shown in Figure 1.9.

FIGURE 1.9 The Sound panel

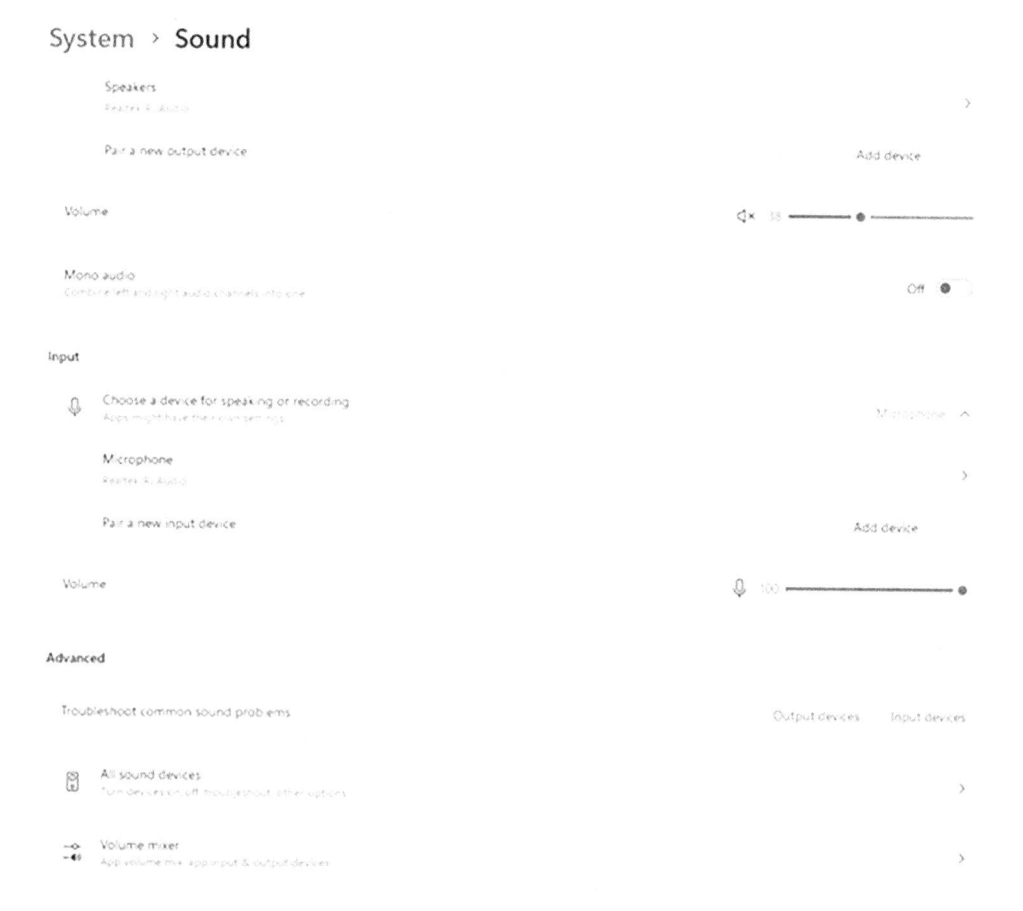

While many desktop systems lack a built-in microphone, almost all laptops have one. In some cases, this microphone will be located on the laptop bottom, but in many cases it will be located in the display next to the webcam or off to the side. If you need to replace it, you will need to take the same steps to get inside the display that you took for the webcam.

When you unhook the lid from the bottom, you will need to unplug several things from the board, and one of those will be the microphone cable. If the microphone is not working (which it probably isn't or you wouldn't be replacing it), take a moment to inspect the cable. Sometimes, the cable can be cut by the constant opening and closing of the case. (It shouldn't, but sometimes it does happen.) You might be able to repair the cable without replacing the microphone.

If that is not the case, remove the microphone and cable and replace both with the new mic and cable. Reverse the steps to get into the display, reconnect the cables to the board, and put the back on the bottom.

Exam essentials

Know where to monitor hardware issues.   Task Manager is the first place to go when you are monitoring hardware issues, such as RAM, HDD, or SSD issues. Use the System panel to see specific device configurations and make adjustments.

Know where to access critical components.   SSDs, HDDs, RAM, keyboards, and wireless cards are the components that are most often replaced. If what you're trying to find does not have an access panel, make sure you know how to find your device's user manual or a YouTube video for further replacement panels.

1.2 Compare and contrast accessories and connectivity options

Your mobile device can be the platform to which you can attach many other devices, wirelessly or through a cable. In many cases, your mobile device can be used as a wireless hotspot. The following topics are covered in Exam Objective 1.2:

- Connection methods
    - Wireless
    - Cables
- Accessories
- Docking station
- Port replicator
- Trackpad/drawing pad/track points

Connection methods

Two primary methods are used to connect other devices to your mobile device: a wireless connection and a wired or cabled connection. Both have several variations, and we will cover them in this section.

Universal serial bus (USB)/USB-C/micro USB/mini USB

We will explore the various types of USB connectors. Pay particular attention to the transfer rates and what the connector looks like. Keep in mind that the most common USB connector for mobile devices today is Type C.

USB is an expansion bus type that is used almost exclusively for external devices. All motherboards today have at least two USB ports. Some advantages of USB include hot plugging (i.e. the ability to plug or unplug a device without shutting the system down) and the capability for up to 127 USB devices to share a single set of system resources. Even if your device has only two USB ports, using a multiport hub will allow you to increase the number of USB devices that you can connect.

Connector types: A, B, mini, micro

USB connectors come in two types and two form factors or sizes. The Type A connector is what is found on USB hubs, on host controllers (i.e. cards plugged into slots to provide USB connections), and on the front and back panels of computers. Type B is the type of USB connector found on the end of the cable that plugs into the devices.

The connectors also come in a mini version and a micro version. The micro version is used on mobile devices, such as mobile phones, GPS units, tablets, and digital cameras, whereas the mini is used to transfer the data between digital devices and computers. The choice between a standard A and B and a mini A and B is dictated by what is present on the device. The cables used cannot exceed 5 m in length. Figure 1.10 shows, from left to right, a standard Type A, a mini Type A, a standard Type B, and a mini Type B. Some manufacturers have chosen to implement a mini connector that is proprietary, choosing not to follow the standard.

USB-C

The USB-C connectors unite with both hosts and devices, replacing various USB-B and USB-A connectors and cables with a standard. This type is distinguished by its twofold rotationally symmetrical connector. The cable is shown in Figure 1.11 next to a USB 3.0 cable.

USB 2.0/3.0

USB 1.1 runs at 12 Mbps, and USB 2.0 runs at 480 Mbps. USB 3.0 has transmission speeds of up to 5 Gbps, significantly reduces the time required for data transmission, reduces power consumption, and is backward-compatible with USB 2.0. Because USB is a serial interface, its width is 1 bit. It is useful to note, however, that a USB 2.0 device will perform at 2.0

FIGURE 1.10 USB connectors

FIGURE 1.11 USB-C and USB 3.0 cable

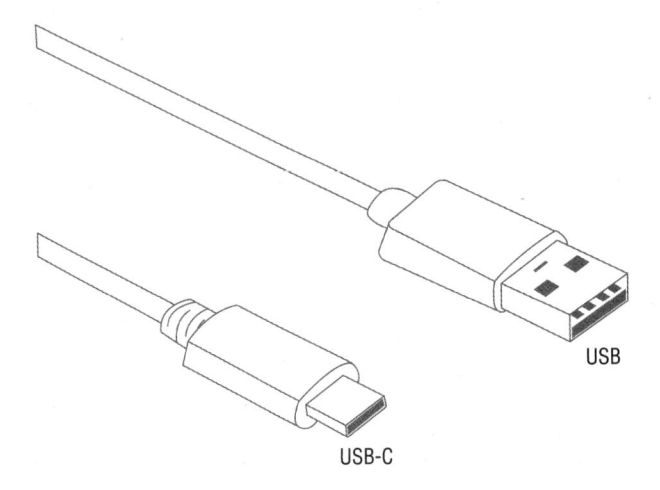

speeds even when connected to a 3.0 port. If you connect a USB 3.0 to a USB 2.0 port, it will also operate at only 2.0 speeds.

By using USB hubs in conjunction with the USB ports available on the local machine, you can connect up to 127 of these devices to a computer. You can daisy-chain up to four external USB hubs to a USB port. Daisy-chaining means that hubs are attached to each other in a line. A USB hub will not function if it is more than four hubs away from the root port.

Lightning

While millions of Apple devices use Lightning connectors for power, Apple is making the transition to USB-C as its primary connector.

Although it makes an adapter to convert a Lightning connector to mini-USB, Apple doesn't encourage its use because of the limitations the adapter places on the functionality of the proprietary connector.

The Lightning connector is an eight-pin connector that, while not standard, has advantages over USB according to Apple. It operates at USB 3.0 speeds of 640 MBps. Following are some of the advantages:

- It can supply more power.
- It can be inserted either way.
- It is physically more durable than USB.
- It can detect and adapt to connected devices.

Figure 1.12 shows a Lightning connector next to a USB cable.

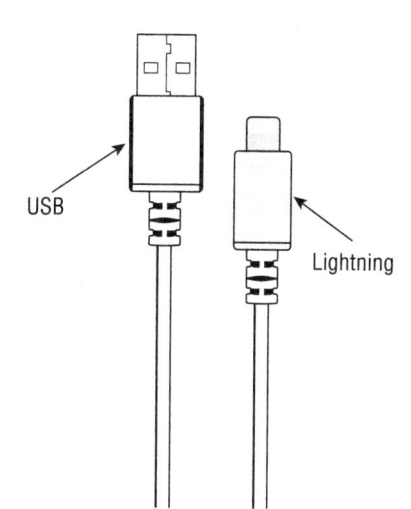

FIGURE 1.12 Lightning connector and a USB cable

Near-field communications (NFC)

Near-field communications (NFC) is a wireless technology that allows smartphones and other equipped devices to communicate when very near one another or when touching. NFC operates at slower speeds than Bluetooth but consumes far less power and doesn't require pairing. It also does not create a personal area network (PAN) like Bluetooth does; rather, the connections are point-to-point. NFC can operate up to 20 cm at a transfer rate of 0.424 Mbps.

NFC is also a standard managed by the International Standards Organization (ISO) and uses tags that are embedded in the device. NFC components include an initiator and a target; the initiator actively generates a radio frequency (RF) field that can power a passive target. This enables NFC targets to take simple form factors, such as tags, stickers, key fobs, or cards that do not require batteries.

You might have noticed these small devices in retail outlets. They communicate wirelessly with NFC cards and smartphones. In some cases, it requires tapping the phone on the device, and in other cases, that is not required. These devices connect using either USB or, in some rare cases, a serial connection. Consult the documentation to determine whether you need a special driver installed.

The technology was first used in radio frequency ID (RFID) tagging and was implemented on mobile devices first as a way to share short-range information and later as a method to make payments at a point of sale. It operates by reading tags, which are small microchips with antennas that can in some cases only be read and that can in other cases be read and written to.

A mobile device must have the support for NFC built in, and many already do. Special applications are available that make it easy to use the technology in various ways:

- Making point-of-sale payments
- Reading information stored in tags in posters and advertisements
- Communicating between toys used in gaming
- Communicating with peripherals

Bluetooth

Bluetooth, like USB, has become ubiquitous as a method to connect devices. Bluetooth has even made its way into automobiles, allowing for things like Apple CarPlay and hands-free cell phone operation. If you have a vehicle that monitors your tire pressure, there is a sensor that uses Bluetooth or RFID to transmit your tire pressure information to the car's computer.

Mobile devices also support Bluetooth wireless connections. Bluetooth is a technology that can connect a printer to a computer at a short range; its absolute maximum range is 100 m (330 ft), and most devices are specified to work within 10 m (33 ft). When printing with a Bluetooth-enabled device (like a tablet or mobile phone) and a Bluetooth-enabled printer, all you need to do is get within range of the device (i.e. move closer), select the print driver from the device, and choose Print. The information is transmitted wirelessly through the air using radio waves and is received by the device. Bluetooth speed depends on version. Table 1.1 details the speeds for the latest versions.

TABLE 1.1 Bluetooth speeds

Version	Speed
2.0	2.1 MB
2.1	2.1 MB
3.0	24 MB (over Wi-Fi connection)
4.0	2.1 MB over Bluetooth and 24 MB over Wi-Fi
4.1	2.1 MB over Bluetooth and 24 MB over Wi-Fi
4.2	2.1 MB over Bluetooth and 24 MB over Wi-Fi
5.0	2.1 MB over Bluetooth and 24 MB over Wi-Fi

Tethering/hotspot

Another way that many mobile devices can connect to other devices is through a hotspot or when tethered to another device. Many mobile devices can act as 802.11 hotspots for other wireless devices in the area. There are also devices dedicated solely to performing as mobile hotspots.

Hotspots are publicly provided points of access to an 802.11 wireless network connected to the Internet. Often, public hotspots in places like cafes have little or no security configured to make it as easy as possible for users to connect. Vendors have also created devices that allow a single device to act as a hotspot for other devices in the area. Sometimes, these are called mobile hotspots. Some mobile devices can be turned into mobile hotspots with a software upgrade or an addition to the service plan.

Accessories

Accessories are items you use with your mobile device to make it more convenient or to increase your productivity. You might want to add a stylus for a tablet, a headset for your mobile phone, or even speakers. We'll take a look at several different accessories.

Stylus

A stylus is an electronic pen that works with a touch screen device. You often see a stylus when you need to sign for purchase at a retail location or a bank. The pen-like device that you "sign" with is a stylus. You can also see a stylus paired with a tablet. The waitstaff in many restaurants use wireless ordering pads, with a stylus to select the menu items tableside.

Headset

There are many headset types that allow you to privately listen to content from your mobile device. Some headsets provide only listening capability, while others have built-in microphones.

There are also specialized headsets for virtual reality (VR) and augmented reality (AR). Both technologies enrich a user's visual experience. AR can be deployed on a smartphone, allowing you to point the smartphone camera at a sign printed in a foreign language and receive instant translation. VR headsets, which look like goggles, immerse the viewer in a 3D environment. Most often seen in gaming systems, VR also has many applications in education, marketing, and e-commerce.

To sum up, headsets provide the ability to take your conversation offline or to listen to your music in private. They can be connected through a wired connection – usually a 3.55 mm audio connector or USB – or by using Bluetooth to pair the device with the headset.

Speakers

On a laptop, you can control many aspects of how the speakers sound by clicking on the speaker icon in the system tray. Figure 1.13 indicates the icon to select to control the sound.

Then, click on the sound controls to raise or lower the sound, as shown in Figure 1.14.

FIGURE 1.13 Sound icon in system tray

FIGURE 1.14 The sound volume control

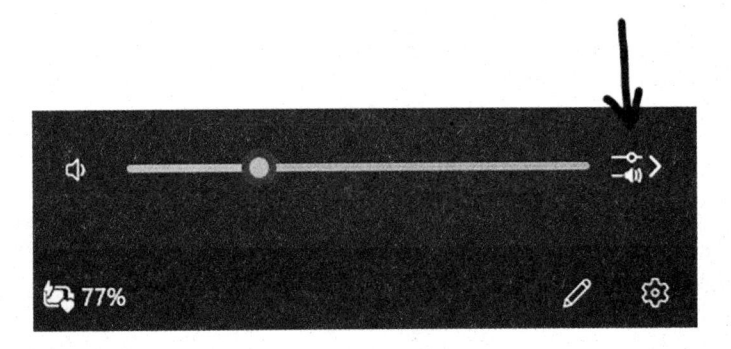

In the pop-up window, you can select your speaker options. Figure 1.15 shows several speaker options.

You can further fine-tune your audio characteristics by clicking on More Volume Settings.

Speakers are used in the same fashion as headsets. They can also be connected using the same options, which include using USB, a 3.55 mm audio plug, or Bluetooth. This includes the speaker systems in many cars, which can now be paired with devices using Bluetooth as well.

Volume settings

On the top row where the keys labeled F1–F12 are located, there are usually a couple of keys (typically F8 and F9) with icons that look like speakers. These keys can be used to raise and lower the volume of the sound. If the icon is blue, you have to hold down the Fn key while pressing the key. Otherwise, you do not need to use the Fn key to activate them. (As a matter of fact, if you hold down the Fn key and use the F8 key, you might be changing the location of the display output.) If these keys are not present, consult the documentation for which keys to use in conjunction with Fn to lower and raise the volume. Most laptops also include a mute button marked as such.

FIGURE 1.15 Speaker options available

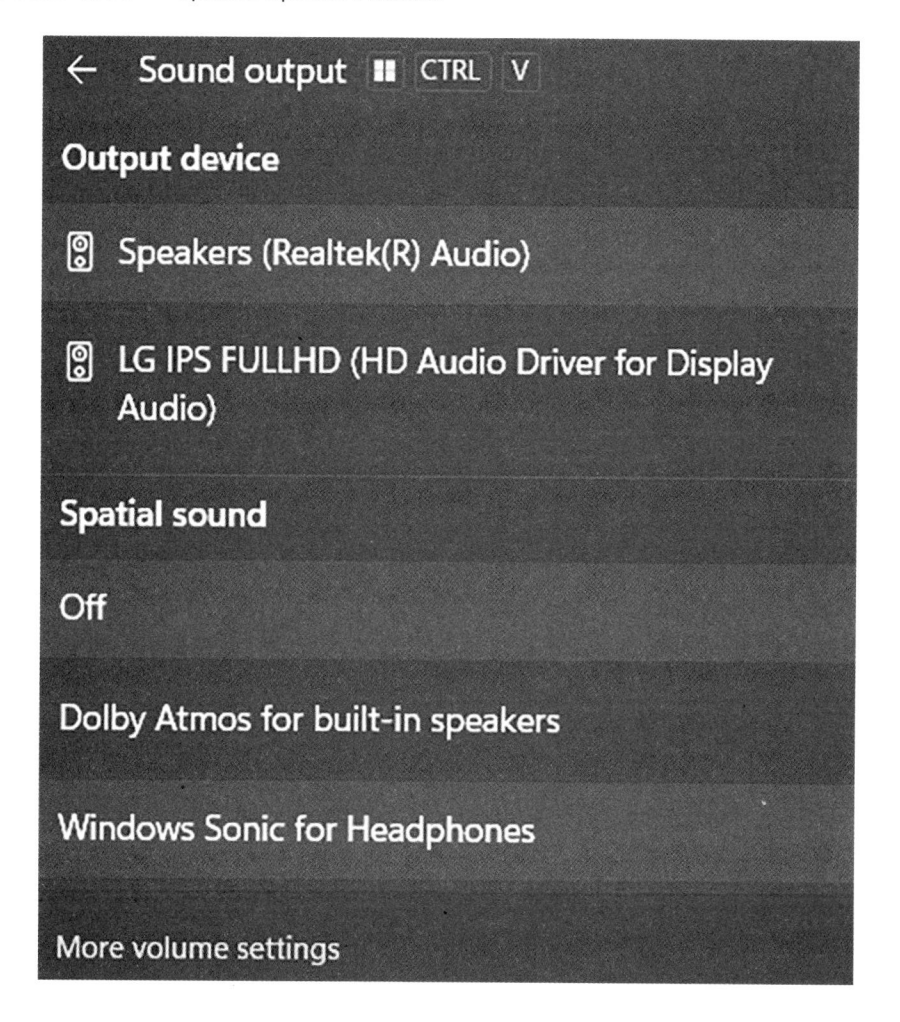

```
← Sound output  ▐▌ CTRL  V

Output device

🔊 Speakers (Realtek(R) Audio)

🔊 LG IPS FULLHD (HD Audio Driver for Display
   Audio)

Spatial sound

Off

Dolby Atmos for built-in speakers

Windows Sonic for Headphones

More volume settings
```

Installation

Installing speakers is more a matter of connecting them properly than installing them. Usually, one of the speakers will connect to a power source, and the other will connect to the powered speaker. Once the speakers are connected to a power source, connect the speaker cable to the proper plug on the PC. These plugs will be marked with icons that indicate which is for a microphone and which is for speakers.

Replacement

To replace speakers, first follow the earlier instructions to remove the hard drive, the battery pack, and all the screws holding the body together.

1. Lift the screen up and separate it from the body. Do not remove the wires connecting the screen to the motherboard.
2. Separate the two pieces of plastic body frame to view the inside of the laptop. Locate the speakers, using the laptop's documentation if necessary.
3. Unscrew the speakers and note where they connect to the motherboard. Disconnect the old speakers and connect the new ones to the same location where the old speakers were removed.
4. Replace all the parts in the reverse order you removed them.

No sound from speakers

When a speaker on a mobile device is not functioning, in most cases it has simply been inadvertently turned off. After checking the settings described later in this section, you can assume that there is a hardware problem. In that case, with smartphones, it is typically advisable to send the device to the manufacturer. However, with laptops, it is possible to replace the internal speakers.

To determine whether the settings are the issue, ensure that the speaker volume is turned up and the speaker is not disabled. On an Android, first test the loudspeaker by following these steps:

1. Go to the Home screen and tap the Phone icon.
2. Type *#7353# into the dialer as though you are dialing a phone number. A list of options will appear.
3. Tap Speaker, and music should start to play. You can tap Speaker again to silence the music.

To test the internal speaker, follow the same steps, but in Step 3, tap Melody. Music should start to play from the earpiece on the phone and allow you to hear whether the speaker that you hold up to your ear to listen to people is working properly as well.

On an iPhone, follow these steps:

1. Go to Settings > Sounds & Haptics and drag the Ringtone and Alerts slider to turn the volume up.
2. If you can hear sound from the speaker, then the speaker works.
3. If the device has a Ring/Silent switch, make sure it's set to ring. If you can see orange, it's set to silent.

Voice-enabled smart speaker/digital assistant

Smart speakers that fulfill your commands are an extension of the digital assistants found in many operating systems today. Alexa, Cortana, and other digital assistants are installed in the speaker. Installing one of these is usually just a matter of turning it on and going through some prompts to enter the wireless network's SSID and password. Then you're up and running.

Webcam

Webcams are built into most mobile devices. When coupled with the appropriate application, webcams allow you to broadcast full-motion video and audio over the Internet. Alternatively, you can record video for editing and subsequent publishing. Webcams are used for videoconferencing, delivery of education, publishing to social media, and much more.

Earlier in this chapter, you learned about webcams. External digital cameras usually connect to the PC with a USB cable. In many cases, the operating system comes with software that may detect the camera and assist you in accessing the pictures and moving them to the computer. In other instances, you may want to install software that came with the camera. Doing so will often allow you to take fuller advantage of the features the camera offers. SD cards can be used to transfer images from the camera if a cable is not available.

Docking station

Some notebook PCs have optional accessories called docking stations or port replicators. They let you quickly connect/disconnect with external peripherals and may also provide extra ports that the notebook PC doesn't normally have.

A docking station essentially allows a laptop computer to be converted to a desktop computer. When plugged into a docking station, the laptop has access to things it doesn't have stand-alone – he network, a workgroup printer, and so on. The cheapest form of docking station (if it can be called that) is a port replicator. Typically, you slide a laptop into the port replicator, and the laptop can then use a full-sized monitor, keyboard (rather than the standard 84 keys on a laptop), mouse, and so on. Extended, or enhanced, replicators add other ports not found on the laptop, such as PC slots, sound ports, and more. The most common difference between port replicators and docking stations is that port replicators duplicate the ports the laptop already has to outside devices, and the docking station expands the laptop to include other ports and devices that the laptop does not natively have.

Laptops can support plug and play at three levels, depending on how dynamically they're able to adapt to changes.

Cold docking The laptop must be turned off and back on for the change to be recognized.

Warm docking The laptop must be put in and out of suspended mode for the change to be recognized.

Hot docking The change can be made and is recognized while running normal operations.

Each docking station works a little differently, but there is usually a button you can press to undock the notebook from the unit. There may also be a manual release lever in case you need to undock when the button is unresponsive. Moreover, the docking station must be purchased from the same vendor you purchased the laptop from, because docking stations are vendor- and model-specific.

FIGURE 1.16 A track point

Port replicator

Port replicators are a form of docking station and were discussed in the "Docking Station" section.

Trackpad/drawing pad/track points

A track point, sometimes called a pointing stick, is a small button on a laptop's keyboard that can be used as a mouse. Figure 1.16 shows a track point.

An optical trackpad is an input device based on an optical sensor, which detects the finger's movement on top of it. This sensor typically is used in smartphones, where it replaces the drawing or D-pad. The main advantages a trackpad has over a D-pad are:

- It can track movements in 360 degrees and with varying speeds.
- It uses space efficiently, without the need for small buttons that are difficult to press.

A drawing pad is a computer input device that enables a user to hand draw images with a special pen-like stylus.

Exam essentials

Identify all types of connection methods. Be able to identify images of the various USB connectors. Know their data transmission rates. Be able to identify a Lightning cable. Know the differences between NFC and Bluetooth. Understand how to tether a mobile device and use it as a hotspot.

Understand the use of accessories. Know how a stylus, headset, speakers, and webcam work. Know where to go to configure the headset and speakers. Understand how docking stations and port replicators are used. Know the difference between trackpads, drawing pads, and track points.

1.3 Given a scenario, configure basic mobile device network connectivity and provide application support

You should be able to configure a mobile device for network connectivity. The following topics are covered in Exam Objective 1.3:

- Wireless/cellular data network (enable/disable)
- Bluetooth
- Location services
- Mobile device management (MDM)
- Mobile device synchronization

Wireless/cellular data network (enable/disable)

Like most computing devices, mobile devices provide more robust functionality when connected to a network (especially if that network is the Internet). Two types of networks can be used to gain access to the Internet: cell phone networks and Wi-Fi networks.

Cell phone networks have in the past been the second choice because the performance has not been as good as an 802.11 Wi-Fi connection. With the introduction of newer technologies like 5G, however, the performance delivered by the cell network has become more competitive.

In either case, most mobile devices will have the ability to make an 802.11 connection or use the cell network. If you want to disable the automatic connection to the cell phone network, or if it was somehow turned off and needs to be turned back on, you can do this through the settings. One example of the steps to access these settings is Settings > Wireless > Mobile > Enable Data (select or deselect this). This is only one navigational example, and you should consult the documentation that came with your device.

3G/4G/5G

Mobile technology and platforms are typically expressed as 3G, 4G, or 5G, with the "G" representing the term "generation." Each has its own performance characteristics. At this writing, 5G is in rollout throughout much of the United States, but there are a significant number of devices that operate in 3G or 4G.

3G

Third generation, or 3G, introduced web browsing, email, video downloading, picture sharing, and other smartphone technologies. The technology of 3G should be capable of handling around 2 Mbps.

4G

Fourth generation, or 4G, is a later cellular technology that specifies 100 Mbps and up to 1 Gbps to pass as 4G. Outside of the covered areas, 4G phones regress to the 3G standards.

5G

With speeds of up to 100 Gbps, 5G is as much as one thousand times faster than 4G. It provides greater network stability to ensure that business-critical mobile functions do not go offline and have the speed necessary to give employees a fully equipped virtual office almost anywhere. Most wireless carriers offer 5G broadband Internet in most big cities.

Hotspot

When the devices using the Internet connection on the cellular device are connected wirelessly using 802.11, it is sometimes called a mobile hotspot. This is also the term used for devices that can act as a hotspot for surrounding Wi-Fi devices. The mobile hotspot device may get its Internet access through either cellular or 802.11. To enable connection to a hotspot, follow these steps:

- Click the Wi-Fi icon in the system tray.
- The hotspot will show up as a wireless connection.
- Select it and enter the password.
- Click Connect.

Wi-Fi

Making a Wi-Fi connection on a mobile device is much like doing so with a laptop. In the device's settings will be a section for Wi-Fi. (On an iPhone, it's called Wi-Fi, and on an Android device, it's called Wireless and Networks.) When you access it, you will see all the Wi-Fi networks within range. Just as you would do with a laptop, select one network and attempt to connect to the Wi-Fi network. If the connection requires a password, you will have to supply it. You also can preconfigure a wireless profile for commonly used secure wireless networks, as well as those where the service set identifier (SSID) has been hidden.

Subscriber identity module (SIM)/eSIM

Subscriber identity module (SIM) cards were originally the size of a credit card but now are the size of a fingernail. SIM cards have a unique number assigned to them that is used to identify the subscriber and validate the device to the mobile network. SIM cards also contain account data like your phone number and other information like text messages and contacts.

SIM cards can be removed from one device and inserted into another, enabling you to keep your phone number when changing devices or phone carriers.

As technology has evolved, the embedded SIM (eSIM) is replacing the SIM on some devices. The eSIM is not a removable card but rather a part of the phone's circuitry. The functionality of the eSim is the same as that of the SIM, just in digital form.

Bluetooth

Bluetooth is a short-range wireless technology that is used to create a wireless connection between digital devices. One application is to create connections between mobile devices and items such as speakers, headphones, external GPS units, and keyboards. Before you can take advantage of this technology, the devices must be configured to connect to one another. This section will discuss how to configure a Bluetooth connection.

Enable Bluetooth

On Android mobile devices, follow these steps:

1. From the Home screen, select the Menu button. From the menu, choose Settings > Connections > Bluetooth.
2. Once Bluetooth is selected, wait until a check mark appears next to Bluetooth. Bluetooth is now enabled.

On iOS mobile devices, follow these steps:

1. On the main page, choose Settings > Bluetooth.
2. Tap the Bluetooth icon so it turns blue.

Enable pairing

Pairing a mobile device with an external device (e.g. a speaker, headphones, and so forth) will enable the two devices to communicate. The first step is to enable pairing, which is much simpler than it sounds. For either mobile operating system, simply turn on the external device and you are ready for the next step. In some cases, you might need to make the external device discoverable. Check the external device's documentation to see whether this is the case and how you can make it discoverable.

Find a device for pairing

Now that the external device is on and transmitting a signal, the mobile device is ready for pairing.

On an Android mobile device, follow these steps:

1. Swipe up on an empty spot on the Home screen to open the Apps tray.
2. Select Settings > Connections.

3. Turn on the Bluetooth switch by tapping it.
4. In the list of Available Devices, tap the Bluetooth device to pair it with the phone.
5. Follow any on-screen instructions.
6. If a password is required, consult the device's documentation or try either 0000 or 1234 (i.e. common passcodes).

On an iOS mobile device, when Bluetooth is enabled, it automatically starts scanning for Bluetooth devices. When your device appears in the list, select it. If a PIN is required, move on to the next step.

Enter the appropriate personal identification number (PIN) code

Many external devices will ask for a PIN code when you select the external device from the list of discovered devices. In many cases, the PIN is 0000, but you should check the external device's manual. In some cases, one device will generate a code, and you must enter that generated code on the other device to complete the pairing.

Test connectivity

Once the previous steps are completed, test communication between the two devices. If you're using a headset, turn on sound and see whether you can hear it in the headphones.

Location services

There are two primary types of location services. Global Positioning System (GPS) uses satellites in geostationary orbits to determine your position. Cellular services locate your position based on your mobile device's proximity to a cell tower. GPS and cellular location services may be used independently or together.

Global Positioning System (GPS) services

GPS uses satellite information to plot the global location of an object and then uses that information to plot the route to a second location. GPS devices are integrated into many mobile devices and are used for many things, but when I use the term for a stand-alone device, I am usually referring to a navigation aid.

These aids have grown in sophistication over time and now can not only plot your route but also help you locate restaurants, lodging, and other services along the way. Another use for these devices is tracking delivery vehicles and rental cars.

Cellular location services

If you use a feature like "Find the nearest gas station," you are using location services. Let's take a look at this feature.

Location services allow the device to determine your location for the purpose of tailoring search results. Location tracking can be disabled on a mobile device. In most cases, disabled location tracking is the default, and users will be asked by certain applications whether they want to enable it. When a user has never enabled this feature or has disabled this feature and it suddenly begins to track the location of the device, it is another indication that the device has been compromised.

Mobile device management (MDM)

In this section, we will cover mobile device management (MDM). Mobile devices with access to the corporate network represent a significant security risk, but this risk may be mitigated through device configurations, policy enforcement, and/or corporate applications.

Device configurations

There are two primary categories of mobile devices that need specific configuration settings to securely access the corporate network: corporate-owned devices and personally owned Bring Your Own Devices (BYODs).

Corporate

If you have a corporate-owned mobile device, your configuration is going to be rather rigid, with minimal opportunities for customization. There are many reasons for these restrictions, such as protecting a company's intellectual property and network security. This is not unlike having a desktop computer, with a standard configuration called an image.

Bring Your Own Device (BYOD)

Many organizations will allow you to use your personal mobile device through a policy called Bring Your Own Device (BYOD). Even though you are using your device, keep in mind that your device has access to sensitive company information and applications. The company will want to ensure that its data and applications are safe on your device. The company may require the installation of a mobile device management (MDM) application to ensure security. MDM is one of a group of centralized MDM tools that are becoming the fastest-growing solution for both organization issues and personal devices.

Some solutions leverage the messaging server's management capabilities, and others are third-party tools that can manage multiple brands of devices. Systems Manager by Cisco is one example that integrates with their Cisco Meraki cloud services. Another example for iOS devices is the Apple Configurator. One of the challenges with implementing such a system is that not all personal devices may support native encryption and/or the management process.

Typically, centralized MDM tools handle company-issued and personal mobile devices differently. For organization-issued devices, a client application typically manages the configuration and security of the entire device. If the device is a personal device allowed through a BYOD initiative, the application typically manages the configuration and security of itself and its data only. The application and its data are sandboxed (i.e. segregated and stored separately) from the other applications and data. The result is that the organization's data is protected if the device is stolen, while the privacy of the user's data is also preserved.

Policy enforcement

Remember, while BYOD allows users to use their own devices to access company resources and data, the company wants to ensure safety and security through MDM. MDM creates policies and helps with company policy enforcement.

MDM policies can be created in Active Directory (AD), or they can be implemented through MDM software. This software allows you to exert control over the mobile devices, even those you do not own if they have the software installed. These policies can force data encryption and data segregation, and they can be used to wipe a stolen device remotely.

Corporate applications

Authenticator applications, such as Google Authenticator, make it possible for a mobile device to use a time-based one-time password (TOTP) algorithm with a site or system that requires such authentication.

An example of a TOTP password is one that is sent via text or email and must be used within a certain time frame. TOTP is often used in password reset requests.

In the setup operation, the site provides a shared secret key to the user over a secure channel to be stored in the authenticator app. This secret key will be used for all future log-ons to the site. The user will enter a username and password into a website or other server, generate a one-time password for the server using TOTP running locally, and type that password into the server as well. The server will then also run TOTP to verify the entered one-time password. While Google makes versions for multiple mobile platforms, there are also other third-party solutions.

Trusted sources vs. untrusted sources

Applications and utilities for mobile devices can come from both trusted and untrusted sources. An example of a trusted source is the official Google Play site or the Apple App Store. That doesn't mean these are the only trusted sources, but users should treat this issue with the same approach they have been taught with regard to desktop and laptop computers.

Any piece of software, be it an application, a tool, or a utility, can come with malware attached. Users should be trained to regard any software downloads with suspicion. It may be advisable to use an enterprise mobility management system to prevent users from downloading any software to a company-owned mobile device. You also might want to deselect the setting shown in Figure 1.17, which is an Android device setting. Apple devices warn users with a pop-up message when they download from an unknown source.

Mobile device synchronization

Keeping information in sync between your desktop or laptop and your mobile device is one feature many users want to take advantage of. There are many types of information that can be synced, applications that can be installed to perform the synchronization, and connection methods that can be used to do it. This section discusses mobile device synchronization.

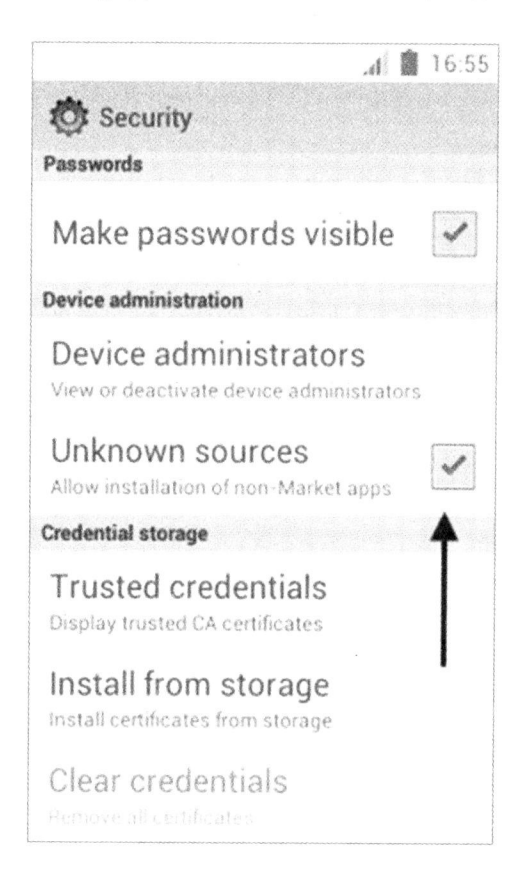

1.3 Given a scenario, configure basic mobile-device network connectivity 35

FIGURE 1.17 Disallowing applications from unknown sources

Synchronization methods

When synchronizing the various data types that we will discuss shortly, there are three basic ways to make this happen: You can synchronize to the cloud, a desktop, or an automobile's computer system. In this section, you'll review all three approaches.

Synchronize to the cloud

One synchronization method is synchronizing all your devices to a cloud server. This provides a central location for your data and settings. This can be set up such that all devices update to the cloud as soon as they attain Internet access.

Synchronize to a desktop

Another approach is to set up a sync process directly between two devices, such as a smartphone and a desktop computer. In this case, the two devices will sync with one another any time they find themselves on the same network, such as a home wireless network.

Synchronize to an automobile

Yes, cars now have computing systems and as such can be synced to a mobile device either by using Bluetooth or by using cables designed by vendors to connect to the car system.

Recognizing data caps

It is very important to know whether your mobile device plan has a data cap, which is the daily or monthly limit on the data you can use. If you travel internationally, it is also important to know how the plan handles data when you cross borders.

Many smartphone accounts have a data cap. Regulating data use is complicated because most users have no idea how much data they're using by streaming video or getting turn-by-turn directions. To identify current use, follow these steps:

On an iPhone:

1. Open Settings.
2. Tap Cellular (or Mobile Data, depending on the model).
3. Tap on Usage or Data Plan, depending on the model. Review the Data Usage report.

On an Android device:

1. Open your Android's Settings.
2. Tap Data Usage. You should now see the total amount of mobile data used in the current month at the top of the screen.

Calendar

The Calendar application on the iPhone allows for syncing events from several different calendars and displays them in one central place. This feature allows you to manage your time for virtual and in-person meetings, doctor visits, speaking engagements, and things that you really don't want to forget, like birthdays and anniversaries.

The calendar is a critical application for both work and play. All mobile devices support syncing the calendar between devices. In some cases, it may require a small application, especially when the email system—which the calendar is part of—is in a different ecosystem (e.g. Google Mail and an iPhone).

Contacts

Synchronizing the contacts on your mobile device offers a whole new level of productivity with the Bluetooth capabilities in newer cars and applications like Apple CarPlay. I can make a call simply by saying "Call …" and a contact name. I can also dictate a text message to a contact or even dictate an email. I often dictate an email to myself while driving, when I remember something I have to do or an idea I want to follow up on. This paragraph, in fact, is a result of a dictated email with the subject "Remember to talk about dictating emails in Chapter 1."

No one wants to enter a long list of contacts into a mobile device when that same list already exists in their email account. Using push synchronization (push means it's automatic and requires no effort on the part of the user), you ensure that any changes made to the contact list either on the mobile device or on the desktop will be sent (pushed) to the other device the next time you connect to that email account from the other device. It will also update if the mobile device makes a direct connection to the desktop.

Business applications

You will want to synchronize your business applications, primarily mail and cloud storage.

Mail

Let's have a brief discussion about incoming email protocols. Incoming email uses one of two protocols: POP3 (which uses port 110) or IMAP (which uses port 143). With Post Office Protocol 3 (POP3), emails are downloaded onto the device requesting new emails and removed from the server, which is fine if you check your email on only one device. Internet Message Access Protocol (IMAP), on the other hand, delivers a copy of the email to the device requesting it but keeps the original on the server. This allows you to see all of your emails on whatever device you use to open them. With IMAP, I can check my email on my phone before a flight and then use the hotel's public computer to work on a critical email. When I open the email application on that public computer, I will be able to see all of my emails.

For many people, having access to their business email on their mobile device is critical. This is particularly true as the lines between "work hours" and "personal hours" become blurred. You also want to ensure that the mail on your mobile device is synced with your primary work computer, which helps with flagging and/or prioritizing emails you need to attend to once you get to the office.

You probably also want to set up your personal email on a device from a commercial provider. This section will review some of the major email systems that you might encounter.

iCloud

To set up iCloud email on an Android device, follow these instructions:

1. Swipe up or Done in the Home screen to access the Apps screen.
2. In Settings, select Accounts, then Add an Account.
3. Click on the account type.
4. If prompted, select the account subtype.
5. After entering the email address, select Next.
6. After entering the password, select Next.
7. If promoted for the username, password, or server name, enter them and select Next.

8. Enter the fully qualified domain name (FQDN) of the Simple Mail Transfer Protocol (SMTP) server, port number, and outgoing server and select Next. Think of the SMTP server as the Internet version of your local post office, which picks up your mail and forwards it to the next post office in the delivery path.

9. After configuring any account options desired (e.g. Sync Frequency, Inbox Download Size, and so on), click Next.

10. Address any additional options you encounter and select Next.

11. Enter an account name for outgoing messages.

As you can imagine, setting up iCloud email on an iOS device is simple because the applications all reside in the Apple ecosystem. First set up an iCloud email account. If you have an email address that ends with @mac.com or @me.com, you already have an equivalent address that's the same, except it ends with @icloud.com. On your IOS device, go to Settings, tap your name, and then select iCloud. Then tap Mail and select Use on This [device].

Gmail

On an Android mobile device, follow these steps:

1. Select the Gmail icon.
2. Select Already Have a Google account.
3. In the Sign In with Your Google Account field, enter your username and password and select Sign In.

On an iOS mobile device, follow these steps:

1. Select Settings > Apps > Mail > Mail Accounts > Add Account.
2. Select Gmail.
3. Fill in your name, email address, password, and description if desired. Click Next.
4. Verify that the address has been carried over from the last page. Click Next.
5. Select the items you want to sync automatically with the email server and click Done.

Outlook

To set up Outlook on Android, first, if required, install Outlook for Android. Follow these steps:

1. On the Android device, select the Email icon.
2. After entering the email address and password, select Manual Setting.
3. Complete the Domain\Username field.
4. After entering the password for the Exchange server, select Use Secure Connection (SSL) and then Next.
5. In the Account Options interface, select a frequency for checking email and click Next.

6. Finally, if desired, enter a name for the account in the Give This Account a Name field and select Done.

On iOS, follow these steps:

1. Add your Exchange account by tapping Settings > Apps > Mail > Mail Accounts > Add Account > Exchange.
2. Enter your email address.
3. Choose either Configure Manually or Sign In to connect to your Exchange server.

If you select Configure Manually, you can set up an Exchange account with basic authentication. Enter your email password. You might also be prompted to enter additional server information.

If you select Sign In, your email address is sent to Microsoft to discover your Exchange account information. If your account uses multifactor authentication, you'll be guided through a custom authentication workflow.

Yahoo

Because Yahoo recommends using IMAP as an email client, these are the instructions for setting up IMAP on Android systems:

1. Swipe up or Done on the Home screen to access the Apps screen.
2. In Settings, select Accounts and then Add an Account.
3. After selecting the account type, select the subtype if required.
4. Enter the email address and then select Next.
5. After entering the password, select Next.
6. If prompted, enter the username, password, or server and click Next.
7. Configure the SMTP server, port number, and outgoing server and click Next.
8. Select any account options desired, such as Sync Frequency, Inbox Download Size, and so on, and select Next.
9. If prompted, enter an account name and an account for outgoing messages.

On an iOS device, use these instructions:

1. Tap Settings > Apps > Mail > Mail Accounts > Add Account.
2. Tap Add Account.
3. Tap Yahoo.
4. Enter your name, email address, email password, and a description and then tap Next.
5. Optionally, disable aspects of Yahoo Mail from syncing (to decrease the amount of data syncing, which will improve performance).
6. Tap Save.

Cloud storage

Several cloud storage solutions are available that allow you to create, store, and edit documents and spreadsheets as well as store images and video. The biggest advantage to cloud storage is that you have access to your items from anywhere and any device with an Internet connection. With cloud storage, you don't have to remember on which device a document or picture is located. You can share your materials with others should you choose, and many cloud services even offer online collaboration.

We have already covered iCloud. Some other examples of these cloud storage solutions include:

- Dropbox
- Google Drive
- Microsoft OneDrive

Exam essentials

Enable Bluetooth and pair a Bluetooth device with a mobile network. Describe the process for both the iOS and Android operating systems.

Configure email on a mobile device. Detail the process of configuring email, including both Exchange and Gmail for both the iOS and Android operating systems.

Review Questions

You can find the answers in the appendix.

1. Which email client does Yahoo recommend when setting up Yahoo email?
   A. SMTP
   B. IMAP
   C. POP3
   D. S/MIME

2. Which action can invalidate a laptop warranty?
   A. Reinstalling the OS
   B. Opening the laptop's case
   C. Flashing the BIOS
   D. Performing a remote wipe

3. What special screwdriver is typically required to work on a notebook?
   A. Phillips head
   B. T8 Torx
   C. Hex
   D. Metric

4. If you have an email address that ends with @mac.com or @me.com, you already have an equivalent address that's the same, except it ends with which of the following?
   A. @iapple
   B. @icloud
   C. @iemail
   D. @istorage

5. Which component, if damaged, can render the hard drive useless?
   A. The caddy
   B. The rails
   C. The signal pins
   D. The chassis

6. What was the smallest hard drive covered in this chapter?
   A. 1.8
   B. 2.5
   C. 3.0
   D. 3.5

7. Which is *not* an advantage of solid-state drives?
   A. Cheaper
   B. Not as susceptible to damage
   C. Faster
   D. No moving parts

8. Which of the following makes it possible for a mobile device to use a time-based one-time password (TOTP) algorithm with a site or system that requires such authentication?
   A. Hardware security modules
   B. Non-transitive trust
   C. Authenticator applications
   D. In-plane switching

9. Adding which of the following will almost always improve performance?
   A. CPU
   B. Disk
   C. Network card
   D. Memory

10. Which of the following will you *not* need to set up corporate email?
    A. FQDN of your SMTP server
    B. IP address of your SMTP server
    C. Port numbers used for both server types
    D. FQDN of your POP3 server or IMAP server

11. In what mode of plug and play must the laptop be turned off and back on for the change to be recognized?
    A. Hot docking
    B. Warm docking
    C. Cold docking
    D. Open docking

12. What small cards have a unique number assigned to them that is used to identify the subscriber and validate the device to the mobile network?
    A. SIM
    B. SPIM
    C. vCard
    D. iMobile

13. Which of the following uses satellite information to plot the global location of an object and uses that same information to plot the route to a second location?
    A. GPS
    B. Geofencing
    C. Remote wipe
    D. Local wipe

14. Which of the following provides centralized device management for company-issued and personal mobile devices?
    A. MDM
    B. DFS
    C. PCM
    D. PS/2

15. Which is the most common PIN code when selecting discovered Bluetooth devices?
    A. 0000
    B. 5555
    C. 1111
    D. 0135

16. When setting up POP3, which of the following is the default port number to enter?
    A. 25
    B. 53
    C. 110
    D. 443

17. Which of the following storage systems monitors the data being read from the hard drive and caches the most frequently accessed bits to the high-speed flash memory?
    A. SSD
    B. HDD
    C. Hybrid drive
    D. Virtual

18. Which of the following describes the use of physical factors of authentication?
    A. Mutual authentication
    B. SSO
    C. Multifactor authentication
    D. Biometrics

Chapter 2

Networking

COMPTIA A+ 220-1201 EXAM OBJECTIVES COVERED IN THIS CHAPTER:

✔ **2.1 Compare and contrast Transmission Control Protocol (TCP) and User Datagram Protocol (UDP) ports, protocols, and their purposes**

- Ports and protocols
  - 20–21 – File Transfer Protocol (FTP)
  - 22 – Secure Shell (SSH)
  - 23 – Telnet
  - 25 – Simple Mail Transfer Protocol (SMTP)
  - 53 – Domain Name System (DNS)
  - 67/68 – Dynamic Host Configuration Protocol (DHCP)
  - 80 – Hypertext Transfer Protocol (HTTP)
  - 110 – Post Office Protocol 3 (POP3)
  - 143 – Internet Mail Access Protocol (IMAP)
  - 137–139 Network Basic Input/Output System (NetBIOS)/NetBIOS over TCP/IP (NetBT)
  - 389 – Lightweight Directory Access Protocol (LDAP)
  - 443 – Hypertext Transfer Protocol Secure (HTTPS)
  - 445 – Server Message Block (SMB)/Common Internet File System (CIFS)
  - 3389 – Remote Desktop Protocol (RDP)
- TCP vs. UDP
  - Connectionless protocols
  - Connection-oriented protocols

✔ **2.2 Explain wireless networking technologies**

- Frequencies
  - 2.4 GHz
  - 5 GHz
  - 6 GHz
- Channels
  - Regulations
  - Channel selection
    - Widths
    - Frequencies
    - Bands
- Bluetooth
- 802.11 standards
  - a
  - b
  - g
  - n
  - ac (Wi-Fi 5)
  - ax (Wi-Fi 6)
  - NFC
  - Radio-frequency identification (RFID)

✔ **2.3 Summarize services provided by networked hosts**

- Server roles
  - DNS
  - DHCP
  - Fileshare
  - Print servers
  - Mail servers
  - Syslog
  - Web servers
  - Authentication, authorization, and accounting (AAA)

- Database servers
- Network Time Protocol (NTP)
- Internet appliances
  - Spam gateways
  - Unified threat management (UTM)
  - Load balancers
  - Proxy servers
- Legacy/embedded systems
  - Supervisory control and data acquisition (SCADA)
- Internet of Things (IoT) devices
  - Thermostat
  - Light switches
  - Security cameras
  - Door locks

✔ 2.4 Explain common network configuration concepts

- DNS
  - IPv4 address (A)
  - IPv6 address (AAAA)
  - Canonical name (CNAME)
  - Mail exchanger (MX)
  - Text (TXT)
  - Name server (NS)
  - Spam management
    - DomainKeys Identified Mail (DKIM)
    - Sender Policy Framework (SPF)
    - Domain-based Message Authentication, Reporting, and Conformance (DMARC)
- DHCP
  - Leases
  - Reservations
  - Scope
  - Exclusions

- Virtual LAN (VLAN)
- Virtual private network (VPN)

✔ 2.5 Compare and contrast common networking hardware devices

- Routers
- Switches
  - Managed
  - Unmanaged
- Access points
- Patch panel
- Firewall
- Power over Ethernet (PoE)
  - Injectors
  - Switch
  - PoE standards
- Cable modem
- Digital subscriber line (DSL)
- Optical network terminal (ONT)
- Network interface card
  - Physical media access control (MAC) address

✔ 2.6 Given a scenario, configure basic wired/wireless small office/home office (SOHO) networks

- Internet Protocol (IP) addressing
  - IPv4
    - Class A
    - Class B
    - Class C
    - Private addresses
    - Public addresses
  - IPV6
- Automatic Private IP Addressing (APIPA)

- Static vs. dynamic
- Subnet mask
- Gateway

✔ **2.7 Compare and contrast Internet connection types, network types, and their characteristics**

- Internet connection types
  - Satellite
  - Fiber
  - Cable/DSL
  - Cellular
  - Wireless Internet service provider (WISP)
- Network types
  - Local area network (LAN)
  - Wide area network (WAN)
  - Personal area network (PAN)
  - Metropolitan area network (MAN)
  - Storage area network (SAN)
  - Wireless local area network (WLAN)

✔ **2.8 Explain networking tools and their purposes**

- Crimper
- Cable stripper
- Wi-Fi analyzer
- Toner probe
- Punchdown tool
- Cable tester
- Loopback plug
- Network tap

CompTIA offers a number of other exams and certifications on networking (Network+, Server+, and so on), but to become A+ certified, you must have good knowledge of basic networking skills. Not only do you need to know the basics of cabling and connectors, but you also need to know how to install and configure a wireless/wired router, apply appropriate settings, and use some basic tools. There are eight objectives for this domain.

2.1 Compare and contrast Transmission Control Protocol (TCP) and User Datagram Protocol (UDP) ports, protocols, and their purposes

Communication across a TCP/IP-based network takes place using various protocols, such as FTP to transfer files, HTTP to view web pages, and POP3 or IMAP to work with email. Each of these protocols has a default port associated with it, and CompTIA expects you to be familiar with them for this exam.

Both Transmission Control Protocol (TCP) and User Datagram Protocol (UDP) use port numbers to listen for and respond to requests for communication using various protocols. There are a number of protocols and their port numbers that you must know for this exam, as well as the differences between TCP and UDP.

Ports and protocols

There are two transport layer protocols in the TCP/IP stack. TCP provides guaranteed, connection-oriented delivery, while UDP provides nonguaranteed, connectionless delivery. Internet Protocol (IP) is the protocol that provides Layer 3 (network layer) routing for packets containing either type of transport protocol. Each protocol or service uses one of the two transport protocols (and, in some cases, both). There will be additional information later in this chapter on TCP and UDP.

TCP and UDP both use port numbers to listen for and respond to requests for communications. RFC 1060 defines *common ports* for a number of services routinely found in use, and these all have low numbers – up to 1,024. You can, however, reconfigure your service to use another port number (preferably much higher) if you're concerned about security and you don't want your site to be available to anonymous traffic.

20–21 – File Transfer Protocol (FTP)

File Transfer Protocol (FTP) is a TCP/IP protocol that permits the transferring of files between computer systems. You use a software package called an FTP client application to actually make the transfer. Because FTP has been implemented on numerous types of computer systems, files can be transferred between disparate systems (e.g. a personal computer and a minicomputer). It uses ports 20 and 21 by default. It can be configured to allow or deny access to specific IP addresses and can be configured to work with exceptions. While the protocol can be run within most browsers, a number of FTP applications are available, with FileZilla (filezilla-project.org) being one of the most popular.

It is valuable to note that FTP is not secure, and if confidentiality is required, you should use either SFTP (FTP encrypted with Secure Shell [SSH]) or FTPS (encrypted with Secure Sockets Layer [SSL]).

22 – SSH

Secure Shell (SSH) is a remote administration tool that can serve as a secure alternative to using Telnet to remotely access and configure a device like a router or switch. Although it requires a bit more setup than Telnet, SSH provides an encrypted command-line session for managing devices remotely.

23 – Telnet

Telnet is a protocol that functions at the application layer of the Open Systems Interconnection (OSI) model, providing terminal-emulation capabilities. Telnet runs on port 23 but has lost favor to SSH because Telnet sends data – including passwords – in plain-text format.

25 – SMTP

Simple Mail Transfer Protocol (SMTP) is a protocol for sending email between SMTP servers. Clients typically use either IMAP or POP to access their email server for incoming mail and use SMTP to send email. SMTP uses port 25 by default.

53 – DNS

Domain Name System (DNS) is used to translate hostnames into IP addresses. DNS is an example of a protocol that uses both UDP and TCP.

67/68 – DHCP

Dynamic Host Configuration Protocol (DHCP) serves a useful purpose of issuing IP addresses and other network-related configuration values to clients to allow them to operate on the network. It uses ports 67 and 68.

80 – HTTP

Hypertext Transfer Protocol (HTTP) is the protocol used for communication between a web server and web browser. It uses port 80 by default.

110 – POP3

The Post Office Protocol (POP) is a protocol for receiving email from a mail server. It runs on port 110. The current version of the protocol is 3 (POP3), and the alternative to it is Internet Message Access Protocol (IMAP).

137–139 – NetBIOS/NetBT

NetBIOS/NetBT is an early networking protocol that used a flat namespace, unlike the hierarchal one found in DNS. Computers register their services with the other devices and locate one another using NetBIOS names. It uses ports 137–139.

> **Definition**
>
> A *flat namespace* is one in which all items are on the same level and there is no hierarchy to the namespace, meaning there are no parent or child objects in the namespace.

143 – IMAP

IMAP is a protocol with a store-and-forward capability. It can also allow messages to be stored on an email server, instead of being downloaded to the client. The current version of the protocol is 4 (IMAP4), and the alternative to it is POP, whose current version is POP3. IMAP runs on port 143.

161/162 – SNMP

Simple Network Management Protocol (SNMP) is a protocol that facilitates network management functionality. It is not, in itself, a network management system (NMS); it is simply the protocol that makes them possible. It uses ports 161 and 162.

389 – LDAP

Lightweight Directory Access Protocol (LDAP) is a protocol that provides a mechanism to access and query directory services systems. These systems are most likely to be Microsoft's Active Directory but could also be Novell Directory Services (NDS). Although LDAP supports command-line queries executed directly against the directory database, most LDAP interactions are via utilities such as an authentication program (e.g. network logon) or a search engine that locates a resource in the directory. LDAP uses port 389.

443 – HTTPS

Hypertext Transfer Protocol over Secure Sockets Layer (HTTPS) is a protocol used to make a secure connection. It uses port 443 by default.

445 – SMB/CIFS

Server Message Block (SMB) is an application layer protocol used to provide shared access to resources. The Common Internet File System (CIFS) protocol is a dialect of SMB. It is primarily used in Windows systems. The latest version is 3.1.1, which was released to support Windows 10 and Windows Server 2016. SMB now supports Windows Server 2022. It operates as a client-server application. It uses port 445.

3389 – RDP

Remote Desktop Protocol (RDP) is used in a Windows environment to make remote desktop communications possible. It presents the user with the graphical interface of the remote device, rather than a command line as in Telnet or SSH.

TCP vs. UDP

Operating at the transport layer of the TCP/IP stack are two key protocols: TCP and UDP. The biggest difference between these two is that one is connection-based (TCP), and the other works in the absence of a dedicated connection (UDP). Both are needed and serve key roles.

If you are sending credit card information to a website, you need a dedicated connection between your host and the server, so TCP handles that task. An example of UDP is DHCP. When a client sends a request for any DHCP server listening to give it an address, the transmission is *not* directed at any specific system. It is a broadcast to all systems—one that will be answered only by DHCP servers.

Connectionless protocols

Connectionless protocols are those that use UDP as the transport protocol and therefore do not go through the establishment of a connection prior to sending data. In this section, you'll learn about two such protocols.

DHCP

Earlier in this chapter, you learned about DHCP. This protocol forgoes the overhead of TCP and gives up error recovery in the process. However, like DNS, it has its own mechanisms for recovering from errors. So, if a response is not forthcoming, the DHCP client will make multiple attempts to contact the DHCP server.

TFTP

Trivial File Transfer Protocol (TFTP) is a version of FTP that uses UDP instead of TCP and is thus called the lightweight version of FTP, as it doesn't generate the overhead from establishing a connection. It is used in any scenario where speed of the process is key. Some typical uses are:

- To transfer operating systems and images to routers and switches
- To send configuration files to IP phones

Connection-oriented protocols

Connection-oriented protocols are those that use TCP as the transport protocol and therefore do go through the establishment of a connection prior to sending data. In this section, you'll learn about two such protocols.

HTTPS

HTTP is the protocol used on the web to transmit website data between a web server and web client. With each new address that is entered into the web browser, whether from initial user entry or by clicking a link on the page displayed, a new connection is established because HTTP is a stateless protocol.

HTTP Secure (HTTPS) is the implementation of HTTP running over the Secure Sockets Layer/Transport Layer Security (SSL/TLS) protocol, which establishes a secure session using the server's digital certificate. SSL/TLS keeps the session open by using a secure channel. HTTPS websites will always include the https:// designation at the beginning.

Although it sounds very similar, Secure HTTP (S-HTTP) protects HTTP communication in a different manner. S-HTTP encrypts only a single communication message, not an entire session (or conversation). S-HTTP is not as common as HTTPS.

SSH

If you don't need access to the graphical interface and just want to operate at the command line, you have two options: Telnet and SSH. While Telnet works just fine, it transmits all the data in clear text, which obviously would be a security issue. Therefore, the connection tool of choice has become SSH. It's not as easy to set up because it encrypts all the transmissions, and that is not possible without an encryption key.

While the commands will be somewhat different based on the operating system, you must generate a key, which is produced using some unique information about the server as seed information, so that the key will be unique to the server (the encryption algorithm will be well-known). Once configured, the connection process will be similar to using Telnet, with the exception, of course, that the transmissions will be protected.

Exam essentials

Know the default ports. There are a number of protocols whose default ports you need to know: FTP (20/21), Telnet (23), SMTP (25), DNS (53), HTTP (80), POP3 (110), IMAP (143), HTTPS (443), and RDP (3389).

Know what the protocols do. In addition to the protocols for which ports are given, know what DHCP, DNS, LDAP, SNMP, and SSH do.

2.2 Explain wireless networking technologies

More often, networks are using wireless as the medium of choice. It is much easier to implement, reconfigure, upgrade, and use than wired networks. Unfortunately, there can be downsides, with security being one of the largest.

The IEEE 802.11 standard applies to wireless networking, and there have been many versions/types of it released; the main ones are a, b, g, n, ac, and ax. Encryption has gone from very weak Wired Equivalent Privacy (WEP) to much stronger with increments along the way, including Wi-Fi Protected Access (WPA), WPA2, WPA3, and implementations of Temporal Key Integrity Protocol (TKIP) and the Advanced Encryption Standard (AES).

The IEEE 802.11x family of protocols provides for wireless communications using radio frequency transmissions. The frequencies in use for 802.11 standards are the 860/900 MHz, 2.4 GHz, 3.6 GHz, 4.9 GHz, 5 GHz, and 6 GHz frequency spectrums. Several standards and bandwidths have been defined for use in wireless environments, and they aren't extremely compatible with each other.

Frequencies

Table 2.1 compares the speed, distance, and frequency of each of the 802.11 standards.

TABLE 2.1 Comparison of 802.11 standards

Standard	Speed	Distance (ft) (indoors)	Frequency (GHz)
802.11a	Up to 54 Mbps	Up to 115	5
802.11b	Up to 11 Mbps	Up to 115	2.4
802.11g	Up to 54 Mbps	Up to 125	2.4
802.11n	Up to 600 Mbps	Up to 380	2.4/5
802.11ac	Up to 6.9 Gbps	Up to 115	5
802.11ax	Up to 9.6 Gbps	230 indoors 820 outdoors	2.4/5/6

2.4 GHz

As you can see in Table 2.1, the 2.4 GHz frequency is used by 802.11b, g, n, and ax. The 2.4 GHz band can transmit over longer distances than the 5.0 or 6.0 bands but offers slower speeds due to the data modulation methods in use – the more crowded nature of the frequency and the greater susceptibility to interference from other 2.4 GHz stations.

5 GHz

The 5 GHz frequency is used by 802.11 a, n, ac, and ax. While it does not transmit as far as the 2.4 GHz band, it offers faster speeds due to the more sophisticated data modulation methods in use.

6 GHz

The 6 GHz band is used only by 802.11ax and only when the devices support Wi-Fi 6e or Wi-Fi 7 (802.11be). The 6 GHz band is from 5.925 GHz to 7.125 GHz. With the new spectrum, Wi-Fi has access 59 20-MHz channels, 29 40-MHz channels, 14 80-MHz channels, and 7 160-MHz channels.

Channels

Wireless routers can be set to use different channels, which are numbered 1 through 11 (1, 6, and 11 are those commonly used in the United States) for the 2.4 GHz band.

Each channel represents a different frequency. You can change the channel to avoid interference – either from another network nearby or from devices also using that frequency.

The channel change is made only on the router because each client should automatically detect and change to the new channel. If you locate access points (APs) close to one another, they should be on different channels to prevent them interfering with one another.

Regulations

Every country has their own set of regulations regarding the frequencies or channels that can be used for 802.11 transmission. While the focus here has thus far been on the 2.4 GHz and 5.0 GHz frequencies, they are not the only ones allowed in the United States. There are 14 channels designated in the 2.4 GHz range, which are spaced 5 MHz apart (with the exception of a 12 MHz spacing before Channel 14). As the protocol requires 25 MHz of channel separation, adjacent channels overlap and interfere with each other. Consequently, using only Channels 1, 6, 11, and 14 is recommended to avoid interference. In North America, while use of Channel 14 is not allowed, use of Channels 12 and 13 is actually allowed under low-powered conditions.

Channel selection

The channels that will be available for selection will depend on the wireless local area network (WLAN) standard in use. For example, if you are using 802.11g, the channels available will be those that lie in the 2.4 GHz frequency. Table 2.1 lists the frequencies that can be used for each standard. Each frequency can be further divided into bands or channels.

Widths

Channels or bands come in different sizes called widths. Wider bands can hold and transmit more data at a time. There are three common channel widths used in Wi-Fi networks:

- **20 MHz:** The standard width in both the 2.4 GHz and 5 GHz bands. A 20 MHz channel width provides a balance between data transfer rates and the potential for interference.
- **40 MHz:** Available in both the 2.4 GHz and 5 GHz bands. Using a 40 MHz channel width can result in higher data transfer rates compared to a 20 MHz channel, but at the cost of increased potential for interference, especially in the 2.4 GHz band.
- **80 MHz and 160 MHz:** Widths are used in the 5 GHz band and supported by more recent standards, such as 802.11ac and 802.11ax (Wi-Fi 6). These wider channels provide even faster data transfer rates and are ideal for applications that require high bandwidth, such as video streaming, online gaming, and large file transfers.

Frequencies

Channels are defined by the range of frequencies over which they operate. For example, available channels in the 2.4 GHz band in the United States are shown in Table 2.2.

Bands

There are three main frequency bands used by 802.11 WLANs. They were discussed previously in this chapter, in the section "Frequencies." Their capabilities were covered in Table 2.1.

Bluetooth

In Chapter 1, you learned about Bluetooth. Please review that section.

TABLE 2.2 GHz channel frequencies

Channel	Frequency range	Center frequency
1	2.402–2.422	2.412
2	2.407–2.427	2.417
3	2.412–2.432	2.422
4	2.417–2.437	2.427

(Continued)

TABLE 2.2 (Continued)

Channel	Frequency range	Center frequency
5	2.422–2.442	2.432
6	2.427–2.447	2.437
7	2.432–2.452	2.442
8	2.437–2.457	2.447
9	2.442–2.462	2.452
10	2.447–2.467	2.457
11	2.452–2.472	2.462
12	2.457–2.477	2.467
13	2.462–2.482	2.472

802.11 standards

There have been several amendments that apply to 802.11 technology. Each amendment describes some improvement in the design or operation of 802.11 networks. In this section, you'll learn about the major amendments.

a

The 802.11a standard provides WLAN bandwidth of up to 54 Mbps in the 5 GHz frequency spectrum. The 802.11a standard also uses orthogonal frequency-division multiplexing (OFDM) for encoding, rather than frequency-hopping spread spectrum (FHSS) or direct-sequence spread spectrum (DSSS).

b

The 802.11b standard provides for bandwidths of up to 11 Mbps (with fallback rates of 5.5, 2, and 1 Mbps) in the 2.4 GHz frequency spectrum. This standard is also called Wi-Fi, or the 802.11 high rate. The 802.11b standard uses only DSSS for data encoding.

g

The 802.11g standard operates in the 2.4 GHz frequency spectrum. This offers a maximum rate of 54 Mbps and is backward compatible with 802.11b. To achieve 54 Mbps, it also uses OFDM for encoding, rather than FHSS or DSSS.

n

The goal of the 802.11n standard is to significantly increase throughput in both the 2.4 GHz and 5 GHz frequency ranges. The standard's baseline goal was to reach speeds of 100 Mbps, but given the right conditions, it is estimated that the 802.11n speeds might be able to reach 600 Mbps. In practical operation, 802.11n speeds will be much slower.

The 802.11n standard achieves some of the higher speeds by using multiple antennas on the AP and station, a feature called multiple in/multiple out (MIMO).

ac (Wi-Fi 5)

The 802.11ac standard, or Wi-Fi 5 as it is also called, builds upon the features of 802.11n and improves on them in the following ways:

- Wider channels (e.g. 40 MHz, 80 MHz, and 160 MHz)
- New modulation (256 quadrature amplitude modulation [QAM], which has the potential to provide a 30% increase in speed)
- More spatial streams (up to eight spatial streams)
- Improved MIMO and beamforming with the use of multiuser MIMO, allowing an AP to transmit a signal to multiple client stations on the same channel simultaneously if the client stations are in different physical areas

With 802.11ac, which operates only in the 5 GHz frequency range, it is possible to achieve a data rate of almost 2 Gbps if the AP and the station have enough antennas.

ax (Wi-Fi 6)

The 802.11ax standard, or Wi-Fi 6 as it is also called, is designed to operate in license-exempt bands between 1 and 7.125 GHz, including the 2.4 and 5 GHz bands already in common use, as well as the much wider 6 GHz band (5.925–7.125 GHz in the United States).

It focuses on improving performance in high-density areas. It is estimated that it improves performance over 802.11ac by 37%. Over an entire network, however, the improvement can be up to 400%. This is accomplished by using OFDM, deploying power-control methods to avoid interference with neighboring networks, and introducing higher order 1024-QAM modulation.

NFC

You learned about near-field communications (NFC) in Chapter 1, in the section "Near-field communications (NFC)." Please review that section.

RFID

RFID is a wireless, no-contact technology that uses RF chips and readers to manage inventory, track animals, and perform many other tasks. The chips are placed on individual pieces or pallets of inventory. RFID readers are placed throughout the location to communicate with the chips. Identification and location information are collected as part of the RFID communication. Organizations can customize the information that is stored on an RFID chip to suit their needs.

RFID chips can be read only if they are within a certain proximity of the RFID reader. Different RFID systems are available for different wireless frequencies. If your organization decides to implement RFID, it is important that you fully research the advantages and disadvantages of different frequencies.

Exam essentials

Identify the frequencies used in 802.11 networks.   The frequencies in use for 802.11 standards are the 2.4 GHz and 5 GHz frequency spectrums.

Describe the characteristics of the 802.11 amendments.   These include 802.11a, 802.11b, 802.11g, 802.11n, 802.11ac, and 802.11ax.

2.3 Summarize services provided by networked hosts

To configure and provide service to a network, you must be versed in the various roles that servers may play in the network. Armed with this knowledge, you can better ensure the proper function of these servers.

Server roles

Servers are computers that provide some type of shared service to the hosts on the network. There are many roles that servers can play, but this section will discuss some of the more common server roles, focusing on those you are most likely to find in your network.

DNS

DNS servers resolve device and domain names (i.e. website names) to IP addresses and vice versa. They make it possible to connect to either without knowing the IP address of the device or of the server hosting the website. Clients are configured with the IP address of a DNS server (usually through DHCP) and make requests of the server using what are called queries. The organization's DNS server will be configured to perform the lookup of IP addresses for which it has no entry in its database, by making requests of the DNS servers on the Internet, which are organized in a hierarchy that allows these servers to more efficiently provide the answer. When they have completed their lookup, they return the IP address to the client so the client can make a direct connection using the IP address.

DHCP

DHCP servers are used to automate the process of providing an IP configuration to devices in a network. These servers respond to broadcast-based requests for a configuration by offering an IP address, a subnet mask, and a default gateway to the DHCP client. While these options provide basic network connectivity, many other options can also be provided, such as the IP address of a TFTP server that IP phones can contact to download a configuration file.

Fileshare

File servers are used to store files that can be accessed by users in a network. Typically, users are encouraged, or even required, to store any important data on these servers rather than on their local hard drives, because these servers are typically backed up on a regular basis, whereas the user machines typically are not. These servers will have significant amounts of storage space and may even have multiple hard drives configured in a redundant array of independent disks (RAID) system to provide quicker recovery from a drive crash than could be provided by recovering with the backup.

Print servers

Print servers are used to manage printers, and in cases where that is their only role, they will manage multiple printers. This type of server provides the spooler service to the printers that it manages, and when you view the print queue, you are viewing it on the print server. Many enterprise printers come with a built-in print server, which makes using a dedicated machine for the role unnecessary.

Mail servers

Mail servers run email server software and use SMTP to send and receive email on behalf of users who possess mailboxes on the server. Those users will use a client email protocol to retrieve their email from the server. Two of the most common are POP3, which is a retrieve-only protocol, and IMAP4, which has more functionality and can be used to manage the email on the server.

Syslog

All infrastructure devices, such as firewalls, routers, and switches, have logs where events of various types are recorded. These logs can contain information valuable for troubleshooting both security and performance of systems. You can direct these event messages to a central server called a syslog server. In doing so, you create a single system for access to all event logs. A syslog server also makes it easier to correlate events on various devices by combining the events into a single log. To ensure proper sequencing of events, all devices should have their time synchronized from a single source using a Network Time Protocol (NTP) server.

Web servers

Web servers are used to provide access to information for users connecting to the server using a web browser, which is the client part of the application. The browser uses HTTP as its transfer mechanism. These servers can be contained within a network and available only within the network (called an intranet server), or they can be connected to the Internet, where they can be reached from anywhere. To provide security, a web server can be configured to require and use HTTPS, which uses SSL/TLS to encrypt the connection with no effort on the part of the user.

Authentication, authorization, and accounting (AAA)

An authentication, authorization, and accounting (AAA) server is one that centralizes the authentication process, while providing the additional services of managing the authorization of rights and the accounting of all that takes place. The server accepts authentication and authorization requests that are relayed from entry devices such as access points and VPN servers, performs the process, and returns the result back to the entry devices. You will learn much more about this service later in this chapter.

Database servers

Databases have become the technology of choice for storing, organizing, and analyzing large sets of data. Users generally access a database though a client interface. As the need arises to provide access to entities outside the enterprise, the opportunities for misuse increase.

Information that resides in a database is usually stored in tables. The database tables are usually divided into columns and rows. In a table, the columns specify the information category and the data type, and the rows hold the actual information. This structure is chosen for its ease of use – it can be easily indexed, accessed, or modified.

Network Time Protocol (NTP)

As you learned earlier, in the section on syslog servers, all devices should have their time synchronized from a single source using an NTP server. These servers obtain time from a trusted source, such as an Internet clock, and keep all NTP client machines synchronized.

As you also learned earlier, this ensures that entries in the syslog server are arranged in the order in which they occurred, making analysis much easier. Many other network operations also depend on proper time synchronization, such as the following:

- File time stamps
- Directory services
- Access security and authentication
- Distributed computing
- Scheduled operations

Internet appliances

Beyond the roles that you can assign to servers by installing server software, there are network appliances that are dedicated to performing particular functions. In many cases, they perform better than a similar product that is software-based. This section will look at several of the most common ones.

Spam gateways

A spam gateway is an appliance through which all email is examined, and all spam is removed or at least segregated from non-spam items. These small rack-mounted devices are connected to the network, and email is routed through them prior to being delivered to mailboxes. Software bundled with the appliance makes managing and customizing the process to meet organizational needs easy.

Unified threat management (UTM)

Unified threat management (UTM) is an approach that involves performing multiple security functions within the same device or appliance. The functions may include the following:

- Network firewalling
- Network intrusion prevention
- Gateway antivirus
- Gateway antispam
- Virtual private network (VPN)
- Content filtering
- Load balancing
- Data leak prevention
- On-appliance reporting

UTM makes administering multiple systems unnecessary. However, some feel that UTM creates a single point of failure and instead favor creating multiple device layers as a more secure approach.

Load balancers

A form of fault tolerance that focuses more on providing high resource availability is load balancing. In load balancing, a front-end device or service receives work requests and allocates the requests to a number of back-end servers. This type of fault tolerance is recommended for applications that do not have long-running in-memory state or frequently updated data. Web servers are good candidates for load balancing. The load-balancing device or service can use several methods to allocate the work, including round robin, DNS delegation, and random.

Proxy servers

A proxy server is one that makes Internet connections on behalf of users in a network. In doing so, it prevents them from making direct connections to the Internet and provides a point of exit at which you can control their access in a variety of ways. For example, you may allow certain users to have complete access to the Internet with no restrictions, while other groups of users may be restricted to the sites they can visit and the activities in which they may participate.

An additional feature of these servers is their role in web caching. Web caching is the process of retrieving a web page for a user and then caching that web page so that another request for the page by the same users or other users can be served locally without returning to the Internet to retrieve the page. It results in faster page retrievals in cases where the page has been cached.

Legacy/embedded systems

An embedded system is a computer system with a specific function within a larger device. Embedded systems are present in many Internet-connected devices, such as Voice over Internet Protocol (VoIP) phones and routers, but they are also increasingly found in devices like home appliances and automobiles. Legacy embedded systems are those that have been handed down from one version of a system to another with no major revision.

Supervisory control and data acquisition (SCADA)

Industrial control system (ICS) is a general term that encompasses several types of control systems used in industrial production. The most widespread is supervisory control and data acquisition (SCADA). SCADA is a system operating with coded signals over communication channels so as to provide control of remote equipment. ICS includes the following components:

- **Human interface:** Such an interface presents data to the operator.
- **Programmable logic controllers (PLCs):** PLCs connect to the sensors and convert sensor data to digital data; they do not include telemetry hardware.
- **Remote Terminal Units (RTUs):** RTUs connect to the sensors and convert sensor data to digital data, including telemetry hardware.
- **Sensors:** Sensors typically have digital or analog input/output (I/O) and are not in a form that can be easily communicated over long distances.
- **Telemetry system:** Such a system connects RTUs and PLCs to control centers and the enterprise.

Internet of Things (IoT) devices

If you don't already have an Internet of Things (IoT) device in your home or office, you probably will soon. These are any devices that can be connected to the small office/home office (SOHO) network and managed from a smartphone or desktop application.

Thermostat

When IoT-enabled thermostats are installed, they connect to the local wireless network. At some point during their configuration, you will enter the service set identifier (SSID) of the network and the password or key. For example, Nest, one of the most popular systems, will display a home screen after the first time you power on the system after wiring it up. (Be sure to follow the manufacturer's directions.) The system will prompt you for language, wireless information, and other settings covering how high and how low you want the temperature to range and whether you want heat, air conditioning, or auto. When the installation is complete, install the app on your phone and follow the directions there for connecting to your thermostat.

Light switches

Lighting systems can also be IoT-enabled. Many of today's systems can be controlled by your personal assistant (e.g. Alexa, Cortana, and similar devices). Kasa is a company that makes plugs you introduce between the light and the power outlet that communicate wirelessly with your wireless network. You install a smartphone app and use that to control the light from anywhere you have the Internet.

Security cameras

Security camera systems that can be managed over the Internet are also available and use smartphone apps, much like the light switch and thermostat. These systems come with a video recorder to record video for later viewing. After the wireless cameras are physically placed and installed, they typically link up with the video system upon startup. After installing the smartphone app, you can manage and view the cameras from anywhere you have Internet. Follow the specific directions from your system to take advantage of their features.

Door locks

Smart door locks replace the manual lock system in doors and can be managed remotely. They communicate wirelessly with your network and in some cases may be part of a total package that includes security system and lights. After physical installation of the lock assembly in the doors, follow the directions in the system to install the smartphone app, connect to the doors, and manage the locks.

Exam essentials

Identify examples of Internet of Things (IoT) devices. These include thermostats, door locks, cameras, light switches, and heating and cooling systems.

Know the major roles played by servers. These include DNS, DHCP, mail, file, AAA, and print servers.

2.4 Explain common network configuration concepts

Later in this chapter, you will learn about configuring IP addressing on a system. In this section, we'll cover other common configurations and settings required to get a system up and running.

DNS

Every computer, interface, or device on a TCP/IP network is issued a unique identifier known as an IP address that resembles 192.168.12.123. Because of the Internet, TCP/IP is the most commonly used networking protocol today. You can easily see that it's difficult for most users to memorize these numbers, so hostnames are used in their place. Hostnames are alphanumeric values assigned to a host; any host may have more than one hostname.

For example, the host 192.168.12.123 may be known to all users as Gemini, or it may be known to the sales department as Gemini and to the marketing department as Apollo9. All that is needed is a means by which the alphanumeric name can be translated into its IP address. There are a number of methods of doing so, but for this exam, you need to know only one: DNS. On a large network, you can add a server to be referenced by all hosts for the name resolution. The server runs DNS and resolves a fully qualified domain name (FQDN) like www.entrepreneurshipcamp.com into its IP address. Multiple DNS servers can serve an area and provide fault tolerance for one another. In all cases, the DNS servers divide their area into zones; every zone has a primary server and any number of secondary servers. DNS works with any operating system and any version.

DNS records are organized by type. The following sections cover some of the key record types, and Table 2.3 shows DNS record types and their functions.

IPv4 address (A)

A records are also called host records and comprise the host name IPv4 address mapping.

IPv6 address (AAAA)

AAAA records are also called host records and comprise the host name IPv6 address mapping.

Canonical name (CNAME)

An alias or canonical name is a record that represents an additional hostname mapped to an IPv4 address that already has an A record mapped.

TABLE 2.3 DNS record types

Record type	Function
A	A host record that represents the mapping of a single device to an IPv4 address
AAAA	A host record that represents the mapping of a single device to an IPv6 address
CNAME	An alias record that represents an additional hostname mapped to an IPv4 address that already has an A record mapped
NS	A name server record that represents a DNS server mapped to an IPv4 address
MX	A mail exchanger record that represents an email server mapped to an IPv4 address
SOA	A start of authority record that represents a DNS server that is authoritative for a DNS namespace
TXT	Provides text information for sources outside of the DNS domain

Mail exchanger (MX)

An MX record is one that maps a mail exchanger server to an IPv4 address. This allows others to contact your DNS server for name resolution.

Text (TXT)

TXT records provide text information for sources outside of your domain. You add these records to your domain settings. You can use TXT records for various purposes. For example, some use them to verify domain ownership and to ensure email security. Let's investigate these record types more closely.

Name server (NS)

A name sever (NS) record represents a DNS server that serves a domain. While all SOA servers are NS servers, there is only one SOA server for a domain, and all others serving the domain are simply NS servers.

Spam management

TXT records can be part of the campaign to mitigate email security issues. For example, they can be used to reduce spam, which often contains attractive phishing emails.

DomainKeys Identified Mail (DKIM)

DomainKeys Identified Mail (DKIM) allows you to verify an email's source. It provides a method for validating a domain name identity that is associated with a message through cryptographic authentication. The email server verifies the domain name (called the DKIM signature) with the DNS server first, before delivering the email. DKIM works by digitally signing each email using a public-private key pair. The public key is hosted in a TXT record associated with the domain.

Sender Policy Framework (SPF)

Another possible mitigation technique is to implement a Sender Policy Framework (SPF). An SPF is an email validation system that works by using DNS to determine whether an email sent by someone has been sent by a host sanctioned by that domain's administrator. If it can't be validated, it is not delivered to the recipient's box. SPF TXT records list all the servers that are authorized to send email messages from a domain.

Domain-based Message Authentication, Reporting, and Conformance (DMARC)

Domain-based Message Authentication, Reporting, and Conformance (DMARC) is an email authentication and reporting protocol that improves email security within federal agencies. All federal agencies are required to implement this standard, which improves email security. Protocols (e.g. SPF and DKIM) authenticate emails to ensure they are coming from a valid source. DMARC TXT records can be set up once DKIM and SPF are configured. A DMARC TXT record should be stored under the title _dmarc.example.com, with example.com replaced with the actual domain name. The "value" of the record is the domain's DMARC policy.

DHCP

You learned about the function of a DHCP server earlier in this chapter. Rather than an administrator having to configure a unique IP address for every host added on a network (and default gateway and subnet mask), they can use a DHCP server to issue these values.

DHCP is built on the older Bootstrap Protocol (BOOTP) that was used to allow diskless workstations to boot and connect to a server that provided them with an operating system and applications. The client uses broadcasts to request the data and thus – normally – can't communicate with DHCP servers beyond their own subnet. (Broadcasts don't route.) A DHCP relay agent, usually installed on the router, however, can be employed to allow DHCP broadcasts to go from one network to another.

While the primary purpose of DHCP is to lease IP addresses to hosts, when it gives the IP address, it also often includes the additional configuration information: DNS server, router information, and so on.

Leases

The server takes one of the numbers it has available and leases it to the client for a length of time. If the client is still using the configuration data when 50% of the lease has expired, it requests a renewal of the lease from the server; under normal operating conditions, the request is granted. When the client is no longer using the address, the address goes back in the scope and can be issued to another client.

Reservations

While by default DHCP randomly assigns IP addresses, it is possible to reserve a dynamic IP address for a device. This is advisable when you want the device to keep the same IP address all the time, but you still want the device to participate in DHCP, so you can keep the device abreast of any changes in the address of the DNS server or the default gateway address.

Scope

The DHCP server is given a number of addresses in a range that it can supply to clients, called a scope. For example, the server may be given the IP range 192.168.12.1 to 192.168.12.200. When a client boots, it sends out a request for the server to issue it an address (and any other configuration data) from that scope.

Exclusions

In some cases, you want to prevent DHCP from issuing a particular IP address to a system. Perhaps the address has been assigned statically to a router or to a web server. IP address exclusions are used to accomplish this goal.

Virtual LAN (VLAN)

Virtual local area networks (VLANs) are logical subdivisions of a switch that segregate ports from one another as if they were in different LANs. VLANs offer another way to add a layer of separation between sensitive devices and the rest of the network. For example, if only one device should be able to connect to the finance server, the device and the finance server could be placed in a VLAN separate from the other VLANs. As traffic between VLANs can occur only through a router, access control lists (ACLs) can be used to control the traffic allowed between VLANs.

These VLANs can also span multiple switches, meaning that devices connected to switches in different parts of a network can be placed in the same VLAN, regardless of physical location.

VLANs have many advantages and few disadvantages, which are listed in Table 2.4.

Virtual private network (VPN)

VPN connections are remote access connections that allow users to securely connect to the enterprise network and work as if they were in the office. These connections use special tunneling protocols that encrypt the information being transferred between the user and the corporate network. Anywhere users, business partners, or vendors are allowed remote access to the network, VPN connections should be used.

TABLE 2.4 Advantages of VLANs

Advantages	Disadvantages
Cost: Switched networks with VLANs are less costly than routed networks, as routers cost more than switches.	Managerial overhead securing VLANs.
Performance: By creating smaller broadcast domains (each VLAN is a broadcast domain), performance improves.	
Flexibility: VLANs remove the requirement that devices in the same LAN (or in this case, VLAN) be in the same location.	
Security: VLANs provide one more layer of separation at Layer 2 and 3.	

VPN connections use an untrusted carrier network but provide protection of the information through strong authentication protocols and encryption mechanisms. While we typically use the most untrusted network – the Internet – as the classic example, and most VPNs do travel through the Internet, a VPN can be used with interior networks as well whenever traffic needs to be protected from prying eyes.

In VPN operations, entire protocols wrap around other protocols when this process occurs. They include the following:

- A LAN protocol (required)
- A remote access or line protocol (required)
- An authentication protocol (optional)
- An encryption protocol (optional)

A device that terminates multiple VPN connections is called a VPN concentrator. VPN concentrators incorporate the most advanced encryption and authentication techniques available.

VPN connections can be used to provide remote access to teleworkers or traveling users (called remote-access VPNs) and can also be used to securely connect two locations (called site-to-site VPNs). The implementation process is conceptually different for these two. In the former, the tunnel that is created has as its endpoints the user's computer and the VPN concentrator. In this case, only traffic traveling from the user computer to the VPN concentrator uses this tunnel.

In the case of two office locations, the tunnel endpoints are the two VPN routers, one in each office. With this configuration, all traffic that goes between the offices will use the tunnel, regardless of the source or destination. The endpoints are defined during the creation of the VPN connection and thus must be set correctly according to the type of remote access link being used.

Exam essentials

Know the capabilities and limitations of VLANs. VLANs are logical subdivisions of a switch that segregate ports from one another as if they were in different LANs. VLANs offer another way to add a layer of separation between sensitive devices and the rest of the network.

Know the requirements to create a VPN link. Requirements and optional components include:

- A LAN protocol (required)
- A remote access or line protocol (required)
- An authentication protocol (optional)
- An encryption protocol (optional)

2.5 Compare and contrast common networking hardware devices

To make a network, you need a number of devices. The most common of those devices are tested on the A+ exam and discussed in this section. Networks are built using multiple devices. For those covered in this section, you should know enough to be able to answer questions on the exam about their functions and features.

Routers

A router is used to connect LANs; you can even use a router to connect dissimilar topologies that use the same protocol, because physical specifications don't apply. A router can be a dedicated hardware device or a computer system with more than one network interface and the appropriate routing software. All modern network operating systems include the functionality to act as a router.

Switches

Like routers, switches are the connectivity points of an Ethernet network. Devices connect to switches via twisted-pair cabling, one cable for each device. The difference between hubs and switches is in how the devices deal with the data they receive. Whereas a hub forwards the data it receives to all the ports on the device, a switch forwards it to only the port that connects to the destination device. It does this by learning the media access control (MAC) address of the devices attached to it and then matching the destination MAC address in the data it receives.

Managed

Managed switches are those used in an enterprise network. These switches can be configured with advanced features such as VLANs, discussed under Objective 2.6 later in this chapter, and EtherChannel links. They are managed remotely, using either a command-line interface or in some cases a GUI management interface.

Unmanaged

Unmanaged switches are those that cannot be managed remotely, and while they can provide basic switching services (e.g. full duplex service and the like), they cannot be configured with the more advanced services of a managed switch.

Access points

Access points (APs) are transmitter and receiver (transceiver) devices used to create a wireless LAN (WLAN). An AP is typically a separate network device with a built-in antenna, transmitter, and adapter. APs use the wireless infrastructure network mode to provide a connection point between WLANs and a wired Ethernet LAN. APs also typically have several ports, giving you a way to expand the network to support additional clients.

Depending on the network's size, one or more APs might be required. Additional APs are used to allow access to more wireless clients and to expand the range of the wireless network. Each AP is limited by a transmission range – the distance a client can be from an AP and still obtain a usable signal. The actual distance depends on the wireless standard being used and the obstructions and environmental conditions between the client and the AP.

Patch panel

A patch panel a device to which the cables running through the walls from the hosts are connected. Then shorter cables called *patch cables* run from the patch panel to the switch or hub. Figure 2.1 shows three types of patch panels.

Firewall

A firewall is a server that sits between the internal network and the rest of the world (or between a public and a private network) and filters what goes between the two. While the filtering can be done on programs, most filtering is performed on ports because applications and protocols use ports that are recognized. Open ports are those that allow traffic, whereas closed ports are those that block traffic. The firewall can be software- or hardware-based, and most incorporate both. The firewall may incorporate a proxy, a gateway, and a filter.

Power over Ethernet (POE)

Many times, when installing devices, the device needs to be located far from an available power outlet. On switches that support Power over Ethernet (PoE), the switch can supply power using an adjacent pair of wires in the same data cable used to connect to the device. So, if you get the device within 100 m of a switch, you can eliminate the need to install costly power outlets.

Injectors

A PoE injector is a device that can be used to provide PoE to a device when the switch does not support PoE. It plugs into the wall, then a line providing data and PoE is run to the device, and another cable runs to the switch, as shown in Figure 2.2.

FIGURE 2.1 Patch panels

(JPE004F) Patch panel type A

(JPE005F) Patch panel type B

(JPE006F) Patch panel type C

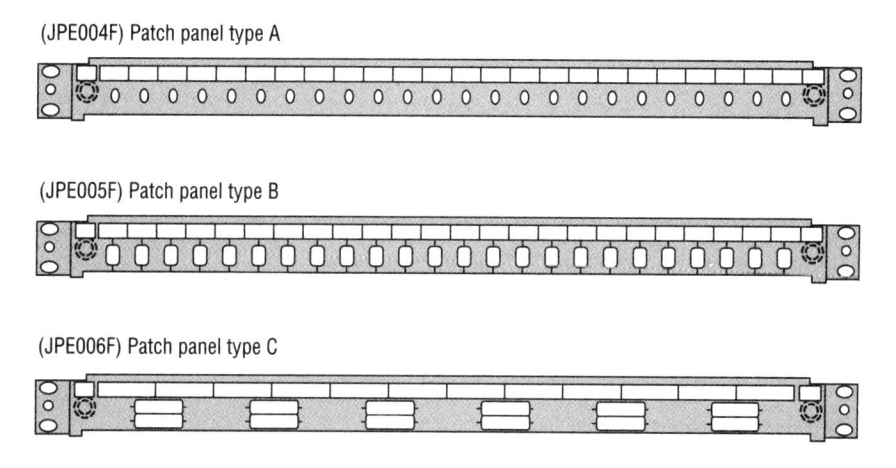

FIGURE 2.2 Power over Ethernet (PoE)

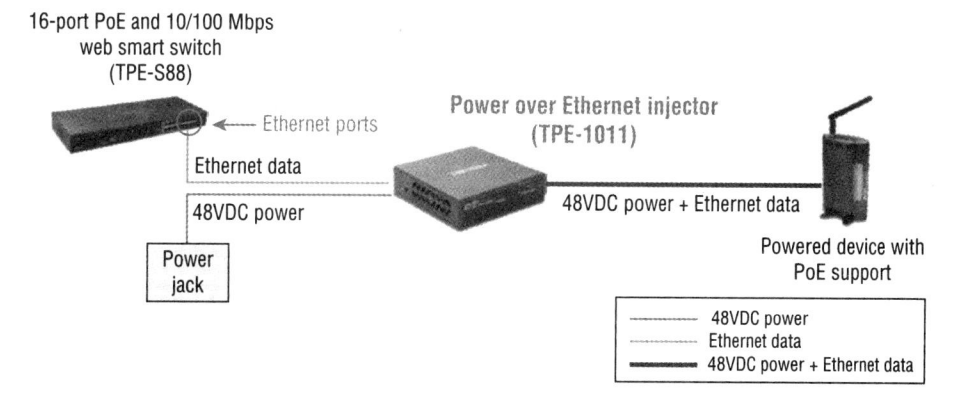

Switch

Enterprise-grade switches, such as Cisco switches, can also come equipped with PoE ports. These ports can be set to provide power to the devices connected.

PoE standards

There have been a number of standards created for providing power over a data cable. These standards differ in several ways:

- Minimum power per port provided to the device
- Maximum power per port provided by the power-sourcing device
- Required cable category
- Power over which wire pairs
- Released date

The standards and their characteristics are shown in Table 2.5.

Cable modem

A modem, short for modulator/demodulator, is a device that converts the digital signals generated by a computer into analog signals that can travel over conventional phone lines. The modem at the receiving end converts the signal back into a format that the computer can understand. Modems can be used to connect to an ISP or as a mechanism for dialing up a LAN.

TABLE 2.5 PoE standards

Type	Standard	PD min. power per port (W)	PSE max. power per port (W)	Cable category	Power over pairs	Released
Type 1	IEEE 802.3af	12.95	15.4	Cat5e	2 pairs	2003
Type 2	IEEE 802.3at	25	30	Cat5e	2 pairs	2009
Type 3	IEEE 802.3bt	51–60	60	Cat5e	2 or 4 pairs class 0–4, 4 pairs class 5–6	2018
Type 4	IEEE 802.3bt	71–90	100	Cat5e	4 pairs class 7–8	2018

Digital subscriber line (DSL)

Digital subscriber line (DSL) uses existing phone lines with a DSL modem and a network card. A standard RJ-45 connector is used to connect the network card to the DSL modem, and a phone cord with RJ-11 connectors is used to connect the DSL modem to the phone jack. Multiple types of DSL exist; the most popular are high bit-rate DSL (HDSL), symmetric DSL (SDSL), very high bit-rate DSL (VHDSL), rate-adaptive DSL (RADSL), and asymmetric DSL (ADSL). The latter provides slower upload than download speed and is the most common for home use.

Optical network terminal (ONT)

In the same way that a cable modem provides Internet access from an Ethernet network, optical network terminals (ONTs) provide Internet access from a fiber network. It can be provided by an ISP. The positioning of the ONT is shown in Figure 2.3. In the fiber line running to a multidwelling unit, each unit will have a splitter, such as the one in the fiber line running to a single-family home that splits the data signal from the phone line.

Network interface card

Network interface cards (NICs) are expansion cards that are installed into slots in a desktop computer and connect the computer to a network. In most cases today, devices large and small have integrated or built-in network interfaces.

FIGURE 2.3   Optical network terminal (ONT)

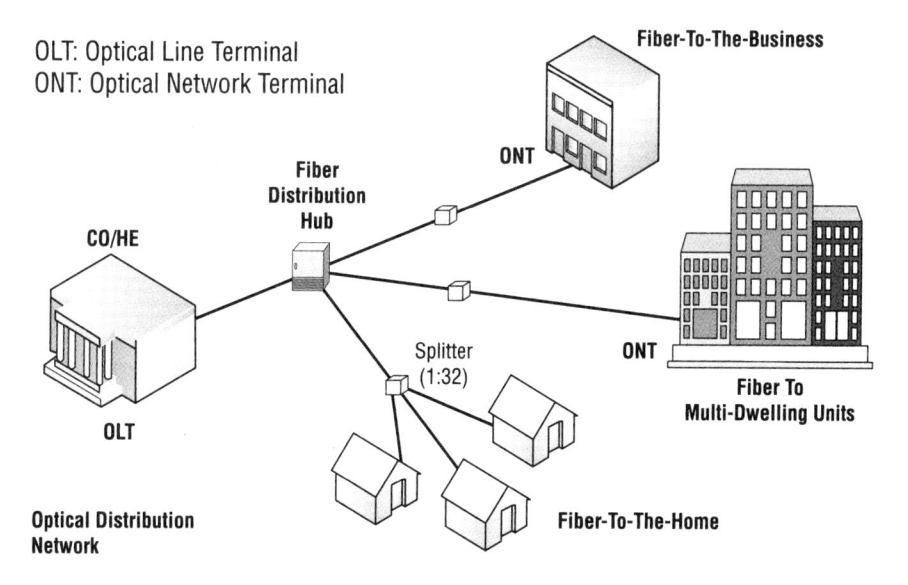

Physical media access control (MAC) address

Both network interface cards and integrated network interfaces possess a physical address (sometimes called a burned-in address because it is installed at the factory). Earlier in this chapter, you learned that switches populate the MAC address table with these addresses and rely on the table to send *only* frames (yes, they are called frames at Layer 2) addressed to a MAC address to the port where that address resides.

They are also called physical addresses because these 48-bit addresses expressed in hexadecimal are permanently assigned to the network interfaces of devices. Here is an example of a MAC address: 01:23:45:67:89:ab

As a packet is transferred across a network at every router hop and then again when it arrives at the destination network, the source and destination MAC addresses change. Address Resolution Protocol (ARP) resolves the next hop address to a MAC address using a process called the ARP broadcast. MAC addresses are unique. This comes from the fact that each manufacturer has a different set of values assigned to it at the beginning of the address called the organizationally unique identifier (OUI). Each manufacturer ensures that it assigns no duplicate within its OUI. The OUI is the first three bytes of the MAC address.

Exam essentials

Know the two types of switches.   Switches can be managed or unmanaged. Managed switches can be configured with advanced features such as VLANs.

Be able to recognize a firewall.   A firewall is a server that sits between the internal network and the rest of the world and filters what goes between the two.

2.6 Given a scenario, configure basic wired/wireless small office/home office (SOHO) networks

The protocol of the Internet is TCP/IP, and because of this, TCP/IP has become the de facto protocol of most networks as well. Far from the only networking protocol available, TCP/IP meets the needs of most organizations and is becoming more and more the one protocol suite that administrators must understand in order to do their jobs. In this section, we'll cover the common configurations and settings required to get TCP/IP up and running.

Internet Protocol (IP) addressing

A host is any machine or interface that participates in a TCP/IP network – whether as a client or as a server. Every interface on a TCP/IP network that must be issued an IP address is considered a host. Those addresses can be manually entered or provided dynamically to the host by a DHCP server. (If IPv4 is in use, the addresses fall into three classes – A, B, and C.) The other values needed, besides the IP address, are the subnet mask (identifying the scope of the network on which the host resides) and the default gateway (the router interfacing with the outside world). A default gateway is the address of the local router and serves as the gateway to other networks. Because memorizing complex numerical addresses can be difficult to do, DNS is used to translate hostnames into IP addresses as needed. In this section, you'll learn about both IPv4 and IPv6 IP addressing.

IPv4

Although there is no official IP class objective, it is helpful to understand IP classes in the real world, and knowing about them also enriches your understanding of various CompTIA objectives.

IPv4 addresses (IPv6 is discussed later) are 32-bit binary numbers. Because numbers of such magnitude are difficult to work with, they're divided into four octets (8 bits) and converted to decimal. Thus, 01010101 becomes 85. This is important because the limits on the size of the decimal number exist because they are representations of binary numbers. The range must be from 0 (00000000) to 255 (11111111) per octet, making the lowest possible IP address 0.0.0.0 and the highest 255.255.255.255. Many IP addresses aren't available because they're reserved for diagnostic purposes, private addressing, or some other function.

Three classes of IP addresses are available for assignment to hosts; they're identified by the first octet. Table 2.6 shows the class, and the range the first octet must fall into to be within that class. The entire 127.0.0.0 network is missing because that network has been set aside or reserved for diagnostics.

TABLE 2.6   IP address classes

Class	Range
A	1–126
B	128–191
C	192–223

> **Note:** Five classes exist. Class D (multicast) and Class E (experimental) are not assigned to hosts.

Class A

If you're given a Class A address, then you're assigned a number such as 125. With a few exceptions, this means you can use any number between 0 and 255 in the second octet, any number between 0 and 255 in the third octet, and any number between 0 and 255 in the fourth octet. This gives you a total number of hosts that you can have on your network in excess of 16 million. The default subnet mask is 255.0.0.0.

Class B

If you're given a Class B address, then you're assigned a number such as 152.119. With a few exceptions, this means you can use any number between 0 and 255 in the third octet and any number between 0 and 255 in the fourth octet. This gives you a total number of hosts that you can have on your network in excess of 65,000. The default subnet mask is 255.255.0.0.

Class C

If you're given a Class C address, then you're assigned a number such as 205.19.15. You can use any number between 1 and 254 in the fourth octet for a total of 254 possible hosts (0 and 255 are reserved). The default subnet mask is 255.255.255.0.

The class, therefore, makes a tremendous difference in the number of hosts your network can have. In most cases, the odds of having all hosts at one location are small. Assuming you have a Class B address, will there be 65,000 hosts in one room, or will they be in several locations? Most often, it's the latter.

Private addresses

Within each of the three major classes of IP addresses, there is a range set aside for private addresses. These are addresses that do not communicate directly with the Internet (often using a proxy server or network address translation to do so), so each host's address needs to be unique only within the realm of that network. Table 2.7 lists the private address ranges for Class A, B, and C addresses.

TABLE 2.7 Private address ranges

Class	Range
A	10.0.0.0 to 10.255.255.255
B	172.16.0.0 to 172.31.255.255
C	192.168.0.0 to 192.168.255.255

Public addresses

Public addresses are those that are allowed to be routed to the Internet. These addresses must be obtained from the Network Information Center (NIC) or the Internet Assigned Numbers Authority (IANA). Issuance by a central body ensures there are no duplicates. These addresses come from the ranges depicted in Table 2.8.

IPv4 configuration

If you're not using DHCP on the router/switch, you'll have to configure the IP addresses of the computers manually. When you do this, ensure the following:

- Each wired interface needs to have an IP address in the same network, with the address of the router Ethernet address. Also, the default gateway needs to be set to the address of the router. Finally, configure the IP address of the DNS server so name resolution can occur.
- Each wireless interface needs to have an IP address in the same network with the address of the router/switch wireless interface. Also, the default gateway needs to be set to that same address. Finally, configure the IP address of the DNS server so that name resolution can occur.

Note, the requirements are the same for wired and wireless interfaces.

NIC configuration

The end user device will need to have the network interface, either wired or wireless, configured to operate on the network. The most common configuration dialog box is that in Windows 11, shown in Figure 2.4. Other operating systems are quite similar.

TABLE 2.8 Public IP addresses

Class	Public IP ranges
Class A	1.0.0.0 to 9.255.255.255 11.0.0.0 to 126.255.255.255
Class B	128.0.0.0 to 169.253.255.255 169.255.0.0 to 172.15.255.255 172.32.0.0 to 191.255.255.255
Class C	192.0.0.0 to 192.167.255.255 192.169.0.0 to 223.255.255.255
Class D	224.0.0.0 to 239.255.255.255 Multicast addresses
Class E	240.0.0.0 to 255.255.255.254 Experimental use

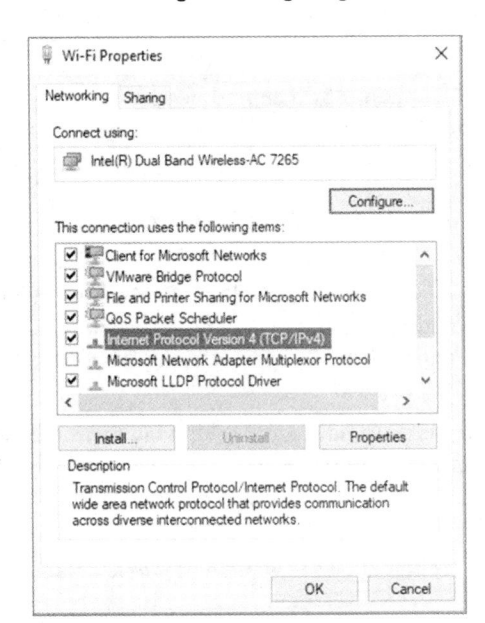

FIGURE 2.4   The Windows 11 dialog for configuring a NIC

Wired

As a representative procedure, you would take the following steps to configure a NIC in Windows 11:

1. Start by navigating to Control Panel > Network and Internet > Network And Sharing Center > Change Adapter Settings.
2. Right-click the interface you would like to configure and select Properties. You will see the dialog box in Figure 2.4.
3. Highlight Internet Protocol Version 4 and select Properties. You will see the dialog box in Figure 2.5.
4. If using a DHCP server, leave both selections as shown in Figure 2.5 to obtain IP and DNS server addresses automatically.
5. If using static IP addressing, select the radio button Use the Following IP Address and enter the IP address, subnet mask, and default gateway. The gateway address should be the IP address of the router.
6. In the bottom section, select Use the Following DNS Server Address and enter the IP address of the DNS server. In a SOHO, this will probably be the address of the router/switch.
7. Click OK on all dialog boxes as you close them.

FIGURE 2.5 TCP/IP Properties dialog box

Wireless

Configuring the IP configuration on the wireless NIC will be the same as just described for the wired NIC.

IPv6

IPv4 uses a 32-bit addressing scheme that provides for more than 4 billion unique addresses. Unfortunately, there are a lot of IP-enabled devices added to the Internet every day—not to mention, not all of the addresses that can be created are used by public networks. (Many are reserved in classes D and above and are unavailable for public use.) This reduces the number of addresses that can be allocated as public Internet addresses.

IPv6 offers a number of improvements, the most notable of which is its ability to handle growth in public networks. IPv6 uses a 128-bit addressing scheme, allowing a huge number of possible addresses: 340, 282, 366, 920, 938, 463, 463, 374, 607, 431, 768, 211, and 456. Table 2.9 compares IPv4 to IPv6.

> **NOTE** In IPv6 addresses, repeating zeros can be left out so that colons next to each other in the address indicate one or more sets of zeros for that section.

Automatic Private IP Addressing (APIPA)

Within each of the three major classes of IP addresses, there is a range set aside for private addresses. These are addresses that do not communicate directly with the Internet (often using a proxy server or network address translation to do so), so each host's address needs to be unique only within the realm of that network. Table 2.10 lists the private address ranges for Class A, B, and C addresses.

Automatic Private IP Addressing (APIPA) is a TCP/IP feature Microsoft added to its operating systems. If a DHCP server cannot be found and the clients are configured to obtain IP addresses automatically, the clients automatically assign themselves an IP address, somewhat randomly, in the 169.254.*x.x* range with a subnet mask of 255.255.0.0. This allows them to communicate with other hosts that have similarly configured themselves, but they are unable to connect to the Internet. If a computer is using an APIPA address, it will have trouble communicating with other clients if those clients do not use APIPA addresses.

Classless Inter-Domain Routing (CIDR) notation is another way to represent the IP address and the subnet mask. The number of bits in the mask is shown after the address and preceded by a slash. For example, the address 192.168.5.5 with a mask of 255.255.255.0 can be written 192.168.5.5/24.

TABLE 2.9 IPv4 vs. IPv6

Feature	IPv4	IPv6
Loopback address	127.0.0.1	0:0:0:0:0:0:0:1 (::1)
Private ranges	10.0.0.0 172.16.0.0 to 172.31.0.0 192.168.0.0	FEC0:: (proposed)
Autoconfigured addresses	169.254.0.0	FE80::

TABLE 2.10 Private address ranges

Class	Range
A	10.0.0.0 to 10.255.255.255
B	172.16.0.0 to 172.31.255.255
C	192.168.0.0 to 192.168.255.255

Static vs. dynamic

The two methods of entering address information for a host are static and dynamic. Static means that you manually enter the information for the host and that it does not change. Dynamic means that DHCP is used for the host to lease information from.

While DHCP can be a godsend, a SOHO network is small enough that you can get by without it issuing IP addresses to each host. The advantage to assigning the IP addresses statically is that you can make certain which host is associated with which IP address and then utilize filtering to limit network access to only those hosts.

While static IP addressing may not be scalable in a wired network with many devices, in a small network, using static IP addressing will make it impossible for someone to just plug into your network without knowing your IP address scheme.

Subnet mask

Subnetting your network is the process of taking the total number of hosts available to you and dividing them into smaller networks. When you configure TCP/IP on a host, you typically need give only three values: a unique IP address, a default gateway (router) address, and a subnet mask. Table 2.11 shows the default subnet mask for each class of network.

> **NOTE** Purists may argue that you don't need a default gateway. Technically this is true if your network is small, and you don't communicate beyond it. For all practical purposes, though, most networks need a default gateway.

When you use the default subnet mask, you're allowing for all hosts to be at one site and not subdividing your network. This is called *classful* subnetting. Any deviation from the default signifies that you're dividing the network into multiple subnetworks, which is called *classless* subnetting.

TABLE 2.11 Default subnet values

Class	Default subnet mask
A	255.0.0.0
B	255.255.0.0
C	255.255.255.0

The problem with classful subnetting is that it allows for only three sizes of networks: Class A (16,777,216 hosts), Class B (65,536 hosts), and Class C (254 hosts). Two of these are too large to operate efficiently in the real world, and when enterprises were issued public network IDs that were larger than they needed, many public IP addresses were wasted. For this reason and simply to allow for the creation of smaller networks that operate better, the concept of classless routing, or CIDR, was born.

Using CIDR, administrators can create smaller networks called *subnets* by manipulating the subnet mask of a larger classless or major network ID. This allows you to create a subnet that is much closer in size to what you need, thus wasting fewer IP addresses and improving performance in each subnet as a result of the reduced broadcast traffic generated in each subnet.

CIDR notation is another way to represent the IP address and the subnet mask. The number of bits in the mask is shown after the address and preceded by a slash. For example, the address 192.168.5.5 with a mask of 255.255.255.0 can be written 192.168.5.5/24.

A gateway can have two meanings. In TCP/IP, a gateway is the address of the machine to send data to that is not intended for a host on the network (in other words, a default gateway). A gateway is also a physical device operating between the transport and application layers of the OSI model that can send data between dissimilar systems. The best example of the latter is a mail gateway – it doesn't matter which two networks are communicating; the gateway allows them to exchange email.

Gateway

A gateway, as it is tested on the exam, is the server (i.e. router) that allows traffic beyond the internal network. Hosts are configured with the address of a gateway (called the default gateway), and if they need to correspond with a host outside the internal network, the data is sent to the gateway to facilitate this correspondence. When you configure TCP/IP on a host, one of the fields that should be provided is a gateway field, which specifies where data not intended for this network is sent in order to be able to communicate with the rest of the world.

Exam essentials

Identify the private IP address ranges in IPv4. The three ranges are 10.0.0.0 to 10.255.255.255, 172.16.0.0 to 172.31.255.255, and 192.168.0.0 to 192.168.255.255.

Describe the purpose of a default gateway. A gateway, as it is tested on the exam, is the server (router) that allows traffic beyond the internal network. Hosts are configured with the address of a gateway (called the default gateway), and if they need to correspond with a host outside the internal network, the data is sent to the gateway to facilitate it.

2.7 Compare and contrast internet connection types, network types, and their characteristics

Your network can connect to the Internet in a number of ways. These can range from a slow dial-up connection, which is established only when you need it to be established, to a high-speed fiber connection that is always on. This section looks at many of the options available and all that you need to know for this objective on the A+ exam.

Internet connection types

When discussing ways to connect to the Internet, most of the focus is on broadband network techniques. It is imperative that you understand the various types of networks, including broadband. The sections that follow will focus on the key issues associated with connecting to the Internet.

Satellite

Whereas the other broadband technologies discussed require the use of physical wiring, with satellite broadband the service provider sends a microwave signal from a dish to an orbiting satellite and back. One satellite can service many receivers, so this is commonly known as point-to-multipoint technology. As a general rule, satellite connections are slower than the other broadband technologies you need to know for the exam, and they are adversely affected by weather and atmospheric conditions.

> **Note:** With satellite, download speed is much faster than upload speed.

Fiber

Fiber optic cabling provides excellent speed and bandwidth but is expensive. Not only are the cables that you use costly, but the light-emitting/receiving hardware costs also make this an expensive undertaking. Because of the cost involved, fiber is often an option for businesses only when it comes to broadband access.

Fiber to the Home (FTTH) is an attempt some communities are undertaking to offer high-speed connectivity to residential dwellings as well. Verizon's fiber optic service (Fios), a similar implementation, runs single-mode optical fiber to homes and includes phone and television service along with Internet access.

Cable/DSL

Two of the most popular methods of connecting to the Internet today are using DSL and cable. DSL and cable were covered earlier in this chapter.

Cellular

Smartphones have made cellular networking popular, though they are not the only devices capable of using networking; for example, a cellular modem can also be quickly added to a laptop. Cellular networking was covered in Chapter 1.

Wireless Internet service provider (WISP)

Wireless Internet service providers (WISPs) provide Internet access to regions where running cables is not cost effective, as in mountainous areas. Some use 802.11 standards, while others use proprietary technologies.

Network types

You should know the terminology used for networking as well as the major topologies that are available. Networks consist of servers and clients. A server is a dedicated machine offering services such as file and print sharing. A client is any individual workstation accessing the network. A workstation is a client machine that accesses services elsewhere (normally from a server).

Networks differ in size and scope. The size of the network on which servers and clients operate can range significantly.

Local area network (LAN)

A LAN is a network that is geographically confined within a small space – a room, a building, and so on. Because it's confined and does not have to span a great distance, it can normally offer higher speeds.

With Ethernet, you can often use the network type to compute the required length and speed of your cabling. For example, 100Base-T tells you three things:

- **100:** The speed of the network, or 100 Mbps
- **Base:** The technology used (either baseband or broadband)
- **T:** Twisted-pair cabling; in the case of 100Base-T, it's generally unshielded twisted pair (UTP)

When you configure a network, one of the first places to turn your attention is the routers and access points – they are the hardware components on which network access can rely. Because it must always be possible to find these devices, I suggest that you not use DHCP to issue them addresses but instead configure their addresses statically.

To increase security, devices should be placed behind a firewall, and you should always change the administrative username and password that comes preconfigured with these devices to ones that adhere to stringent password policies (i.e. a mixture of uppercase and lowercase alphabet, numbers, and special characters), and you should keep the firmware updated.

With wireless access points, you should change the SSID from its default value (if one is preconfigured) and disable broadcasts. MAC filtering can be used on a wireless network, for example, to prevent certain clients from accessing the Internet. You can choose to deny service to a set list of MAC addresses (and allow all others) or allow service only to a set of MAC addresses (and deny all others).

Wide area network (WAN)

A wide area network (WAN) is a collection of two or more LANs that are typically connected by routers and dedicated leased lines (not to mention complicated implementations). The geographic limitation is removed, but WAN speeds are traditionally less than LAN speeds.

Personal area network (PAN)

A personal area network (PAN) is a LAN created by personal devices. Often, personal devices include networking capabilities and can communicate directly with one another. Wireless technologies have introduced a new term: wireless personal area network (WPAN). This refers to the technologies involved in connecting devices in close proximity to exchange data or resources. An example is connecting a laptop with a personal digital assistant (PDA) to synchronize an address book. Because of their small size and the nature of the data exchange, WPAN devices lend themselves well to ad hoc wireless networking. Ad hoc wireless networks are those that have devices connect to each other directly, not through a wireless access point.

Metropolitan area network (MAN)

Occasionally, a WAN will be described as a metropolitan area network (MAN) when it is confined to a certain geographic area, such as a university campus or city. No formal guidelines dictate the differences between a MAN and a WAN; technically, a MAN is a WAN. Perhaps for this reason, the term MAN is used less frequently than WAN. If any distinction exists, it's that a MAN is smaller than a WAN. A MAN is almost always bigger than a LAN and usually is smaller than or equal to a WAN. MANs utilize an ISP or telecommunications (telco) provider.

Storage area network (SAN)

Storage area networks (SANs) are comprised of high-capacity storage devices that are connected by a high-speed private network (separate from the LAN) using storage-specific switches. This storage information architecture addresses the collection, management, and use of data. In a SAN, only devices that can use the fiber channel Small Computer System Interface (SCSI) network can access the data, so it is typically done though a server.

Wireless local area network (WLAN)

A WLAN is simply a wireless network that uses one of the 802.11 standards. The use of 802.11 was discussed earlier in this chapter.

Exam essentials

Differentiate the types of networks.   These include local area networks (LANs), wide area networks (WANs), personal area networks (PANs), metropolitan area networks (MANs), storage area networks (SANs), and wireless local area networks (WLANs).

Describe Internet connection types.   These include satellite, fiber, cable, DSL, cellular, and WISPs.

2.8 Explain networking tools and their purposes

To create a network and solve problems with it, you need a toolbox. While some of the tools you use will be in software form, many others are hardware, and those are the focus of this objective.

No networking administrators worth their pay would try to troubleshoot a problem without a set of tools. The tools that should be readily on hand include a crimper for fixing connectors, a multimeter for checking signals, a toner probe to find breaks in a cable, a cable tester, a loopback plug, and a punchdown tool, among others.

Crimper

Wire crimpers look like pliers but are used to attach media connectors to the ends of cables. For instance, you use one type of wire crimper to attach RJ-45 connectors on an unshielded twisted pair (UTP) cable. You use a different type of wire crimper to attach a Bayonet Neill-Concelman (BNC) connector to coaxial cabling.

Cable stripper

A cable stripper is used to remove the cable's outer covering to get to the wire pairs within. You place the end of the cable in the mouth of the device, close the mouth, and then circle the cable, cutting away the outer sheath without damaging the wire pairs within. Figure 2.6 shows a cable stripper.

FIGURE 2.6 Cable stripper

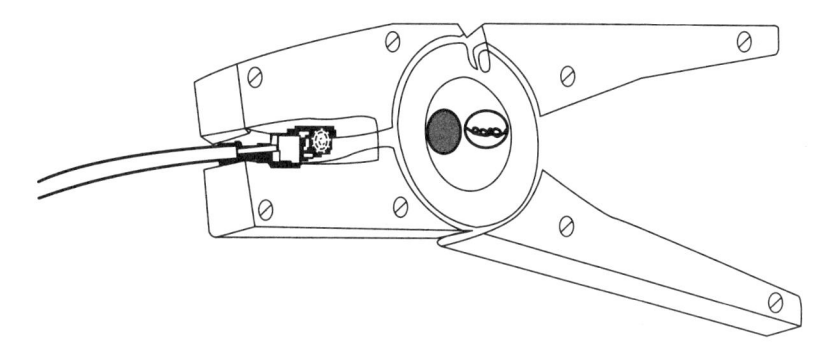

Wi-Fi analyzer

A Wi-Fi analyzer is a tool that gathers information of all sorts about the RF medium in the area. These may be handheld hardware devices or software that is installed on a laptop and uses the wireless card in the laptop to gather information. These analyzers vary widely in what type of information they are capable of generating and their price points.

The following are among the functions that these analyzers offer:

- Noise and inference detection and location
- Channel information
- Signal strength
- List of APs in the area

Toner probe

A toner probe has two parts: the tone generator (called the toner) and the tone locator (called the probe). The toner sends the tone, and at the other end of the cable the probe receives the toner's signal. This tool makes it easier to find the beginning and end of a cable.

The purpose of the toner probe is to generate a signal that is transmitted on the wire you are attempting to locate. At the other end, you press the probe against individual wires. When it makes contact with the wire that has the signal on it, the locator emits an audible signal or tone.

> **NOTE** A toner probe can be used to find breaks in a cable. It converts electrical signals into audible sound, and by moving the device down the cable, one will hear a drop in the sound where the break is located.

Punchdown tool

Punchdown tools are used to attach twisted-pair network cables to connectors within a patch panel. Specifically, they connect twisted-pair wires to the insulation displacement connector (IDC).

Cable tester

Cable testers (sometimes called media testers) are used to verify that the cable you are using is good. Commonly used with network cabling, they enable you to perform many of the same tests as a multimeter does. Any tool that facilitates the testing of a cable can be deemed a cable tester, but a media tester allows administrators to test a segment of cable, looking for shorts, improperly attached connectors, or other cable faults. All media testers have a way of telling you whether the cable is working correctly and where the problem in the cable might be.

Loopback plug

Also called wrap plugs, loopback plugs take the signal going out and essentially echo it back. This allows you to test ports to make certain they're working correctly.

> To simply test an implementation of TCP/IP on a host, you can always use the loopback address of 127.0.0.1. This is often used with ping (discussed in Chapter 6, "Operating Systems").

Network tap

A network tap is a hardware device with (at least) three ports: an input port, an output port, and a monitor port. The tap is inserted between the input and output ports and passes all traffic (i.e. send and receive data streams) through unimpeded in real time but also copies that same data to its monitor port, enabling you to capture all traffic for inspection. The copied traffic can then be directed from the network tap to security devices, such as an intrusion prevention system (.), for examination.

Exam essentials

Know the tools for working with networks. A good administrator's toolbox will include wire crimpers, a multimeter, a toner probe, a cable tester, loopback plugs, and a punchdown tool.

Know the two parts of a toner probe. A toner probe has two parts: the tone generator (the toner) and the tone locator (the probe).

Review Questions

You can find the answers in the appendix.

1. Which of the following uses port 110?
   A. FTP
   B. SSH
   C. Telnet
   D. POP3

2. Which of the following uses two ports?
   A. FTP
   B. SSH
   C. Telnet
   D. POP3

3. Which of the following uses port 22?
   A. FTP
   B. SSH
   C. Telnet
   D. POP3

4. Which device operates at layer 2?
   A. Router
   B. Switch
   C. Repeater
   D. Hub

5. Which device operates at layer 1?
   A. Router
   B. Switch
   C. Bridge
   D. Hub

6. Which device operates at layer 2?
   A. Router
   B. Switch
   C. Repeater
   D. Hub

7. Which of the following is *not* a private IP address range?
   A. 10.0.0.0–10.255.255.255
   B. 172.16.0.0–172.16.255.255
   C. 192.168.0.0–192.168.255.255
   D. 192.168.5.5–192.168.255.255

8. Which of the following delivers an upload speed equal to the download speed?
   A. SDSL
   B. VDSL
   C. VHDSL
   D. RADSL

9. Which of the following is a system operating with coded signals over communication channels so as to provide control of remote equipment?
   A. NAT
   B. ICS
   C. SCADA
   D. IPS

10. Which of the following operates in the 5.0 GHz range?
    A. 802.11a
    B. 802.11b
    C. 802.11g
    D. 802.11

11. Which of the following operates at a maximum of 2 Mbps?
    A. 802.11a
    B. 802.11b
    C. 802.11g
    D. 802.11

12. Which of the following has the largest cell size?
    A. 802.11a
    B. 802.11b
    C. 802.11g
    D. 802.11

13. Which type of server resolves IP addresses to hostnames?
    A. HTTP
    B. DNS
    C. DHCP
    D. SQL

14. Which type of server provides automatic IP configurations?
    A. HTTP
    B. DNS
    C. DHCP
    D. SQL

15. Which type of server is used to store system messages and errors from multiple devices?
    A. HTTP
    B. DNS
    C. DHCP
    D. Syslog

16. Which of the following is a Class B address?
    A. 192.168.5.5
    B. 10.6.6.3
    C. 172.6.8.9
    D. 201.69.3.2

17. Which of the following is a Class A address?
    A. 192.168.5.5
    B. 10.6.6.3
    C. 172.6.8.9
    D. 201.69.3.2

18. Which of the following is a Class C address?
    A. 192.168.5.5
    B. 10.6.6.3
    C. 172.6.8.9
    D. 224.69.3.2

19. When personal devices include networking capabilities and can communicate directly with one another, they create which type of network?
    A. WAN
    B. MAN
    C. PAN
    D. WMN

20. Which of the following is a collection of two or more LANs, typically connected by routers and dedicated leased lines, and is confined to a certain geographic area such as a university campus or city?
    A. WAN
    B. MAN
    C. PAN
    D. WMN

21. Which of the following is a collection of two or more LANs, typically connected by routers and dedicated leased lines?
    A. WAN
    B. MAN
    C. PAN
    D. WMN

22. Which of the following is used to attach media connectors to the ends of cables?
    A. Crimper
    B. Cable stripper
    C. Injector
    D. Tone generator

23. Which of the following is used to remove the cable's outer covering to get to the wire pairs within?
    A. Crimper
    B. Cable stripper
    C. Injector
    D. Tone generator

24. Which of the following makes it easier to find the beginning and end of a cable?
    A. Crimper
    B. Cable stripper
    C. Injector
    D. Tone generator

Chapter 3

Hardware

COMPTIA A+ CERTIFICATION EXAM CORE 1 (220-1201) OBJECTIVES COVERED IN THIS CHAPTER:

✔ **3.1 Compare and contrast display components and attributes**

- Types
    - Liquid crystal display (LCD)
        - In-plane switching (IPS)
        - Twisted nematic (TN)
        - Vertical alignment (VA)
    - Organic light-emitting diode (OLED)
    - Mini light-emitting diode (mini-LED)
- Touch screen/digitizer
- Inverter
- Attributes
    - Pixel quality
    - Refresh rates
    - Screen resolution
    - Color gamut

✔ **3.2 Summarize basic cable types and their connectors, features, and purposes**

- Network cables
    - Copper
        - Categories
        - Coaxial
        - Shielded twisted pair (STP)
        - Direct burial
        - Unshielded twisted pair (UTP)

- Plenum-rated
- Optical
  - Fiber
  - Single-mode
  - Multi-mode
- Peripheral cables
  - USB 2.0
  - USB 3.0
  - Serial
- Thunderbolt
- Video cables
  - High-Definition Multimedia Interface (HDMI)
- DisplayPort
  - Digital Visual Interface (DVI)
    - DVI-D
    - DVI-I
    - DVI-A
  - Video Graphics Array (VGA)
  - USB-C
- Hard drive cables
  - Serial Advanced Technology Attachment (SATA)
  - External SATA (eSATA)
- Adapters
  - DVI to HDMI
  - USB to Ethernet
  - DVI to VGA
- Connector types
  - RJ-11
  - RJ-45
  - F-type
  - Straight tip (ST)
  - Subscriber connector (SC)

- Lucent connector (LC)
- Punchdown block
- Micro-USB and Mini-USB
- USB-C
- Molex
- Lightning
- DB9

✔ 3.3 Compare and contrast RAM characteristics

- Form factors
  - Small outline dual inline memory module (SoDIMM)
  - Dual inline memory module (DIMM)
- Double data rate (DDR) iterations
  - DDR SDRAM
  - DDR3
  - DDR4
  - DDR5
- Error correction code (ECC) vs. non-ECC RAM
- Channel configurations
  - Dual-channel
  - Triple-channel
  - Quad-channel

✔ 3.4 Compare and contrast storage devices

- Hard drives
  - Spindle speeds
    - 5,400 rpm
    - 7,200 rpm
    - 10,000 rpm
    - 15,000 rpm
  - Form factors
    - 2.5 inch
    - 3.5 inch

- Solid-state drives (SSDs)
- Communications interfaces
  - Non-Volatile Memory Express (NVMe)
    - SATA
    - Peripheral Component Interconnect Express (PCIe)
    - Serial Attached Small Computer System Interface [SCSI] (SAS)
  - Form factors
    - M.2
    - Mini-Serial Advanced Technology Attachment (mSATA)
- Drive configurations
  - Redundant Array of Independent Disks (RAID) 0,1,5,6,10
    - RAID 0
    - RAID 1
    - RAID 5
    - RAID 6
    - RAID 10
- Removable storage
  - Flash drives
  - Memory cards
    - SD card
    - CompactFlash (CF)
    - microSD card
    - miniSD card
    - xD
- Optical drives
  - CD-ROM/CD-RW
  - DVD-ROM/DVD-RW/DVD-RW DL
  - Blu-ray
  - BD-R
  - BD-RE

✔ **3.5 Given a scenario, install and configure motherboards, central processing units (CPUs), and add-on cards**

- Motherboard form factors
  - Advanced Technology Extended (ATX)
  - Micro-ATX
  - Information Technology eXtended (ITX)
- Motherboard connector types
  - Peripheral Component Interconnect (PCI)
  - PCIe
  - Power connectors
  - SATA
  - eSATA
  - SAN
  - Headers
  - M.2
- Motherboard compatibility
  - CPU socket types
    - Advanced Micro Devices, Inc. (AMD)
    - Intel
  - Multisocket
- Basic Input/Output System/Unified Extensible Firmware Interface (BIOS/UEFI) settings
- Boot options
  - USB permissions
  - Trusted Platform Module (TPM) security features
  - Fan considerations
  - Secure Boot
  - Boot password
  - BIOS password
  - Temperature monitoring
- Virtualization support
- Encryption

- TPM
- Hardware Security Module (HSM)
- CPU Architecture
  - X86/x64
  - Advanced RISC Machine (ARM)
  - Core configurations
- Expansion cards
  - Sound card
  - Video card
    - Onboard
    - Add-on card
  - Capture card
  - Network interface card (NIC)
- Cooling
  - Fans
  - Heat sink
  - Thermal paste/pads
  - Liquid

✔ **3.6 Given a scenario, install the appropriate power supply**

- Input 110–120 VAC vs. 220–240 VAC
- Output 3.3V vs. 5V vs. 12V
- 20+4 pin motherboard connector
- Redundant power supply
- Modular power supply
- Wattage rating
- Energy efficiency

✔ **3.7 Given a scenario, deploy and configure multifunction devices/printers and settings**

- Properly unbox device and consider setup location
- Use appropriate drivers for a given operating system
  - Printer Control Language (PCL) vs. PostScript

- Firmware
- Device connectivity
  - USB
  - Ethernet
  - Wireless
    - Bluetooth
    - 802.11 (a, b, g, n, ac, ax)
- Public/shared devices
  - Printer share
  - Print server
- Configuration settings
  - Duplex
  - Orientation
  - Tray settings
  - Quality
- Security
  - User authentication
  - Badging
  - Audit logs
  - Secured prints
- Network scan services
  - Email
  - SMB
  - Cloud services
  - Automatic document feeder (ADF)/flatbed scanner

✔ **3.8 Given a scenario, perform appropriate printer maintenance**

- Laser
  - Maintenance: replace toner, apply maintenance kit, calibrate, and clean
    - Replace toner
    - Apply a maintenance kit

- Calibrate
- Clean
- Inkjet
  - Ink cartridge, printhead, roller, and feeder
    - Ink cartridge
    - Printhead
    - Roller
    - Feeder
  - Maintenance: clean printheads, replace cartridges, calibrate, and clear jams
    - Clean printheads
    - Replace cartridges
    - Calibrate
    - Clear jams
- Thermal
  - Feed assembly
    - Thermal wax transfer
    - Dye sublimation
    - Feed assembly
    - Heating element
  - Special thermal paper
  - Maintenance: replace paper, clean heating element, remove debris
    - Replace paper
    - Clean heating element
    - Remove debris
- Impact
  - Multipart paper
  - Maintenance: replace ribbon, printhead and paper
    - Replace ribbon
    - Replace printhead
    - Replace paper

This chapter will focus on the exam topics related to hardware. It will follow the structure of the CompTIA A+ 220-1201 exam blueprint, Objective 3, and cover the eight subobjectives that you will need to master before taking the exam. The hardware domain represents 25 percent of the total exam.

3.1 Compare and contrast display components and attributes

There are several types of displays, also known as monitors, as well as components that help project the image on the screen. In this section, I'll discuss these components and, in some cases, cover competing technologies. The following topics are addressed in Exam Objective 3.1:

- Types
- Touch screen/digitizer
- Inverter
- Attributes

Types

There are three types of displays covered on the CompTIA A+ 2201-1201 exam: liquid crystal display (LCD), organic light-emitting diode (OLED), and mini light-emitting diode (Mini-LED). I'll cover each of these types in this section.

Liquid crystal display (LCD)

Liquid crystal displays (LCDs) have completely replaced older glass monitors (i.e. cathode ray tubes [CRTs]) as the default display type for both laptops and desktops. Three major types of LCDs are used today: in-plane switching (IPS), twisted nematic (NM), and vertical alignment (VA). Their main differences lie in the quality of the image. They all use fluorescent tubes to backlight the screen, with the alignment of the crystals determining the quality of the picture.

In-plane switching (IPS)

IPS is the most common technology for computer monitors. The crystals are parallel with the glass, and they rotate to let the light pass through to the screen. It also provides better color quality than NM. Newer versions like Super-IPS (SIPS) make improvements on the original response times found in IPS.

Twisted nematic (TN)

TN is the older of these major technologies for flat-panel displays. While it provides the shortest response time, has high brightness, and draws less power than competing technologies, it suffers from poor quality when viewed from wide angles. It suffers color distortions when viewed from above or from the sides. When compared to IPS and VA monitors, the quality of TN monitors is out of date.

Vertical alignment (VA)

The third type is an LED that uses vertical alignment. In VA, when no electric current is running through the liquid crystal cells, the cells naturally align vertically between two substrate panes of glass, which blocks the transmission of light from the backlight. This renders the crystals opaque and results in a black display screen. When an electric current is applied, the liquid crystal cells shift to a horizontal position between the substrates, allowing light to pass through, resulting in a white display screen. Monitors with VA LCD panels provide the advantages of wide viewing angles and high-contrast ratios and reproduce colors well. VA is the most common type used in TVs. The operation of VA is shown in Figure 3.1.

Organic light-emitting diode (OLED)

OLED is another type of LED technology. It uses an emissive electroluminescent layer of organic compounds that emit light in response to an electric current. An interesting characteristic of these displays is their flexibility and transparency. This means they can roll up for storage (like a mat), and you can see through the display to objects behind the display. These carry a higher price and are considered high-performance units for monitors and TVs.

Mini light-emitting diode (mini-LED)

LED monitors use either one large or a couple of dozen fluorescent backlights. Mini-LED, on the other hand, uses thousands of LED backlights. Because of this, mini-LED has an advantage when displaying pure black and is superior in contrast and brightness.

FIGURE 3.1 Vertical alignment

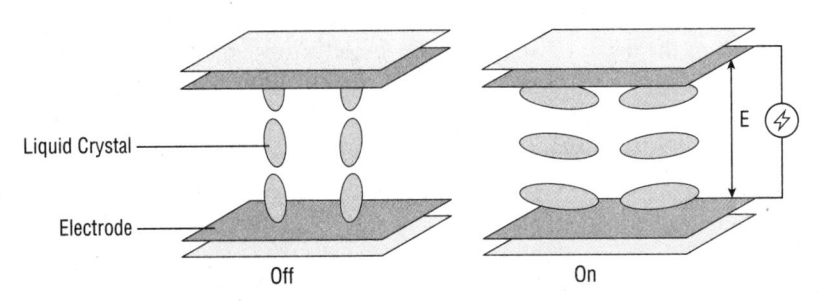

Touch screen/digitizer

Touch screens are primarily found on mobile devices but can also be found in desktop LCD monitors. These types of displays provide for easy navigation without the use of a mouse. They allow for screen control by tapping to select an application, pinching and squeezing to zoom in/out, or swiping left/right to navigate between screens.

Digitizers read pressure applied to the surface of the display and are what make touch screens work. In some cases, they work with a stylus or small pen-like device; in others, you simply touch the screen with your finger. The digitizer is a thin piece of clear material that fits on top of the display. If you have ever electronically signed for a purchase or a package delivery, you have used a digitizer!

Inverter

An inverter is a component that takes DC power and converts it to AC, which can be used by the LCD screen. It is implemented as a circuit board that is located behind the LCD or under the keyboard of a laptop. If problems with flickering display begin or the display dims, the inverter is a prime suspect. If the inverter needs to be replaced, you should be aware that it might contain stored energy, so it might need to be discharged to be safe.

Attributes

When you are comparing displays to purchase, there are several characteristics or attributes to consider. Let's discuss some of the more critical attributes: pixel quality, refresh rates, screen resolution, and color gamut.

Pixel quality

First, let's define what a pixel is. The display screen is made of millions of small dots called *pixels*. These small dots light up when an electrical signal is applied and display some combination of red, green, and blue colors along with a brightness (i.e. intensity) setting.

Pixels represent color through a combination of red, green, and blue (RGB) colors. Each color can have up to 256 shades, providing more than 16 million colors (16,777,216, to be exact). You might see colors represented as an RGB value, such as (255,255,255) for white, or a hex value like #FFFFFF. Brown can be expressed as (165,42,42) or #A52A2A, meaning the color is composed of shade #165 of red, shade #42 of green, and shade #42 of blue.

Refresh rates

The refresh rate is the number of times per second that the display repaints, or refreshes, the screen. If you have a 60-Hz refresh rate, that means the display is refreshed 60 times per second. While 60-Hz monitors are a baseline or standard, larger-display monitors, higher-resolution monitors, and gaming monitors might have higher refresh rates, such as 120 Hz, 144 Hz, and 240 Hz. If your hardware (and budget) can support it, you might want a high-performance monitor with a refresh rate of 280 Hz or 360 Hz.

Screen resolution

Screen resolution is how many pixels are available. As you increase the number of pixels, you increase the quality of the picture displayed. The number of pixels is expressed as screen resolution, usually as the number of pixels horizontally across the screen × the number of pixels vertically on the screen. HD television is 1920 × 1080 (i.e. 1,920 pixels across and 1,080 pixels up and down), while 4K is 3840 × 2160, and 8K is 7680 × 4320.

Color gamut

We touched on colors when we discussed pixel quality. Color gamut is the range of colors that a device can display. Graphic designers, photographers, engineers, and others might need to use very specific and highly accurate colorations for accurate reproduction. They would ensure that their colors are expressed using a color standard, such as Adobe RGB, CMYK for printing, and RGB for monitors, and each of these is a color gamut.

Exam essentials

Identify characteristics or attributes to consider when selecting a display. These considerations include pixel quality, refresh rate, screen resolution, and color gamut.

Identify the location and function of the inverter. An inverter is a component that takes DC power and converts it to a form that can be used by the LCD screen. It is implemented as a circuit board behind the LCD.

Understand the attributes of a display. The different terms that can be used to describe the capabilities of a display are pixel quality, refresh rates, screen resolution, and color gamut.

3.2 Summarize basic cable types and their connectors, features, and purposes

You're expected to know the basic concepts of networking as well as the different types of cabling that can be used. For the latter, you should be able to identify connectors and cables from figures even if those figures are crude line art (think shadows) appearing in pop-up boxes. This section covers cables and connectors of all types.

Network cables

For this exam, you must know the three specific types of network cables (i.e. fiber, twisted pair, and coaxial) and the connectors associated with each. Fiber is the most expensive of the three and can run the longest distance. A number of types of connectors can work with fiber, but three you must know are the subscriber connector (SC), straight tip (ST), and Lucent connector (LC).

Twisted-pair cable is commonly used in office settings to connect workstations to hubs or switches. This cable comes in two varieties: unshielded (UTP) and shielded (STP). The two types of connectors commonly used are RJ-11 (i.e. four wires and popular with landline telephones and DSL) and RJ-45 (i.e. eight wires and used with xBaseT networks—100Base-T, 1000Base-T, etc.). Two common wiring standards are T568A and T568B. Coaxial cabling for networking is not as popular as it once was, but it's still used with cable television, security cameras, and some legacy networks. The two most regularly used connectors are F connectors (for television cabling) and Bayonet Neill-Concelman (BNC) (i.e. 10Base2 coax and so on).

Copper

Ethernet is a popular method of networking computers in a local area network (LAN) using copper cabling. It is used in a variety of scenarios, such as connecting patch panels to switches in the form of patch cables, connecting a wall outlet to a desktop, and connecting infrastructure devices such as routers and switches. In this section, we'll look at its various implementations.

Categories

Ethernet cabling is classified by category numbers such as Cat 5, Cat 5e, Cat 6, and Cat 7. Each has different characteristics and performance specifications:

Cat 5

Cat 5 transmits data at speeds up to 100 Mbps and was used with Fast Ethernet (operating at 100 Mbps), with a transmission range of 100 m. It contains four twisted pairs of copper wire to give the most protection. Although it had its share of popularity (it's used primarily for 10/100 Ethernet networking), it is now an outdated standard. Newer implementations use the 5e standard.

Cat 5e

Cat 5e transmits data at speeds up to 1 Gbps (1,000 Mbps). Category 5e cabling can be used up to 100 m, depending on the implementation and standard used, and provides a minimum of 100 MHz of bandwidth. It also contains four twisted pairs of copper wire, but they're physically separated and contain more twists per foot than Category 5 to provide maximum interference protection.

Cat 6

Cat 6 transmits data at speeds up to 10 Gbps, has a minimum of 250 MHz of bandwidth, and specifies cable lengths up to 100 m (using Cat 6a). It contains four twisted pairs of copper wire and is used in 10GBase-T networks. Category 6 cable typically is made up of four twisted pairs of copper wire, but its capabilities far exceed those of other cable types. Category 6 twisted pair uses a longitudinal separator, which separates each of the four pairs of wires from each other and reduces the amount of crosstalk possible.

Cat 6a

Cat 6a cable has improved alien crosstalk characteristics, allowing 10GBase-T to be run for the same 330 ft (100 m) maximum distance as previous Ethernet variants.

Cat 7

Cat 7 cable provides better shielding on individual wires, so it helps reduce interference and does a better job at higher speeds approaching 10 Gbps. It still has the same 100 m limitation. Cat 7 does not use RJ-45 connectors, but rather GG45, ARJ45, or TERA connectors.

Cat 7a

Cat 7a is an enhancement to Cat 7. It allows for 10 Gbps over 100 m but also allows for 40 Gbps over 50 m. This is an excellent cabling system for data centers.

T568A/T568B standards

Two wiring standards are commonly used with twisted-pair cabling: T568A and T568B (sometimes referred to simply as 568A and 568B). These are telecommunications standards from the Electronic Industries Alliance (EIA) and the Telecommunications Industry Association (TIA) that specify the pin arrangements for the RJ-45 connectors on UTP or STP cables. The number 568 refers to the order in which the wires within the Cat 5 cable are terminated and attached to the connector. The signal is identical for both.

T568A was the first standard, released in 1991. Ten years later, in 2001, T568B was released. Figure 3.2 shows the pin number assignments for the 568A and 568B standards. Pin numbers are read left to right, with the connector tab facing down. Notice that the pinouts stay the same, and the only difference is in the color coding of the wiring.

The bottom line here is that if the same standard is used on each end, the cable will be a crossover cable, and if a different standard is used on either end, it will be a straight-through cable. Crossover cables are used to connect like systems, such as two computers or two switches or two routers.

FIGURE 3.2 Pin assignments for T568A and T568B

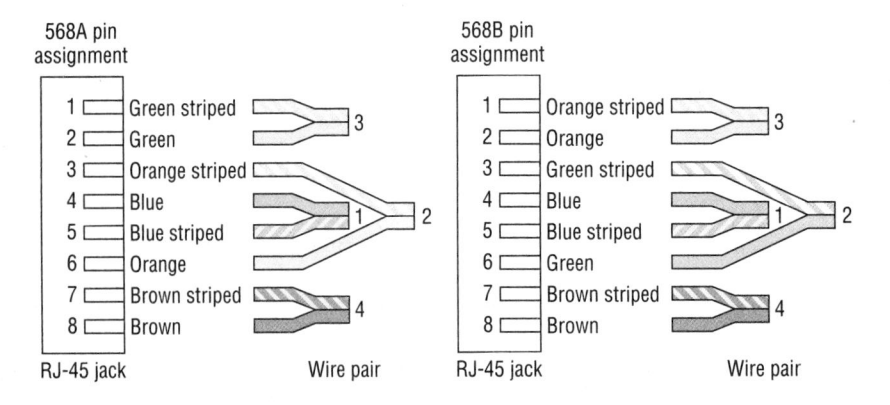

568A pin assignment

Pin	Wire
1	Green striped
2	Green
3	Orange striped
4	Blue
5	Blue striped
6	Orange
7	Brown striped
8	Brown

568B pin assignment

Pin	Wire
1	Orange striped
2	Orange
3	Green striped
4	Blue
5	Blue striped
6	Green
7	Brown striped
8	Brown

3.2 Summarize basic cable types and their connectors, features, and purposes

> **Note:** Mixing cable types can cause communication problems on a network. Before installing a network or adding a new component, make sure the cable being used is in the correct wiring standard.

Coaxial

Coaxial cable, or coax, is one of the oldest media used in networks. Coax is built around a center conductor or core that is used to carry data from point to point. The center conductor has an insulator wrapped around it, a shield over the insulator, and a nonconductive sheath around the shielding. This construction, depicted in Figure 3.3, allows the conducting core to be relatively free from outside interference. The shielding also prevents the conducting core from emanating signals externally from the cable.

> **Note:** In today's environment, RG-6 is almost exclusively used for cable TV connections. That said, you do need to know about coax for this exam.

FIGURE 3.3 Coax cable

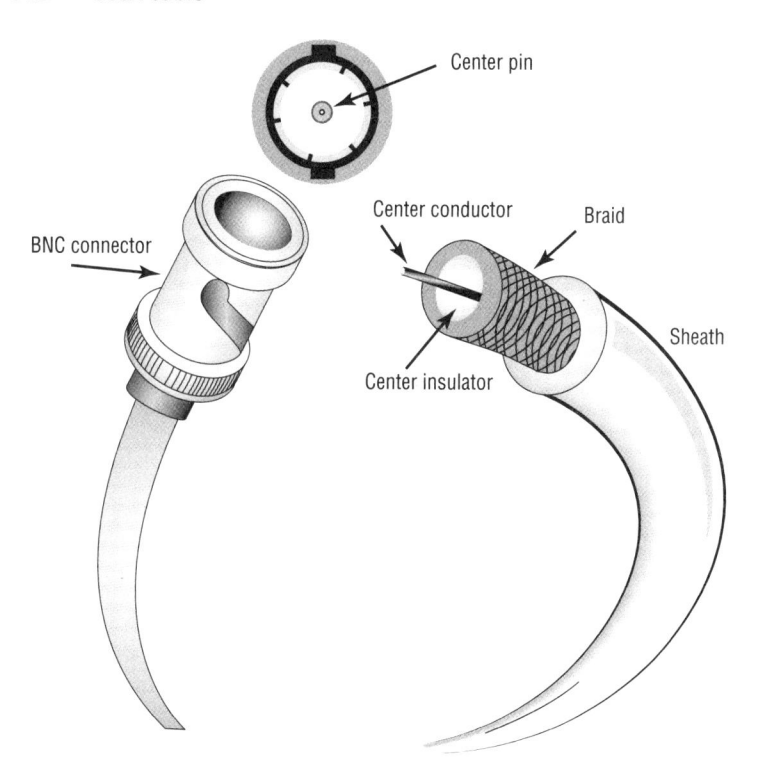

Shielded twisted pair (STP)

STP differs from UTP only in the presence of the shielding, which resembles aluminum foil directly beneath the outer insulation. The shielding adds to the cost of the cable and eliminates interference from outside the cable. As a rule of thumb, based on current prices, STP is 30% more expensive than UTP for the same length of cable.

Direct burial

Direct burial cabling (DBC), typically used for coaxial or fiber runs, is cable made to be buried with no outer covering. DBC consists of multiple layers of heavy metallic-banded sheathing, reinforced by heavy rubber covers for shock absorption.

Unshielded twisted pair (UTP)

UTP is the most popular twisted-pair cabling in use and should be used in any scenario where external interference is not an issue.

Plenum-rated

Plenum cable is a specific type of cable that is rated for use in plenum spaces—those spaces in a building used for heating and air-conditioning systems or above ceiling tiles. Most cables cannot be used in the plenum because of the danger of fire (or the fumes the cables give off as they burn). While it is more expensive, plenum cable is fire-rated and meets the necessary standards, which makes it acceptable to use in these locations. It replaces PVC with a Teflon-like material.

Optical

Optical transmission of data using either lasers or LEDs offers a secure and speedy way to move traffic. In this section, you'll learn about the cables used in optical transmission.

Fiber

Fiber-optic cabling provides excellent speed and bandwidth but is expensive. Not only are the cables that you use costly, but the light-emitting/receiving hardware costs also make this an expensive undertaking.

Because of the cost involved, fiber is often an option for businesses only when it comes to broadband access. Fiber to the Home (FTTH) is being rolled out, as some communities are undertaking to offer high-speed connectivity to residential dwellings as well. Verizon's fiber-optic service (Fios), a similar implementation, runs single-mode optical fiber to homes and includes phone and television service along with Internet access.

Fiber-optic cabling has a glass core within a rubber outer coating and uses beams of light rather than electrical signals to relay data (see Figure 3.4). Because light doesn't diminish over distance the way electrical signals do through attenuation, this cable can run for distances measured in kilometers with transmission speeds from 1 Gbps up to 100 Gbps or higher.

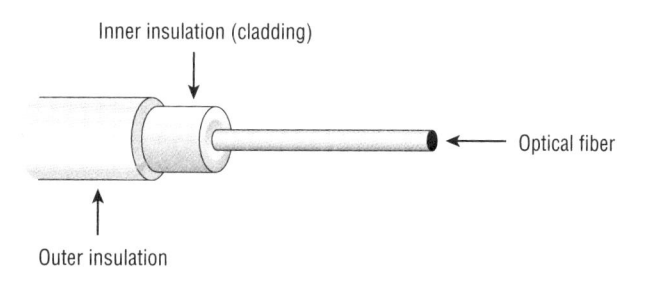

FIGURE 3.4 Fiber-optic cable

Single-mode
Single-mode fiber sends a single light pulse through the cable. It is most often used in distances over 500 m, even up to 40 km. You will see single-mode fiber used in connections between buildings and in wide area networks (WANs). Bandwidth can exceed 100 Gbps.

Multi-mode
Multi-mode fiber sends multiple signals over the same optical cable. You most often see multi-mode fiber within buildings, covering short distances less than 500 m. Bandwidth, depending on the exact cable type, ranges from 10 Gbps to 400 Gbps.

Peripheral cables

Many connection methods have come and gone with respect to external ports on devices. In this section, you'll learn about the most common ones found in today's mobile devices.

USB 2.0
Universal serial bus (USB) is the most common (hence, "universal") connector. USB 2.0 is the most basic general-purpose connector today, running at 480 Mbps.

USB 3.0
USB 3.0 has transmission speeds of up to 5 Gbps, significantly reduces the time required for data transmission, reduces power consumption, and is backward-compatible with USB 2.0. Because USB is a serial interface, its width is 1 bit. It is useful to note, however, that a USB 2.0 device will perform at 2.0 speeds even when connected to a 3.0 port. If you connect a USB 3.0 to a USB 2.0 port, it will also operate at only 2.0 speeds.

Serial
Although an older cable type, a serial connector may be found connecting some peripherals to the serial connection on the system. This connector is shown in Figure 3.5. The maximum speed is 115,200 bps.

FIGURE 3.5 Serial connector

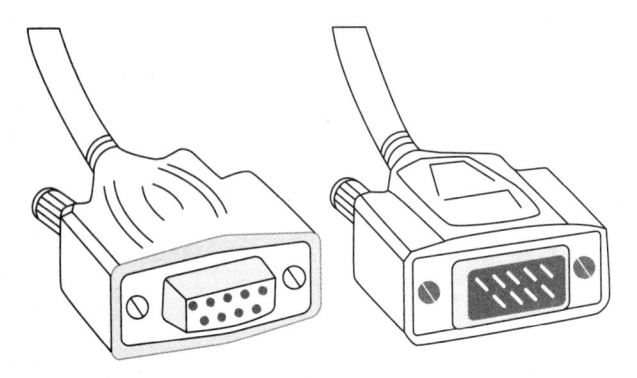

FIGURE 3.6 Thunderbolt port

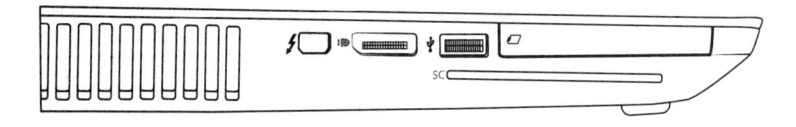

FIGURE 3.7 Thunderbolt cable

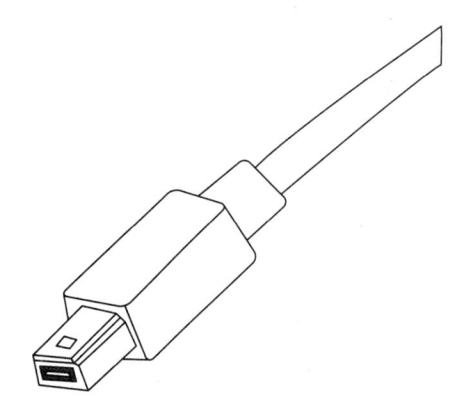

Thunderbolt

Thunderbolt ports are most likely to be found on Apple laptops, but they are now showing up on other devices as well. Figure 3.6 shows a Thunderbolt port on an HP laptop. Notice the "thunderbolt" icon next to the port. Thunderbolt has a maximum speed of 10 Gbps, Thunderbolt 2 has a maximum speed of 20 Gbps, and Thunderbolt 3 has a maximum speed of 40 Gbps, compared to 800 Mbps for FireWire 800, 5 Gbps for USB 3.0, and 10 Gbps for USB 3.1.

The Thunderbolt cable is shown in Figure 3.7.

FIGURE 3.8 HDMI connectors

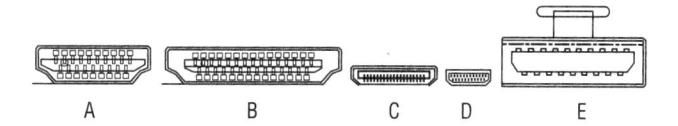

A   B   C   D   E

TABLE 3.1 HDMI versions

Version	1.0	1.1	1.2	1.3	1.4	2.0
Maximum throughput (Gbps)	3.96	3.96	3.96	10.2	10.2	6
Maximum color depth (bit/px)	24	24	24	48	48	48
Maximum audio throughput (Mbps)	36.86	36.86	36.86	36.86	36.86	49.152

Video cables

You might require one of a variety of cable types for video or display. In this section, we'll survey the types of video cables you might encounter.

High-Definition Multimedia Interface (HDMI)

High-Definition Multimedia Interface (HDMI) connectors are used to connect compatible digital items (e.g. DVD players and conference-room projectors). The Type A connector has 19 pins and is backward-compatible with Digital Visual Interface (DVI) (discussed later in this chapter). Type B connectors have 29 pins and aren't backward-compatible with DVI, but they support greater resolutions. Type C connectors are a smaller version of Type A for portable devices. Type D is an even smaller micro version that resembles a micro-USB connector. Type E is planned for use in automotive applications. HDMI has a theoretical cable length limit of 45 ft or 15 m. Figure 3.8 shows all HDMI types.

There are several versions of HDMI, as described in Table 3.1.

DisplayPort

DisplayPort is a digital interface standard produced by the Video Electronics Standards Association (VESA), used for audio and video. The interface is primarily used to connect a video source to a display device, such as a computer monitor or television set. It resembles a USB connector (see Figure 3.9). It supports a 1.62-, 2.7-, 5.4-, or 8.1-Gbps data rate per lane; 1, 2, or 4 lanes; effective total 5.184, 8.64, 17.28, or 25.92 Gbps for 4-lane link; and 1 Mbps or 720 Mbps for the auxiliary channel.

FIGURE 3.9 DisplayPort

FIGURE 3.10 DVI connectors

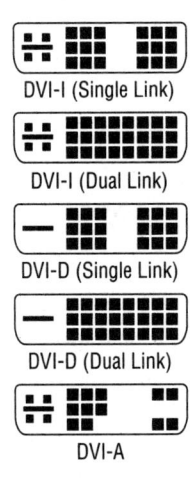

DVI-I (Single Link)

DVI-I (Dual Link)

DVI-D (Single Link)

DVI-D (Dual Link)

DVI-A

Digital Visual Interface (DVI)

There are several types of DVI pin configurations, but all connectors are D-shaped. The wiring differs based on whether the connector is single-linked or dual-linked (extra pins are used for the dual link). DVI differs from everything else in that it includes both digital and analog signals at the same time, which makes it popular for LCD and plasma TVs. Maximum cable length is 16 ft (5 m).

DVI connectors can come in several forms, known as DVI-D, DVI-I, and DVI-A. DVI can sometimes do analog and digital at the same time. Figure 3.10 shows the various types of DVI plugs discussed in this section.

3.2 Summarize basic cable types and their connectors, features, and purposes

The single-link maximum data rate, including 8b/10b overhead is 4.95 Gbps at 165 MHz. With the 8b/10b overhead subtracted, the maximum data rate is 3.96 Gbps.

> **8b/10b overhead**
>
> In DVI, the 8b/10b overhead is used for DC balancing. The b stands for balancing. DC balancing refers to ensuring an equal balance of 1 or 0 in a stream of data. It is used in communications systems to prevent bit errors when passing through circuits with capacitive coupling or transformers.

Dual-link maximum data rate is twice that of single-link. Including 8b/10b overhead, the maximum data rate is 9.90 Gbps at 165 MHz. With the 8b/10b overhead subtracted, the maximum data rate is 7.92 Gbps.

DVI-D

DVI-D (the -D stands for digital) connectors supply digital signals only. These can also come in a single- or dual-link format. A dual-link format allows for a second data link.

DVI-I

A DVI-I connector (the -I stands for integrated) has pins that can provide analog and digital. These can also come in a single- or dual-link format.

DVI-A

A DVI-A connector (the -A stands for analog) has pins that can provide analog and digital. This type comes in a single-link format only.

Video Graphics Array (VGA)

The Video Graphics Array (VGA) is the traditional connector for the display of a computer, and it is shaped like a D. It has three rows of five pins each, for a total of 15 pins. This is also often called the HD-15 (also known as DB-15) connector. A VGA cable carries analog signals. The cable length utilized will affect the resolution achieved: 1024 × 768 would operate more effectively with 30 ft or less of cable length. As the need for resolution increases, the allowable maximum cable length decreases. Figure 3.11 shows a VGA port.

FIGURE 3.11 VGA port

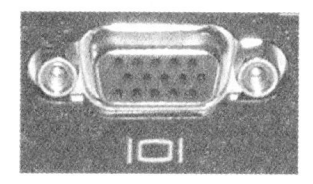

USB-C

The USB-C connectors connect to both hosts and devices, replacing various USB-B and USB-A connectors and cables with a standard connection. This connector type was discussed and illustrated in Chapter 1, in the section "Connection methods."

Hard drive cables

When drives are connected internally or externally, there are several options, and the options available on your PC will be a function of how old it is and, in the case of SCSI, whether it is a computer designed to operate as a server.

Serial Advanced Technology Attachment (SATA)

Serial Advanced Technology Attachment (SATA) drives are Advanced Technology Attachment (ATA) drives that use serial transmission as opposed to parallel, which is why they use a different cable. It is not a ribbon cable but a smaller cable. Both implementations can operate up to 16 GB. Figure 3.12 shows the data cable and its connector.

Internal SATA storage devices have 7-pin data cables and a 15-pin power cable. eSATA cables may be either flat or round and can be only 6 ft (2 m) in length. An eSATA connector is shown in Figure 3.13.

FIGURE 3.12 Serial ATA data cable and connector

FIGURE 3.13 eSATA cable

eSATA connectors

Standard internal SATA connectors

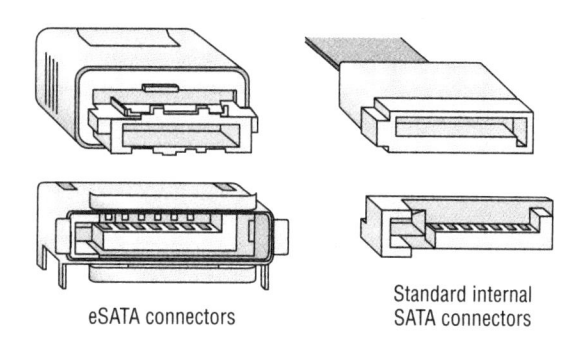

TABLE 3.2 SATA speeds

Standard	Transfer Speed
SATA 1.0	150 MBps
SATA 2.0	300 MBps
SATA 3.0	600 MBps
SATA 3.2	1,969 MBps
eSATA	6 GBps

External SATA (eSATA)

Connections for storage devices can be either Serial AT Attachment (SATA) or Integrated Drive Electronics (IDE). IDE is an interface created for IBM computers by Western Digital and Compaq in 1986. IDE was the only option early on, and then SATA came on the scene in the early 2000s. SATA came out as a standard and was first adopted in desktops and then laptops. Whereas ATA had always been an interface that sent 16 bits at a time, SATA sends only one bit at a time. The benefit is that the cable used can be much smaller, and faster cycling can actually increase performance. SATA uses a 7-wire cable that can be up to about 3 ft (1 m) in length. eSATA cables can be up to about 6 ft (2 m). Figure 3.12 earlier showed the SATA connector, and Figure 3.13 shows the eSATA cable.

Table 3.2 lists the speeds of the options.

Adapters

In many cases, you will need to attach a device to a computer on which the correct connectors are not present. In these cases, there are adapters (i.e. converters) and connectors that can be used to connect the device to a connector type for which it was not designed. In this section, you'll look at some of the more common adapters.

DVI to HDMI

These adapters connect from HDMI to DVI and come in a number of gender combinations (e.g. male DVI to female HDMI, male DVI to male HDMI, female DVI to male HDMI, etc.) and as either a cable or simply an inline connector. Figure 3.14 shows an inline connector.

USB to Ethernet

These converters allow you to use a USB port as a network interface. They come both as cables and as inline connectors. Figure 3.15 shows an example of a USB-to-Ethernet adapter.

DVI to VGA

In cases where you need to convert DVI to VGA, you can use a DVI-to-VGA adapter. These come as cable or inline connectors and also come in a variety of gender combinations. Figure 3.16 shows an example of the ends of this adapter.

FIGURE 3.14 HDMI to DVI

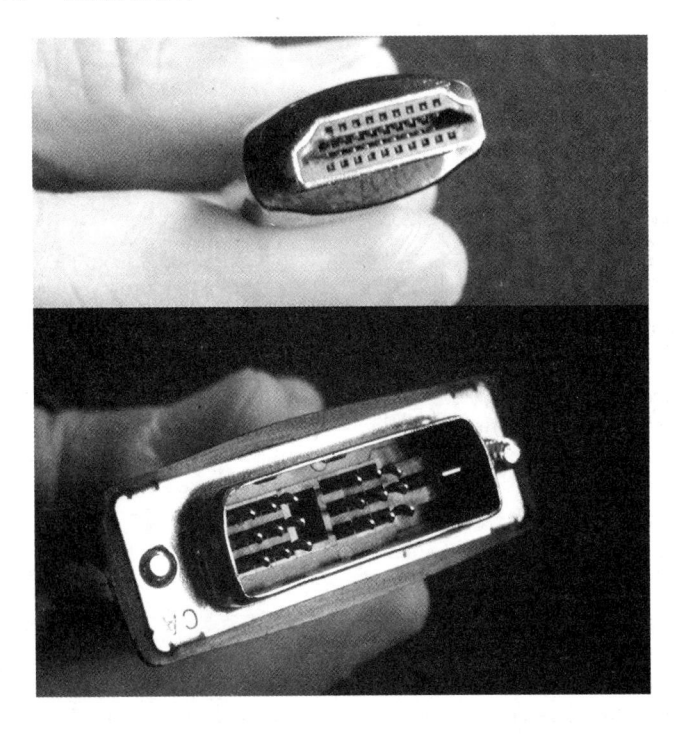

FIGURE 3.15 USB to Ethernet

FIGURE 3.16 DVI to VGA

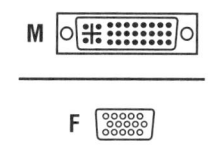

Connector types

A computer's peripheral ports are the physical connectors on the outside of the computer. Cables of various types are designed to plug into these ports and create a connection between the PC and the external devices that may be attached to it. A successful IT technician should have an in-depth knowledge of ports and cables.

Because the peripheral components need to be upgraded frequently, either to keep pace with technological change or to replace broken devices, a well-rounded familiarity with the ports and their associated cabling is required. In this section, you'll learn about connector types.

RJ-11

A registered jack (RJ) is a plastic plug with small metal tabs, like a telephone cord plug. RJ-11 has two metal tabs. An RJ-11 connector, as shown in Figure 3.17, is a standard connector for a landline telephone and is most commonly used to connect a DSL modem to a phone line. It looks much like an RJ-45 but is noticeably smaller.

RJ-45

RJ-45 has eight tabs and is used for Ethernet 10Base-T/100Base-T, 1000Base, and 10GBase networking. The maximum cable length is about 300 ft (100 m) but can vary slightly based on the category of cabling used. Figure 3.17 shows both RJ-11 and RJ-45 connectors.

FIGURE 3.17 RJ-11 (left) and RJ-45 (right) jacks

F-type

The RG-59 connector, also called an F-type connector, is used with a coaxial cable and is normally used to generate low-power video connections for security cameras. This cable cannot be used over long distances because of its high-frequency power losses. In such cases, RG-6 cables are used instead.

RG-6 is another connector normally used with coaxial cabling. It is often used for cable TV and cable modems. It can run longer distances than RG-59 and support digital signals.

Straight tip (ST)

An ST is used with fiber cables. They are spring-loaded, which means they are easily inserted and removed, but one also has to make sure that they are seated properly to ensure that there is no light loss.

Subscriber connector (SC)

SC is a standard-duplex fiber-optic connector with a square molded plastic body and push-pull locking features.

Lucent connector (LC)

The LC connector was first developed by Lucent Technology for telecommunications (telco) uses. These LC connectors utilize traditional components of the standard connector but with a 1.25 mm ceramic ferrule. All three fiber connector types are shown in Figure 3.18.

FIGURE 3.18 From top to bottom, SC, LC, and ST

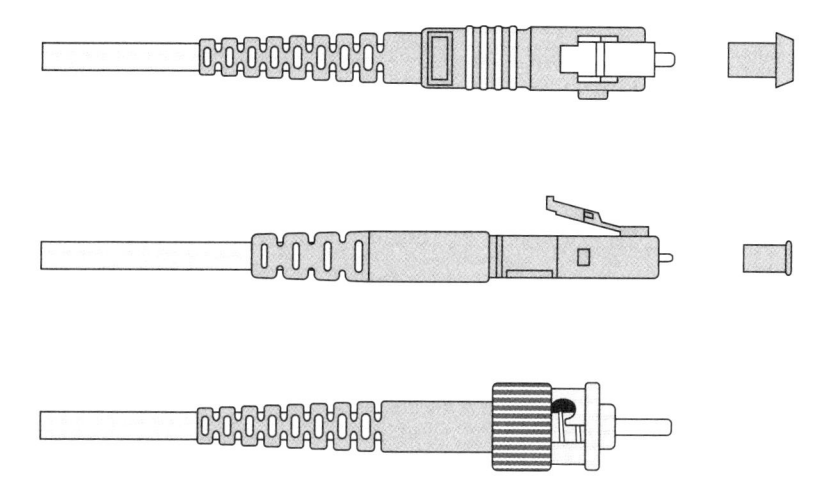

FIGURE 3.19 Punchdown block

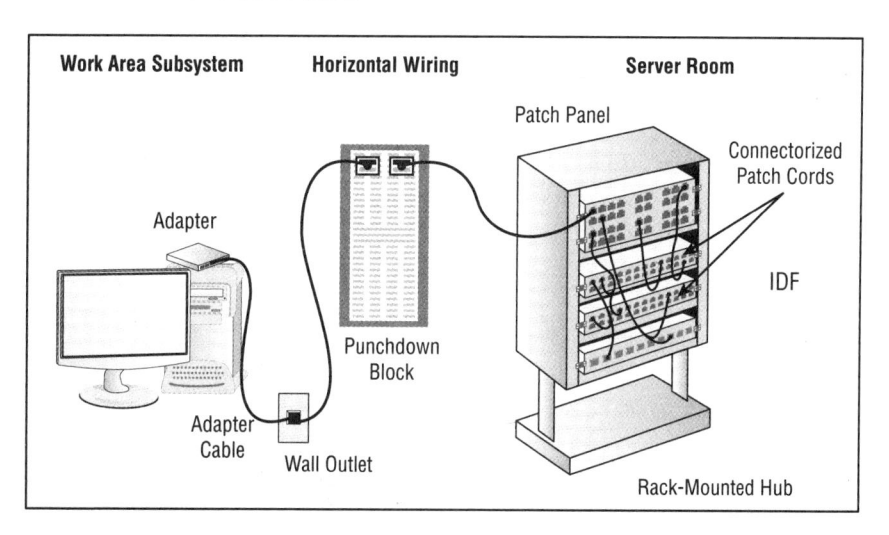

Punchdown block

A punchdown block is a panel owned by the telco where solid copper wires are "punched down" into short open-ended slots, which are a type of insulation-displacement connector. You learned about the tool used to do this back in Chapter 2, in the section "Punchdown tool." Figure 3.19 shows the relationship of the punchdown block to the computers and to the intermediate distribution frame (IDF) in the server room.

Micro-USB and Mini-USB

USB connectors also come in a mini version and a micro version. The micro version is used on mobile devices, such as mobile phones, GPS units, tablets, and digital cameras, whereas the mini is used for data transfer between digital devices and computers. The choice between a standard A and B and a mini A and B will be dictated by what is present on the device. The cables used cannot exceed about 15 ft (5 m) in length. Figure 3.20 shows standard Types A and B, in addition to mini Types A and B.

Some manufacturers have chosen to implement a mini connector that is proprietary, choosing not to follow the standard.

USB-C

The USB-C connectors connect to both hosts and devices, replacing various USB-B and USB-A connectors and cables with a standard connection. This connector type was discussed and illustrated earlier in Chapter 1, in the section "Connector types: A, B, mini, micro."

Molex

Connectors usually used for computer fans are called Molex connectors, and there can be several types. The following are some examples:

- A 3-pin Molex connector is used when connecting a fan to the motherboard or other circuit board. Figure 3.21 shows the 3-pin Molex.
- A 4-pin Molex connector includes an additional pin used for a pulse-width modulation signal to provide variable speed control. These connectors can be plugged into 3-pin headers but will lose their fan speed control. Figure 3.22 shows the 4-pin Molex connector.

FIGURE 3.20 USB connectors (from left to right) a standard Type A, a mini Type A, a standard Type B, and a mini Type B

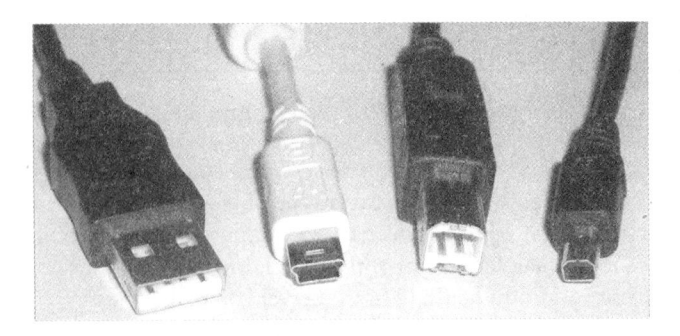

FIGURE 3.21 Three-pin Molex

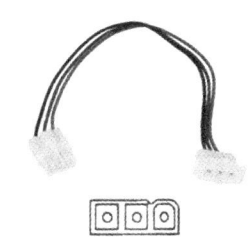

FIGURE 3.22 Four-pin Molex

Lightning

The Lightning connector from Apple is an 8-pin connector that, while not standard, has advantages over USB, according to Apple. Following are some of these advantages:

- It can supply more power.
- It can be inserted either way.
- It is physically more durable than USB.
- It can detect and adapt to connected devices.
- It operates at USB 3.0 speeds.

Figure 3.23 shows a Lightning connector next to a USB cable.

DB9

A DB9 cable is one of several form factors for serial connections and is shown in Figure 3.24.

FIGURE 3.23 Lightning connector and USB

USB

Lightning

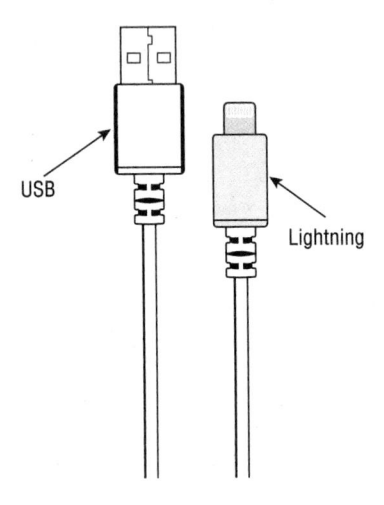

FIGURE 3.24 Serial cable

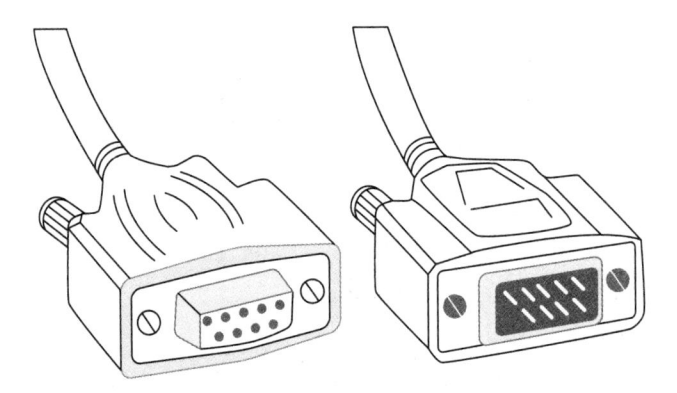

Exam essentials

Identify display connectors, their associated cables, and the maximum cable lengths. This includes, but is not limited to, DVI in all variants, DisplayPort, HD-15 (or DB-15), and mini HDMI.

Identify hard drive cables and adapters. These include SATA, eSATA, and SCSI. They also include adapters such as DVI to HDMI, USB to Ethernet, and DVI to VGA.

3.3 Compare and contrast RAM characteristics

RAM slots contain memory chips. There are many and varied types of memory for PCs today, which are outlined in this section.

PCs use memory chips arranged on a small circuit board. These circuit boards (often called RAM sticks) are characterized as single inline memory modules (SIMMs) or dual inline memory modules (DIMMs). DIMMs utilize connectors on both sides of the board, whereas SIMMS utilize single connectors that are mirrored on both sides. DIMM is 64-bit and SIMM is 32-bit.

Form factors

Memory modules/RAM sticks come in a variety of physical sizes and numbers of pins. These physical characteristics are called a *form factor*. Along with chip placement, memory modules also differ in the number of conductors, or pins, that the particular module uses. The number of pins used directly affects the overall size of the memory slot. Slot sizes include 30-pin, 72-pin, 168-pin, 184-pin, and 288-pin. Laptop memory comes in smaller form factors known as small outline DIMMs (SoDIMMs).

Figure 3.25 shows the form factors for the most popular memory chips. Notice that they basically look the same, but the memory module sizes are different.

Small outline dual inline memory module (SoDIMM)

Portable computers (e.g. notebooks and subnotebooks) require smaller sticks of RAM because of their smaller size. SoDIMM DDR can have 200, 204, or 260 pins. Figure 3.25 showed the form factors for 72- and 144-pin SODIMMs.

FIGURE 3.25 Various memory module form factors

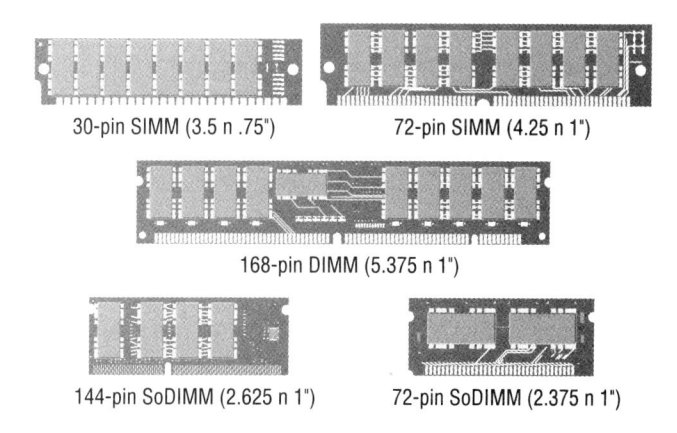

30-pin SIMM (3.5 n .75") 72-pin SIMM (4.25 n 1")

168-pin DIMM (5.375 n 1")

144-pin SoDIMM (2.625 n 1") 72-pin SoDIMM (2.375 n 1")

Dual inline memory module (DIMM)

DIMMs utilize connectors on both sides of the board.

Double data rate (DDR) iterations

Double data rate (DDR) is clock-doubled synchronous dynamic random-access memory (SDRAM). The memory chip can perform reads and writes on both sides of any clock cycle (the up, or start, and the down, or ending), thus doubling the effective memory executions per second. So, if you're using DDR SDRAM with a 100-MHz memory bus, the memory will execute reads and writes at 200 MHz and transfer the data to the processor at 100 MHz. The advantage of DDR over regular SDRAM is increased throughput and thus increased overall system speed.

DDR has gone through a number of iterations over the years, so let's discuss them.

DDR SDRAM

DDR SDRAM is double data rate 2 (DDR2). This allows for two memory accesses for each rising and falling clock and effectively doubles the speed of DDR. DDR2-667 chips work with speeds at 667 MHz and are also referred to as PC2-5300 modules.

DDR3

The primary benefit of DDR3 over DDR2 is that it transfers data at twice the rate of DDR2 (i.e. eight times the speed of its internal memory arrays), enabling higher bandwidth or peak data rates. By performing two transfers per cycle of a quadrupled clock, a 64-bit-wide DDR3 module may achieve a transfer rate of up to 64 times the memory clock speed in megabytes per second. In addition, the DDR3 standard permits chip capacities of up to 8 GB.

DDR4

DDR4 SDRAM is an abbreviation for double data rate fourth-generation synchronous dynamic random-access memory. DDR4 is not compatible with any earlier type of RAM. The DDR4 standard allows for DIMMs of up to 64 GB in capacity, compared to DDR3's maximum of 8 GB per DIMM. Higher bandwidths are achieved by sending more read/write commands per second. To allow this, the standard divides the DRAM banks into two or four selectable bank groups, so that transfers to different bank groups may be done more rapidly. Table 3.3 lists the selected memory standards, speeds, and formats.

DDR5

DDR5 makes several changes over DDR4. Among them:

- It reduces memory voltage to 1.1 V, thus reducing power consumption.
- It supports a speed of 51.2 GBps per module and 2 memory channels per module.
- It requires additional active circuitry, making the interface to the DIMM different from the interface to the RAM chips themselves.

TABLE 3.3 Selected memory details

Module Standard	Speed (MBps)	Format
DDR500	4,000	PC4000
DDR533	4,266	PC4200
DDR2-667	5,333	PC2-5300
DDR2-750	6,000	PC2-6000
DDR2-800	6,400	PC2-6400
DDR3-800	6,400	PC3-6400
DDR3-1600	12,800	PC3-12800
DDR4-1866M	14,933	PC4-14900
DDR4-2133P	17,066.67	PC4-17000
DDR4-2400R	19,200	PC4-19200
DDR4-2666U	21,333	PC4-21333
DDR4-2933W	23,466	PC4-23466
DDR4-3200W	25,600	PC4-25600

- Command encoding was significantly rearranged.
- The addressing range is slightly extended.

Error correcting code (ECC) vs. non-ECC RAM

A type of RAM error correction is error correcting code (ECC). RAM with ECC can detect and correct errors. As with parity RAM, additional information needs to be stored, and more processing needs to be done, making ECC RAM more expensive and a little slower than non-parity and parity RAM. Both ECC and parity memory work in ECC mode. However, ECC memory does not work in plain parity checking mode because the extra bits cannot be individually accessed when ECC memory is used. This type of parity RAM is now obsolete. While most RAM today is non-ECC, you will see ECC RAM in servers.

Channel configurations

Depending on the motherboard configuration, RAM can be arranged in channels of two, three, or four RAM sticks. These multiple channels allow data to be transferred at a higher rate. When taking advantage of the increased speeds of dual-channel or quad-channel, it is important to remember that the RAM modules installed in the channel must be identical.

Utilizing multiple channels between the RAM and memory controller increases the transfer speed between these two components. Single-channel RAM does not take advantage of this concept, but dual-channel memory does and creates two 64-bit data channels. Do not confuse this with DDR. DDR doubles the rate by accessing the memory module twice per clock cycle.

Dual-channel

This strategy requires a motherboard that supports it and two or more memory modules. The modules are inserted in separate color-coded banks, as shown in Figure 3.26.

Triple-channel

Triple-channel architecture adds a third memory module and reduces memory latency by interleaving or accessing each module sequentially with smaller bits of data, rather than completely filling up one module before accessing the next one. Data is spread among the modules alternatingly, with the potential to triple bandwidth as opposed to storing the data all on one module.

Quad-channel

As you might expect from the name, this type possesses four channels for moving data. The architecture can be used only when all four memory modules (or a multiple of four) are identical in capacity and speed and are placed in quad-channel slots.

FIGURE 3.26 Dual-channel memory slots

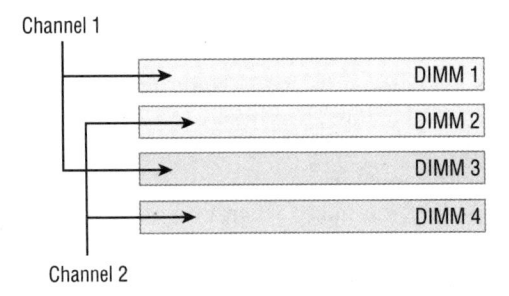

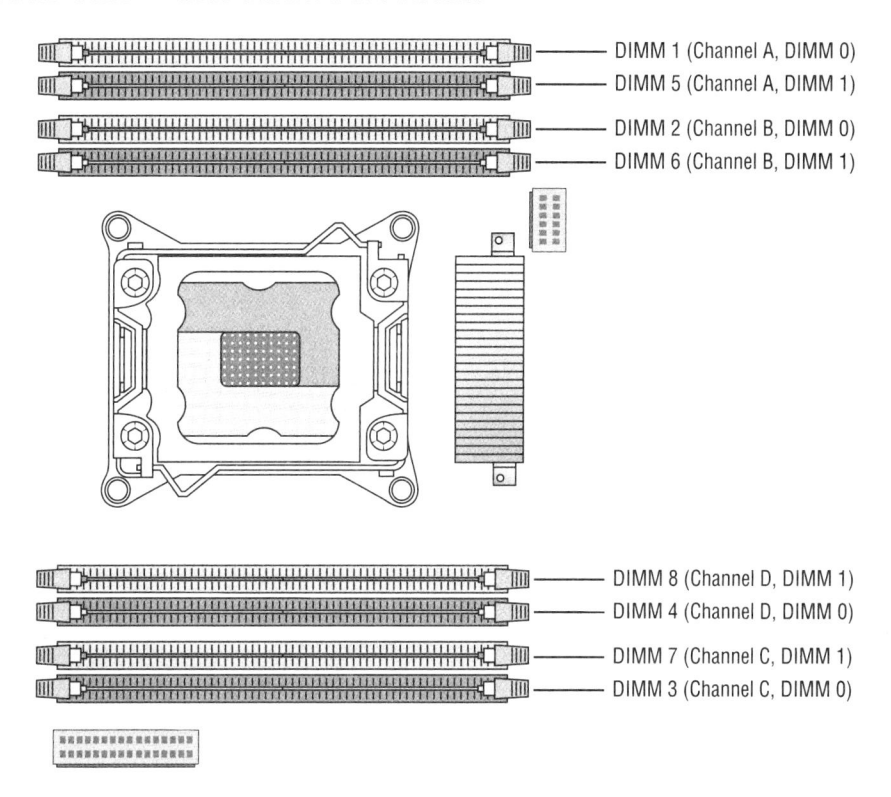

FIGURE 3.27 Quad-channel with 8 modules

- DIMM 1 (Channel A, DIMM 0)
- DIMM 5 (Channel A, DIMM 1)
- DIMM 2 (Channel B, DIMM 0)
- DIMM 6 (Channel B, DIMM 1)

- DIMM 8 (Channel D, DIMM 1)
- DIMM 4 (Channel D, DIMM 0)
- DIMM 7 (Channel C, DIMM 1)
- DIMM 3 (Channel C, DIMM 0)

Eight modules can be used on motherboards with eight memory sockets, and each group of four modules can have different capacities, but the modules inside the same group must be identical. This arrangement is shown in Figure 3.27.

Exam essentials

Identify the types of memory.   Types of memory include SDRAM, DDR, DDR2, DDR3, and DDR4. These types differ in their data rates. Memory can also differ in packaging. There are SIMMS (single module) and DIMMs (double modules). They also can use either parity or ECC for error checking and can be single-, dual-, or triple-channel, with multiple channels widening the path between the memory and the memory controller.

Follow RAM speed and compatibility guidelines.   Faster memory can be added to a PC with slower memory installed, but the system will operate only at the speed of the slowest module present. RAM types cannot be mixed.

3.4 Compare and contrast storage devices

Storage media hold the data being accessed as well as the files the system needs to operate and the data that needs to be saved. The various types of storage differ in terms of capacity, the access time, and the physical media being used. This section provides a comparison of various storage devices.

Hard drives

Before the development and use of solid-state drives (SSDs), magnetic drives were the main type of hard drive used. The drive itself is a mechanical device that spins a stack of disks or platters and uses a magnetic head to read and write data to the surface of the disks. One of the advantages of SSDs (discussed in the next section) is the absence of mechanical parts that can malfunction. Figure 3.28 shows the parts of a magnetic hard drive.

The basic hard disk geometry consists of three components: the number of sectors that each track contains, the number of read/write heads in the disk assembly, and the number of cylinders in the assembly. This set of values is known as CHS (for cylinders/heads/sectors). A *cylinder* is the set of tracks of the same number on all the writable surfaces of the assembly. It is called a cylinder because the collection of all same-number tracks on all writable surfaces of the hard disk assembly looks like a geometric cylinder when connected vertically. Therefore, Cylinder 1, for instance, on an assembly that contains three platters comprises six tracks (one on each side of each platter), each labeled Track 1 on its respective surface. Figure 3.29 illustrates the key terms presented in this discussion.

FIGURE 3.28 Magnetic hard drive

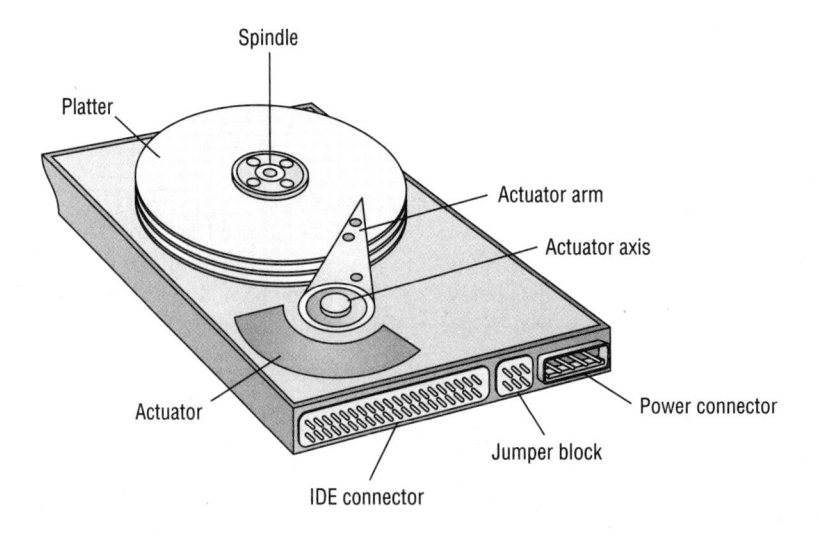

FIGURE 3.29 Cylinders, heads, and sections

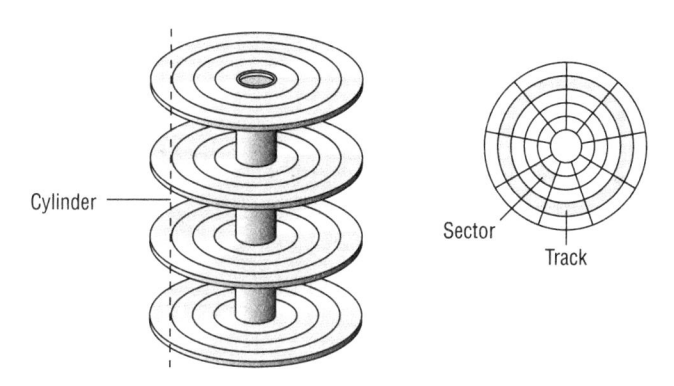

Spindle speeds

Spindle speed is the rotational speed of the disk or platter. Spindle speed has a direct influence on how quickly the drive can locate any specific disk sector on the drive. This locational delay is called *latency* and is measured in milliseconds (ms). Rotation is measured in revolutions per minute (rpm). As rpm increase, latency decreases. The most common speeds are in the following sections.

5,400 rpm

A drive operating at 5,400 rpm will experience about 5.5 ms of latency.

7,200 rpm

Drives that operate at 7,200 rpm will experience about 4.16 ms of latency. A typical 7,200 rpm desktop hard drive has a sustained data transfer rate up to 1,030 Mbps. This rate depends on the track's location, so it will be higher for data on the outer tracks and lower toward the inner tracks.

10,000 rpm

At 10,000 rpm, the latency will decrease to about 3 ms. Data transfer rates also generally go up with a higher rotational speed but are influenced by the density of the disk (i.e. the number of tracks and sectors present in a given area).

15,000 rpm

Drives that operate at 15,000 rpm are higher-end drives and suffer only 2 ms of latency. These drives also generate more heat, requiring more cooling to the case. They also offer faster data transfer rates for the same areal density.

Form factors

Form factor describes the size of the drive enclosure. Magnetic hard drives come in two sizes, 2.5 inch and 3.5 inch. Smaller drives are typically found in laptops, while the larger size is found in desktop computers. Figure 3.30 shows the comparison of a 2.5 inch drive to a 3.5 inch drive.

FIGURE 3.30 3.5 vs. 2.5 form factor

2.5 inch

The 2.5 inch drives are most commonly used in laptops, where the physical space required is a primary consideration. As of this writing, 2.5 inch drive storage capacity is approximately 6 TB.

3.5 inch

The 3.5 inch drives are primarily used in desktop computers and servers. As of this writing, 3.5 inch drive storage capacity is approximately 32 TB.

Solid-state drives (SSD)

SSDs retain data in nonvolatile memory chips and contain no moving parts. Compared to electromechanical hard disk drives (HDDs), SSDs are typically less susceptible to physical shock, are silent, have much lower access time and latency, and use less power, but are more expensive per gigabyte. A good thing to keep in mind is that because SSDs have no moving parts, they are far less susceptible to failure when compared with mechanical hard drives.

Communications interfaces

Drives can use various interface types to connect to the system. This section looks at these communication interface technologies.

Non-Volatile Memory Express (NVMe)

NVM Express (NVMe), or Non-Volatile Memory Host Controller Interface Specification (NVMHCIS), is an open logical device interface specification for accessing nonvolatile storage media attached via a PCI Express (PCIe) bus. It allows host hardware and software to fully exploit the levels of parallelism possible in modern SSDs. The latest version is 2.1.

SATA

Earlier in this chapter, you learned about the SATA drive interface. SATA 6, also known as SATA3 or SATA III, is the most recent generation of SATA, and the full version was released in 2009. SATA 6 communicates at the rate of up to 6 Gbps, and its bandwidth throughput is 4.8 Gbps (600 MBps), which doubles that of SATA 2. SATA 3 is backward-compatible with both SATA 1 and SATA 2.

Peripheral Component Interconnect Express (PCIe)

PCI Express (PCIE, PCI-E, or PCIe) uses a network of serial interconnects that operate at high speed. It's based on the PCI system; you can convert a PCIe slot to PCI using an adapter plug-in card, but you cannot convert a PCI slot to PCIe. Intended as a replacement for Accelerated Graphics Port (AGP) and Peripheral Component Interconnect (PCI), PCIe has the capability of being faster than AGP while maintaining the flexibility of PCI. There are five versions of PCIe: Version 1 is up to 8 GBps, version 2 is up to 16 GBps, version 3 is up to 32 GBps, version 4 is up to 64 GBps, and version 5 is up to 128 GBps. Figure 3.31 shows the slots discussed so far in this section.

Serial Attached Small Computer System Interface [SCSI] (SAS)

Serial Attached SCSI (SAS) is a point-to-point method of data transfer between devices, where the two devices are connected by a cable. This technology is primarily used for bulk transfer to external hard drives or tape drives. It allows 255 direct connections to storage devices, host computers, or expanders. Each expander can also support 255 connections, meaning that an SAS system can have as many as 65,535 (255 × 255) connections.

Form factors

SSDs come in two form factors, which are covered in the following sections.

FIGURE 3.31 PCI slots

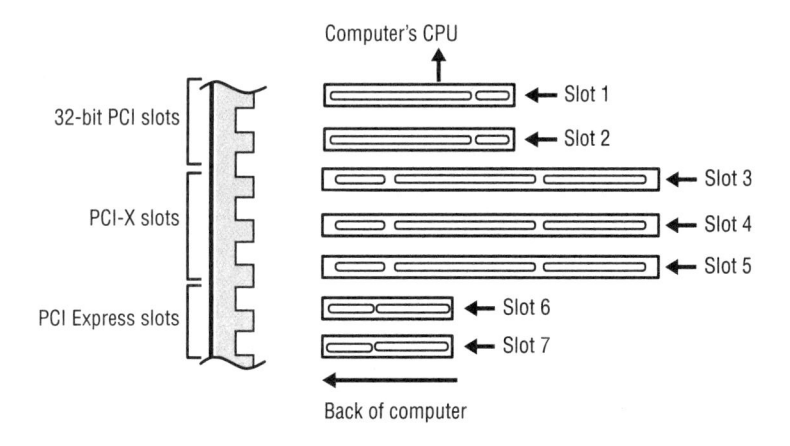

M.2

M.2, formerly known as the Next Generation Form Factor (NGFF), is a specification for internally mounted computer expansion cards and associated connectors. It replaces the mSATA standard. M.2 modules are rectangular, with an edge connector on one side and a semicircular mounting hole at the center of the opposite edge. They can use PCIe, SATA, and USB 3 connectors. The M.2 standard allows module widths of 12, 16, 22, and 30 mm and lengths of 16, 26, 30, 38, 42, 60, 80, and 110 mm.

Mini-Serial Advanced Technology Attachment (mSATA)

This type of SSD has a smaller form factor than SATA SSDs. Apart from having a small form, this drive also features low power consumption. The capacity of mSATA SSD is up to 1 TB.

Drive configurations

There are some special configuration scenarios that you should understand. Drives can be set up in configurations that offer performance benefits and in configurations that provide fault tolerance. We'll look at some of these configurations, including Redundant Array of Independent (or Inexpensive) Disks (RAID) arrays. In this section, you'll learn about five forms of RAID.

Redundant Array of Independent Disks (RAID) 0,1,5,6,10

RAID is a way of combining the storage power of more than one hard disk for a special purpose, such as increased performance or fault tolerance. RAID is more commonly done with SCSI drives, but it can be done with IDE or SATA drives. This section outlines the most common types of RAID. Because of the methods used to provide fault tolerance, the total amount of usable space in the array will vary, as discussed for each type.

RAID 0

RAID 0 is also known as *disk striping*. This is technically not RAID because it doesn't provide fault tolerance. Data is written across multiple drives, so one drive can be reading or writing while the next drive's read/write head is moving. This makes for faster data access. However, if any one of the drives fails, all content is lost. In RAID 0, because there is no fault tolerance, the usable space in the drive is equal to the total space on all the drives. So, if the two drives in an array have 250 GB each of space, 500 GB will be the available drive space. RAID 0 is shown in Figure 3.32.

RAID 1

RAID 1 is also known as *disk mirroring*. This is a method of producing fault tolerance by writing all data simultaneously to two separate drives. Drive #2 will have the same data as Drive #1. If one drive fails, the other drive contains all the data and may also be used as a data source. However, disk mirroring doesn't help access speed, and the cost is double that of a single drive. Because RAID 1 repeats the data on two drives, only one-half of the total

FIGURE 3.32 RAID 0

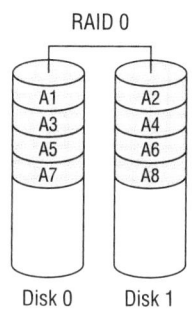

FIGURE 3.33 RAID 1

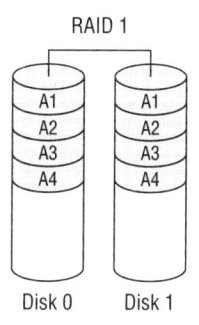

drive space is available for data. So, if two 250-GB drives are used in the array, 250 GB will be the available drive space. RAID 1 is shown in Figure 3.33.

RAID 5

RAID 5 combines the benefits of RAID 0 and RAID 1 and is also known as *striping with parity*. It uses a parity block distributed across all the drives in the array, in addition to striping the data across them. That way, if one drive fails, the parity information can be used to recover what was on the failed drive. A minimum of three drives is required. RAID 5 uses $1/n$ (n = the number of drives in the array) of each drive for parity information (e.g. one-third of the space in a three-drive array), and only 1 ($1/n$) is available for data. So, if three 250-GB drives are used in the array (for a total of 750 GB), 500 GB will be the available drive space. Likewise, with four 250-GB drives in the array, 750 GB will be available for storage. RAID 5 is shown in Figure 3.34.

RAID 6

RAID 6 fixes a potential flaw in the event of a failure of two disks in a RAID 5 array. RAID 5 repairs the disk if one disk fails but cannot rebuild the array if two disks fail. That's where RAID 6 comes in.

RAID 6 adds a second parity drive for rebuilding the array and is shown in Figure 3.35.

FIGURE 3.34 RAID 5

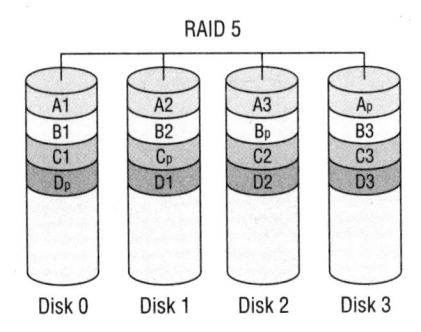

FIGURE 3.35 RAID 6

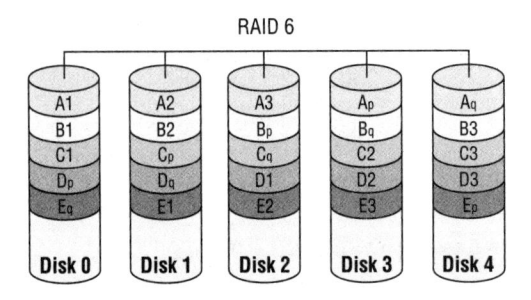

RAID 10

RAID 10 is also known as RAID 1+0. Striped sets are mirrored (a minimum of four drives, and the number of drives must be even). It provides fault tolerance and improved performance but increases complexity. Because this is effectively a mirrored stripe set and a stripe set gets 100% use of the drive without mirroring, this array will provide half of the total drive space in the array as available drive space. For example, if there are four 250-GB drives in a RAID 10 array (for a total of 1 TB), the available drive space will be 500 GB. RAID 10 is shown in Figure 3.36.

Removable storage

Drives that connect as peripherals are called *removable storage*. In this section, you'll learn about these devices.

Flash drives

Thumb drives are USB flash drives that have become extremely popular for transporting files. Figure 3.37 shows three thumb drives (also known as keychain drives) next to a pack of gum for size comparison.

FIGURE 3.36 xRAID 10

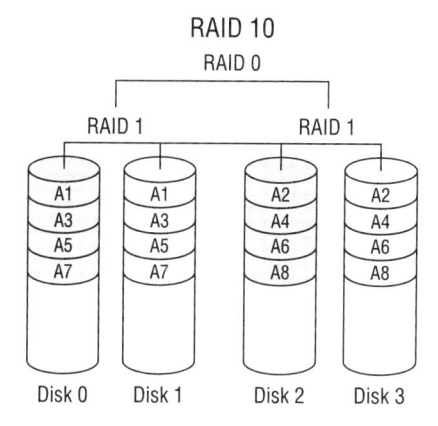

FIGURE 3.37 USB flash

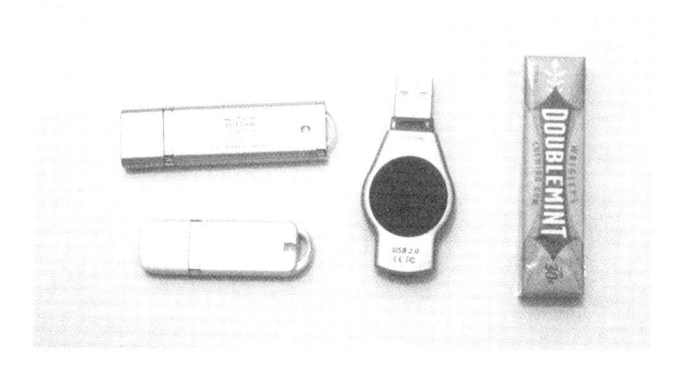

Flash drives (which are SSD) have been growing in popularity for years because they offer swift access to data and faster read and write speeds.

Memory cards

Flash technology is ideally suited for use not only with computers but also with many other things—digital cameras, smartphones, and so on. The next section discusses various forms of these drives.

SD card

Secure Digital (SD) cards are just one type of flash card; there are many others. The maximum capacity of a standard SD card is 2 TB, and there are two other standards that go beyond this: Secure Digital High Capacity (SDHC) can go to 32 GB, and Secure Digital Extra Capacity (SDXC) to 2 TB. Figure 3.38 shows a CompactFlash card (the larger of the two) and an SD card along with an eight-in-one card reader/writer. The reader shown

FIGURE 3.38   SD and CompactFlash

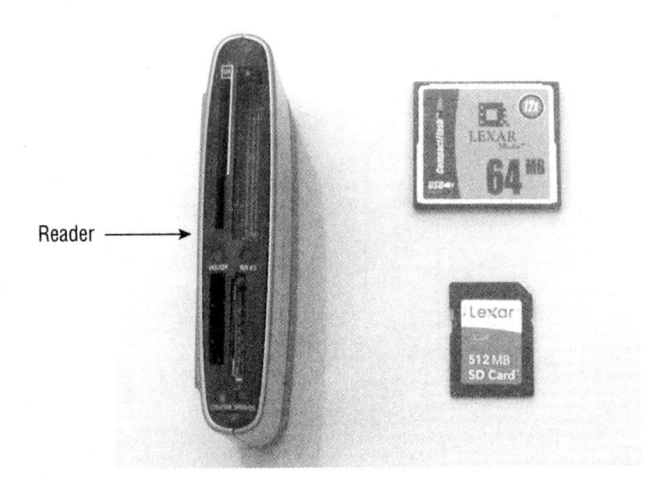

connects to the USB port and then interacts with CompactFlash, CompactFlash II, Memory Stick, Memory Stick PRO, xD-Picture, SD, and multimedia cards. The SD card specification defines three physical sizes, discussed in the following sections.

CompactFlash (CF)

CompactFlash (CF) cards are a widely used form of solid-state storage. There are two main subdivisions of CF cards: Type I (3.3 mm thick) and the thicker Type II (CF2) cards (5 mm thick). CF cards can be used directly in a PC card slot with a plug adapter, used as an ATA (IDE) or Personal Computer Memory Card International Association (PCMCIA) storage device with a passive adapter or with a reader, or attached to other types of ports, such as USB or FireWire. Figure 3.38 shows a CF card.

microSD card

microSD is the smallest of the three. It is 11 mm × 15 mm × 1 mm. microSD cards are commonly used to expand the storage capacity of smartphones.

miniSD card

miniSD is the middle child of the three SD form factors shown in Figure 3.39. It is 20 mm × 21.5 mm × 1.4 mm.

xD

An xD-Picture card is a flash memory card format used mainly in older digital cameras. xD stands for eXtreme Digital. xD cards are available in capacities from 16 MB up to 2 GB. Pictures are transferred from a digital camera's xD card to a PC by plugging the camera into the USB or IEEE 1394 (FireWire) cable or by removing the card from the camera and inserting it into a card reader. Figure 3.40 shows an xD card.

Optical drives

Optical drives work by using a laser rather than magnetism to change the characteristics of the storage medium. This is true for CD-ROM drives, DVD drives, and Blu-ray, all of which are discussed in the following sections.

FIGURE 3.39 SD, microSD, and miniSD

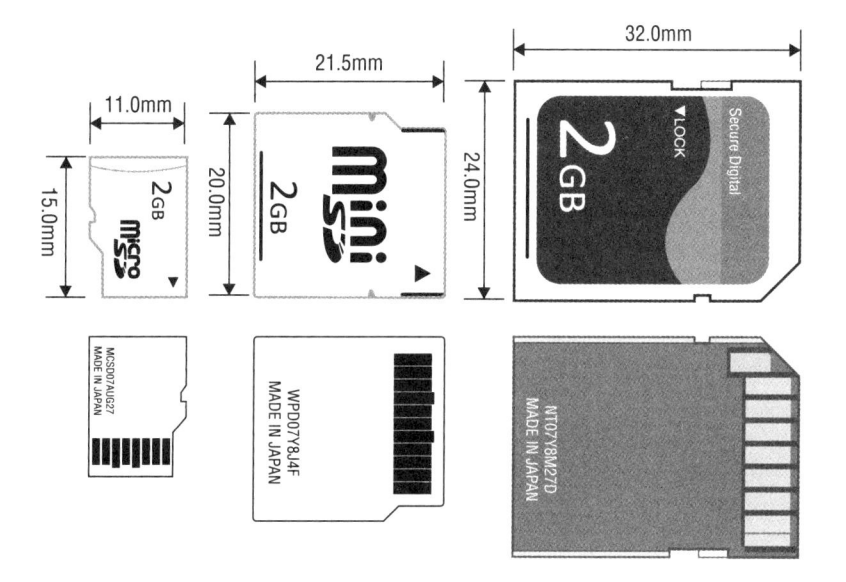

FIGURE 3.40 xD card

CD-ROM/CD-RW

CD-ROM stands for Compact Disc Read-Only Memory. The CD-ROM media is used for long-term storage of data. CD-ROM media is read-only, meaning that once information is written to a CD, it can't be erased or changed. Access time for CD-ROM drives is considerably slower than for a hard drive. Standard CDs normally hold 650 MB to 700 MB of data and use the ISO 9660 standard, which allows them to be used on multiple platforms.

Compact Disc-ReWritable (CD-RW) media are rewritable optical discs. A CD-RW drive requires more sensitive laser optics. It can write data to the disc but also has the ability to erase that data and write more data to the disc. It does this by liquefying the layer where the data resides (removing the reflectivity placed there by the writing process used to create the old data) and then creating new reflectivity in the same layer upon writing again that represents the new data. Two states of reflectivity are used to represent the 0s and 1s for the data. CD-RWs cannot be read in some CD-ROM drives built prior to 1997.

DVD-ROM/DVD-RW/DVD-RW DL

Because DVD-ROM drives use slightly different technology than CD-ROM drives, they can store up to 4.7 GB of data in a single-layer configuration. A single DVD, in a double-sided, double-layered configuration, can hold as much as 17 GB (as much as 26 regular CDs).

As you might expect, the primary advantage of DVD-RW drives over DVD-R drives is the ability to erase and rewrite to a DVD-RW disc. In these drives, a layer of metal alloy on the disk is manipulated to erase and write the data, rather than burning into the disc itself, similar to the operation of CD-RW.

A dual-layer DVD-RW disc employs a second physical layer within the disc itself. The drive with dual-layer capability accesses the second layer by shining the laser through the first semitransparent layer.

Blu-ray

Blu-ray recorders have been available since 2006 and they have the ability to record more information than a standard DVD using similar optical technology. In recent years, Blu-ray has been more synonymous with recording television and movie files than data, but the Blu-ray specification (1.0) includes two data formats: BD-R for write-once and BD-RE for rewritable media (more later in this section). BD-J is capable of more sophisticated bonus features than provided by standard DVD, including network access, picture-in-picture, and access to expanded local storage. With the exception of the Internet access component, these features are called Bonus View. The addition of Internet access is called BD Live.

> In the official specification, as noted on the Blu-ray Disc Association website (http://us.blu-raydisc.com/), the *r* is lowercase. CompTIA favors the uppercase R.

The current capacity of a Blu-ray is 100 GB. As a final note, there was a long-running (but finally complete) battle between Blu-ray and HD DVD to be the format of the future, and Blu-ray won.

BD-R

Blu-ray players have two data formats: BD-R for recording computer data and BD-RE for rewritable media. BD-R can be written to only one time.

BD-RE

Blu-ray Disc Recordable Erasable (BD-RE) can be erased and written to multiple times. Disc capacities are 25 GB for single-layer discs, 50 GB for double-layer discs, 100 GB for triple-layer discs, and 128 GB for quad-layer discs.

Exam essentials

Identify and differentiate the optical drive options for the long-term storage of data. Those options include CD-ROM, DVD-ROM, and Blu-ray. When the ability to erase and rewrite to the disk is required, the options include CD-RW, DVD-RW, Dual-Layer (DL) DVD-RW, and BD-RE.

Describe the types of interfaces to connect a drive to the system. Drives can be connected externally using USB, FireWire (IEEE 1394), eSATA, and Ethernet. Internally the connection types are SATA and SCSI.

3.5 Given a scenario, install and configure motherboards, central processing units (CPUs), and add-on cards

When working with motherboards, CPUs, and add-on cards, you are working with the basic components of a PC. In this section, we'll look at installing and configuring these basic components.

Motherboard form factors

The motherboard is the physical platform through which all the connected components communicate. The motherboard provides basic services needed for the machine to operate and provides communication channels through which connected devices, such as the processor, memory, disk drives, and expansion devices, communicate.

> The figures in this section are representative of what can be expected. Minor variations depend on the motherboard manufacturer. Consult the documentation for your motherboard.

The spine of the computer is the *system board*, or *motherboard*. This component is made of green or brown fiberglass and is placed in the bottom or side of the case. It's the most important component in the computer because it connects all the other components of a PC together. On the system board, you'll find the central processing unit (CPU), underlying circuitry, expansion slots, video components, RAM slots, and a variety of other chips. There are a number of different sizes or *form factors* of motherboards, which will be discussed in this section.

Advanced Technology Extended (ATX)

An older but still used form factor, Advanced Technology Extended (ATX), provided many design improvements over the previous version, AT. These improvements include I/O ports built directly into the side of the motherboard, the CPU positioned so that the power-supply fan helps cool it, and the ability for the PC to be turned on and off via software. It uses a PS/2-style connector for the keyboard and mouse, which is rarely used today because USB keyboards are used. Newer ATX models have removed PS/2 connectors. The expansion slots are parallel to the narrow edge of the board. See Figure 3.41 for an example of an ATX motherboard.

Micro-ATX

The micro-ATX motherboard typically measures 9.6 × 9.6 in. It usually has four PCI/PCIe slots for limited expansion as compared to ATX motherboards. Also, there are generally two to four RAM slots. It's a budget-friendly motherboard. See Figure 3.42 for an example of a micro-ATX motherboard.

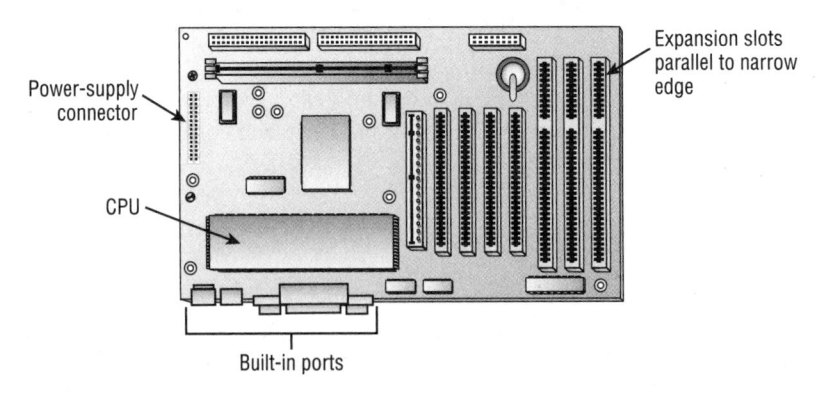

FIGURE 3.41 An ATX-style motherboard

FIGURE 3.42 Micro-ATX motherboard

Information Technology eXtended (ITX)

The Information Technology eXtended (ITX) motherboards—the mini-ITX, nano-ITX, and pico-ITX—were proposed by VIA Technologies. The mini-ITX fits in the same case as the micro-ATX; uses low power, which means it can be passively cooled (i.e. no fan); and has one expansion slot. The nano-ITX is even smaller; it is used for set-top boxes, media centers, and car computers. The pico-ITX is even smaller again, half the size of the nano-ITX. It uses daughter cards (extensions of the motherboard) to supply additional functionality.

Figure 3.43 compares common motherboard types and their sizes.

Motherboard connector types

Expansion slots exist on a motherboard to allow for the addition of new interfaces, peripherals, or new technologies without replacing the motherboard. If expansion slots did not exist, you would have to buy a new motherboard every time you wanted to add a new device that uses an interface to the board. This section reviews various types of expansion slots as well as connecters on the board for components, such as drives, panel lights, and the USB connector.

Peripheral Component Interconnect (PCI)

The PCI bus is a fast (33 MHz), wide (32-bit or 64-bit) expansion bus that was a modern standard in motherboards for general-purpose expansion devices. Its slots are typically white.

FIGURE 3.43 Motherboard sizes

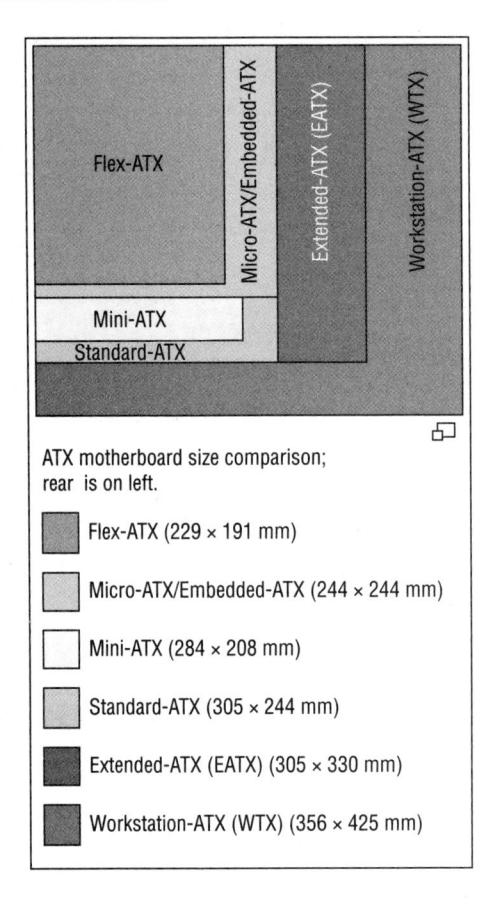

ATX motherboard size comparison; rear is on left.

- Flex-ATX (229 × 191 mm)
- Micro-ATX/Embedded-ATX (244 × 244 mm)
- Mini-ATX (284 × 208 mm)
- Standard-ATX (305 × 244 mm)
- Extended-ATX (EATX) (305 × 330 mm)
- Workstation-ATX (WTX) (356 × 425 mm)

PCI devices can share interrupt requests (IRQs) and other system resources with one another in some cases. You might see two PCI slots, but most motherboards have gone to newer standards. Figure 3.44 shows some PCI slots.

PCI cards that are 32-bit with 33 MHz operate up to 133 MBps, whereas 32-bit cards with 64 MHz operate up to 264 MBps. PCI cards that are 64-bit with 33 MHz operate up to 266 MBps, whereas 64-bit cards with 66 MHz operate up to 538 MBps.

PCIe

PCIe was discussed earlier in this chapter, in the section "Peripheral Component Interconnect Express (PCIe)." Please review that section. Figure 3.45 shows the slots discussed in this chapter.

FIGURE 3.44 PCI bus connectors

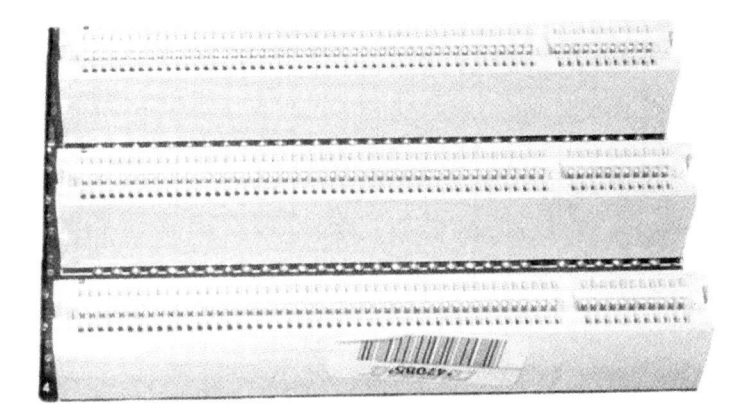

FIGURE 3.45 PCI slots

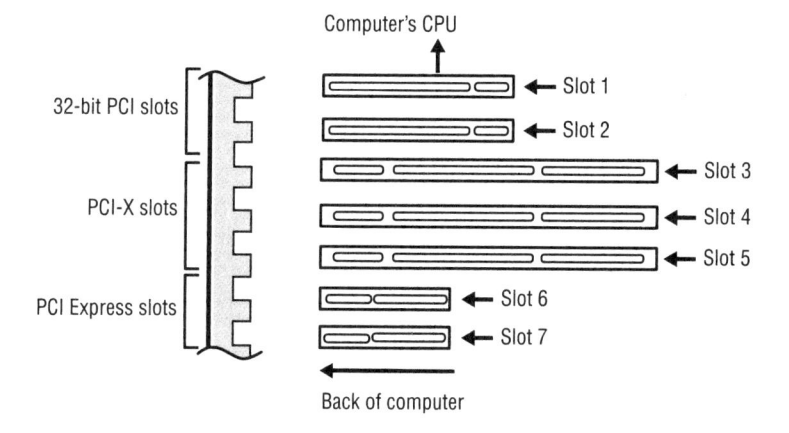

Power connectors

Various components in the case must receive power from the power supply. While you'll learn about power supplies later in this chapter, in this section you'll learn about the cables that run from the power supply to each component.

SATA

The SATA power connector has 15 pins, with 3 pins designated for 3.3 V, 5 V, and 12 V, and with each pin carrying 1.5 A. This results in a total draw of 4.95 W + 7.5 W + 18 W, or about 30 W. Figure 3.46 shows the SATA power connector.

FIGURE 3.46 SATA power connector

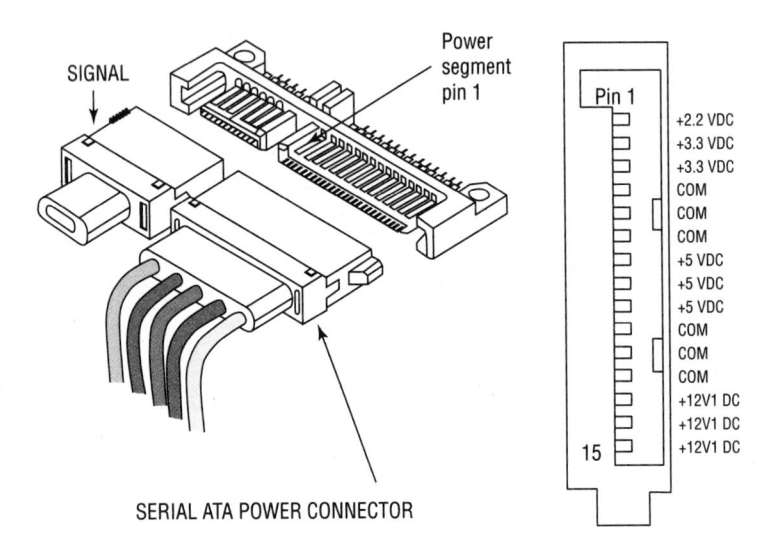

eSATA

eSATA provides a form of SATA meant for external connectivity. As compared to SATA (discussed more completely earlier in the section), eSATA is used for drive connections internally on many PCs. eSATA uses a more robust connector, longer shielded cables, and stricter (but backward-compatible) electrical standards. The interface resembles that of USB and IEEE 1394 (FireWire), but the cable cannot be as long, and the cable does not supply power to the device. The advantage it has over the other technologies is speed—it is approximately three times as fast as either FireWire or USB 2.0 (although USB 3.0 is faster).

SAN

You learned about Storage Area Networks (SAN) in Chapter 2 in the section "Network types." When a server is connected to a SAN, a cable connects the SAN to a host adapter through a host bus adaptor. The connections for the fiber cables can be seen on the end of the card shown in Figure 3.47.

Headers

Headers is simply another name for the connections or plugs found on a motherboard that send power to other components, such as USB connections, case lights, the speaker for beeps/error codes, fans, and so forth. So, a USB connector might also be called a USB header, and a fan power connector might also be called a fan header.

M.2

You learned about the M.2 form factor for drives earlier in this chapter. They can interface to the motherboard using either SATA, PCI, or PCIe slots.

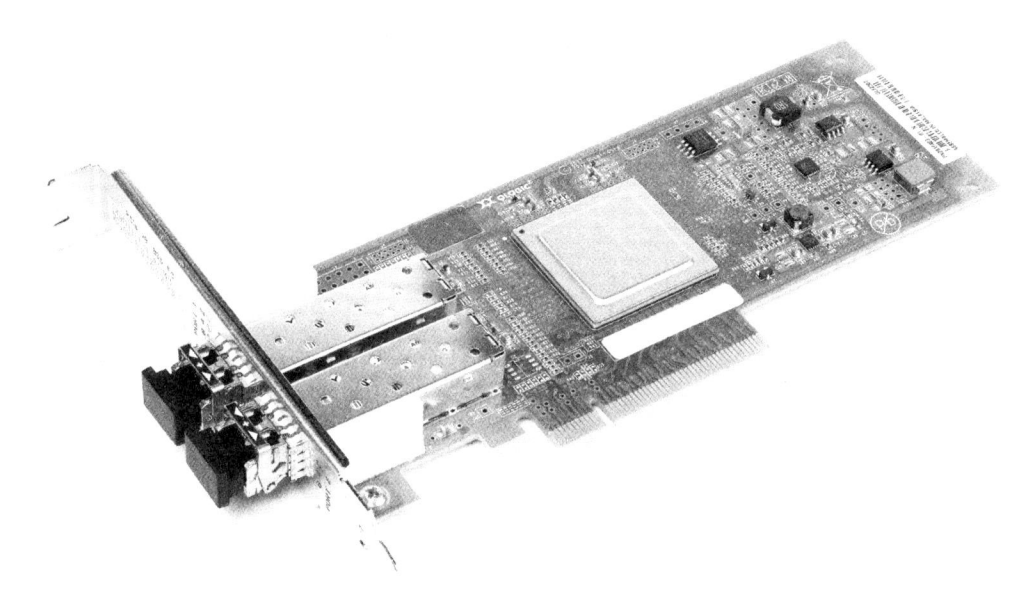

FIGURE 3.47   SAN host bus adapter (HBA)

Motherboard compatibility

When adding or replacing components on a motherboard, one must ensure that the components are compatible with the board. In some cases the slot will make it obvious, but in other scenarios you might need to consult documentation. In this section, you'll learn about components where compatibility is a key issue.

CPU socket types

Processors (i.e. CPUs) must be compatible with the sockets in which you install them. Let's take a closer look at sockets, compatibility, and the two major CPU types.

The CPU slot permits the attachment of the CPU to the motherboard, allowing the CPU to use the other components of the system. There are many different types of processors, meaning there are many types of CPU connectors.

The CPU slot can take on several different forms. In the past, the CPU slot was a rectangular box called a pin grid array (PGA) socket, with many small holes to accommodate the pins on the bottom of the chip. With the release of new and more powerful chips, additional holes were added, changing the configuration of the slot and its designator or number. Figure 3.48 shows a typical PGA-type CPU socket.

With the release of the Pentium II, the architecture of the slot went from a rectangle to more of an expansion-slot style of interface called a Single Edge Contact Cartridge (SECC). This style of CPU slot includes Slot 1 and Slot 2 for Intel CPUs and Slot A for Athlon (AMD)

FIGURE 3.48   A PGA CPU socket

FIGURE 3.49   SECC

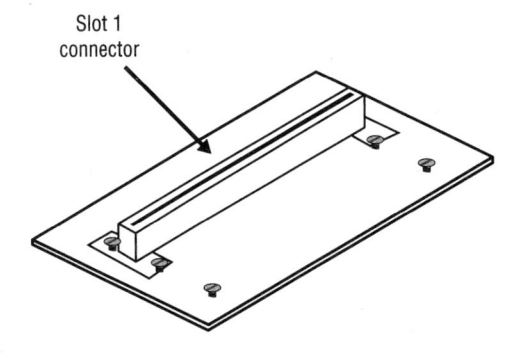

CPUs. This slot type looks much like an expansion slot, but it's located in a different place on the motherboard from the other expansion slots. Figure 3.49 shows an SECC.

To see which socket type is used for which processors, examine Table 3.4. This list is not exhaustive. Some slots may fit processors that are not specifically listed.

Sockets are the interface with which CPUs are plugged into the motherboard. These sockets have evolved over the years along with the changes in CPU architecture and design. There are three form factors for CPU chips: PGA, SECC, and land grid array (LGA). The PGA style is a flat square or rectangular ceramic chip with an array of pins in the bottom. The actual CPU is a silicon wafer embedded inside that ceramic chip. The SECC style is a circuit board with the silicon wafer mounted on it. The circuit board is then surrounded by a plastic cartridge for protection; the circuit board sticks out of the cartridge along one edge. This edge fits into a slot in the motherboard.

Advanced Micro Devices, Inc. (AMD)

Advanced Micro Devices (AMD) is one of two major processor vendors in the world. Athlon models are AMD processors. See Table 3.4 for models and socket compatibility.

TABLE 3.4 Socket types and the processors they support

Connector Type	Processor
Socket 1	486 SX/SX2, 486 DX/DX2, 486 DX4 Overdrive
Socket 2	486 SX/SX2, 486 DX/DX2, 486 DX4 Overdrive, 486 Pentium Overdrive
Socket 3	486 SX/SX2, 486 DX/DX2, 486 DX4 486 Pentium Overdrive
Socket 4	Pentium 60/66, Pentium 60/66 Overdrive
Socket 5	Pentium 75-133, Pentium 75+ Overdrive
Socket 6	DX4, 486 Pentium Overdrive
Socket 7	Pentium 75-200, Pentium 75+ Overdrive
Socket 8	Pentium Pro
Socket 370	Pentium III
Socket 423	Pentium 4
Socket 478	Pentium 4 and Celeron 4
SECC (Type I), Slot 1	Pentium II
SECC2 (Type II), Slot 2	Pentium III
Slot A	Athlon
Socket 603	Xeon
Socket 754	AMD Athlon 64
Socket 939	Some versions of Athlon 64
Socket 940	Some versions of Athlon 64 and Opteron

(Continued)

TABLE 3.4 (Continued)

Connector Type	Processor
Socket LGA 775	Core 2 Duo/Quad
Socket AM2	Athlon 64 family (replacing earlier socket usage)
Socket F	Opteron
Socket AM2+	AMD Athlon64, X2, Phenom, and Phenom II
Socket P	Intel Core2
Socket 441	Intel Atom
Socket LGA 1366/B	Intel Core i7, Xeon (35xx, 36xx, 55xx, 56xx series)
G1/G2/rPGA 988A/B	Intel Core i7, i5, i3, P6000, P4000
Socket AM3	AMD Phenom, Athlon II, Sempron
Socket H/LGA 1156	Intel Core i7, i5, Xeon, Pentium G5000, G1000
Socket G34	AMD Opteron 6000 series
Socket C32	AMD Opteron 4000 series
LGA 1150	Intel Haswell, Haswell Refresh, and Broadwell
Socket AM3+	AMD FX Vishera, AMD FX Zambezi, AMD Phenom II, AMD Athlon II, AMD Sempron
Socket FM2	AMD Trinity Processors
Socket FM2+	AMD Kaveri
LGA 1248	Intel Titanium 9300 series
LGA 1567	Intel Xeon 6500/7500 series
Socket H2/LGA 1155	Intel Sandy Bridge-DT
Socket R/LGA 2011	Intel Sandy Bridge B2 (also referred to as Xeon E5)
Socket FM1	AMD Llano (also referred to as A-series)

Intel

The market leader in chip manufacturing is Intel Corporation, with Advanced Micro Devices (AMD) gaining a market share in the home PC market. Here's a quick list of socket types from both manufacturers you may encounter:

Intel: LGA 775, 1155, 1156, 1366, 1150, 2011   Earlier in this chapter, Table 3.4 listed the various Intel CPU slots and sockets you might find in a motherboard and explained which CPUs will fit into them.

AMD: AM3, AM3+, FM1, FM2, FM2+   Table 3.4 also listed the various AMD CPU slots and sockets you might find in a motherboard and which CPUs will fit into them. These later-generation AMD sockets were launched as the successor to Socket AM2+. In 2009, AMD3 was released alongside the initial grouping of Phenom II processors designed for it. The principal change from AM2+ to AM3 is support for DDR3 SDRAM. The AM3+ socket has been designed for the AMD FX series Zambezi processors based on the Bulldozer architecture. Socket FM2 is a CPU socket launched in September 2012. Motherboards using the FM2 utilize AMD's new A85X chipset. The FM2+ uses three PCI Express cores: one 2 × 16 core and two 5 × 8 cores, for a total of 64 lanes.

Multisocket

CPUs can have a single core, or they can be dual-core, quad-core, or even dual-quad-core (eight CPUs total). When multiple cores exist, they operate as individual processors, so the more the better. The largest boost in performance will likely be noticed in improved response time while running CPU-intensive processes, such as virus scans, ripping/burning media (requiring file conversion), or file searching.

The addition of more cores does not have a linear effect on performance. The potential impact of multiple cores also depends on the amount of cache or memory present to serve the CPU. When a computer is designed for the processor, this will have been taken into consideration, but when adding a multicore processor to a PC, it is an issue to consider.

Multicore Processors

Multicore processors, available from Intel as well as AMD, essentially combine multiple processors into one chip. Instead of adding two more processors to a machine (making it a multiprocessor system), you have one chip splitting operations and essentially performing as if it is two or more processors to get better performance. A *multicore* architecture simply has multiple completely separate processor dies (small blocks of semiconducting material on which a given functional circuit is fabricated) in the same package, whether it's dual, triple, or quad core. The OS and applications see multicore processors in the same way that they see multiple processors in separate sockets. Both dual- and quad-core processors are common cases for the multicore technology. Most multicore processors from Intel come in even numbers, whereas AMD's Phenom series can contain odd numbers (such as the triple-core processor).

Basic Input/Output System/Unified Extensible Firmware Interface (BIOS/UEFI) settings

PCs and other devices that use an OS usually also contain firmware that provides low-level instructions to the device even in the OS's absence. This firmware, called either the Basic Input/Output System (BIOS) or the Unified Extensible Firmware Interface (UEFI), contains settings that can be manipulated as well as diagnostic utilities that can be used to monitor the device. This section discusses those settings and utilities.

Boot options

Each system has a default boot order, which is the order in which it checks the drives for a valid OS to which it can boot. Usually, this order is set for the hard disk and then CD-ROM (if the device still has one of these) or boot over the network, but these components can be placed in any boot order. For example, you might set CD-ROM first to boot from a disk that already contains an OS. If you receive an error message when booting, always check the CD-ROM, and if a non-system disk is present, remove it and reboot.

USB permissions

One of the more difficult security measures to enforce is a restriction on the use of USB devices. While the reasons for it are clear (prevention of the introduction of malware to the network), users don't have a good track record for complying. One step you can take is to disable the USB ports in the BIOS. As you can see in Figure 3.50, it's simply a matter of disabling them in Settings.

Trusted Platform Module (TPM) security features

Many operating systems provide the ability to encrypt an entire volume or drive, protecting a mobile device's data in the event of theft. A good example of this is BitLocker, which is available beginning with Windows 10. The drives are encrypted with encryption keys, and the proper keys are required to boot the device and access the data.

BitLocker can be used with a Trusted Platform, but it is not required. When this feature is in effect with no TPM chip, the keys are stored on a USB drive, which must be presented during startup to allow access to the drives. Without the USB drive holding the key, the device will not boot.

FIGURE 3.50 Disabling USB ports

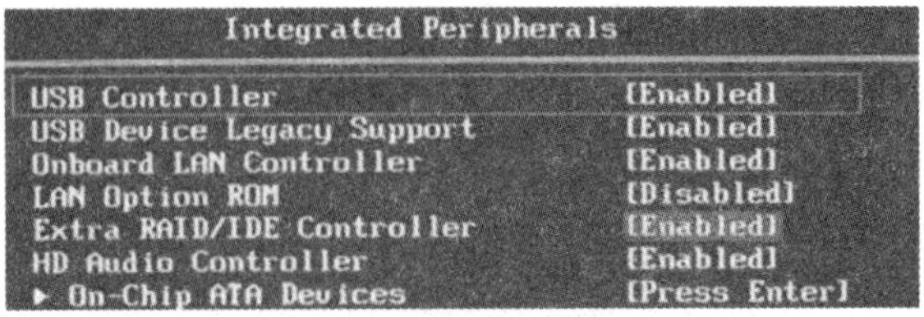

Fan considerations

As you will learn later in this book, overheating causes significant issues with many of the components inside the case, especially the CPU. The BIOS has settings that impact the fan operations. Some BIOS menus allow you to specify the speed or percentage at which the fan operates. In some cases, you might be able to specify at what temperature different fan speeds or power percentages activate. You might find that by altering the fan settings, you suffer fewer overheating issues.

Secure Boot

Secure Boot is a standard adopted by many vendors that requires the OS to check the integrity of all system files before allowing the boot process to proceed. This process protects against the alteration or corruption of system files. As with any emerging technology, issues have already been discovered that can enable a hacker not only to bypass Secure Boot but also to change a key value in the settings that will "brick" the device (i.e. render it useless).

Boot password

The boot password, when the option is set, comes up as a prompt after power-on self-test (POST) has been completed but before the OS begins loading. It's there to ensure that only authorized users can proceed to the OS boot process. Sometimes, it is referred to as the user password in some BIOS/UEFI versions.

BIOS password

While you can set a BIOS password when using a TPM chip in most CMOS Setup programs, as explained previously, you can also set a supervisor password. This activates the requirement that a password must be entered in order to use the CMOS Setup program, effectively locking out users from making changes to it. You might also be able to set a user password, which restricts the PC from booting unless the password is entered.

To reset a forgotten password, you can remove the CMOS battery to reset everything. There also may be a reset jumper (a small switch that can be moved between two positions, one of which removes the password) on the motherboard. The CMOS battery is shown in Figure 3.51.

FIGURE 3.51   CMOS battery

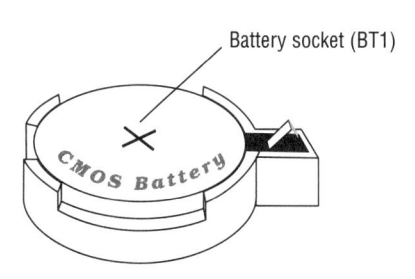

Temperature monitoring

Temperature monitoring in the BIOS/UEFI allows you to keep track of the heat generated by critical components. It's a great tool to ensure your system is running within safe operating ranges and to prevent overheating. It can check temperatures on the CPU, motherboard/chipset, and GPU. You can set it to issue an alarm or warning when the temperature gets too high. This is a critical feature if you are overclocking!

> **Overclocking**
>
> Overclocking is the process of increasing a component's clock rate, running it at a higher speed than it was designed to run. While it will speed up the system, it can cause overheating.

Virtualization support

When using virtualization technology, a fuller realization of its benefits can be achieved when the processor supports this concept. The benefit derived from this support is to allow the virtualization product (also called a *hypervisor*) to use hardware-assisted virtualization. This allows the hypervisor to dynamically allocate CPU to the virtual machines (VMs) as required. Both AMD and Intel offer CPUs that support hardware virtualization.

Encryption

A number of security features are built into most BIOSes. As you've learned, these features include drive encryption. In this section, you'll learn about performing encryption without placing an additional strain on the system's CPU.

TPM

BitLocker can be used with a TPM chip (discussed in the next paragraph), but it is not required. When this feature is in effect with no TPM chip, the keys are stored on a USB drive that must be presented during startup to allow access to the drives. Without the USB drive holding the key, the device will not boot.

When the device has a TPM chip present on the motherboard, additional security and options become available. First, the chip contains the keys that unlock the drives. When the computer boots, the TPM chip unlocks the drive only after it compares hashes of the drive to snapshots of the drive taken earlier. If any changes have been made or tampering has been done to the Windows installation, the TPM chip will not unlock the drives.

Moreover, you can (and should) combine this with a PIN entered at startup or a key located in a USB drive. In this scenario, the computer will not start unless the hashes pass the test and the personal identification number (PIN) or key is provided.

Hardware security module (HSM)

A hardware security module (HSM) is an appliance that safeguards and manages digital keys used with strong authentication and provides crypto processing. It attaches directly to a computer or server. Among the functions of an HSM are:

- Onboard secure cryptographic key generation
- Onboard secure cryptographic key storage and management
- Use of cryptographic and sensitive data material
- Offloading of application servers for complete asymmetric and symmetric cryptography

   There are some drawbacks to an HSM, including the following:

- High cost
- Lack of a standard for the strength of the number generator
- Difficulty in upgrading

CPU architecture

Computer architecture describes the set of rules, methods, and physical structures used in the CPU. There have been many different architectures over the years. In this section, you will learn about them.

x86/x64

CPUs can be either 32-bit (x86) or 64-bit (x64). This value describes what is called the *word size* of the processor. Having 64 bits offers two important benefits. Data can be processed in larger chunks, which also means with greater precision. Moreover, the system can point to or address a larger number of locations in physical memory. A key consideration is the OS. If the OS is not 64-bit, you cannot take advantage of the 64-bit processor.

Advanced RISC Machine (ARM)

The Advanced reduced instruction set computer (RISC) Machine (ARM) architecture uses a reduced set of CPU instruction and will only run an OS designed to support it. They come in both 32-bit and 64-bit versions.

Core configurations

You learned about single and multicore processors earlier in this chapter.

Expansion cards

Expansion cards allow you to add functionality to the PC. In this section, I'll discuss the types of cards and the functionality they provide. I'll also talk about installing and configuring them properly.

Newer cards will be installed in the PCI or PCIe slots and will probably be detected by the OS. If it already contains the driver for the device in its preinstalled driver library, the process will be done as soon as you restart the PC. If the driver is not present in the driver cache, you will have to install the driver that came with it.

Sound card

Most computers these days come with an integrated sound card, but for more robust sound or advanced features, you might need to install a sound card. Sound cards can be either internal or external. Internal cards require opening the case and installing the card in a slot. External cards plug into the USB socket.

In some cases, an audio cable will be connected from the card to the optical drive, but this is rarely required these days. Figure 3.52 shows the connectors present on most sound cards today.

Video card

PCs today also contain internal video cards, but as with sound cards, you can achieve better video quality with more expensive video cards. This is especially true when the video card has its own dedicated memory.

Onboard

In earlier times, most internal cards were vastly inferior to the cards you could buy, but that is much less the case today, when users have learned to expect better video quality.

Newer OSes like Windows 10 have helped raise the bar for internal cards as well, in that they require a card with a minimum set of features and a minimum amount of dedicated RAM to appreciate the OS's visual capabilities.

FIGURE 3.52 Sound card connectors

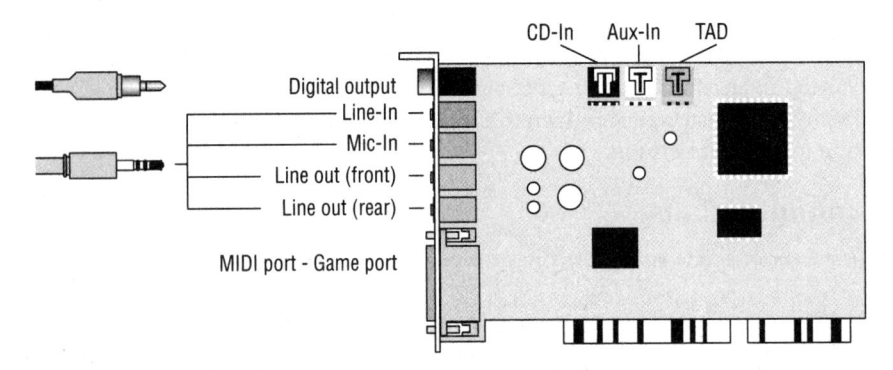

3.5 Install and configure motherboards, CPUs, and add-on cards

WARNING If you decide to install an add-on card in a system that has an onboard card, the technician will need to disable the onboard card (using UEFI).

Add-on card

Video cards can be installed in the AGP, PCI, and PCIe slots. At one point, the best choice was clear, and that was the AGP slot. However, the newer PCIe slots provide more bandwidth. AGP provides a wider data path because it's parallel, whereas PCIe is serial. But PCIe now goes up to 16,000 MBps as compared to AGP, which is 2,000 MBps. Figure 3.53 shows the AGP slot next to some slots about which you have already learned.

Some of the special functions you might get with a more expensive video card are 3D imaging, Moving Picture Experts Group (MPEG) decoding (decoding simply means it can interpret this file type), and TV output. The ability to use multiple monitors is also built into many cards.

Capture card

Many video- and audio-editing software packages come with a special capture card that works in concert with the accompanying software to provide ease of use. For example, it might be an internal PCI card that captures video from any analog or DV source, like you would when transferring older VCR tapes to digital formats. You can also output video to a DVD recorder or an analog or DV camcorder from this card. They require a high-end audio and video card as well, plus plenty of memory and a processor that might not have quite the requirements of computer-aided design/computer-aided manufacturing (CAD/CAM), but still the GPU should be 2.4 GHz or higher.

FIGURE 3.53 AGP and PCI slots

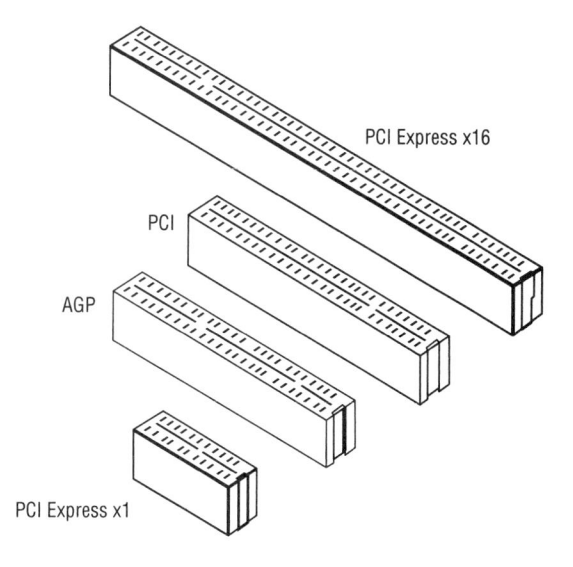

Network interface card (NIC)

Network cards do exactly what you would think; they provide a connection for the PC to a network. In general, network interface cards (NICs) are added to a PC via an expansion slot, or they are integrated into the motherboard, but they might also be added through a USB or PCMCIA slot (also known as PC card). The most common issue that prevents network connectivity is a bad or unplugged patch cable.

Network cards are made for Ethernet, fiber-optic, token ring (rarely used now), and 802.11 (wireless) connections. The Ethernet, token ring, and fiber-optic cards accept the appropriate cable, and the wireless cards have radio transmitters and antennas.

The most obvious difference between network cards is the speed of which they are capable. Most networks today operate at 100 MBps or 1 GBps. Regardless of other components, the PC will operate at the speed of the slowest component, so if the card is capable of 1 GBps, but the cable is capable of only 100 MBps, the PC will transmit only at 100 MBps.

Another significant feature to be aware of is the card's ability to perform autosensing. This feature allows the card to sense whether the connection is capable of full duplex and to operate in that manner with no action required.

There is another type of autosensing, in which the card is capable of detecting what type of device is on the other end and changing the use of the wire pairs accordingly. For example, normally a PC connected to another PC requires a crossover cable, but if both ends can perform this sensing, that is not required. These types of cards are called auto-medium-dependent interface crossover (MDIX).

Cooling

CPUs produce heat, and the more powerful the CPU, the more heat it produces. Heat is generally an enemy to the PC because it causes problems such as random reboots. Methods of cooling the CPU—and, in turn, the overall interior of the case—have evolved with the increasing need to remove this heat. This section covers options that are used.

Among methods of cooling, technology that transfers heat away from components uses thermoelectric cooling, which comprises a solid-state active heat pump that transfers heat from one side of the device to the other. Components that perform this function are called *Peltier components*. Heat sinks, cooling fans, and cooling fins are Peltier components. Liquid cooling, on the other hand, cools not by transferring heat away from components but by circulating a cool liquid around them.

Fans

Active heat sinks have a fan that sits atop the heat sink. It pulls the heat out of the heat sink and away from it. Then the case fan shoots the heat out the back or side of the case.

Heat sink

A heat sink's cooling can be either active or passive. A *passive heat sink* is a block of heat-conductive material that sits close to the CPU and wicks away the heat into the air. An *active heat sink* contains a fan that pulls the hot air away from the CPU. The heat sink sits atop the CPU in many cases, obscuring it from view entirely.

Thermal paste/pads

Most passive heat sinks are attached to the CPU using a glue-like thermal compound (called *thermal glue*, *thermal compound*, or *thermal paste*). This makes the connection between the heat sink and the CPU more seamless and direct. Thermal compound can be used on active heat sinks too, but generally it isn't because of the possibility that the fan may stop working and need to be replaced. Thermal compound improves thermal transfer by eliminating tiny air pockets between the heat sink and CPU (or other device, like a north bridge or video chipset). Thermal compound both provides improved thermal transfer and adds bonding for heat sinks when there are no mounting holes to clamp the heat sink to the device to be cooled.

Liquid

Liquid-based cooling cases are available that use circulating water rather than fans to keep components cool. These cases are typically more expensive than standard ones and may be more difficult for a technician untrained in this technology to work on, but they result in an almost completely silent system.

Issues with liquid-based cooling machines can include problems with hoses or fittings, the pump, or the coolant. A failure of the pump can keep the liquid from flowing and cause the system to overheat. A liquid-based cooling system should also be checked every so often for leaks or corrosion on the hoses and fittings, and the reservoir should be examined to make sure it is full and does not contain contaminants. Liquid-based cooling is more expensive, less noisy, and more efficient than Peltier components.

Exam essentials

Differentiate the motherboard form factors.   The ATX is the oldest and largest of motherboard sizes still being manufactured. The micro-ATX is for smaller and cheaper systems. The smaller ITX motherboards come in three sizes: the mini-ITX, the nano-ITX, and the pico-ITX.

Identify expansion slot types.   PCI slots are the standard for general-purpose cards. PCIe is a newer high-speed slot based on the PCI system. Mini PCI slots are used in laptops.

Locate the CPU socket on the motherboard.   The CPU socket can take on several different forms. In the past, the CPU socket was a rectangular box called a PGA socket, with many small holes to accommodate the pins on the bottom of the chip. With the release of the Pentium II, the architecture of the socket went from a rectangle to more of an expansion-slot style of interface called an SECC.

3.6 Given a scenario, install the appropriate power supply

The power supply provides a number of connectors for various devices as well as a plug for the motherboard. It is important to understand these connector types and to appreciate the power drawn by various devices. Knowledge of the power needs of the devices can allow the technician to choose a power supply that provides the total power needs of the PC.

Input 110–120 VAC vs. 220–240 VAC

Most power supplies have a recessed, two-position slider switch (often a red one) on the rear that is exposed through the case. Selections read 110 and 220, 115 and 230, or 120 and 240. This voltage selector switch is used to select the voltage level used in the country where the computer is in service. For example, in the United States, the power grid supplies anywhere from 110 VAC to 120 VAC. However, in Europe, for instance, the voltage supplied is double, ranging from 220 VAC to 240 VAC.

Output 3.3V vs. 5V vs. 12V

In 2004, the ATX 12V 2.0 (now 2.03) standard was passed, changing the main connector from 20 pins to 24. The additional pins provide +3.3V, +5V, and +12V (the fourth pin is a ground) for use by PCIe cards. When a 24-pin connector is used, there is no need for the optional 4- or 6-pin auxiliary power connectors.

20+4 pin motherboard connector

A power connector allows the motherboard to be connected to the power supply. On an ATX, there is a single power connector consisting of a block of 20 holes (in two rows). On an AT, there is a block consisting of 12 pins sticking up; these pins are covered by two connectors with six holes each.

Figure 3.54 shows a versatile motherboard with both kinds so you can compare them. The upper connector is for ATX, and the lower one is for AT.

When using the AT power connector, the power cable coming from the power supply will have two separate connectors, labeled P8 and P9. When you are attaching the two parts to the motherboard, the black wires on one should be next to the black wires on the other for proper function.

Redundant power supply

Data centers usually deploy redundant power sources to maintain constant power. Redundancy can be provided in several ways:

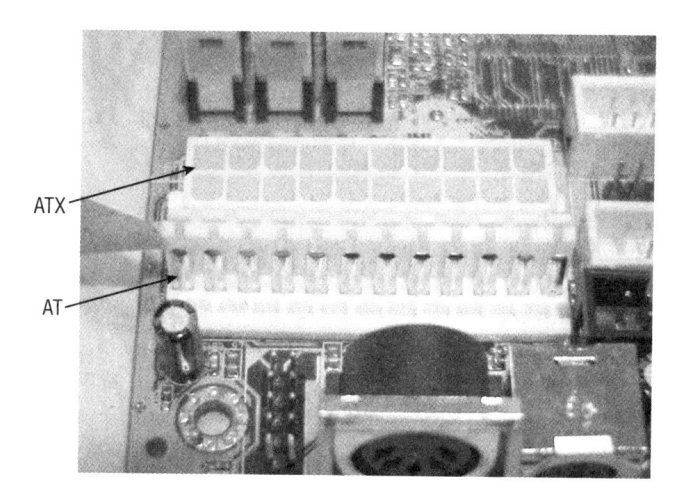

FIGURE 3.54 Power connectors on a motherboard

- Parallel redundancy or the N+1 option describes an architecture where there is always a single extra uninterruptible power supply (UPS) available (that's the +1), and the N simply indicates the total number of UPSes required for the data center. Because the system runs in two feeds and there is only one redundant UPS, this system can still suffer failures.
- Redundancy of 2N means the data center provides double the power it requires, by providing two power supplies with one as backup. This ensures that the system is fully redundant.

Redundancy also refers to using redundant power supplies on the devices. Many servers come with two supplies, and you can buy additional power supplies as well. Always ensure that the power supply you buy can accommodate all the needs of the server.

Modular power supply

A modular power supply differs from a nonmodular one in that cables or wires that run from the supply to each component on the board are not permanently attached. This allows you to use only the cable you need. The presence of such a unit will allow you to install it even in a mini-ATX case without losing space in the system unit. Typically, the cost of a modular power supply for a computer is more expensive than the price of a regular one. This is the biggest drawback of a full modular power supply unit (PSU).

Wattage rating

When you add up the wattage needs of each device, as well as the motherboard and CPU, you will know the wattage that the power supply must provide. A power supply has a rated output capacity in watts, and when you fill a system with power-hungry devices, you must ensure that its maximum capacity isn't exceeded. Otherwise, problems with power can occur, creating lockups or spontaneous reboots. Most power supplies provide between 250 W and 1,200 W. It's always a good idea to have more than the minimum required for the devices that are present, so that additional devices can be added in the future.

Energy efficiency

Power supplies are voluntarily rated by their efficiency, expressed as a percentage. This percentage indicates how much of the AC coming from the electric wall outlet is converted to DC and how much is lost to heat. If a power supply is rated at 80%, that means 80% of the AC is delivered as DC power, and the other 20% is lost as heat.

Power supplies will often have an 80-Plus certification level of Bronze, Silver, Gold, Platinum, or Titanium. These ratings indicate an efficiency level ranging from 80% to 92%.

A more efficient power supply consumes less AC power to deliver DC to the motherboard. For comparison, a budget power supply might cost $165 per year to operate, while a Gold-rated power supply might cost $110 per year. Why does this matter? For the consumer with a single computer, this doesn't mean a lot. However, if your organization has thousands of computers, this cost savings could be considerable!

Exam essentials

Identify common power connector types and their voltages. These include but are not limited to SATA, Molex, 4- to 8-pin 12V, PCIe 6- to 8-pin, 20-pin, and 24-pin connectors.

Understand the specifications of power supplies. Differentiate power supplies by wattage, size, number of connectors, and design (ATX or mini-ATX).

Describe a dual-wattage power supply. This is a supply that can be set to accept either 110 V or 220 V.

3.7 Given a scenario, deploy and configure multifunction devices/printers and settings

Printers are one of the most common elements in any computing environment, from home to office. The range they cover is phenomenal—everything from a free printer included by a vendor with the purchase of a PC, up to a monolith in a large office churning out hundreds of pages a minute. Regardless of where a printer falls in that spectrum, they are all the same in that they must be installed and properly configured to be of use. Moreover, most printing devices today are multifunction devices. They print, scan, and fax in various combinations.

Properly unbox device and consider setup location

When a new printer arrives, the setup starts with proper unboxing of the unit. Keep in mind that the device might not function properly and might need to be returned. Until acceptable operation is validated, you should keep all packing materials so you can reuse them. Also, be very careful when using knives and other sharp instruments to cut into the packaging. You don't want to cut a cable or damage a component.

The location of the print device is also an important consideration. If it is a shared device, you should place it in a location convenient for the bulk of users rather than making it convenient for you or for any single person. Also locate the paper, toner cartridges, and other maintenance items in the same location.

Use appropriate drivers for a given operating system

Besides understanding the printer's operation, for the exam you need to understand how these devices communicate with a computer. The driver software controls how the printer processes the print job. When you install a printer driver for the printer that you are using, it allows the computer to print to that printer correctly (assuming you have the correct interface configured between the computer and printer). Also keep in mind that drivers are OS-specific, so you need to select one that is for both the correct printer and the correct OS.

An interface is the collection of hardware and software that allows the device to communicate with a computer. Each printer, for example, has at least one interface, but some printers have several to make them more flexible in a multiplatform environment. If a printer has several interfaces, it can usually switch between them on the fly, so that several computers can print at the same time.

Printer Control Language (PCL) vs. PostScript

For a printer to work with a particular OS, a driver must be installed for it. This driver specifies the page description language (PDL) the printer understands as well as information about the printer's characteristics (e.g. paper trays, maximum resolution, etc.). For laser printers, there are two popular PDLs: Adobe PostScript (PS) and Hewlett-Packard Printer Control Language (PCL). Almost all laser printers use one or both of these.

Firmware

Firmware (on any device) is the software that makes that device operate. In the case of a printer or multifunction device, the firmware determines how the paper feeds, the lights or messages that are displayed, the controls for how the printhead moves across the page, and how it accepts a signal from a wired network, Wi-Fi, or a physical cable.

Drivers are used to translate print commands coming from a computer's OS into the manufacturer's firmware language. As an analogy, let's say a Brother printer understands the "BrotherSpeak" firmware language, and a Lexmark printer understands "LexmarkSpeak" firmware language. This would make sense, as they are made in different factories by different companies. A Windows 11 machine issues a printer command in "WindowsPrint" language. A driver is what is used to translate "WindowsPrint" into "BrotherSpeak" firmware or "LexmarkSpeak" firmware.

Device connectivity

The forms of connection this exam tests on are USB, Ethernet, and wireless. Each is addressed in the following sections.

USB

The most popular type of printer interface as this book is being written is USB. It's the most popular interface for just about every peripheral. The benefits for printers are that USB has a higher transfer rate than either serial or parallel, and it automatically recognizes new devices. USB is also fully plug and play, and it allows several printers to be connected at once without adding ports or using up additional system resources.

Ethernet

Most large-environment printers (primarily laser and LED printers) have a special interface that allows them to be hooked directly to a network. These printers have a NIC as well as ROM-based software that lets them communicate with networks, servers, and workstations.

Wireless

The wireless connections for multifunction devices are Bluetooth and 802.11x. Each is addressed in the following sections.

Bluetooth

Bluetooth is a wireless technology that can connect a printer to a computer at a short range; its absolute maximum range is 330 ft (100 m), and most devices are specified to work within 33 ft (10 m). When printing with a Bluetooth-enabled device (such as a mobile phone) and a Bluetooth-enabled printer, all you need to do is get within range of the device (i.e. move closer), select the print driver from the device, and choose Print. The information is transmitted wirelessly through the air using radio waves and is received by the device.

802.11 (a, b, g, n, ac, ax)

A network-enabled printer that has a wireless adapter can participate in a wireless Ethernet (e.g. IEEE 802.11b, a, g, n, ac, or ax) network, just as it would as a wired network client.

Public/shared devices

All OSes allow you to share a local printer or connect over the network to one that has been shared. To connect to a printer in Windows 11, choose Start > Control Panel > Hardware and Sound > Devices and Printers, and it will show the currently recognized printers (see Figure 3.55) and allow you to add new ones.

In Figure 3.55, the checkbox on the first instance of the Samsung M2070 shows that it is the current default printer, and the image of two people on the second instance of the device means that it is a shared printer. The Add Printer wizard is shown in Figure 3.56.

FIGURE 3.55 The Devices and Printers window in Windows 10

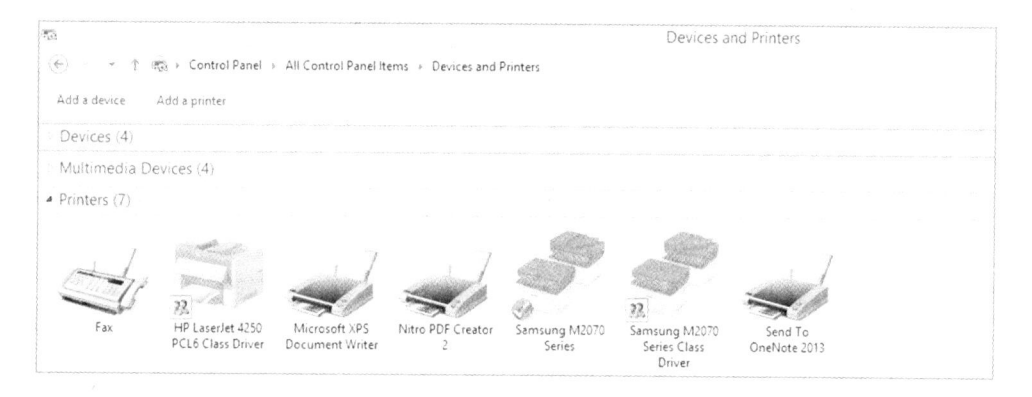

FIGURE 3.56 Adding a printer

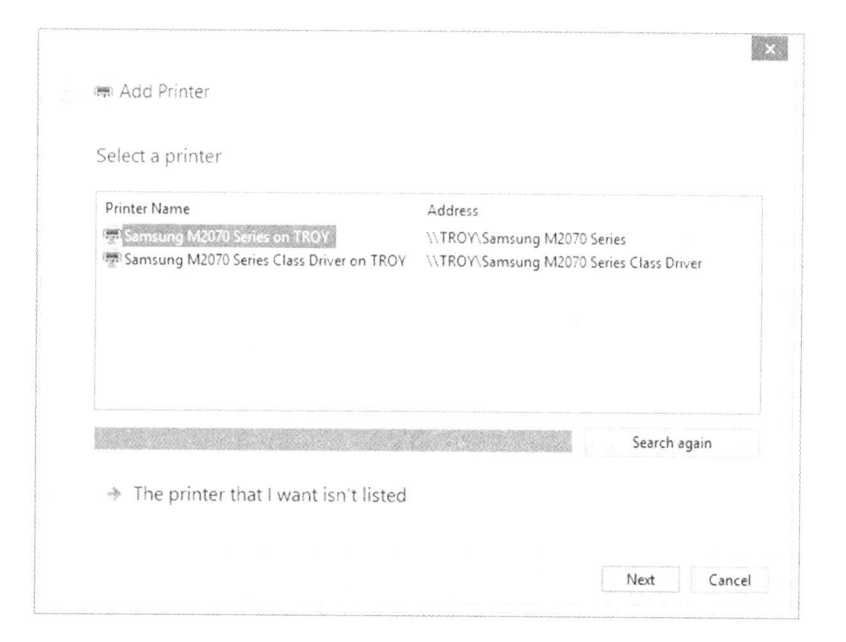

Printer share

To share a local/networked printer via the Windows OS, right-click the icon for the printer (beneath Devices and Printers or Printers and Faxes, depending on your OS) and choose Printer Properties. Next, click the Sharing tab.

Select Share This Printer and provide a name that the printer will be known by on the network. This is the name that will appear when adding a new network printer on a client, and it can also be referenced by the entire qualified name using the syntax `\host\share_name`, where `share_name` is the name that you have assigned to the printer.

Print server

A print server is a popular option for adding a printer to the network and not adding a host computer. To be a print server, the NIC in the printer differs from a NIC in a computer, in that it has a processor on it to perform the management of the NIC interface, and it is made by the same manufacturer as the printer.

For a printer to qualify as a print server, when someone on the network prints, the print job must go directly to the printer and not through any third-party device. This tends to make printing to that printer faster and more efficient—that NIC is dedicated to receiving print jobs and sending printer status to clients.

Configuration settings

You need to be familiar with the various settings that are available and what these settings do. This section covers the more common settings, features, and characteristics of printers.

Duplex

An optional component that can be added to printers (usually laser but also inkjet) is a duplexer. This can be an optional assembly added to the printer or built into it, but the sole purpose of duplexing is to turn the printed sheet over so it can be run back through the printer and allow printing on both sides.

Orientation

The orientation of a document refers to how the printed matter is laid out on the page. In landscape orientation, the printing is written across the paper turned on its long side, while in portrait the paper is turned up vertically and printed on from top to bottom.

Tray settings

Many printers can hold multiple types and sizes of paper in multiple trays. Tray settings allow you to choose the type of paper, and then the printer will use paper found in that tray. Of course, for this system to work, users must be trained to load the proper paper in the proper tray when reloading the machine. Situations where this is most helpful include printing the first page of a multipage document on letterhead or printing on different colors of paper.

Quality

Print quality is a description of the look of the printing, its sharpness, and its color depth. It is impacted by the quality of the paper, the speed of the printing process, and the resolution settings. It can also be affected by the dots per inch (DPI) setting. This setting controls the size of objects on the page and therefore their sharpness. As you increase an object's size, its quality will usually decrease a bit unless you increase the DPI.

Security

Printers can be a source of data exfiltration if not secured properly. In this section, you'll learn security concepts and best practices regarding printers.

User authentication

While nearly all enterprise-grade multifunction devices support user authentication, it might be easier and make more sense in a large network to perform this on the print server and use domain credentials to take advantage of single sign-on. In any case, user authentication forms the bedrock for auditing.

Badging

Badging can be used to demonstrate the knowledge and skill required to manage a particular printer type. This might be extremely important for specialty printers, such as 3D printers or printers that print ID badges. You can also use badging to restrict access to certain printers or to assign printing costs to a certain department.

Audit logs

As you have learned, all devices have a log listing all that has occurred. These logs can be very useful in identifying issues that need to be solved. Also, issues regarding access can be solved by examining the Windows security log.

Secured prints

In some cases, you are printing a document that is so secure that random users visiting the printer to pick up their finished print jobs cannot see it. Many printers have the ability to hold the print job until you enter a PIN or present another credential, such as a badge, that releases the job to be printed while you physically monitor the process. These are called *secure prints*.

Network scan services

Many multifunction devices can also scan documents of various types. In this section, you'll learn about scanning of emails and about connection methods used to access the scanner.

Email

Many multifunction devices can scan a document and then send that scanned file as an attachment to an email. To do so, you typically must use the printer control panel (one you might have to install and use to manage the printer) to create an email account for each user that will be doing this. For example, the HP OfficeJet Pro 9015e All-in-One printer can do this. When set up properly, there will be an option available to Scan to Email.

SMB

Print jobs can also be submitted through the Server Message Block (SMB) protocol. The SMB printing function is used to print data by directly specifying this machine on the computer. From an application that has the ability to print from within the application, this is done at the command line. For example, to print a document where FILE is a local file containing print job data, SERVER is the name of the server, and PRINTQ is the name of a shared print queue, the command would be: `copy /b FILE \\SERVER\PRINTQ`

Keep in mind that you might need to enable SMB printing and configure some other settings for this to function properly.

Cloud services

Using cloud services to print can follow one of two paradigms. One is the home user who uses cloud services to access a printer at home from anywhere. The other is the professional printing service done using cloud technologies to tie together multiple facilities to carry out a print job. For example, it could be the printing, binding, and boxing of books for sale.

Automatic document feeder (ADF)/flatbed scanner

Scanners are used to convert paper documents or photographs to digital files, so they can be stored on a PC and transmitted as files across the network. The installation process is much like that for a print device. Because so many of these now are USB, plugging them in will install the driver. In cases where that does not work (usually when it is a new model and the operating system is older), visit the manufacturer website and download and install the driver. To make functions such as collating and organizing sets of documents possible, the device must have an automatic document feeder (ADF) that performs these actions. Scanning on both sides is another function that requires a feeder that supports it.

Exam essentials

Identify the available printer languages. This print driver specifies the page description language (PDL) the printer understands. For laser printers, there are two popular PDLs: Adobe PostScript (PS) and Hewlett-Packard Printer Control Language (PCL).

Describe the printer interface types. These include Ethernet, wireless, and USB.

Identify printer configurations. These include duplex, orientation, tray settings, and quality.

3.8 Given a scenario, perform appropriate printer maintenance

This objective tests your knowledge of four types of printers: laser, inkjet (sometimes called ink dispersion), thermal, and impact. Make certain you understand the imaging process associated with each of these printer types. The A+ certification exams have traditionally focused heavily on laser printers, but you can expect to also see questions about other printer types.

Laser

Laser printers are referred to as *page printers* because they receive their print job instructions one page at a time. They're sheet-fed, nonimpact printers. Another name for a laser printer is an *electrophotographic* (EP) printer.

> **NOTE** LED printers are much like laser printers except they use light-emitting diodes (LEDs) instead of lasers. Their process is similar to that of laser printers.

Maintenance: replace toner, apply maintenance kit, calibrate, and clean

Just as laser printers are the most complicated of the types (and offer the most capabilities), they also have the most things that can go awry. A thermal fuse is included to keep the system from overheating, and if it becomes faulty, it can prevent the printer from printing. Many high-capacity laser printers also include an ozone filter to prevent the corona's ozone output from reaching too high a level. On these printers, the filter should be changed as part of regular maintenance.

Replace toner

Toner represents the consumable within the laser printer. Toner cartridges are used by laser printers to store toner. Use toner that is recommended for your printer. Using bad supplies could ruin your printer and void your warranty. Remove the toner before moving or shipping a printer to avoid spills.

Apply a maintenance kit

Maintenance kits are marketed by the manufacturer. Each kit varies in contents based on the printer in question but typically consists of a fuser, a transfer roller, and feed/separation rollers. A counter on the laser printer often identifies when the maintenance kit is needed, and you can reset the counter after applying the new kit.

Calibrate

With laser printers and inkjets, there is often a need to calibrate. Calibration is the process by which the result produced matches what was created. All the hardware, including the monitor, scanner, and printer, need to match on color, margins, and so forth.

The calibration process is different for each manufacturer but is usually similar to the following:

1. During installation of the software, you are asked (by the installation wizard) if you want to calibrate now. (Say Yes.)
2. The printer prints multiple sets of numbered lines. Each set of lines represents an alignment instance, and you are asked which set looks the best.
3. You enter the set number and click OK. In some cases, the alignment ends here. In other cases, the alignment page is reprinted to verify that the settings are correct, and you are given a chance to change.
4. You exit the alignment routine.

Clean

It is important to keep the printer and the area around it clean. Each time you replace the toner or perform any maintenance, be sure to clean the debris. A good idea is to purchase a special vacuum cleaner designed for toner particles.

Inkjet

Inkjet printers are one of the most popular types in use today. This type of printer sprays ink on the page to print text or graphics. It's a nonimpact, sheet-fed printer. Figure 3.57 shows an ink cartridge.

There are two kinds of inkjet printers: *thermal* and *piezoelectric*. These terms refer to the way the ink is sprayed onto the paper. A thermal inkjet printer heats the ink to about 400° Fahrenheit, creating vapor bubbles that force the ink out of the cartridge. Thermal inkjets are also sometimes called *bubble jets*. A piezoelectric printer does the same thing but with electricity instead of heat.

Inkjet printers are popular because they can print in color and are inexpensive. However, their speed isn't quite as good as that of a laser printer, and the per-page ink cost can be higher than for a laser printer. Therefore, most businesses prefer laser printers for their main printing needs, perhaps keeping one or two inkjet printers around for situations requiring color printing.

FIGURE 3.57 A typical ink cartridge

Ink cartridge, printhead, roller, and feeder

Components of an inkjet printer, which include the ink cartridge, printhead, roller, and feeder, are covered in the following sections.

Ink cartridge

These cartridges contain printer ink. Some cartridges contain the printhead for that color of ink; you get a new printhead each time you replace the cartridge. On other printer models, the ink cartridge is just an ink reservoir, and the heads don't need replacing.

Printhead

The printhead has a series of nozzles from which the ink is sprayed onto the paper. They may be attached to the ink cartridge, or those two components (i.e. head and nozzle) may be separate. In cases where they are one piece, you will be getting a new printhead each time you get a new ink cartridge.

Roller

Just as on a laser printer, rollers are used to pull the paper in from the tray or feeder and advance the paper when the printhead assembly is ready for another pass. As is the case with any rollers, they will need to be replaced when they lose their ability to "grab" the paper.

Feeder

The feeder looks like a tray and is where you load paper. It is from here that the paper is pulled into the printer when a new sheet is required. These feeders do not usually hold as much paper as a printer tray will.

Maintenance: clean printheads, replace cartridges, calibrate, and clear jams

While inkjet printers use a different technology to print, they require many of the same maintenance procedures. These procedures are discussed briefly in this section.

Clean printheads

Two maintenance tasks apply to the printheads. If your colors don't look the same or your blacks are getting a bronze look, you need to clean the nozzles. This can be done with the head-cleaning cycle, which will clean out the nozzles. The second task is head alignment. If you see white repeating lines or a grid-like pattern in the printing, the head is misaligned. While some newer printers have an automatic alignment and cleaning function, you might need to do this manually using the printer documentation.

Replace cartridges

When ink runs low (and most printers will alert you before you run out), you must remove the old cartridge and replace it with a new one. The procedure is as follows:

1. Open the printer cover and locate the button that is used to place the cartridge in the replacement position.
2. Open the cover that may be over the cartridge.
3. Grasp and remove the empty cartridge.
4. Take the new cartridge out of its packaging.
5. Place the new cartridge in the empty position left by the old cartridge. It should click into place.
6. Replace the cartridge cover.
7. Use the same button you used to place the cartridge into the replacement position to move it back to its home position.

Calibrate

Calibration is a task usually performed by accessing the properties of the printer and looking for the calibration function either on the General tab or on the Advanced tab. Select it and the printer will perform a calibration. Often, the printer will print a sheet with multiple images, and you will tell it which image is not properly aligned or incorrect. It is also useful to know that in most cases, calibration is done whenever you replace one of the cartridges.

Clear jams

While keeping in mind that many paper jams are a result of using poor-quality paper, there will be times when you suffer jams with good paper. To clear a jam, do the following:

1. Check the paper tray. If you see a piece protruding from where the paper is picked up, pull it out gently.
2. If there is still a jam, remove the rear access door and look into the printer. If you see any paper stuck inside, pull it out, ensuring you remove all the pieces.
3. Check the front door of the printer and see whether any pieces are stuck in that section; if so, gently pull them out.
4. At any point in this process, you can select the Resume button, and if you have cleared the jam, the print process will resume.

Please keep in mind that some printers will show the procedures to clear a jam on the printer's control screen.

Thermal

Thermal printers print on a waxy paper that comes on a roll; the paper turns black when heat passes over it. These are also found on many handheld package tracking and point-of-sale (POS) devices, such as credit card terminals. These printers should not be used for documents that need long-term storage, as the printed image quickly degrades (i.e. disappears) so you are just left with a blank sheet of paper. This is especially true of receipts that need to be retained for tax purposes.

Feed assembly

Thermal printers work by using a printhead the width of the paper. When it needs to print, the printhead heats and cools spots on the printhead. The paper below the heated printhead turns black in those heated spots. As the paper moves through the printer, the pattern of blackened spots forms an image on the page of what is being printed.

Another type of thermal printer uses a heat-sensitive ribbon instead of heat-sensitive paper. A thermal printhead melts wax-based ink from the ribbon onto the paper. These are called *thermal transfer* or *thermal wax-transfer* printers.

Thermal direct printers typically have long lives because they have few moving parts. However, the paper is somewhat expensive, doesn't last long, and produces poorer-quality images (that tend to fade over time) than most of the other printing technologies.

Some variations of thermal printing exist. They're all high-end color graphics printers designed for specialty professional usage. Four popular ones are discussed here.

Thermal wax transfer

This is a color, nonimpact printer that uses solid wax. A heater melts the wax and then sprays it onto the page, somewhat like an inkjet. The quality is very high, but so is the price.

Dye sublimation

This is another color, nonimpact line printer. This one converts a solid ink into a gas that is then applied to the paper. Color is applied in a continuous tone, rather than in individual dots, and the colors are applied one at a time. The ink comes on film rolls. The paper is expensive, as is the ink. Print speeds are low. The quality is extremely high. This type of printer might be used to print a company logo on mugs.

Feed assembly

Feed assemblies, commonly called *feeders*, are available to allow you to feed in the media you are printing on (e.g. paper, cards, etc.). Some feeders allow you to switch between multiple feeds, which is helpful if you need to alternate printing on different types of stock.

Heating element

The heating element for a thermal printer is what generates the heat and does the actual printing. It is often the most expensive component.

Special thermal paper

To print with a thermal printer, you need to use heat-sensitive paper designed for the thermal printer, as opposed to paper for any other type of printer. Rolls of thermal paper are available in a variety of sizes and colors.

Maintenance: replace paper, clean heating element, remove debris

The amount of maintenance required on a thermal printer pales in comparison to laser because there are fewer moving parts. The following sections look at the key items to be aware of related to thermal printers as you study for the exam.

Replace paper

Replace the thermal paper as it is needed; be sure to keep the paper feed area clean of paper slivers and other debris.

Clean heating element

Before even looking at a heating element, always unplug the printer and make certain it is cool. Thermal printer cleaning cards, cleaning pens, and kits are available and recommended for cleaning.

Remove debris

Keep the printer free of dust and debris. Any particulates that get into the printer can interfere with the paper feeding properly or can affect the print quality. Use compressed air or a computer vacuum to remove any debris.

Impact

A dot-matrix printer is an impact printer; it prints by physically striking an inked ribbon, much like how a typewriter can. It's an impact, continuous-feed printer.

The printhead on a dot-matrix printer consists of a block of metal pins that extend and retract. These pins are triggered to extend in patterns that form letters and numbers as the printhead moves across the paper. Early models, known as near letter-quality (NLQ), printed using only nine pins. Later models used 24 pins and produced much better letter-quality (LQ) output.

The main advantage of dot matrix is its impact (i.e. physical striking of the paper). Because it strikes the paper, you can use it to print on multipart forms. Nonimpact printers can't do that. Dot-matrix printers aren't commonly found in most offices these days because of their disadvantages, including noise, slow speed, and poor print quality.

> Dot-matrix printers are still found in many warehouses and other businesses like auto repair shops, where multipart forms are used or where continuous feed is required.

Multipart paper

Because an impact printer works by striking characters onto pressure-sensitive paper, it is particularly suited to printing on multipart paper. This type of paper has more than one sheet to a page, stacked together, so that you print multiple copies at the same time. These are often used where one copy goes to the customer, another copy (e.g. yellow) goes to the service technician in the shop, and a third copy (e.g. pink) goes to accounting. An impact printer uses continuous-feed paper fed to it by the tractor feed unit, where spokes on the tractor wheel line up with holes on the sides of the paper that pull the paper through. Figure 3.58 shows multipart paper.

Maintenance: replace ribbon, printhead, and paper

A dot-matrix printhead reaches high temperatures, and care must be taken to avoid a user or technician touching it and getting burned. Most dot-matrix printers include a temperature sensor to tell whether the printhead is getting too hot. The sensor interrupts printing to let

FIGURE 3.58 Multipart paper

the printhead cool down and then allows printing to start again. If this sensor becomes faulty, it can cause the printer to print a few lines, stop for a while, print more, stop, and so forth. The following sections look at the key items to be aware of related to impact printers, as you study for the exam.

Replace ribbon

A common culprit with poor printing is the ribbon. A tight ribbon, or one that isn't advancing properly, will cause smudges or an overly light printout. To solve this problem, replace the ribbon.

Replace printhead

The printhead should never be lubricated, but you can clean off any debris with a cotton swab and denatured alcohol. Print pins missing from the printhead will cause incomplete images or characters or white lines running through the text. This can be remedied by replacing the printhead.

If the printhead isn't at fault, make certain it's close enough to the platen (i.e. the surface on which typing occurs) to make the right image. The printhead can be moved closer to and farther from the platen depending on the thickness of the paper and other considerations.

Replace paper

Preventive maintenance includes not only keeping the printhead dry and clean but also vacuuming paper shreds from inside the machine. This should be done more often if needed, but always when you replace the paper.

Exam essentials

Know the maintenance functions of laser, inkjet, thermal, and impact printers.

Review Questions

You can find the answers in the appendix.

1. Which cable type comes in two varieties: unshielded and shielded?
   A. Fiber optic
   B. Coaxial
   C. Twisted pair
   D. Serial

2. Which cable type transmits data at speeds up to 100 Mbps and was used with Fast Ethernet (operating at 100 Mbps) with a transmission range of 100 m?
   A. Cat 4
   B. Cat 5
   C. Cat 5e
   D. Cat 6

3. Which cable type has a glass core within a rubber outer coating?
   A. Fiber-optic
   B. Coaxial
   C. Twisted pair
   D. Serial

4. Which connector is used for telephone cord?
   A. RJ-11
   B. RJ-45
   C. RS-232
   D. BNC

5. Which standard has been commonly used in computer serial ports for a telephone landline?
   A. RJ-11
   B. RJ-45
   C. RS-232
   D. BNC

6. Which connectors are sometimes used in networking?
   A. RJ-11
   B. RJ-45
   C. RS-232
   D. BNC

7. Which RAM type is used in laptops?
   A. DIMM
   B. SoDIMM
   C. Rambus
   D. BNC

8. Which RAM type allows for two memory accesses for each rising and falling clock?
   A. DIMM
   B. SoDIMM
   C. DDR3
   D. DDR2

9. Which RAM type is not compatible with any earlier type of random-access memory?
   A. DDR5
   B. DDR4
   C. DDR3
   D. DDR2

10. Which of the following is a rewritable optical disc?
    A. CD
    B. CD-RW
    C. DVD
    D. CD-ROM

11. Which of the following is a specification for internally mounted computer expansion cards and associated connectors that replaces the mSATA?
    A. M.2
    B. NVMe
    C. SATA
    D. SATA 2.5

12. At what speed will latency on a magnetic drive decrease to about 3 ms?
    A. 5,400 rpm
    B. 7,200 rpm
    C. 10,000 rpm
    D. 15,000 rpm

13. Laptops and other portable devices utilize which expansion card?
- **A.** Mini PCI
- **B.** PCIe
- **C.** PCI
- **D.** SATA

14. Which of the following is a standard firmware interface for PCs, designed to replace BIOS?
- **A.** UEFI
- **B.** NVRAM
- **C.** CMOS
- **D.** CHS

15. Which type of printer has pins in the printhead?
- **A.** Impact
- **B.** 3D
- **C.** Thermal
- **D.** Laser

16. What is the most expensive part of a thermal printer?
- **A.** Feed assembly
- **B.** Heating element
- **C.** Printhead
- **D.** Print bed

17. Which of the following is the process of ensuring that there is proper alignment of the cartridges to one another and to the paper so that high quality is maintained?
- **A.** Orientation
- **B.** Alignment
- **C.** Calibration
- **D.** Tuning

18. Ghosting—repeating text or images on the page—is usually caused by which of the following?
- **A.** Wrong paper
- **B.** Wrong driver
- **C.** No connectivity
- **D.** Cartridge needs replacement

19. In 2004, the ATX 12V 2.0 (now 2.03) standard was passed, changing the main connector from 20 pins to how many?
    A. 16
    B. 22
    C. 24
    D. 28

20. Which of the following is *not* part of printer maintenance?
    A. Replace toner
    B. Apply maintenance kit
    C. Calibrate
    D. Test power supply

21. The SATA power connector has how many pins?
    A. 8
    B. 12
    C. 15
    D. 18

22. Which of the following causes blank pages in a laser printer?
    A. Empty toner cartridge
    B. No connectivity
    C. Scratched drum
    D. Wrong paper

23. Which RAID implementation offers speed but no fault tolerance?
    A. RAID 0
    B. RAID 1
    C. RAID 5
    D. RAID 10

24. Which laser printer component applies a +600V charge to the paper?
    A. High-voltage power supply
    B. DC power supply
    C. Transfer corona
    D. Fusing assembly

25. To submit an SMB print job, where FILE is a local file containing print job data, SERVER is the name of the server, and PRINTQ is the name of a shared print queue, what would the command be?
    A. `copy /b FILE \\\PRINTQ/SERVER`
    B. `copy /b FILE \\SERVER\PRINTQ`
    C. `copy FILE \\SERVER\PRINTQ`
    D. `copy /b \\SERVER\PRINTQ`

26. What type of printing process holds the print job until you enter a PIN that releases the job to be printed while you physically monitor the process?
    A. Locked prints
    B. Printer hold
    C. Secured prints
    D. Privileged print

27. Which of the following is a technology that can connect a printer to a computer at a short range; its absolute maximum range is 330 ft (100 m), and most devices are specified to work within 33 ft (10 m)?
    A. 802.11
    B. RFID
    C. Bluetooth
    D. Ethernet

28. What software controls how the printer processes the print job?
    A. Driver
    B. Interface
    C. Network
    D. Line

29. What printer component turns the printed sheet over so it can be run back through the printer and allow printing on both sides?
    A. Driver
    B. Duplexer
    C. Orientation
    D. Collator

30. Which of the following refers to how the printed matter is laid out on the page?
    A. Driver
    B. Duplex
    C. Orientation
    D. Collate

31. Which of the following paper types feeds through the printer using a system of sprockets and tractors?
    A. Continuous feed
    B. Sheet fed
    C. Impact
    D. Thermal

32. Which of the following should not be used more than once?
    A. Toner
    B. Paper
    C. Cable
    D. Inkjets

33. Which of the following is a large circuit board that acts as the motherboard for the printer?
    A. Printer controller
    B. Imaging drum
    C. Toner cartridge
    D. Maintenance kit

Chapter 4

Virtualization and Cloud Computing

COMPTIA A+ 220-1201 EXAM OBJECTIVES COVERED IN THIS CHAPTER:

✓ **4.1 Explain virtualization concepts**
- Purpose of virtual machines
  - Sandbox
  - Test development
  - Application virtualization
    - Legacy software/OS
    - Cross-platform virtualization
- Requirements
  - Emulators and hypervisors
  - Security
  - Network
  - Storage
- Desktop virtualization
  - Virtual desktop infrastructure (VDI)
  - VDI in the cloud
- Containers
- Hypervisors
  - Type 1
  - Type 2

✓ **4.2 Summarize cloud computing concepts**
- Common cloud models
  - Public vs. private vs. hybrid vs. community
  - Infrastructure as a Service (IaaS)

- Software as a Service (SaaS)
- Platform as a Service (PaaS)
- Cloud characteristics
  - Shared resources vs. dedicated resources
  - Metered utilization
    - Ingress/egress
  - Elasticity
  - Availability
  - File synchronization
  - Multitenancy

This chapter will focus on the exam topics related to virtualization and cloud computing. It will follow the structure of the CompTIA A+ 220-1201 exam blueprint, Objective 4, and it will explore the two subobjectives that you will need to master before taking the exam.

4.1 Explain virtualization concepts

Cloud computing and its underlying technology, virtualization, have moved beyond the "new" stage and are now becoming ubiquitous. This section will focus on the exam topics related to virtualization. It will discuss virtual machines (VMs) and the hypervisor software that makes them possible. It will also cover some of the uses of VMs and security issues that accompany the use of virtualization.

Purpose of virtual machines

Traditionally, workstations can have multiple operating systems installed on them but run only one at a time. By running virtualization software, the same workstation can be running Windows 11 along with Windows Server 2022 and Red Hat Enterprise Linux (or almost any other operating system) at the same time, allowing a developer to test code in various environments as well as cut and paste between VMs.

So, what is a VM? In essence, a VM can be considered a fully functional operating system or computer, running within an app called a hypervisor. You can have many VMs running at the same time, as described previously. From a networking standpoint, each VM will typically need full network access, and configuring the permissions for each can sometimes be tricky. Let's look at some of the scenarios where virtualization can play a role.

Sandbox

Sandboxing is the segregation of virtual environments for security purposes. Sandboxed appliances have been used in the past to supplement the network's security features. These appliances are used to test suspicious files in a protected environment.

Malware sandboxing aims to detect malware code by running it in a computer to analyze it for behavior and traits that indicate malware. One of its goals is to spot zero-day malware, which is malware that has not yet been identified by commercial anti-malware systems and for which there is not yet a cure.

Test development

Another great use of a virtual environment is in the development of applications or in the testing of network configurations. Using a virtual version of your infrastructure, issues that may occur when rolling out any of the following changes can be determined safely without impacting the production environment:

- New security devices
- New applications
- Automation scripts
- Updates
- Security patches

Application virtualization

Just as operating systems can be provided on demand with technologies like virtual desktop infrastructure (VDI), applications can also be provided to users from a central location. Two models used to implement this include:

- **Server-based application virtualization (terminal services):** In server-based application virtualization, an application runs on servers. Users receive the application environment display through a remote client protocol, such as Microsoft Remote Desktop Protocol (RDP) or Citrix Independent Computing Architecture (ICA). Examples of terminal services include Remote Desktop Services and Citrix Presentation Server.
- **Client-based application virtualization (application streaming):** In client-based application virtualization, the target application is packaged and streamed to the client PC. It has its own application computing environment, which is isolated from the client OS and other applications. A representative example is Microsoft Application Virtualization (App-V). Figure 4.1 compares these two approaches.

FIGURE 4.1   Application streaming and terminal services

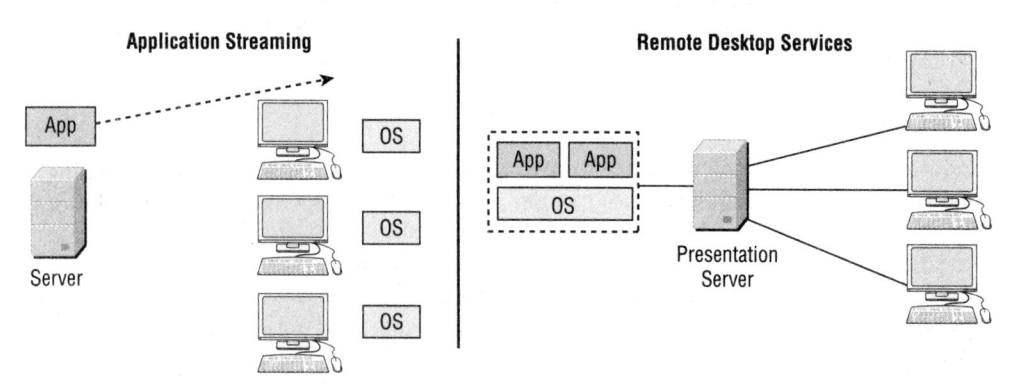

Legacy software/OS

In many cases, the organization may use an application that runs on only a certain operating system. Often, that operating system is a legacy system, meaning it is no longer supported by the vendor. Moreover, all other workstations in the network may have already been upgraded to another operating system.

In this scenario, you can configure a VM with the legacy operating system and use it to run the application. Since legacy operating systems no longer receive security patches from their vendor, you can also take advantage of sandboxing (covered earlier) to isolate the system from the rest of your network and the Internet.

Cross-platform virtualization

Another scenario in which virtualization can solve a problem is when an application runs on an operating system that you currently don't use in the network. Perhaps your environment is Windows, and an application requires Linux or Apple's macOS. You can configure a VM with one of the necessary operating systems installed and use that to run the application.

Requirements

The resource requirements for virtualization are largely based on what environments you are creating. The machine's hardware must have enough memory, hard drive space, and processor capability to support virtualization. For example, if you were installing a Windows 11 VM, that VM would still need a minimum of 4 GB of RAM and 64 GB of drive space from the host computer. You also need the software to make virtualization possible (which is discussed in the next section). Two types of software make virtualization possible, emulators and hypervisors. Let's look at both.

Emulators and hypervisors

Emulators require a software layer (i.e. the emulator) to interact with the hardware. These are also called Type 2 hypervisors, and examples include VMware Workstation and Oracle's VirtualBox. Type 1 hypervisors interact directly with the hardware (more later in this section). Some virtualization products, such as Microsoft's Hyper-V and Windows 11 Client Hyper-V, require that the motherboard support hardware-assisted virtualization. The benefit derived from using hardware-assisted virtualization is that it reduces overhead and improves performance.

Security

Tales of security woes that can occur with attackers jumping out of one VM and accessing another have been exaggerated. Although such threats are possible, most software solutions include sufficient protection to reduce the possibility to a small one.

Most virtualization-specific threats focus on the hypervisor (i.e. the software upon which the VMs run). If the hypervisor can be successfully attacked, the attacker can gain root-level access to all virtual systems. While this is a legitimate issue – and one that has been demonstrated to be possible in most systems – it is one that has been patched each time it has appeared. The solution to most virtualization threats is to always apply the most recent patches and keep the systems up to date.

It is much easier to attack a virtual machine than a hypervisor because admins do not think about the security of each individual VM. It is also important to ensure that all VMs are updated with patches for both the OS and all applications. If VMs are allowed to run with an outdated OS or software, known vulnerabilities will exist, and an attacker will take advantage of these.

Keep in mind that in any virtual environment, each virtual server that is hosted on the physical server must be configured with its own security mechanisms. These mechanisms include antivirus software and all the latest service packs and security updates for all the software hosted on the VM.

Network

The network requirements of the virtual environment depend on its purpose. Within the environment, VMs have virtual network interface cards (vNICs) that can be assigned IP configurations, which will then enable them to communicate with one another through a virtual network switch. In a sandbox environment, communication outside this virtual network is not possible, which in the case of malware analysis prevents the infection from spreading to the production network.

In some cases, you *do* want network access from the virtual network to the production network and perhaps even on to the Internet. In that case, the virtual switch will have one interface that connects to a physical network card on the host. In cases where access to the Internet is desired for the virtual systems, a network address translation (NAT) device will convert the private IP addresses in use in the virtual network to public IP addresses required for the Internet. This design is shown in Figure 4.2.

Storage

The virtualization host will provide its hard drive as storage for the VMs and their applications and data. Therefore, it is critical that sufficient space be available. The VMs and the server host must share this disk space. Each VM will have an assigned portion called its virtual machine

FIGURE 4.2 Virtual network

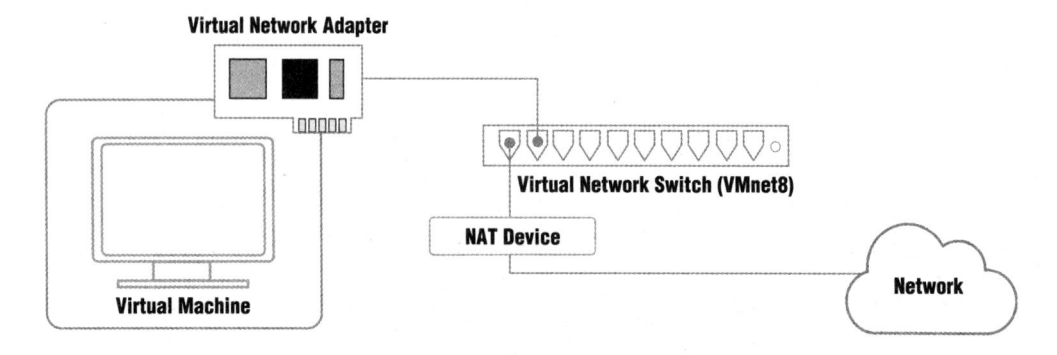

disk (VMDK). Commercial hypervisor products such as VMware provide the ability to use what are called disk shares to assign disk priorities to the various VMs.

Desktop virtualization

VDIs host desktop operating systems within a virtual environment in a centralized server. Users access the desktops and run them from the server. There are two on-site models and one off-site model for implementing VDI.

Virtual desktop infrastructure (VDI)

When hosted on-site there are two approaches to VDI:

- **Centralized:** All desktop instances are stored in a single server, requiring significant processing power on the server.
- **Remote virtual desktops:** An image is copied to the local machine, making a constant network connection unnecessary.

VDI in the cloud

Also called hosted desktops, these virtual desktops are maintained by a service provider in a cloud environment. This model eliminates capital cost and is instead subject to operation cost.

Containers

Another approach to virtualization is referred to as container-based virtualization, also called operating system virtualization. This kind of server virtualization uses a technique in which the kernel (i.e. the core of the operating system) allows for multiple isolated user space instances. The instances are known as containers, virtual private servers, or virtual environments.

In this model, the hypervisor is replaced with operating system–level virtualization, where the kernel of an operating system allows multiple isolated user spaces or containers. A virtual machine is not a complete operating system instance but rather a partial instance of the same operating system. The containers in Figure 4.3 are the boxes just above the container engine. Container-based virtualization is used mostly in Linux environments.

Hypervisors

There are two types of hypervisors. Let's look at their differences.

Type 1

The hypervisor that manages the distribution of the physical server's resources can be either Type 1 or Type 2. A guest operating system runs on another level above the hypervisor. Examples of Type 1 hypervisors are Citrix XenServer, Microsoft Hyper-V, and VMware vSphere. Type 1 hypervisors are installed directly on the host hardware and are considered "bare metal" hypervisors.

Type 2

A Type 2 hypervisor runs as an application on a conventional operating system environment. With the hypervisor layer as a distinct second software level, guest operating systems run at the third level above the hardware. VMware Workstation and Oracle VirtualBox exemplify Type 2 hypervisors. A comparison of the two approaches is shown in Figure 4.4.

FIGURE 4.3 Containerization

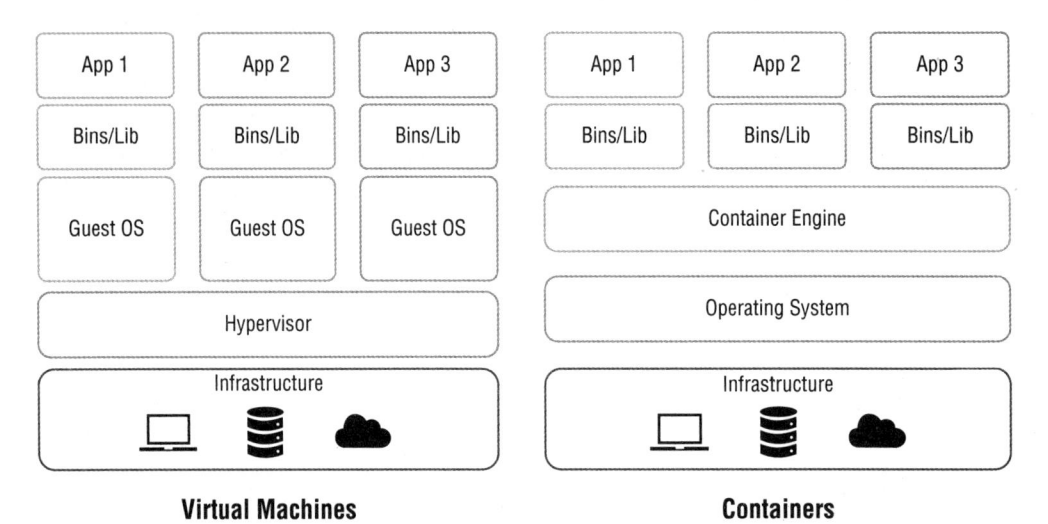

FIGURE 4.4 Hypervisor types

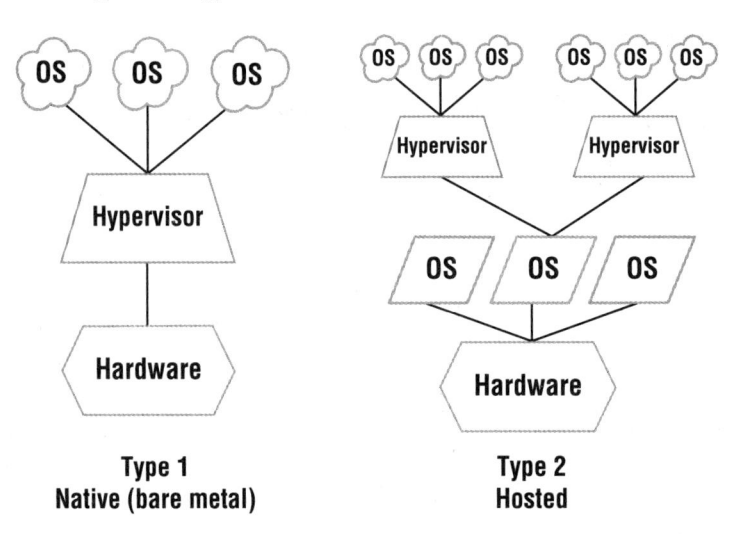

Exam essentials

Be familiar with virtualization terminology. The hypervisor is the software that allows the VMs to exist. VMs are separate instances of an operating system, and they function independently of one another on a host physical machine.

Know security concerns related to virtualization. Most virtualization-specific threats focus on the hypervisor. If the hypervisor can be successfully attacked, the attacker can gain root-level access to all virtual systems.

4.2 Summarize cloud computing concepts

Cloud computing can be deployed in different architectural models and can be used to support multiple service models. In this section, we'll discuss these concepts as well as the requirements of cloud computing. Finally, we'll look at the characteristics and capabilities of cloud computing.

Common cloud models

Increasingly, organizations are utilizing cloud-based storage instead of storing data in local data centers. The advantages to this approach include the ability to access the data from anywhere, the ability to scale computing resources to meet demand, and robust fault tolerance options. This section will look at various cloud models and some of the concepts that make cloud models a viable option for the enterprise.

Public vs. private vs. hybrid vs. community

When a company pays another company to host and manage this environment, it is called a public cloud solution. If the company hosts this environment itself, it is a private cloud solution.

There is trade-off when a decision must be made between the two architectures. The private solution provides the most control over the safety of your data but also requires the staff and the knowledge to deploy, manage, and secure the solution. A public cloud puts your data's safety in the hands of a third party, but that party is often more capable and knowledgeable about protecting data in this environment and managing the cloud environment.

When the solution is partly private and partly public, the solution is called a hybrid solution. It may be that the organization keeps some data in the public cloud but also may keep more sensitive data in a private cloud, or the organization may have a private cloud that when overtaxed may utilize a public cloud for additional storage space or additional computing resources.

Finally, a community cloud is one that is shared by multiple organizations for some common purpose. This could be to share data for a joint project, for example.

Infrastructure as a Service (IaaS)

Infrastructure as a Service (IaaS) involves the vendor providing the hardware platform and the customer installing and managing their own operating systems and application systems. The vendor simply provides access to the data center and maintains that access.

Software as a Service (SaaS)

When an enterprise contracts with a third party to provide cloud services, there is a range of options, differing mostly in the division of responsibilities between the vendor and the client. Software as a Service (SaaS) involves the vendor providing the entire solution. This includes the operating system, the infrastructure software, and the application. The company may provide you with an email system, for example, whereby it hosts and manages everything for you.

Platform as a Service (PaaS)

Platform as a Service (PaaS) involves the vendor providing the hardware platform or data center and the software running on the platform. This includes the operating systems and infrastructure software. The customer is still involved in managing the system.

Cloud characteristics

There are certain aspects to using a cloud environment that are unique to virtualization. In this section, you'll learn about these characteristics.

Shared resources vs. dedicated resources

The handling of resources is largely dependent on the hosting model in use. In a public or community cloud, multiple tenants share the same server resources, including disk space, processing power, and bandwidth. This means that resources are divided among all the users on the server. On the other hand, with a private cloud, you have full control over an entire server's resources because it is exclusively yours to use.

Devices in a cloud data center are VMs that share the resources of the underlying host. VMs represent virtual instances of an operating system that exist as files on the physical host. Technicians can appropriate these resources in whichever relative percentages they are comfortable with. One benefit of hypervisor-driven virtualization is the ability of the hypervisor to recognize momentary needs for more resources by one of the VMs and then react by shifting some percentage of the resource in contention to the overloaded VM.

Metered utilization

Metered utilization means that you pay for only what you use and is sometimes called pay-as-you-go. Usage metering tracks information about CPU, GPU, TPU, memory, storage, and optionally network egress usage.

This is compared to services that are prepaid. The fixed price of nonmetered services means that your price won't fluctuate, regardless of your cloud usage, but you may not use all you pay for.

Ingress/egress

Metering is typically performed on ingress traffic, but it can also be based on egress traffic. One focuses more on connections (ingress) while the other focuses more on data downloaded (egress).

Elasticity

One advantage of a cloud environment is the ability to add resources as needed on the fly and to release those resources when they are no longer required. This makes for more efficient use of resources, allocating them where needed at any particular point in time. These include CPU and memory resources. This is called rapid elasticity because it occurs automatically according to the rules for resource sharing that have been deployed.

Availability

Due to the use of rapid elasticity and shared resources, the cloud is a highly available environment. You can even have a new VM spun up to address capacity issues, or in cases where a system is down, another can easily be brought up without users losing connections or data.

File synchronization

Most cloud storage services come with an application that can be used to keep the files in the cloud synchronized with local copies of the same files. These apps can automate the synchronization process for you. Moreover, they typically provide versioning services as well, allowing you to recover from any accidental edits or deletions.

Multitenancy

Earlier in this section, you learned that in a community or public cloud, the cloud is shared with other customers of the provider. This is called multitenancy. In these scenarios, you are sharing the resources with other tenants.

Exam essentials

Describe the cloud service models. These include SaaS, PaaS, and IaaS. Differentiate the models with respect to the various responsibilities of the vendor and the customer.

Differentiate cloud architectures. Describe the architectural differences in the private, public, hybrid, and community cloud models.

Identify the basic terms describing some of the benefits of cloud computing. These include rapid elasticity, on-demand computing, and measured service.

Review Questions

You can find the answers in the appendix.

1. Which of the following involves the vendor providing the entire solution?
   A. IaaS
   B. SaaS
   C. PaaS
   D. SIEM

2. When a company pays another company to host and manage a cloud environment, it is called what?
   A. Public cloud
   B. Hybrid cloud
   C. Community cloud
   D. Private cloud

3. Which of the following describes the ability to add resources as needed on the fly and release those resources when they are no longer required?
   A. On-demand
   B. Rapid elasticity
   C. Virtual sharing
   D. Stretched resources

4. In which VDI model are all desktop instances stored in a single server, requiring significant processing power on the server?
   A. Centralized
   B. Hosted
   C. Remote
   D. Local

5. Which of the following involves the vendor providing the hardware platform and the software running on the platform?
   A. IaaS
   B. SaaS
   C. PaaS
   D. DaaS

6. What is the benefit derived from using hardware-assisted virtualization?
   A. Better performance
   B. Better security
   C. Less power consumption
   D. Easier troubleshooting

7. Which of the following is the software that allows the VMs to exist?
   A. DIMM
   B. Hypervisor
   C. Azureware
   D. NAT

8. Which of the following involves the vendor providing only the hardware?
   A. IaaS
   B. SaaS
   C. PaaS
   D. SIEM

9. Which of the following hosts desktop operating systems within a virtual environment in a centralized server?
   A. VDI
   B. RDP
   C. SSH
   D. OVC

10. Which of the following is an example of a Type 1 hypervisor?
    A. VMware Workstation
    B. Windows 11 Client Hyper-V
    C. Oracle VirtualBox
    D. VMware vSphere

Chapter 5

Hardware and Network Troubleshooting

COMPTIA A+ 220-1201 EXAM OBJECTIVES COVERED IN THIS CHAPTER:

✓ **5.1 Given a scenario, troubleshoot motherboards, RAM, CPUs, and power**

- Common symptoms
  - Power-On Self-Test (POST) beeps
  - Proprietary crash screens
    - BSOD
    - Pinwheel
  - Blank screen
  - No power
  - Sluggish performance
  - Overheating
  - Burning smell
  - Random shutdown
  - Application crashes
  - Unusual noise
  - Capacitor swelling
  - Inaccurate system date/time

✓ **5.2 Given a scenario, troubleshoot drive and RAID issues**

- Common symptoms
  - Light-emitting diode (LED) status indicators
  - Grinding noises
  - Clicking sounds

- Bootable device not found
  - OS not found
- Data loss/corruption
- RAID failure
  - RAID stops working
- Self-Monitoring, Analysis, and Reporting Technology (S.M.A.R.T.) failure
- Extended read/write times
- Input/output operations per second (IOPS)
- Missing drives in OS
- Array missing
- Audible alarms

✓ **5.3 Given a scenario, troubleshoot video, projector, and display issues**

- Common symptoms
  - Incorrect input source
  - Physical cabling issues
  - Burnt-out bulb
  - Fuzzy image
  - Display burn-in
  - Dead pixels
  - Flashing screen
  - Incorrect color display
  - Audio issues
  - Dim images
  - Intermittent projector shutdown
  - Sizing issues
  - Distorted image

✓ **5.4 Given a scenario, troubleshoot common mobile device issues**
- Common symptoms
  - Poor battery health
  - Swollen battery
  - Broken screen
    - Touch flow
    - Multitouch
  - Improper charging
  - Poor/no connectivity
  - Liquid damage
  - Overheating
  - Digitizer issues
  - Physically damaged ports
  - Malware
  - Cursor drift/touch calibration
  - Unable to install new applications
  - Stylus does not work
  - Degraded performance

✓ **5.5 Given a scenario, troubleshoot network issues**
- Common symptoms
  - Intermittent wireless connectivity
  - Slow network speeds
  - Limited connectivity
  - Jitter
  - Poor Voice over Internet Protocol (VoIP) quality
  - Port flapping
  - High latency
  - External interference
  - Authentication failures
  - Intermittent Internet connectivity

✓ 5.6 Given a scenario, troubleshoot printer issues

- Lines down the printed pages
  - Vertical black lines on the page
  - Vertical white lines on the page
- Garbled print
- Paper jams
- Faded prints
- Paper not feeding
- Multipage misfeed
- Multiple prints pending in queue
- Speckling on printed pages
- Double/echo images on the print
- Grinding noise
- Finishing issues
  - Staple jams
  - Hole punch
- Incorrect page orientation
- Tray not recognized
- Connectivity issues
- Frozen print queue

This chapter will focus on the exam topics related to troubleshooting. It will follow the structure of the CompTIA A+ 220-1201 exam blueprint, Objective 5, and it will explore the six subobjectives that you will need to master before taking the exam.

5.1 Given a scenario, troubleshoot motherboards, RAM, CPUs, and power

While problems can occur with an operating system (OS) with little or no physical warning, that is rarely the case when it comes to hardware problems. Your senses will often alert you that something is wrong based on what you hear, smell, or see. This section discusses common issues with the main players.

Common symptoms

Once you have performed troubleshooting for some time, you will notice a pattern. With some exceptions, the same issues occur repeatedly and usually give you the same warnings each time. This section covers common symptoms or warning signs you might encounter. When you learn what these symptoms are trying to tell you, they will make your job easier.

Power-On Self-Test (POST) beeps

During the bootup of the system, a Power-On Self-Test (POST) occurs, and each device is checked for functionality. If the system boots to the point where the video driver is loaded and the display is operational, any problems will be reported with a numeric error code on the display.

If the system cannot boot to that point, problems will be reported with a series of beeps called a *beep code*. Although each motherboard manufacturer's set of beep codes and their interpretations can be found in the documentation for the system or on the website of the Basic Input/Output System/Unified Extensible Firmware Interface (BIOS/UEFI) manufacturer, one short beep always means everything is OK. Some examples of items tested during this process include the following:

- Random-access memory (RAM)
- Video card
- Motherboard

> **Tip:** To interpret the beep codes in a case where you cannot read the error codes on the screen, use the chart provided at www.computerhope.com/beep.htm.

During start-up, problems with devices that fail to be recognized properly, services that fail to start, and other start-up issues are written to the system log and can also be viewed with Event Viewer in Microsoft or in the Console in Mac. If no POST error code prevents a successful boot, this utility provides information about what's been going on system-wise to help you troubleshoot problems. Event Viewer shows warnings, error messages, and records of things happening successfully. You can access it through Computer Management, or you can access it directly from the Administrative Tools in Control Panel.

Proprietary crash screens

Some OSes have a proprietary method of notifying the user that the worst may have just happened. In this section, you'll look at two of the most widely known methods.

BSOD

Once a regular occurrence when working with Windows, blue screens (aka the blue screen of death [BSOD]) have become much less frequent since Windows 2000. Occasionally, systems will lock up, and you can usually examine the log files to discover what was happening when this occurred and then take the necessary steps to correct it. For example, if you see that a driver or an application was loading before the crash, you can begin to isolate it as a possible problem. The details included in the BSOD error that come up can help in troubleshooting the problem. It is often easy to query Microsoft's Knowledge Base with the first part of the BSOD numeric error message to discover the component causing the problem. Often, the Knowledge Base article gives a detailed explanation of how to fix the problem as well. An example code is shown in Figure 5.1.

In more recent versions of Windows, such as Windows 11, information from such crashes is written to XML files by the OS. When the system becomes stable, a prompt usually appears asking for approval to send this information to Microsoft. The goal that Microsoft has in collecting this data is to be able to identify drivers that cause such problems and work with vendors to correct these issues.

FIGURE 5.1   BSOD with error code.

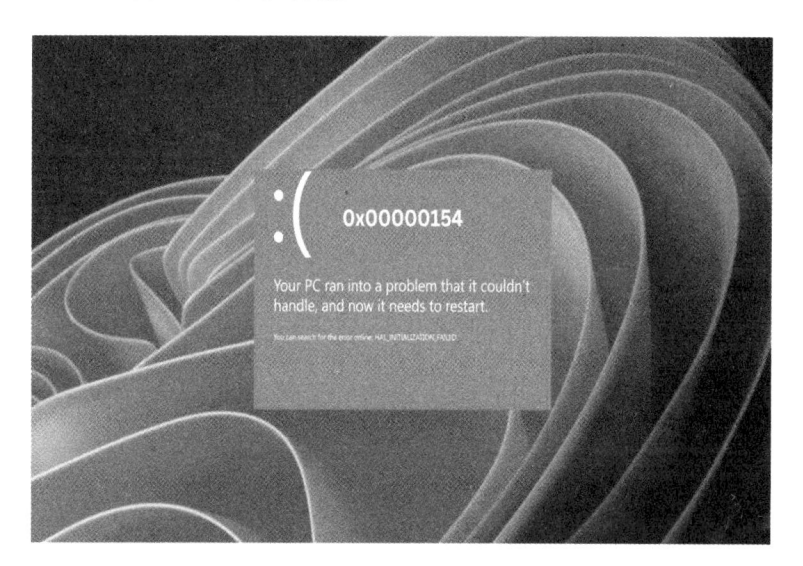

Better-known error messages include the following:

Data_Bus_Error   This error is described on the Microsoft website: "The most common cause of this error message is a hardware problem. It usually occurs after the installation of faulty hardware, or when existing hardware fails. The problem is frequently related to defective RAM, L2 RAM cache, or video RAM. If hardware has recently been added to the system, remove it and test to see if the error still occurs." See `https://learn.microsoft.com/en-us/windows-hardware/drivers/debugger/bug-check-0x2e--data-bus-error`.

Unexpected_Kernel_Mode_Trap   This error is described on the Microsoft website: "If hardware was recently added to the system, remove it to see if the error recurs. If existing hardware has failed, remove or replace the faulty component. Run hardware diagnostics supplied by the system manufacturer, especially the memory scanner, to determine which hardware component has failed. For details on these procedures, see the owner's manual for your computer. Setting the CPU to run at speeds above the rated specification (known as overclocking the CPU) can also cause this error." See `https://learn.microsoft.com/en-us/windows-hardware/drivers/debugger/bug-check-0x7f--unexpected-kernel-mode-trap`.

Page_Fault_in_nonpaged_area   This error is described on the Microsoft website: "This Stop message usually occurs after the installation of faulty hardware or in the event of failure of installed hardware (usually related to defective RAM, either main memory, L2 RAM cache, or video RAM). If hardware has been added to the system recently, remove it to see if the error recurs. If existing hardware has failed, remove or replace the faulty component. Run hardware diagnostics supplied by the system manufacturer. For details on these procedures, see the owner's manual for your computer."

See `https://learn.microsoft.com/en-us/windows-hardware/drivers/debugger/bug-check-0x50--page-fault-in-nonpaged-area`.

irq1_not_less_or_equal   This error is described on the Microsoft website: "This Stop message indicates that a kernel-mode process or driver attempted to access a memory address to which it did not have permission to access. The most common cause of this error is an incorrect or corrupted pointer that references an incorrect location in memory. A pointer is a variable used by a program to refer to a block of memory. If the variable has an incorrect value in it, the program tries to access memory that it should not. When this occurs in a user-mode application, it generates an access violation. When it occurs in kernel mode, it generates a STOP 0x0000000A message. If you encounter this error while upgrading to a newer version of Windows, it might be caused by a device driver, a system service, a virus scanner, or a backup tool that is incompatible with the new version." See `https://learn.microsoft.com/en-us/windows-hardware/drivers/debugger/bug-check-0xa--irql-not-less-or-equal`.

Pinwheel

While Microsoft users have the BSOD to deal with, Apple users have similarly come to have the same negative feelings about the pinwheel of death (PWOD). This multicolored pinwheel mouse pointer (shown in Figure 5.2) signifies a temporary delay while the system "thinks." In the death scenario, waiting until doomsday will yield no relief to the user.

FIGURE 5.2   The Apple PWOD.

In many cases, the situation may not be as dire as it appears. It can be that a single application is holding the device captive. If this is the case, either clicking the desktop or bringing another application to the front will return control to the user. While that will solve the issue for the moment, there is some reason why that application caused the lockup, and it will probably occur again. Two things can be done to prevent a problem from recurring.

First, it could be that the system permissions associated with the application and the files it uses have become corrupted. You can use Disk Utility to perform a "permissions repair," which restores file or folder permissions to the state in which the OS and applications expect them to be.

Second, it may help to clear the dynamic link editor cache. This is a cache of recently used entry points to the dynamic link library. If this cache becomes corrupted, it can cause the PWOD. To clear the cache, follow these steps:

1. Launch Terminal, located at `/Applications/Utilities/`.
2. At the Terminal prompt, enter the following command. Please note this is a single line; some browsers may show this command spanning multiple lines.

   `sudo update_dyld_shared_cache -force`
3. Press Enter or Return.
4. Enter the administrator account password.
5. Terminal might display warnings about mismatches in the `dyld` cache. These are normal, and you can proceed.

On the other hand, if you are experiencing this spinning wheel at start-up, the problem is more severe. It means that the system is corrupted. The recovery options will be found by booting to the recovery hard drive, which is a partition created for this purpose in OS X. To do this, start the device and, after the chime, press and hold Command+R until a menu appears. Then select to boot to the recovery partition. Figure 5.3 shows the menu that will appear. You have four options:

1. Restore the system from a Time Machine backup by selecting Restore From Time Machine Backup. Then use a backup to restore the system.
2. Boot to the Apple servers, which can be done only on newer systems. To do this, select Reinstall OS X. Of course, this will require an Internet connection to work.
3. If you choose Get Help Online, you can use Safari to browse to the Apple support site. This will require an Internet connection to work as well.
4. Repair the hard drive and permissions. To do this, select Disk Utility from the menu. Click the First Aid tab and select Repair.

If none of the options discussed so far works, you might need to delete the recovery partition. Use the following steps to do that:

1. Confirm the presence of the recovery partition. Open the Terminal app and enter **diskutil list** to do so.
2. Assuming you see a recovery partition listed on the screen that appears, go back to the Terminal app and enter the following:

FIGURE 5.3 OS X Utilities.

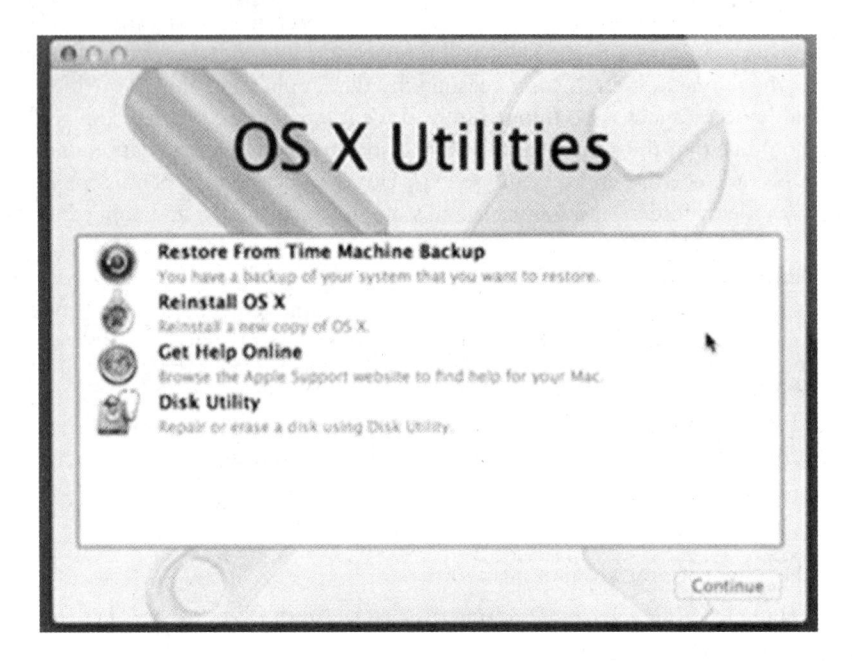

```
defaults write com.apple.DiskUtility DUDebugMenuEnabled 1
```

3. Open the Disk Utility app. In the menu bar at the top, select Debug > Show Every Partition.
4. Select Recovery HD and click the Mount icon to make it active.
5. Once the Recovery HD option is no longer grayed out, you can right-click to delete it or use Control+click and select Erase.
6. There is still an empty partition, so select the Partition tab and click the Recovery HD partition to select it. Then click the minus sign to remove it.

Blank screen

When the screen is blank after boot-up and there are signs that the system has power and some functionality (perhaps you can hear the fan or see lights on the system), the problem could lie in several areas. Consider these possibilities:

- Make sure the monitor is turned on. It has a power switch, so check it.
- If you hear the fan but the system doesn't boot, it could be the power to the motherboard. Check and reseat the power cable to the motherboard.
- Make sure the cable from the monitor to the system is connected properly and try changing it out with a known good cable.

- Try a known good video card to rule out a bad card.
- Ensure that the brightness setting is set high enough.
- In cases where a laptop has been used to direct output to a second display, ensure that the image is being sent to the main display and not just to the external monitor.
- As a last solution, try replacing the monitor.

No power

Power problems usually involve the following issues and scenarios:

- Check the power cord. If it's plugged into a power strip or uninterruptible power supply (UPS), ensure that the strip is plugged in (and if it has a breaker, check to see whether it was tripped by a surge or whether the switch that turns off the entire strip has been inadvertently turned to the off position). In the case of a UPS, check whether the UPS's battery is dead. If the cord and UPS are OK, also try a second wall outlet.
- Try replacing the power supply with a known good unit to see whether the power supply failed.

Sluggish performance

Sluggish performance can be caused by many different issues, including the following:

- Malware consumes resources and may cause it.
- A full system drive can cause slow performance.
- Drive fragmentation will slow performance.
- Insufficient RAM can cause slow performance.
- Overheating is occurring.
- Outdated drivers and software need to be updated.
- Pirated software is being used.

Overheating

Under normal conditions, the PC cools itself by pulling in air. That air is used to dissipate the heat created by the processor and the graphics card (and absorbed by the heat sinks). When airflow is restricted by clogged ports, a bad fan, and so on, heat can build up inside the unit and cause problems. Chip creep—the unseating of components, causing them to move—is one of the more common byproducts of a cycle of overheating and cooling of the inside of a system.

Because air is being pulled into the machine, excessive heat can originate from outside the PC as well, due to a hot working environment. This heat can be pulled in and cause the same problems. Take care to keep the ambient air within normal ranges (approximately 60–90° Fahrenheit) and at a consistent temperature.

Replacing expansion slot covers is vital. Computers are designed to circulate air with slot covers in place or cards plugged into the ports. Leaving slots on the back of the computer open alters the air circulation and causes more dust to be pulled into the system.

Finally, note whether the fan is working; if it stops, that is a major cause of overheating.

Burning smell

A burning smell usually accompanies smoke but could be present after the smoke has ended because the burning component is now dead. Try to identify the damaged component through a visual inspection; if that is not possible, try to determine the damaged component by replacing parts one by one until functionality returns.

Random shutdown

Among the most vexing issues to troubleshoot is any issue that is intermittent. When presented with this type of behavior, consider the following possibilities:

- Try replacing the problem component with a known good one.
- A bad motherboard can cause these types of problems when there are issues with its circuitry. Try replacing the motherboard with a known good motherboard.
- Check the CPU's fan. If the fan is not working, the system will shut down when it reaches a critical CPU temperature.

Application crashes

Application crashes can be an issue with software, but hardware issues can also cause applications to crash. Among the culprits are:

- Voltage spikes or transients
- Heat buildup around a faulty component
- Faulty (partly) memory
- Surface of a hard disk platter hit by the read/write head(s)

Unusual noise

Unusual noises (usually a grinding noise) can be one of two things:

- Blades on the PC's fans could be hitting each other, as they do not necessarily spin at an even pace, therefore resulting in a grinding noise.
- A grinding noise from the hard drive is a symptom of failure in the future. This indicates that hard drive components have turned faulty. Back up your hard drive quickly!

Capacitor swelling

A swollen or distended capacitor on the motherboard does not always indicate a failed or failing capacitor, but at the least it indicates one that is in poor health and should be replaced. A distended capacitor will look normal on the side, but the top of it will be swollen a bit, and there may be brown residue coming out of the top of the capacitor. This is caused by gassing of the electrolyte, meaning that the electrolyte has been broken down into gas and is no longer contributing to the capacitance of the capacitor. The symptoms of this are a system that reboots intermittently and will start only intermittently or not at all.

While replacing a failed capacitor is not easy compared to replacing the motherboard—and in some cases not worth the time and effort—to replace a failed capacitor, follow these steps:

1. Locate the failed capacitor. Look for those that exhibit any of the physical symptoms shown in Figure 5.4.
2. Procure a replacement capacitor. It should have the following:
   - Same voltage
   - Same or larger capacity (look for a number followed by uF)
   - Same external size

   While you can use a capacitor that has a higher voltage or a larger capacity, it is best to use one that matches the one you are replacing.
3. Remove the battery from the board.
4. Use a soldering iron to heat the connection to the board until you can remove the old capacitor. Be careful not to heat the board so much that you damage the connections of other components.

FIGURE 5.4 Failed capacitors.

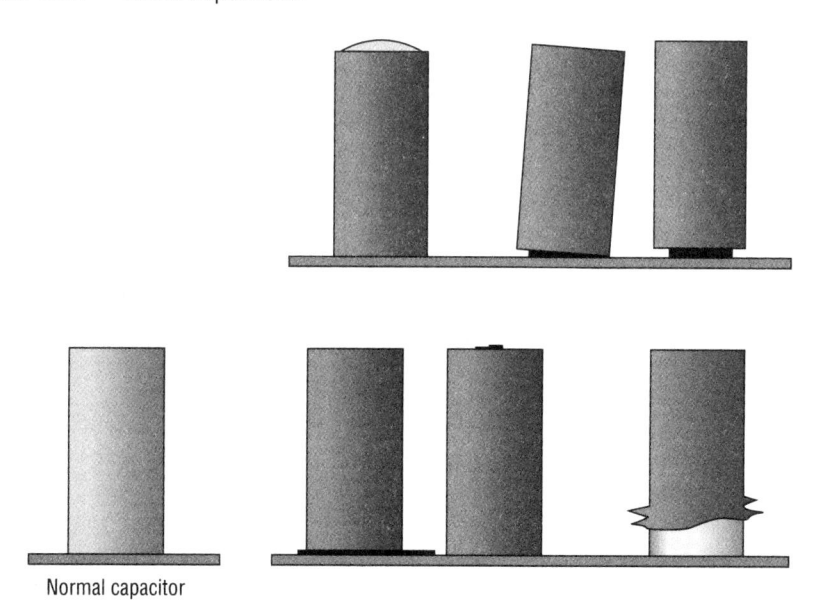

5. Clean the remaining hole and, if necessary, use a pin to enlarge the hole for the new capacitor.
6. Insert the new capacitor. Heat some solder and allow it to flow into the hole to seal. Try to keep the remaining drop on the outside as small as possible. This should be performed only by an experienced technician. Soldering incorrectly can ruin the motherboard.

Inaccurate system date/time

If you find that you are continually resetting the system's time, it could be that the complementary metal-oxide semiconductor (CMOS) battery is dying. Sometimes, a symptom of this is that the hard drive and other settings stored in the BIOS are lost. In the absence of an external time source, the time in the BIOS is where the system gets its cue for the date and time. Change the CMOS battery and the problem should be solved.

Exam essentials

Describe the common symptoms of hardware problems   These symptoms include unexpected shutdowns, lockups, and reboots; POST code beeps; blank screens on boot-up; loss of system timekeeping; attempts to boot to an incorrect device; overheating; loss of power; loud noises; intermittent device failures; smoke; a burning smell; and BSODs.

5.2 Given a scenario, troubleshoot drive and RAID issues

Hard drive and Redundant Array of Independent Disks (RAID) issues should be considered serious, as they can put the data residing on these drives at risk. While RAID drives or arrays exist for the purpose of providing recoverability from issues, these systems are not perfect. When issues do occur, recognizing them and applying the appropriate solution(s) can be a data- (and job-)saving move!

Common symptoms

Hard drives and RAID arrays typically exhibit symptoms before they fail. Learning to read these clues is critical to troubleshooting. The following are the most common of these clues and symptoms.

Light-emitting diode (LED) status indicators

Most storage devices have light-emitting diodes (LEDs) on them that indicate certain things. Every device is different, and referring to their documentation is the best way to learn to interpret these indicators. Just as an example, Table 5.1 shows the meaning of the front panel LEDs on a My Cloud Mirror storage device from Western Digital.

Grinding noises

A grinding noise will be produced if the read head hits the hard drive platter without freezing its rotation. It can be caused by a number of things:

- Power failure that causes the head to stay still over the platter and collapse on it. The friction produced by the moving platter and the stuck head may produce a grinding noise.
- Jerking movements or falls may cause the head to stick to the platter, resulting in a grinding noise.
- The hard drive arm may be so thin that overheating may deform it. Due to this deformity, the head, which is attached to the arm, may come in contact with the platter, causing a grinding noise.

TABLE 5.1 My Cloud Mirror front panel indicators

State	Color	Appearance	Description
Power down	Not lit	N/A	Device is off.
Power up	Blue	Blinking	Device is powering on or in the process of updating firmware.
Power up	Blue	Solid	Device is powered up and ready.
System failure	Red	Blinking	System fault (e.g. firmware update failed, system hang, fan not working, etc.).
Standby	Blue	Pulsing (slowly on and off)	System is in standby.
User attention required	Red	Solid	Device is powered up, but user attention is needed.

Clicking sounds

A loud clicking noise, sometimes referred to as the *click of death*, is caused by the read/write heads contacting the platters. After that happens, both the heads and the platters become damaged, and the system becomes unable to establish a successful starting point to read the drive. This serious damage cannot be repaired. Back up all the data if it's still possible. If the drive is no longer readable, the only option to recover the data is with the help of a professional data recovery service. At that point, you must balance the recovery's cost with the value of the data. This is a case where performing regular backups saves the day!

Bootable device not found

A failure of the system to boot can be caused by a number of issues:

- Failure of the system to locate the boot files.
- If you are presented with an "IDE drive not ready" message at start-up, the drive may not be spinning fast enough to be read. Enable or increase the hard disk predelay time.
- If you receive the message "Immediately back up all your data and replace your hard drive. A fault may be imminent," take it seriously. It means that the drive is using self-monitoring, analysis, and reporting technology to predict failure.
- The hard drive data cable or power cable may have become unseated. Sometimes, even if the cable appears to be seated properly, reseating it can have a positive effect. Also, ensure that the data cable has not been reversed.

OS not found

When you receive the "Operating system not found" message, it's usually a software error rather than a hardware error. It could be that the master boot record or the active partition cannot be located. These issues can be corrected in Windows by rebooting the computer into recovery mode and executing one of several commands at the command line of the recovery environment.

Data loss/corruption

Read/write failures occur when areas of the hard drive require repeated attempts before successful reads or writes occur. This is because these areas are at least partially damaged, although perhaps not enough to be marked as bad sectors. You should perform a hard drive scan using an OS utility to determine whether there are lots of bad sectors. If over time the bad sectors increase, it is an indication that drive failure is imminent, and the drive should be replaced. Make sure to back up your data!

RAID failure

RAID can be either software- or hardware-based. When hardware-based RAID is implemented, a RAID controller card is installed into a slot, and the RAID drives connect to that controller card. You might recall from Chapter 3 in the section "Drive Configurations" that this collection of drives is called a RAID array. When the controller cannot locate the RAID array, usually it's a problem with the controller card.

One item to check after you first install the RAID controller card is that RAID is correctly set in the BIOS. It is also possible that the computer has a built-in RAID controller. If that is the case, there will be ports for the drives in the motherboard. Ensure that the two (or three) hard drives are connected to the same port group.

If the RAID system has been operational, check that all the cables are connecting the drives to the motherboard, reseating them to ensure a good connection. Also, ensure that the BIOS/UEFI is still set to RAID.

If there is no integrated RAID controller and the controller card is installed in a slot, ensure that the card is seated properly (reseating it if needed). Also, ensure that all the drives are securely connected to the ribbon cable coming from the controller card.

RAID stops working

In some cases, one of the drives in the RAID array will cease to function and, depending on the RAID type, can cause the entire array to be unavailable.

If this is a RAID 1 or a mirrored set, you should still be able to access the other drive. To determine which drive is bad, remove each drive one by one and reboot until you have identified the bad drive. Replace the bad drive and use the RAID software to rebuild the array.

If this is a RAID 5 array, follow the same procedure. The bad news is that if more than one drive has failed, you will not be able to rebuild the array. You will need to create the array again after replacing the bad drives and then restore the data from backup.

Once the bad drives have been replaced, the system may rearrange the drives such that the drive with the OS cannot be found. Use the RAID setup program that you access during bootup to set the boot order of the drives in the array, with the drive with the OS first in the list.

Self-Monitoring, Analysis, and Reporting Technology (S.M.A.R.T.) failure

Self-Monitoring, Analysis, and Reporting Technology (often written as S.M.A.R.T.) is a system included in both hard and solid-state drives that detects and reports on drive reliability, with a goal of anticipating hardware failures. It requires software on the computer (located in a protected part of the operating system) to read the data from the drives and performs its analysis during start-up.

Errors reported by S.M.A.R.T. should be accepted as predictions that the drive will soon fail, and you should back up all the data as soon as possible, even if the drive appears to be performing normally and passes other disk checks that you might run. One error that you might be able to mitigate is overheating. If you can increase ventilation such that the error disappears, you are probably safe to continue using the drive.

Extended read/write times

Another symptom of hard drive issues is slow access to the drive. Oddly, one of the potential causes of this is insufficient memory. When this is the case, it causes excessive paging. (Paging occurs when the system does not hold the requested data in memory and therefore must go to the hard drive to retrieve it. Because hard drive access is slower than memory access, this slows the system.)

Another potential cause is that the drive needs to be defragmented. When a drive is fragmented, it takes much longer for all the parts of a file to be located before the file will open. Other issues that cause slow performance are controller cards that need updating, improper data cables, and slower devices sharing the same cable with the hard drive. Finally, insufficient drive space alone will slow performance.

Input/output operations per second (IOPS)

Disk input/output operations per second (IOPS) represents the number of reads and writes that can be performed in a second. One of the advantages of newer solid-state drives (SSDs) is that they exhibit much higher IOPS values than traditional hard disk drives. For example, a 15,000 rpm Serial Advanced Technology Attachment (SATA) drive with a 3 Gbps interface is listed to deliver approximately 175–210 IOPS, whereas an SSD with a SATA 3 Gbps interface is listed at approximately 8,600 IOPS (and that is one of the slower SSD drives).

Missing drives in OS

If the system does not recognize the drive, the problem could be one of the following:

- The hard drive data cable or power cable may have become unseated.
- If you just added a drive, ensure that both drives have not been set to master or slave and that the boot drive is set as master on the first channel.
- If the system uses SATA and you just added a drive, ensure that all the onboard SATA ports are enabled.
- If you just added a drive, ensure that there is no conflict between the new drive and another device.

If you receive the "No boot device available, strike F1 to retry boot, F2 for setup utility" message, the cause could be incorrect drive geometry (probably not the case if this drive was functioning properly before), a bad CMOS battery, or an inability to locate the active partition or master boot record.

Array missing

As mentioned earlier in the section "RAID failure," when the RAID array cannot be located, usually it's a problem with the controller card. Please review that section.

Audible alarms

While it will require reviewing the documentation that came with the RAID array or disk system, many systems use audible alarms to inform the technician of an issue. For example, the Intel RAID Controller audible alarm beeps when a drive fails and during a rebuild. Different patterns indicate different issues as follows:

- **Degraded array:** Short tone, one second on, one second off. Array has degraded, but no data has been lost.
- **Failed array:** Long tone, three seconds on, one second off. Array has failed, and there's a high likelihood that data has been lost.

Please review the documentation that came with the RAID array or disk system in question.

Exam essentials

Identify the most common symptoms of hard drive issues   These include, but are not limited to, read/write failures, slow performance, loud clicking noises, boot failures, unrecognizable drives, missing OSes, and blue screens of death.

List symptoms of RAID array issues   These include missing arrays and RAID arrays that stop functioning.

5.3 Given a scenario, troubleshoot video, projector, and display issues

Video, projector, and display problems may not rate at the top of the priority list for technicians (unless the display is not functioning at all), but to a user, problems with their display may seem like a huge issue. This section discusses common video- and display-related symptoms and their possible sources.

Common symptoms

Display monitors and projectors can exhibit a wide range of symptoms when video-related problems arise. Some are as obvious as no signal whatsoever, whereas other symptoms can be so slight as to almost defy detection. This section discusses common symptoms and some approaches to dealing with these issues.

Incorrect input source

Sometimes, the images you see in the display or being represented by the projector or video are not what you expect. Check the input. You might be connected to the incorrect input source. Most projectors have multiple inputs for VGA, HDMI, HDMI1, HDMI2, Computer 1, Computer 2, and so on. Switch from input to input using the input button on the projector.

You also might need to hit the Fn key and a function button with a monitor icon on your laptop to get the picture to project from your projector. It varies from laptop to laptop.

Physical cabling issues

When there is no image on the screen, the display either has no power, is not functioning at all, or is simply not receiving a signal from the computer. Check the cable from the back of the PC to the monitor, ensuring it is tightly screwed in place, and reseat the cable if required. Also ensure that the monitor is plugged into a functional power outlet and that the brightness settings are high enough. Finally, for a laptop, you should use the appropriate Fn key to ensure that the signal isn't being sent to an external monitor.

To eliminate the video card as the problem, connect a known good display to the computer and see whether the same problem exists. If so, then the problem is not the display. If it works fine, then the problem is the display. Displays do die and usually are not cost-effective to repair. The usual solution is to replace the display.

If the card is the problem, try reseating it. If that provides no relief, insert a known good card. Operating in the same fashion as you did with the display, you can determine whether the video card is the problem.

Burnt-out bulb

When projectors have a dim image, it can be that the bulb is going bad. All projector bulbs have a stated lifetime, which can be found in the projector's documentation. The hours of lifetime that you find stated in the documentation have usually been stretched a bit, meaning that toward the end of the bulb's lifetime it will start to fade in its brightness.

Fuzzy image

A fuzzy image on a projector can be caused by:

- A dirty lens
- Improper alignment between the screen and the projector
- The lens cap still on
- The lens being out of focus
- A defective lens

With regard to the computer display, adjusting the resolution may help. You might also try updating the graphics driver software. Finally, try downloading and installing the latest BIOS for your system.

Display burn-in

Burn-in is a condition that affected cathode ray tube (CRT) monitors and still affects plasma and organic light-emitting diode (OLED) displays. LCDs are generally not affected. The condition occurs when images are left for extended time periods on the screen. Early screensavers were designed to prevent this in unattended displays by displaying a constantly changing image.

Software and utilities can be used to remedy burn-in conditions but will have little effect if it is severe. It is also useful to know that the display will be most susceptible to burn-in when the display is new and in its first few hours of operation. DVDs can be purchased that will "break in" a screen, and in some cases they can even eliminate existing burn-in conditions if they are not severe.

Dead pixels

Pixels are small dots on the screen that are filled with a color; as a group, they present the image you see on the screen. Two conditions can occur with the pixels: stuck pixels and bad or dead pixels.

Stuck pixels have been filled with a color and are not changing as required to display changes in the image. Dead pixels are simply black with no color in them.

When there are few of these and they are not clustered in the same spot, you might not even be able to notice them. When they build to the point where they are noticeable, they cannot be fixed and the monitor must be replaced. You might be able to get some satisfaction from the manufacturer depending on how old the monitor is and the policy of the vendor.

Flashing screen

When the image is flickering or flashing, check the cables and ensure they are seated properly. If that doesn't help, try different cables because it could be a problem with the cable itself.

Another possible reason is a mismatch between the resolution settings and the refresh rate. If this is the problem, it will occur only when using the higher resolutions. You should increase the refresh rate to support higher resolutions.

Incorrect color display

When the image displayed uses incorrect color patterns or is garbled, the root of the problem could depend on when the condition first presented itself. If the screen looked fine during the POST but then goes bad when Windows starts to load, it is probably because of an incorrect video card setting. For example, the display may be set to do something the card is incapable of doing. Restart the system in safe mode (which will cause it to use the VGA driver) and check all the settings of the card while ensuring that it is not set for a resolution level the card or the monitor is not capable of. You might also try updating the driver if a new one is available.

If this problem occurs from the moment you turn the system on, the problem is hardware, and you should check the monitor, cable, and card, replacing each with a known good piece until you isolate the bad component.

Audio issues

In some cases, you have no sound when playing a video that is using a data source, such as the DisplayPort or High-Definition Media Interface (HDMI). While these interfaces are designed to also carry audio, in some cases the system may change the default audio playback device to the audio-supported cable, assuming that another audio device is being used. An issue may occur when a laptop is coming out of sleep mode, as the system is first detecting the audio-capable cable.

To change the default sound playback device in Windows 10 or 11:

1. Click Start and then click Settings (i.e. the gear icon).
2. Click System.
3. On the left menu, click Sound.
4. Under Choose Your Output Device, select the audio device that you want to use.

Dim images

If the image is fine but dim, first check the brightness setting, usually found on the front of the monitor. If this is a laptop, remember there are function keys that when hit inadvertently will dim the screen as well. Check that.

If the display is an LCD, the backlight may be going bad. You learned earlier that these are pencil-sized lights that go behind the screen. They can be replaced on a laptop by following the procedure for opening the laptop lid (where the display resides) and replacing the backlight. Keep in mind that opening the case voids the warranty, so if you still have warranty left, make use of that option.

If it is the backlight on a desktop LCD, the backlight can be replaced for about $20, so it makes a repair worth doing if you want to open the monitor. See the documentation or the vendor website for details on opening the case.

Intermittent projector shutdown

When projector bulbs are overheating, they may shut down to cool down. Simply waiting until the bulb has cooled and then restarting the projector will usually solve the problem. It may also be helpful to inform users that many projectors will not allow the bulb to be restarted soon after you turn it off, so they may want to consider that if they intend to restart the projector soon after shutting it down.

Sizing issues

Sometimes the screen size is either too small or too large, which in either case can make the display difficult if not impossible to work with. There are several settings you can use to try to fix the issue. Among them are:

- **Adjust resolution:** In the Display Settings menu, scroll down to the Resolution dropdown. Select a resolution that best fits your screen. Common resolutions include 1920 × 1080 (full HD) and 1366 × 768.
- **Adjust scaling:** Scroll down to the Scale and Layout section. Adjust the scaling percentage to make text and other items larger or smaller. Common settings include 100%, 125%, and 150%.

Distorted image

The approach to addressing a distorted image is the same as addressing a dim or flashing display. Projectors may be adjusted to remove the keystone effect. A *keystone effect* is the distortion of an image from projecting it onto an angled surface. It makes a typically square image look like a trapezoid—the shape of an architectural keystone, hence the name of the feature. Keystone correction is a standard feature that allows you to compensate for the angled surface and present the normal square projection. Please review the sections on dim and flashing displays.

Exam essentials

List the common symptoms of display problems and the appropriate troubleshooting technique for each   These include, but are not limited to, no image, overheating, dead pixels, incorrect color patterns, and dim, flickering, or distorted images. Resolution techniques include updating drivers, changing resolution settings, and replacing the monitor.

5.4 Given a scenario, troubleshoot common mobile device issues

Mobile devices have their own unique sets of issues that may not be encountered with desktop computers. This section discusses common issues and their solutions. Mobile devices require a different set of procedures for opening the case while protecting the integrity of the unit. It is important to note that updates to the OSes of mobile devices (updates happen frequently) may change the location and look of tools used to fix/adjust settings.

Common symptoms

Not all mobile device issues are unique to mobile devices. They suffer from many of the same issues as desktop machines. However, some problems are unique to laptops and mobile devices or at least are more prone to occur with laptops, as you will learn in this section.

Poor battery health

When battery life is not what it should be in a mobile device, there are several possible reasons. The following are some things that can drain a good battery:

- Display brightness continuously too high
- Constantly enabled wireless connections
- Constantly enabled location services
- Constantly enabled background data services

You might detect a trend in this list, and that is leaving things on! All those services eat the battery's charge. Setting the device to Airplane mode stops all that battery drain. Yes, you might have to manually turn it on to check email, but the convenience is draining your battery.

In other cases, the battery is nearing the end of life (EOL). If using Airplane mode doesn't help, it's probably time for a new battery. All batteries have a limited number of recharges in them. Check the device's documentation for guidance on it. If the battery does suddenly die shortly after a charge, it's a red flag.

Swollen battery

Just as swollen capacitors are a bad thing, so are swollen batteries. A swollen battery occurs when the battery's cells are overcharged, because lithium-ion batteries react unfavorably to overcharging. When you encounter a swollen battery, the only solution is to replace it. You should practice the following safe battery-handling procedures, however, when dealing with swollen batteries:

- Be careful not to puncture a swollen battery. The casing is under stress from the built-up gasses within, and it could explode.
- If the swollen state makes the battery difficult to remove, take the device to an expert for removal.
- If you are able to safely remove the swollen battery, store it in a safe, cool container and take it to an authorized acceptance center. Do not throw it in the trash. Batteries contain toxic chemicals. If a battery gets punctured, crushed, or otherwise damaged, it can cause these chemicals to leach out of them.

To avoid a swollen battery altogether, follow the guidelines in the section "Poor battery health" to extend the life of batteries.

5.4 Given a scenario, troubleshoot common mobile device issues 221

Broken screen

Tablets and smartphones use a touchscreen interface that eliminates the need for a keyboard. Touchscreen monitors use two technologies: touch flow and multitouch. Before we dive into solving a nonresponsive touchscreen, let's review these technologies.

Touch flow

Touch flow, or TouchFLO, is a user interface feature designed by HTC. It is used by dragging your finger up and down or left and right to access common tasks on the screen. This movement is akin to scrolling the screen up and down or scrolling the screen left and right.

Multitouch

Multitouch allows the screen to recognize multiple simultaneous screen touches. It allows for movements such as those used for expanding or enlarging pictures with two fingers and then reducing them back again with the reverse movement.

    The first thing that all documentation will tell you to try is to restart the device; this does actually solve the issue in many cases. Unfortunately, if the screen is broken or the wires are cut, this will not help, but you should always try this first.

    Devices with the Android OS have a Device Diagnostics tool, which can test the touchscreen, among other things. To access this tool, use a special key sequence (see the device's documentation) on the same keypad where you dial phone numbers. When you hit the proper sequence, the menu for the tool will appear; Figure 5.5 shows the menu for the

FIGURE 5.5 Samsung Device Diagnostics menu.

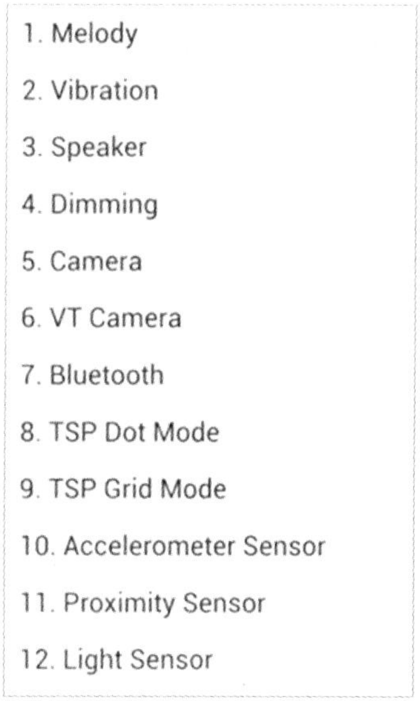

1. Melody
2. Vibration
3. Speaker
4. Dimming
5. Camera
6. VT Camera
7. Bluetooth
8. TSP Dot Mode
9. TSP Grid Mode
10. Accelerometer Sensor
11. Proximity Sensor
12. Light Sensor

Device Diagnostics tool for the Samsung S4. There are two tests found here that apply to the touchscreen: the Touch Screen Panel (TSP) Dot Mode and the TSP Grid Mode.

TSP Dot Mode allows you to verify that the screen is reading your touch. It will place a dot on the screen everywhere you touch it, where it is reading the input. The TSP Grid Mode allows you to test each section (or grid) of the screen. You can drag your finger across the screen and identify any dead spots that may be present.

If the device passes both of these tests, you have no problem with the screen; you have an issue with software, not hardware. Try removing the battery while the device is on (aka performing a soft reset). If the device doesn't allow this, it will typically have an operation you can execute called a *simulated battery* (a technique used to simulate the process of removing and reinserting the battery). If neither of these steps helps, the next step is to reboot the device to safe mode.

If booting to safe mode solves the issue, the issue lies in your application. It may be outdated or corrupt, so try reinstalling the latest version. But if none of these techniques works, you are ready to get more extreme and perform a hard reset, which returns the device to the factory settings. Don't do this until you have backed up all the data on the device. Also, do not do this if the device exhibited any hardware issues when you ran the diagnostics test. You will need it to work properly when you finish the reset, so you can set up the phone again.

If the device fails the diagnostic test, you have a hardware issue. If the damage is from liquids, submerge the phone in 99% isopropyl alcohol. Dry the phone completely and turn it on. This has actually fixed some phones with water damage. Unfortunately, in most cases, when the diagnostic test fails, you have to replace the screen.

These same options are also available with touchscreens on devices like the Microsoft Surface. The same general approach applies with some variation (i.e. clean screen, restart, recalibrate the screen, install the latest updates, restore from backup, refresh, reset). The terms *refresh* and *reset* mean the same here as when dealing with laptops and desktops.

Improper charging

Most nickel cadmium (NiCd) batteries build up memory, and that memory can prevent a battery from offering a full charge. The biggest issue with DC power problems is a battery's inability to power the laptop as long as it should. If a feature is available to fully drain the battery's power, you should use it to eliminate the memory (i.e. letting the laptop run on the battery on a regular basis greatly helps). If you can't drain the battery and eliminate the memory effect, you should replace the battery.

Poor/no connectivity

When there is no wireless connectivity, the cause is usually one of two things:

- The wireless capability is disabled (enabling and disabling this function is usually done with a key combination or Fn key); this is easy to disable inadvertently. This can also be a hardware switch on the side, front, or back of the case.
- The wireless antenna is bad, or the cable needs to be reseated.

Bluetooth is also enabled and disabled with a key combination and can be disabled easily. The first thing to try is to reenable it. The second thing to try is to reseat the antenna cable. If all else fails, try a new antenna. Like the wireless local area network (WLAN) network interface card (NIC), this can also be a hardware switch on the side, front, or back of the case.

Liquid damage

Exposure to even small amounts of liquid can cause batteries to function erratically, charger ports to charge intermittently, software to corrupt, or even total battery power failure to occur. If this happens:

1. Turn off your device and remove the battery.
2. Place the battery in rice to reduce drying time.

If this doesn't work completely, disassemble your device and clean all remnants of the damage, including corrosion, contaminants, and rust. Replace components that were too badly damaged.

Overheating

When a mobile device is getting hot (and I'm talking very hot here, not just warm), the cause can be the battery. If you find that is the source of the heat, replace the battery. Beyond that, some issues that can cause or contribute to overheating are as follows:

- Excessive gaming
- Excessive browsing
- Using the device while charging the device

On a laptop, excessive heat can indicate that the vents are blocked. It also can be a case of running too many things at once. Clean a device's vents often and ensure they are not blocked when it is on. Laptops need a hard, even surface so that the vents can expel heat. This is why running a device on your lap produces so much heat.

Digitizer issues

In Chapter 3, in the "Touch screen/digitizer" section, you learned that digitizers read pressure applied to the display's surface and are what make touchscreens work. Symptoms of digitizer problems include:

- Erratic touchscreen behavior
- Poor touchscreen response
- Dead touchscreen spots
- Random opening of applications
- No touch response

Replacing the digitizer is the solution. For some devices, that is a field-replaceable unit (FRU). However, for other devices, it might mean replacing the entire screen.

Physically damaged ports

There are not many physical ports on most smartphones, while laptops can have a wide range of interfaces. The port that usually gets the most use on a smartphone is the charging port. Th easiest possible fix is to clean the port out using a toothpick. Replacement charging ports can be purchased directly from phone part suppliers like Repairs Universe, Injured Gadgets, and iFixit. Though it's possible to replace the standalone charging port with soldering, it's typically easier to replace the entire flex cable. Doing so will also ensure the charging port is completely repaired in the event that the issue is with the flex cable itself.

When physical interfaces break on a laptop, on the other hand, they are usually replaceable without buying a new motherboard. Replacing a bad DC jack usually requires soldering. If this is not a skill you possess, just replace the motherboard. If you want to attempt it, remove all the parts to get to the motherboard. In some cases, the old DC jack can still be used; it just needs to have the old solder removed and replaced. If that is not the case, remove the old DC jack by unsoldering it from the connector. Then put the new jack in place and solder it to the connectors. Replace all the parts and pieces you removed to get to the board. In general, a bad DC jack usually means a new board.

Malware

When system performance drops, the first thing to check is for the presence of a virus. If the system seems to have an overabundance of disk activity, scan it for viruses, using a virus program that resides externally on a CD/DVD or a memory stick.

Cursor drift/touch calibration

A second, or ghost, cursor can be caused when the laptop has a trackpad that is too sensitive. Some laptops and tablets also vent warm air through the keyboard, and when the lid is left down, it heats up the trackpad and causes this type of cursor behavior. Updating the driver for the touchpad has been known to help this problem. Another approach is to disable the touchpad completely and use an external mouse.

Pointer drift occurs when the mouse cursor slowly drifts across the screen with no user assistance. In some cases, it occurs only on a second or third monitor and not the main monitor. If that is the case, there is a setting in the display properties that may solve the issue. In Windows 10, navigate to the display properties by right-clicking the display and selecting Display Settings. In the menu at the bottom left of the resulting screen, choose Display. On the Display Settings page, select the checkbox next to Let Me Choose One Scaling Level for All My Displays.

In other cases, the problem is not related to multiple monitors at all. If you find that it is occurring only with certain applications, it may be neither a pointer nor a device problem at all, but rather an application issue. Finally, on some laptops and other small devices that use trackpads, you or the user may be leaving your hand resting on a part of the device very close to the trackpad, and it is picking that up and causing the pointer to move.

Touchscreens sometimes need calibration. Calibration is a process that varies by vendor, but it usually requires touching the screen in certain places when it tells you to. See the device's documentation for the exact method.

Unable to install new applications

In some cases, users will discover they run into issues when attempting to install a new application. Potential reasons and possible solutions depend on the type of mobile device. First, let's look at laptops, with causes and solutions listed in Table 5.2.

A different set of issues may confront users who are having smartphone installation issues. Table 5.3 includes some of these issues.

TABLE 5.2 Laptop installation issues

Cause	Solution
Misconfigured power settings	Disable Fast Startup.
Background processes conflicting with the installation	Use Task Manager to end the Windows installer process.
Incorrect system setting	Disable the setting that allows apps only from the Microsoft Store.
Running an outdated version of the OS	Update the system.
Lack of rights	Log in as administrator.

TABLE 5.3 Smartphone app installation issues

Cause	Possible solution(s)
Pending downloads	Cancel pending downloads.
Issues with app store	Clear the cache. Force stop (an option that is used to completely stop a running app and prevent it from running in the background). Uninstall updates. Authenticate to the store.
System service issues	Clear package installer, downloads, and Download Manager cache.

Stylus does not work

When a stylus stops working, there are several potential causes. Causes and possible solutions are covered in Table 5.4.

Degraded performance

When mobile devices suffer from degraded performance, the source is usually a lack of system resources—but not always. Causes and possible solutions are listed in Table 5.5.

Exam essentials

Identify common symptoms of mobile device issues   Some of the symptoms include dimming, flickering, or blank display; sticking keys; intermittent or nonexistent wireless or Bluetooth connectivity; battery and power issues; and ghost cursors.

TABLE 5.4   Stylus issues and solutions

Cause	Possible solution
System glitch	Restart the device.
Sensitivity issues caused by phone cover or screen protector	Remove the phone cover or screen protector.
Inoperable nib/tip	Replace the nib/tip.
Inoperable stylus	Replace the stylus.
Outdated software	Update the software.

TABLE 5.5   Causes of degraded performance

Cause	Possible solution
Loss of battery capacity	Replace the battery.
Lack of memory	Clear memory and cache.
App bloat	Remove unnecessary apps.
Normal wear and tear	Replace the device.

5.5 Given a scenario, troubleshoot network issues

At one time, wireless networks were considered an extravagant and insecure addition to the enterprise network, but now users expect wireless access. No longer is it a business advantage; now it is a business requirement. This section discusses troubleshooting both wired and wireless networks.

Common symptoms

Network problems, usually manifesting themselves as an inability to connect to resources, can arise from many different sources. This section discusses some common symptoms of networking issues.

Intermittent wireless connectivity

When a connectivity issue comes and goes, it can be a hardware issue or a software issue. The following hardware components should be checked for functionality:

Network cable A damaged cable connecting the access point (AP) to the network can cause intermittent connectivity.

Network interface card In cases where the WLAN card is not integrated, if the WLAN NIC is not properly seated or has worked its way partially out of its slot, it can cause intermittent connections.

Interference On a wireless network, cordless phones, microwave ovens, and other wireless networks can interfere with transmissions. Also, users who stray too far from the AP can experience a signal that comes and goes.

The following are software issues that can cause intermittent connectivity:

DHCP issues When the Dynamic Host Configuration Protocol (DHCP) server is down or out of IP addresses, the problem will not manifest itself to those users who already have an IP address until their lease expires and they need a new address. In this case, some users will be fine and others will not, and then users who were fine earlier in the day may have problems later when their IP address lease expires. An IP address beginning with 169.254 (known as an Automatic Private Internet Protocol Addressing [APIPA] address) indicates a DHCP issue.

DNS problems If the Domain Name System (DNS) server is down or malfunctioning, it will cause problems for DNS clients who need name resolution requests answered. For users who have already connected to resources in the last hour before the outage, connectivity to those resources will still be possible until the IP address mapping name is removed from the client's DNS resolver cache.

Slow network speeds

Slow network transmission can be caused by hardware and software issues. Some physical issues that can cause slow performance are as follows:

Incorrect cabling   The network can go only as fast as its slowest component. Using Category 3 (CAT3) cabling, for example, will allow the network to operate at only 10 Mbps even if all the network cards are capable of 10 Gbps.

Malfunctioning NIC   NICs can malfunction and cause a broadcast storm. These broadcast packets fill the network with traffic that slows performance for all users. Use a protocol analyzer to determine the media access control (MAC) address of the offending computer.

From a software standpoint, the following issues can result in less-than-ideal performance:

Router misconfiguration   If the router is incorrectly configured, it can cause slow performance because of less than optimal routing paths. Escalate the issue to the appropriate administrators.

Switch misconfiguration   An improperly implemented redundant switch network can result in switching loops that cause slow performance. Escalate the issue to the appropriate administrators.

Limited connectivity

In some cases, the computer has connectivity to some but not all resources. When this is the case, issues that may reside on other layers of the Open Systems Interconnection (OSI) model should come under consideration. These include the following:

Authentication issues   Does the user have permission to access the resource?

DNS issues   You may be able to ping the entire network using IP addresses, but most access is done by name, not IP address. If you can't ping resources by name and the DNS is not functional, it means that either the DNS server is down or the local machine is not configured with the correct IP address of the DNS server. If recent changes have occurred in the DNS mappings or if your connection to the destination device has recently failed because of a temporary network issue that has been solved, you might need to clear the local DNS cache using the `ipconfig /flushdns` command.

Remote problem   Don't forget that establishing a connection is a two-way street, and if the remote device has an issue, communication cannot occur. Always check the remote device as well. Any interconnecting device between the computer and the resource, such as a switch or router, should also be checked for functionality.

Jitter

When there is a variation in the amount of packet delay, it is called *jitter*. This fluctuation in delay causes congestion in the network. It can also cause packets at the end of the queue to get dropped, requiring retransmissions that cause further delay. Solutions might be as follows:

- Upgrade the router.
- Increase the bandwidth.
- Implement a jitter buffer.

Poor Voice over Internet Protocol (VoIP) quality

Although voice over the public switched telephone network (PSTN) or landline communication is circuit-switched, voice can also be encapsulated in packets and sent across packet-switching networks. When this is done over an IP network, it is called Voice over IP (VoIP). Where circuit-switching networks use the Signaling System 7 (SS7) protocol to set up, control, and disconnect a call, VoIP uses Session Initiation Protocol (SIP) to break up the call sessions. When VoIP quality is poor, it is usually a matter of network congestion. In VoIP implementations, quality of service (QoS) is implemented to ensure that certain traffic (especially voice) is given preferential treatment over the network.

SIP is an application-layer protocol that can operate over either Transmission Control Protocol (TCP) or User Datagram Protocol (UDP). Addressing is in terms of IP addresses, and the voice traffic uses the same network used for regular data. Because latency is always possible on these networks, protocols have been implemented to reduce the impact, as this type of traffic is much more affected by delays. Applications such as voice and video need to have protocols and devices that can provide an isochronous network. Isochronous networks guarantee continuous bandwidth without interruption. Isochronous networks don't use an internal clock source or start and stop bits. All bits are of equal importance and are anticipated to occur at regular intervals.

Port flapping

Port flapping is a situation in which a physical interface on the switch continually goes up and down, caused by bad, unsupported, or nonstandard cable or other link synchronization issues. Some network devices allow you to set link flap prevention settings on a switch that err-disables (i.e. shuts down) a flapping port. If you have a redundant network (multiple routes to destinations through multiple interfaces), this feature will help. Otherwise, it will make the situation even worse because there will be no alternate route to the destination.

The root cause must be discovered. While it can be symptomatic of hardware issues, keep in mind that in cases where two ends of a link require a compatible setting or require authentication, the settings are not compatible or the authentication is failing.

High latency

High latency simply means the network is slow. It's rare that the entire network is slow. It's usually one or two sections (i.e. subnets). Use `tracert` to determine where the slow subnet(s) reside(s) and then concentrate your troubleshooting effort there. You will learn more about using both `ping` and `tracert` in Chapter 6, in the section "Network."

External interference

Both wireless and wired networks can be affected by electromagnetic interference (EMI) and radio frequency interference (RFI). EMI will degrade network performance. This can be identified by the poor operation you might experience. Be sure to run cables around (not over) ballasts and other items that can cause EMI. RFI is a similar issue introduced by radio waves. Wireless networks suffer even more from both issues.

Authentication failures

In some cases, access to the network is impossible because the user is unable to identify themself and provide required credentials. As discussed in the section on intermittent connectivity, the user *must* have the permission to access the resource or the network in question. The solution is to verify the user's rights and address the failing credentials issue.

Intermittent Internet connectivity

Troubleshooting Internet connectivity issues is very similar to addressing intermittent network issues. Please review that section, especially the sections on DNS and DHCP issues. With respect to the Internet, however, there can be an additional consideration. Is the Internet service provider (ISP) down? If your ISP is down, there will be nothing you can do to solve the issue. This is why it is advisable to provision a second (or third) ISP connection to provide redundancy.

Exam essentials

Identify common symptoms of network issues and their potential causes   Examples include limited, intermittent, or no connectivity; slow transfer speeds; and low RF signal.

5.6 Given a scenario, troubleshoot printer issues

In the real world, you'll find that a large portion of all service calls relate to printing problems. This section will give you some general guidelines and common printing solutions to resolve printing problems.

Lines down the printed pages

Vertical lines can appear in either of two forms.

Vertical black lines on the page

With laser printers, a groove or scratch in the enterprise portal (EP) drum can cause the problem of vertical black lines running down all or part of the page. Because a scratch is lower than the surface, it doesn't receive as much (if any) of a charge as the other areas. The result is that toner sticks to it as though it were discharged. Because the groove may go around the circumference of the drum, the line may go all the way down the page.

Another possible cause of vertical black lines is a dirty charge corona wire, which prevents a sufficient charge from being placed on the EP drum. Because the EP drum has almost zero charge, toner sticks to the areas that correspond to the dirty areas on the charge corona wire.

The solution to the first problem is, as always, to replace the toner cartridge (or EP drum, if your printer uses a separate EP drum and toner). You can also solve the second problem with a new toner cartridge, but in this case that would be an extreme solution. It's easier to clean the charge corona with the brush supplied with the cartridge.

When dealing with inkjet printers, vertical black lines on the page can mean the printhead needs cleaning or that the print cartridge needs to be replaced.

Vertical white lines on the page

With laser printers, vertical white lines running down all or part of the page are a relatively common problem on older printers, especially ones that see little maintenance. They're caused by foreign matter (more than likely toner) caught on the transfer corona wire. The dirty spots keep the toner from being transmitted to the paper at those locations, with the result being that streaks form as the paper progresses past the transfer corona wire.

The solution is to clean the corona wires. Some printers come with a small corona-wire brush to help with this procedure. To use it, remove the toner cartridge and run the brush in the charge corona groove on top of the toner cartridge. Replace the cartridge and use the brush to brush away any foreign deposits on the transfer corona. Be sure to put it back in its holder when you're finished.

For inkjet printers, clean the printhead first (or run the built-in cleaning cycle) and then try replacing the cartridge. This behavior is usually caused by dust or debris.

Garbled print

Many problems with a printer that won't work with the system or that prints the wrong characters can be traced to problems with its software. Computers and printers can't talk to each other by themselves. They need interface software known as *drivers* to translate software commands into commands that the printer can understand.

For a printer to work with a particular OS, a driver must be installed for it. In Chapter 3, in the section "Printer Control Language (PCL) vs. PostScript," you learned about the page description languages (PDL) and drivers. Please review that section.

If the wrong printer driver is selected, the computer will send commands in the wrong language. If that occurs, the printer will print several pages of garbage (even if only one page of information was sent). This "garbage" isn't garbage at all, but the printer PDL commands printed literally as text instead of being interpreted as control commands.

In situations where the printer is physically connected and you have verified that the proper drivers are in place, consider reseating the cable connecting the printer and computer.

Paper jams

Laser printers today run at copier speeds. As a result, their most common problem is paper jams. Paper can get jammed in a printer for several reasons. First, feed jams happen when the paper-feed rollers get worn. The solution to this problem is easy: Replace the worn rollers.

> If your paper-feed jams are caused by worn pickup rollers, there is something you can do to get your printer working while you're waiting for the replacement pickup rollers. Scuff the feed rollers with a pot scrubber pad (or something similar) to roughen up the surfaces. This trick works only once. After that, the rollers aren't thick enough to touch the paper.

Another cause of feed jams is related to the drive of the pickup roller. The drive gear (or clutch) may be broken or have teeth missing. Again, the solution is to replace it. To determine whether the problem is a broken gear or worn rollers, print a test page but leave out the paper tray. Look into the paper-feed opening with a flashlight to see whether the paper pickup rollers are turning evenly and don't skip. If they turn evenly, the problem is more than likely worn rollers.

Worn exit rollers can also cause paper jams. These rollers guide the paper out of the printer into the paper-receiving tray. If they're worn or damaged, the paper may catch on its way out of the printer. These jam types are characterized by a paper jam that occurs just as the paper is getting to the exit rollers. If the paper jams, open the rear door and see where the paper is. If the paper is close to the exit roller, the exit rollers are probably the problem.

The solution is to replace all the exit rollers. You must replace all of them at the same time, because even one worn exit roller can cause the paper to jam. Besides, they're inexpensive. Don't be cheap and skimp on these parts if you need to have them replaced.

Paper jams can be the fault of the paper. If your printer consistently tries to feed multiple pages into the printer, the paper isn't dry enough. If you live in an area with high humidity, this could be a problem. Some solutions are pretty extreme but may work (such as keeping the paper in a Tupperware-type airtight container or microwaving it to remove moisture). The best all-around solution, however, is humidity control and keeping the paper wrapped until it's needed. Keep the humidity around 50% or lower (but greater than 25% if you can, to avoid problems with electrostatic discharge). Poor paper quality can also cause this problem.

Finally, a metal, grounded strip, called the *static eliminator strip*, inside the printer drains the corona charge away from the paper after it has been used to transfer toner from the EP cartridge. If that strip is missing, broken, or damaged, the charge will remain on the paper and may cause it to stick to the EP cartridge, causing a jam. If the paper jams after reaching the corona assembly, this may be the cause.

Faded prints

In laser printers, faded output usually indicates that the toner cartridge is just about empty. You can usually remove it, shake it, and replace it, and then get a bit more life out of it before it is completely empty, but this is a signal that you are near the end.

Another possibility is that the ink cartridge has dried out from a lack of use. That's why the manufacturers include a small suction pump inside the printer that primes the ink cartridge before each print cycle. If this priming pump is broken or malfunctioning, this problem will manifest itself, and the pump will need to be replaced.

For dot-matrix printers, faded printing means you need to replace the ribbon, which is the source of ink in that printer type.

Paper not feeding

When the paper is not feeding into the printer, it means the pickup rollers have hardened and lost their ability to pick up the paper. Replacing these rollers usually fixes the problem.

In some cases, it's not the rollers but a dirty paper-feed sensor. It is designed to tell the printer when it is out of paper. Always try cleaning the sensor first before replacing it. High humidity can also cause the paper to not feed properly.

Multipage misfeed

Another issue that is usually traced to the pickup rollers is when multiple pages are fed at a time rather than a single page. It can also be caused by the paper. Paper-feed issues might result from dusty, torn, wrinkled, wet, or folded paper in the tray. Finally, it also occurs when the paper trays are overloaded.

Multiple prints pending in queue

Sometimes the printer will not print, and all attempts to delete print jobs or clear the print queue fail. It's almost as if the printer is just frozen. When this occurs, the best thing to do is to restart the print spooler service on the computer that is acting as the print server. Unfortunately, all users will have to resend their print jobs after this, but at least the printer will be functional again.

Speckling on printed pages

A faulty ink or toner cartridge is one reason that ink specks may appear on documents; paper dust and ink particles on the printer's internal components can also cause this problem. If you are using a laser printer, toner specks can also be caused by a faulty photoconductor unit. A buildup of paper dust and ink particles inside your printer can also cause specks on your printed output as well as on blank paper.

If these are white specks, then it could be the following:

- The appropriate paper is not being used.
- Damp paper is being used.
- The drum in the toner cartridge is deteriorated.

Double/echo images on the print

A problem unique to laser printers, *ghosting*, occurs when you can see light images of previously printed pages on the current page. This is caused by one or two things: bad erasure lamps or a broken cleaning blade. If the erasure lamps are bad, the previous electrostatic discharges aren't completely wiped away. When the electrophotographic (EP) drum rotates toward the developing roller, some toner sticks to the slightly discharged areas. A broken cleaning blade, on the other hand, causes old toner to build up on the EP drum and consequently present itself in the next printed image.

Replacing the toner cartridge solves the second problem. Solving the first problem involves replacing the erasure lamps in the printer. Because the toner cartridge is the least expensive cure, you should try that first. Usually, replacing the toner cartridge will solve the problem. If it doesn't, you'll then have to replace the erasure lamps.

Grinding noise

If there is a grinding noise when you either start the printer or print a job, it is either a carriage stall or a paper jam. The carriage assembly, which holds the ink cartridges, may be stalled at the left side of the printer. A paper jam may have occurred previously. The cause of the problem may be that the printer's clutch actuator is disengaged.

Locate the metal gear assembly at the left side of the printer. Directly above the metal gear is the clutch actuator. The arrow on the clutch actuator should be in the space to the right of the metal gear and plastic half-gear just below the clutch actuator.

If the arrow on the clutch actuator is stuck between the metal gear and plastic half-gear, lift the clutch actuator and move the arrow to the right of the plastic half-gear. Once the arrow on the clutch actuator is to the right of the gears, the clutch actuator should move freely.

Finishing issues

The finishing process is when pages are stapled together and holes are punched, if so configured. In this section, you'll learn about finishing issues.

Staple jams

Printers that staple will hold the staples in what is sometimes called the *stapling mailbox*. When staples get jammed, follow this procedure:

1. Press the button to release the stapling mailbox and slide it away from the printer.
2. Press the latch to release the stapler door.
3. Open the stapler door.
4. Lift the green tab on the staple cartridge upward and then pull the staple cartridge straight out of its slot.
5. Lift up on the small lever at the back of the staple cartridge.
6. Remove the jammed staples from the staple cartridge.
7. Load the new staples and reverse the steps to put the printer back together.

Hole punch

The hole punch system can get jammed if the hole-punch waste container used to hold the small pieces punched out of each sheet is full. To empty it:

1. Open the finisher door.
2. Slide the hole-punch waste container out of the finisher.
3. Dispose of the paper waste.
4. Insert the emptied hole-punch waste container into the printer.

Incorrect page orientation

Page orientation specifies whether to print landscape or portrait. This is a choice you can make when sending the print job, so if incorrectly chosen, it will result in this behavior. But it can also be the result of an incorrect or corrupt printer driver.

Tray not recognized

As you learned in Chapter 3, in the section "Configuration settings," many printers can hold multiple types and sizes of paper in multiple trays. Tray settings allow you to choose the type of paper, and then the printer will use paper found in that tray. When you select a tray and receive the message "Tray not recognized," try the following steps:

- **Check the paper tray settings:** Ensure it is configured correctly for the paper type and size you are using.
- **Power cycle the printer:** Turn it off, wait 10 seconds, and turn it back on.
- **Check for paper or foreign objects:** Make sure the paper tray is inserted correctly and free of any obstructions.

Connectivity issues

If a network printer is not able to receive jobs, the issue may be with the IP address that it has (or, more correctly, does not have). Often, the printer will need to be manually assigned an IP address to ensure that it has the same one each time. Read the manufacturer's documentation for assigning an IP address to the printer and walk through the steps to do so.

Frozen print queue

In the previous section "Multiple prints pending in queue," you learned about dealing with a frozen print queue. Please review that section.

Exam essentials

Identify the most common symptoms of printing problems   These include streaks, faded prints, ghost images, incompletely fused toner, creased paper, paper jams, and feeding issues; no connectivity; garbled characters; vertical lines; print queue issues; and incorrect print colors.

Review Questions

You can find the answers in the appendix.

1. Which of the following is the final step in the CompTIA troubleshooting method?
    A. Establish a plan of action to resolve the problem and implement the solution.
    B. Document findings, actions, and outcomes.
    C. Establish a theory of probable cause (question the obvious).
    D. Identify the problem.

2. Which of the following is the first step in the CompTIA troubleshooting method?
    A. Establish a plan of action to resolve the problem and implement the solution.
    B. Document findings, actions, and outcomes.
    C. Establish a theory of probable cause (question the obvious).
    D. Identify the problem.

3. What is the most common reason for an unexpected reboot?
    A. Overheating
    B. ESD damage
    C. RFI
    D. Memory leak

4. Which of the following is typically not a cause of system lockups?
    A. Memory issues
    B. Virus
    C. Video driver
    D. Bad NIC driver

5. What are proprietary screen crashes called in Windows?
    A. Pinwheel
    B. BSOD
    C. Bomb screen
    D. PSOID

6. Which operating system uses the pinwheel of death as a proprietary screen crash?
    A. Apple
    B. Linux
    C. Windows
    D. UNIX

7. What are the small dots on the screen that are filled with a color?
   A. Pixels
   B. Hypervisors
   C. Cells
   D. Capacitors

8. Which of the following is NOT a cause of sluggish system performance?
   A. Malware
   B. Overheating
   C. Incorrect subnet mask
   D. Outdated drivers

9. What is the light in the device that powers the LCD screen?
   A. Backlight
   B. Inverter
   C. Charger
   D. Reflector

10. Which of the following is a user interface feature designed by HTC?
    A. Type I
    B. TouchFLO
    C. Type II
    D. Container-based

11. Which of the following indicates that the fuser is not fusing the toner properly on the paper?
    A. Black spots
    B. Streaks
    C. Blank spots
    D. Garbled output

12. Which of the following indicates that the toner cartridge is just about empty?
    A. Black spots
    B. Streaks
    C. Faded prints
    D. Garbled output

13. If you can ping resources by IP address but not by name, which service is not functional?
    A. HTTP
    B. DNS
    C. DHCP
    D. ARP

14. Which of the following should be set to the IP address of the router interface connecting to the local network?
    A. IP address
    B. Subnet mask
    C. Default gateway
    D. DHCP server

CompTIA A+ Core 2 Exam 220-1202

PART II

Chapter 6   Operating Systems

Chapter 7   Security

Chapter 8   Software Troubleshooting

Chapter 9   Operational Procedures

Chapter 6

Operating Systems

COMPTIA A+ 220-1202 EXAM OBJECTIVES COVERED IN THIS CHAPTER:

✔ **1.1 Explain common operating system (OS) types and their purposes.**

- Workstation systems (OSes)
  - Windows
  - Linux
  - macOS
  - Chrome OS
- Mobile OSes
  - iPadOS
  - iOS
  - Android
- Various file system types
  - New Technology File System (NTFS)
  - File Allocation Table 32 (FAT32)
  - Resilient File System (ReFS)
  - Fourth Extended File System (ext4)
  - Extended File System (XFS)
  - Apple File System (APFS)
  - Extensible File Allocation Table (exFAT)
- Vendor life-cycle limitations
  - End of life (EOL)
  - Update limitations
- Compatibility concerns between operating systems

✓ **1.2 Given a scenario, perform OS installations and upgrades in a diverse environment.**

- Boot methods
  - Universal serial bus (USB)
  - Network
    - Preboot Execution Environment (PXE)
    - NetBoot
  - Solid-state/flash drives
  - Internet-based
  - External/hot-swappable drive
  - Internal hard drive (partition)
  - Multiboot
- Types of installations
  - Clean install
    - Unattended/attended clean install
  - Upgrade
  - Image deployment
    - Creating an image
    - Image deployment
  - Remote network installation
  - Zero-touch deployment
  - Recovery partition
  - Repair installation
  - Other considerations
    - Third-party drivers
- Partitioning
  - Dynamic
  - Basic
  - Primary
  - Extended
  - Logical

- GUID (globally unique identifier) Partition Table (GPT)
- Master boot record
- Drive format
- Upgrade considerations
  - Backup files and user preferences
  - Application and driver support/backward compatibility
  - OS compatibility/upgrade path
  - Hardware compatibility
- Feature updates
  - Product life cycle

✔ **1.3 Compare and contrast basic features of Microsoft Windows editions.**

- Windows 10 editions
  - Home
  - Pro
  - Pro for Workstations
  - Enterprise
- Windows 11 editions
  - Home
  - Pro
  - Enterprise
- N versions
- Feature differences
  - Domain vs. workgroup
  - Desktop styles/user interface
  - Availability of Remote Desktop Protocol (RDP)
  - Random-access memory (RAM) support limitations
  - BitLocker
  - gpedit.msc
- Upgrade paths
  - In-place upgrade

- Upgrading to Windows 10
  - Windows Upgrade OS Advisor
- Clean install
- Hardware requirements
  - Trusted Platform Module (TPM)
  - Unified Extensible Firmware Interface (UEFI)

✔ 1.4 Given a scenario, use Microsoft Windows operating system features and tools.

- Task Manager
  - Services
  - Startup
  - Performance
  - Processes
  - Users
- Microsoft Management Console (MMC) snap-in
  - Event Viewer (eventvwr.msc)
  - Disk Management (diskmgmt.msc)
    - Drive status
    - Mounting
    - Initializing
    - Extending partitions
    - Splitting partitions
    - Shrinking partitions
    - Assigning/changing drive letters
    - Adding drives
    - Adding arrays
    - Storage spaces
  - Task Scheduler (taskschd.msc)
  - Device Manager (devmgmt.msc)
  - Certificate Manager (certmgr.msc)
  - Local User and Groups (lusrmgr.msc)
  - Performance Monitor (perfmon.msc)

- Group Policy Editor (gpedit.msc)
- Additional tools
  - System Information (msinfo32.exe)
  - Resource Monitor (resmon.exe)
  - System Configuration (msconfig.exe)
    - General
    - Boot
    - Services
    - Startup
    - Tools
  - Disk Cleanup (cleanmgr.exe)
  - Disk Defragment (dfrgui.exe)
  - Registry Editor (regedit.exe)

✔ **1.5 Given a scenario, use the appropriate Microsoft command-line tools.**

- Navigation
  - cd
  - dir
- Network
  - ipconfig
  - ping
  - netstat
  - nslookup
  - net use
  - tracert
  - pathping
- Disk management
  - chkdsk
  - Format
  - diskpart

- File management
  - md
  - rmdir
  - robocopy
- Informational
  - hostname
  - netuser
  - winver
  - whoami
  - [command name] /?
- OS management
  - gpupdate
  - gpresult
  - sfc

✔ **1.6 Given a scenario, configure Microsoft Windows Settings.**

- Internet options
  - Connections
  - Security
  - General
  - Privacy
  - Programs
  - Advanced
- Devices and Printers
- Program and Features
- Network and Sharing Center
- System
  - Performance (virtual memory)
  - Remote settings
  - System protection
- Windows Defender Firewall
- Mail

- Sound
- User Accounts
- Device Manager
- Indexing Options
- Administrative Tools
- File Explorer Options
  - View Hidden Files
  - Hide Extensions
  - General Options
  - View Options
- Power Options
  - Hibernate
  - Power plans
  - Sleep/suspend
  - Standby
  - Choose what closing the lid does
  - Turn on Fast Startup
  - USB Selective Suspend
  - Ease of Access
- Time and Language
- Update and Security
- Personalization
- Apps
- Privacy
- System
- Devices
- Network and Internet
- Gaming
- Accounts

✔ **1.7 Given a scenario, configure Microsoft Windows networking features on a client/desktop.**
- Domain joined vs. workgroup
  - Domain setup
  - Shared resources
  - Printers
  - File servers
  - Mapped drives
- Local OS firewall settings
  - Application restrictions and exceptions
  - Configuration
  - Enabling/disabling Windows Firewall
- Client network configuration
- Establish network connections
  - VPN
  - Wireless
  - Wired
  - Wireless wide area network (WWAN)/cellular network
- Proxy settings
- Public network vs. private network
- File Explorer navigation–network paths
- Metered connections and limitations

✔ **1.8 Explain common features and tools of the macOS/desktop operating system.**
- Installation and uninstallation of applications
  - File types
    - .dmg
    - .pkg
    - .app
  - App Store
  - Uninstallation process

- System folders
  - /Applications
  - /Users
  - /Library
  - /System
  - /Users/Library
- Apple ID and corporate restrictions
- Best practices
  - Backups
  - Antivirus
  - Update/patches
  - Rapid Security Response (RSR)
- System Preferences
  - Display
  - Network
  - Printers and Scanners
  - Privacy
  - Accessibility
  - Time Machine
- Features
  - Multiple desktops
  - Mission Control
  - Keychain
  - Spotlight
  - iCloud
  - iMessage
  - FaceTime
  - Drive
  - Gestures
  - Finder
  - Dock

- Disk Utility
  - Disk maintenance utilities
  - FileVault
  - Terminal
  - Force Quit

✔ **1.9 Identify common features and tools of the Linux client/desktop operating system.**

- Common commands
- File management
  - ls
  - pwd vs. passwd
  - mv
  - cp
  - rm
  - chmod
  - chown
  - grep
  - find
- Filesystem management
  - fsck
  - mount
- Administrative
  - su/sudo
- Package management
  - apt
  - yum
  - dnf
- Network
  - ip
  - ping
  - curl

- dig
- traceroute
- Informational
  - man
  - cat
  - top
  - ps
  - du
  - df
- Text editors
  - nano
- Common configuration files
  - /etc/passwd
  - /etc/shadow
  - /etc/hosts
  - /etc/fstab
  - /etc/resolv.conf
- OS components
  - systemd
  - kernel
  - bootloader
- Root account

✔ 1.10 Given a scenario, install applications according to requirements.

- System requirements for applications
  - 32-bit vs. 64-bit dependent application requirements
  - Dedicated vs. integrated graphics card
  - Video random-access memory (VRAM) requirements
  - RAM requirements
  - Central processing unit (CPU) requirements
  - External hardware tokens

- Storage requirements
- Application to OS compatibility
    - 32-bit vs. 64-bit OS
- Distribution methods
    - Physical media vs. mountable ISO file
        - Local (CD/USB)
        - Network-based
    - ISO-mountable
    - Downloadable package
    - Image deployment
- Impact considerations for new applications
    - Device
    - Network
    - Operation
    - Business

✓ **1.11 Given a scenario, install and configure cloud-based productivity tools.**

- Email systems
- Storage
    - Sync/folder settings
- Collaboration tools
    - Spreadsheets
    - Videoconferencing
    - Presentation tools
    - Word processing tools
    - Instant messaging
- Identity synchronization
- Licensing assignment

This chapter focuses on exam topics related to operating systems (OSes). It follows the structure of the CompTIA A+ 220-1202 exam blueprint, Objective 1, and it explores the 11 subobjectives that you need to master before taking the exam.

> **NOTE**
> This book covers Windows 10 and Windows 11, but most of the examples use Windows 10. We will call out differences when necessary. Microsoft announced that support for Windows 10 ends in October 2025.

1.1 Explain common operating system (OS) types and their purpose

While the overwhelming percentage of the workstations you will come into contact with will be Windows devices, you will also encounter other operating systems (OSes). The Linux OS and the macOS are increasingly found in enterprise networks in situations where their strengths can be leveraged. There are also many other technologies that you might not be directly managing, but you should still be familiar with them and understand their purpose. This first section will focus on these areas, as well as other OSes, such as those found on smartphones and tablets.

Workstation systems (OSes)

Workstations are the most common device types in our networks. These are the user machines, both laptop and desktops. There are four main OSes used on workstations: Windows, Apple (macOS), Linux, and Chrome OS.

Windows

While there are many Windows OSes available, this exam asks that you know the intricacies of only Windows 10 and Windows 11. You will learn more about Windows 10 in this chapter. We will call out where major differences exist.

Linux

Linux is probably used more often than macOS in enterprise networks, in part because many proprietary OSes that reside on devices, such as access points, switches, routers, and firewalls, are Linux-based. Linux systems also predominate in the software development area.

macOS

In your career, you are almost certain to encounter the macOS OSes. Even though these systems constitute only a small percentage of the total number of devices found in enterprise environments, there are certain environments where they dominate and excel, such as music and graphics.

Chrome OS

Chrome is an OS developed by Google that runs on its Chromebook. Based on the Linux kernel, it uses the Chrome browser as an interface. Originally it ran Chrome apps, but now Android apps have been made to run on it.

Mobile OSes

Computer OSes are not the only type of OS with which you will come into contact. Many tablets, smartphones, and other small devices will have OSes that are designed to run on devices that have different resource capabilities and therefore require different systems. This section will look at OSes for such mobile devices.

iPadOS

The iPadOS is a rebranded variant of iOS, the OS used by Apple's iPhones. It differs by supporting multitasking capabilities and keyboard use. The current version is iPadOS 18.7 released in 2025.

iOS

Apple iOS is a vendor-specific system made by Apple for mobile devices. Developers must use the software development kit (SDK) from Apple and register as Apple developers.

Android

The Android OS from Google is built on a Linux kernel with a core set of libraries that are written in Java. It is an open-source OS, which means that developers have full access to the same framework application programming interfaces (APIs) used by the core applications.

Various file system types

While New Technology File System (NTFS) is available with Windows, Windows also recognizes and supports File Allocation Table 32 (FAT32). Linux and macOS use different systems. This section lists the major file systems and the differences among them.

New Technology File System (NTFS)

Introduced along with Windows NT, NTFS is a much more advanced file system in almost every way than all versions of the FAT file system. It includes features such as individual file security and compression, Redundant Array of Independent Disks (RAID) support, support for extremely large file and partition sizes, and disk transaction monitoring. It is the file system of choice for higher-performance computing. Finally, it supports both file compression and file encryption.

File Allocation Table 32 (FAT32)

FAT is an acronym for the file on a file system used to keep track of where files are stored. It's also the name given to this type of file system, introduced in 1981. The largest FAT disk partition that could be created was approximately 2 GB. FAT32 was introduced along with Windows 95 Original Equipment Manufacturer (OEM) Service Release 2. As disk sizes grew, so did the need to be able to format a partition larger than 2 GB. FAT32 was based more on Virtual File Allocation Table (VFAT) than on FAT16. It allowed 32-bit cluster addressing, which in turn provided for a maximum partition size of 2 TB (i.e. 2,048 GB). It also included smaller cluster sizes to avoid wasted space. FAT32 support is included in current Windows versions.

Resilient File System (ReFS)

The Resilient File System (ReFS) is Microsoft's newest file system. It seeks to address an expanding set of storage scenarios and establish a foundation for future innovations. A comparison of FAT32, NTFS, and ReFS can be found in Table 6.1.

TABLE 6.1 Windows file system comparison

Comparison	ReFS	NTFS	FAT32
Compatibility	Windows Server 2022, 2019, 2016, 2012 R2, and Windows Server 2012	Windows 2000/XP; Windows 2003/Vista/7/8/8.1/10,11; Windows Server 2008/2008 R2/2012; GNU/Linux; macOS X	All Windows versions; Linux; macOS; gaming consoles such as the Xbox One, PS3/4, and the Steam Deck
Max. volume size	32 PB	8 PB	32 GB
Max. file size	35 PB	16 TB	4 GB

Fourth Extended File System (ext4)

ext4 is a Linux file system. While ext4 has advantages, it should be noted that it is *not* compatible with Windows. The following are the strengths of ext4:

- It supports individual file sizes up to 16 TB.
- The overall maximum ext4 file system size is 1 EB (exabyte); 1 EB = 1,024 PB (petabyte), and 1 PB = 1,024 TB (terabyte).
- The directory can contain 64,000 subdirectories.

In ext4, you also have the option of turning off the journaling feature. A journaling file system is a file system that keeps track of changes not yet committed to the file system.

Extended File System (XFS)

Originally designed at Silicon Graphics, Inc. Extended File System (XFS) is the default file system for Red Hat Enterprise Linux 7. When large files must be stored and retrieved, the XFS file system is the most beneficial.

Its features include:

- Metadata journaling, facilitating quicker crash recovery.
- Ability to be defragmented and enlarged while mounted and active.
- Support for backup and restore utilities specific to XFS.

Apple File System (APFS)

The Apple File System (APFS) is the successor to the Hierarchical File System (HFS) developed by Apple for use in computer systems running macOS. Designed for floppy and hard disks, it can also be found on read-only media such as CD-ROMs.

AFPS was developed and deployed for macOS Sierra (10.12.4) and, later, iOS 10.3. APFS is optimized for solid-state drive storage and supports encryption, snapshots, and increased data integrity, among other capabilities.

Extensible File Allocation Table (exFAT)

Extended File Allocation Table (exFAT) is a Microsoft file system optimized for flash drives. It is proprietary and has also been adopted by the Standard Definition (SD) Association as the default file system for Secure Digital eXtended Capacity (SDXC) cards larger than 32 GB. The proprietary nature and licensing requirements make this file system difficult to use in any open-source or commercial software. This file system is supported in Windows 10 and 11.

Vendor life-cycle limitations

Vendors of OSes impose certain restrictions and limitations on the support provided to their systems. Two of the more important of these are covered in this section: end-of-life and update limitations.

End of life (EOL)

Whenever a vendor sets an end-of-life (EOL) date, it means that after that date, they will no longer offer help and support for that product. After that date, you are on your own regarding errors and troubleshooting. Even worse, there will be no more security patches and updates provided. For example, EOL for Windows 10 is October 14, 2025.

Update limitations

When Microsoft and possibly other vendors release OS updates, they sometimes make the update package available only to those who purchased a full copy of the previous version. In cases like this, the update package will be cheaper than the full OS, with the idea being to give the customer credit for the purchase of the previous system. Those without the previous system must pay full price for a new installation of the updated OS.

Compatibility concerns between operating systems

While using a mix of desktop operating systems in an organization is not recommended, you might find yourself in that scenario. If that is the case, you might also find yourself supporting many more applications, as they are specific to the OS and sometimes even to an OS version, such as Windows 10. Be aware that you might encounter compatibility issues between the systems and between the documents produced by the applications. Always research online about these issues, as someone has probably already solved the issue!

Exam essentials

Describe the major differences between the Android and iOS operating systems. Android is an open-source OS, and iOS is a vendor-specific system made by Apple. Apps for Android systems can be obtained from Google Play or many other sites, whereas iOS apps are available only on the App Store site.

1.2 Given a scenario, perform OS installations and upgrades in a diverse environment

While most administrators will agree that there are benefits to operating in an environment where all systems are the same version and make, you might be installing and supporting multiple OS types in a diverse environment. In this section, you'll learn about installation considerations.

Boot methods

You can begin the installation or upgrade process by booting from a number of sources. In this section, you'll learn methods of getting the destination system booted up and moving the installation files to the devices.

Universal serial bus (USB)

Most systems will allow you to boot from a universal serial bus (USB) device, but you must often change the Basic Input/Output System (BIOS) settings to look for the USB first. Using a large USB drive, you can store all the necessary installation files on one device and save the time needed to swap media.

Network

It is also possible to boot a system over the network and then perform the installation over the network. This is a much more efficient way to do this, as you can boot up and subsequently install multiple systems at once. Let's look at two methods: PXE and NetBoot.

Preboot Execution Environment (PXE)

Booting the computer from the network without using a local device creates a Preboot Execution Environment (PXE). Once it is up, it is common to load the Windows Preinstallation Environment (WinPE) into random-access memory (RAM) as a stub operating system and install the OS image to the hard drive.

WinPE can be installed onto a bootable CD, USB, or network drive using the `copype.cmd` command. This environment can be used in conjunction with a Windows deployment from a server for unattended installations.

NetBoot

NetBoot is a method developed by Apple that allows an Apple device to boot from a network location rather than from the hard drive. The device uses Dynamic Host Configuration Protocol (DHCP) to receive a network configuration and to receive the IP address of a Trivial File Transport Protocol (TFTP) server, from which the device will download an OS image from a server. This entire process is similar to the way an Internet Protocol (IP) phone learns through DHCP the IP address of the server, from which it downloads its configuration file.

Solid-state/flash drives

If boot and installation files are located on a solid-state drive (SSD) or flash drive and the device is set to look on those drives for boot files, you can boot from these devices and install the OS in the same way that you boot from a CD or DVD drive.

Internet-based

It is also possible to download and install the OS from an Internet location, such as a vendor site where you purchase an OS. Moreover, a tool called Windows Installer accepts a uniform resource locator (URL) as a valid source for installation. Windows Installer can install packages, patches, and transforms from a URL location.

Purchasing and then downloading and installing to a single system at a time is inefficient and probably *not* the way you will be doing this. Instead, using a tool such as Windows Installer to provision multiple systems at a time is more likely. For more information on Windows Installer, see the `https://docs.microsoft.com/en-us/windows/win32/msi/windows-installer-portal`.

External/hot-swappable drive

Just as boot files can be located on a USB drive, CD, DVD, and flash drive, they can also be located on an external hard drive. Most of these drives are also hot-swappable (i.e. you can connect and remove them with the devices on). As always, you will probably have to alter the device's boot order so that it looks on the external drive before the other drives if boot files are also located in these locations.

Internal hard drive (partition)

Finally, the most common location of boot files is on the internal hard drive. These files are placed there during the installation and will be executed as long as the device is set to look for them there. By default, most systems are set to look on the internal hard drive first, and even if the device is not set to look there first, it will eventually boot to those files if there are no boot files located on any of the other drives or boot sources.

Multiboot

A multiboot system is one that has two or more OSes installed. These systems must be installed on separate hard drives or on separate volumes or partitions on the same hard drive. When two or more operating systems are installed, one of the OSes will be the default and will be the system to which the computer will boot without intervention.

However, by accessing the Boot menu while the system is booting up (i.e. pressing the F8 key before Windows starts), you can select the OS you want to use. If you have multiple OSes installed, this key sequence will present the boot menu when you start your computer.

Types of installations

There are several types of operating system installations. In this section we'll discuss how these various methods differ.

Clean install

A clean installation is one in which:

- The target drive is empty
- The operating system on the target drive is deleted and wiped.

Unattended/attended clean install

Clean OS installations can be lumped into two generic methods: attended or unattended. During an attended installation, you walk through the installation and answer the questions as prompted. Questions typically ask for the product key, the directory in which you want to install the OS, and relevant network settings.

Answering the questions posed by Windows Setup doesn't qualify as exciting work for most people. Fortunately, there is a way to answer the questions automatically: through an unattended installation. In this type of installation, an *answer file* is supplied with all the correct parameters (i.e. time zone, regional settings, administrator username, etc.), so no one needs to be there to tell the computer what to choose or to hit Next 500 times.

Unattended installations are great because they can be used to upgrade OSes identically on multiple computers. The first step is to create an answer file. This XML file, which must be named `unattend.xml`, contains configuration settings specific to the computer on which you are installing the OS, which means that for every installation, the answer file will be unique. See the following for details on these settings: https://docs.microsoft.com/en-us/windows-hardware/manufacture/desktop/update-windows-settings-and-scripts-create-your-own-answer-file-sxs.

Generally speaking, you'll want to run a test installation using that answer file first, before deploying it on a large scale, because you'll probably need to make some tweaks to it. After you create your answer file, place it on a network share that will be accessible from the target computer. (Most people put it in the same place as the Windows installation files for convenience.)

Boot the computer that you want to install on using a boot disk or CD and establish the network connection. Once you start the setup process, everything should run automatically.

Table 6.2 shows you four common unattended installation methods and when they can be used.

Another decision you must make is which method you are going to use to access the Windows installation files. It is possible to boot to the installation DVD and begin the installation process. However, your system must have a system BIOS that is capable of supporting bootable media.

TABLE 6.2 Windows unattended installation methods

Method	Clean installation	Upgrade
Unattended install	Yes	Yes
Bootable media	Yes	No
Sysprep	Yes	No
Remote install	Yes	No

If you don't have a bootable DVD, you must first boot the computer using some other bootable media, which then loads the disk driver so that you can access the installation program on the DVD. Boot methods were covered earlier in this chapter.

Upgrade

An upgrade involves moving from one OS to another and retaining as many of the settings as possible. An example of an upgrade would be changing the OS on a laptop computer from Windows 10 to Windows 11 and keeping the user accounts that existed.

It is also possible to upgrade from one OS edition to another—for example, from Windows 10 Professional to Windows 10 Enterprise.

To begin the upgrade, execute the installation program after you download it, and the Setup program should automatically begin. (If it doesn't, run `setup.exe` from the root folder.) From the menu that appears, choose Install Now and then select Upgrade when the Which Type of Installation Do You Want? screen appears. Answer the prompts to walk through the upgrade.

Booting from the DVD is also possible but recommended only if the method just described does not work. When you boot, you will get a message upon startup that says Press Any Key to Boot from CD, and at that point you simply press a key. (Don't worry that it is a DVD and not a CD.)

Image deployment

Systems can also be deployed as images. In this section, you'll learn about creating an image and installing it.

Creating an image

Creating an image isn't an objective, but it is something important that you'll need to know how to do in the real world. Creating an image involves taking a snapshot of a model system (often called a *reference computer*) and then applying it to other systems (see the upcoming section "Image deployment"). A number of third-party vendors offer packages that can be used to create images, and you can use the system preparation tool, or *Sysprep*. The Sysprep utility works by making an exact image (or replica) of the reference computer (sometimes also called the *master computer*) to be installed on other computers. Sysprep removes the master computer's security ID (a process sometimes called *generalization*), and will generate new IDs for each computer where the image is used to install.

> **NOTE** Sysprep only creates the system image. You still need a cloning utility to copy the image to other computers.

Perhaps the biggest caveat to using Sysprep is that because you are making an exact image of an installed computer (including drivers and settings), all the computers on which you will be installing the image need to be identical (or close) to the configuration of the master computer.

Otherwise, you would have to go through and fix driver problems on every computer installed. Sysprep images can be installed across a network or copied to a CD or DVD for local installation. Sysprep cannot be used to upgrade a system; plan on all data on the system (if there is any) being lost after a format.

Several third-party vendors provide similar services, and you'll often hear the process referred to as *disk imaging* or *drive imaging*. The third-party utility makes the image, and then the image file is transferred to the computer that does not have an OS. You boot the new system with the imaging software and start the image download. The new system's disk drive is made into an exact sector-by-sector copy of the original system.

Imaging has major upsides. The biggest one is speed. In larger networks with multiple new computers, you can configure tens to hundreds of computers by using imaging in just hours, rather than the days it would take to individually install the OS, applications, and drivers.

Image deployment

System images created with Sysprep and other tools can be deployed for installation on hosts across the network. The Windows Automated Installation Kit (AIK) can be useful for this purpose.

Remote network installation

Older Windows Server OSes had a feature called Remote Installation Services (RIS), which allowed you to perform several network installations at one time. Beginning with Windows Server 2003 SP2, RIS was replaced by Windows Deployment Services (WDS). This utility offers the same functionality as RIS.

A *network installation* is handy when you have many installs to do and installing manually is too much work. In a network installation, the installation program is copied to a shared network location. Then individual workstations boot and access the network share. The workstations can boot either through a boot disk or through a built-in network boot device known as a Preboot Execution Environment Read-Only Memory (PXE ROM). Boot ROMs essentially download a small file that contains an OS and network drivers and has enough information to boot the computer in a limited fashion. At the very least, it can boot the computer so it can access the network share and begin the installation.

Zero-touch deployment

Zero-touch deployment is a Microsoft process for quickly deploying systems across the Enterprise automatically. It works in conjunction with another Microsoft component, Autopilot, and with processes embedded in Windows 10 and Windows 11.

With Autopilot, systems can be unboxed and deployed automatically. The process is illustrated in Figure 6.1. The administrator configures the profile for the system(s) in Intune. Microsoft Intune (formerly Windows Intune) is a Microsoft cloud-based unified endpoint management service for both corporate and bring your own device (BYOD) devices. The hardware vendor supplies the device ID(s) to Windows Autopilot, and when the employee

1.2 Given a scenario, perform OS installations and upgrades in a diverse environment

FIGURE 6.1 Zero-touch deployment

Windows Autopilot overview

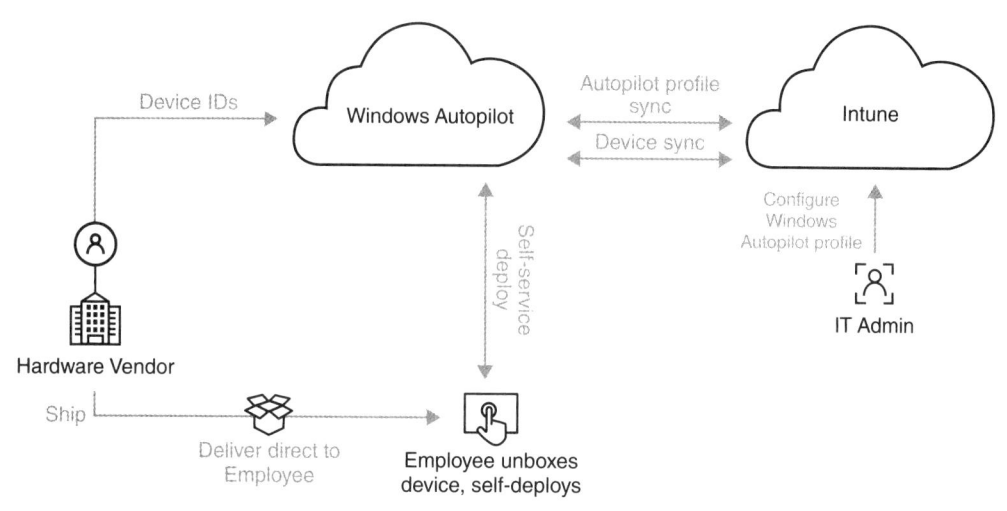

unboxes and starts the device, it is identified by its device ID by Autopilot and, using the profile provided by Intune, self-deploys itself. Note that both Intune and Autopilot are cloud-based tools.

Recovery partition

In the past, many devices that were purchased with the OS installed by the original equipment manufacturer (OEM) came with recovery media, which could be used to boot the device and recover (or replace) the OS if needed. Now, many come with an additional partition on the drive called a *recovery partition*. The users could use a specific key sequence during bootup that would cause the device to boot to the recovery partition and make available tools to either recover the installation or replace it. The downside of this approach is that if the hard drive fails or if the partition is overwritten, the recovery partition is useless. In an effort to address this concern, many OEMs now make available recovery media if requested by the user.

Repair installation

A repair installation overwrites system files with a copy of new ones from the same OS version and edition. For example, a laptop running Windows 10 is hanging on boot, and the cause is traced to a corrupted system file. A repair installation can replace that corrupted file with a new one (from the DVD or other source), without changing the OS or settings (i.e. for configuration, accounts, etc.).

Other considerations

There are some other scenarios that you might encounter during installation that require your consideration. In this section, you'll learn about other installation considerations.

Third-party drivers

During the installation, it might be necessary to load a third-party driver that you update later. The goal during installation is to get the OS up and running and in a state where you can interact with it. To add a mass storage driver (which is what you need to access the drive), you hit the F7 key when you are prompted during the installation.

In addition, you will be presented with the option to download any required updates and new driver packages that may have become available since the time the installation DVD was created. If the device will have an active Internet connection, you might want to take advantage of this because it will download the required files and make them part of the installation. If this is not an option, you can always perform this step by visiting Windows Update after the installation.

Partitioning

For a hard disk to be able to hold files and programs, it has to be partitioned and formatted. *Partitioning* is the process of creating logical divisions on a hard drive. A hard drive can have one or more partitions. You can think of them as rooms within a house. *Formatting* is the process of creating and configuring a file allocation table and creating the root directory. Several file system types are supported by the various versions of Windows, such as FAT32 and NTFS. (Partitions are explored later, in the discussion of disk management.)

The partition that the OS boots from must be designated as *active*. Only one partition on a disk may be marked active. Each hard disk can be divided into a total of four partitions, either four primary partitions or three primary and one extended partition.

Dynamic

Partitions can be made dynamic, which—as the name implies—means they can be configured and reconfigured on the fly. The big benefits they offer are that they can increase in size (without reformatting) and can span multiple physical disks. Dynamic partitions can be simple, spanned, or striped.

Dynamic partitions that are simple are similar to primary partitions and logical drives (which exist on basic partitions, discussed next). This is often the route you choose when you have only one dynamic disk and want the ability to change allocated space as needed.

Choosing spanned partitions means that you want space from a number of disks (up to 32) to appear as a single logical volume to users. A minimum of two disks must be used, and no fault tolerance is provided by this option.

Striped partitions are similar to spanned in that multiple disks are used, but the big difference is that data is written (in fixed-size stripes) across the disk set to increase I/O performance. Although read operations are faster, a concern is that if one disk fails, none of the data is retrievable. (Like spanned, the striped option provides no fault tolerance.)

Basic

With basic storage, Windows drives can be partitioned with *primary* or *logical* partitions. Basic partitions are a fixed size and are always on a single physical disk. This is the simplest storage solution and has been the traditional method of storing data for many years.

You can change the size of primary and logical drives by *extending* them into additional space on the same disk. You can create up to four partitions on a basic disk, either four primary or three primary and one extended.

Primary

A primary partition contains the boot files for an OS. In the past, the OS had to also be on that partition, but with the Windows versions you need to know for this exam that the OS files can be located elsewhere as long as the boot files are in that primary partition.

Primary partitions cannot be further subdivided.

Extended

Extended partitions differ from primary partitions in that they can be divided into one or more logical drives, each of which can be assigned a drive letter.

Logical

In reality, all partitions are logical in the sense that they don't necessarily correspond to one physical disk. One disk can have several logical divisions (i.e. partitions). A logical partition is any partition that has a drive letter.

> **Note:** Sometimes, you will also hear of a logical partition as one that spans multiple physical disks. For example, a network drive that you know as Drive H might actually be located on several physical disks on a server. To the user, these are seen as one drive, or H.

GUID (globally unique identifier) Partition Table (GPT)

Devices that use the Unified Extensible Firmware Interface (UEFI) specification instead of a BIOS also use a partitioning standard called a GUID Partition Table (GPT). Since 2010, most OSes support this and using a master boot record (MBR), which is the alternative method of booting to a legacy BIOS firmware interface. Today, almost all OSes support it, and many *only* support booting from a GPT rather than from an MBR. You will learn more about BIOS and UEFI password security in Chapter 7.

Moreover, a GPT is also used on some BIOS systems because of the limitations of MBR partition tables, which was the original driver for the development of UEFI and GPT. MBR works with disks up to 2 TB in size, but it can't handle larger disks. MBR also supports only up to four primary partitions, so to have more than four, you had to set one of your primary partitions as an "extended partition" and create logical partitions inside it. GPT removes both of these limitations. It allows up to 128 partitions on a GPT drive.

Master boot record

Master boot record was discussed in the previous section. Please review the previous section.

Drive format

File systems available when formatting were covered earlier in this chapter in "Various file system types." Please review that section for more information about the systems available. Formatting options were also covered earlier in this chapter, under "Partitioning." Please review that section for more information on the various partition types.

Upgrade considerations

When upgrading a system from one edition to another or from one version to another, you must think about certain upgrade considerations before you jump in. You'll learn about upgrade considerations in this section.

Backup files and user preferences

In Chapter 5, "Hardware and Network Troubleshooting," you learned the importance of backing up files prior to making changes to a system with an issue. This is also advisable prior to performing an upgrade, just in case something goes wrong.

When doing so, you want to back up not only all of the machine's user files but also the user's preferences. Doing so will save the user aggravation from having to create all the settings again. You will learn much more about the types of backups in Chapter 9, "Operational Procedures."

Application and driver support/backward compatibility

This area is another where some prior research can be invaluable. Applications are made to work on specific OSes. While you'll have fewer problems with an upgrade, a new installation, especially when going from one vendor to another (e.g. Windows to Apple) might result in application incompatibility. The upgrade advisors mentioned earlier can also assess your application's compatibility.

OS compatibility/upgrade path

Keep in mind that some upgrades are not possible and will require new installations. Later in this chapter, in the section "Compare and contrast basic features of Microsoft Windows editions," you will learn more about allowable upgrade paths.

Hardware compatibility

Prior to installing or upgrading an OS, it is advisable to ensure that the system supports all the hardware prerequisites (provided earlier in this chapter). It also is a good idea to check whether any additional hardware is compatible with the system. The upgrade advisors provided with many upgrade programs can assist with this as well. If you don't check ahead of time, the installation or upgrade may fail when you attempt it.

Feature updates

Features are Windows tools and utilities that are provided to make certain operations easier. Often when updating a system, features may updated, which may result in users being trained on the new feature. When Windows updates occur, you can choose *not* to download feature updates. These will be listed as optional updates.

Product life cycle

All products have a life-cycle policy. An example is the Microsoft Fixed Lifecycle Policy. This is only policy and does not apply to all products. The policy describes when the product is end of life (EOL) and when it is end of support (EOS). EOS means no more help with troubleshooting, and EOL means no more security updates.

Exam essentials

Identify methods of installation and deployment. These methods include local (CD/USB), network-based, flash drives, over the Internet, and internal hard drive.

Identify operating system log-in options. These include username and password, personal identification number (PIN), biometrics, SSO, and passwordless/Windows Hello.

1.3 Compare and contrast basic features of Microsoft Windows editions

This section contains numerous tables because of the nature of the information it covers. It is imperative that you be familiar with Windows 10 and Windows 11. Make certain you understand the features available in each of the editions of Windows 10 and 11 that are available.

Windows 10 editions

As with most previous versions of Windows, Windows 10 is available in multiple editions. These editions vary in the features that are available, because they are designed for different scenarios. In this section, you'll learn about these various editions.

Home

Windows 10 Home edition is designed for use in a noncorporate setting and thus lacks many features that you might need in an enterprise setting. For example, it does not offer BitLocker as some other editions do. Following the coverage of the general use of each edition, Table 6.3 will compare the editions on the basis of Windows features, all of which will be discussed later in this chapter.

Pro

Windows 10 Pro offers many features required to use the system in a domain-based corporate environment, while lacking some of the advanced security features that one might require in a higher-security environment. These features will be found in the Enterprise edition (covered later in this section).

Pro for Workstations

Some applications require significantly more power as compared to typical office applications. When editing videos or using computer-aided design tools or performing extremely difficult mathematics, more power is needed. Windows 10 Pro for Workstations is designed to operate in these types of environments.

Enterprise

As was mentioned earlier, when an organization wants all features required for a domain-based enterprise and they require high security functions, Windows Enterprise is the edition of choice. With the exception of workstations that run resource-hungry applications (in which Windows 10 Pro for Workstations is indicated), this system is appropriate for all Enterprise workstations.

Windows 11 editions

Microsoft described Windows 11 as an "operating system as a service" that would receive ongoing updates to its features and functionality. It was released in October 2021. There are three versions: Home, Pro, and Enterprise. In this section, we will discuss only the differences between Windows 10 and Windows 11 features.

Home

Windows 11 Home edition, like the Windows 10 version, is designed for use in a noncorporate setting and thus also lacks many of the features that you might need in an enterprise setting. Following the coverage of the general use of each edition, Table 6.4 will compare the editions on the basis of Windows features, all of which will be discussed later in this chapter.

Pro

Windows 11 Pro, like Windows 10 Pro, offers many of the features required to use the system in a domain-based corporate environment, while lacking some of the advanced security features that one might require in a higher-security environment. These features will be found in the Enterprise edition.

Enterprise

When an organization wants all features required for a domain-based enterprise and they require high security functions, Windows 11 Enterprise is the edition of choice. Table 6.4 compares feature support in the editions of Windows 11.

N versions

Versions of Windows carrying the "N" designation lack Windows Media Player. (N stands for No Media Player.) Saying Microsoft had a monopoly on the media market, the European Union fined Microsoft €500 million in 2004 and ordered it to create a version of Windows that did not include built-in multimedia features. Consequently, Microsoft created this version.

Feature differences

The features found in Tables 6.3 and 6.4 are examined in this section. It is important not only that you understand these features and their purpose, but also that you know which editions offer which features. As an IT professional, you may be involved in the selection of the proper edition for the scenario.

TABLE 6.3 Features across Windows 10 editions

	Domain access	Desktop styles/user interface	RDP	RAM min	BitLocker	gpedit.msc
Home	No	No	No	64-bit: 2 GB 32-bit: 1 GB	No	No
Pro	Yes	No	Yes	64-bit: 2 GB 32-bit: 1 GB	Yes	Yes
Pro for Workstations	Yes	No	Yes	64-bit: 2 GB 32-bit: 1 GB	No	Yes
Enterprise	Yes	Yes	Yes	64-bit: 2 GB 32-bit: 1 GB	Yes	Yes

TABLE 6.4 Features across Windows 11 editions

	Domain access	User Experience Virtualization (UE-V).	Windows Virtual Desktop (WVD) user rights	RDP	RAM min	BitLocker	gpedit.msc
Home	No	No	No	No	64-bit: 4 GB	No	No
Pro	Yes	No	Yes	Yes	64-bit: 4 GB	Yes	Yes
Enterprise	Yes	Yes	Yes	Yes	64-bit: 4 GB	Yes	Yes

Domain vs. workgroup

A workgroup is a collection of systems that each maintain their own security system. Workgroups primarily use peer-to-peer networking. Local security means that to log into a system in a workgroup, you need an account created on that machine as a local account. Therefore, each system is its own "castle" and in charge of its own security.

In a domain, the systems are all related in that domain-based accounts are used to log into these systems (although local accounts can still be created). These domain accounts are not tethered to the individual systems, meaning that a user with a domain account can log into any system that is a member of the domain. Later in this chapter, you'll learn how to join a computer to a domain.

Microsoft provides the Join a Domain option on three versions of Windows 10 and two of Windows 11. See Tables 6.3 and 6.4.

Desktop styles/user interface

Windows once offered a feature in some editions called Windows Virtual Desktop User Rights. It was meant to be used when providing virtual desktops (you learned about these in Chapter 4) from a cloud platform such as Windows Azure. Microsoft retired this feature in 2021. However, Azure Virtual Desktop, the successor to Windows Virtual Desktop, offers robust access management through Azure role-based access control (RBAC) and licensing options tailored for various use cases.

A related feature is User Experience Virtualization (UE-V) for Windows 10, which captures user-customized Windows and application settings and stores them on a centrally managed network file share. This is again tied to the use of virtual desktops and is available only in certain editions.

Availability of Remote Desktop Protocol (RDP)

In Chapter 2, you learned about the Remote Desktop Protocol (RDP). It allows members of the Administrators group to gain access to the workstation. (You can specifically allow other users as well.) While any edition of Windows 10 can act as Remote Desktop Client, to host a remote session you need to be running Windows 10 Pro or Enterprise. For Windows 11, you need Pro or Enterprise.

Random-access memory (RAM) support limitations

Each edition of Windows 10 and Windows 11 places a minimum requirement on the memory required to run the OS. This is valuable to know when selecting an OS for a device. Please refer to Tables 6.3 and 6.4 for details. Windows 11 requires at least 4 GB of memory.

BitLocker

In Chapter 3, in the section "Encryption," you learned about the concept of drive encryption and Trusted Platform Module (TPM) chips. The Windows feature that makes use of TPM chips and provides whole drive encryption is BitLocker. BitLocker is the whole drive encryption tool that can also seal a device such that it will not boot if any system files are altered. It can also lock the drive to a particular machine, preventing anyone from stealing the drive and connecting it to another device. You will learn more about implementing BitLocker later in this chapter and in Chapter 7. See Tables 6.3 and 6.4 for availability in the various editions.

gpedit.msc

Group policies can be used in certain editions to exert control over both security and desktop settings. This configuration is done with a tool called the Group Policy Editor. This tool can be added to an interface called the Microsoft Management Console (MMC). The underlying program you are invoking when you open this tool is called gpedit.msc and is available only in certain editions. You will learn more about the Group Policy Editor later in this chapter and again in Chapter 7, in the section "Applying group policy." For availability across editions, see Tables 6.3 and 6.4.

Upgrade paths

When installing or upgrading an OS, it is important to know what is possible and what is not. Not all systems can be directly upgraded to the newest version. Some must be completely reinstalled. There are several things to be aware of regarding upgrade paths, including the differences between in-place upgrades, the available compatibility tools, and the Windows Upgrade Assistant. In this section, we'll look at some possible upgrade paths and other installation considerations.

In-place upgrade

One Windows OS can often be upgraded to another, if compatible. When you are faced with a scenario in which you cannot upgrade, you can always do a clean installation (covered later, in the section "Clean install"). There's one more thing to consider when evaluating installation methods. Some methods work only if you're performing a clean installation and not an upgrade. Table 6.5 lists the minimum system requirements for Windows 10. If your

TABLE 6.5 Minimum system requirements for Windows 10

Hardware	Minimum requirements supported for all editions of Windows 10
Processor	1 GHz with support for Physical Address Extension (PAE), No eXecute (NX), and Security Service Edge (SSE)
Memory	1 GB for 32-bit, 2 GB for 64-bit
Free hard disk space	16 GB free for 32-bit, 20 GB free for 64-bit
CD-ROM or DVD	DVD-ROM
Video	DirectX 9 with Windows Display Driver Model (WDDM) 1.0 (or higher) driver

existing Windows 10 PC is running the current version of Windows 10 and meets the minimum hardware specifications to run Windows 11, it will be able to upgrade.

If there is one thing to be learned from Table 6.5, it is that Microsoft is nothing if not optimistic. For your own sanity, though, I strongly suggest you always take the minimum requirements with a grain of salt. They are the minimums needed to get the OS to run and will not provide good performance. Even the recommended requirements should be considered minimums. Bottom line: Ensure you have a good margin between your system's performance and the minimum requirements listed. Always run Windows on more hardware, rather than less!

Upgrading to Windows 10

With Windows 10, the in-place upgrade is now a first-class deployment option and the preferred approach for Windows 10 deployment—even in enterprises. It allows Windows 10 installations to be initiated from within an existing Windows OS. Upgrading to Windows 11 from Windows 10 is also allowed, as long as the system supports the new hardware requirements.

Windows 11 Installation Assistant

The Windows 11 Installation Assistant can be useful in any upgrade process. It will check your system, verify that it can run the desired OS, and give you a report of any identified compatibility issues.

Clean install

A clean installation is one in which you delete everything that might be present on the hard drive and start with a clean (i.e. empty) drive. A clean installation can be either attended or unattended. With an attended installation, a human will need to be present to answer the questions presented during the setup.

With a clean installation, you delete the volume where the old OS existed and place a new one there. An example of a clean installation would be changing the OS on a laptop from Windows 10 to Windows 11. The user accounts and other settings that existed with Windows 10 would be removed in the process and need to be recreated under Windows 11.

As simple as attended installations may be, they're time-consuming and administrator-intensive in that they require someone to fill in a fair number of fields to move through the process.

Hardware requirements

The hardware requirements of Windows 10 and Windows 11 were covered in Tables 6.3 and 6.4. Please review that section. Two other hardware considerations are covered in the rest of this section.

Trusted Platform Module (TPM)

As you learned in Chapter 3, when the device has a TPM chip present on the motherboard, additional security and options become available. The chip contains keys that can lock and unlock the drives. When the computer boots, if any changes have been made or tampering has been done to the Windows installation, the TPM chip will not unlock the drives. TPM support varies by Windows edition, as shown in Table 6.3 and 6.4.

Unified Extensible Firmware Interface (UEFI)

As you learned in Chapter 3, UEFI is a standard firmware interface for PCs, designed to replace BIOS. UEFI support varies by Windows edition, as shown in Tables 6.3 and 6.4.

Exam essentials

Describe the method used to install a new Windows edition.   These include performing a clean install, removing the old system, and doing an in-place update that preserves accounts and settings.

Identify the hardware requirements for Windows 11 Enterprise.   The requirements are:

Hardware	Minimum requirements supported for all editions of Windows 10
Processor	1 GHz with support for Physical Address Extension (PAE), No eXecute (NX), and Security Service Edge (SSE)
Memory	1 GB for 32-bit, 2 GB for 64-bit
Free hard disk space	16 GB free for 32-bit, 20 GB free for 64-bit

(Continued)

(Continued)

Hardware	Minimum requirements supported for all editions of Windows 10
CD-ROM or DVD	DVD-ROM
Video	DirectX 9 with Windows Display Driver Model (WDDM) 1.0 (or higher) driver

1.4 Given a scenario, use Microsoft Windows operating system features and tools

This objective requires you to know how to work at the command line and run common command-line utilities available with the Windows-based OSes as well as use administrative tools. Some material here overlaps with other objectives, but you'll want to make certain you know each utility discussed.

Although most of the information presented about Windows utilities and administration should seem second nature to you (on-the-job experience is expected for A+ certification), you should read these sections thoroughly to make certain you can answer any questions that may appear around them.

Task Manager

This tool lets you shut down nonresponsive applications selectively in all Windows versions. In current Windows versions, it can do much more. Task Manager allows you to see which processes and applications are using the most system resources, view network usage, see connected users, and so on. To display Task Manager, press Ctrl+Alt+Del and click the Task Manager button. You can also right-click an empty spot in the taskbar and choose Task Manager from the pop-up menu that appears.

> To get to the Task Manager directly in any Windows version, press Ctrl+Shift+Esc.

In Windows 10 and 11, Task Manager has seven tabs: App History, Processes, Performance, Details, Startup, Services, and Users. The Users tab is displayed only if the computer you are working on is a member of a workgroup or is a stand-alone computer. The Users tab is unavailable on computers that are members of a network domain. Let's look at the tabs as shown in Figure 6.2.

FIGURE 6.2 Task Manager

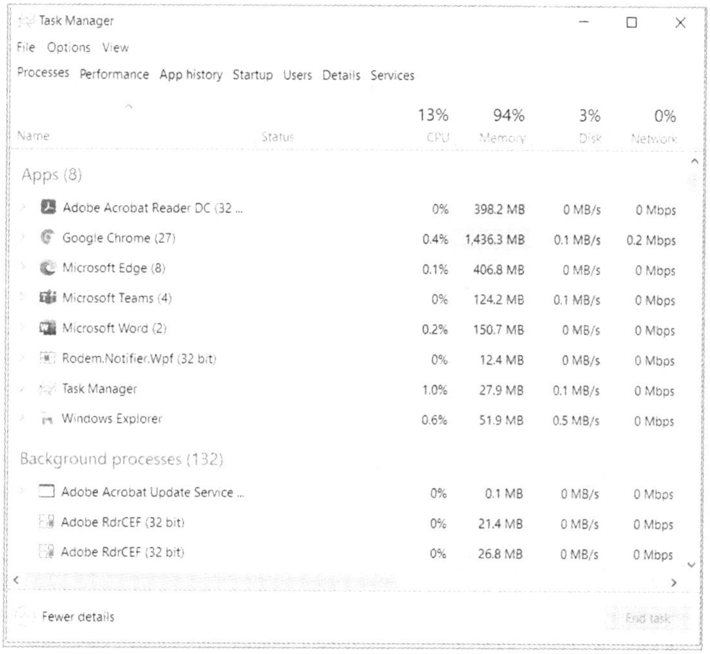

Services

The Services tab (shown in Figure 6.3) lists the name of each running service, as well as the process ID associated with it, its description, its status, and its group. A button labeled Open Services appears on this tab, and clicking it will open the MMC console for Services where you can configure each service. Within Task Manager, right-clicking a service will open a context menu listing three choices: Start Service, Stop Service, and Go to Process (which takes you to the Processes tab).

Startup

The Startup tab displays programs that will start automatically when the computer is booted up. It is also will indicate the impact on performance if that function is enabled. As you can see in Figure 6.4, this function is not enabled and thus is not measuring impact.

Performance

The Performance tab (shown in Figure 6.5) contains a variety of information, including overall central processing unit (CPU) usage percentage, a graphical display of the CPU's usage history, page-file usage in megabytes, and a graphical display of page-file usage. Figure 6.6 shows the Performance tab of Windows 11.

278 Chapter 6 ▪ Operating Systems

FIGURE 6.3 The Services tab

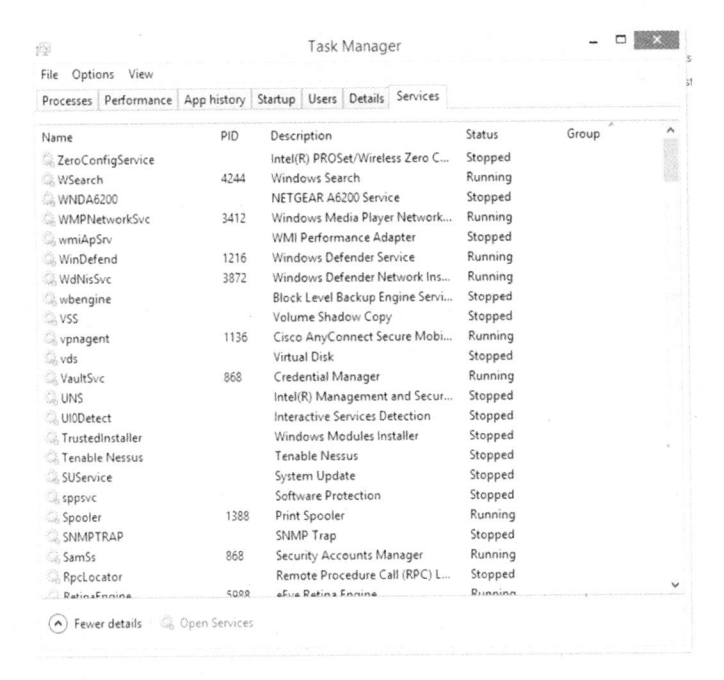

FIGURE 6.4 The Startup tab

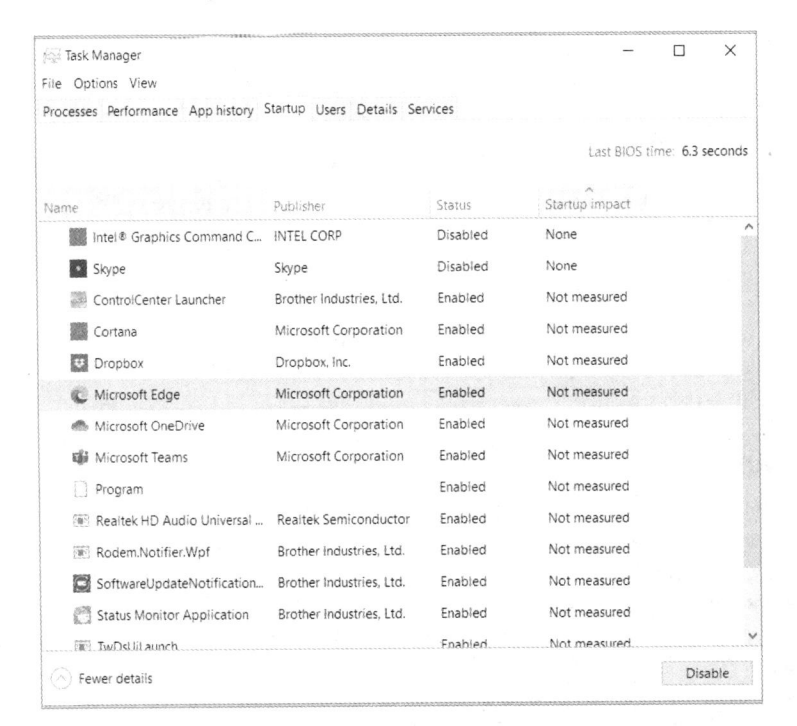

1.4 Given a scenario, use Microsoft Windows OS features and tools

FIGURE 6.5   The Performance tab of Windows 10

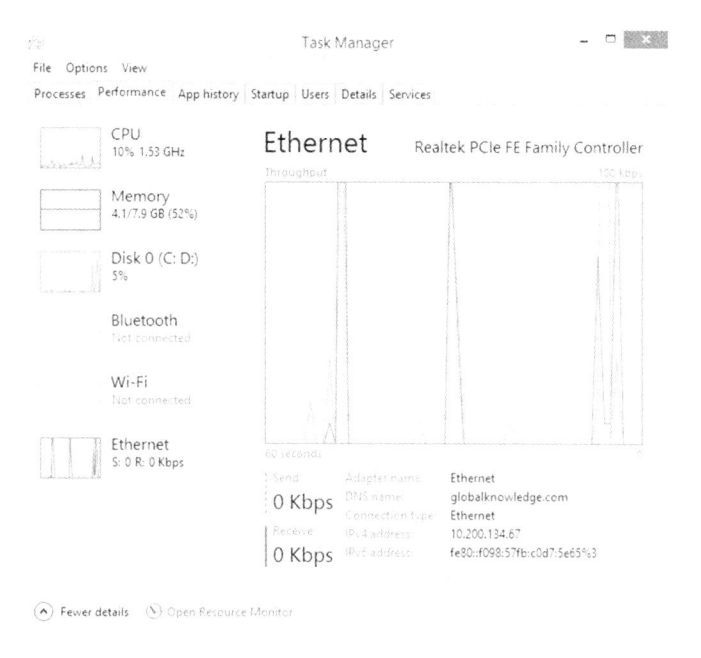

FIGURE 6.6   The Performance tab of Windows 11

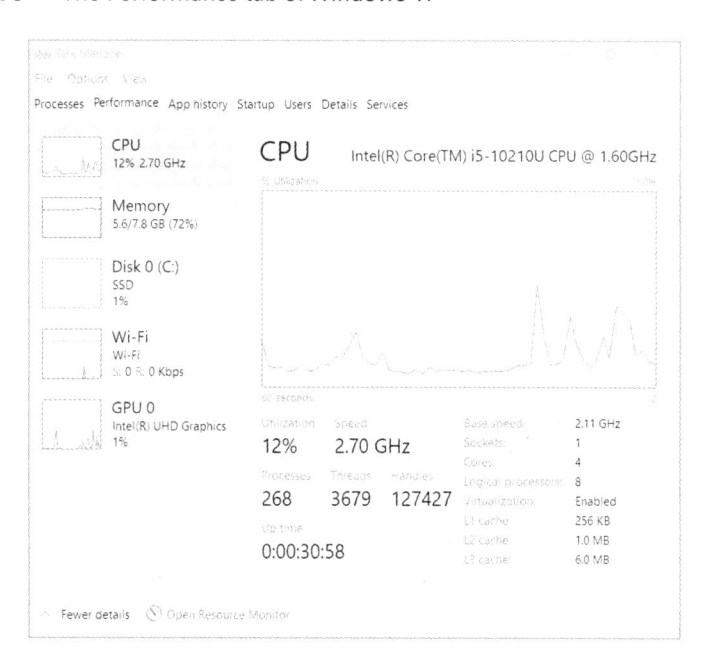

280 Chapter 6 ▪ Operating Systems

This tab also provides you with additional memory-related information, such as physical and kernel memory usage as well as the total number of handles, threads, and processes. Total, limit, and peak commit-charge information also displays. Some of these items are beyond the scope of this book, but it's good to know that you can use the Performance tab to keep track of system performance. Note that the number of processes, CPU usage percentage, and commit charge always displays at the bottom of the Task Manager window, regardless of which tab you have currently selected.

Processes

The Processes tab (shown in Figure 6.7) lets you see the names of all the processes running on the machine. You also see the user account that's running the process as well as how much CPU and RAM resources each process is using. To end a process, select it in the list and then click End Task. Be careful with this choice, because ending some processes can cause Windows to shut down. If you don't know what a particular process does, you can look for it in any search engine and find several sites that will explain it.

FIGURE 6.7 The Processes tab

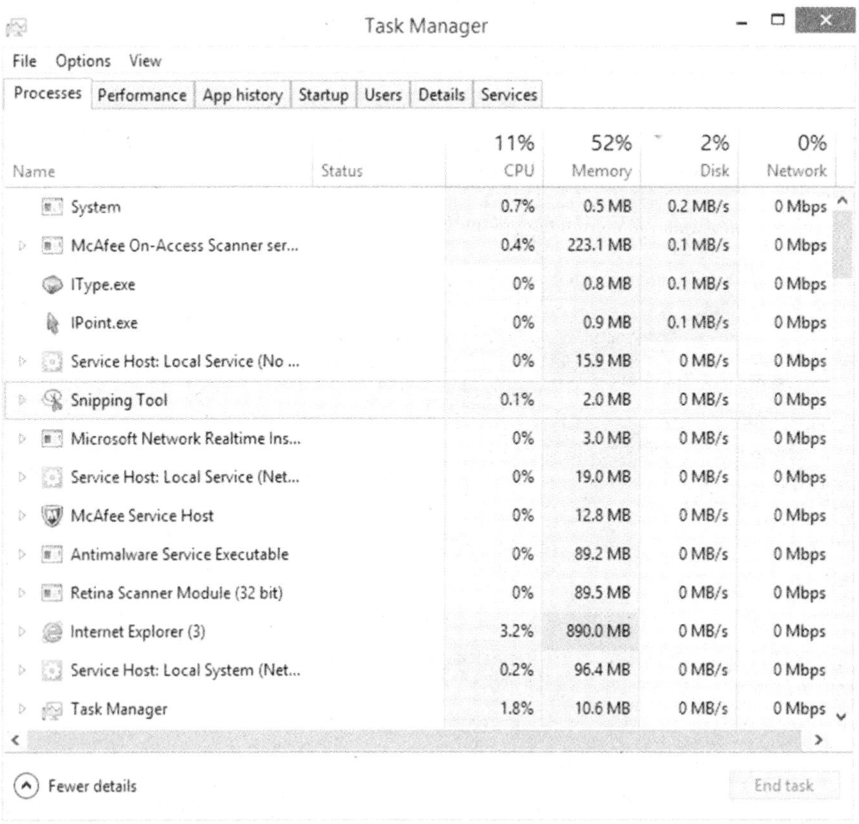

Name	Status	11% CPU	52% Memory	2% Disk	0% Network
System		0.7%	0.5 MB	0.2 MB/s	0 Mbps
McAfee On-Access Scanner ser...		0.4%	223.1 MB	0.1 MB/s	0 Mbps
IType.exe		0%	0.8 MB	0.1 MB/s	0 Mbps
IPoint.exe		0%	0.9 MB	0.1 MB/s	0 Mbps
Service Host: Local Service (No ...		0%	15.9 MB	0 MB/s	0 Mbps
Snipping Tool		0.1%	2.0 MB	0 MB/s	0 Mbps
Microsoft Network Realtime Ins...		0%	3.0 MB	0 MB/s	0 Mbps
Service Host: Local Service (Net...		0%	19.0 MB	0 MB/s	0 Mbps
McAfee Service Host		0%	12.8 MB	0 MB/s	0 Mbps
Antimalware Service Executable		0%	89.2 MB	0 MB/s	0 Mbps
Retina Scanner Module (32 bit)		0%	89.5 MB	0 MB/s	0 Mbps
Internet Explorer (3)		3.2%	890.0 MB	0 MB/s	0 Mbps
Service Host: Local System (Net...		0.2%	96.4 MB	0 MB/s	0 Mbps
Task Manager		1.8%	10.6 MB	0 MB/s	0 Mbps

You can also change the priority of a process on the Details tab. The six priorities, from lowest to highest, are as follows:

Low For applications that need to complete at some point but that you don't want interfering with other applications. On a numerical scale from 0 to 31, this equates to a base priority of 4.

Below Normal For applications that don't need to drop all the way down to Low. This equates to a base priority of 6.

Normal The default priority for most applications. This equates to a base priority of 8.

Above Normal For applications that don't need to boost all the way to High. This equates to a base priority of 10.

High For applications that must complete soon, when you don't want other applications to interfere with the application's performance. This equates to a base priority of 13.

Realtime For applications that must have the processor's attention to handle time-critical tasks. Applications can be run at this priority only by a member of the Administrators group. This equates to a base priority of 24.

If you decide to change the priority of an application, you'll be warned that changing the priority of an application might make it unstable. You can generally ignore this warning when changing the priority to Low, Below Normal, Above Normal, or High, but you should heed it when changing applications to the Realtime priority. Realtime means that the processor gives precedence to this process over all others—over security processes, over spooling, over everything—and is sure to make the system unstable.

Task Manager changes the priority only for that instance of the running application. The next time the process is started, priorities revert to that of the base (typically Normal).

Users

The Users tab (shown in Figure 6.8) provides you with information about the users connected to the local machine. You'll see the username, ID, status, client name, and session type. You can right-click any connected user to perform a variety of functions, including disconnecting the user.

Use Task Manager whenever the system seems bogged down by an unresponsive application. By ending processes and services that are hung up, performance can be restored.

Details

The Details tab provides deeper information about the processes running on your system. Some examples include process name, PID (process ID, a unique identifier for each process), status (running, suspended, etc.), CPU, memory, disk, network usage, and the user account running the process.

FIGURE 6.8 The Users tab

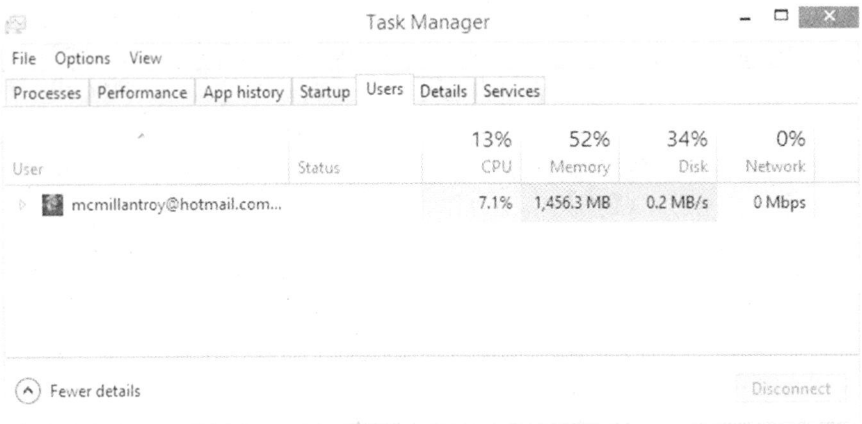

App History

The App History tab provides a summary of resource usage for apps over time. Information provided includes the name of the app, the amount of processor time used, the total network data consumed, and the data usage on metered networks.

Microsoft Management Console (MMC) snap-in

Microsoft Management Consoles (MMC) are preconfigured dashboards for various functions that can be combined into a single console or invoked in a dedicated console. An MMC with no tools added is shown in Figure 6.9. As you see, you can add a tool (called a snap-in) using the menu.

In this section, you'll learn about key utilities and tools you can add to an MMC.

Event Viewer (eventvwr.msc)

Windows employs comprehensive error and informational logging routines. Every program and process theoretically could have its own logging utility, but Microsoft has come up with a rather slick utility, Event Viewer, which tracks all events on a particular Windows computer through log files. Normally, though, you must be an administrator or a member of the Administrators group to have access to Event Viewer.

The process for starting Event Viewer differs based on the OS you are running, but always log in as an administrator (or equivalent). Choose Start Programs > Administrative Tools > Event Viewer (or you can right-click the computer desktop icon and choose Manage Event Viewer). In the resulting window (shown in Figure 6.10), you can view the System,

1.4 Given a scenario, use Microsoft Windows OS features and tools

FIGURE 6.9 The Microsoft Management Console

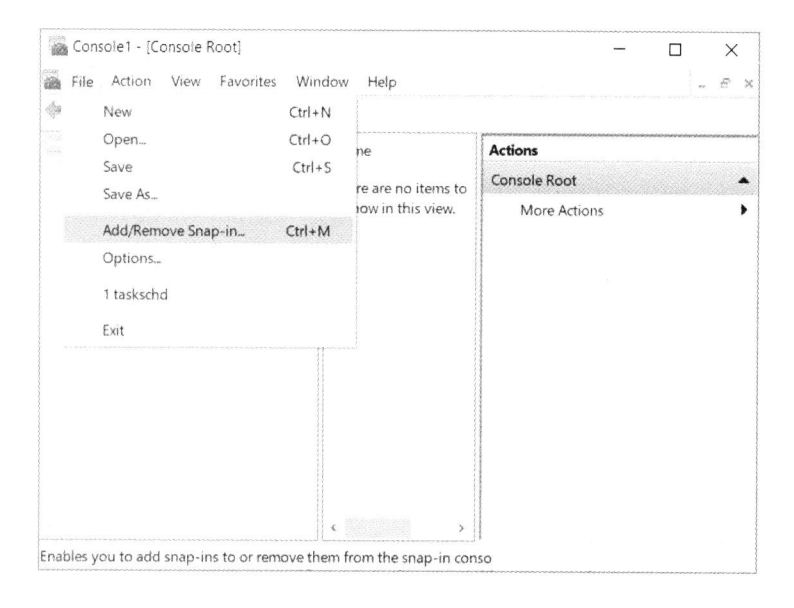

FIGURE 6.10 The opening interface of Event Viewer

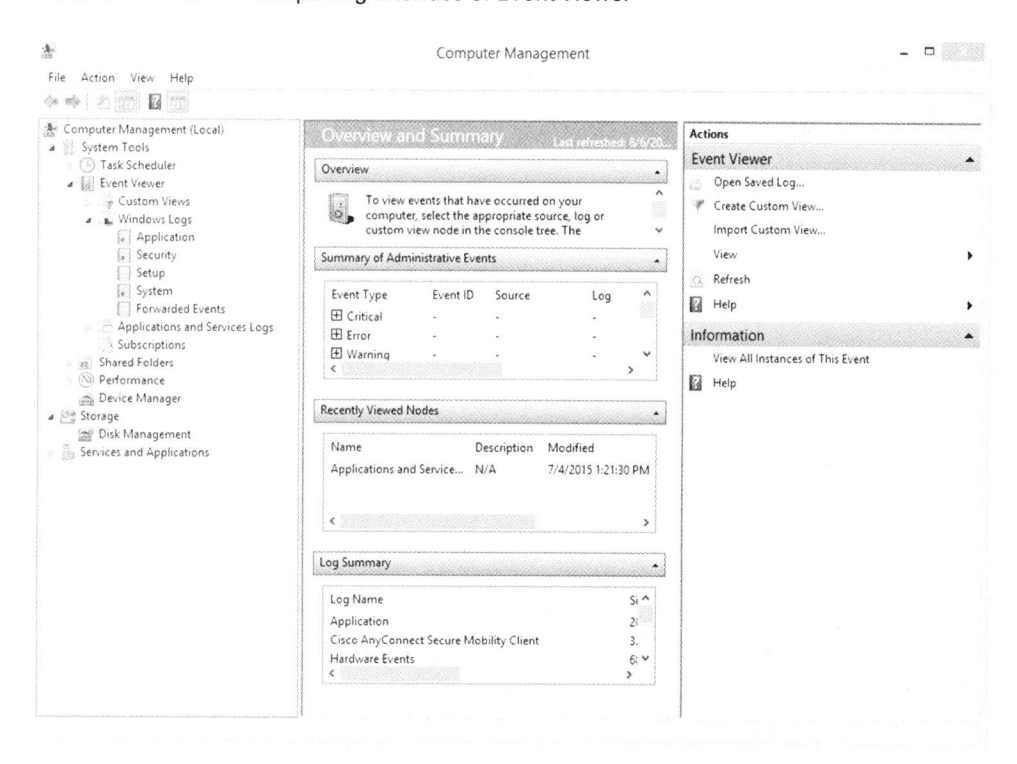

Application, Security, Setup, and Forwarded Events log files. The System log file displays alerts that pertain to the general operation of Windows.

- The Application log file logs application errors.
- The Security log file logs security events, such as login successes and failures.
- The Setup log will appear on domain controllers and will contain events specific to them.
- The Forwarded Events log contains events that have been forwarded to this log by other computers.
- The System Log records all OS events.

These log files can give a general indication of a Windows computer's health.

One situation that does occur with Event Viewer is that the log files get full. Although this isn't really a problem, it can make viewing log files confusing because there are so many entries. Even though each event is time- and date-stamped, you should clear Event Viewer every so often. To do this, open Event Viewer, right-click the log, choose Properties, and click the Clear Log button. Doing so erases all events in the current log file, allowing you to see new events more easily when they occur. You can set maximum log size by right-clicking the log and choosing Properties. By default, when a log fills to its maximum size, old entries are deleted in a first in, first out (FIFO) order. Clearing the log, setting maximum log size, and setting how the log is handled when full are done in the Log Properties dialog box, as shown in Figure 6.11.

> **TIP** You can save the log files before erasing them. The saved files can be stored on a cloud drive. Often, you are required to save the files to CD or DVD if you are working in a company that adheres to strict regulatory standards.

In addition to just erasing logs, you can configure three different settings for what you want to occur when the file does reach its maximum size. The first option is Overwrite Events as Needed (i.e. oldest events first), which replaces the older events with the new entries. The second option is Archive the Log When Full, Do Not Overwrite Events, which will create another log file as soon as the current one runs out of space. The third option, Do Not Overwrite Events (i.e. clear logs manually), will not record any additional events once the file is full.

A scenario for using Event Viewer would be in the case of an attempted improper login. You could use the log to identity the time, machine, and other information concerning the attempt.

Disk Management (diskmgmt.msc)

In Windows, you can manage your hard drives using the Disk Management tool. To access Disk Management, access the Control Panel and double-click Administrative Tools, then double-click Computer Management, and finally double-click Disk Management.

FIGURE 6.11 The Log Properties dialog box

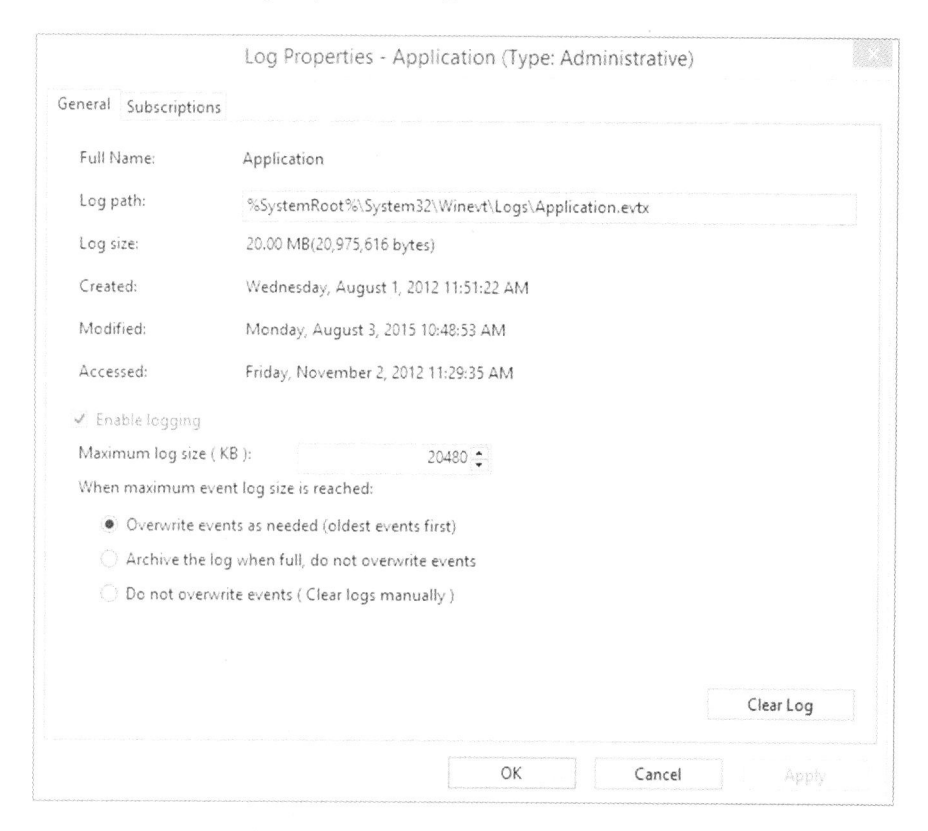

The Disk Management screen lets you view a lot of information regarding all the drives installed in your system, including CD-ROM and DVD drives. The list of devices in the top portion of the screen shows you additional information for each partition on each drive, such as the file system used, status, free space, and so on. If you right-click a partition in either area, you can perform a variety of functions, such as formatting the partition and changing the name and drive letter assignment. For additional options and information, you can also access the properties of a partition by right-clicking it and selecting Properties.

The basic unit of storage is the disk. Disks are partitioned (e.g. primary, logical, extended) and then formatted for use. With the Windows OSes this exam focuses on, you can choose to use either FAT32 or NTFS; the advantage of the latter is that it offers security and many other features that FAT32 can't handle.

> If you're using FAT32 and want to change to NTFS, the `convert` utility will allow you to do so. For example, to change the E: drive to NTFS, the command is `convert e: /FS:NTFS`.

Once the disk is formatted, the next building block is the directory structure, in which you divide the partition into logical locations for storing data. Whether these storage units are called directories or folders is a matter of semantics—they tend to be called *folders* when viewed in the graphical user interface (GUI) and *directories* when viewed from the command line.

Drive status

The status of a drive can have a number of variables associated with it (e.g. system, boot, etc.), but what really matters is whether it falls into the category of *healthy* or *unhealthy*. As the title implies, if it is healthy, it is properly working, and if it is unhealthy, you need to attend to it and correct problems. In Figure 6.12, you can see in the Status column of Disk Management that all drives are healthy.

Mounting

Drives must be mounted before they can be used. Mounting means to make files and directories available to users. Within Windows, most removable media (i.e. flash drives, CDs, etc.) are recognized when attached and mounted. Volumes on basic disks, however, are not automatically mounted and assigned drive letters by default. To mount them, you must manually assign them drive letters or create mount points in Disk Management.

FIGURE 6.12 Status in Disk Management

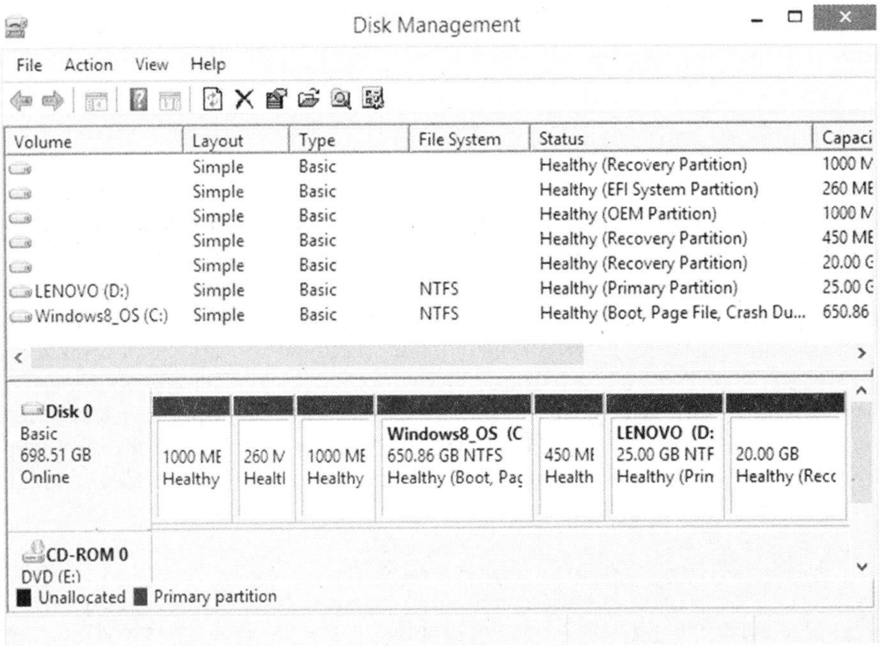

> You can also mount from the command line using either the Diskpart or Mountvol utility.

Initializing

Initializing a disk makes it available to the Disk Management system, and in most cases, the drive will not show up until you do this. Once the drive has been connected or installed, it should be initialized. Initializing the drive can be done at the command line using `diskpart` or in the Disk Management tool. Be aware that initialization will wipe out any drive contents! To use `diskpart` to perform the initialization on 2 TB drives and smaller, follow these steps:

1. Open the Start menu and enter **diskpart**.
2. Enter **list disk**.
3. Enter **select disk X** (where *X* is the number your drive shows up as).
4. Enter **clean**.
5. Enter **create partition primary**.
6. Enter **format quick fs=ntfs**.
7. Enter **assign**.
8. Enter **exit**.

To use `diskpart` to perform the initialization on drives that are 2.5 TB or larger, follow these steps:

1. Open the Start menu and enter **diskpart**.
2. Enter **list disk**.
3. Enter **select disk X** (where *X* is the number your drive shows up as)
4. Enter **clean**.
5. Enter **convert gpt**.
6. Enter **create partition primary**.
7. Enter **format quick fs=ntfs**.
8. Enter **assign**.
9. Enter **exit**.

To use Disk Management, follow this procedure:

1. Install the drive and reboot the device.
2. In the search line, enter **Disk Management**. With the drive connected, you will get the pop-up box shown in Figure 6.13.
3. If you received the pop-up box, choose either MBR or GPT and click OK.

FIGURE 6.13   The Initialize Disk pop-up

FIGURE 6.14   The Initialize Disk option

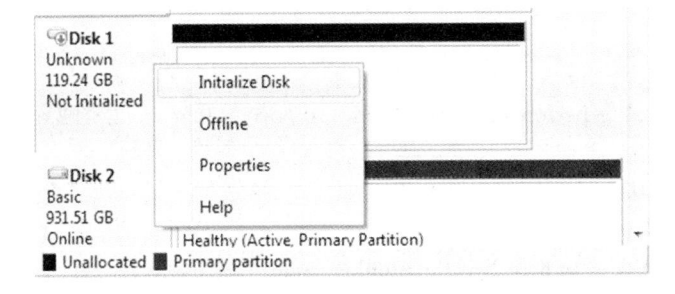

If you didn't get the pop-up, right-click and select to initialize the newly added drive under where it says Disk 1, as shown in Figure 6.14.

Extending partitions

It is possible to add more space to partitions (and logical drives) by extending them into unallocated space. This is done in Disk Management by right-clicking and choosing Extend or using the Diskpart utility. Please note: Extending a partition does not add additional space to the drive. It simply "moves the wall" to allow more space for your "room."

Splitting partitions

Just as you can extend a partition, you can also reduce the size of it. While this operation is generically known as *splitting* the partition, the menu option in Disk Management is Shrink. By shrinking an existing partition, you are creating another with unallocated space that can then be used for other purposes. You can shrink only basic volumes that use the NTFS file system (and space exists) or that do not have a file system.

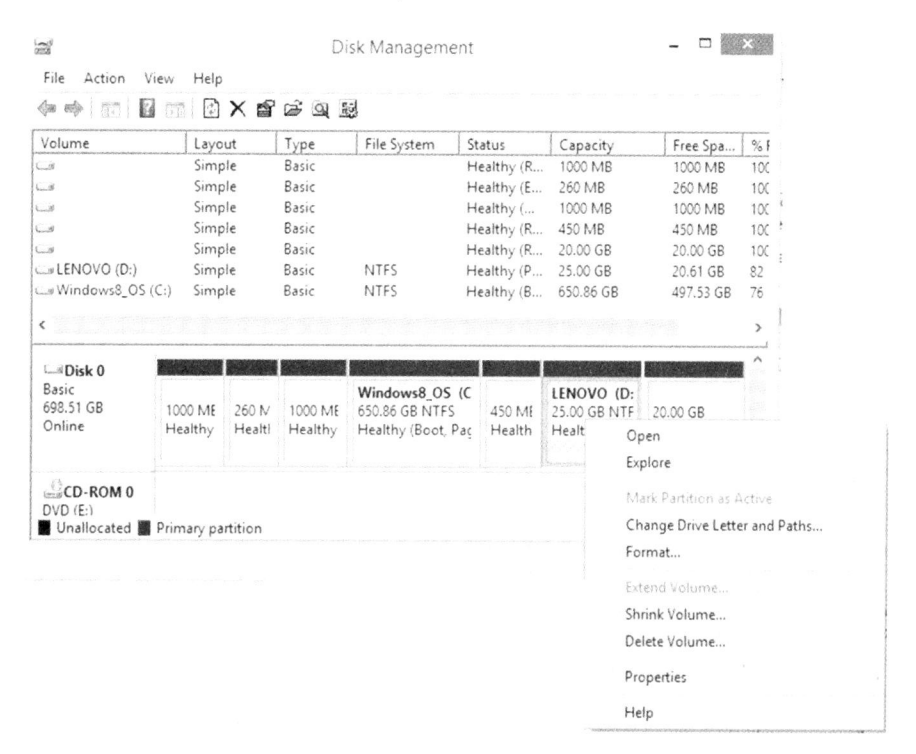

FIGURE 6.15 The Shrink Volume option

Shrinking partitions

It is also possible to shrink a volume from its size at creation. To do so in Disk Management, access the volume in question, right-click the volume, and select Shrink Volume, as shown in Figure 6.15.

Selecting Shrink Volume will open another box that will allow you to control how much you want to shrink the volume, as shown in Figure 6.16.

Assigning/changing drive letters

Mounting drives and assigning drive letters are two tasks that go hand in hand. When you mount a drive, you typically assign it a drive letter to be able to access it. Right-clicking on a volume in Disk Management gives the option Change Drive Letter and Paths, as shown in Figure 6.17.

Adding drives

When removable drives are added, the Windows OS is configured, by default, to identify them and assign a drive letter. When nonremovable drives are added, you must mount them and assign a drive letter, as mentioned earlier, in the section "Assigning/changing drive letters."

FIGURE 6.16 Setting the volume size

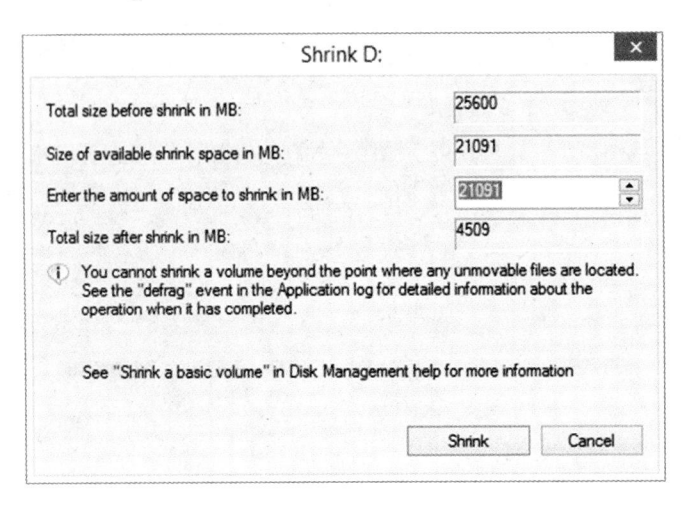

FIGURE 6.17 Changing the drive letter

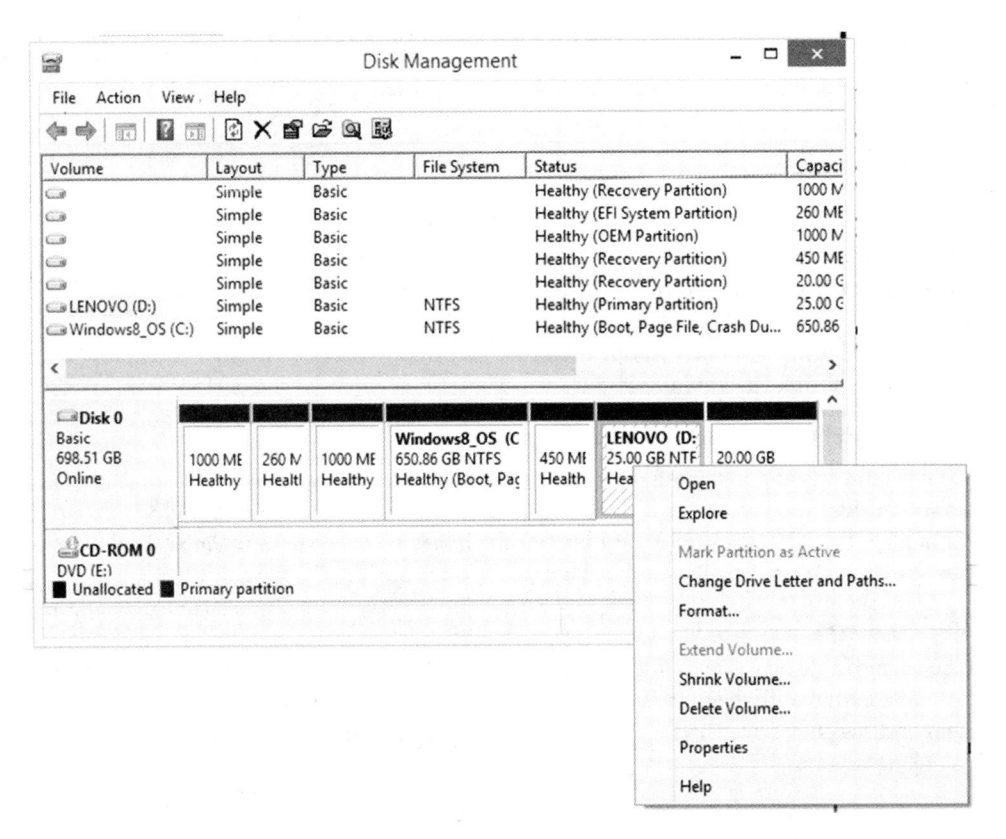

Adding arrays

Arrays of drives are added to increase fault tolerance (using RAID 5) or performance (striping using RAID 0). Disk Management allows you to create and modify arrays as needed.

Storage spaces

Configuring storage spaces is a fault tolerance and capacity expansion technique that can be used as an alternative to the techniques described earlier when discussing dynamic volume types. It enables you to virtualize storage by grouping industry-standard disks into storage pools, and then creating virtual disks called *storage spaces* from the available capacity in the storage pools. This means that, at a high level, you have to do three tasks to use storage spaces:

1. Create a storage pool, which is a collection of physical disks.
2. From the storage pool, create a storage space, which can also be thought of as a virtual disk.
3. Create one or more volumes on the storage space.

First let's look at creating the pool from several physical disks. Each of the disks must be at least 4 GB in size and should not have any volumes in it. The number of disks required depends on the type of resiliency you want to provide to the resulting storage space. *Resiliency* refers to the type of fault tolerance desired. Use the following guidelines:

- For simple resiliency (i.e. no fault tolerance), only a single disk is required for the pool.
- For mirror resiliency, two drives are required.
- For parity resiliency (i.e. RAID 5), three drives are required.

To create the pool, access the Control Panel using any of the methods discussed so far and click the applet Storage Spaces. On the resulting page, select the option Create a New Pool and Storage Space. On the Select Drives to Create Storage Pools page, the drives that are available and supported for storage pools will appear, as shown in Figure 6.18.

In this case, only one drive is eligible, so you can create only a simple pool. Check the drive and click the Create Pool button at the bottom of the page. On the next page, give the space a name, select a drive letter, and choose the file system (i.e. NTFS or ReFS), the resiliency type (in this case, you can select only Simple), and the size of the pool. Figure 6.19 shows the pool as Myspace, with a drive letter of F, an NTFS file system, simple resiliency, and a maximum size of 100 GB. When you click Create Storage Space, the space will be created. Be aware that any data on the physical drive will be erased in this process!

When the process is finished, the new space will appear on the Manage Storage Spaces page. Now, you have a pool and a space derived from the pool. The last step is to create a volume in the storage space. If you now access Disk Management, you will see a new virtual disk called Myspace. It will be a basic disk, but you can convert it to dynamic by right-clicking it and selecting Convert to Dynamic Disk. This will allow you to shrink or delete the existing volume if you desire.

FIGURE 6.18 The Select Drives to Create a Storage Pool page

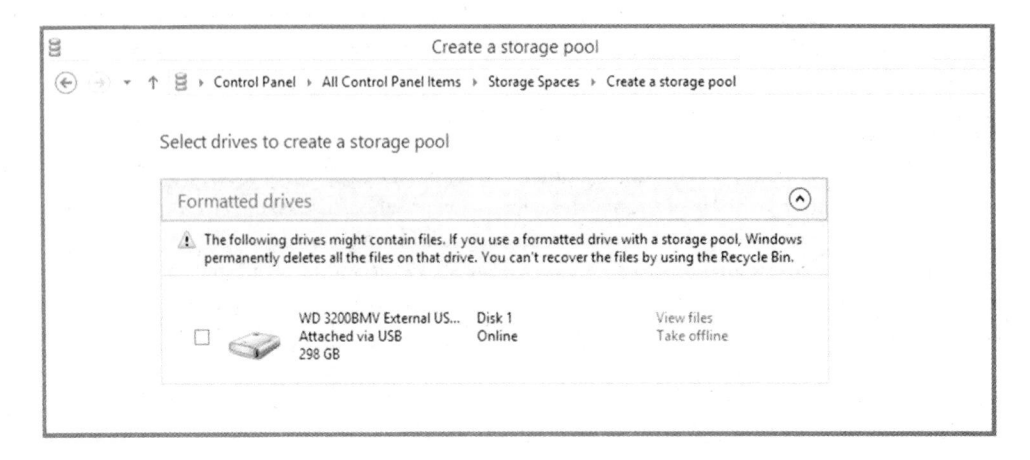

FIGURE 6.19 Creating a storage space

A scenario for using `diskpart` is to extend a partition that is getting full.

1. In the command prompt, enter **diskpart**.
2. At the Diskpart prompt, enter **list disk**.
3. Then enter **select disk n** where *n* is the partition you want to extend.
4. Enter **list partition**.
5. Select the partition you want to extend. Enter **partition n,** where *n* is the partition you want to extend.
6. Enter **extend size=n**, where *n* is the size in megabytes you want to add to the partition.

Task Scheduler (taskschd.msc)

Task Scheduler allows you to configure jobs to automatically run unattended. For the run frequency, you can choose any of the following options: Daily, Weekly, Monthly, One Time Only, When the Computer Starts, or When You Log On. You can access a job's advanced properties any time after the job has been created. To do so, double-click the icon for the job in the Scheduled Tasks screen. In the resulting dialog box, you can configure such things as the username and password associated with the job, the actual command line used to start the job (in case you need to add parameters to it), and the working directory. At any time, you can delete a scheduled job by deleting its icon, or you can simply disable a job by removing the check mark from the Enabled box on the Task tab of the task's Properties dialog box. For jobs that are scheduled to run, a picture of a clock appears in the bottom-left corner of the icon; jobs not scheduled to run do not have that clock. This tool is shown in Figure 6.20.

Device Manager (devmgmt.msc)

Device Manager shows a list of all installed hardware and lets you add items, remove items, update drivers, and more. This tool is shown in Figure 6.21.

Certificate Manager (certmgr.msc)

Certificate Manager is a tool for managing all certificate issues. You can view currently held certificates and their details, and you can request, export, and import certificates. A common scenario is when a user is presented with a certificate, and the system rejects it because the certificate of the root server, which issued the certification being rejected, is not found in the local certificate store. Importing the root certificate into the proper location will solve the issue. The tool is shown in Figure 6.22. To open the tool in Windows 11, execute the command `certmgr.msc` at the command line.

Local Users and Groups (lusrmgr.msc)

If Local Users and Groups is not visible in the left pane of MMC, choose File Add/Remove Snap-In and select Local Users and Groups from the list of possible snap-ins. You can choose to manage the local computer or another computer (requiring you to provide its address).

FIGURE 6.20 Task Scheduler

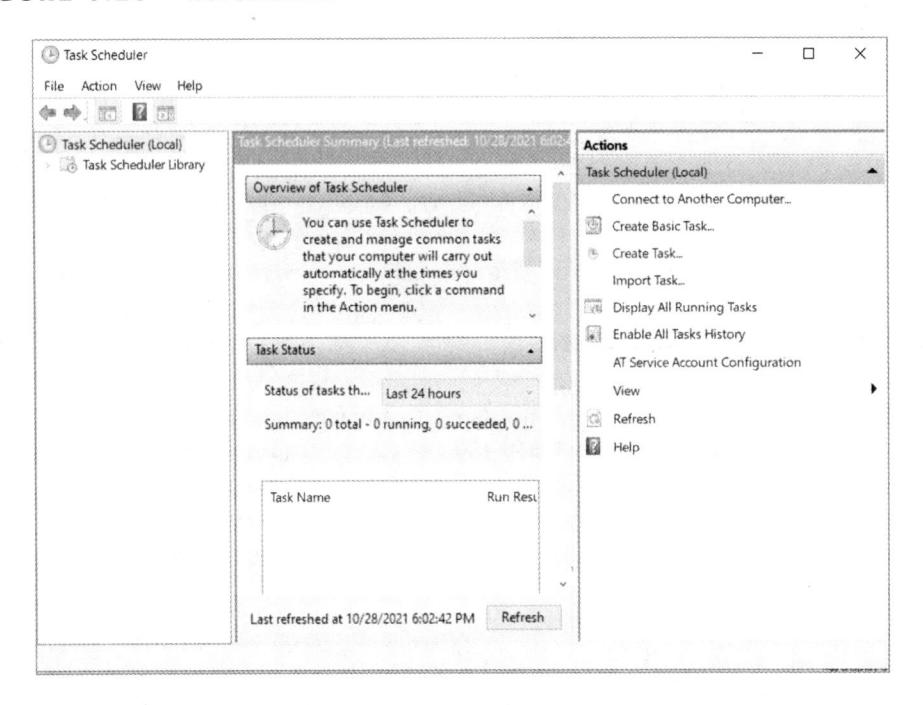

FIGURE 6.21 Device Manager

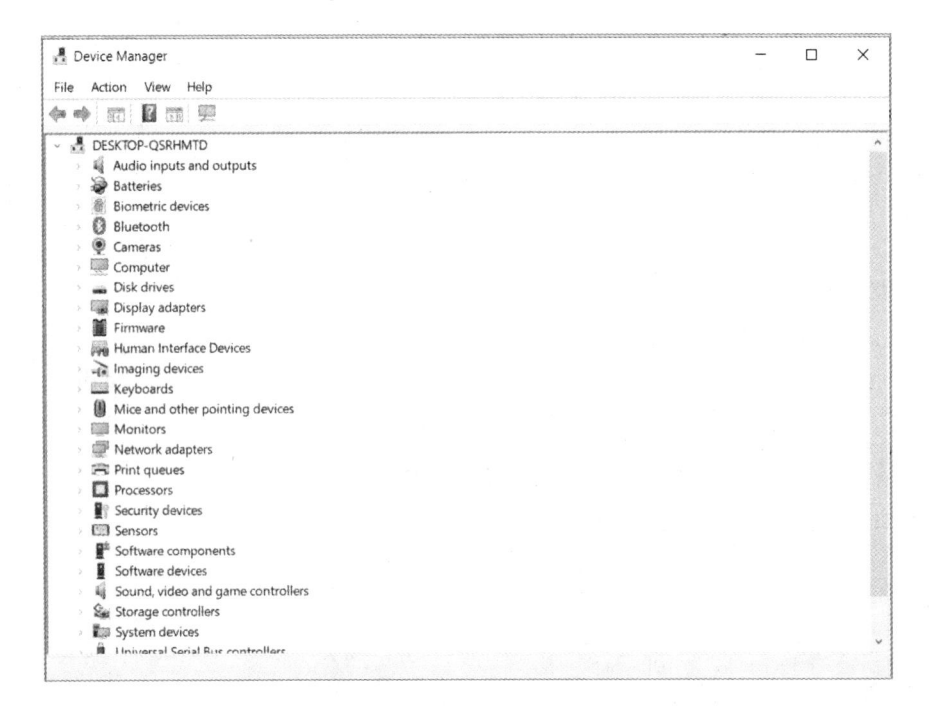

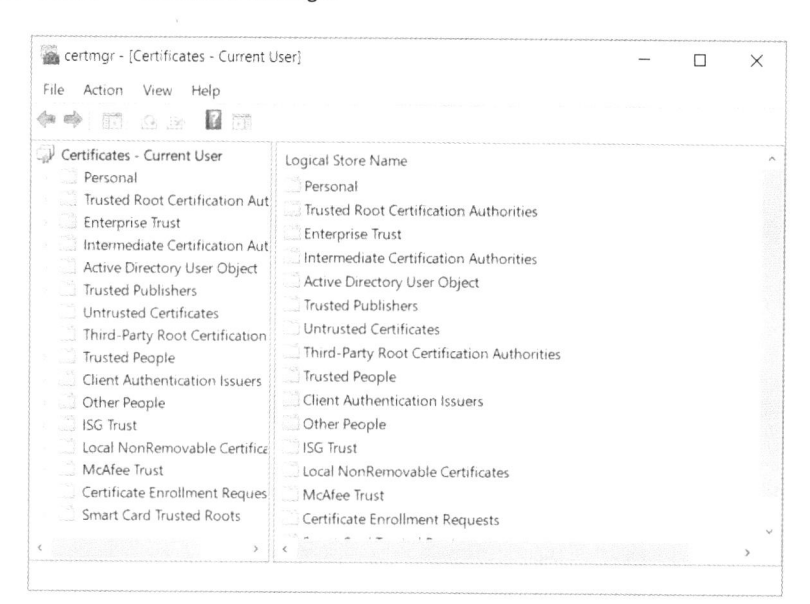

FIGURE 6.22 Certificate Manager

The built-in groups for a domain are a superset of local groups. You must manage user accounts using the User Accounts applet in the Control Panel, and you cannot create or manage groups. The default users created are Administrator, Guest, and the administrative account created during the install. This tool is shown in Figure 6.23.

Performance Monitor (perfmon.msc)

Performance Monitor is invoked by executing `perfmon.msc` in the Run box or by adding its snap-in. It contains monitoring tools, including Resource Monitor, which can help you see how your system resources are being used; System Reliability Monitor, which allows you to view the performance impact of software updates and installations; and Performance Monitor (or real-time statistics), which gives you the ability to create data sets of values that you would like to monitor over time. This tool is shown in Figure 6.24, where it is focused on the Performance Monitor tool that is currently monitoring the real-time use of the processor.

Group Policy Editor (gpedit.msc)

As you learned earlier in this chapter, group policies can be used in certain editions to exert control over both security and desktop settings. This configuration is done with a tool called the Group Policy Editor, which is invoked by executing `gpedit.msc` in the Run box or by adding its snap-in. Please review the earlier section "gpedit.msc." The tool is shown in Figure 6.25.

FIGURE 6.23 Local Users and Groups

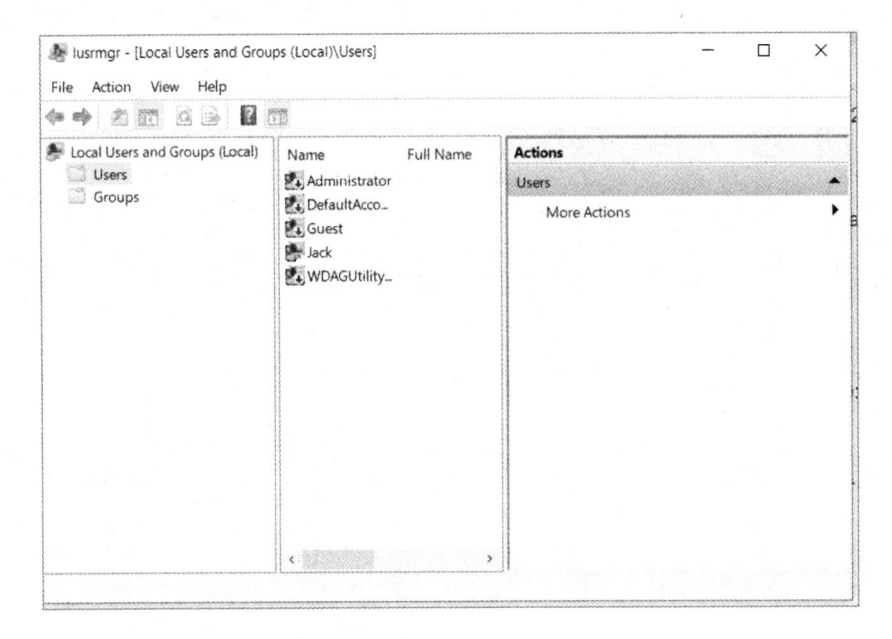

FIGURE 6.24 Performance Monitor

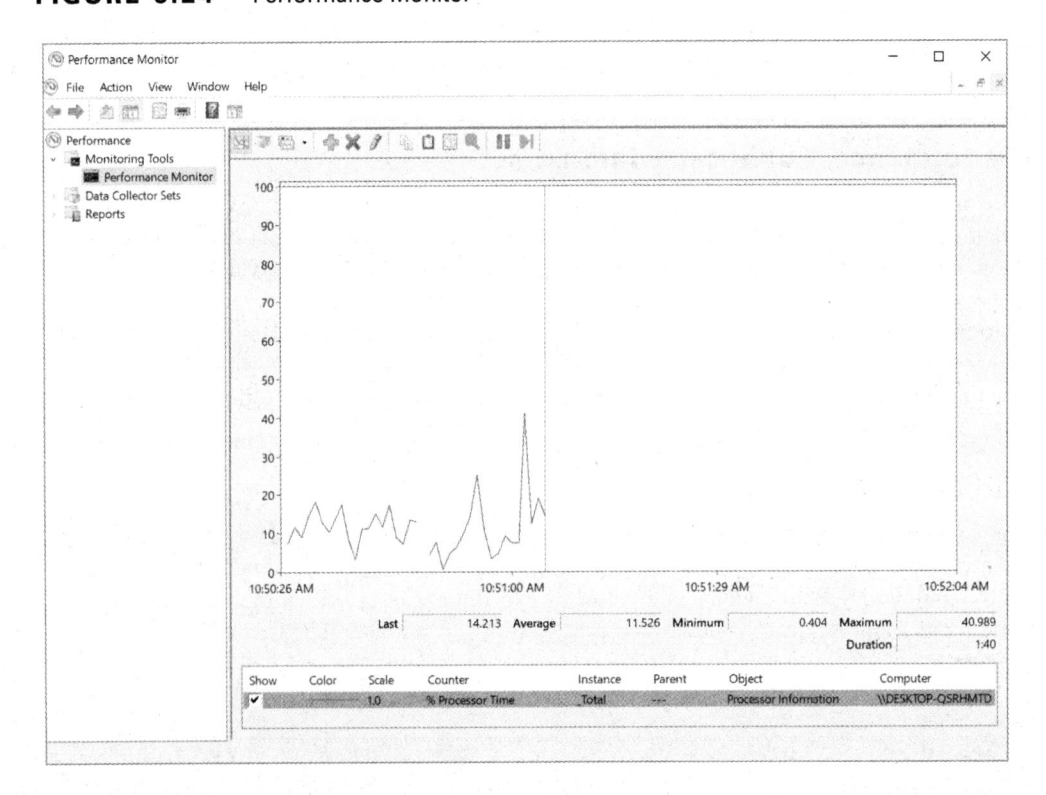

FIGURE 6.25   Group Policy Editor

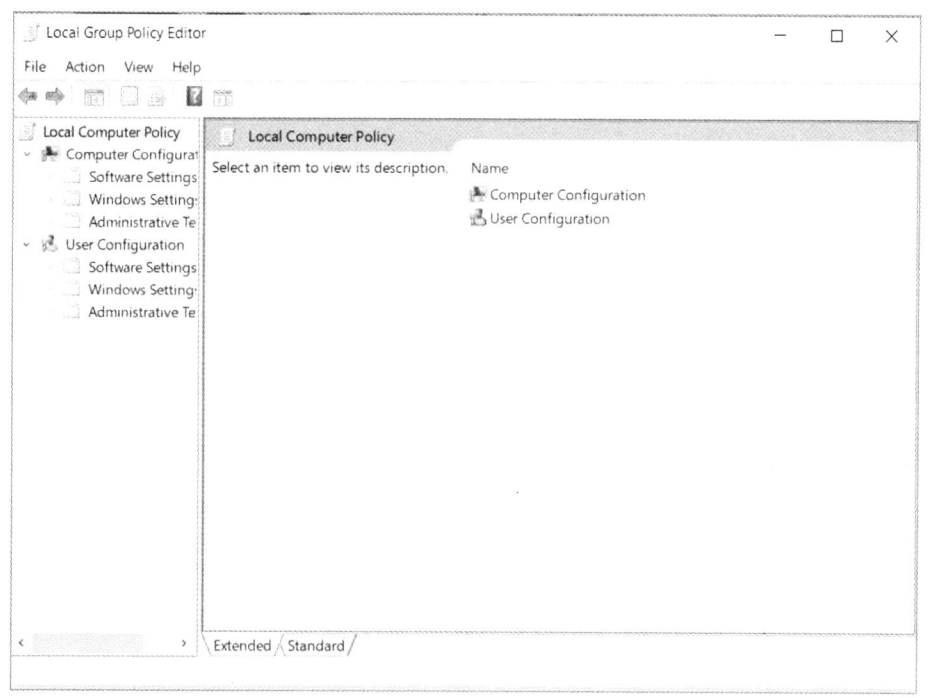

Group Policy can be used to control the behavior of both users and computers and has a section for each type of policy. Policies that impact users will be effective on any machine they log into that is a member of the domain. Likewise, policies impacting computers will be effective, regardless of who logs into the machine. In cases where these policies don't agree, administrators have the ability to configure the superior policy.

Policies are not applied to security groups but are applied to containers in Active Directory (i.e. domain, organizational unit (OU), child OU, etc.) An organizational unit is a subdivision of a domain. By organizing domains into OUs, the OUs can be used to apply different policies to different OUs within the same domain. Policies also leverage the concept of inheritance, which means a policy applied to a domain will be inherited by all OUs in the domain. This inheritance is also under the control of the administrators, meaning it can be enabled and disabled as needed.

Additional tools

Both Windows 10 and 11 have plenty of tools to make management easier. In this section, you'll learn about the additional tools at your disposal.

FIGURE 6.26 System Information

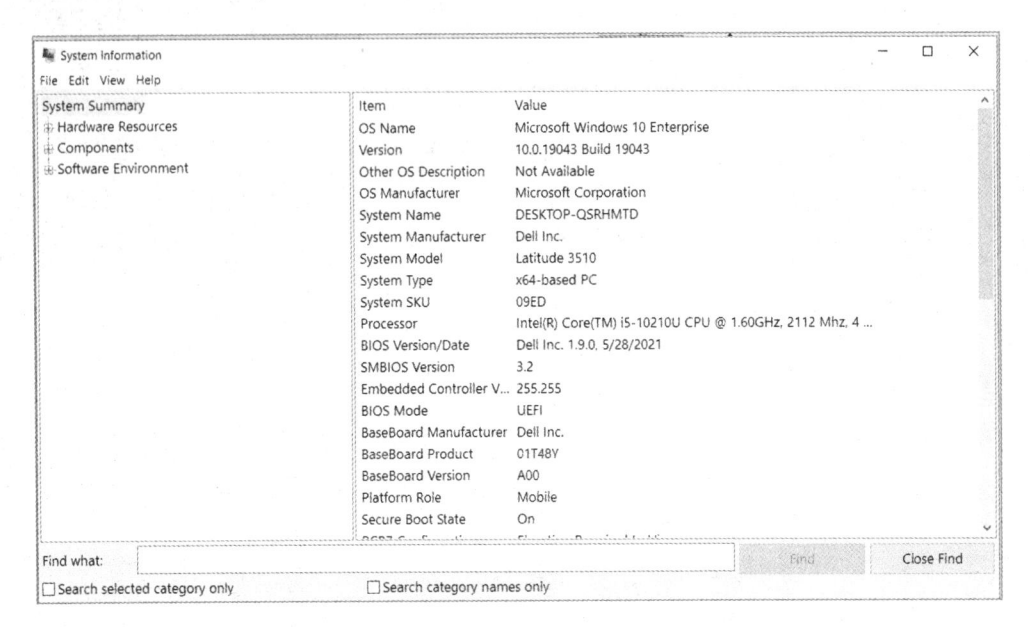

![System Information dialog box showing System Summary with details: OS Name Microsoft Windows 10 Enterprise, Version 10.0.19043 Build 19043, OS Manufacturer Microsoft Corporation, System Name DESKTOP-QSRHMTD, System Manufacturer Dell Inc., System Model Latitude 3510, System Type x64-based PC, System SKU 09ED, Processor Intel(R) Core(TM) i5-10210U CPU @ 1.60GHz, 2112 Mhz, 4..., BIOS Version/Date Dell Inc. 1.9.0, 5/28/2021, SMBIOS Version 3.2, Embedded Controller V... 255.255, BIOS Mode UEFI, BaseBoard Manufacturer Dell Inc., BaseBoard Product 01T48Y, BaseBoard Version A00, Platform Role Mobile, Secure Boot State On]

System Information (msinfo32.exe)

The System Information dialog box displays a thorough list of settings on the machine. You cannot change any values from here, but you can search, export, save, and run a number of utilities. The tool is primarily used during diagnostics because it is an easy way to display settings such as interrupt requests (IRQs) and direct memory access (DMA). This dialog box is shown in Figure 6.26, where it is currently displaying general information about the system, including the OS version.

Resource Monitor (resmon.exe)

This tool displays information about the use of hardware (e.g. CPU, memory, disk, and network) and software (e.g. file handles and modules) resources in real time. While this can also be done with Performance, this tool organizes the information to focus on the use of these four hardware resources in real time. It is shown in Figure 6.27, where it is focused on the Overview tab with a graph for each resource at the right. By selecting the tabs for a resource, you can focus on just this resource.

System Configuration (msconfig.exe)

MSConfig, known as the System Configuration utility, helps you troubleshoot startup problems by allowing you to selectively disable individual items that normally are executed at startup. The MSConfig system configuration tool features five tabs—General, Boot, Services, Startup, and Tools—which are discussed next.

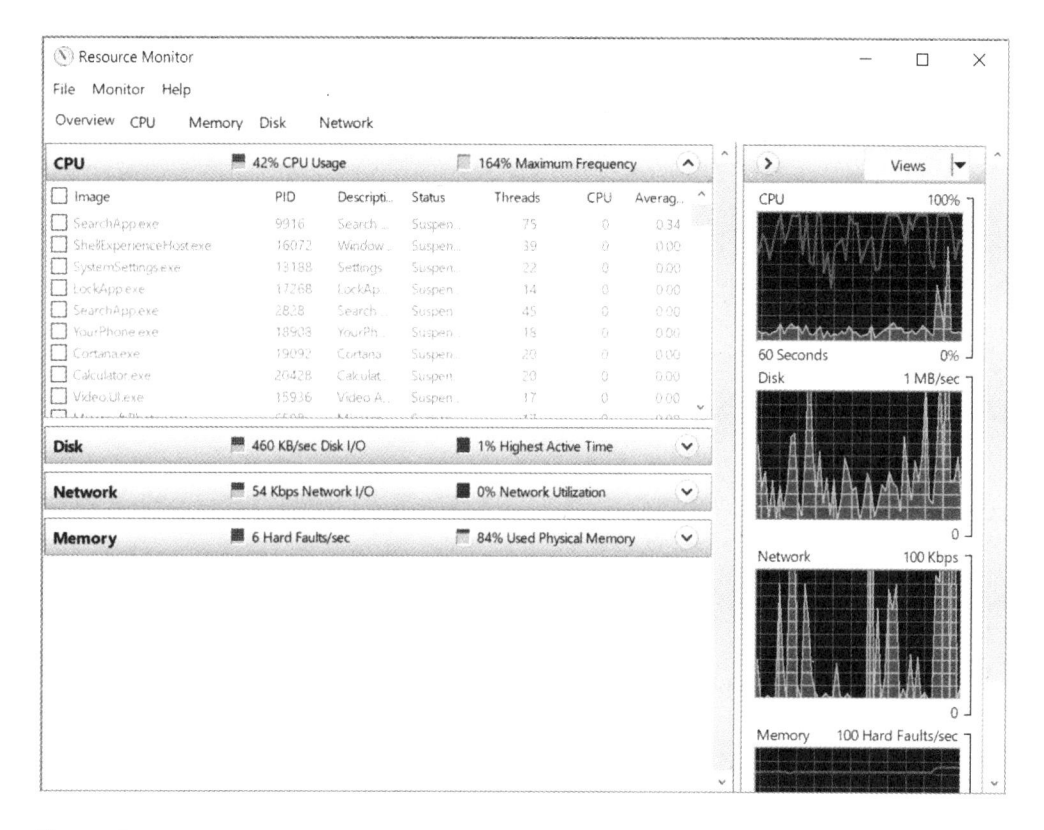

FIGURE 6.27   Resource Monitor

General

On the General tab, you can choose the startup type. There are three options: Normal, Diagnostic, and Selective. A normal startup loads all drivers and services, whereas a diagnostic startup loads only the basic drivers and services. Between the two extremes is the selective startup, which gives you limited options on what to load. Figure 6.28 shows the General tab.

Boot

The Boot tab shows the boot menu and allows you to configure parameters, such as the number of seconds the menu should appear before the default option is chosen and whether you want to go to safe boot. You can toggle on/off the display of drivers as they load during startup and choose to log the boot, go with basic video settings, and similar options. Figure 6.29 shows the Boot tab.

Services

The Services tab shows the services configured and their current status. From here, you can enable or disable all and hide Microsoft services from the display (which greatly reduces the display in most cases). Figure 6.30 shows the Services tab.

FIGURE 6.28 The General tab

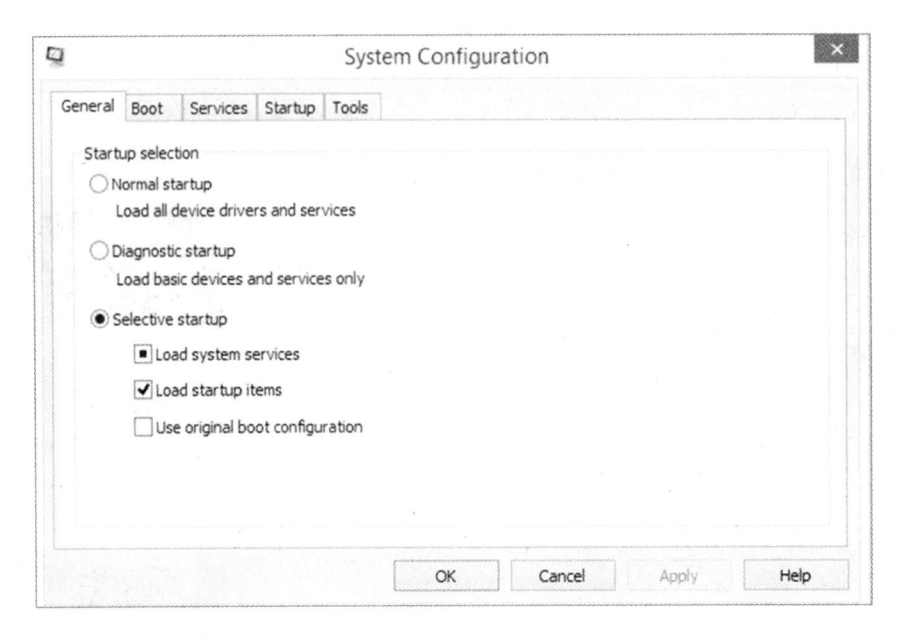

FIGURE 6.29 The Boot tab

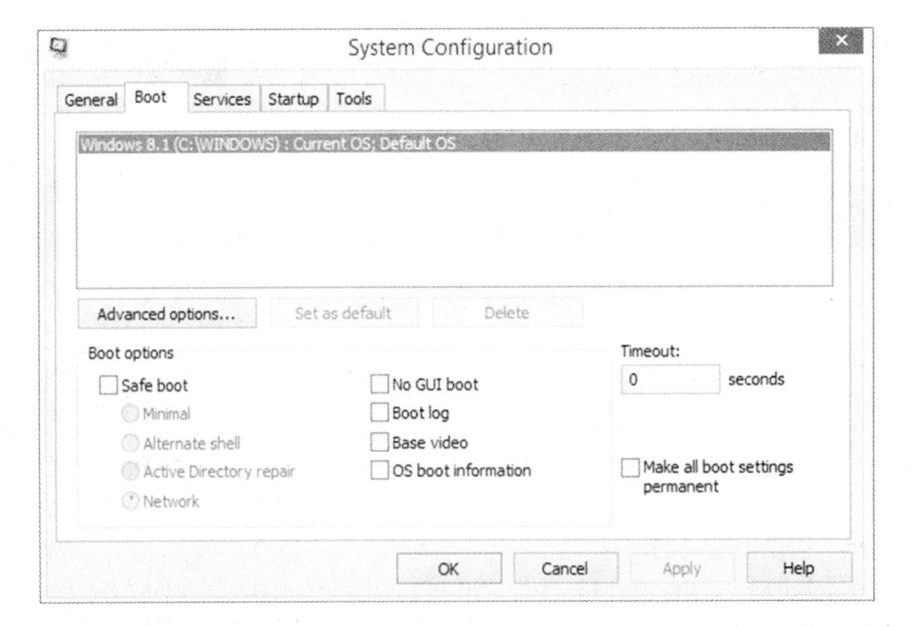

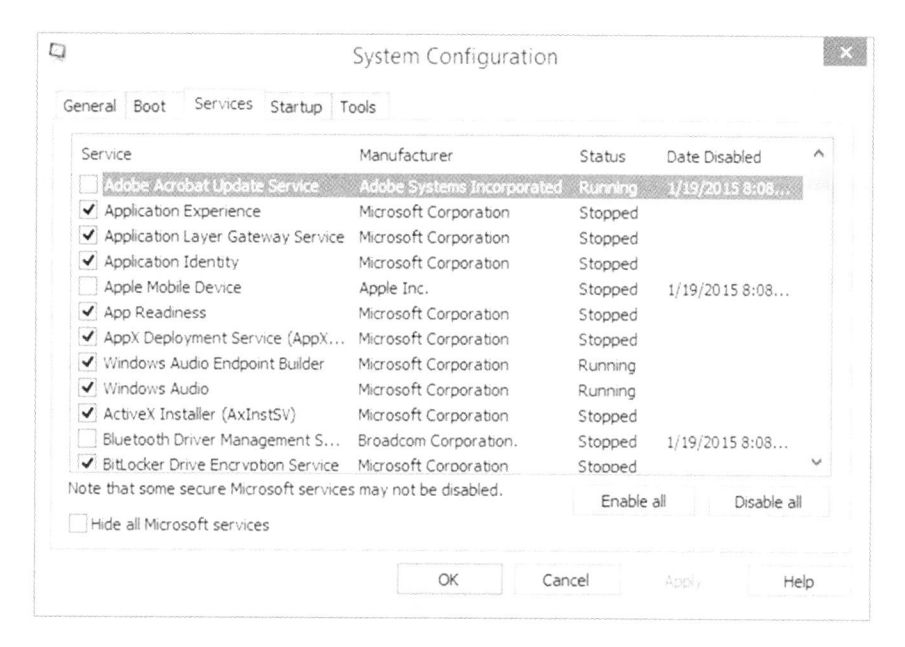

FIGURE 6.30 The Services tab

Startup

The Startup tab is only a reference point to the Startup section of Task Manager, as shown in Figure 6.31.

Tools

The Tools tab contains quick access to some of the most useful diagnostic tools in Windows. You can launch such items as the Registry Editor as well as many Control Panel applets, and you can enable or disable User Account Control (UAC). Figure 6.32 shows the Tools tab.

A scenario for using MSConfig would be when a device is performing slowly; you can check to see what applications and services are starting at boot, and you might find spyware and other software loading that is causing the performance hit.

Disk Cleanup (cleanmgr.exe)

Disk Cleanup, invoked at the Run box by executing `cleanmgr.exe`, provides a utility for removing the data clutter that is hindering performance and not providing any benefits. It will suggest data locations where data is typically safe to delete, such as the Recycle Bin and Temp folders. The tool is shown in Figure 6.33.

Disk Defragment (dfrgui.exe)

Microsoft Drive Optimizer (formerly Disk Defragmenter) is a utility used to eliminate the fragmentation of data on a drive, which makes it more difficult for data to be located when requested and thus slowing performance. Fragmentation occurs when Windows stores pieces of files wherever it can find empty disk space. This utility rearranges the data so that there is no fragmentation and the files are contiguous. Running this from time to time will improve performance. The tool is shown in Figure 6.34.

FIGURE 6.31 The Startup tab

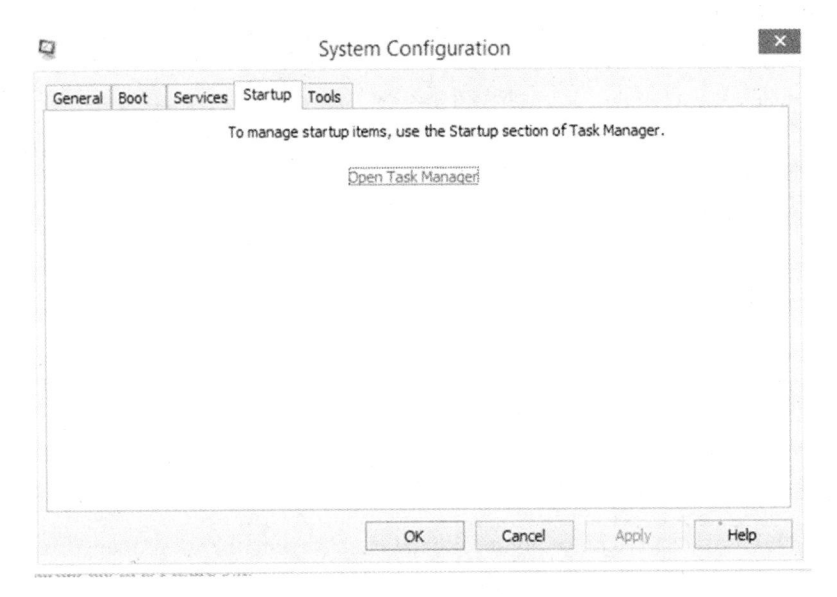

FIGURE 6.32 The Tools tab

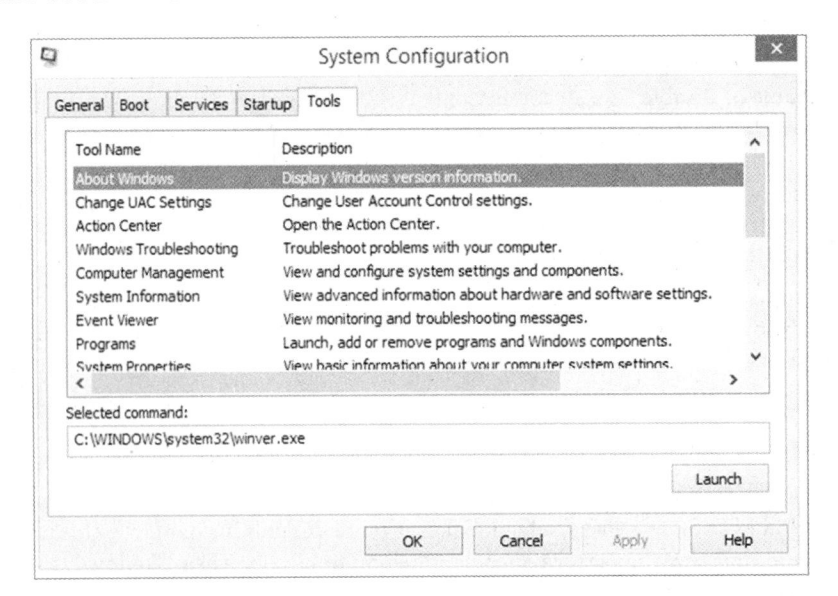

FIGURE 6.33 Disk Cleanup

FIGURE 6.34 Disk Defragmenter

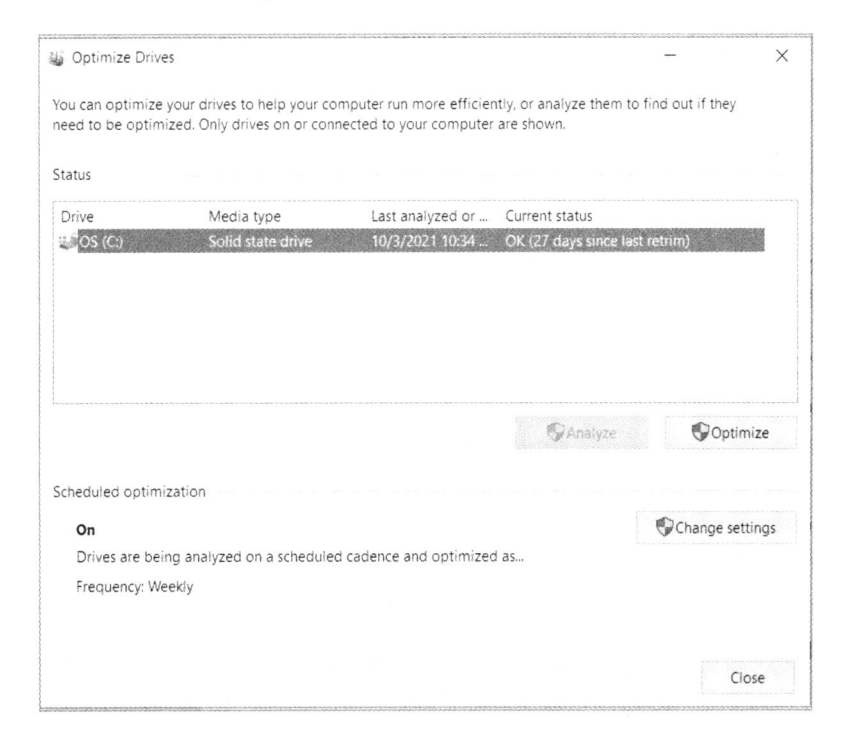

Registry Editor (regedit.exe)

Registry Editor is used to open and edit the Registry. Regedit does not have save or undo features (though you can import and export); once you make a change, you've made the change for better or worse, and the Registry is not a place to play around in if you're not sure what you're doing. The Registry is divided into five "hives" that hold all settings. The two main hives are HKEY_USERS (which contains settings for all users) and HKEY_LOCAL_MACHINE (which contains settings for the machine itself). HKEY_CURRENT_USER is a subset of HKEY_USERS, holding information only on the current user. HKEY_CURRENT_CONFIG and HKEY_CLASSES_ROOT are both subsets of HKEY_LOCAL_MACHINE for the current configuration. The tool is shown in Figure 6.35.

> **WARNING**
>
> Use extreme caution when using Regedit. Changes happen in real time. There is no undo or revert option. An incorrect value can cause serious system instability.

Exam essentials

Describe the administrative tools in Windows. These tools include Computer Management, Device Manager, Users and Groups, Local Security Policy, Performance Monitor, Services, System Configuration, and Task Scheduler.

FIGURE 6.35 Registry Editor

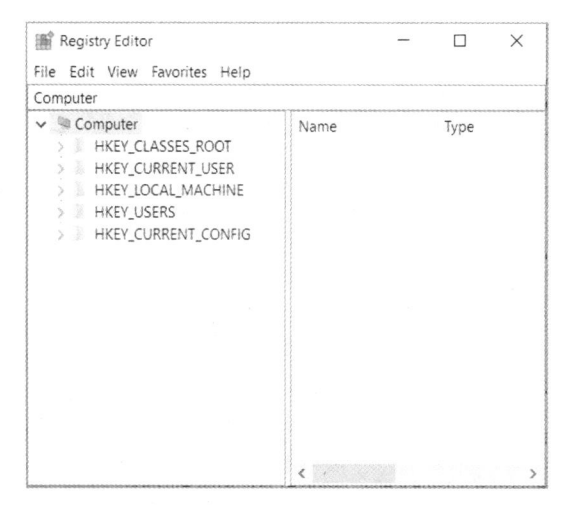

1.5 Given a scenario, use the appropriate Microsoft command-line tools

Although the exam is on the Windows OSes, it tests many concepts that carry over from the earlier Microsoft Disk Operating System (MS-DOS), which was never meant to be extremely friendly. Its roots are in Control Program/Monitor (CP/M), which was based on the command line, and so is MS-DOS. In other words, these systems use long strings of commands typed in at the computer keyboard to perform operations. Some people prefer this type of interaction with their computers, including many folks with technical backgrounds (such as yours truly). Although Windows has left the full command-line interface behind, it still contains a bit of DOS, and you get to it through the command prompt.

Although you can't tell from looking at it, the Windows command prompt is a Windows program that is intentionally designed to have the look and feel of a DOS command line. Despite its appearance as a Windows program, the command prompt provides all the stability and configurability you expect from Windows. You can access a command prompt by running CMD.EXE.

A number of diagnostic utilities are often run at the command prompt. Because knowledge of each is required for the exam, they are discussed here in this section.

Navigation

Some commands are used to navigate the file system. The two commands covered in this section are used for that purpose.

cd

The change directory (cd) command is used to move to another folder or directory. It is used in both Linux and Windows. Parameters are shown in Table 6.6.

TABLE 6.6 change directory (cd) command

LINUX	Action
cd or cd ~	Puts you in your Home directory
cd .	Leaves you in the same directory you are currently in
cd ~username	Puts you in username's Home directory
cd dir (without a /)	Puts you in a subdirectory
cd -	Switches you to the previous directory
cd ..	Moves you up one directory

(Continued)

TABLE 6.6   (Continued)

DOS and Windows	Action
no attributes	Prints the full path of the current directory
-p	Prints the final directory stack
-n	Entries are wrapped before they reach the screen's edge
-v	Entries are printed one per line, preceded by their stack positions
cd\	Returns to the root directory
..	Moves you up one directory

dir

The DIR command is simply used to view a listing of the files and folders that exist within a directory, subdirectory, or folder. The following is the syntax:

```
dir [Drive:][Path][FileName] [...] [/p] [/q] [/w] [/d]
[/a[[:]attributes]][/o[[:]SortOrder]] [/t[[:]TimeField]] [/s] [/b]
[/l] [/n] [/x] [/c] [/4]
```

The parameters are as follows in Table 6.7.

Network

While navigation commands are used to move through the command structure, network commands are used to manage and configure network settings. We'll explore seven such commands in this section.

ipconfig

The ipconfig command is used to view the IP configuration of a device and, when combined with certain switches or parameters, can be used to release and renew the lease of an IP address obtained from a DHCP server and to flush the DNS resolver cache. Its most common use is to view the current configuration. Figure 6.36 shows its execution with the /all switch, which results in a display of a wealth of information about the IP configuration.

A scenario in which this command would be valuable is when you are dealing with a device you have never touched before that is having communication issues. This command would show a wealth of information with its output.

TABLE 6.7 DIR command

Command	Action
`[Drive:][Path]`	Specifies the drive and directory for which you want to see a listing.
`[FileName]`	Specifies a particular file (or group of files) for which you want to see a listing.
`/p`	Displays one screen of the listing at a time. To see the next screen, press any key on the keyboard.
`/q`	Displays file ownership information.
`/w`	Displays the listing in wide format, with as many as five filenames or directory names on each line.
`D`	Same as /w but files are sorted by column.
`I`	Displays only the names of those directories and files with the attributes you specify.
`/o [[:]SortOrder]`	Controls the order in which DIR sorts and displays directory names and filenames.
`/t [[:]TimeField]`	Specifies which time field to display or use for sorting.
`/s`	Lists every occurrence, in the specified directory and all subdirectories, of the specified filename.
`/b`	Lists each directory name or filename, one per line, including the filename extension. /b does not display heading information or a summary. /b overrides /w.
`/l`	Displays unsorted directory names and filenames in lowercase. /l does not convert extended characters to lowercase.
`/n`	Displays a long list format with filenames on the far right of the screen.
`/x`	Displays the short names generated for files on NTFS and FAT volumes. The display is the same as the display for /n, but short names are displayed after the long name.
`/c`	Displays the thousand separator in file sizes.
`/4`	Displays the four-digit year format.

FIGURE 6.36 Using ipconfig

```
C:\Users\tmcmillan>ipconfig/all
Windows IP Configuration

    Host Name . . . . . . . . . . . . : tmcmillan
    Primary Dns Suffix  . . . . . . . : alpha.kaplaninc.com
    Node Type . . . . . . . . . . . . : Hybrid
    IP Routing Enabled. . . . . . . . : No
    WINS Proxy Enabled. . . . . . . . : No
    DNS Suffix Search List. . . . . . : alpha.kaplaninc.com
                                        kaplaninc.com

Ethernet adapter Local Area Connection:

    Connection-specific DNS Suffix  . : alpha.kaplaninc.com
    Description . . . . . . . . . . . : Broadcom NetXtreme 57xx Gigabit Controller
    Physical Address. . . . . . . . . : 00-1A-A0-E1-95-AB
    DHCP Enabled. . . . . . . . . . . : Yes
    Autoconfiguration Enabled . . . . : Yes
    Link-local IPv6 Address . . . . . : fe80::ada3:8b73:a66e:6bc0%10(Preferred)
    IPv4 Address. . . . . . . . . . . : 10.88.2.103(Preferred)
    Subnet Mask . . . . . . . . . . . : 255.255.254.0
    Lease Obtained. . . . . . . . . . : Monday, January 30, 2012 9:38:37 AM
    Lease Expires . . . . . . . . . . : Tuesday, January 31, 2012 9:38:37 AM
    Default Gateway . . . . . . . . . : 10.88.2.6
    DHCP Server . . . . . . . . . . . : 10.88.10.48
    DHCPv6 IAID . . . . . . . . . . . : 234887840
    DHCPv6 Client DUID. . . . . . . . : 00-01-00-01-14-EE-0F-98-00-1A-A0-E1-95-AB

    DNS Servers . . . . . . . . . . . : 10.88.10.48
                                        10.75.139.18
    NetBIOS over Tcpip. . . . . . . . : Enabled
```

You can use `ipconfig` to release and then renew a configuration obtained from a DHCP server by issuing the following commands:

```
ipconfig /release
ipconfig /renew
```

It is also helpful to know that when you have just corrected a configuration error (such as an IP address) on a destination device, you should ensure that the device registers its new IP address with the DNS server by executing the `ipconfig /registerdns` command.

It may also be necessary to clear incorrect IP addresses to hostname mappings, which might still exist on the devices that were attempting to access the destination device. This can be done by executing the `ipconfig /flushdns` command.

If you are using a macOS or Linux system, the command is not `ipconfig` but `ifconfig`. Figure 6.37 shows an example of the command and its output. The `ifconfig` command with the `-a` option shows all network interface information, even if the network interface is down.

ping

The `ping` command makes use of the Internet Control Message Protocol (ICMP) to test connectivity between two devices and is one of the most useful commands in the TCP/IP suite. It sends a series of packets to another system, which in turn sends a response. The `ping` command can be extremely useful for troubleshooting problems with remote hosts.

FIGURE 6.37   Using ifconfig

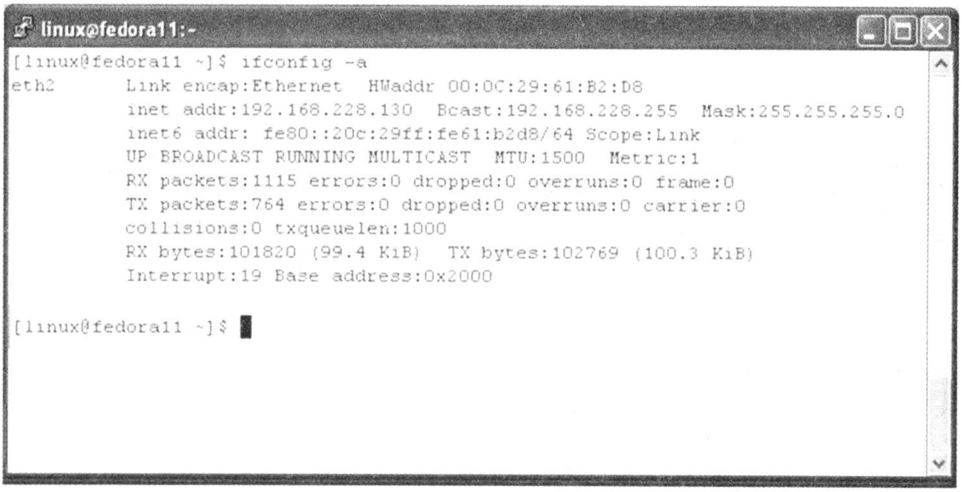

```
[linux@fedora11 ~]$ ifconfig -a
eth2      Link encap:Ethernet  HWaddr 00:0C:29:61:B2:D8
          inet addr:192.168.228.130  Bcast:192.168.228.255  Mask:255.255.255.0
          inet6 addr: fe80::20c:29ff:fe61:b2d8/64 Scope:Link
          UP BROADCAST RUNNING MULTICAST  MTU:1500  Metric:1
          RX packets:1115 errors:0 dropped:0 overruns:0 frame:0
          TX packets:764 errors:0 dropped:0 overruns:0 carrier:0
          collisions:0 txqueuelen:1000
          RX bytes:101820 (99.4 KiB)  TX bytes:102769 (100.3 KiB)
          Interrupt:19 Base address:0x2000

[linux@fedora11 ~]$
```

FIGURE 6.38   The ping command

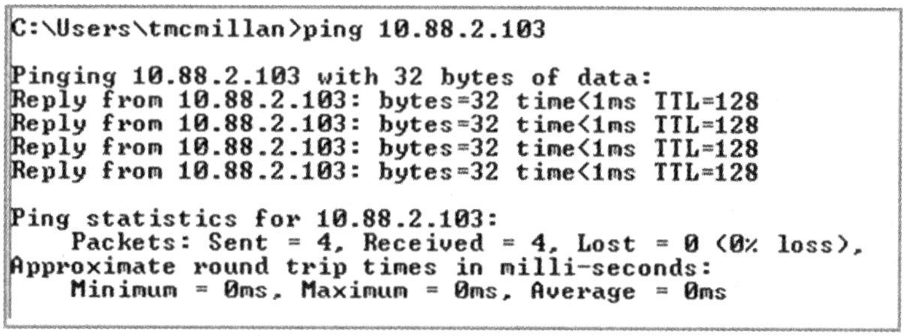

```
C:\Users\tmcmillan>ping 10.88.2.103

Pinging 10.88.2.103 with 32 bytes of data:
Reply from 10.88.2.103: bytes=32 time<1ms TTL=128
Reply from 10.88.2.103: bytes=32 time<1ms TTL=128
Reply from 10.88.2.103: bytes=32 time<1ms TTL=128
Reply from 10.88.2.103: bytes=32 time<1ms TTL=128

Ping statistics for 10.88.2.103:
    Packets: Sent = 4, Received = 4, Lost = 0 (0% loss),
Approximate round trip times in milli-seconds:
    Minimum = 0ms, Maximum = 0ms, Average = 0ms
```

The ping command indicates whether the host can be reached and how long it took for the host to send a return packet. On a local area network (LAN), the time is indicated as less than 10 milliseconds. Across wide area network (WAN) links, however, this value can be much greater. When the -a parameter is included, it will also attempt to resolve the hostname associated with the IP address. Figure 6.38 shows an example of a successful ping.

A common scenario for using ping is when you need to determine whether the network settings are correct. If you can ping another device that is correctly configured, the settings are correct. The syntax is as follows:

```
ping [-t] [-a] [-n count] [-l size] [-f] [-i TTL] [-v TOS]
[-r count] [-s count] [-w timeout] [-R] [-S srcaddr]
[-p] [-4] [-6] target [/?]
```

TABLE 6.8 ping switches

Switch	Purpose
T	Pings the target until you force it to stop by using Ctrl+C
-a	Resolves, if possible, the hostname of an IP address target
-n count	Sets the number of ICMP echo requests to send (4 by default)
-l size	Sets the size, in bytes, of the echo request packet (32 by default)
-f	Prevents ICMP echo requests from being fragmented by routers between you and the target
-i TTL	Sets the Time to Live (TTL) value, the maximum of which is 255
-r count	Specifies the number of hops between your computer and the target computer
-s count	Reports the time, in Internet Timestamp format, that each echo request is received and when an echo reply is sent

Some switches used with ping are in Table 6.8.

netstat

The netstat command (i.e. network status command) is used to see what ports are listening to on the TCP/IP-based system. The -a option is used to show all ports, and /? is used to show what other options are available (i.e. the options differ based on the OS you are using). When executed with no switches, the command displays the current connections, as shown in Figure 6.39.

A common scenario for using netstat is when you suspect that a host is "calling home" to a malicious server. If so, the connection would appear in the output.

The syntax is as follows:

```
ping [-t] [-a] [-n count] [-l size] [-f] [-i TTL] [-v TOS]
[-r count] [-s count] [-w timeout] [-R] [-S srcaddr]
[-p proto] [-4] [-6] target [/?]
```

Table 6.9 shows some switches used with netstat.

1.5 Given a scenario, use the appropriate Microsoft command-line tools

FIGURE 6.39 Using netstat

```
C:\Users\tmcmillan>netstat

Active Connections

  Proto  Local Address          Foreign Address          State
  TCP    10.88.2.103:51273      64.94.18.154:https       ESTABLISHED
  TCP    10.88.2.103:51525      srat1060:microsoft-ds    ESTABLISHED
  TCP    10.88.2.103:51529      gmonsalvatge:microsoft-ds ESTABLISHED
  TCP    10.88.2.103:51573      sjc-not18:http           ESTABLISHED
  TCP    10.88.2.103:51716      schexv02:2785            ESTABLISHED
  TCP    10.88.2.103:51720      schvoip01:epmap          ESTABLISHED
  TCP    10.88.2.103:51721      schvoip01:1297           ESTABLISHED
  TCP    10.88.2.103:51722      schvoip01:1299           ESTABLISHED
  TCP    10.88.2.103:51824      69.31.116.27:http        CLOSE_WAIT
  TCP    10.88.2.103:51965      dcalpsch2:1026           ESTABLISHED
  TCP    10.88.2.103:53865      cs219p3:5050             ESTABLISHED
  TCP    10.88.2.103:53871      sip109:http              ESTABLISHED
  TCP    10.88.2.103:62522      ord08s08-in-f22:https    ESTABLISHED
  TCP    10.88.2.103:62567      ord08s08-in-f22:https    CLOSE_WAIT
  TCP    10.88.2.103:62682      by2msg3010613:http       ESTABLISHED
  TCP    10.88.2.103:63554      baymsg1020213:msnp       ESTABLISHED
  TCP    10.88.2.103:63770      v-client-2b:https        CLOSE_WAIT
  TCP    10.88.2.103:63771      ec2-174-129-205-197:https CLOSE_WAIT
  TCP    10.88.2.103:63772      v-client-2b:https        CLOSE_WAIT
  TCP    10.88.2.103:63773      65.55.121.231:http       ESTABLISHED
  TCP    10.88.2.103:63774      168.75.207.20:http       ESTABLISHED
  TCP    10.88.2.103:63777      65.55.17.30:http         ESTABLISHED
  TCP    10.88.2.103:63779      70.37.131.11:http        ESTABLISHED
  TCP    10.88.2.103:63781      65.124.174.56:http       ESTABLISHED
  TCP    10.88.2.103:63788      69.31.76.41:http         ESTABLISHED
  TCP    10.88.2.103:63791      207.46.140.46:http       ESTABLISHED
  TCP    10.88.2.103:63792      64.4.21.39:http          ESTABLISHED
  TCP    127.0.0.1:2002         tmcmillan:51543          ESTABLISHED
  TCP    127.0.0.1:19872        tmcmillan:51571          ESTABLISHED
  TCP    127.0.0.1:51543        tmcmillan:2002           ESTABLISHED
  TCP    127.0.0.1:51549        tmcmillan:51550          ESTABLISHED
  TCP    127.0.0.1:51550        tmcmillan:51549          ESTABLISHED
  TCP    127.0.0.1:51571        tmcmillan:19872          ESTABLISHED
  TCP    127.0.0.1:53869        tmcmillan:53870          ESTABLISHED
  TCP    127.0.0.1:53870        tmcmillan:53869          ESTABLISHED
  TCP    127.0.0.1:63557        tmcmillan:63574          ESTABLISHED
  TCP    127.0.0.1:63574        tmcmillan:63557          ESTABLISHED

C:\Users\tmcmillan>
```

TABLE 6.9 netstat switches

Switch	Purpose
-a	Displays all connections and listening ports
-b	Displays the executable involved in creating each connection or listening port
-e	Displays Ethernet statistics
-n	Displays addresses and port numbers in numerical form
-o	Displays the owning process ID associated with each connection
-p proto	Shows connections for the protocol specified by *proto*
-r	Displays the routing table

nslookup

The `nslookup` command is a command-line administrative tool for testing and troubleshooting DNS servers. It can be run in two modes, interactive and noninteractive. While noninteractive mode is useful when only a single piece of data needs to be returned, interactive allows you to query for either an IP address for a name or a name for an IP address without leaving `nslookup` mode.

A common scenario for using `nslookup` is when a system cannot resolve names, and you need to see what DNS server it is using.

The command syntax is as follows:

```
nslookup [-option] [hostname] [server]
```

Table 6.10 shows selected switches used with `nslookup`.

To enter interactive mode, simply enter `nslookup` as shown:

```
C:\> nslookup
Default Server: nameserver1.domain.com
Address: 10.0.0.1
```

When you do this, by default it will identify the IP address and name of the DNS server that the local machine is configured to use, if any, and then will go to the > prompt. At this prompt, you can enter either an IP address or a name, and the system will attempt to resolve the IP address to a name or the name to an IP address.

TABLE 6.10   nslookup switches

Switch	Purpose
All	Prints all options, current server, and host info
[no]debug	Provides debugging info
[no]d2	Provides exhaustive debugging info
[no]defname	Appends a domain name to each query
[no]recurse	Asks for a recursive answer to the query
[no]search	Uses the domain to search the list
[no]vc	Always uses a virtual circuit
domain=name	Sets the default domain name to *name*

The following are other queries that can be run and may prove helpful when troubleshooting name resolution issues:

- **Looking up different data types in the database (such as Microsoft records).** For example, the following command will filter for mail server records:

```
C: Nslookup
Set Type=mx
```

- **Querying directly from another name server (different from the one the local device is configured to use).** The command for the DNS server named some.dns.server in the somewhere.com domain is as follows:

```
nslookup somewhere.com some.dns.server
```

- **Performing a zone transfer.** This example is from wayne.net to dns.wayne.net:

```
C: nslookup
set Type=any
> ls -d wayne.net > dns.wayne.net
> exit
```

net use

Network shares can be mapped to drives to appear as if the resources are local. The net use command is used to establish network connections via a command prompt. For example, to connect to a shared network drive and make it your M drive, you would use the syntax net use m: \\server\share. Figure 6.40 shows an example of mapped drives. This can also be done in File Explorer, as shown in Figure 6.41.

net use can also be used to connect to a shared printer: net use lpt1: \\printername.

FIGURE 6.40   Mapped network drives

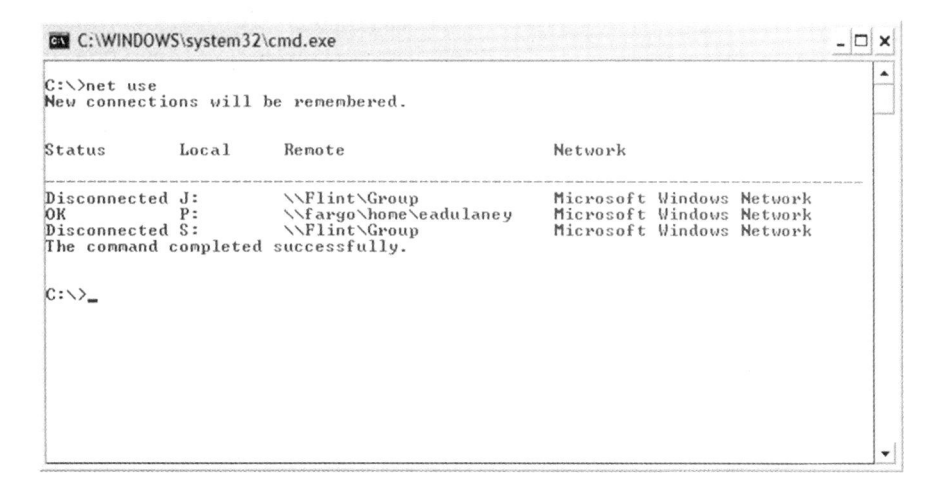

FIGURE 6.41 Mapping a drive

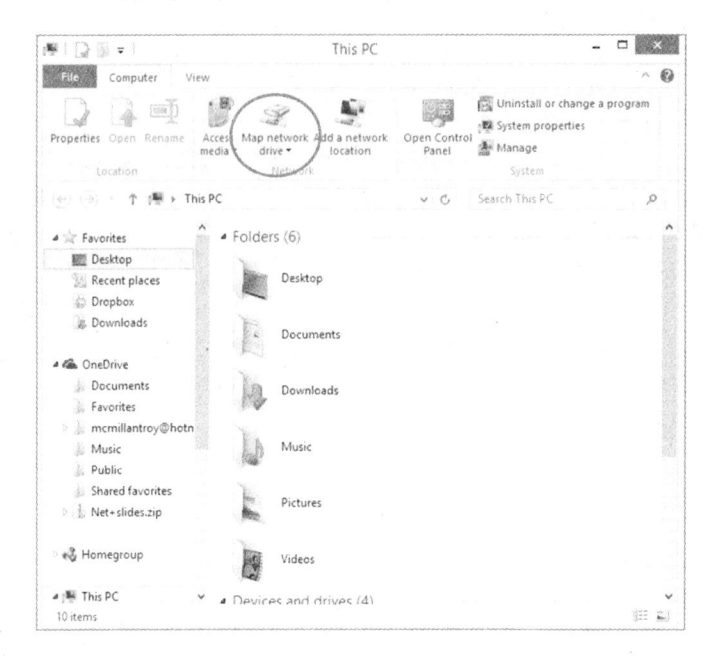

tracert

The `tracert` command (called `traceroute` in Linux) is used to trace the path of a packet through the network. Its best use is in determining exactly where in the network the packet is being dropped. It will show each hop (i.e. router) the packet crosses and how long it takes to do so. Figure 6.42 shows a partial display of a traced route to www.msn.com.

A common scenario for using `tracert` is when there is a slow remote connection, and you would like to find out which part of the path is problematic.

The syntax used is as follows:

```
tracert [-d] [-h MaxHops] [-w TimeOut] [-4] [-6] target [/?]
```

Table 6.11 shows some selected switches used with `tracert`.

pathping

This command displays information about network latency and network loss at intermediate hops between a source and destination—meaning it works in a similar fashion to `tracert`. An example of output is shown in Figure 6.43, showing the latency in the path to www.nascar.com.

1.5 Given a scenario, use the appropriate Microsoft command-line tools

FIGURE 6.42 Using tracert

```
C:\Users\tmcmillan>tracert www.msn.com
Tracing route to us.co1.cb3.glbdns.microsoft.com [70.37.131.153]
over a maximum of 30 hops:

  1    11 ms     1 ms     1 ms  10.88.2.6
  2     2 ms     2 ms     1 ms  208-47-7-130.dia.static.qwest.net [208.47.7.130]
  3     7 ms     7 ms     7 ms  frp-edge-04.inet.qwest.net [205.168.14.213]
  4     7 ms     7 ms     7 ms  frp-core-02.inet.qwest.net [205.171.22.49]
  5    22 ms    22 ms    22 ms  chx-edge-03.inet.qwest.net [67.14.38.1]
  6    22 ms    22 ms    23 ms  63-234-10-14.dia.static.qwest.net [63.234.10.14]
  7    23 ms    23 ms    23 ms  xe-0-1-2-0.ch1-16c-1b.ntwk.msn.net [207.46.43.204]
  8    24 ms    24 ms    24 ms  xe-0-1-0-0.ch1-96c-1a.ntwk.msn.net [207.46.46.133]
  9    34 ms    34 ms    34 ms  ge-2-1-0-0.ash-64cb-1b.ntwk.msn.net [207.46.45.14]
 10    38 ms    38 ms    38 ms  ge-4-0-0-0.nyc-64cb-1b.ntwk.msn.net [207.46.46.57]
 11    39 ms    38 ms    38 ms  xe-3-1-0-0.ewr-96cbe-1b.ntwk.msn.net [207.46.47.2]
 12    39 ms     *       39 ms  xe-3-0-0-0.ewr-96cbe-1a.ntwk.msn.net [207.46.43.250]
 13
```

TABLE 6.11 tracert switches

Switch	Purpose
-d	Prevents tracert from resolving IP addresses to hostnames
-h MaxHops	Specifies the maximum number of hops in the search for the target (30 by default)
-w TimeOut	Specifies the time, in milliseconds, to allow each reply before timeout using this tracert option
-4	Forces tracert to use IPv4 only
-6	Forces tracert to use IPv6 only
Target	Designates the destination, either an IP address or a hostname
/?	Shows detailed help about the command

Disk management

While the Disk Management utility can be used to manage the disk system, the command line can also be used to view and configure the system. Let's look at three important commands in that category.

FIGURE 6.43   pathping

```
C:\>hostname
DESKTOP-QSRHMTD

C:\>pathping www.nascar.com

Tracing route to e7436.g.akamaiedge.net [104.127.157.226]
over a maximum of 30 hops:
  0  DESKTOP-QSRHMTD.home [192.168.1.23]
  1  192.168.1.1
  2  *        *        *
Computing statistics for 25 seconds...
             Source to Here   This Node/Link
Hop  RTT    Lost/Sent = Pct  Lost/Sent = Pct  Address
 0                                             DESKTOP-QSRHMTD.home [192.168.1.23]
                              0/ 100 =  0%   |
 1   4ms    0/ 100 =  0%      0/ 100 =  0%   192.168.1.1

Trace complete.
```

chkdsk

You can use the Windows CHKDSK utility to create and display status reports for the hard disk. CHKDSK can also correct file system problems (such as cross-linked files) and scan for and attempt to repair disk errors. CHKDSK can be run from the command line by executing chkdsk, or you can use a version in File Explorer.

To use the File Explorer version, right-click the problem disk and select Properties. This will bring up the Properties dialog box for that disk, which shows the current status of the selected disk drive. By clicking the Tools tab at the top of the dialog box and then clicking the Check button in the Error Checking section, you can start CHKDSK.

Format

The FORMAT command is used to wipe data off disks and prepare them for new use. Before a hard disk can be formatted, it must have partitions created on it. (Partitioning is done in Windows using DISKPART, which was discussed earlier and in the next section.) The syntax for FORMAT is as follows:

```
FORMAT [volume] [switches]
```

The volume parameter describes the drive letter (e.g. D:), mount point, or volume name. Table 6.12 lists some common FORMAT switches.

There are other options as well to specify allocation sizes, the number of sectors per track, and the number of tracks per disk size. However, I don't recommend you use these unless you have a specific need. The defaults are just fine.

So, if you wanted to format your D: drive as NTFS with the name of HDD2, you would enter the following:

```
FORMAT D: /FS:NTFS /V:HDD2
```

1.5 Given a scenario, use the appropriate Microsoft command-line tools

TABLE 6.12 FORMAT switches

Switch	Purpose
`/FS:[filesystem]`	Specifies the type of file system to use (e.g. FAT, FAT32, or NTFS)
`/V:[label]`	Specifies the new volume label
`/Q`	Executes a quick format

TABLE 6.13 diskpart parameters

Parameter	Purpose
`ACTIVE`	Marks the selected partition as active
`ADD`	Adds a mirror to a simple volume
`ATTRIBUTES`	Manipulates volume or disk attributes
`ASSIGN`	Assigns a drive letter or mount point to the selected volume
`ATTACH`	Attaches a virtual disk file
`AUTOMOUNT`	Enables and disables automatic mounting of basic volumes
`BREAK`	Breaks a mirror set
`Osk dCLEAN`	Clears the configuration information or all information

> **WARNING:** Before you format anything, be sure you have it backed up, or be prepared to lose whatever is on that drive!

diskpart

The `diskpart` command shows the partitions and lets you manage them on the computer's hard drives. It's a universal tool for working with hard drives from the command line. It allows you to convert between disk types, extend/shrink volumes, and format partitions and volumes as well as list them, create them, and so on. The `diskpart` command sets the command prompt at the `diskpart` prompt as follows:

```
Diskpart>
```

Subcommands like those in listed Table 6.13 are then used.

TABLE 6.14   md command

Command	Purpose
`<drive>:`	Specifies the drive on which you want to create the new directory.
`<path>`	Specifies the name and location of the new directory. The maximum length of any single path is determined by the file system. This is a required parameter.
`/?`	Displays help at the command prompt.

This is only the beginning. You can find a list of all the available commands at http://technet.microsoft.com/en-us/library/bb490893.aspx.

File management

Some commands are used for file management tasks. Specifically, we'll cover three important commands.

md

The `md` command is the shorthand version of the `mkdir` command and is used to create a new folder (originally called a directory). Its syntax is:

```
md [<drive>:]<path>
```

The parameters are listed in Table 6.14.

rmdir

The remove directory command (i.e. `rmdir` command) deletes an existing directory. This command is the same as the `rd` command. Its syntax is:

```
rmdir [<drive>:]<path> [/s [/q]]
```

The parameters are in Table 6.15.

> **WARNING** When you run in quiet mode, the entire directory tree is deleted without confirmation. Ensure that important files are moved or backed up before using the `/q` command-line option.

1.5 Given a scenario, use the appropriate Microsoft command-line tools

TABLE 6.15 rmdir command

Command	Purpose
[<drive>:]<path>	Specifies the location and the name of the directory that you want to delete. Path is required. If you include a backslash (\) at the beginning of the specified path, then the path starts at the root directory (regardless of the current directory).
/s	Deletes a directory tree (the specified directory and all its subdirectories, including all files).
q	Specifies quiet mode. Does not prompt for confirmation when deleting a directory tree. The /q parameter works only if /s is also specified.
/?	Displays help at the command prompt.

robocopy

The `robocopy` command (Robust File Copy for Windows) is included with Windows 10 and 11 and has the big advantage of being able to accept a plethora of specifications and keep NTFS permissions intact in its operations. The /MIR switch, for example, can be used to mirror a complete directory tree.

You can find an excellent TechNet article on how to use `robocopy` at https://learn.microsoft.com/en-us/windows-server/administration/windows-commands/robocopy.

The syntax is as follows:

```
robocopy <Source> <Destination> [<File>[ ...]] [<Options>]
```

Some of the more common switches when using the copy option are in listed Table 6.16.

Informational

Some commands are used to collect information about settings and performance. In this section, you'll learn about four such commands, and you'll learn how to get information about using a command with which you might not be familiar.

hostname

You can use the `hostname` command to find out the name of the computer. This prints only the NetBIOS name of the PC. Following is an example of using the command; the hostname of the system is DESKTOP-QSRHMTD. After displaying the name, it returns to the previous prompt.

```
C:\>hostname
DESKTOP-QSRHMTD

C:\>
```

net user

The `net user` command is used to add, remove, and make changes to the user accounts on a computer—all from the command prompt. It has the following command syntax:

```
netuser [username [password | *] [/add] [options]] [/domain]]
[username [/delete] [/domain]] [/help] [/?]
```

TABLE 6.16   robocopy switches

Switch	Purpose
/s	Copies subdirectories. Note that this option excludes empty directories.
/e	Copies subdirectories. Note that this option includes empty directories.
/lev:<N>	Copies only the top *N* levels of the source directory tree.
/z	Copies files in restartable mode.
/b	Copies files in backup mode.
/efsraw	Copies all encrypted files in EFS RAW mode.
/copy:<copyflags>	Specifies the file properties to be copied. The following are the valid values for this option:
D	Data
A	Attributes
T	Time stamps
S	NTFS access control list (ACL)
O	Owner information
U	Auditing information
/dcopy:<copyflags>	Defines what to copy for directories. Default is DA. Options are D = data, A = attributes, and T = timestamps.

1.5 Given a scenario, use the appropriate Microsoft command-line tools

TABLE 6.17   netuse parameters

Parameter	Purpose
netuser	Displays a simple list of every user account, active or not, on the computer you're currently using
username	Displays the name of the user account
password	Modifies an existing password or assigns one when creating a new username
*	Used in place of a password to force the entering of a password in the Command Prompt window after executing the net user command
/add	Adds a new username on the system
/domain	Forces net user to execute on the current domain controller instead of the local computer
/delete	Removes the specified username from the system
/help	Displays detailed information

Parameters are in Table 6.17.

winver

The winver command shows details on the OS version running. Figure 6.44 shows an example. When the command is executed, the system will open a GUI dialog box, as shown, that tells all about the version of Windows running.

whoami

The whoami command is used to obtain username and group information along with security identifiers (SID), privileges, and logon identifiers (logon ID) for the current user (access token) on the local system. The syntax is:

```
whoami/parameter
```

The parameters are shown in Table 6.18.

[command name] /?

You can also get help information by typing /? after a command.

FIGURE 6.44 The winver command

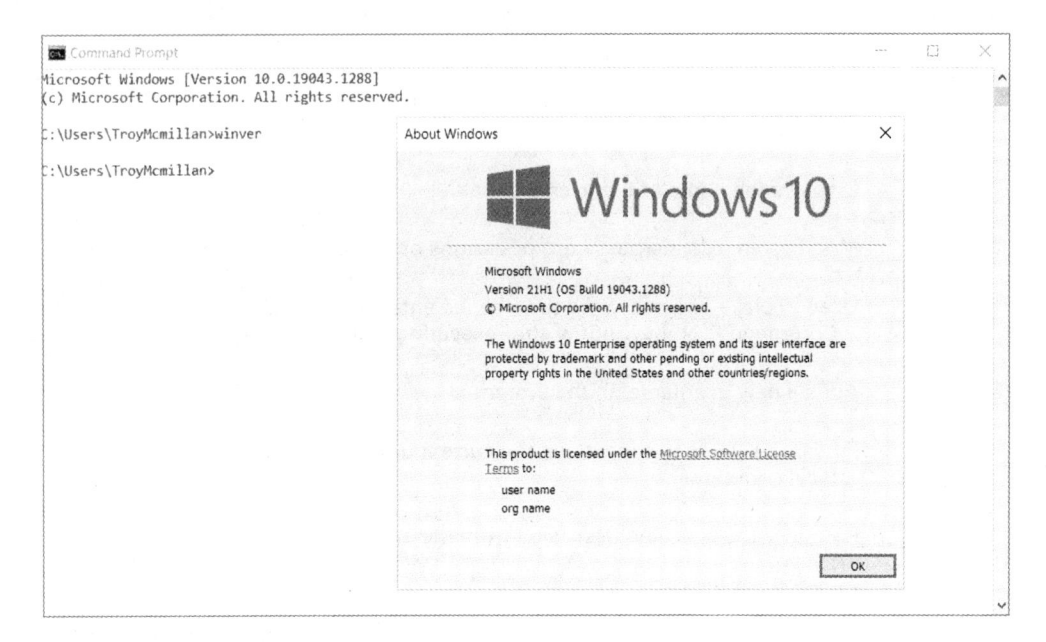

TABLE 6.18 whoami parameters

Parameter	Explanation
UPN	Displays the username in the user principal name (UPN) format.
FQDN	Displays the username in fully qualified domain name (FQDN) format.
/USER	Displays information on the current user along with the security identifier (SID).
/GROUPS	Displays group membership for current user, type of account, SIDs, and attributes.
/PRIV	Displays security privileges of the current user.
/LOGONID	Displays the logon ID of the current user.
/ALL	Displays the current username, groups belonged to along with SIDs, and privileges for the current user access token.
/FO format	Specifies the output format to be displayed. Valid values are TABLE, LIST, CSV. Column headings are not displayed with CSV format. The default format is TABLE.

Parameter	Explanation
/NH	Specifies that the column header should not be displayed in the output. This is valid only for TABLE and CSV formats.
/?	Displays description of the tool and guidance on its usage.

> **Note:** The /? switch is slightly faster and provides more information than the HELP command. HELP provides information only for system commands. (It does not include network commands.) For example, if you enter **help ipconfig** at a command prompt, you get no useful information (except to try /?); however, typing **ipconfig /?** provides the help file for the ipconfig command.

OS management

Finally, there are commands that are used to interact with and manage the OS. While there are many GUI tools that also perform these actions, many administrators prefer using the command line.

gpupdate

Configuration settings on Windows devices can be controlled through the use of policies. These policies can be applied on a local basis or on a domain and organizational unit basis when a device is a member of an Active Directory domain. When changes are made by an administrator to these policies, some types of changes will not take effect until the next scheduled refresh time.

An administrator can force a device to update its policies after a change by executing the gpupdate ("group policy update") command on the device. This is the syntax of the command:

```
gpupdate [/target:{computer|user}] [/force] [/wait:value] [/logoff] [/boot]
```

The parameters are found in Table 6.19.

gpresult

Group policies can be applied to Windows devices at the local, OU, and domain levels, and when the policies are applied to the device, the results can be somewhat confusing because of variables that can affect how the policies interact with one another. If you need to determine

TABLE 6.19 gpupdate parameters

Parameter	Explanation
/target: {computer | user }	Processes only the `computer` settings or the current `user` settings. By default, both the computer settings and the user settings are processed.
/force	Ignores all processing optimizations and reapplies all settings.
/wait: value	Number of seconds that policy processing waits to finish. The default is 600 seconds. 0 means "no wait," and -1 means "wait indefinitely."
/logoff	Logs off after the refresh has completed. This is required for those Group Policy client-side extensions that do not process on a background refresh cycle, but that do process when the user logs on, such as user Software Installation and Folder Redirection. This option has no effect if there are no extensions called that require the user to log off.
/boot	Restarts the computer after the refresh has completed. This is required for those Group Policy client-side extensions that do not process on a background refresh cycle but do process when the computer starts up, such as computer Software Installation. This option has no effect if there are no extensions called that require the computer to be restarted.

the policies that are in effect for a particular device, you can execute the `gpresult` command on the device, and it will list the currently applied and defective policies. This is the command syntax:

```
gpresult [/s <COMPUTER> [/u <USERNAME> [/p [<PASSWORD>]]]] [/user
[<TARGETDOMAIN>\]<TARGETUSER>] [/scope {user | computer}]
{/r | /v | /z | [/x | /h] <c06f0xx.png> [/f] | /?}
```

The parameters are covered in Table 6.20.

sfc

The System File Checker (SFC) is a command line–based utility that checks and verifies the versions of system files on your computer. If system files are corrupted, the SFC will replace the corrupted files with correct versions.

The syntax for the `SFC` command is as follows:

```
SFC [switch]
```

TABLE 6.20 gpresult parameters

Parameter	Explanation
/s <COMPUTER>	Specifies the name or IP address of a remote computer. Do not use backslashes. The default is the local computer.
/u <USERNAME>	Uses the credentials of the specified user to run the command. The default user is the user who is logged on to the computer that issues the command.
/p [<Password>]	Specifies the password of the user account that is provided in the /u parameter. If /p is omitted, gpresult prompts for the password. /p cannot be used with /x or /h.
/user [<TARGETDOMAIN>\]<TARGETUSER>	Specifies the remote user whose data is to be displayed.
/scope {user | computer}	Displays data for either the user or the computer. If /scope is omitted, gpresult displays data for both the user and the computer.
[/x | /h] <c06f0xx.png>	Saves the report in either XML (/x) or HTML (/h) format at the location and with the filename that is specified by the c06f0xx.png parameter. This cannot be used with /u, /p, /r, /v, or /z.
/f	Forces gpresult to overwrite the filename that is specified in the /x or /h option.
/r	Displays summary data.
/v	Displays verbose policy information. This includes detailed settings that were applied with a precedence of 1.
/z:	Displays all available information about Group Policy. This includes detailed settings that were applied with a precedence of 1 and higher.

While the switches vary a bit between different versions of Windows, Table 6.21 lists the most common ones available for SFC.

To run the SFC, you must be logged in as an administrator or have administrative privileges. If the SFC discovers a corrupted system file, it will automatically overwrite the file by using a copy held in the %systemroot%\system32\dllcache directory. If you believe that the dllcache directory is corrupted, you can use SFC /SCANNOW, SFC /SCANONCE, SFC /SCANBOOT, or SFC /PURGECACHE, depending on your needs, as described in Table 6.21, to repair its contents.

TABLE 6.21 SFC switches

Switch	Purpose
/CACHESIZE=X	Sets the Windows File Protection cache size in megabytes
/PURGECACHE	Purges the Windows File Protection cache and scans all protected system files immediately
/REVERT	Reverts SFC to its default operation
/SCANFILE (Windows 7 and Vista only)	Scans a file that you specify and fixes problems if they are found
/SCANNOW	Immediately scans all protected system files
/SCANONCE	Scans all protected system files once
/SCANBOOT	Scans all protected system files every time the computer is rebooted
/VERIFYONLY	Scans protected system files and does not make any repairs or changes
/VERIFYFILE	Identifies the integrity of the file specified and makes any repairs or changes
/OFFBOOTDIR	Does a repair of an offline boot directory
/OFFFWINDIR	Does a repair of an offline Windows directory

> **Tip:** The C:\Windows\System32 directory is where many of the Windows system files reside.

If you attempt to run SFC or many other utilities from a standard command prompt, you will be told that you must be an administrator running a console session to continue. Rather than opening a standard command prompt, choose Start > All Programs > Accessories and then right-click Command Prompt and choose Run as Administrator. The UAC will prompt you to continue, and then you can run SFC without a problem.

Exam essentials

Use command-line tools and their switches. These tools include `ipconfig`, `ping`, `tracert`, `netstat`, `shutdown`, `sfc`, `chkdsk`, `diskpart`, `gpupdate`, `gpresult`, `format`, `copy`, `xcopy`, `robocopy`, `net use`, and `net user`.

1.6 Given a scenario, configure Microsoft Windows settings

While most Windows settings can be managed through the applets contained in the Control Panel (and should be the first place to turn for configuration settings), other tools can be used for specific tasks.

Among the applets that every version of Windows has in common, CompTIA specifically singles out a few of them for you to know. In this section, you'll learn about these applets and other tools used to manage Windows settings.

Internet options

The configuration settings for Internet options provide a number of Internet connectivity possibilities. The tabs here include Connections, Security, General, Privacy, Content, Programs, and Advanced.

Content

The Content tab is used to manage content-related settings for the browser. Things you can do there include viewing and managing digital certificates; configuring settings for saving and suggesting usernames, passwords, and other form entries using Autocomplete; setting restrictions on web content using Content Advisor; managing settings for RSS feeds; and adjusting SSL and TLS settings for a secure connection.

Connections

As the name implies, from this tab you can configure connections for an Internet connection, a dial-up or virtual private network (VPN) connection, and LAN settings, as shown in Figure 6.45.

A scenario for using this tool would be when a user needs you to configure their laptop with a VPN connection to the office.

FIGURE 6.45 The Connections tab

Security

On the Security tab, as shown in Figure 6.46, you can choose both a zone and a security level for the zone. The zones include Internet, Local Intranet, Trusted Sites, and Restricted Sites. The default security level for most of the zones is between High and Medium-High, but you can also select lower levels.

A scenario in which you would use this tool is when a user wants more secure settings on their Internet connection while loosening the settings somewhat for their home network.

General

On the General tab, as shown in Figure 6.47, you can configure the home page that appears when the browser starts or a new tab is opened. You can also configure the history settings, search defaults, what happens by default when new tabs are opened, and the appearance of the browser (i.e. colors, languages, fonts, and accessibility). The General tab in Windows 11 is shown in Figure 6.48.

1.6 Given a scenario, configure Microsoft Windows settings 329

FIGURE 6.46 The Security tab

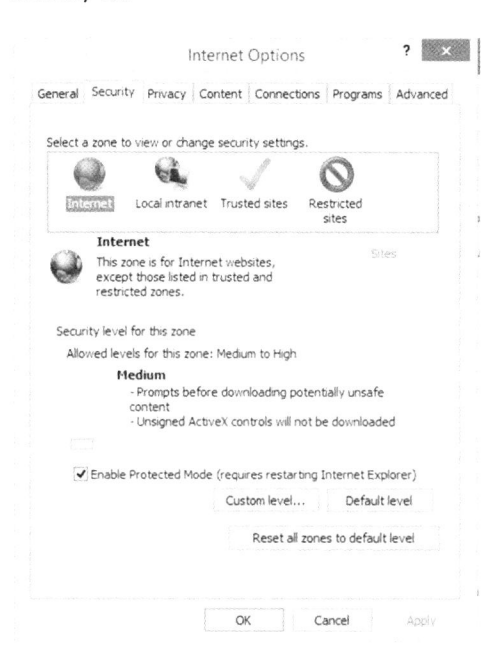

FIGURE 6.47 The General tab in Windows 10

FIGURE 6.48 The General tab in Windows 11

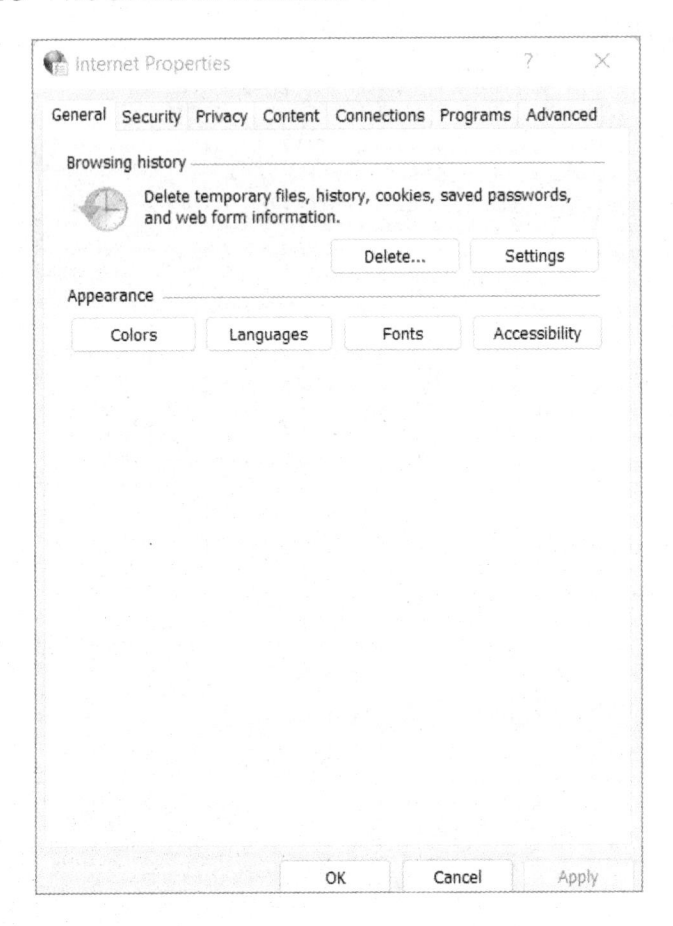

A scenario for using this tool is when a user would like to change their home page to their company intranet site.

Privacy

Privacy settings, as shown in Figure 6.49, allow you to configure the privacy level, choose whether you want to provide location information, use a pop-up blocker, and disable toolbars (and extensions) when InPrivate Browsing starts. The Privacy tab in Windows 11 is shown in Figure 6.50.

A scenario for using this tool would be when a user needs to disable pop-ups for a site that requires them to function properly.

FIGURE 6.49 The Privacy tab in Windows 10

FIGURE 6.50 The Privacy tab in Windows 11

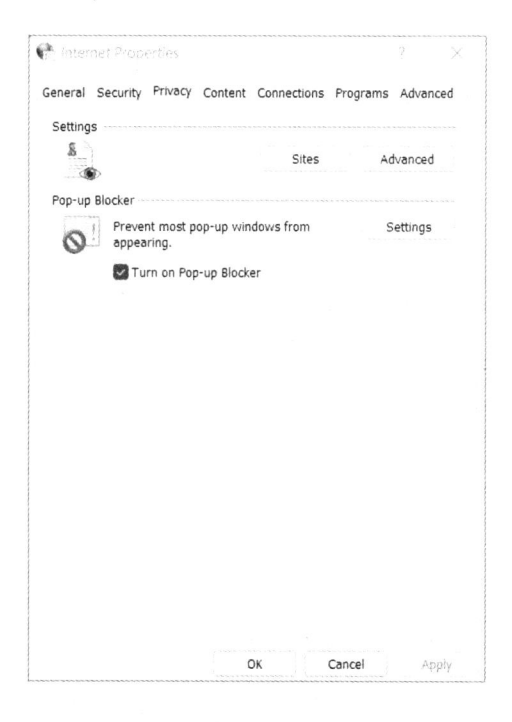

Programs

On the Programs tab in Windows 10, as shown in Figure 6.51, you specify which browser you want to be the default browser, what editor to use if HTML needs editing, and what programs to associate with various file types. You can also manage add-ons from here. The Programs tab in Windows 11 is shown in Figure 6.52.

A scenario for using this tool is when a user has an unusual file type that their system doesn't recognize. You could use this tool to associate the file type with the application that opens it.

Advanced

On the Advanced tab, as shown in Figure 6.53, you can reset settings to their default options. You can also toggle configuration settings for granular settings not found on other tabs.

FIGURE 6.51 The Programs tab in Windows 10

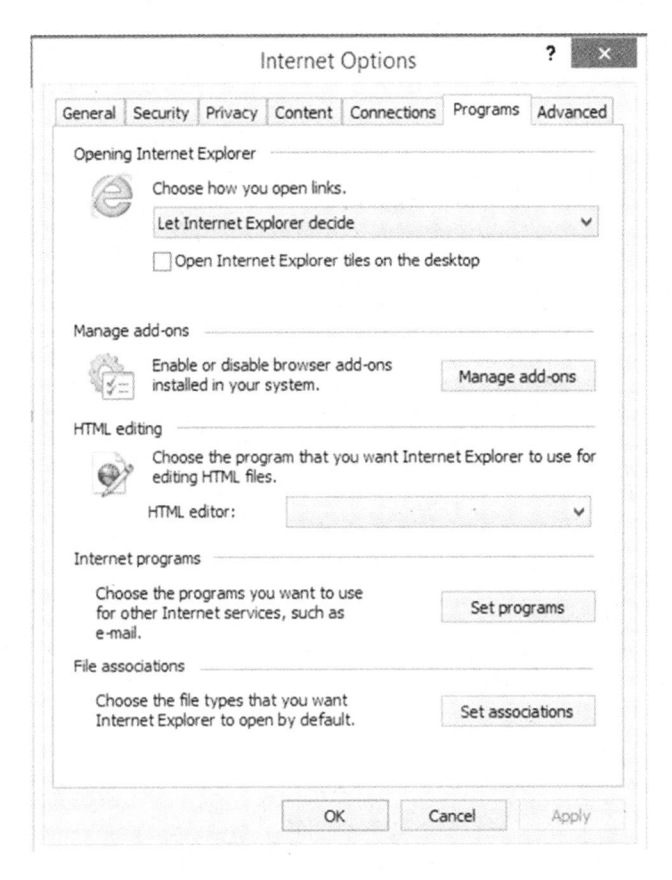

FIGURE 6.52 The Programs tab in Windows 11

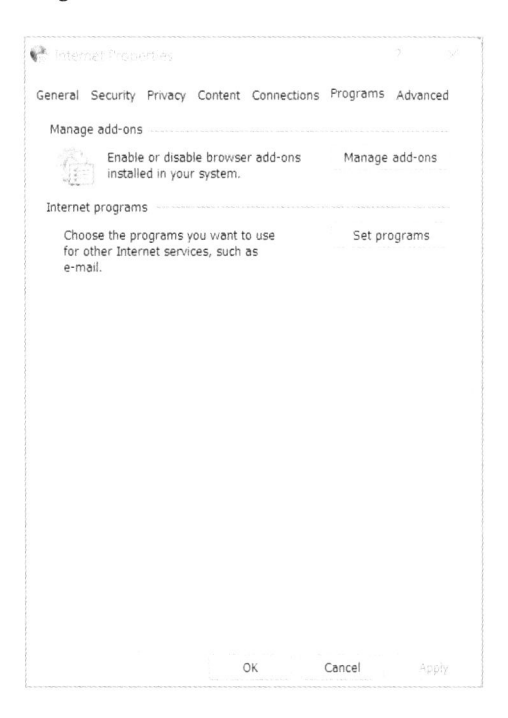

FIGURE 6.53 The Advanced tab

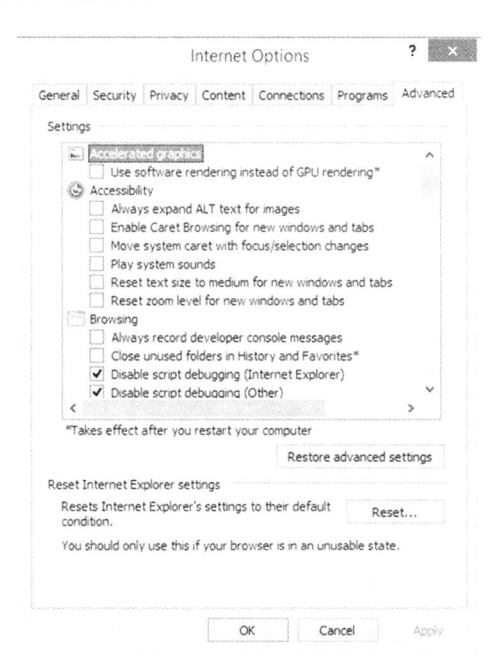

A scenario for using this tab would be when a user has played with the settings and would like to move them back to the default settings; this tool will do it.

Devices and Printers

The Devices and Printers applet is the place where printers and other devices are managed. This tool is divided into three sections, with printers in one, multimedia devices in another, and other devices in a third section, as shown in Figure 6.54. To manage any device, you right-click the device and select its properties. The printers also can be double-clicked, and you can see what's printing, manage the print queue, and adjust additional settings. The Devices and Printers applet in Windows 11 is shown in Figure 6.55.

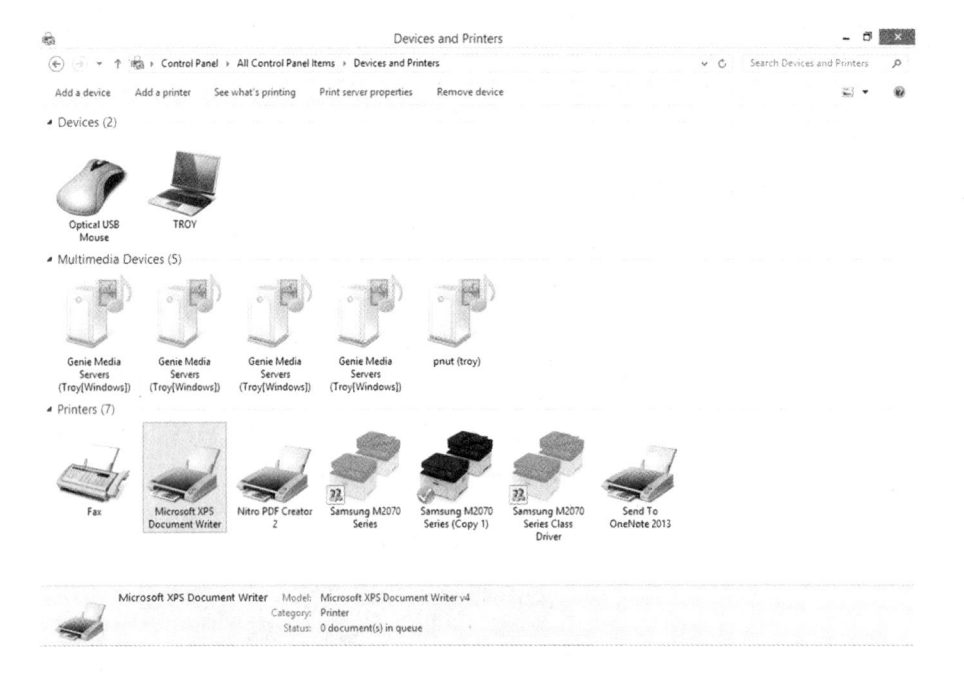

Programs and Features

Formerly known as Add/Remove Programs, this tool allows you to manage the programs running on the machine and the Windows features as well. Windows features are tools and utilities that come with the systems, which may or may not be installed and running. You can uninstall any program you have installed here. When you select Turn Windows Features On or Off from the menu on the left, you get a box that allows you to enable and disable Windows features, as shown in Figure 6.56.

FIGURE 6.54 The Devices and Printers applet in Windows 10

1.6 Given a scenario, configure Microsoft Windows settings 335

FIGURE 6.55 The Devices and Printers applet in Windows 11

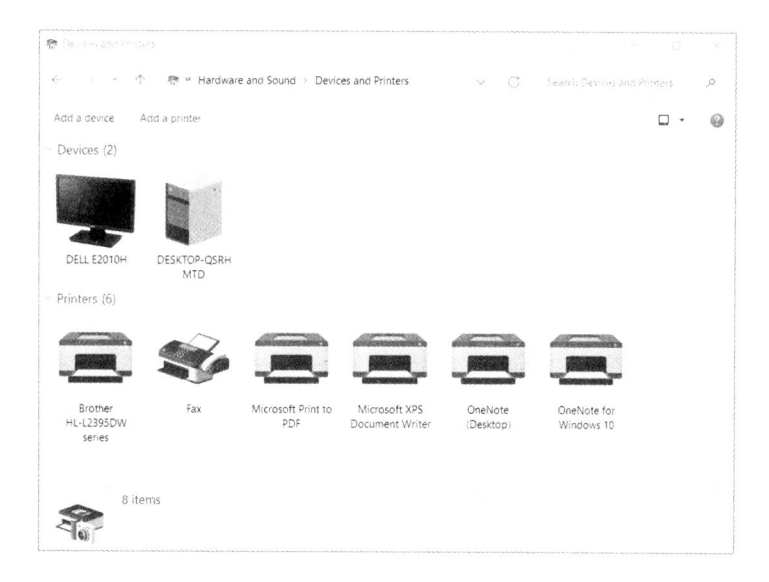

FIGURE 6.56 Programs and features

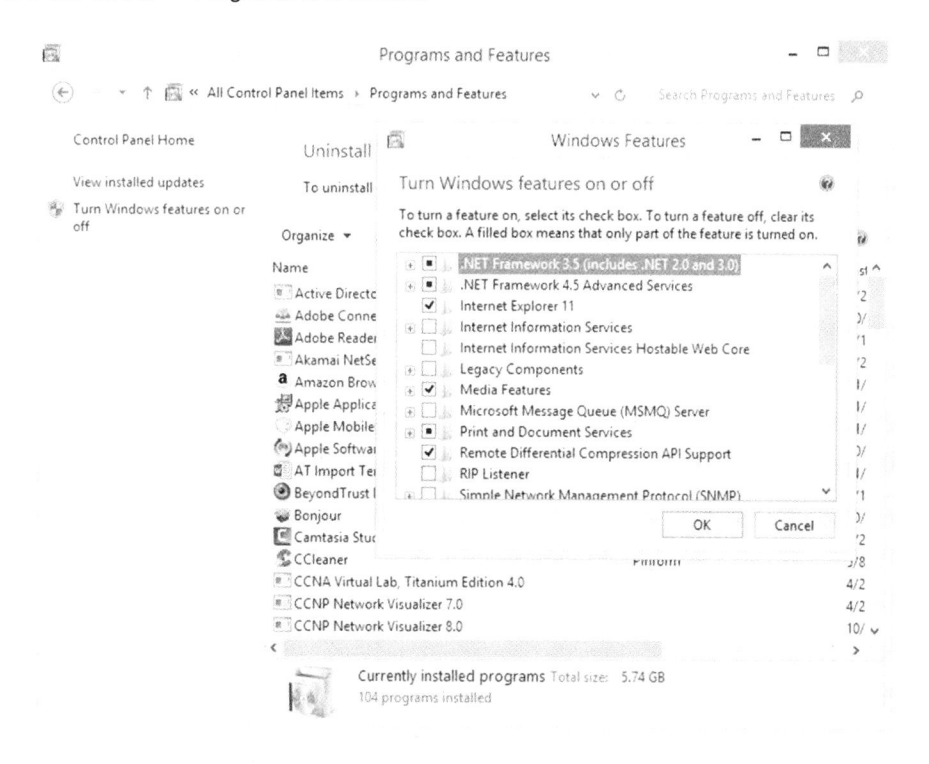

Network and Sharing Center

All network settings have been combined in an applet called Network and Sharing Center, where many sharing functions have also been relocated. While most of the tools are dedicated to creating and managing both wireless and wired network connections, some Advanced Sharing functions are available in this applet. Figure 6.57 shows this applet.

System

The System utility allows you to view and configure various system elements. From within this one relatively innocuous panel, you can make a large number of configuration changes to a Windows machine. The different Windows versions have different options available in this panel, but they will include some of the following: General, Network Identification, Device Manager, Hardware, Hardware Profiles, User Profiles, Environment, Startup/Shutdown, Performance, System Restore, Automatic Updates, Remote, Computer Name, and Advanced. System is found in the Control Panel.

The General tab gives you an overview of the system, such as OS version, registration information, basic hardware levels (of the processor and RAM), and the service pack level that's installed, if any.

FIGURE 6.57 The Network and Sharing Center applet

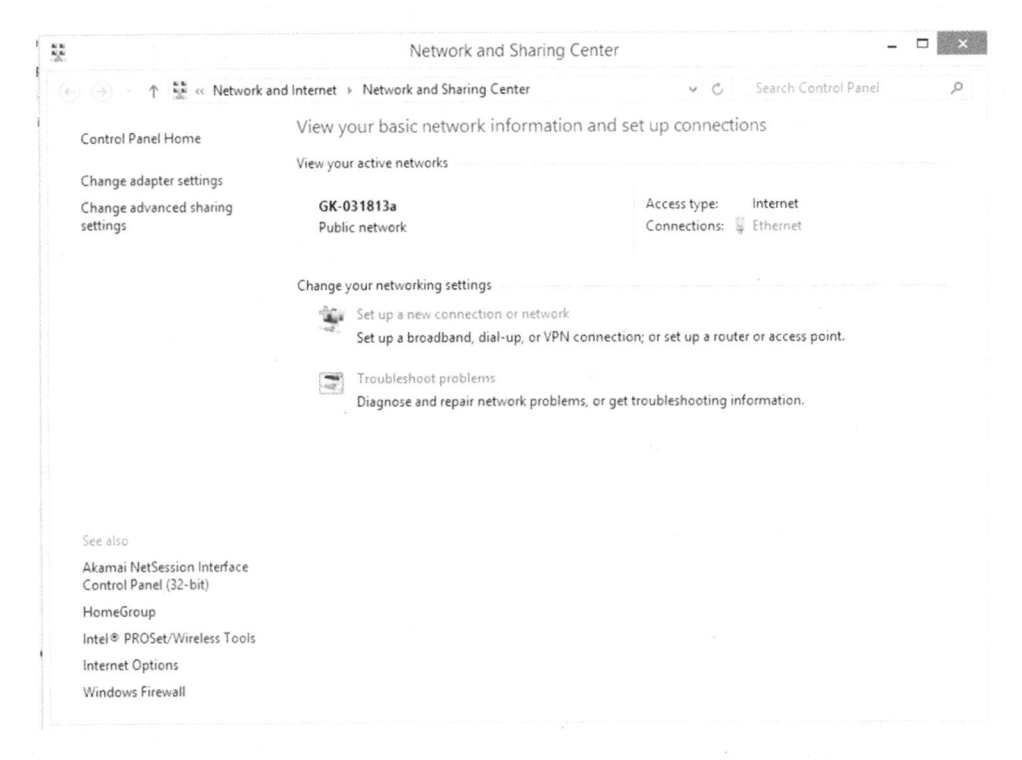

1.6 Given a scenario, configure Microsoft Windows settings 337

> **General**
>
> To access System Properties in Windows 11, enter **SystemPropertiesHardware.exe** in the search bar.

Performance (virtual memory)

Performance settings are configured on the Advanced tab, as shown in Figure 6.58. Clicking the Settings button allows you to change the visual effects used on the system and configure Data Execution Prevention (DEP), which is a security feature that prevents the execution of certain processes in key files. You can also configure virtual memory on the Advanced tab. Virtual memory is the paging file used by Windows as RAM.

In most cases, you should never change the Virtual Memory section, but in cases where performance is lagging, you can try to dedicate more disk space for this function.

FIGURE 6.58   The Advanced tab

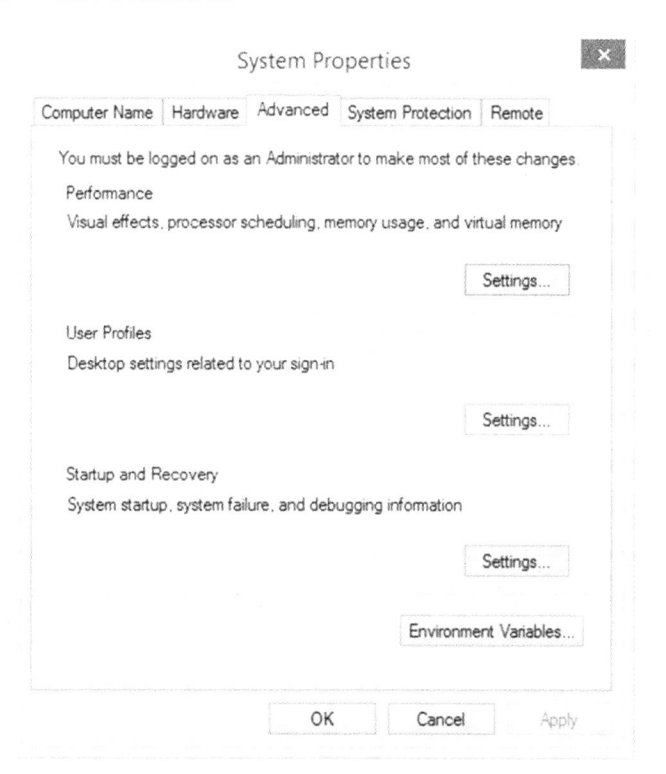

Remote settings

On the Remote tab, as shown in Figure 6.59, you can choose whether to allow Remote Assistance to be enabled. The Remote tab in Windows 11 is shown in Figure 6.60.

System Protection

On the System Protection tab, as shown in Figure 6.61, you can choose to do a System Restore as well as create a manual restore point and see the date and time associated with the most recent automatic restore point.

Windows Defender Firewall

As the name implies, the Windows Defender Firewall applet can be used to manage the firewall included with the OS. Figure 6.62 shows an example. In this case, the computer's firewall settings are being managed by the domain administrator. When the computer is outside of that network, the firewall settings are available to the user of the computer.

FIGURE 6.59 The Remote tab in Windows 10

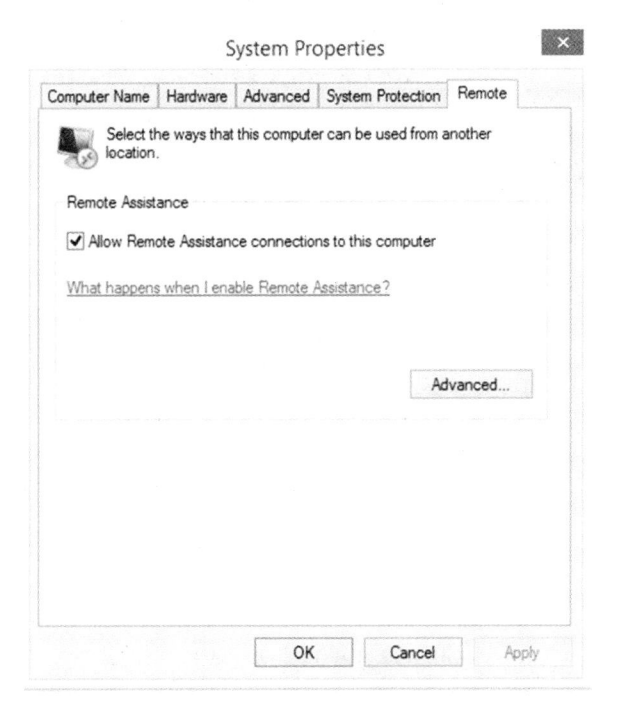

1.6 Given a scenario, configure Microsoft Windows settings 339

FIGURE 6.60 The Remote tab in Windows 11

FIGURE 6.61 The System Protection tab

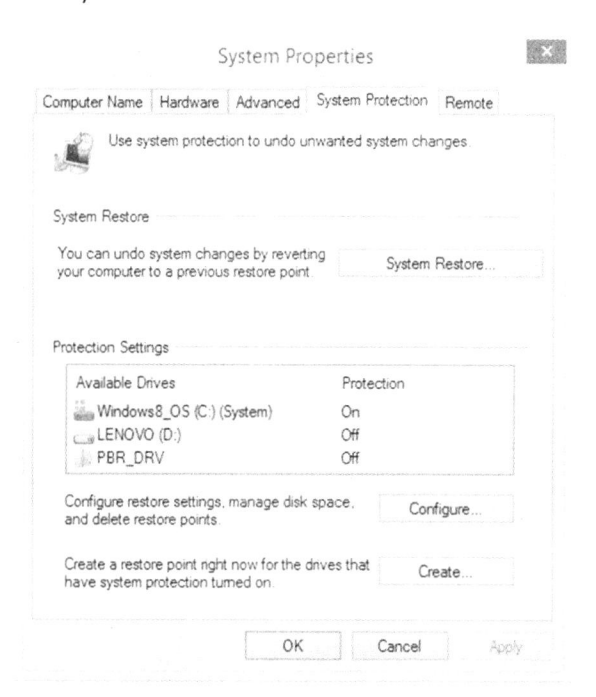

FIGURE 6.62 The Windows Firewall

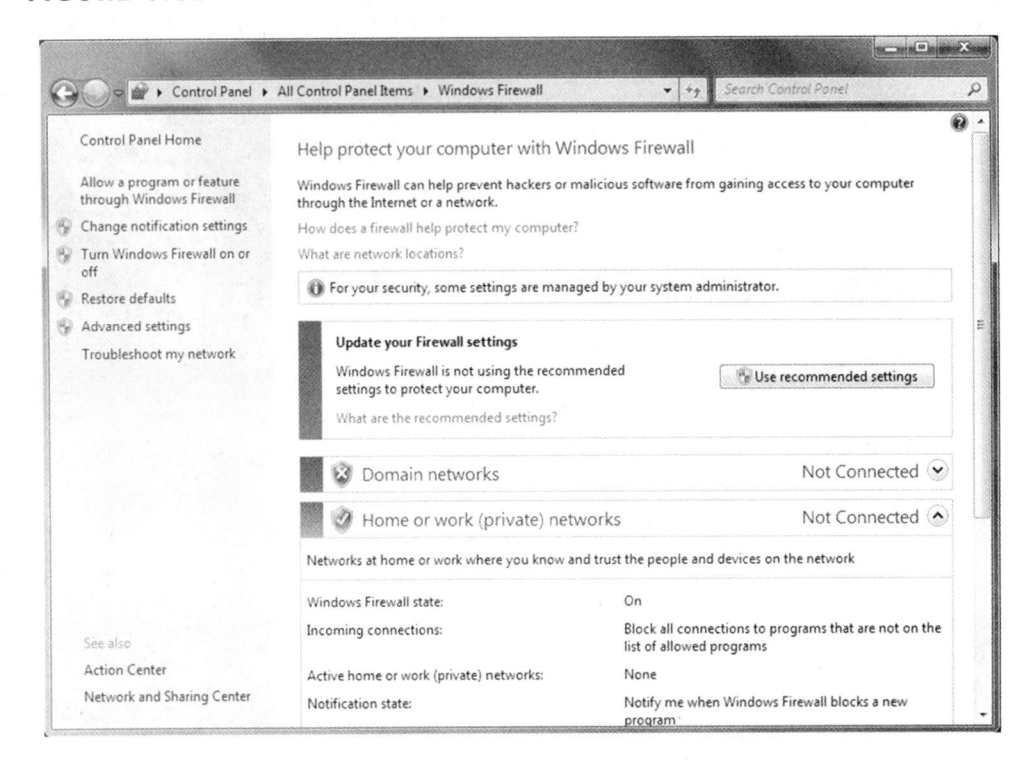

Mail

Mail, formerly known as Windows Mail, is the email client built into Windows 10 and 11. It contains preset server configurations for Outlook.com, Office 365, Gmail, iCloud, Yahoo! Mail, and AOL Mail, as well as other Exchange Server and Internet Message Access Protocol (IMAP) accounts. Figure 6.63 shows the interface.

Sound

Windows 10 and 11 have a Control Panel item called Sound that is used to manage all sound settings. You can manage the input devices (i.e. microphones, lines in, etc.) and the output devices (i.e. speakers, headphones, etc.) in one place. Moreover, you can enable and disable the various Windows sounds that you hear when certain events occur. Figure 6.64 shows the Sound applet.

> **NOTE**
> To open the classic Sounds applet in Windows 11, first enter **sound**s in the search bar and then select Sound Settings. Then go to the bootup of the next page and select More Sound Settings.

FIGURE 6.63 Mail

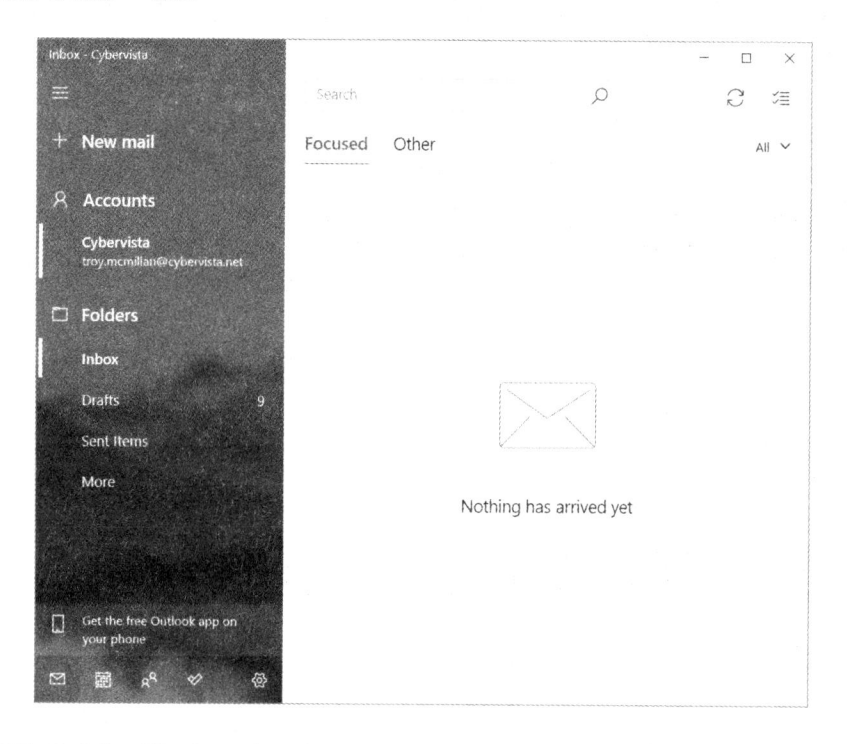

FIGURE 6.64 The Sound applet

User Accounts

The User Accounts dialog box lets you create and manage user accounts, parental controls, and related settings. The default users created are Administrator, Guest, and the administrative account created during the install. It is shown in Figure 6.65. This applet has the same functions but looks different in Windows 11, as shown in Figure 6.66.

Device Manager

You learned about using Device Manager to troubleshoot device issues earlier in this chapter, in the section "Device Manager (devmgmt.msc)." The interface is shown in Figure 6.67.

Indexing Options

The Indexing Options applet allows you to index data, resulting in faster searches. While it will automatically index certain common locations on your drive, such as offline files, Start menu, user profile, and Edge browsing history, you can have it index other data sets as well. In some cases, rebuilding the index may be required when you are failing to find certain items that you know are there. The Indexing Options applet is shown in Figure 6.68.

Administrative Tools

Table 6.22 lists the Windows Administrative Tools, and the purpose for each, which you need to know for this objective. The majority of these run in the MMC.

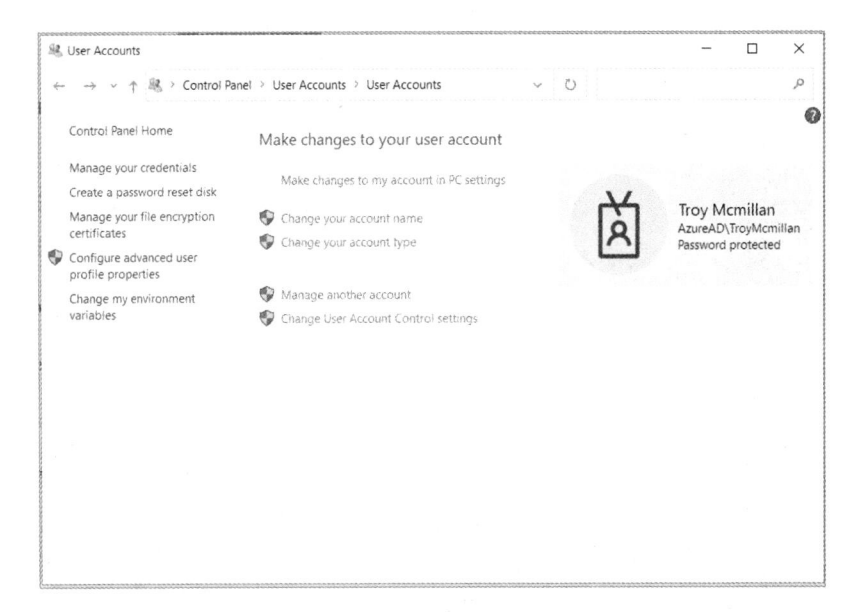

FIGURE 6.65 User Accounts in Windows 10

FIGURE 6.66 User Accounts in Windows 11

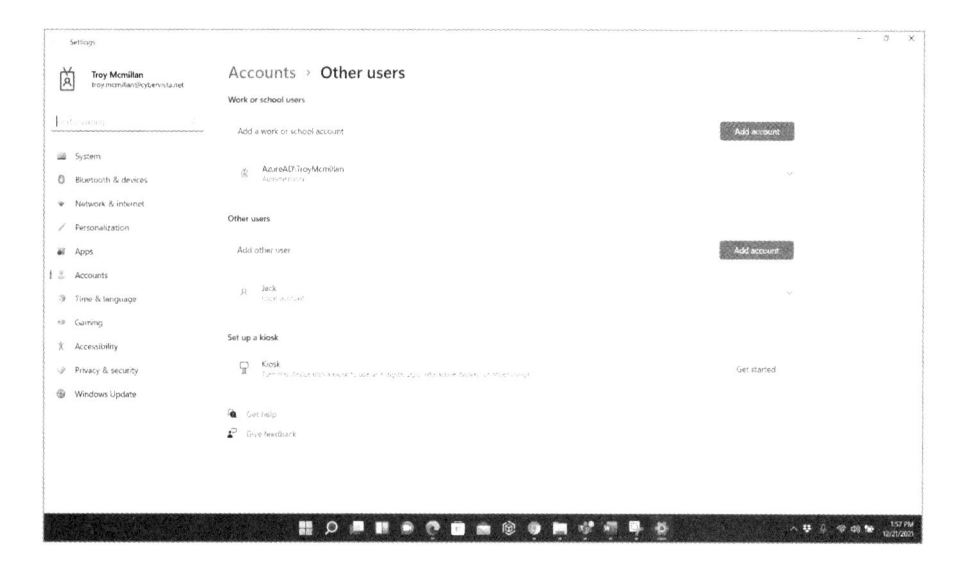

FIGURE 6.67 The Device Manager

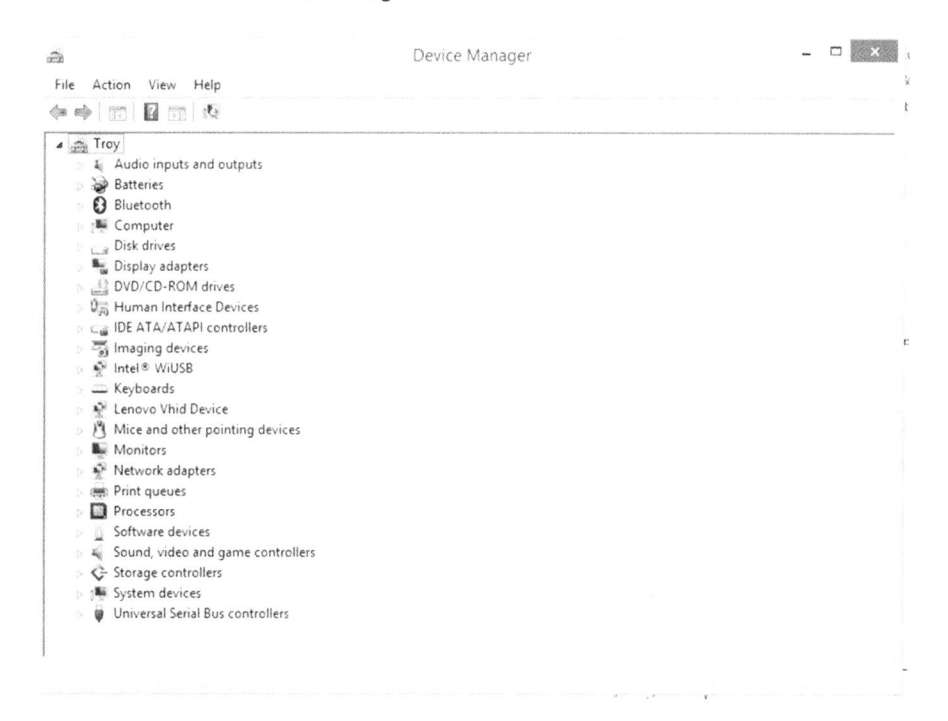

FIGURE 6.68 Indexing Options

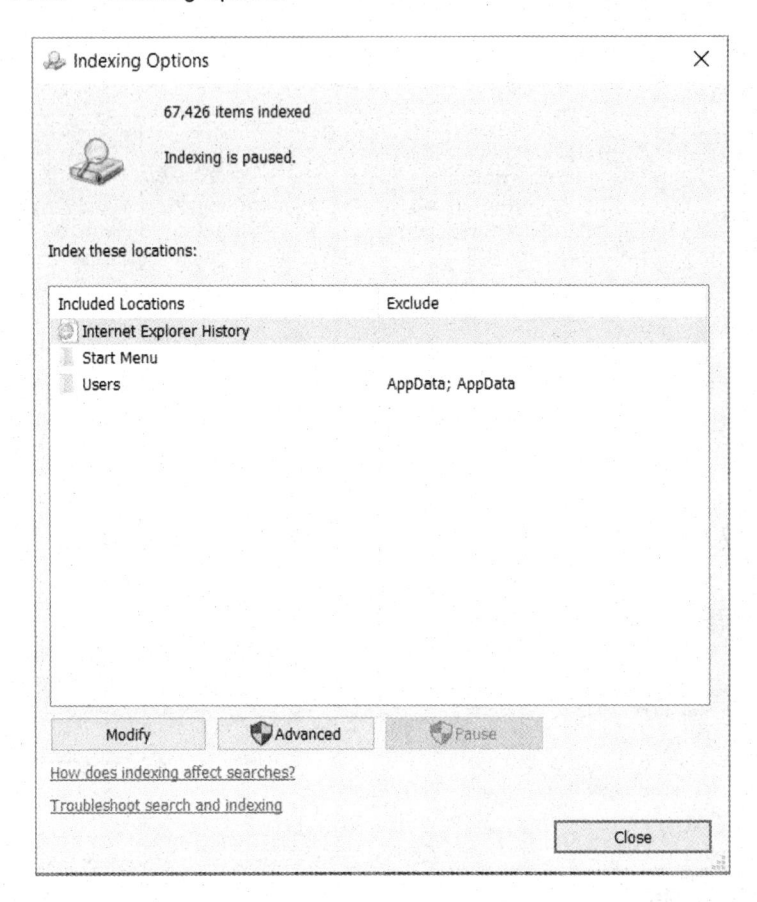

TABLE 6.22 Windows Administrative Tools

Tool	Purpose
Computer Management	The Computer Management Console includes the following system tools: Device Manager, Event Viewer, Shared Folders, and Performance/Performance Logs and Alerts. (Based on the OS you are running, you might also see Local Users and Groups or Task Scheduler.) Computer Management also has the Storage area, which lets you manage removable media, defragment your hard drives, and manage partitions through the Disk Management utility. Finally, you can manage system services and applications through Computer Management as well.
Device Manager	Device Manager shows a list of all installed hardware and lets you add and remove items, update drivers, and more.

1.6 Given a scenario, configure Microsoft Windows settings

Tool	Purpose
Local Users and Groups	If Local Users and Groups is not visible in the left pane of MMC, choose File > Add/Remove Snap-In and select Local Users and Groups from the list of possible snap-ins. You can choose to manage the local computer or another computer (requiring you to provide its address). The built-in groups for a domain are a superset of local groups. The default users created are Administrator, Guest, and the administrative account created during the install.
Performance Monitor	Performance Monitor displays performance counters. Two tools are available—System Monitor and Performance Logs and Alerts. System Monitor will show the performance counters in graphical format. The Performance Logs and Alerts utility collects the counter information and then sends it to a console (such as the one in front of the admin, so they can be aware of the problem) or an event log.
Services	The Services utility can be added to the MMC. This tool was discussed earlier in this chapter, in the "Task Manager" section.
System Configuration	MSConfig, known as the System Configuration utility, helps you troubleshoot startup problems by allowing you to selectively disable individual items that normally are executed at startup. It works in all versions of Windows, although the interface window is slightly different among each version.
Task Scheduler	Task Scheduler allows you to configure jobs to automatically run unattended. For the Run frequency, you can choose any of the following options: Daily, Weekly, Monthly, One Time Only, When the Computer Starts, or When You Log On. You can access a job's advanced properties any time after the job has been created. To do so, double-click the icon for the job in the Scheduled Tasks screen. In the resulting dialog box, you can configure such things as the username and password associated with the job, the actual command line used to start the job (in case you need to add parameters to it), and the working directory. At any time, you can delete a scheduled job by deleting its icon, or you can simply disable a job by removing the check mark from the Enabled box on the Task tab of the task's Properties dialog box. For jobs scheduled to run, a picture of a clock appears in the bottom-left corner of the icon; jobs not scheduled to run do not have that clock.
Component Services	Component Services is an MMC snap-in that allows you to administer as well as deploy component services and to configure behavior such as security. (Component Services is located beneath Administrative Tools.)
Data Sources	Open Database Connectivity (ODBC) Data Source Administrator (located beneath Administrative Tools) allows you to interact with database management systems.

(Continued)

TABLE 6.22 (Continued)

Tool	Purpose
Windows Memory Diagnostics	The Windows Memory Diagnostic Tool (located beneath Administrative Tools) can be used to check a system for memory problems. For the tool to work, the system must be restarted. The two options that it offers are to restart the computer now and check for problems or wait and check for problems on the next restart. Upon reboot, the test will take several minutes, and the display screen will show which pass number is being run and the overall status of the test (i.e. percentage complete). When the memory test concludes, the system will restart again, and nothing related to it is apparent until you log in. If the test is without error, you'll see a message that no errors were found. If anything else is found, the results will be displayed.
Windows Firewall	Windows Firewall (Start > Control Panel > Windows Firewall) is used to block access from the network. While host-based firewalls are not as secure as other types of firewalls, this provides much better protection than previously and is turned on by default. It is also included in the Security component of the Action Center and can be tweaked significantly using the Advanced Settings.
Advanced Security	Continuing the discussion of Windows Firewall, once you click Advanced Settings, Windows Firewall with Advanced Security opens. Here, you can configure inbound and outbound rules as well as import and export policies and perform monitoring. Monitoring is not confined only to the firewall; you can also monitor security associations and connection security rules. Not only can this MMC snap-in do simple configuration, but it can also configure remote computers and work with Group Policy.
User Account Management	Used to create, delete, and configure properties of user accounts.

File Explorer Options

The File Explorer Options dialog box allows you to configure how folders are displayed in File Explorer. It has three tabs and a collection of settings on each tab. Let's look at these tabs and their settings.

View Hidden Files

Many important system files are hidden normally to prevent inadvertent deletions by users. On the View tab, shown in Figure 6.69, beneath Advanced Settings, you can choose the option Show Hidden Files, Folders, and Drives, which when enabled will allow you to see those items. The opposite of this—the default setting—is Don't Show Hidden Files, Folders, or Drives. Radio buttons allow you to choose only one of these options.

FIGURE 6.69 The View tab

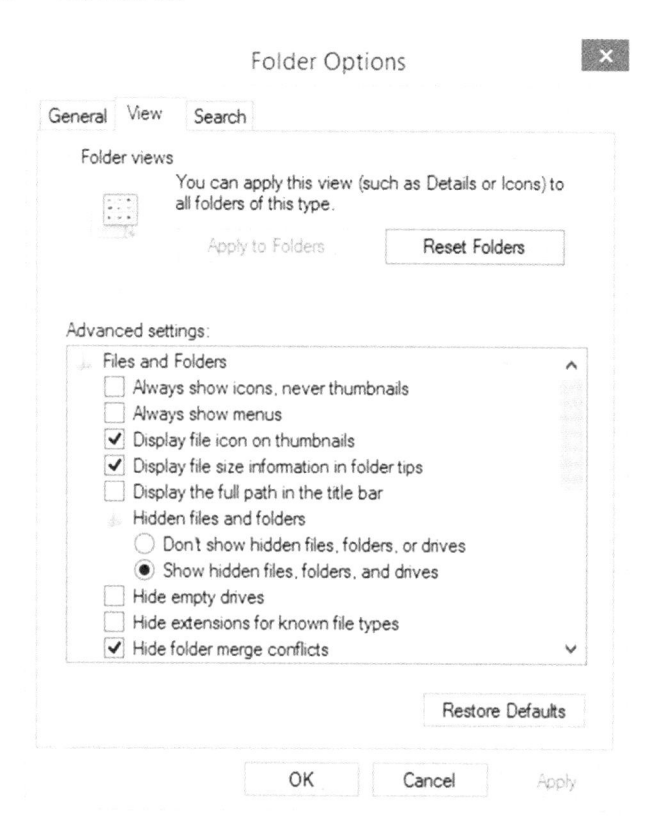

[Screenshot of Folder Options dialog, View tab, showing Advanced settings for Files and Folders including checkboxes for showing hidden files, hiding extensions, etc.]

A related checkbox that you should also clear in order to see all files is Hide Protected Operating System Files (recommended). When this checkbox is cleared, those files will also appear in the view you are seeing.

Hiding these files is recommended so that users do not inadvertently delete or change these critical files. Hiding them is the default setting.

Hide Extensions

On the View tab, shown in Figure 6.69, you must clear the checkbox Hide Extensions for Known File Types in order for the extensions to be shown with the files.

General Options

You can configure the layout on the General tab of Folder Options (shown in Figure 6.70). Browsing options allow you to choose whether each folder will open in its own folder or the same folder. The Navigation Pane setting allows you to control what items are included in the tree structure that appears to the left when using File Explorer.

FIGURE 6.70 The General tab

View Options

Along with the setting that allows you to hide or show file extensions and to show hidden files are a number of other settings that affect what you see when you use File Explorer (as shown in Figure 6.69 earlier). They include the following:

Always Show Icons, Never Thumbnails   Always show icons rather than thumbnail previews of files. Use this setting if thumbnail previews are slowing down your computer.

Always Show Menus   Always show menus above the toolbar. Use this setting if you want access to the classic menus, which are hidden by default.

Display File Icon on Thumbnails   Always shows the icon for a file, in addition to the thumbnail (for easier access to a related program).

Display File Size Information in Folder Tips   See the size of a folder in a tip when you point to the folder.

Hide Protected Operating System Files See all system files that are usually hidden from view.

Hide Empty Drives in the Computer Folder Show removable media drives (such as card readers) in the Computer folder, even if they currently don't have media inserted.

Launch Folder Windows in a Separate Process Increase the stability of Windows by opening every folder in a separate part of memory.

Restore Previous Folder Windows at Logon Automatically open the folders that you were using when you last shut down Windows whenever you start your computer.

Show Drive Letters Hide or show the drive letter of each drive or device in the Computer folder.

Show Encrypted or Compressed NTFS Files in Color Display encrypted or compressed NTFS files with unique color coding to identify them.

Show Pop-Up Description for Folder and Desktop Items Turn off the tips that display file information when you point to files.

Show Preview Handlers in Preview Pane Never show or always show the contents of files in the Preview pane. Use this setting to improve your computer's performance or if you don't want to use the Preview pane.

Use Check Boxes to Select Items Add checkboxes to file views for easier selection of several files at once. This can be useful if it's difficult for you to hold down the Ctrl key while clicking to select multiple files.

When typing into list view, there are two radio buttons: Automatically Type into the Search Box and Select the Type Item in the View. They are explained below.

Automatically Type into the Search Box Automatically places the cursor in the Search box when you start typing.

Select the Type Item in the View Does not automatically put the cursor in the Search box when you start typing.

Power Options

In Power Options, you can configure different power schemes to adjust power consumption, dictating when devices—the display and the computer—will turn off or be put to sleep. Through the Advanced Settings, you can configure the need to enter a password to revive the devices, as well as configure wireless adapter settings, Internet options (namely, JavaScript), and the system's Sleep policy. Common choices are covered in the following sections.

Hibernate

Hibernate saves your workspace (i.e. all your open windows) and then turns the computer off.

Power plans

Power plans are collections of power settings that determine when various components in the device are shut down. There are some built-in plans available, or you can create your own. There are three default plans: Balanced, which strikes a balance between performance and saving power; Power Saver, which errs on the side of saving power at the expense of performance; and High Performance, which errs on the side of performance over power saving. These options appear on the opening page when you open Power Options, as shown in Figure 6.71. To create a power plan, select Create a Power Plan from the tree menu on the left. To open this box in Windows11, enter **power** in the Search box and select Edit Power Plan.

Sleep/suspend

Sleep/suspend places your computer into an even deeper energy-saving mode than Standby, where it uses even less power.

FIGURE 6.71 Power Options in Windows 10

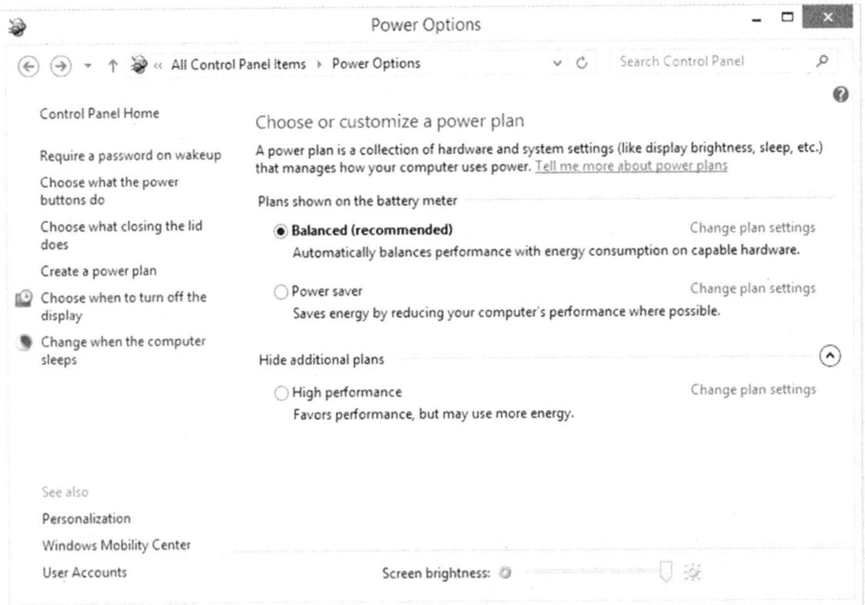

Standby

Standby places your computer into energy-saving mode, where it uses little power.

Choose what closing the lid does

This setting, which can contain different settings for when the system is plugged in and when on battery, allows for configuring the behavior when closed. The choices are shown in Figure 6.72.

Turn on Fast Startup

This setting that Microsoft recommends saves some data to the hard drive, which makes startup much faster. Be aware this setting can cause issues in the following scenarios and may need to be disabled:

- Computer cannot perform a regular shutdown: Because you are required to shut down your PC when applying new system updates, new system updates will be affected because of Fast Startup. You will need to disable Fast Startup to allow the restart required by the update.
- Windows hard disk will be locked, so if configured to dual-boot and you boot in another OS and then access or modify items on the disk or partition of the hibernating Windows PC, it can result in corruption.
- When you turn down a computer with Fast Startup enabled, you will fail to access the BIOS/UEFI settings on some systems.

FIGURE 6.72 Choosing what closing the lid does

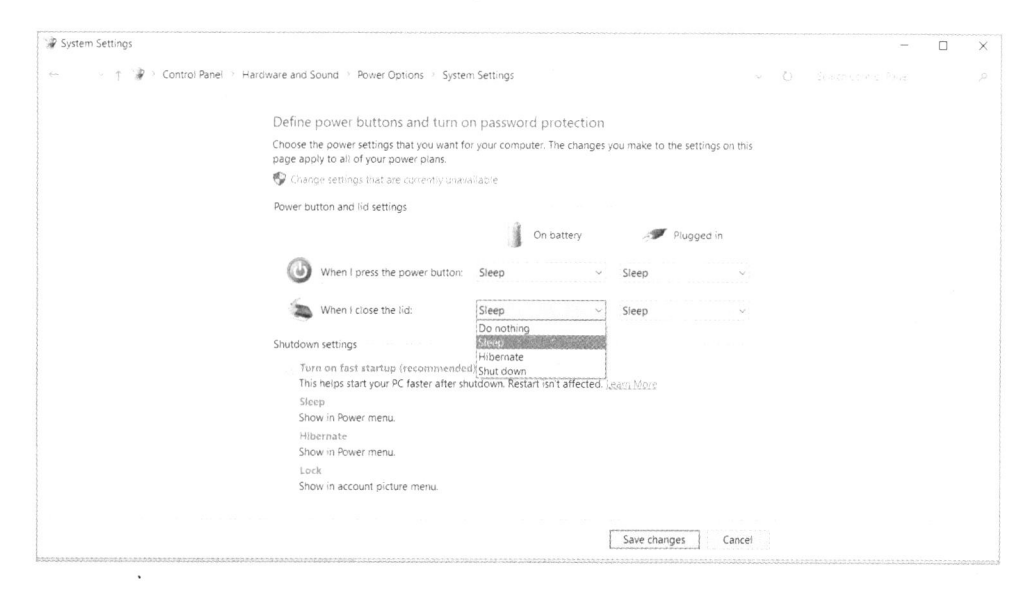

USB Selective Suspend

The USB 3.0 specification allows a device to enter suspended state when not in use. This mechanism is known as USB Selective Suspend and requires the software to cancel all transfers to the device and then sends the device to the suspended state.

Ease of Access

Ease of Access is a collection of settings that may make using the system a bit easier for those with disabilities. These include settings to add additional brightness, narrate screen readings, and enlarge the cursor. Selected settings are shown in Figure 6.73.

Time and Language

When you click on the Time and Language tile in the Settings applet, you will be presented with the screen shown in Figure 6.74. This box looks different in Windows 11, as shown in Figure 6.75, but offers the same functions.

Here you can create settings for the date time and time zone. While not the focus of this section, notice you can also set the region in which you're located and the languages(s) you need to support. Finally, there is a section for setting up the microphone and the voice that is used if the system is reading or talking to you.

FIGURE 6.73 Ease of Access

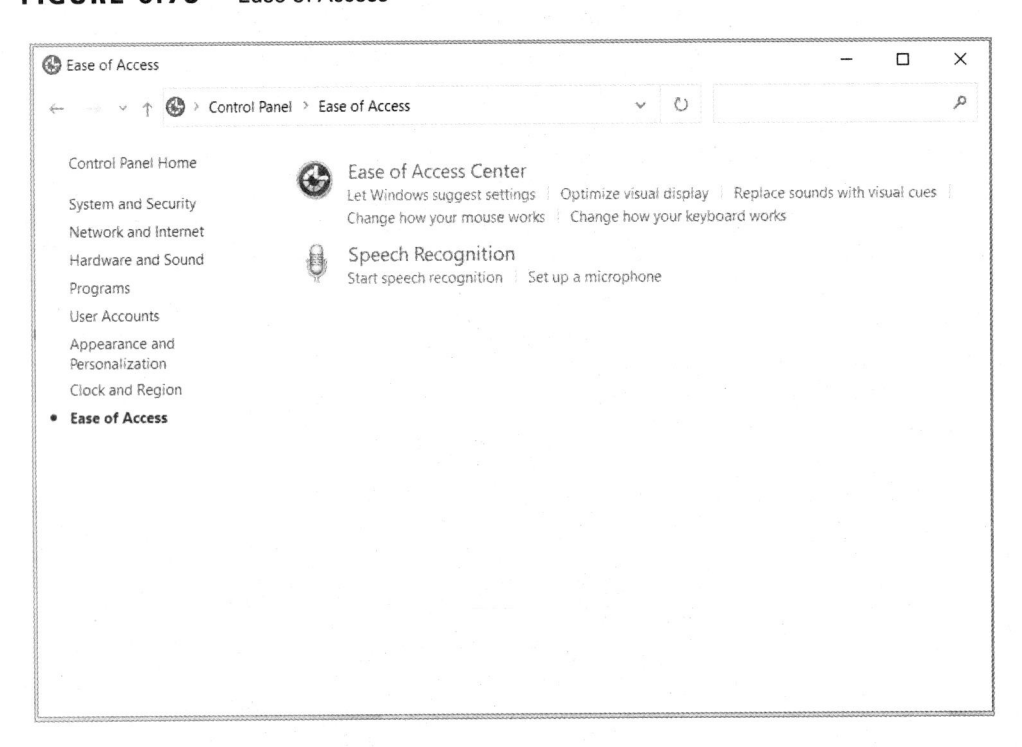

1.6 Given a scenario, configure Microsoft Windows settings 353

FIGURE 6.74 Time and Language in Windows 10

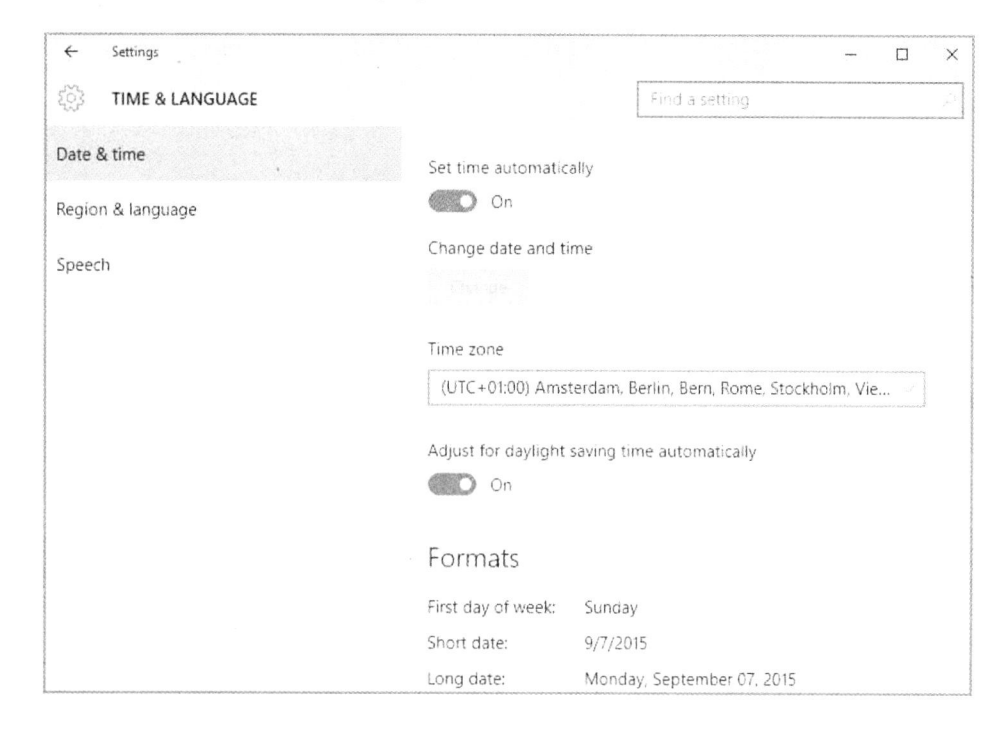

FIGURE 6.75 Time and Language in Windows 11

Update and Security

This section, shown in Figure 6.76, is called Update and Security, but it does much more. In this tool, you can manage the behavior of the update process and configure how the updates are downloaded. Other settings are used to manage backups and security issues.

Table 6.23 shows what can be done in each section.

FIGURE 6.76 Update and Security

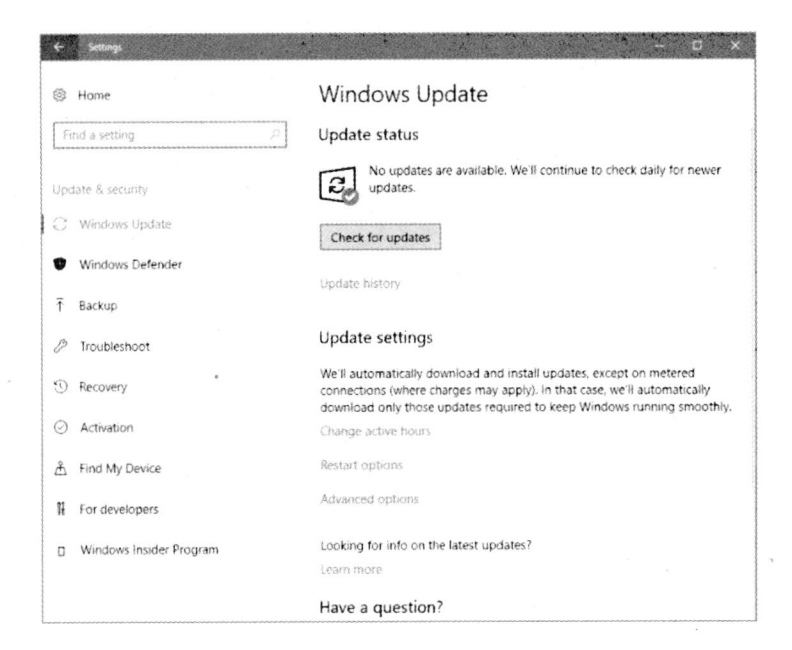

TABLE 6.23 Update and Security settings

Setting	Purpose
Update	Sets the behavior of Windows Updates.
Deliver Optimization	Settings for allowing updates from other computers.
Windows Security	A wide range of settings, including setting up virus protection, account security, application and browser security, and more.
Backup	Sets up an external drive for backup.
Troubleshoot	Offers automated troubleshooting scripts.
Recovery	Contains settings to reset the PC and to boot to advanced options when there are boot issues.

Setting	Purpose
Activation	Displays activation status and offers the ability to attempt activation.
Find My Device	If enabled, this tracks the location of your device. If the device is on a work or school network, this setting is disabled.
For Developers	Contains certain settings that are typically used by software developers, including settings for Remote Desktop and PowerShell.
Windows Insiders Program	Where you can join a group that receives a preview build in order to review it and provide input.
Device Encryption	Where device encryption can be enabled, helping to protect the data if the device is stolen.

FIGURE 6.77 Privacy and security in Windows 11

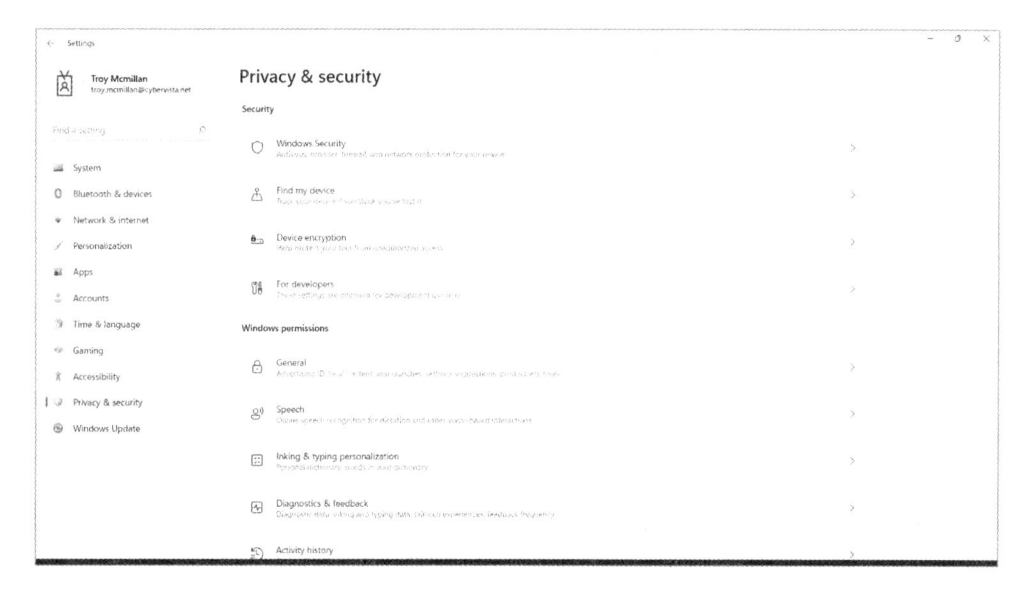

In Windows 11, there are two different applets located in the Control Panel. Privacy and Security is shown in Figure 6.77, and Windows Update is shown in Figure 6.78.

FIGURE 6.78 Windows Update in Windows 11

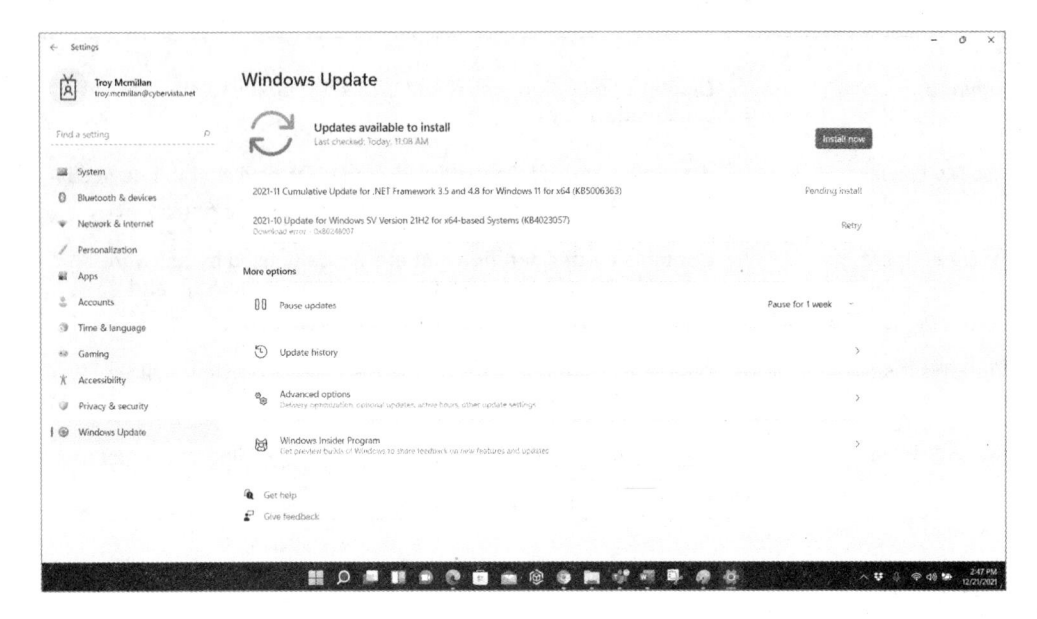

Personalization

The Personalization settings mostly apply to the display. As you can see in Figure 6.79, you can set the background of the desktop, the colors used in various boxes, a screen lock that can appear when you step away, theme settings (i.e. a collection of display settings that follow a "theme," size, and font style), the layout of the Start menu, and the location and layout of the taskbar. The Windows 11 version is shown in Figure 6.80.

Apps

The Apps section is concerned with the download and installation of applications. It displays the apps currently available and offers a section to set the default application used for various file types, a section to download maps to use when the Internet is not available, a section to associate a website with a particular browser or application, a section for the behavior of videos when played on the system, and finally one more location where you can specify applications that start when you start the system. Apps in Windows 10 is shown in Figure 6.81. The Windows 11 version is shown in Figure 6.82.

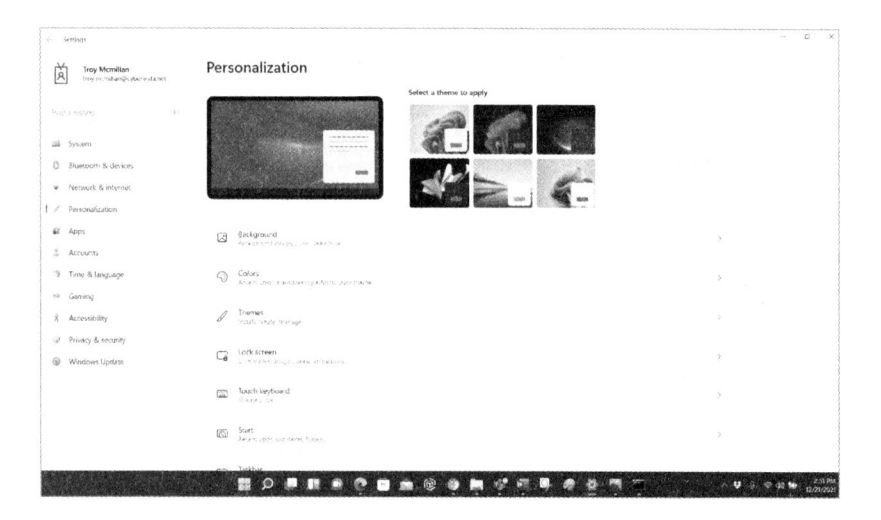

FIGURE 6.79   Personalization in Windows 10

FIGURE 6.80   Personalization in Windows 11

FIGURE 6.81 Apps in Windows 10

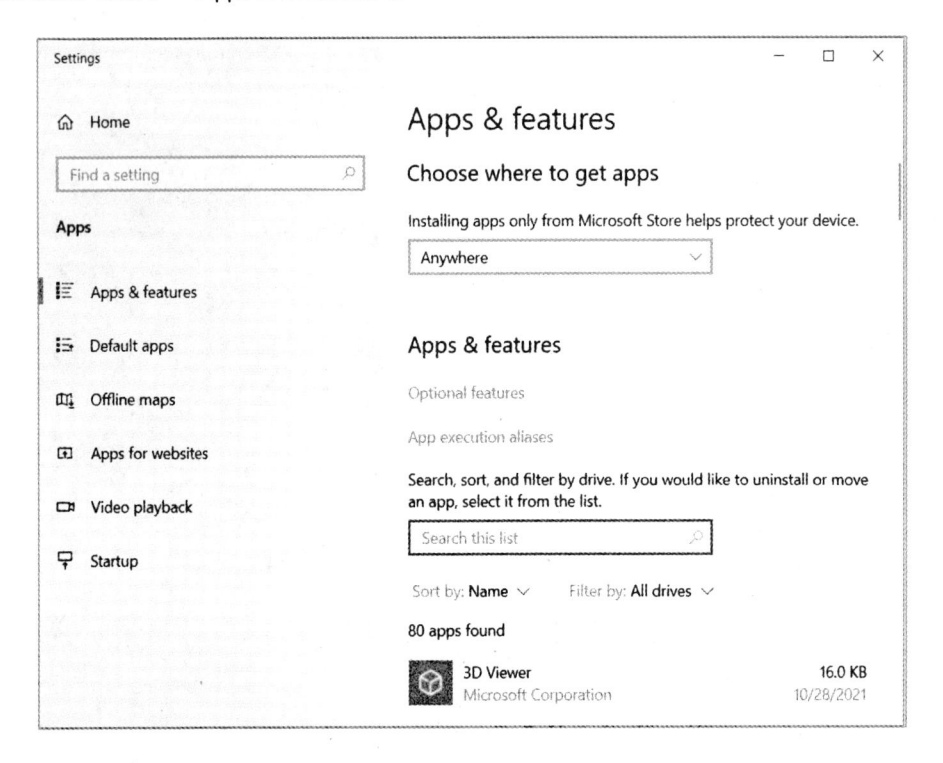

FIGURE 6.82 Apps in Windows 11

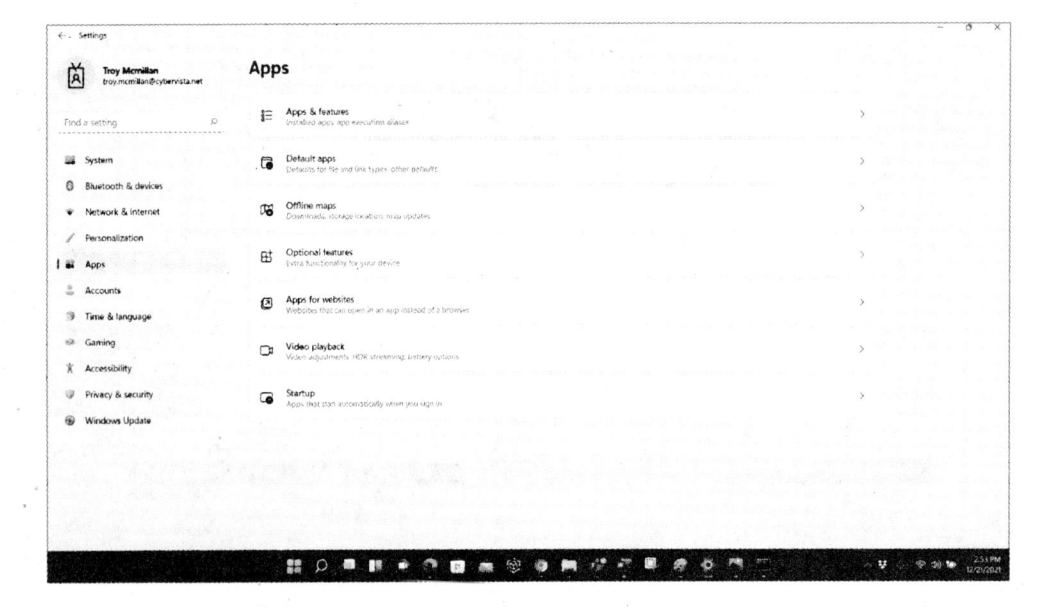

Privacy

As you might suspect, this tool contains settings that are used to maintain the privacy of your data. It also contains many other settings as well, including but not limited to the following:

- Enable speech recognition
- Enable typing and handwriting history so the system can make suggestions
- Allow or disallow sending diagnostic information to Microsoft
- Enable storing activity history on the device
- Enable app location tracking
- Allow app access to the camera
- Allow app access to the mic
- Allow apps to use voice activation

Privacy is shown in Figure 6.83. In Windows 11, these functions are in the Privacy and Security applet shown earlier, in the section "Update and Security."

FIGURE 6.83 Privacy settings

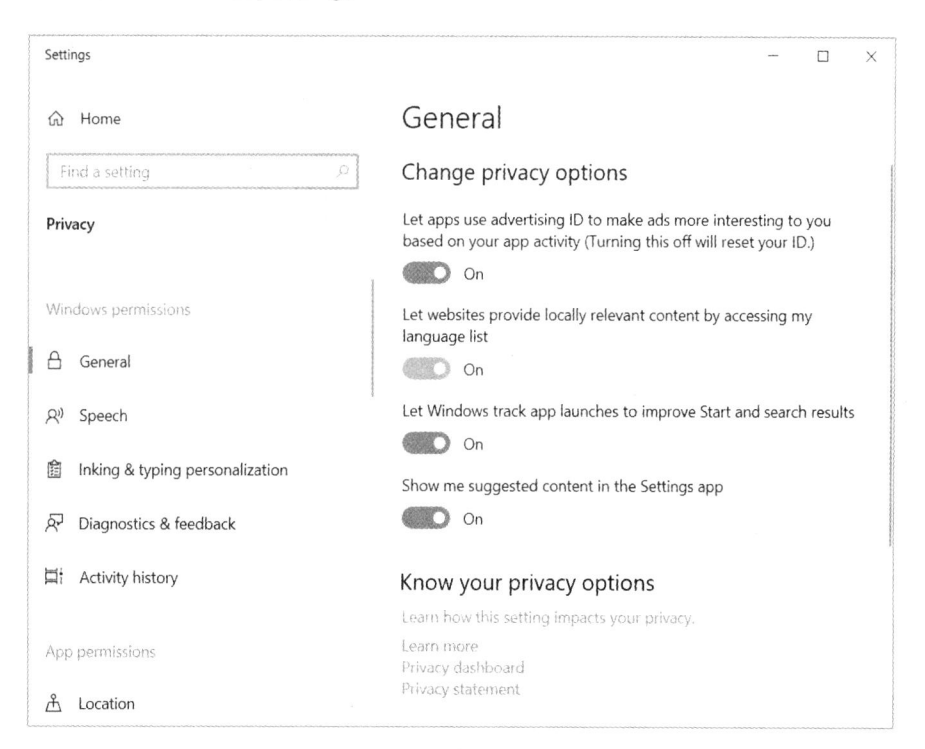

System

System contains a wide array of settings, many of which are also found in other locations as well. Most System settings in Windows 10 are shown in Figure 6.84. The Windows 11 version is shown in Figure 6.85.

FIGURE 6.84   System in Windows 10

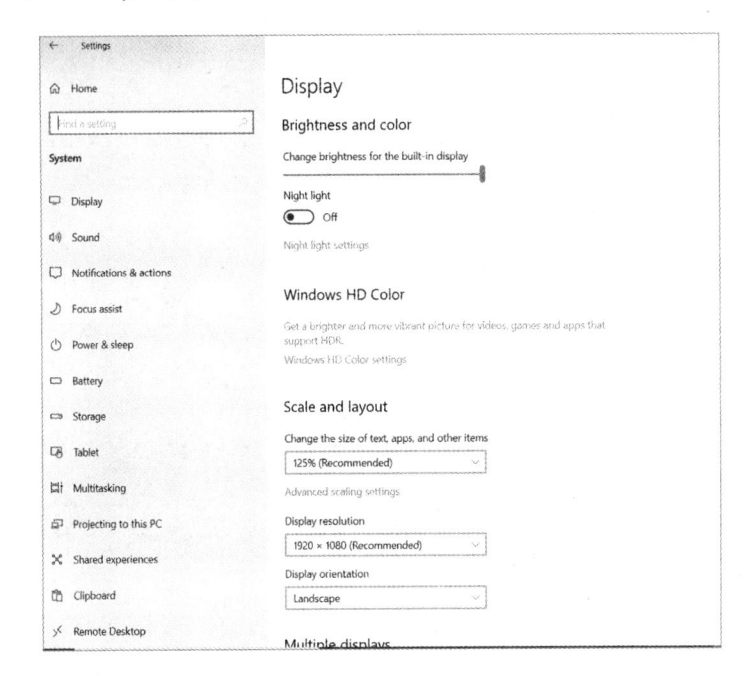

FIGURE 6.85   System in Windows 11

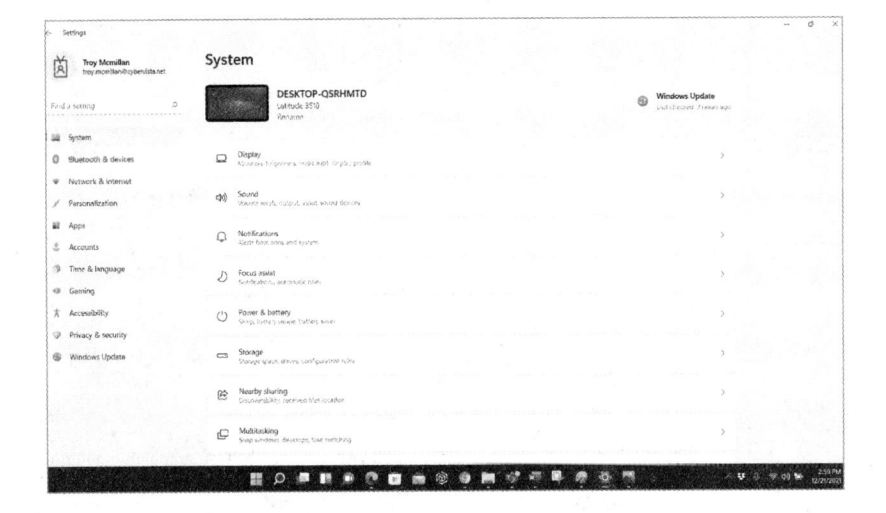

FIGURE 6.86   Devices

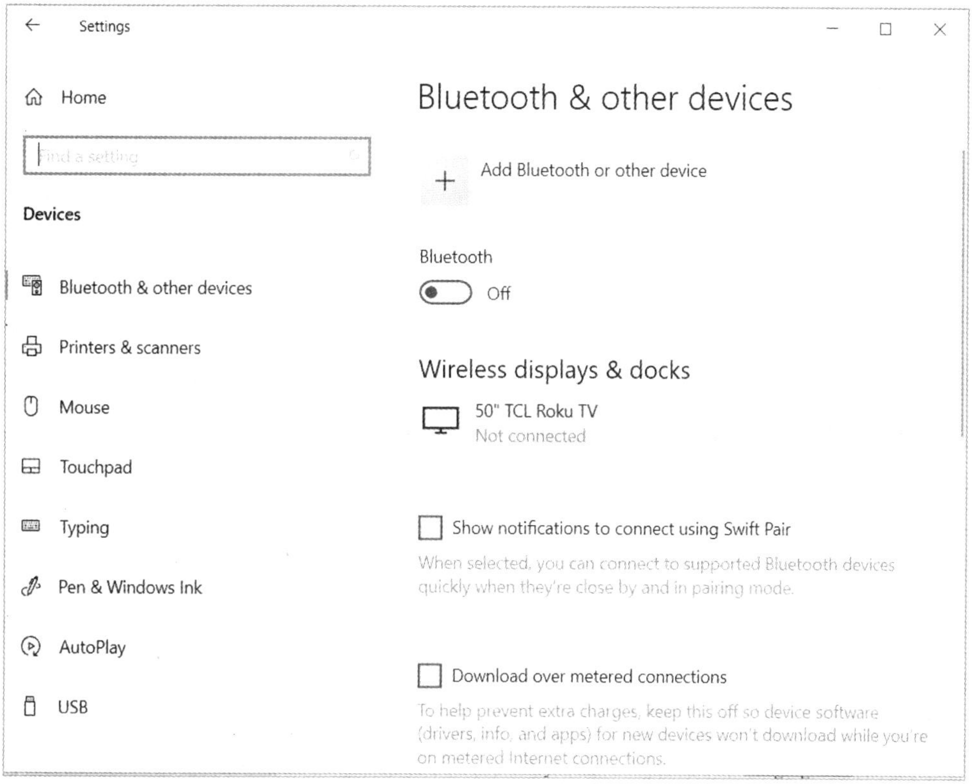

Devices

Devices contains settings for the external devices and peripherals that are connected to the system. Devices is shown in Figure 6.86. In Windows 11, devices are managed in Printers and Scanners, covered earlier in this chapter, in the section "Printers/Scanners."

Network and Internet

This section is for setting and configuring network connections of all types including:

- Ethernet
- WLAN
- Dial-up
- VPN

Chapter 6 ▪ Operating Systems

It also is where you can set your WLAN interface for Airplane mode, set up a mobile hotspot, and configure a proxy server. Network and Internet in Windows 10 is shown in Figure 6.87. The Windows 11 version is shown in Figure 6.88.

FIGURE 6.87   Network and Internet in Windows 10

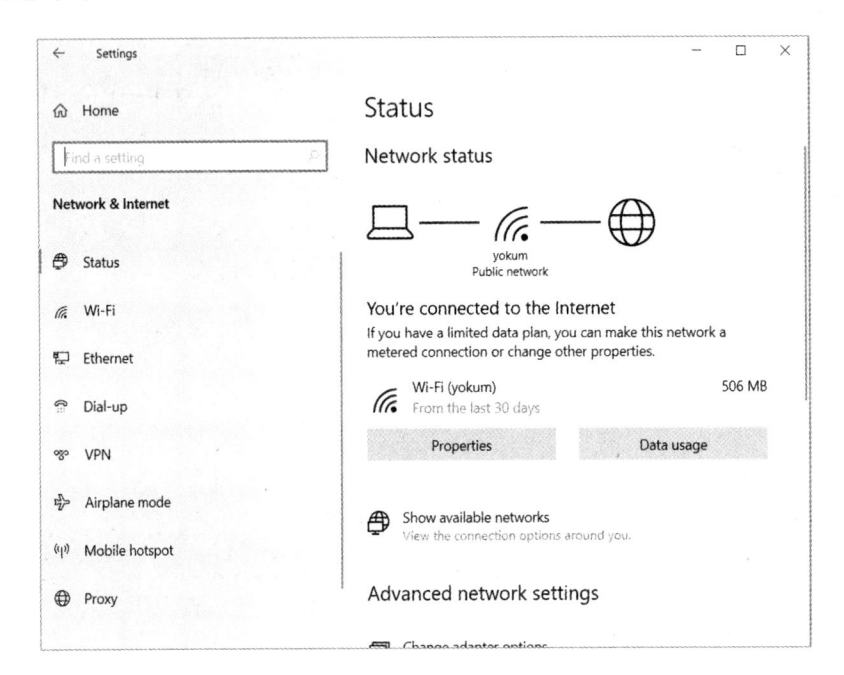

FIGURE 6.88   Network and Internet in Windows 11

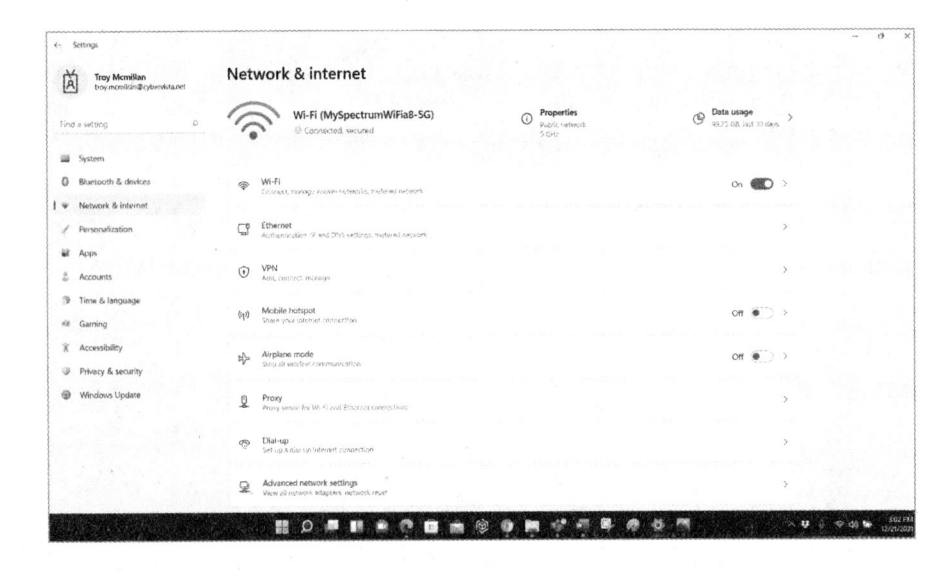

Gaming

If you are into gaming, then you will visit this section often. Here you can make settings that affect the gaming experience. You can control the Xbox Game Bar, set the system to record screenshots of games, enable game mode (optimizes performance), and view the amount of packet loss and latency. Gaming in Windows 10 is shown in Figure 6.89. The Windows 11 version is shown in Figure 6.90.

FIGURE 6.89 Gaming in Windows 10

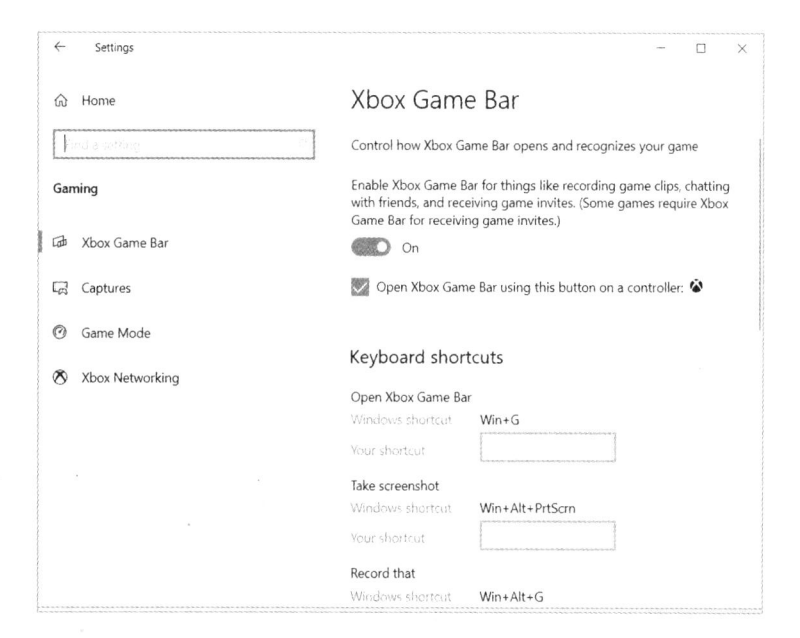

FIGURE 6.90 Gaming in Windows 11

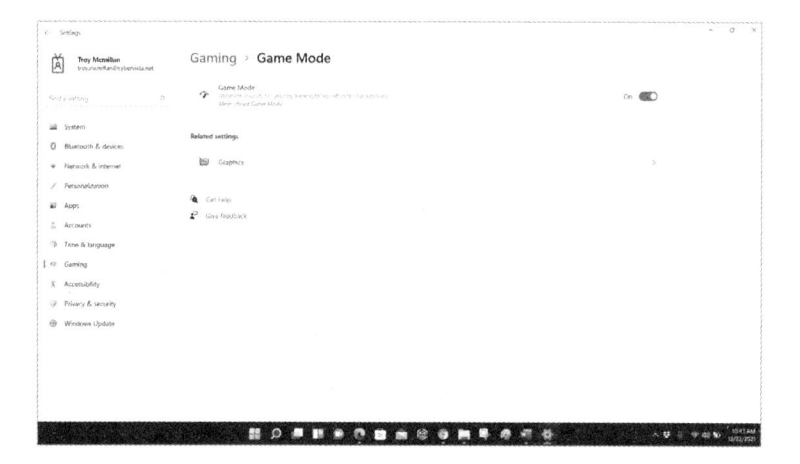

Accounts

Accounts displays information of the currently logged on user and also has sections to do the following:

- Manage the sign-on process
- Set default email
- Access a school or work network
- Add a work or school user account and grant access
- Manage settings to sync data across devices

Accounts in Windows 10 is shown in Figure 6.91. The Windows 11 version is shown in Figure 6.92.

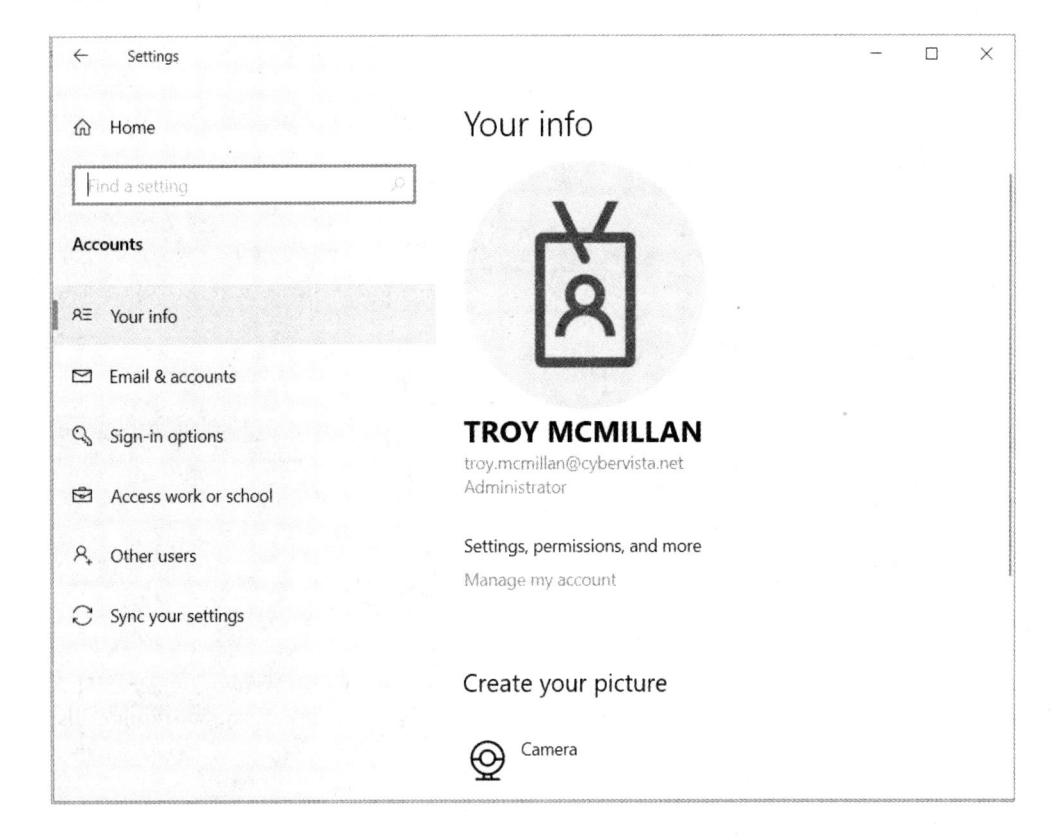

FIGURE 6.91 Accounts in Windows 10

FIGURE 6.92 Accounts in Windows 11

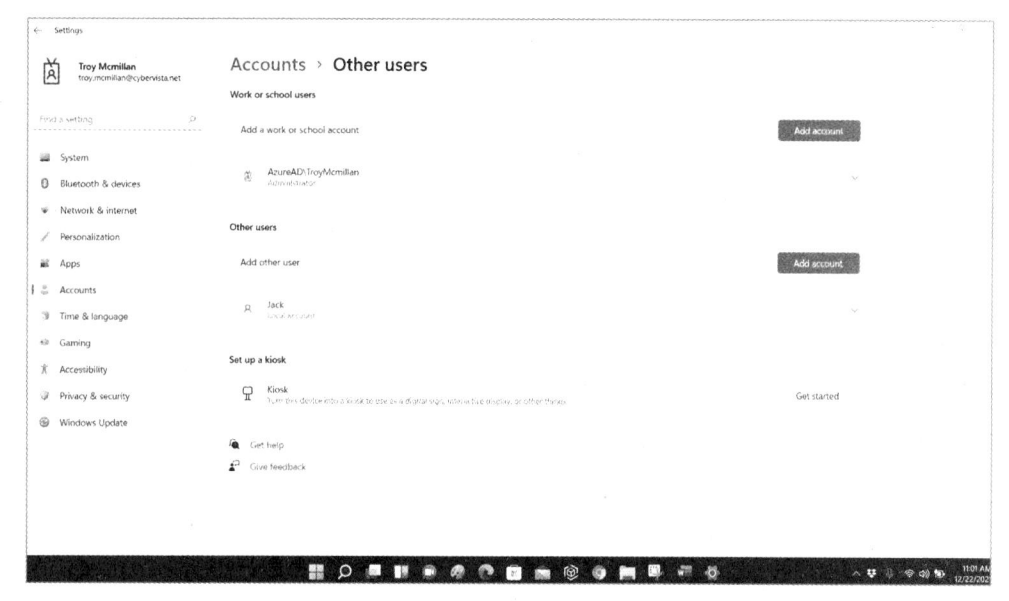

Exam essentials

Identify Settings tiles. These commands include Time and Language, Update and Security, Personalization, Apps, Privacy System, Devices, Network and Internet, Gaming, and Accounts.

1.7 Given a scenario, configure Microsoft Windows networking features on a client/desktop

CompTIA offers several exams and certifications on networking (e.g. Network+, Server+, etc.), but to become A+ certified, you must have good knowledge of basic networking skills as they relate to the Windows OS.

It's important to know how network addressing works and the features offered in the Windows OSes to simplify configuration. CompTIA expects you to have a broad range of knowledge in this category, including some less-common features (such as quality of service [QoS]).

Domain joined vs. workgroup

A peer-to-peer network, one of two network types you can create in Windows (also known as a *workgroup*), consists of a few workstations (2 or more, and generally fewer than 10) that share resources among themselves. The resources shared are traditionally file and print access, and every computer has the capacity to act as a workstation (by accessing resources from another machine) and as a server (by offering resources to other machines).

The other network type is client-server (or a domain). The primary distinction between workgroups and client-server networks is where security is controlled: locally on each workstation or centrally on a server. A domain is a group of computers that are centrally managed by a server, and physical proximity does not matter; the computers within a domain may all be on the same LAN or spread across a WAN.

The advantage of a peer-to-peer network is that the cost is lower; you need only add cards and cables to the computers you already have if you're running an OS that allows such modifications. With a server-based network, you must buy a server—a dedicated machine—and thus the costs are higher. It's never recommended that a peer-to-peer network be used for more than 10 workstations because the administration and management become so significant that a server-based network makes far greater sense.

Domain setup

In a domain (also known as a *client-server network*), users log on to the server by supplying a username and password. They're then authenticated for the duration of their session. Rather than requiring users to give a password for every resource they want to access (which would be share-level), security is based on how they authenticated themselves at the beginning of their session. This is known as *user-level* security, and it's much more powerful than share-level security.

Enterprise networks join servers, workstations, and other devices into security associations called *domains* or *realms*. These associations are made possible through the use of directory services such as Active Directory. These associations are what make the concept of single sign-on possible. This means that any user can log into the network using any device that is a domain member and receive all their assigned rights and privileges by using a single logon.

Joining a computer to the domain can be done during the installation in some cases, but most administrators do this after a successful OS installation. An example of how this is done in Windows 10 is shown in Figure 6.93. This is done through the Computer Name tab of System Properties, by clicking the Change button. To navigate to System Properties, open the Control Panel and select the System icon (using icon view). Then select Advanced System Settings from the menu on the left side of the page. This opens the System Properties dialog box shown in Figure 6.93.

Shared resources

An *administrative share* is one that is hidden to those file browsing. To connect to these drives, you must reference the name of the drive. While you can create a hidden drive at any time, simply by adding a dollar sign at the end of its name, there are some default administrative drives.

Table 6.24 gives information on the default administrative drives.

FIGURE 6.93 Joining the server to the domain

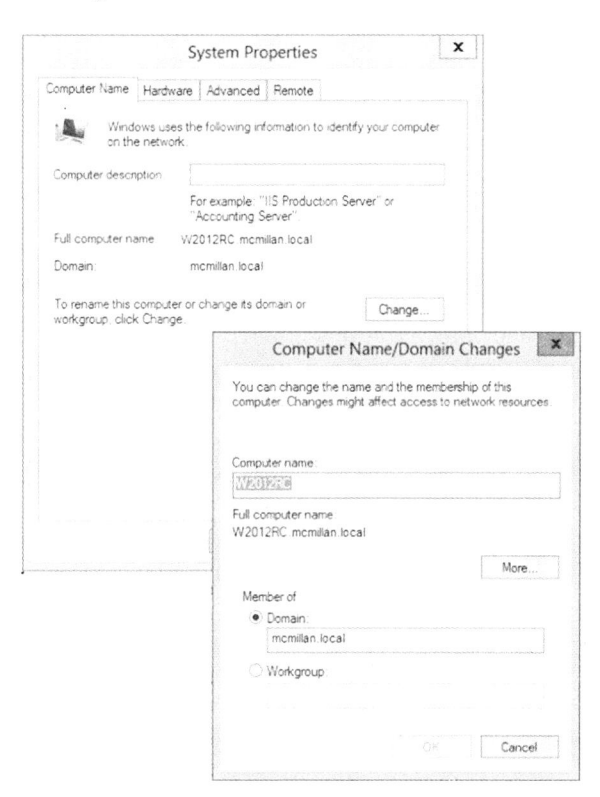

TABLE 6.24 Default administrative drives

Share name	Location	Purpose
ADMIN$	%SystemRoot%	Remote administration
IPC$	N/A	Remote interprocess communication
print$	%SystemRoot%\System32\spool\drivers	Access to printer drivers
C$, D$, E$, and so on	The root of any drive	Remote administration

Printers

In Chapter 3, in the section "Public/Shared Devices," you learned how to share a printer that is connected locally to a computer. It is also possible to connect to a network printer that is not tied to a computer but has its own IP address and probably built-in print server. To connect (or map) a user's device to one of these devices, follow the procedure to add a shared printer, and on the page you normally enter the Universal Naming Convention (UNC) path to the shared printer, select the option Add a Printer Using a TCP/IP Address or Hostname, as shown in Figure 6.94, and click Next.

Enter the IP address or the hostname of the printer, as shown in Figure 6.95, and click Next.

If the IP address is correct and can be reached, the printer driver will download, and the printer will be added to the printers area of the Control Panel.

File servers

In Chapter 2, you learned about the role of fileshare servers in the network. Shares are typically created on these devices that make resources such as files and folders available to users, while controlling their specific access with permissions. Review the "Fileshare" section in Chapter 2.

Mapped drives

Network shares can be mapped to drives to appear as if the resources are local. The `net use` command is used to establish network connections via a command prompt. For example, to

FIGURE 6.94 Adding a printer using a TCP/IP address

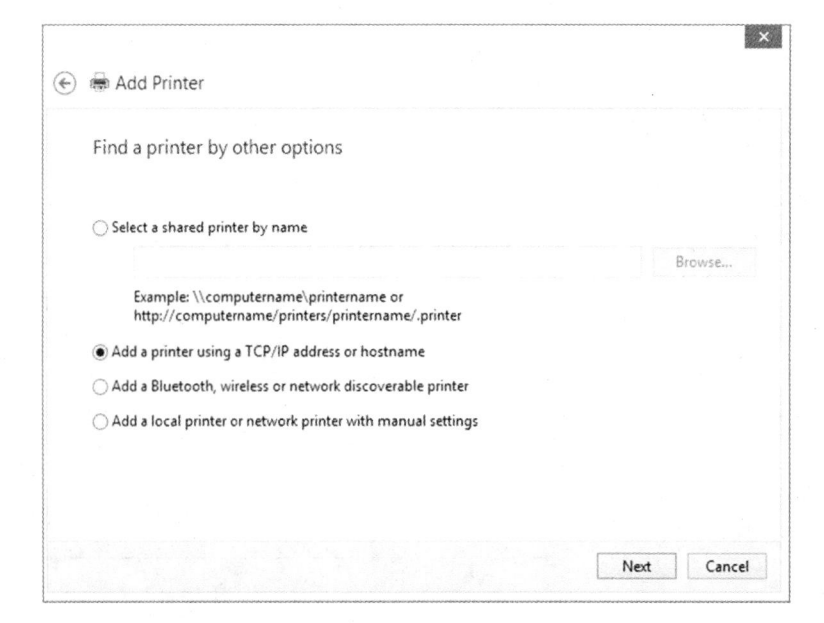

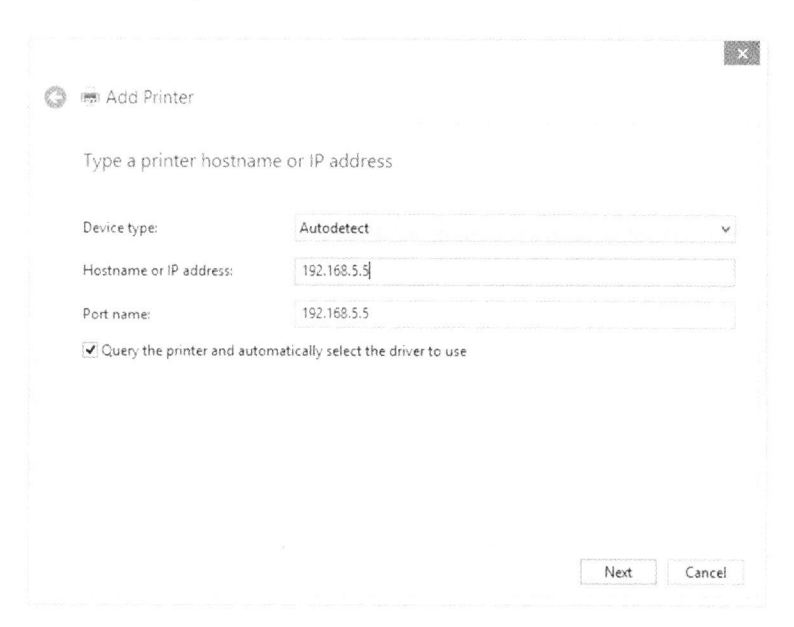

FIGURE 6.95 Adding the printer's IP address

connect to a shared network drive and make it your M drive, you would type the syntax **net use m: \\server\share**. This can also be done in File Explorer.

Local OS firewall settings

Windows Firewall (Start > Control Panel > Windows Firewall) is used to block access from the network. It is divided into separate settings for private networks and public networks.

Application restrictions and exceptions

Exceptions are configured as variations from the rules. Windows Firewall will block incoming network connections except for the programs and services that you choose to allow into the network. For example, you can make an exception for Remote Assistance to allow communication from other computers when you need help. (Note, the scope of the exception can be set to allow any computer, only those on the network, or a custom list of allowed addresses you create.) Exceptions can include programs as well as individual ports.

A scenario for using exceptions would be when you want to block all traffic with the exception of *only* required traffic. You define each allowed traffic type as an exception and disallow all others by default.

Restrictions prevent an application from sending traffic though the interfaces of the firewall. A scenario for using this would be when you need to prevent malicious traffic of a particular type.

Configuration

Most configuration is done as network connection settings. You can configure both ICMP and Services settings. Examples of ICMP settings include allowing incoming echo requests, allowing incoming router requests, and allowing redirects. Examples of services often configured include File Transfer Protocol (FTP) server, Post Office Protocol Version 3 (POP3), and web server (HTTP).

A scenario for using this setting is to disallow ICMP traffic to prevent ping sweeps. This type of network probing is used to discover the devices in your network.

Enabling/disabling Windows Firewall

On the General tab of Windows Firewall, it is possible to choose the radio button Off (not recommended). As the name implies, this turns Windows Firewall completely off. The other radio button option, On (recommended), enables the firewall. You can also toggle the checkbox Don't Allow Exceptions. This option should be enabled when you're connecting to a public network in an unsecure location (such as an airport or library), and it will then ignore any exceptions that were configured.

A scenario where you might choose to turn off the firewall is when you are using another firewall product instead. You want to use only one firewall. The box used in Window 11 is shown in Figure 6.96.

FIGURE 6.96 Enabling Defender Firewall

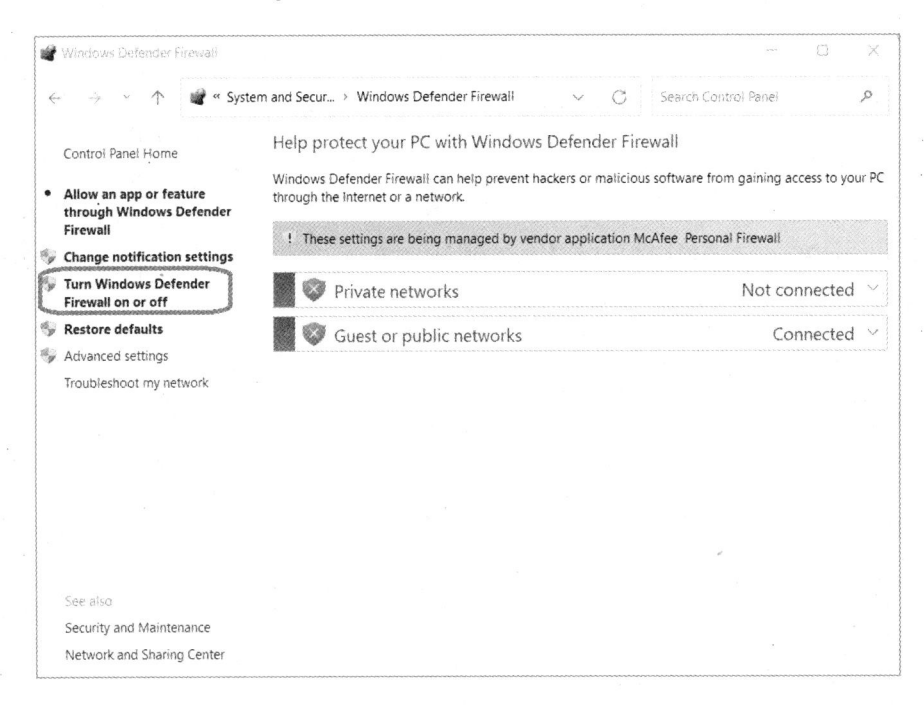

Client network configuration

In Chapter 2, you learned about the concepts covered in this section of the A+ objectives. These include coverage of the following:

- IP addressing scheme
- Domain Name System (DNS) settings
- Subnet mask
- Gateway
- Static vs. dynamic

Please review Chapter 2, as these are critical objectives for the A+ exam.

Establish network connections

When configuring the connection method for accessing the Internet, the three choices that Windows offers are This Computer Connects Directly to the Internet, This Computer Connects Through a Residential Gateway or Another Computer, and Other. If you choose the first option, you can turn on Internet Connection Sharing and allow this machine to serve as a proxy. The network connection you configure can be wireless or wired, dial-up, or a VPN. In Windows 11, the choices are all there, but the boxes look as shown in Figure 6.97.

FIGURE 6.97 Network connections in Windows 11

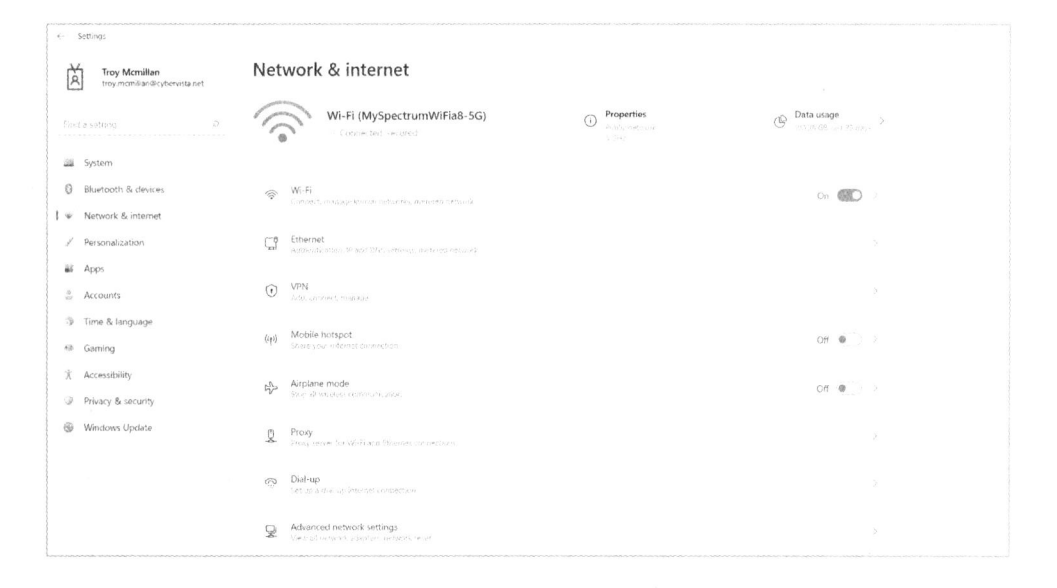

VPN

A VPN is used when you want to connect from a remote location (such as home) to your company's network (authenticating the user and encrypting the data).

Wireless

A wireless connection uses one of the 802.11 technologies, along with encryption, to connect to the network.

Wired

A wired connection uses a wire to connect the computer to the network. Typically, this is an Ethernet cable, such as 100Base-T, which connects to a hub or switch and offers network access to the host.

Wireless wide area network (WWAN)/cellular network

A wireless wide area network (WWAN) connection is one that uses a cellular connection to connect the host to the network. A wireless service provider (e.g. AT&T, Sprint, or T-Mobile) will provide a card that plugs into the host to make the cellular connection possible.

Options available are shown in Table 6.25.

Regardless of which option you choose, you will need to fill out the appropriate fields for the device to be able to communicate on the network. With TCP/IP, required values are an IP address for the host, subnet mask, address for the gateway, and DNS information.

Proxy settings

Proxy settings identify the proxy server to be used to gain Internet access. The proxy server is responsible for making Internet access possible and may utilize network address

TABLE 6.25 Network connection options

Option	Purpose
Connect to the Internet	Used for connection to a proxy server or other device intended to provide Internet access. This includes wireless, broadband, and dial-up access.
Set Up a New Network	Used to set a new WLAN router or access point.
Manually Connect to a Wireless Network	If you have a wireless network already in place and the device (such as the router) is not directly connected to this machine, use this option.
Connect to a Workplace	If you need to dial into a VPN from a remote location, this is the option to use.

FIGURE 6.98 LAN settings

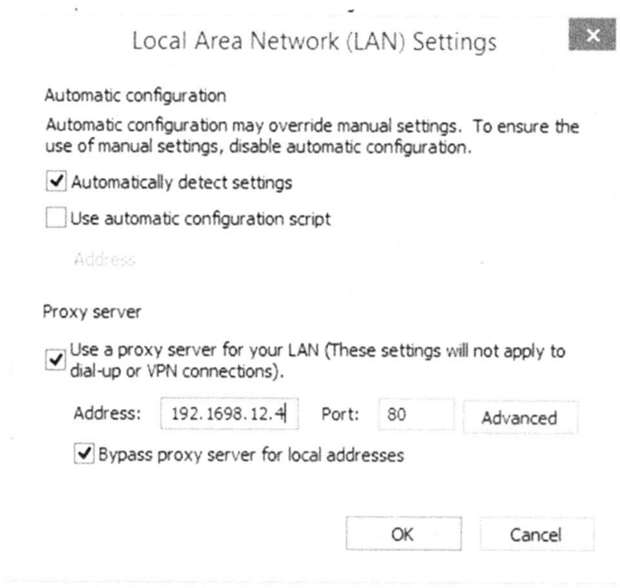

translation (NAT) to translate between the public network (i.e. Internet) and the private network (i.e. where the host sits). These settings are configured by using the LAN Settings button in the Connections tab to open the dialog box shown in Figure 6.98. Proxy settings for Windows 11 are shown in Figure 6.97 (i.e. network connections).

Public network vs. private network

In Windows 10, when you make a new connection, you are asked to identify whether it is a private or public network. If you choose one of the first two, network discovery is on by default, allowing you to see other computers and other computers to see you. If you choose Public, network discovery is turned off.

Network discovery, when enabled, is a security issue, and this function should not be used on untrusted networks, like those found in coffee shops and airports.

In Figure 6.99, you can see that the device is connected to a public network. The Windows 11 version is shown in Figure 6.100.

File Explorer navigation—network paths

Earlier in this chapter, in the section "Mapped drives," you learned about network paths, mapped drives, and the use of File Explorer in creating and accessing these. Please review that section.

FIGURE 6.99 Public network

FIGURE 6.100 Public network in Windows 11

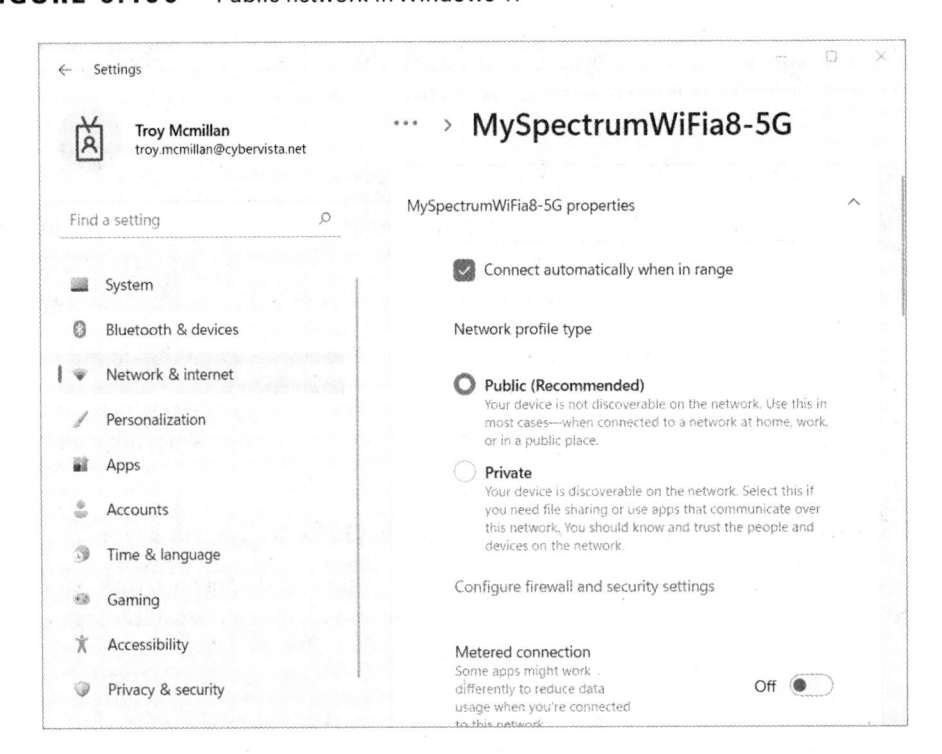

Metered connections and limitations

In Chapter 4, in the section "Metered utilization," you learned about metered connections and metered services. Please review that chapter.

Exam essentials

Join a computer to a domain. Describe the steps involved in placing a computer in a domain using a directory service such as Active Directory.

1.8 Explain common features and tools of the macOS/desktop operating system

While the overwhelming percentage of devices you will come into contact with will be Windows devices, you will also encounter other OSes. Linux OS and macOS are increasingly found in enterprise networks in situations where their strengths can be leveraged. There are also many other technologies that you may not be directly managing, but you should still be familiar with them and understand their purpose. This section will focus on these areas.

Installation and uninstallation of applications

When new to macOS, it might seem that installing applications is confusing, as there are various file types and sources of applications. In this section, you'll learn about the file types involved in installation, where to get applications, and the process for uninstalling.

File types

When installing applications on macOS, you might encounter several different types of files. In this section, you'll learn about three file types you may come across: .dmg, .pkg, and .app.

.dmg

Files with a .dmg extension are called Apple Disk Image files or macOS disk image files. These are digital reconstructions of a physical disk. Only versions of Mac newer than OS X 9 support these files. Older systems use the .img file type (covered later in this section). This is a mountable image used to distribute software to macOS.

To open a .dmg file on a Mac, simply double-click it. It will use the Disk Image Mounter utility that comes with macOS to open it. Then it will mount a virtual disk and open an Apple Finder window as if it were a CD or a USB flash drive that was just inserted into the computer.

Windows can open a .dmg file with any compression/decompression program that supports the format. Opening these files in Linux is dependent on Linux supporting HFS as a disk file system format. To enable HFS and HFS+ support on your Linux machine, you will need to install HFS tools and kernel modules.

.pkg

Package or .pkg files are very similar to the .msi files used to install software in Windows. These files will install by simply double-clicking the file or by choosing Open with installer.app from the context menu. If you simply want see what's inside without installing it, choose Show Package Content from the context menu.

- In Windows, if you know which application uses the .pkg file, use it to open the .pkg file.
- If the .pkg file is in macOS installation file format, you should use a macOS machine to open it.
- In Linux, you will have to convert the .pkg file to another format that is supported by Linux.

.app

These files are executable application program files and are similar to the Windows EXE file format. To open these files, you will need a program compatible with the specific file. Because these are made for macOS, you can interact with them in a similar way to how you treat .dmg files. You can right-click and select Show Package Contents to view the files contained in the package and open it by double-clicking it.

App Store

The App Store is the recommended and safest location to discover and download apps. Other Apple products, including laptops, smartphones, and all accessories, are also available for purchase in the Apple Store. Downloading apps from other locations is discouraged because you don't know the actual source and contents of the app.

Uninstallation process

Surprisingly, there is no uninstall function built into Mac as there is in Windows. To uninstall, you can simply drag the icon of the app to the Trash. Be aware that some apps store files in multiple locations rather than all in one place (i.e. bundled files). This means that some files will be left behind. You might try seeing if the app has its own uninstall program that will do a better job of cleaning up. Many software programs can clean up for you. Popular examples include AppTrap, AppCleaner, and AppZapper.

System folders

System folders contain data that the OS uses in its operation. Some of these folders can contain items you've created (such as a new user account), and others contain only items created automatically by the system. Let's look at some important system folders.

/Applications

As you might imagine, this folder holds the applications with two Application directories:

- **/Applications** – a systemwide folder accessible to all users. It is located at the root of your system disk.
- **/Users/[your username]/Applications** – a folder exclusive to a user account. Applications installed there are available only to your user, not to the other users of the machine.

/Users

This folder contains the user accounts that exist in the system. When a new user account is added on Mac, it will generate a corresponding user folder. There are also user accounts in there that are preconfigured and represent default accounts, such as admin, root, and guest user.

/Library

The /Library folder stores user account settings, preference files, caches, and other important data used by the operating system (macOS). Files and folders within this folder are created by the operation of the system. Deleting, changing, moving, editing, or renaming these files and folders inside the /Library folder can cause damage. This is why this folder is hidden by default.

/System

The System folder is the directory in macOS that holds various files required for the system to operate. You might think of this as the engine of the OS.

> **Note:** Do not add to, remove, or modify system folders and files. You can browse safely, but adding, removing, or modifying files or changing the folders themselves can have unpredictable—and sometimes system-breaking—consequences. If you must experiment, make a bootable clone of your Mac before proceeding.

/Users/Library

The /Library folder inside the /Users folder houses systemwide settings and items such as **screensavers, wallpapers, and apps that share their data and settings with other users on your system.** Because Apple doesn't really want you messing with this folder, the User Library folder is hidden by default.

Apple ID and corporate restrictions

Apple ID is an authentication method used to access iPhone, iPad, Mac, and other Apple devices. It's more than just a username; it also contains all your settings and preferences that are applied when you log in.

A company can create Managed Apple IDs for employees to use for business purposes. These IDs don't allow purchases, and unlike personal Apple IDs, IT administrators can manage the services that your Managed Apple ID can access.

Best practices

Like any OS, macOS will function better and with more reliability when given the proper care. This section will discuss some of the best practices that have been developed over the years for using these operating systems, including backups, antivirus products, and updates and patches.

Backups

In macOS, you can also use the `rsync` utility from the command line. The basic syntax is as follows, where the `-a` switch tells `rsync` to work in "archive" mode:

```
rsync -a [source dir] [destination dir]
```

As with any command-line utility, you can create batch files and schedule these backups.

In addition, there is another tool available called Time Machine. With it, you can back up your entire Mac, including system files, apps, music, photos, emails, and documents. When enabled, it automatically backs up your Mac and performs hourly, daily, and weekly backups of your files. You will learn more about Time Machine later in this chapter, in the section "Time Machine."

Antivirus

All the major antivirus and anti-malware vendors create products for both Mac and commercial versions of Linux. Updates to the engines and definitions for these applications are done in a similar fashion to Windows. Checks for updates can be scheduled just as is done in Windows. Regardless of what you might have been told, Apple devices need antivirus protection.

Updates/patches

In macOS, updates can come either directly from Apple or from the Apple Store. To make updates automatic, access Software Update preferences, where you can set it to daily, monthly, or weekly, as shown in Figure 6.101.

1.8 Explain common features and tools of the macOS/desktop operating system 379

FIGURE 6.101   Software Update preferences

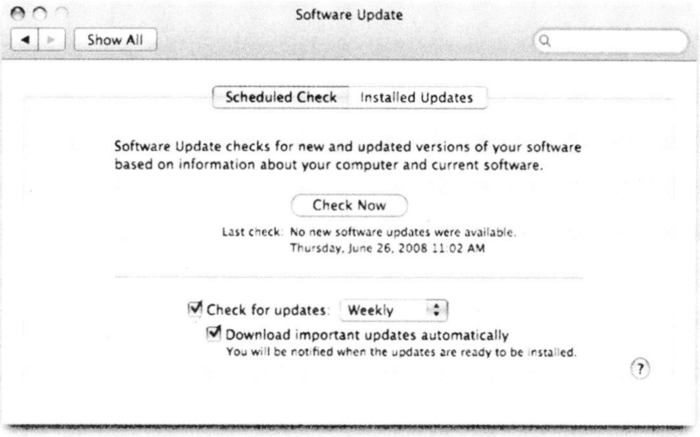

Rapid Security Response (RSR)

Rapid Security Response (RSR) is a new method for applying critical security fixes to Apple devices. These patches are swift releases that come between regular Apple updates. The speed is designed to reduce the time a system is at risk (i.e. what we call "zero day"). These updates are very small downloads, usually installed in less than a minute, and are intended to target urgent security issues that need immediate attention.

System Preferences

System Preferences is a central location where you can set configuration settings, somewhat like the Control Panel in Windows. An example is shown in Figure 6.102.

While the exact icons found in this dialog box can differ, in this section you'll learn about the utility of some of the more common icons or tools used to configure your system.

Display

The Display dialog box, shown in Figure 6.103, is used to adjust the display settings. It has three tabs or buttons: Display, Arrangement, and Color. Display is where you set the resolution, Arrangement is used to manage multiple displays, and Color is for choosing and creating a color profile for your display.

Network

Network is where you can manage your network connections of all types. As you can see in Figure 6.104, all network connections will appear on the left, and by choosing one, you can manage its TCP/IP settings on the right.

FIGURE 6.102　　System Preferences

FIGURE 6.103　　Display

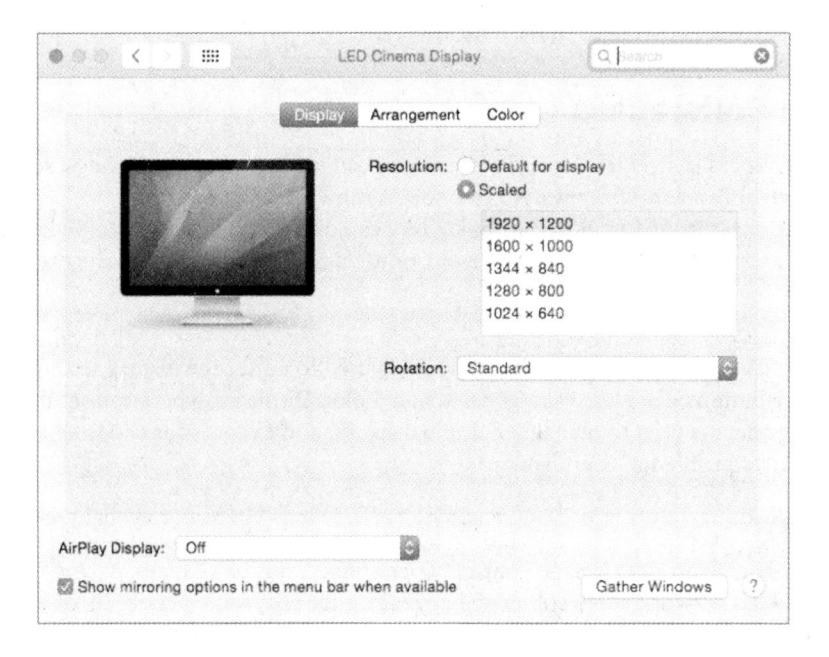

1.8 Explain common features and tools of the macOS/desktop operating system 381

FIGURE 6.104   Network

Printers and Scanners

Printers and scanners are managed in the same dialog box. Figure 6.105 shows the dialog box. All printers and scanners will appear on the left side, and after selecting one, you can manage it on the right side.

Privacy

Privacy settings are located in the Security and Privacy applet in System Preferences. You can decide per application or service how much and what type of your information you would like to share with the application or service. As shown in Figure 6.106, you choose the application or service on the left, and then you are offered options with respect to how that application handles your data.

Accessibility

Some users face challenges with using a computer. They may have poor eyesight, be hearing impaired, or have tremors in their hands. Accessibility offers options to make using the system easier for them by reading things aloud, enlarging the screen font, or offering a keyboard on the screen that can be managed with the mouse. This applet is shown in Figure 6.107.

FIGURE 6.105 Printers and Scanners

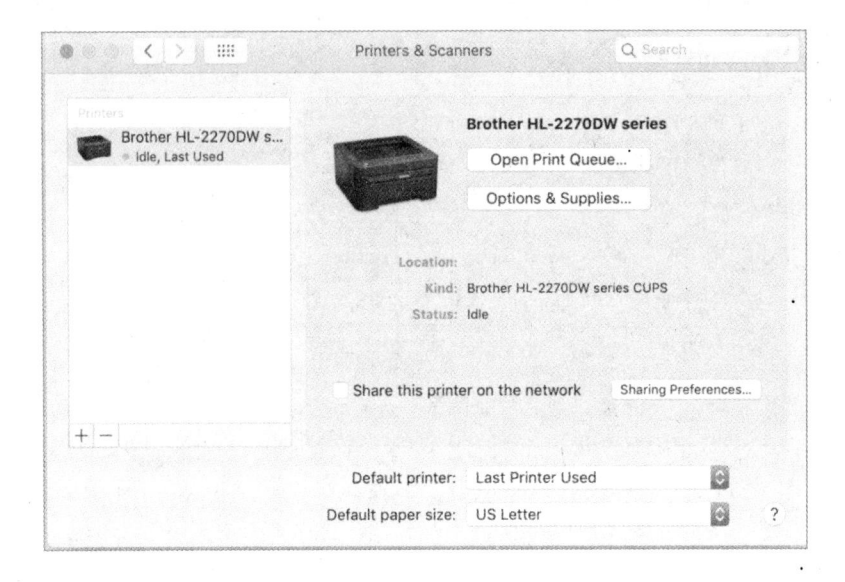

FIGURE 6.106 Security and Privacy

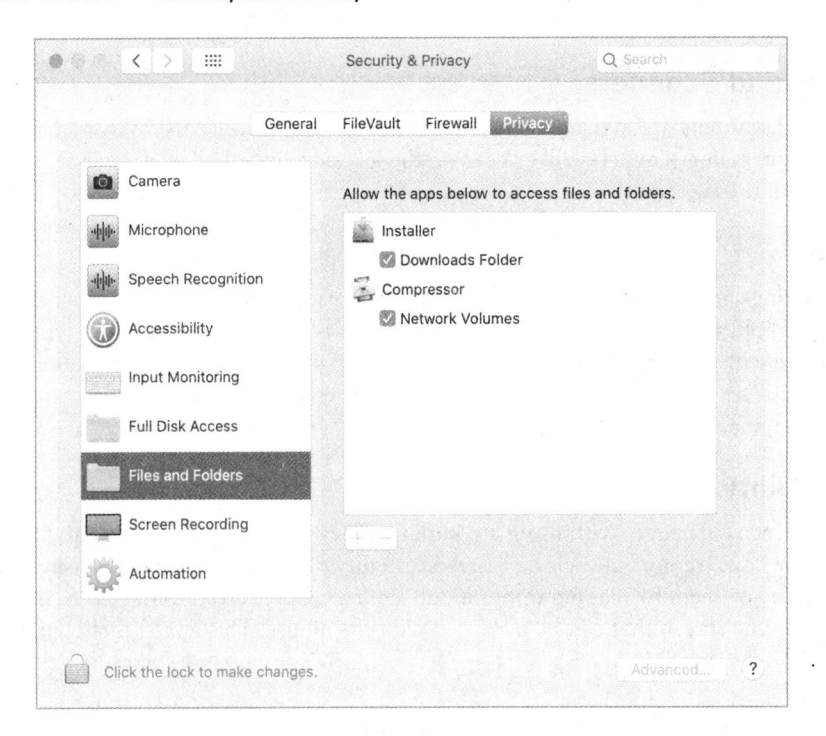

1.8 Explain common features and tools of the macOS/desktop operating system

FIGURE 6.107   Accessibility preferences pane

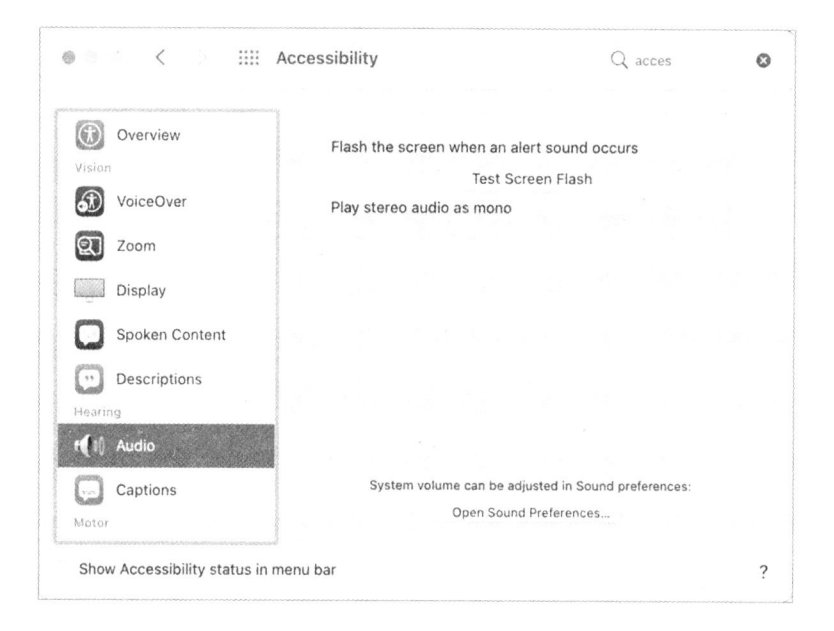

FIGURE 6.108   Time Machine

Time Machine

With Time Machine, shown in Figure 6.108, you can back up your entire Mac, including system files, apps, music, photos, emails, and documents. When Time Machine is enabled, it automatically backs up your Mac and performs hourly, daily, and weekly backups of your files.

Features

Now that you have looked at maintenance on these systems, let's examine some of the key features you will find in the macOS. You can find many of these features in Windows with different names and different combinations of functions.

Multiple desktops

In Apple, Mission Control provides a quick way to see everything that's currently open on your Mac. To use Mission Control, do one of the following:

- Swipe up with three or four fingers on your trackpad.
- Double-tap the surface of your Magic Mouse with two fingers.
- Click the Mission Control icon in the Dock or Launchpad.
- On an Apple keyboard, press the Mission Control key.

Regardless of how you invoke Mission Control, all your open windows and spaces are visible, grouped by app. You can also use the tool to create desktops that are called *spaces* and place certain apps in certain spaces. Moreover, you can switch between the spaces in the same session.

When you enter Mission Control, all your spaces appear along the top of your screen. The desktop you're currently using is shown below the row of spaces. To move an app window to another space, drag it from your current desktop to the space at the top of the screen.

To switch between spaces, do one of the following:

- Enter Mission Control and click the space you want at the top of the Mission Control window.
- Swipe three or four fingers left or right across your trackpad to move to the previous or next space.
- Press Ctrl+Right Arrow or Ctrl+Left Arrow on your keyboard to move through your current spaces. Then click a window to bring it to the front of your view.

Mission Control

Mission Control was covered in the previous section.

Keychain

Keychain is the password management system in macOS. It can contain private keys, certificates, and secure notes. In macOS keychain files are stored in `/Library/Keychains/`, `/Library/Keychains/`, and `/Network/Library/Keychains/`. Keychain Access is a macOS application that allows a user to access the keychain and configure its contents.

Spotlight

Spotlight is a search tool built into Mac systems. To open Spotlight, click the magnifying glass icon in the upper-right corner of the menu bar or press Command+spacebar from any app. Spotlight results can include dictionary definitions, currency conversions, and quick calculations. It will search the web as well, but you can limit its scope to just search the local computer.

iCloud

iCloud is Apple's cloud storage solution, much like OneDrive in Windows. It also allows for the automatic synchronization of information across all devices of the user. In addition, it can be used to locate an iPhone and can be a location to which a backup can be stored. All Mac users are provided with 5 GB of free storage and can purchase additional storage for a monthly fee.

iMessage

iMessage is the instant messaging service developed by Apple and launched in 2011. One interesting feature is its end-to-end encryption that only the sender and recipient can decrypt. No one else, not even Apple itself, can decrypt the messages.

FaceTime

FaceTime is the Apple videotelephony product, which is included for free in iOS and macOS from Mac OS X Lion (10.7) onward. One interesting feature is Center Stage, which allows the camera to follow a user when they are on a FaceTime call.

Drive

Drive (also called iCloud Drive) is a file hosting service that makes it possible to sync files across devices running iOS, macOS, and even Windows 7 and later. This allows users to start their work on one device and continue another device.

Gestures

Gestures are used in Mac to interact with a touchscreen. The system is based on using multitouch, which allows you to touch the screen in more than one place and initiate specific subroutines called *gestures*, such as when expanding or reducing a photo.

Finder

While Finder can also be used on a Mac to search for files, its main function is a file system navigation tool, much like File Explorer. To open a new Finder window, click the Finder icon in the Dock, and then select File > New Finder Window. Figure 6.109 shows a Finder window.

FIGURE 6.109   Finder

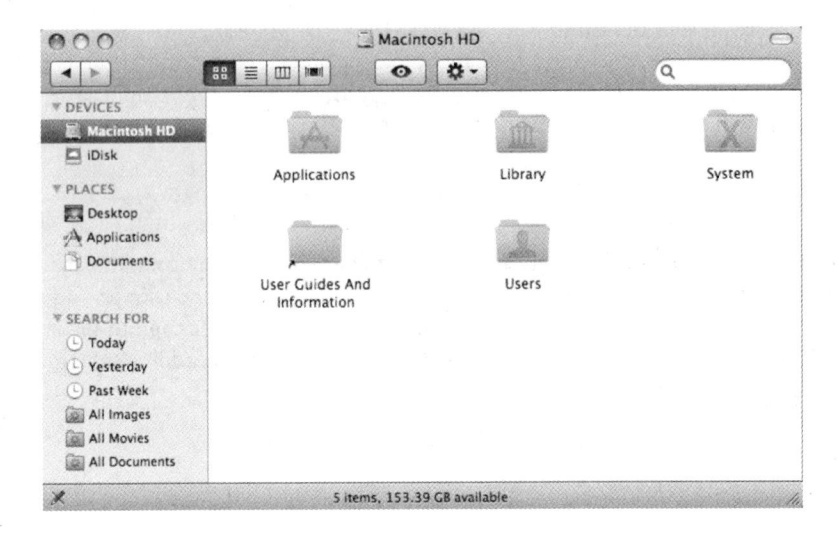

FIGURE 6.110   The Dock

Dock

The Dock is a series of icons that appear usually on the bottom of the screen on a Mac. It provides quick access to applications that come with the Mac, and you can add your own items to the Dock as well. In many ways, it is like the taskbar in Windows. It keeps apps on its left side. Folders, documents, and minimized windows are kept on the right side of the Dock. Figure 6.110 shows the Dock.

Continuity

Continuity is a feature that lets you partner your iPhone with a Mac (or another iOS device). The functionality it provides includes the ability to:

- Make and receive phone calls via an iPad, iPod Touch, or Mac.
- Send and receive text (SMS) or multimedia (MMS) messages via Mac, iPad, and iPod Touch, even to non-Apple users.
- Hand off files between devices (create or open a file on a Mac, an iPad, or iPod Touch, then continue instantly on any other of your Macs or iOS devices).

Disk Utility

Disk Utility is used for a variety of disk-related functions. macOS needs defragmentation in only a small number of cases. If the user creates large numbers of multimedia files and the drive has been filling for quite some time, the system may benefit from defragmentation. However, in most cases, this is not required.

One task that is beneficial to execute from time to time is to check the health of the disk using the Disk Utility's Verify Disk functionality. While many disk operations (including the use of Time Machine) require booting to a different drive to perform the operation on the drive in question, Disk Utility can perform a live verification without doing this.

Recovering an entire image in either system is not different from restoring a single file. On a Mac, you use Disk Utility in conjunction with a backup of the system and the OS media. To do this, follow these steps:

1. Connect the external hard drive that contains the backup to the Mac to which you are restoring.
2. Insert the macOS CD/DVD or thumb drive in the USB port and restart it.
3. Hold down the C key while booting to boot to the macOS CD/DVD or thumb drive and select your language.
4. From the Utilities menu, select Disk Utility.
5. Select the drive the backup is stored on.
6. Select the Restore tab, then select that disk and drag that to the Source window. If you created a .dmg image, you'll need to click the drive you saved the image to (do not drag it), click Image, and select the disk image from the drive on which you stored it.
7. In the left pane of Disk Utility, click your hard drive and drag it to the Destination window.
8. Check the Erase Destination checkbox to erase your old hard drive and replace it with the disk image you've selected as the source.
9. Click Restore. Click OK to verify.

Disk maintenance utilities

While I covered the many disk maintenance utilities in the various sections earlier, Table 6.26 summarizes the tools discussed, along with some additional ones.

TABLE 6.26   Disk maintenance utilities

Tool	Function
rsync	Backs up and restores files
Time Machine	Backs up and restores files and images

(Continued)

TABLE 6.26 (Continued)

Tool	Function
fsck	File system checker
Disk utilities	Verifies disk health and restores images
tar	Backs up files
lvcreate	Creates a snapshot volume

FileVault

FileVault is Apple's form of encryption. Its first implementation was only for files in the user's Home directory, and there it would perform encryption on the fly to everything located there. Now it can also be enabled in the startup disk, a behavior similar to BitLocker in Windows. Mac OS X Lion (10.7) and newer offer FileVault 2, which is a significant redesign. This encrypts the entire macOS startup volume and typically includes the Home directory, abandoning the disk image approach. For this approach to disk encryption, authorized users' information is loaded from a separate nonencrypted boot volume.

Terminal

Shells and terminals both accept commands, but they are two separate programs. The following are some differences:

- A terminal window can run different shells depending on what you have configured.
- Certain interactive applications can be run in the terminal emulator, and they will run in the same window.
- Remote logins, using a program like Secure Shell (SSH), can be run from inside a terminal window.

macOS calls the shell Terminal, and you can find it under Applications > Utilities > Terminal, as shown in Figure 6.111.

Force Quit

Force Quit can be used on a Mac to stop an unresponsive application. To use this function, follow these steps:

1. Choose Force Quit from the Apple menu or press Command+Option+Esc.
2. Select the unresponsive app in the Force Quit Applications window, as shown in Figure 6.112, and then click Force Quit.

1.8 Explain common features and tools of the macOS/desktop operating system   389

FIGURE 6.111   The Mac Terminal

FIGURE 6.112   Force Quit Applications window

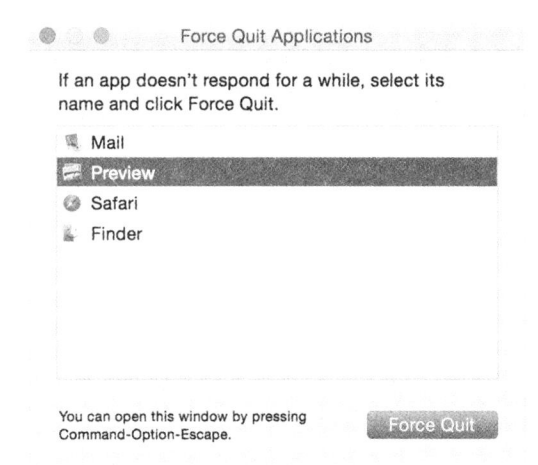

Exam essentials

Identify basic macOS/desktop operating tools.   These tools include System Preferences, Displays, Networks, Printers, Scanners, Privacy, Accessibility, and Time Machine.

1.9 Identify common features and tools of the Linux client/desktop operating system

In your career, you are almost certain to come in contact with the Linux OSes. Linux is probably used more often than Mac, in part because many proprietary OSes that reside on devices, such as access points, switches, routers, and firewalls, are Linux-based. In this section, you will be introduced to some of the common features and functions in this OS.

Common commands

While you may not be expected to be an expert in Linux, you will be responsible for knowing some basic Linux commands. This section will go over the main ones you need to know. In the following descriptions, items in [BRACKETS] are optional portions of the command, also called switches or parameters. Items in *bold italic* are required after the command. Also, please be aware that everything in Linux is case-sensitive.

File management

First, let's start with commands that are used to manage files and folders. This section covers `ls`, `pwd`, `mv`, `cp`, `rm`, `chmod`, `chown`, `grep`, and `find`.

ls

The `ls` command lists information about the files in the current directory. Its syntax is as follows:

`ls [OPTION]... [FILE]...`

For example, to list the contents of the /etc directory, you would type:

`$ ls /etc`

While the file options are too numerous to mention here, they mostly specify the format of the output. For a complete listing and their use, see https://linuxize.com/post/how-to-list-files-in-linux-using-the-ls-command/.

pwd vs. passwd

While the `passwd` command changes passwords for user accounts, the `pwd` command prints the full path name of the current working directory. The syntax for the `passwd` command is as follows:

`passwd [options] [LOGIN]`

1.9 Identify common features and tools of the Linux client/desktop operating system

To change a user's password (tmcmillan) to killmenow, enter:

```
$ sudo passwd tmcmillan killmenow
```

For information on the numerous options that can be used, see https://www.geeksforgeeks.org/pwd-command-in-linux-with-examples/.

The syntax for the `pwd` command is as follows:

```
pwd [OPTION]...
```

To print the current working directory, simply enter:

```
tmcmillan@debian:pwd
```

The options that can be used are found in Table 6.27.

mv

While the `mv` command can be used to move or rename a file in Linux, it's usually used to move a file. In that scenario, the syntax is as follows:

```
mv [OPTION]... [-T] SOURCE DEST
```

Basically, **SOURCE** is what you want to move, and **DEST** is where you want to put it. As an example, this command moves a file into another folder (directory):

```
mv passwordpolicy.txt c:\hr\policies\
```

For information on the parameters that can be used, see https://www.geeksforgeeks.org/mv-command-linux-examples/.

TABLE 6.27 passwd command

Password	Purpose
-L, --logical	If the contents of the environment variable PWD provide an absolute name of the current directory with no . or .. components, then output those contents, even if they contain symbolic links. Otherwise, fall back to the default -P handling.
-P, --physical	This prints a fully resolved name for the current directory in which all components of the name are actual directory names and not symbolic links.
--help	This displays a help message and exits.
--version	This displays version information and exits.

cp

The `cp` command is used to copy files and directories. Its syntax is as follows:

```
cp [OPTION]... SOURCE... DIRECTORY
```

For example, to copy the Sales file to a second file called FinalSales, enter:

```
$ cp Sales FinalSales
```

> **Warning** — Note: If the second file doesn't exist, it is created, and the content is copied into it. However, if the second file already exists, it is overwritten without warning.

For information on the parameters that can be used, see https://www.geeksforgeeks.org/cp-command-linux-examples/.

rm

The `rm` command removes (i.e. deletes) files or directories when it is combined with the `-r` option. The syntax is as follows:

```
rm [OPTION]... FILE...
```

For example, to remove the a.txt file, enter:

```
$ rm a.txt
```

For information on using parameters, see https://www.geeksforgeeks.org/rm-command-linux-examples/.

chmod

The `chmod` command is used to change the permissions of files or directories. Its syntax is as follows:

```
chmod options permissions filename
```

The options variable is used to alter the behavior of the `chmod` command. While these options are not required and are beyond the scope of this discussion, more on them can be found at https://www.tutorialspoint.com/unix_commands/chmod.htm.

The permissions variable is a set of characters, one set of which is entered for the file owner, one set for any group that may have permissions, and one set for any other single user accounts. The characters that are used and their meanings are as follows:

- `-` The file is not readable. You cannot view the file contents.
- `r` The file is readable.
- `-` The file cannot be changed or modified.
- `w` The file can be changed or modified.
- `-` The file cannot be executed.
- `x` The file can be executed.

For example, `rw-r--r--` means that the file owner has read and write permissions (`rw-`), and the group and others have only read permissions (`r--`).

In the following example, the command assigns all the permissions to the owner of the Sales file (using the `u` operator), read and write permissions to the group (using the `g` operator), and only read permissions to other users (using the operator):

```
$ sudo chmod u=rwx,g=rw,o=r Sales
```

For information on using parameters, see https://www.howtogeek.com/437958/how-to-use-the-chmod-command-on-linux/.

chown

The `chown` command is used to change the ownership of a file. The syntax is as follows, where *new_owner* is the username or the numeric user ID (UID) of the new owner and *object* is the name of the target file, directory, or link:

```
chown [options] new_owner object(s)
```

The ownership of any number of objects can be changed simultaneously.
The options are as follows:

- `-R` operates on file system objects recursively.
- `-v` (verbose) provides information about every object processed.
- `-c` reports only when a change is made.

For example, the following command designates the user "master" as the owner of file named file71.txt:

```
$ chown master file71.txt
```

grep

The `grep` command is used to search text or search the given file for lines containing a match to the given strings or words. Its syntax is as follows, where PATTERN is the pattern that you are trying to match:

```
grep [OPTIONS] PATTERN [FILE...]
```

For example, to search for text that includes the three-letter pattern wow in the file named Exclamation, enter:

```
$ grep wow exclamation
```

It has options that govern the matching process as well as options that specify the output. For more information on the options and their use, see https://www.howtogeek.com/496056/how-to-use-the-grep-command-on-linux/.

find

As you might suspect, the find command searches for files and directories in a file system. The syntax is:

```
find [-H] [-L] [-P] [-D debugopts] [-Olevel] [path...] [expression]
```

For example, to search for a file named troyfile, enter the following:

```
find -type f -name troyfile
```

Note: the `-f` variable makes the search for files *only*, not for directories or subdirectories.

For more information on the arguments, see https://www.geeksforgeeks.org/find-command-in-linux-with-examples/#syntax-of-find-command-in-linux-.

Filesystem management

The next two Linux commands are used to check the file system for errors and to attach or associate a file system or storage device to a particular location in the Linux directory tree. Let's look at these commands.

fsck

Because Linux systems manage the disk differently than Windows systems do, they need no defragmentation. There is a maintenance task you might want to schedule in Linux. From time to time, you should run a file system checker called `fsck`. This is a logical file system checker. Do not run `fsck` on a mounted device; you will need to unmount the target first to avoid damage to your files. (See the section on mount in the next section.) The syntax is as follows:

```
fsck <options> <filesystem>
```

For example, to check the filesystem /dev/sda2 enter:

```
sudo fsck /dev/sda2
```

For more information on the arguments, see https://linuxhandbook.com/fsck-command/.

mount

The mount command in Linux is used to attach file systems and removable devices, such as USB flash drives. Its syntax is as follows:

```
mount <options> <device> <mountpoint>
```

For example, to mount all file systems, enter:

```
$ mount
```

To specify a file system, use the -t variable. For example, to mount the ext4 filesystem, enter:

```
$ mount -t ext4
```

For more information on the arguments, see https://linuxconfig.org/Mount.

Administrative

Many commands cannot be run without root privileges. The following commands are used to enter that security context so that a command of this type can be executed.

su/sudo

The sudo commands can be added at the front of a command to execute the command using root privileges. For example, to remove a package with root privileges, the command is as follows:

```
sudo apt-get remove {package-name}
```

The `su` command is used to change from one user account to another. When the command is executed, you will be prompted for the password of the account to which you are switching, as shown here:

```
$ su mact
password:
mact@sandy:□$
```

Package management

Software for Linux is usually distributed in the form of packages, kept in repositories. Working with packages is known as *package management*. These commands are used in this process.

apt

There is a family of `apt` commands that are used in package management. For example, `apt-get` is the command-line tool for working with Advanced Packaging Tool (APT) software packages. These tools install or update packages on your system. The syntax of the command is as follows:

```
apt [...COMMANDS] [...PACKAGES]
```

COMMANDS represent the actions you wish to perform, such as install, update, or remove, and PACKAGES refer to the specific software you want to manage by name.

For example, to install a package named "Troy," enter:

```
apt install Troy
```

For additional information on its use and the options, see https://linuxize.com/post/how-to-use-apt-command/.

yum

This is also a package management command. Yellowdog Updater Modified (`yum`) is the traditional package manager for RedHat-based systems.

The general syntax of the `yum` command is:

```
yum [options] <command> [<args>...]
```

- [options] are optional flags that modify the behavior of the command.
- [command] is the YUM operation you want to perform (e.g. install, update, remove, etc.).
- [package(s)] specify the package(s) you want to work with.

For example, to update the package named Corky, enter:

```
yum update Corky
```

For more on this command, see https://www.geeksforgeeks.org/yum-commands-for-linux-package-management/.

dnf

The DNF command (Dandified `yum`) is the next-generation version of the YUM package manager for RedHat-based systems. It is the default package manager for Fedora 22, CentOS 8, and RHEL 8. It is intended to be a replacement for YUM. Its syntax is:

```
dnf [options] <command> [<args>...]
```

For example, to install a package named mcmillan, enter:

```
# dnf install mcmillan
```

For more on this command, see: https://www.linuxfordevices.com/tutorials/dnf-command.

Network

The commands in this section are used to manage and configure network connections and settings. They include `ip`, `ping`, `curl`, `dig`, and `traceroute`.

ip

The `ip` command is used to configure and manage network interfaces. The syntax is as follows:

```
ip [ OPTIONS ] OBJECT { COMMAND | help }
```

where OBJECT may be:

```
{ link | addr | addrlabel | route | rule | neigh | ntable | tunnel |
tuntap maddr | mroute | mrule | monitor | xfrm | netns | l2tp | tcp_metrics }
```

and OPTIONS may be:

```
{ -V[ersion] | -s[tatistics] | -r[esolve] | -f[amily]
{ inet | inet6 | ipx | dnet | link } | -o[neline] }
```

For example, to assign the IP address 192.168.1.100/24 to the first Ethernet interface in the dev system (interfaces are numbered starting with 0, not 1), enter:

```
sudo ip addr add 192.168.1.100/24 dev eth0
```

For more in this command, see https://www.howtogeek.com/657911/how-to-use-the-ip-command-on-linux/.

ping

The `ping` command you learned about in the section earlier in this chapter serves the same function in Linux. Please review that section. The Linux `ping` uses a different packet size and behaves differently, in that the Linux `ping` does not terminate by default. You must interrupt it (Ctrl-C) to end it and get a summary report.

curl

The `curl` command is a tool for transferring data from or to a server designed to work without user interaction. In its simplest form, when invoked without any option, `curl` displays the specified resource to the standard output.

```
curl [options] [URL]
```

For example, to retrieve the home page of macdaddy.com, enter:

```
$ curl macdaddy.com
```

For more on this command, see https://www.geeksforgeeks.org/curl-command-in-linux-with-examples/.

dig

The `dig` command performs network DNS lookups. It can be used to troubleshoot DNS by interrogating DNS name servers.

The syntax is as follows:

```
dig [@server] [-b address] [-c class] [-f filename] [-k filename] [-m]
[-p port#] [-q name] [-t type] [-x addr] [-y [hmac:]name:key]     [-4] [-6]
[name] [type] [class] [queryopt...]
```

For example, to query (request) all A (host) records for the daddymac.org domain, enter:

```
$ dig daddyman.org
```

For more information on the arguments, see https://www.geeksforgeeks.org/dig-command-in-linux-with-examples/.

traceroute

You learned about the `tracert` command earlier in this section. Please review that section. `traceroute` is the Linux version of this command. One difference is that `traceroute` returns only the number of hops encountered, while `tracert` also provides the IP addresses of all the hops.

Informational

Some commands are used to get information. This section covers man, cat, top, ps, du, and df.

man

This command is used to view the system's reference manuals. The syntax is as follows:

```
man [-C file] [-d] [-D] [--warnings[=warnings]] [-R encoding] [-L locale]
[-m system[,...]] [-M path] [-S list] [-e extension] [-i|-I] [--regex|--
wildcard] [--names-only] [-a] [-u] [--no-subpages] [-P pager] [-r prompt]
[-7] [-E encoding] [--no-hyphenation] [--no-justification] [-p string] [-t]
[-T[device]] [-H[browser]] [-X[dpi]] [-Z] [[section] page ...] ...
```

For example, to view the section of the manual that covers the `ls` command, enter:

```
$ man ls
```

For more information on the arguments, see https://www.geeksforgeeks.org/traceroute-command-in-linux-with-examples/.

cat

The simplest way to display the contents of a file at the command line is with the `cat` command. It can be used to do the following:

- Display text files
- Copy text files into a new document
- Append the contents of a text file to the end of another text file, combining them

Its syntax is as follows:

```
cat [OPTION]... [FILE]...
```

For example, to view the OctSales file, enter:

```
$ cat OctSales
```

top

The command `top` provides a dynamic real-time view of a running system. The syntax is as follows:

```
top -hv | -bcHisS -d delay -n limit -u|U user | -p pid -w [cols]
```

For example, to display all running processes, enter:

```
$ top
```

For more information on the arguments, see https://www.howtogeek.com/668986/how-to-use-the-linux-top-command-and-understand-its-output/.

ps

The `ps` command displays information about a selection of the active processes. Its syntax is as follows:

```
ps [options]
```

For example, to list all processes in the current shell, enter:

```
$ ps
```

For all processes in all shells, enter:

```
$ ps -A
```

For more information on the use of the options, see https://linuxize.com/post/ps-command-in-linux/.

du

The `du` command is a powerful utility that allows users to analyze and report on disk usage within directories and files. Its syntax is as follows:

```
du [options] [directory/file]
```

For example, to get the disk usage of the test folder in the mandeep subdirectory of the home directory, enter:

```
$ du /home/mandeep/test
```

For more information on the arguments, see https://www.geeksforgeeks.org/du-command-linux-examples/.

df

This command is used to assess the disk space used by a file system. The syntax is as follows:

```
df [OPTION]... [FILE]...
```

For example, to use `df` to assess the disk usage of the mcmillan.txt file, enter:

```
$ df mcmillan.txt
```

For more on this command, see https://www.geeksforgeeks.org/df-command-in-linux-with-examples/.

Text editors

While not the only text editor for Linux, nano is probably the one in most use, because it is simple, lightweight (i.e. doesn't use a lot of resources), and fast.

nano

Nano is a terminal-based text editor for Linux. It is functionally the same as another command called `pico`. Its syntax is as follows:

```
nano [ options ] [ file ]
```

For example, to open the file named troy.doc, enter:

```
$ nano troy.doc
```

For more information on the numerous options, see https://linuxize.com/post/how-to-use-nano-text-editor/.

Common configuration files

Settings or configuration of various items are contained within configuration files. Knowing the contents of these files can help in troubleshooting issues. Most global config files (like the ones discussed in this section) are located in the /etc directory.

/etc/passwd

The /etc/passwd file contains information about users, including their username, user ID, group ID, home directory, and shell. This file is available to all users on the system, but it is important to keep it secure to prevent unauthorized access to user accounts.

/etc/shadow

The /etc/shadow file contains encrypted password security information for each user on the system. Unlike /etc/passwd, this file is available *only* to the root user and is therefore much more secure. It is used to store items, such as the last password change, minimum password age, and maximum password age.

/etc/hosts

The /etc/hosts file maps hostnames to IP addresses. This simple text file can be used to specify custom hostnames and IP addresses, bypassing the need to use a DNS server. This file is used to perform local name resolution on a Linux system.

/etc/fstab

The /etc/fstab file controls the mounting of file systems at boot time and during normal system operation. It lists all available file systems and their mount points.

/etc/resolv.conf

The /etc/resolv.conf file is used to specify the system's DNS resolver. It identifies the DNS servers that the system should use for name resolution as well as search domains and options. This file is crucial for proper network communication on a Linux system.

OS components

It is also helpful when troubleshooting to understand the components of the Linux OS. You will learn about three important components, systemd, kernel, and bootlegger, in this section.

systemd

The systemd utility is a system and service manager that replaces several earlier tools for this function, such as SysVInit and BSD init. Like sysvinit, it is the first process started by the kernel when you boot up any Linux computer. Table 6.28 lists some useful systemd utilities along with a brief description of what they do.

1.9 Identify common features and tools of the Linux client/desktop operating system 403

TABLE 6.28 systemd utilities

Utility	Function
systemctl	Controls the systemd system and services
journalctl	Used to manage journal, systemd's own logging system
hostnamectl	Can control hostname
localectl	Helps configure a system's local and keyboard layout
timedatectl	Used to set time and date
systemd-cgls	Shows cgroup contents
systemadm	Is a front-end for systemctl command

kernel

As is the case in Windows, the Linux kernel is the central and most basic part of the OS. The Linux kernel is what is called free and open software, unlike the Windows kernel. The latest supported version of the kernel is 6.13.

Bootloader

Bootloader programs are used to bring the system to life and load the OS into memory so it can be processed. The most popular one in Linux is the GNU Grand Unified Bootloader, which is called GRUB for short. The latest version is called GRUB2. GRUB is both a bootloader (i.e. loads the system into memory) and a boot manager that offers an interface to the user to alter boot behavior.

Root account

We have mentioned things several times in this chapter that can *only* be done with the root account. Roughly like the administrator account in Windows, its security context can be accessed when logged in with a nonroot account by first using the sudo command, discussed in the "su/sudo" section earlier. Please review that section.

Exam essentials

Identify basic Linux commands. These commands include ls, grep, cd, pwd, passwd, mv, cp, rm, chmod, chown, ps, su, sudo, and apt-get.

1.10 Given a scenario, install applications according to requirements

When installing applications, there are a number of considerations to keep in mind. Unless the proper computing environment and resources are available, there will be issues. For example, if the system does not have the required CPU or disk space, the installation will stop and an error will be generated. In this section, you'll learn about these considerations when installing applications.

System requirements for applications

Every application has minimum system requirements with regard to computing resources. Applications also cannot run unless you provide them with the required CPU architecture. In this section, you'll learn about CPU architectures along with other system requirement issues.

32-bit vs. 64-bit dependent application requirements

The primary difference between 32-bit and 64-bit computing is the amount of data the processor (i.e. CPU) is able to process effectively. A 32-bit processor can accept and process 32 "lanes of data" simultaneously, while a 64-bit processor can accept and process 64 "lanes of data" simultaneously. To run a 64-bit version of the OS, you must have a 64-bit processor. To find out whether you are running the 32-bit or 64-bit version of Windows, you can look at the information shown in the System applet in the Control Panel.

Other differences between 64-bit and 32-bit systems are their hardware requirements and the types of applications you can run on them. You can run a 32-bit application on either a 64-bit or 32-bit OS, but you can run 64-bit applications only on a 64-bit system.

Dedicated vs. integrated graphics card

Many applications, such as computer-aided design (CAD), video editing software, and gaming software, require high-end graphics cards not typically installed in systems. Systems today come with integrated cards, which means they are built into the motherboard.

A graphics processing unit (GPU) is a specialized circuit designed to rapidly manipulate and alter memory to accelerate the building of images in a frame buffer intended for output to a display. It improves the graphic abilities of the PC when this feature is present in the CPU.

Some visual features provided by OSes such as Windows 11 are unavailable unless the CPU has dedicated graphics memory or a GPU. For example, the Aero view in Windows 11 requires a card capable of DirectX, which is a technology that requires the DirectCompute API, which in turn requires a GPU.

Video random-access memory (VRAM) requirements

As you can imagine, the video demands of graphics like 3D are much higher than those of common office applications. For example, AutoCAD 2024 requires a 3840 × 2160 (4K) or greater True Color video display adapter; 12 GB VRAM or greater; Pixel Shader 3.0 or greater; and a DirectX-capable workstation-class graphics card.

RAM requirements

The minimum RAM requirement should be viewed as just that, a minimum. Make sure you have more than required for satisfactory performance. While meeting the minimum might work, more memory will always help performance.

Central processing unit (CPU) requirements

In Chapter 3, you learned about processors and their characteristics in the section "CPU architecture." Earlier in this chapter, you learned that all OSes have minimum CPU requirements, and so do applications. For example, Office 2024 requires a 1.1-GHz or faster two-core processor. If this minimum is not met, the application will not install.

External hardware tokens

Physical tokens are anything that a user must have on them to access network resources and are often associated with devices that enable the user to generate a one-time password authenticating their identity. SecurID from RSA is one of the best-known examples of a physical token; learn more at `https://www.rsa.com/products/securid/`.

Storage requirements

Applications need storage space. Storage is another area where if you don't meet requirements, the application will simply *not* install. For example, Office 2024 requires at least 4 GB of space, and that's just the minimum.

Application to OS compatibility

The first requirement that must be met is the proper version of the OS. For example, if the documentation says it requires Windows 11, it may not install or run on Windows 10. Also, ensure that the application is made to run on Windows and not macOS or Linux.

32-bit vs. 64-bit OS

As you know, the primary difference between 32-bit and 64-bit computing is the amount of data the processor (i.e. CPU) can process effectively. As was stated earlier, you can run a 32-bit application on either a 64-bit or a 32-bit OS, but you can run 64-bit applications only on a 64-bit system.

Distribution methods

There are several ways the installation files may be introduced to your system. Let's look at the three of the most common ways for files to be placed on your OS.

Physical media vs. mountable ISO file

The first two ways that files can be introduced into your OS might already be familiar to you: locally or via a network.

Local (CD/USB)

Outside of the enterprise, most installations are done by using the CD that came packaged with the software or by placing these same files on a USB stick and accessing them via the USB drive.

Network-based

In most enterprises, installations are done by placing the install files in a network location and accessing and running them from that network location. Doing so saves the administrative effort involved in visiting each machine manually with an installation CD.

ISO-mountable

You can also install a software program from an International Organization for Standardization (ISO) file. To do so, first you obtain the application as an ISO file or image. Use the following steps.

1. Download the ISO file, then open File Explorer and right-click on the file. From the pop-up menu, select the Mount command. See Figure 6.113.

2. Selecting the Mount command opens a virtual drive from which you can install the software. On that virtual drive, you should find a setup.exe file or a similar file for installing the program. Double-click that file to install it, as shown on Figure 6.114.

3. Open the This PC folder in File Explorer. Right-click on the new virtual drive. Click the Eject command. Doing so removes the virtual drive, though your ISO file is still alive and well.

Downloadable package

A downloadable application package is a collection of files, configurations, and resources that come together to enable the swift and consistent installation of applications across various environments. Many applications are downloaded in this form.

Image deployment

Earlier in this chapter, you learned about tools like PXE in the section "Preboot Execution Environment (PXE)" and NetBoot in the section "NetBoot" that are used to boot a system with no operating systems, and thereafter connect to a server to download an OS image. The

FIGURE 6.113 Mounting an ISO file

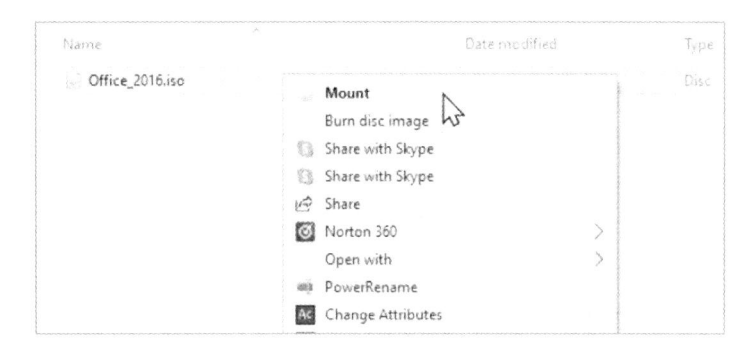

FIGURE 6.114 Running the setup

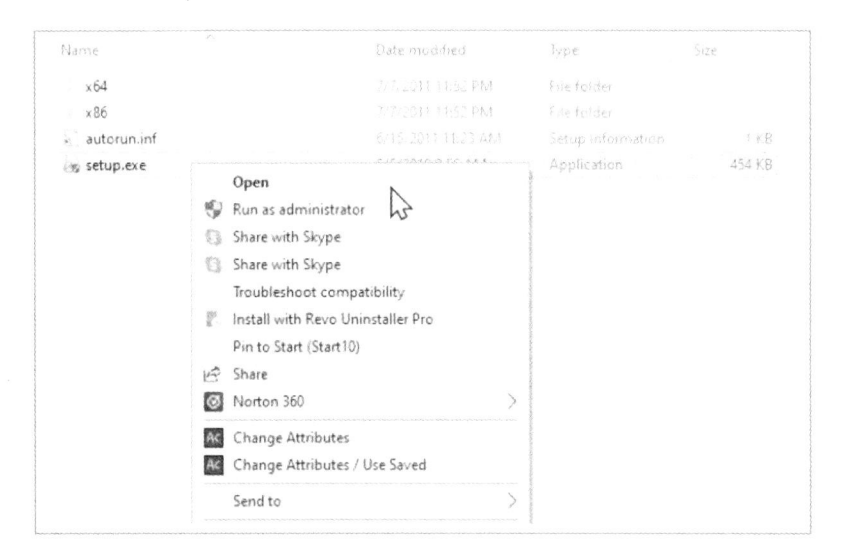

image is created by installing the OS on a system and then using imaging software, such as SmartDeploy, to save the system as an image. The beauty of this process is that you can make numerous application installations and setting configurations prior to taking the image, so that it is fully ready for users when it first boots up.

Impact considerations for new applications

Applications can serve as a security opening to hackers. Always research and consider the relative security of an application before installing it into your system. Also consider how the application may impact nonsecurity issues. For example, can the application handle the workload you expect? Can it output information in a format or syntax that is useful to you? These are issues you should also consider.

Device

Some software can be compromised in such a way as to potentially allow compromise of the entire device. Consider the application's reputation in the industry with regard to such weaknesses. Also consider the impact of the application on the performance of the device, and give consideration to what other applications may be running as well.

Network

While it's bad that a software compromise can lead to device compromise, it can also lead to a compromise of multiple devices on the network. Moreover, you should always consider the level of network traffic this application may create in its operation, because an increase in traffic means slower network performance for all devices.

Operation

While focusing on hardware minimums, security issues, and network traffic, it might be easy to overlook the consideration of the application's impact on operations. How will this new application fit into current workflows? Will it cause disruption, and how long will it last? Will the learning curve be steep for users? Consider all of these issues when choosing applications, as they will have a massive influence on your device's operation.

Business

Always keep in mind that a business may have many missions, but the most critical one for survival is to make money. If an organization is dependent on an application as a revenue source, such as an e-commerce system, the stakes are even higher. These applications should undergo a robust review process and lots of testing to ensure they will have a positive impact on your organization's bottom line.

Exam essentials

Identify methods of installation and deployment.   These methods include local (CD/USB), network-based, and ISO-mountable installation and deployment.

Understand critical system requirements.   Identify the system resources that must be fulfilled during each installation, including RAM, CPU, and disk space.

Understand possible impacts of new applications.   New applications can cause security issues and slow network performance, and disrupt workflows.

1.11 Given a scenario, install and configure cloud-based productivity tools

Not only have many organizations moved data to the cloud, but applications and tools can also be cloud-based. In this section, we'll look at installing various cloud-based productivity tools.

Email systems

Cloud email is a program that's Internet-based. A cloud provides hardware (i.e. storage and servers) and the related electricity, cooling, maintenance, and floor space. It can present big savings on both capital expenditures as well as ongoing expenses. Another unquantifiable benefit is that younger generations of workers (i.e. Gen Z) have grown to expect this type of email. In fact, some school systems require it.

One of the reasons some companies avoid cloud-based email is the same reason that other cloud-based tools might be avoided, and that's security and loss of control. Many organizations don't trust another entity to keep their email secure.

Storage

One of the biggest success stories for cloud providers is the use of the cloud for data storage. Accessible from anywhere one has an Internet connection, it frees the organization from spending big bucks on hardware and storage software, not to mention the cost of the provided support for the infrastructure.

Sync/folder settings

When users access data in the cloud from their local machines, it's always possible that the data in the cloud has changed, while the copy on the user's hard drive has not, or that the data has changed on the user's hard drive but not in the cloud. This can cause inadvertent data loss. For example, a file may have been deleted in the cloud, which causes a deletion of the file on the user's hard drive. Moreover, when users are editing the same document in the cloud, one user could overwrite another user's work.

The solution is a proper setting of the sync/folder settings. An example of some possible settings for FileCloud is shown in Figure 6.115.

An explanation of selected settings is in Table 6.29.

FIGURE 6.115 Sync settings

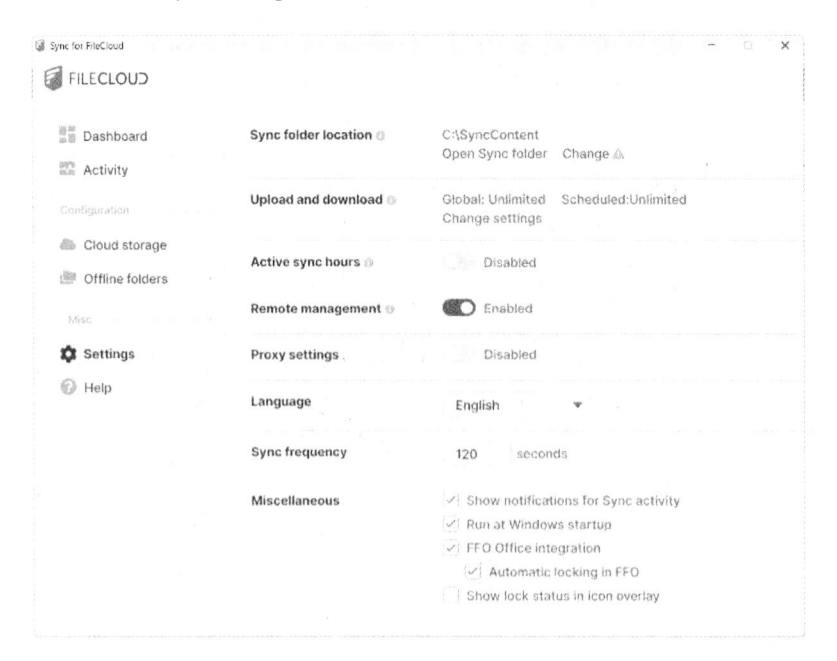

TABLE 6.29 Sync settings explained

Setting	Function
Sync folder location	Click Open Sync Folder to open the Sync directories in your File Explorer. Click Change to select a different location (i.e. a different drive or folder) for your Sync folder in File Explorer.
Upload and download	Limit upload and download rate.
Active sync hours	Limit sync to a schedule.
Remote management	Allows sync users to manage their sync application by overriding an administrator's settings.
Proxy settings	Set and enable proxy server.
Language	Set interface language.
Sync frequency	Change the built-in sync frequency of 120 seconds for cloud storage.

Collaboration tools

One of the other reasons organizations choose cloud-based tools is the ability to provide tools that make collaborating with others easier. When we speak of collaboration, we are talking about several functions:

- Editing the same document
- Using online videoconferencing
- Presenting plans to others online
- Using instant messaging

Spreadsheets

It is possible to connect your spreadsheets to the cloud. For example, with Excel these are all possibilities:

- Saving a workbook to OneDrive to access it from different devices and share with others.
- Using Excel's native Open Database Connectivity (ODBC) driver to connect directly to cloud storage services, such as Snowflake, Databricks, AWS, and Google Cloud.

Videoconferencing

Videoconferencing, which saves lots of money on travel, also improves communication by placing employees face to face, which can eliminate misunderstandings in written documents. The COVID pandemic made videoconferencing essential, and it is now firmly established as the default meeting method. Examples include Zoom, Lifesize, Zoho Meeting, and Google Meet.

Presentation tools

Typically a part of the videoconferencing tool, presentation tools allow one user to share the desktop, a window on the desktop, a video, or a slide deck with others. This makes meetings more productive.

Word processing tools

Many word processing tools, such as MS Word, are now cloud-based. The benefits can include:

- **Availability online.** You can work from anywhere.
- **Collaboration.** Allows multiple persons to edit at the same time.
- **Storage safety.** Many also autosave every time you make a change.

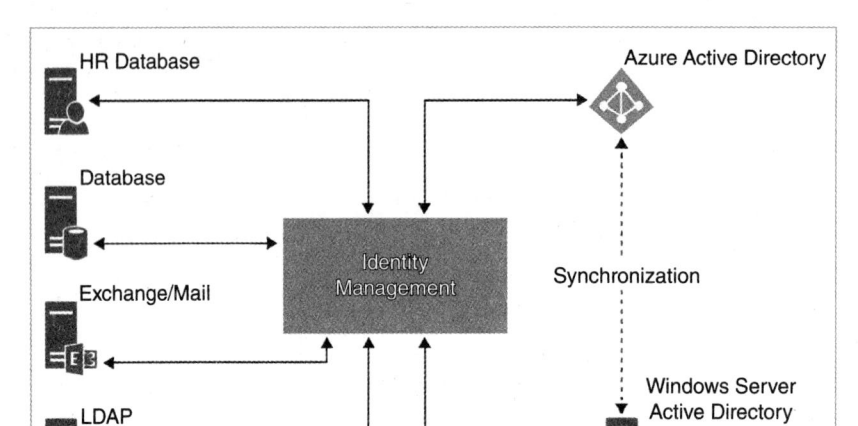

FIGURE 6.116 Identity synchronization

Instant messaging

For some workers email is way too slow for today's communication, as they require instant gratification. Instant messaging tools are how these folks prefer to communicate. Many commercial tools offer encryption.

Identity synchronization

Identity synchronization is part of what makes the synchronization of objects discussed earlier in this section possible. It is the process of bidirectionally synchronizing objects distributed across data sources, so that a change in an object in one source at the attribute level, or for the whole object, can be reflected into many other connected objects.

Another example of this concept is the identity synchronization that occurs between a cloud-based directory service and an on-premises directory service, as shown in Figure 6.116. In this case, the synchronization is focused on keeping the settings of the two services synchronized.

Licensing assignment

License management can also be done with a cloud-based tool. Cloud-based tools such as ezOnboard have many benefits. Among them are:

- **Cost efficiency.** Avoids the upfront expense of traditional license management tools by paying a reasonable subscription fee, which already covers updates, maintenance, and customer support.

- **Easier scalability.** Can grow with your business and easily scale up when you need more software assets, and if your needs decrease, you can scale down just as quickly.
- **Centralized software asset management.** Stores license inventory in one place. It helps you identify unused licenses and reallocate them where needed.
- **Improved license compliance.** Offers a unified view of software licenses, making it easier to track compliance.
- **Faster deployment.** Deployment is quick, and you can get up and running in hours, not weeks.
- **Automatic updates and maintenance.** Automatic updates keep your system current and secure against cyberattacks, and vendors handle all maintenance and updates.

Exam essentials

Identify the benefits of cloud-based license assignments. Thes include cost efficiency, easier scalability, centralized software asset management, improved license compliance, faster deployment, and automatic updates and maintenance.

Review Questions

You can find the answers in the appendix.

1. Which of the following cannot be a member of a domain?
   A. Windows 10 Pro
   B. Windows 10 Enterprise
   C. Windows 10 Pro for Workstations
   D. Windows 10 Home

2. Which command in Windows is used to create a new folder?
   A. md
   B. dir
   C. cd
   D. rd

3. Which tool lets you shut down nonresponsive applications selectively in all Windows versions?
   A. Action Center
   B. Task Manager
   C. Windows Firewall
   D. Defender

4. From which tab in Internet Options do you configure a VPN?
   A. Security
   B. General
   C. Connections
   D. Start

5. Where can you reset Windows 10 to improve performance?
   A. Personalization
   B. Privacy
   C. System
   D. Update and Security

6. In the Windows 10 Firewall, if you set the network as Public, which service is turned off?
   A. Network discovery
   B. ICMP
   C. IPv6
   D. SMB

7. Which Windows command is used to view a listing of the files and folders that exist within a directory, subdirectory, or folder?
   A. `net use`
   B. `dir`
   C. `cd`
   D. `ipconfig`

8. Which Windows command is used to move to another folder or directory?
   A. `net use`
   B. `dir`
   C. `cd`
   D. `ipconfig`

9. Which Windows tool shows a list of all installed hardware and lets you add items, remove items, update drivers, and more?
   A. Device Manager
   B. Event Viewer
   C. Users and Groups
   D. Sync Center

10. Which Windows tool tracks all events on a particular Windows computer?
    A. Device Manager
    B. Event Viewer
    C. Users and Groups
    D. Sync Center

11. Which of the following can be used on a Mac to stop an unresponsive application?
    A. Task Manager
    B. File Vault
    C. Finder
    D. Force Quit

12. Which of the following is true?
    A. You can only run a 32-bit application on a 64-bit operating system.
    B. You can run a 32-bit application on either a 64-bit or a 32-bit operating system, but you can run 64-bit applications only on a 64-bit system.
    C. You can only run a 32-bit application on a 32-bit operating system.
    D. You can run a 64-bit application on either a 64-bit or a 32-bit operating system.

13. Which of the following should you exceed for good performance?
    A. Minimum RAM
    B. Resolution
    C. Disk space
    D. Pixel count

14. Which type of installation is most likely to take place in a SOHO?
    A. Network
    B. RIS
    C. CD
    D. Unattended

15. Many proprietary operating systems that reside on devices such as access points, switches, routers, and firewalls are based on which operating system?
    A. Windows
    B. Mac
    C. Linux
    D. Android

16. Which of the following can be used to connect to a shared printer?
    A. `net use`
    B. `net user`
    C. `robocopy`
    D. `xcopy`

17. Which of the following is a command-line interface in Linux?
    A. `shell`
    B. `domain`
    C. `cmd`
    D. `DOS`

18. Which of the following provides a quick way to see everything that's currently open on your Mac?
    A. Shell
    B. Mission Control
    C. Sandbox
    D. Beeker

Chapter 7

Security

COMPTIA A+ 220-1202 EXAM OBJECTIVES COVERED IN THIS CHAPTER:

✔ **2.1 Summarize various security measures and their purposes**

- Physical security
  - Bollards
  - Access control vestibule
  - Badge reader
  - Video surveillance
  - Alarm systems/motion sensors
  - Door locks
  - Equipment locks
  - Security guards
  - Fences
- Physical access security
  - Key fobs
  - Smart cards
  - Keys
  - Mobile digital key
  - Biometrics
    - Retina scanner
    - Fingerprint scanner
    - Palm print scanner
    - Facial recognition technology (FRT)
    - Voice recognition technology
  - Lighting
    - Types of systems
    - Types of lighting

- Magnetometers
- Logical security
  - Principle of least privilege
  - Zero-trust model
  - Access control lists (ACLs)
  - Multifactor authentication
    - Email
    - Hardware token
    - Authenticator application
    - Short Message Service (SMS)
    - Voice call
    - One-time password/passcode (OTP)
    - Time-based one-time password (TOTP)
  - Security Assertion Markup Language (SAML)
  - Single sign-on (SSO)
  - Just-in-time access
    - Privileged access management (PAM)
  - Mobile device management (MDM)
  - Data loss prevention (DLP)
  - Identity and access management (IAM)
  - Directory services

✔ **2.2 Given a scenario, configure and apply basic Microsoft Windows OS security settings**

- Defender Antivirus
  - Activate/deactivate
  - Update definitions
- Firewall
  - Activate/deactivate
  - Port security
  - Application security
- Users and Groups

- Local vs. Microsoft account
- Standard account/administrator
- Guest user
- Power user
- Login OS options
  - Username and password
  - Personal identification number (PIN)
  - Fingerprint
  - Facial recognition
  - Single sign-on (SSO)
  - Passwordless/Windows Hello
- NTFS vs. share permissions
  - Allow vs. deny
  - Moving vs. copying folders and files
  - File and folder attributes
  - Inheritance
  - Permission propagation
  - Shared files and folders
  - Administrative shares vs. local shares
- Run as administrator vs. standard user
- User Account Control (UAC)
- BitLocker
- BitLocker-To-Go
- Encrypted File System (EFS)
- Active Directory
  - Joining domain
  - Assigning login script
  - Moving objects within organizational units
  - Assigning home folders
  - Applying Group Policy
  - Selecting security groups

- Administrator
- Power User
- Guest
- Standard User
- Configuring folder redirection

✔ **2.3 Compare and contrast wireless security protocols and authentication methods**

- Protocols and encryption
  - Wi-Fi Protected Access 2 (WPA2)
  - Wi-Fi Protected Access 3 (WPA3)
  - Temporal Key Integrity Protocol (TKIP)
  - Advanced Encryption Standard (AES)
- Authentication
  - Remote Authentication Dial-In User Service (RADIUS)/ Terminal Access Controller Access-Control System Plus (TACACS+)
  - Kerberos
  - Multifactor

✔ **2.4 Summarize types of malware and tools/methods for detection, removal, and prevention**

- Malware
  - Trojan
  - Rootkit
  - Virus
    - Symptoms of a virus/malware infection
    - How viruses work
    - Types of viruses
  - Spyware
  - Ransomware
  - Keylogger
  - Boot sector virus
  - Cryptominers

- Stalkerware
- Fileless
- Adware
- Potentially unwanted program (PUP)
- Tools and methods
  - Recovery Console
  - Endpoint Detection and Response (EDR)
  - Managed Detection and Response (MDR)
  - Extended Detection and Response (XDR)
  - MDR vs. EDR vs. XDR: key differences
  - Antivirus/anti-malware
  - Email security gateway
  - Software firewalls
  - User education regarding common threats
    - Anti-phishing training
  - OS reinstallation

✔ 2.5 Compare and contrast common social engineering attacks, threats, and vulnerabilities

- Social engineering
  - Phishing
    - Vishing
    - Smishing
    - QR code phishing
    - Spear phishing/whaling
  - Shoulder surfing
  - Tailgating
  - Impersonation
  - Dumpster diving
- Threats
  - Denial of service (DoS)
  - Distributed denial of service (DDoS)

- Evil twin
- Zero-day attack
- Spoofing
- On-path attack
- Brute-force attack
- Dictionary attack
- Insider threat
  - Intentional
  - Unintentional
- Structured Query Language (SQL) injection
- Cross-site scripting (XSS)
- Business email compromise (BEC)
- Supply chain/pipeline attack
- Vulnerabilities
  - Noncompliant systems
  - Unpatched systems
  - Unprotected systems (missing antivirus/missing firewall)
  - End of life (EOL)
  - Bring your own device (BYOD)

✔ **2.6 Given a scenario, implement procedures for basic small office/home office (SOHO) malware removal**

- Investigate and verify malware symptoms
- Quarantine infected systems
- Disable System Restore in Windows
- Remediate infected systems
  - Update anti-malware software
  - Use wise scanning and removal techniques (e.g. safe mode, preinstallation environment)
  - Reimage/reinstall
- Schedule scans and run updates
- Enable System Restore and create a restore point in Windows
- Educate the end user

✔ **2.7 Given a scenario, apply workstation security options and hardening techniques**

- Data-at-rest encryption
- Password considerations
  - Complexity requirements
  - Expiration
- Basic Input/Output System (BIOS)/Unified Extensible Firmware Interface (UEFI) passwords
- End-user best practices
  - Use screensaver locks
  - Log off when not in use
  - Secure/protect critical hardware (e.g. laptops)
  - Secure personally identifiable information (PII) and passwords
  - Use password managers
- Account management
  - Restrict user permissions
  - Restrict login times
  - Disable guest account
  - Use failed attempts lockout
  - Use timeout/screen lock
  - Apply account expiration dates
  - Change default administrator's user account/password
  - Disable AutoRun
  - Disable unused services

✔ **2.8 Given a scenario, apply common methods for securing mobile devices**

- Hardening techniques
  - Device encryption
  - Screen locks
    - Facial recognition
    - PIN codes
    - Fingerprint

- Pattern
- Swipe
- Configuration Profiles
- Patch management
  - OS updates
  - Application updates
- Endpoint security software
  - Antivirus/anti-malware
  - Content filtering
- Locator applications
- Remote wipes
- Remote backup applications
- Failed login attempts restrictions
- Policies and procedures
  - Mobile device management (MDM)
  - Bring your own device (BYOD) vs. corporate owned
  - Profile security requirements

✔ 2.9 Compare and contrast common data destruction and disposal methods

- Physical destruction of hard drives
  - Drilling/hammer
  - Shredding
  - Degaussing
  - Incineration
- Recycling or repurposing best practices
  - Erasing/wiping
    - Drive wipe
  - Low-level format vs. standard format
- Outsourcing concepts
  - Third-party vendor
  - Certification of destruction/recycling
- Regulatory and environmental requirements

✔ **2.10 Given a scenario, apply security settings on SOHO wireless and wired networks**
- Router settings
  - Change default passwords
  - IP filtering
  - Firmware updates
  - Content filtering
  - Physical placement/secure locations
    - Antenna and access point placement
    - Radio power levels
    - WPS
  - Universal Plug and Play (UPnP)
  - Screened subnet
  - Configure secure management access
- Wireless specific
  - Changing the service set identifier (SSID)
  - Disabling SSID broadcast
  - Encryption settings
  - Configuring guest access
- Firewall settings
  - Disabling unused ports
- Port forwarding/mapping

✔ **2.11 Given a scenario, configure relevant security settings in a browser**
- Browser download/installation
  - Trusted sources/untrusted sources
    - Hashing
- Browser patching
- Extensions and plug-ins
  - Trusted sources/untrusted sources
- Password managers
- Secure connections/sites—valid certificates

- Settings
  - Pop-up blocker
  - Clearing browser data/clearing cache
  - Private-browsing mode
  - Sign-in/browser data synchronization
  - Ad blocker
  - Proxy
  - Secure DNS
- Browser feature management
  - Enable/disable
    - Plug-ins/extensions
    - Features

2.1 Summarize various security measures and their purposes

This chapter focuses on the exam topics related to security. It follows the structure of the CompTIA A+ 220-1202 exam blueprint, Objective 2, and explores the 11 subobjectives that you need to master before taking the exam.

2.1 Summarize various security measures and their purposes

To properly secure a network environment, one must understand the available security mechanisms, along with their purpose and operation. It is also important to be able to match the mitigation technique with the vulnerability it is meant to address. Only then can you ensure you have reduced or eliminated the vulnerability. In this section, you'll learn about security measures and when to implement them.

Physical security

Physical security is a grab bag of elements that can be added to an environment to aid in securing it. It ranges from key fobs to retinal scanners. In this section, you will examine the physical security components as listed by CompTIA.

Bollards

Barriers called *bollards* have become quite common around the perimeter of new office and government buildings. These short vertical posts are placed at the building's entranceway and also line the sidewalks. They help to provide protection from vehicles that might either intentionally or unintentionally crash into or enter the building or injure pedestrians. Bollards can be made from many types of materials. Three types of bollards are shown in Figure 7.1.

Access control vestibule

An access control vestibule, sometimes also called a *mantrap*, is a series of two doors with a small room between them. A user is authenticated at the first door and then allowed into the room. At that point, additional verification will occur (such as a guard visually identifying the person), and then they are allowed through the second door. These doors are normally used only in high-security situations. Mantraps also typically require that the first door is closed prior to enabling the second door to open. Figure 7.2 shows a mantrap design.

FIGURE 7.1 Bollards examples

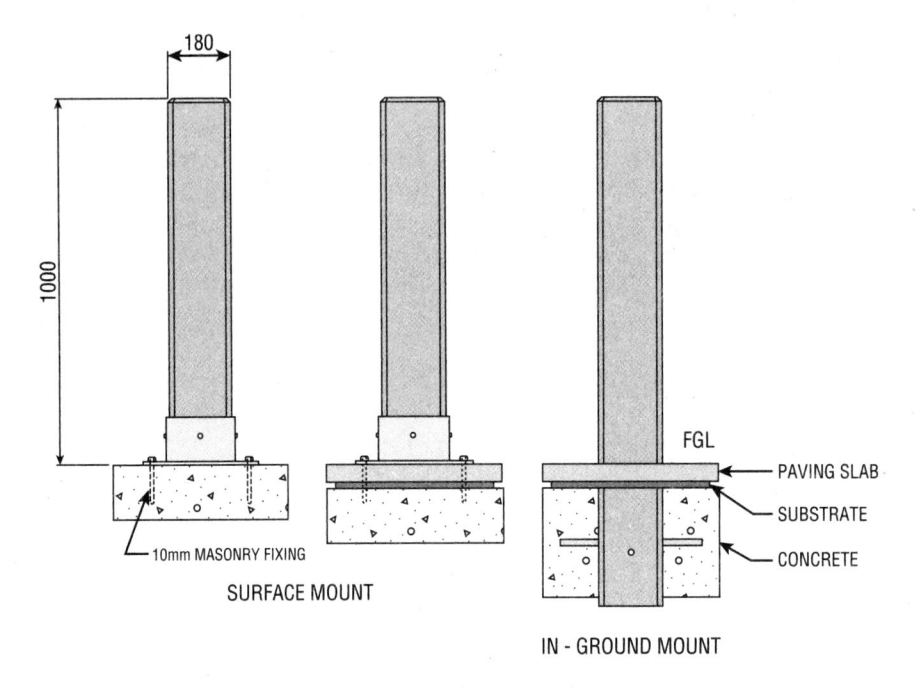

FIGURE 7.2 Aerial view of a mantrap

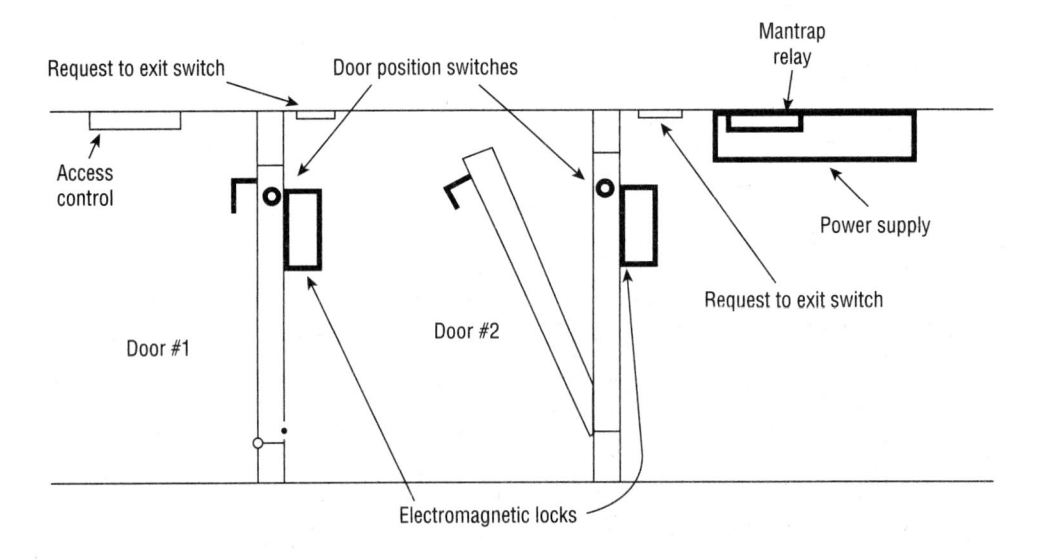

Badge reader

Radio frequency identification (RFID) is a wireless, no-contact technology used with badges or cards and their accompanying reader. The reader is connected to a workstation and validates against the security system. This increases the security of the authentication process, because the user must be in physical possession of the smart card to use the resources. Of course, if the card is lost or stolen, the person who finds the card can access the resources it allows. Badge readers are used not only to provide access to devices but also to provide access to doors.

Video surveillance

IP video systems provide a good example of the benefits of networking applications. These systems can be used for both surveilling a facility and facilitating collaboration. An example of the layout of an IP surveillance system is shown in Figure 7.3.

FIGURE 7.3 IP surveillance

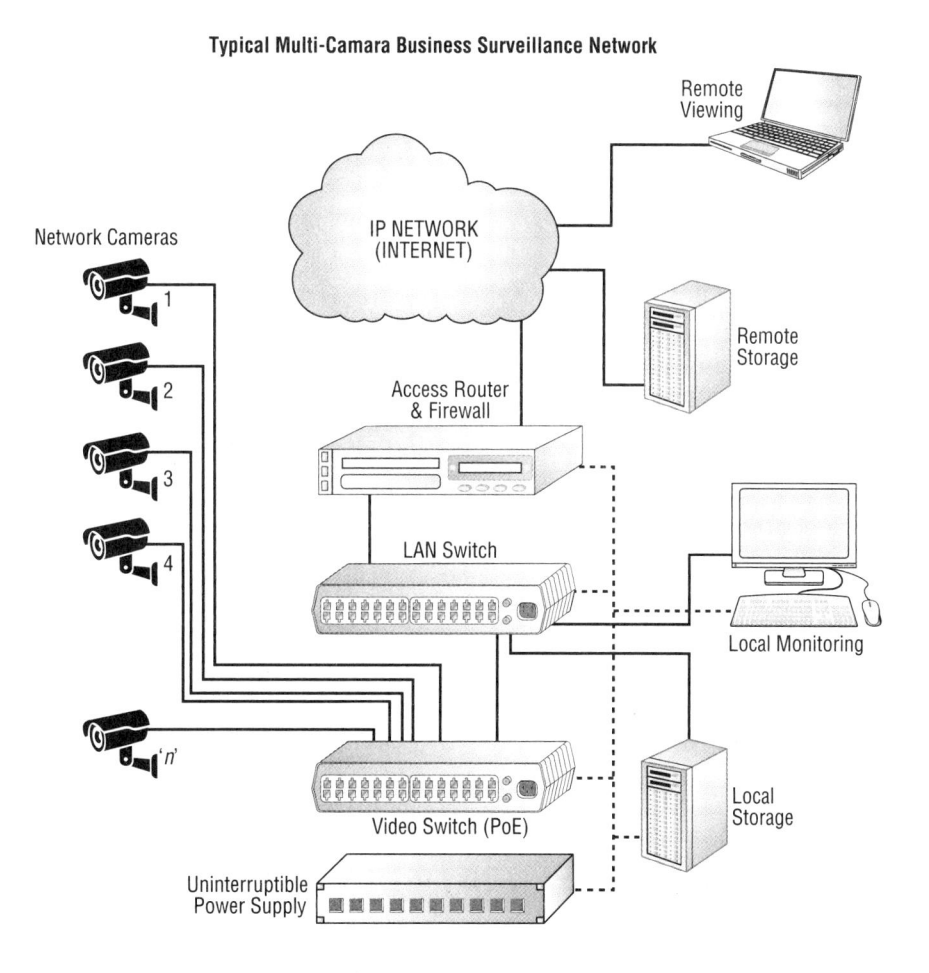

Alarm systems/motion sensors

Alarm systems can alert you when a physical intrusion has occurred. There are various technologies you can deploy, including:

- **Passive infrared (PIR) systems.** These operate by identifying changes in heat waves in an area. Because the presence of an intruder would raise the temperature of the surrounding air particles, this system alerts or sounds an alarm when this occurs.
- **Electromechanical systems.** These operate by detecting a break in an electrical circuit. For example, the circuit might cross a window or door and when the window or door is opened, the circuit is broken, setting off an alarm of some sort. Another example might be a pressure pad placed under the carpet to detect the presence of individuals.
- **Photoelectric systems.** These operate by detecting changes in the light, and thus are used in windowless areas. They send a beam of light across the area, and if the beam is interrupted (e.g. by a person), the alarm is triggered.
- **Acoustical detection systems.** These use strategically placed microphones to detect any sound made during a forced entry. These systems work well only in areas where there is not a lot of surrounding noise. They are typically very sensitive, which would cause many false alarms in a loud area, such as a door next to a busy street.
- **Wave motion detectors.** These generate a wave pattern in the area and detect any motion that disturbs the wave pattern. When the pattern is disturbed, an alarm sounds.
- **Capacitance detectors.** These emit a magnetic field and monitor that field. If the field is disrupted, which will occur when a person enters the area, the alarm will sound.

Door locks

One of the easiest ways to prevent people intent on creating problems from physically entering your environment is to lock your doors and keep them out.

Door locks are the most universal form of *physical barriers*, which are a key aspect of access control. The objective of a physical barrier is to prevent access to computers and network systems. The most effective physical barrier implementations require that more than one physical barrier be crossed to gain access. This type of approach is called a *multiple-barrier system*.

Ideally, your systems should have a minimum of three physical barriers. The first barrier is the external entrance to the building, referred to as a *perimeter*, which is protected by burglar alarms, external walls, fencing, surveillance, and so on. An access list should exist to specifically identify who can enter and be verified by a guard or someone in authority. The second barrier is the building's entrance and could rely on items such as ID badges to gain access. The third barrier is the entrance to the computer server room itself (and could require fobs or keys). Each of these entrances can be individually secured, monitored, and protected with alarm systems.

> Think of the three barriers this way: outer (the fence), middle (guards, locks, and mantraps), and inner (key fobs).

Although these three barriers won't always stop intruders, they will deter them enough that law enforcement can respond before an intrusion is fully developed. Once inside, a truly secure site should be dependent on a physical token for access to the actual network resources.

Equipment locks

While not all devices support this, larger mobile devices such as laptops come with a notch where you can attach a cable lock and lock the device to something solid, as you would lock a bicycle to a rack. This might even be advisable on some desktop systems if those systems are vulnerable to theft and contain sensitive data. Users who carry company devices that support cable locks should be instructed to never leave the device unattended and, if necessary, to lock the device to an immovable object.

Server locks

Both rack and nonrack server systems can come with physical locks that prevent tampering with the server if physical access becomes possible. Having said that, all servers should be locked in a room, but the inclusion of physical server locks as well is an example of defense in depth (an approach in which multiple layers of defense are provided).

Security guards

While many other less manual methods of monitoring are available, nothing takes the place of a human being. Security guards can exercise judgment and common sense, which sometimes an automated system seems to lack, as they encounter issues.

Fences

Fencing is the first line of defense in the concentric circle paradigm shown in Figure 7.4.

FIGURE 7.4 Concentric circles of protection

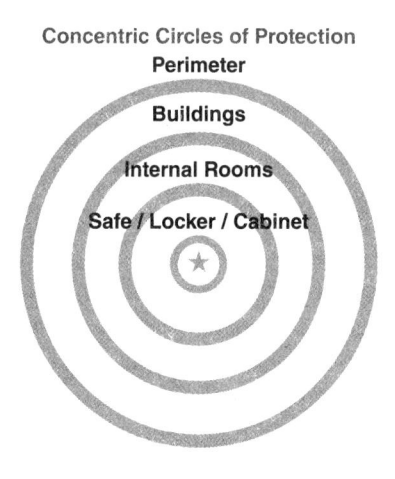

When selecting the type of fencing to install, consider the determination of the individual you are trying to discourage. Use the following guidelines with respect to height:

- Three- to four-foot fences deter only casual intruders.
- Six- to seven-foot fences are too tall to climb easily.
- Eight-foot and taller fences deter more determined intruders, especially when augmented with razor wire to physically deter anyone from climbing over.

Physical access security

Some mitigations or techniques are designed to address staff access to resources and devices. In this section you'll learn about measures designed to allow staff members to do their job but in a secure fashion.

Key fobs

Key fobs are named after the chains used to hold pocket watches to clothes. In today's terms, they resemble car remotes. They are security devices that you carry with you and that display a randomly generated code you can then use for authentication. This code usually changes quickly (every 60 seconds is probably the average), and you combine the code with your personal identification number (PIN) for authentication.

Smart cards

A smart card is a type of badge or card with embedded information that gives you access to resources, including buildings, parking lots, and computers. It contains information about your identity and access privileges. When used, each area or computer has a card scanner or a reader into which you insert your card.

Smart cards are difficult to counterfeit, but they're easy to steal. Once a thief has obtained a smart card, that person has all the access the card allows. To prevent this, many organizations don't put any identifying marks on their smart cards, making it harder for someone to use them. Many modern smart cards require a password or PIN to activate the card, and they employ encryption to protect the card's contents.

Keys

As you learned in the section on door locks, some doors have physical keys that fit into the lock. These keys must be accounted for at all times. It might be advantageous to create a chain-of-custody document that tracks the location of each key at all times. Chain-of-custody documents, as you will learn later in Chapter 9, in the section "Incident response," are used to account for evidence gathered in an investigation. They can also be used in this scenario.

Mobile digital key

Mobile digital keys are keys you can download to a smartphone and then use that smartphone to unlock a car door, a hotel door, or even an office door. Security issues with the keys include:

- Lost or stolen smartphones
- Rolling password attacks, in which the hacker uses a cheap, easy-to-obtain device that can intercept the codes from the smartphone to the car or door, and then uses them to unlock the door or unlock or start the vehicle.

Biometrics

Biometric devices use physical characteristics to identify the user. Such devices are becoming more common in the business environment. Biometric systems include hand scanners, retinal scanners, and, possibly soon, DNA scanners. To gain access to resources, you must pass a physical screening process. In the case of a hand scanner, this may include identifying fingerprints, scars, and markings on your hand. Retinal scanners compare your eye's retinal pattern to a stored retinal pattern to verify your identity. DNA scanners will examine a unique portion of your DNA structure to verify that you are who you say you are.

With the passing of time, the definition of *biometric* is expanding from simply identifying physical attributes about a person to being able to describe patterns in their behavior. Recent advances have been made in the ability to authenticate someone based on the key pattern they use when entering their password (i.e. how long they pause between each key, the amount of time each key is held down, etc.), otherwise known as *keyboard cadence*. A company adopting biometric technologies needs to consider the controversy they may face (as some authentication methods are considered more intrusive than others). It also needs to consider the error rate and that errors can include both false positives and false negatives.

Biometric systems, like most security tools, make mistakes. When the system improperly allows an individual in who should not be, it is called a *false acceptance*, and the rate at which this occurs is called the *false acceptance rate* (FAR). When the system improperly rejects a legitimate user, it is called a *false rejection*, and the rate at which these occur is called the *false rejection rate* (FRR).

Retina scanner

A retina scan examines the retina's blood vessel pattern, which is unique to each person. A retina scan, however, is considered by some to be intrusive, as it can disclose medical conditions.

Fingerprint scanner

A fingerprint scan usually analyzes the ridges of a finger for a matching pattern. A special type of fingerprint scan called *minutiae matching* is more microscopic in that it records the bifurcations (a single ridge that divides itself into two or more branches) and other detailed characteristics. Minutiae matching requires more authentication server space and more processing time than ridge fingerprint scans. Fingerprint scanning systems have a lower user acceptance rate than many systems, because users are concerned with how fingerprint information will be used and shared.

Palm print scanner

A palm or hand scan combines fingerprint and hand geometry technologies. It records fingerprint information from every finger as well as hand geometry information.

Facial recognition technology (FRT)

Facial recognition technology (FRT) uses points on the facial structure to create a map of the face that is as unique as a fingerprint. While it can be used as an authentication mechanism, it faces challenges from those who say it is an invasion of privacy, especially when used without the user's permission.

Voice recognition technology

In a similar manner to FRT, voice recognition technology (VRT) uses voice characteristics to create a sound template that is also as unique as a fingerprint. It can also be used as an authentication mechanism.

Lighting

One of the best ways to deter crime and mischief is to shine a light on the areas of concern. In this section, we look at some types of lighting and some lighting systems that have proven to be effective. Lighting is considered a physical control for physical security.

Types of systems

There are several types of lighting systems:

- **Continuous lighting:** An array of lights that provide an even amount of illumination across an area
- **Standby lighting:** A type of system that illuminates only at certain times or on a schedule
- **Movable lighting:** Lighting that can be repositioned as needed
- **Emergency lighting:** Lighting systems with their own power source to use when power is out

Types of lighting

The following are the most common choices when choosing the illumination source or type of light:

- **Fluorescent:** Very low-pressure mercury-vapor gas-discharge lamp that uses fluorescence to produce visible light

- **Mercury vapor:** Gas-discharge lamp that uses an electric arc through vaporized mercury to produce light
- **Sodium vapor:** Gas-discharge lamp that uses sodium in an excited state to produce light
- **Quartz lamps:** A lamp consisting of an ultraviolet light source, such as mercury vapor, contained in a fused-silica bulb that transmits ultraviolet light with little absorption

Regardless of the light source, it will be rated by its feet of illumination. When positioning the lights, you must take this rating into consideration. For example, if a controlled light fixture mounted on a 16 ft (5 m) pole can illuminate an area 98 ft (30 m) in diameter, for security lighting purposes, the distance between the fixtures should be 30 ft (9 m). Moreover, there should be extensive exterior perimeter lighting of entrances or parking areas to discourage prowlers or casual intruders.

Magnetometers

Handheld wand scanners that check for metal hidden on a person's body are called *magnetometers*. Magnetometers allow you to measure the strength and, depending on the instrument, the direction of a magnetic field at a point in space. So, what does this have to do with security? While they can be used to measure the Earth's magnetic field, used in geographical surveys, and used by the military to detect submarines, our interest is in their ability to detect weapons. Sadly, with the shootings in the workplace that have occurred in recent years, this can be a concern and might be a good addition to perimeter security. They come in both handheld models and as walk-through devices.

Logical security

Whereas physical security focuses on keeping individuals out, digital security focuses mostly on keeping harmful data/malware out. In this section, you'll learn about the principles and techniques involved in logical security.

Principle of least privilege

The concept of least privilege is a simple one: When assigning permissions, give each user only the permissions they need to do their work and no more. This is especially true with administrators. Users who need administrative-level permissions should be assigned two accounts: one for performing nonadministrative, day-to-day tasks, and the other to be used only when performing administrative tasks that specifically require an administrative-level user account. Those users should be educated on how each of the accounts should be used.

The biggest benefit to following this policy is the reduction of risk. The biggest headache is trying to deal with users who may not understand the importance of the policy. A manager, for example, may assert that he should have more permission than those who report to him, but giving those permissions to him also opens up all the possibilities for inadvertently deleting files, crippling accounts, and so forth.

A least-privilege policy should exist and be enforced throughout the enterprise. Users should have only the permissions and privileges needed to do their jobs and no more. ISO standard 27002 (which updates 17799) sums it up well: "Privileges should be allocated to individuals on a need-to-use basis and on an event-by-event basis, i.e., the minimum requirement for their functional role when needed." Adopting this as the policy for your organization is highly recommended.

Zero-trust model

The zero-trust model prescribes trusting no device and no user, even your own users and your own devices.

The introduction of wireless networks, portable network devices, virtualization, and cloud service providers has rendered the network boundary and attack surface increasingly porous. The evolution of security architecture has led to increased security capabilities, the same amount of security risks, and a higher total cost of ownership (TCO) but a smaller corporate data center, on average. In summary, the game has changed because of the impact of deperimeterization (i.e. constantly changing network boundaries). The following sections cover the influence of the zero-trust model in various technology areas.

Access control lists (ACLs)

Access control lists (ACLs) are sets of rules that either control access to a resource or are configured on a router or firewall to control the type of traffic allowed to enter or leave an interface. These lists are what make packet-filtering firewalls work. Using these lists, an administrator can, at a granular level, define who can send specific types of traffic to specific locations. For example, you could prevent a user from using Telnet to connect to the sales server without preventing them from using Telnet to connect to any other devices and without impacting any of their other activities.

Multifactor authentication

Multifactor authentication is a form of authentication that relies not on a single factor of authentication (such as a password) but on multiple factors of authentication. So, what are factors of authentication? These are various methods of proving one's identity. Authentication factors or methods are divided into five broad categories:

- **Knowledge factor authentication:** Something a person knows
- **Ownership factor authentication:** Something a person has
- **Characteristic factor authentication:** Something a person is
- **Location factor authentication:** Somewhere a person is
- **Action factor authentication:** Something a person does

Authentication usually ensures that a user provides at least one factor from these categories, which is referred to as *single-factor authentication*. An example of this would be providing a username and password at login. *Two-factor authentication* ensures that the user provides two of the three factors. An example of two-factor authentication would be providing a username and a password as well as a smart card at login. *Three-factor authentication* ensures that a user provides three factors. An example of three-factor authentication would be providing a username as well as a password, a smart card, and a fingerprint at login. For authentication to be considered strong authentication, a user must provide factors from at least two different categories. (Note that the username is the identification factor, not an authentication factor.)

You should understand that providing multiple authentication factors from the same category is still considered single-factor authentication. For example, if a user provides a username as well as a password and the user's mother's maiden name, single-factor authentication is being used. In this example, the user is still providing only factors that are something the person knows.

Email

When an email account is compromised, it can expose sensitive data that can damage the organization and even lead to additional compromises and data breaches. When an account is secured by multiple factors of authentication, such as a password and a smartcard, it makes the compromise much less likely.

Hardware token

Hardware and software tokens are typically used in multifactor authentication (MFA) mechanisms. A hardware token is a physical device (such as a key fob) that contains authentication information required during authentication. As such, a hardware token, or hard token, represents "something you possess."

Software tokens are cheaper than hardware tokens and do not have a battery that can run down as hardware tokens do. Software tokens reside on devices, such as smartphones or laptops, and unlike hardware tokens, they can be duplicated, so that is a risk to recognize.

Authenticator application

You learned about authenticator applications in Chapter 1, in the section "Corporate applications." Please review that chapter. These applications often implement MFA.

Short Message Service (SMS)

Short Message Service (SMS) is a text-messaging service component of most telephone, World Wide Web, and mobile telephony systems. These systems can also use and benefit from MFA. It is typically implemented as a one-time code that is sent to the user, with the code acting as an additional factor of authentication.

Voice call

Voice calls are one way a second factor of authentication can be delivered to a user attempting to authenticate to a web page or login screen. Instead of a one-time code being sent via text, the user receives a call at a specified number, and when they answer, they are asked to confirm the authentication attempt.

One-time password/passcode (OTP)

A one-time password (OTP) is a value that authenticates a user for a single login attempt or transaction. An algorithm generates a unique value for each one-time password by factoring in contextual information, like time-based data (see the next section) or previous login events. These were previously discussed in the discussion of multifactor authentication earlier in this chapter, in the section "Multifactor authentication." Please review that section.

Time-based one-time password (TOTP)

You learned about time-based one-time passwords (TOTP) in Chapter 1, in the section "Corporate applications." Please review that section.

Security Assertion Markup Language (SAML)

Security Assertion Markup Language (SAML) is an XML-based open standard data format for exchanging authentication and authorization data between parties, between an identity provider and a service provider. The major issue on which it focuses is called the *web browser single sign-on (SSO) problem* (see the next section). SAML's goal is to create a standard for this process.

Single sign-on (SSO)

Single sign-on (SSO) is the ability to authenticate once to access multiple sets of data. SSO at the Internet level is usually accomplished with cookies, but extending the concept beyond the Internet has resulted in many propriety approaches that are not interoperable. You will learn more about SSO later in this chapter, in the section "SSO."

Just-in-time access

Just-in-time (JIT) access refers to the granting of privileged access only for a limited time when needed. Such access terminates after a set duration of time has expired or when certain conditions are met or not met. A JIT access model eliminates persistent privileged access.

Privileged access management (PAM)

The most common implementation of JIT access is privileged access management (PAM). Typically implemented as Software as a Service (SaaS) offering from the cloud, it employs a least-privilege security strategy, allocating time-limited administrative permissions across different systems.

Mobile device management (MDM)

In recent years, mobile device management (MDM) and mobile application management (MAM) systems have become popular in enterprises. They are implemented to ensure that an organization can control mobile device settings, applications, and other parameters when those devices are attached to the enterprise network. In Chapter 1, you learned how MDM polices can be implemented through Active Directory or in the MDM software, in the "Mobile device management (MDM)" section. Please review that chapter.

Data loss prevention (DLP)

Data leakage occurs when sensitive data is disclosed to unauthorized personnel either intentionally or inadvertently. Data loss prevention (DLP) software attempts to prevent data leakage. It does so by maintaining awareness of actions that can and cannot be taken with respect to a document or data.

DLP software uses ingress (incoming) and egress (outgoing) filters to identify sensitive data that is leaving the organization and can prevent such leakage. Ingress filters examine information that is entering the network, while egress filters examine information that is leaving the network. Using an egress filter is one of the main mitigations to data exfiltration, which is the unauthorized transfer of data from a network.

Let's look at an example. Suppose that product plans should be available only to the development group. For that document, you might create a policy that specifies the following:

- It cannot be emailed to anyone other than development group members.
- It cannot be printed.
- It cannot be copied.

Identity and access management (IAM)

Identity and access management (IAM) describes how components and devices work together in an enterprise to secure resource access. It describes a formal set of steps to configure secure access control that allows only authorized users, applications, devices, and systems to access enterprise resources and information. These steps include the following:

1. Identify resources.
2. Identify users.
3. Identify the relationship between users and resources.

Directory services

Directory services are used to organize and locate resources such as users and computers. Later in this chapter, you will learn more in the section "Active Directory."

Exam essentials

Know the difference between single sign-on and multifactor authentication. Single sign-on (SSO) is the concept of having the user be authenticated on all services they access after logging in once. Multifactor authentication (MFA) is not the opposite of single sign-on but merely requires more than one entity to be authenticated for security purposes.

2.2 Given a scenario, configure and apply basic Microsoft Windows OS security settings

There is an entire domain dedicated to security for A+. Add to that, CompTIA also provides security certifications with Security+ and CompTIA Advanced Security Practitioner+ (CASP+), so you can see how important this topic is to those creating the exam. Because of that, make sure you have a good understanding of the topics covered here.

You want to make certain that your Windows systems and the data within them are kept as secure as possible. This security prevents others from changing the data, destroying it, or inadvertently harming it. This can be done by assigning users the least privileges possible and hardening as much of the environment as possible.

Defender Antivirus

Microsoft Defender Antivirus is an antivirus tool that can be downloaded for Windows 11. There is also a version that works on Macs. In this section, you will learn how to activate or deactivate it and update definitions.

Activate/deactivate

While you can use only Microsoft Defender for protection, you can still use another product at the same time. To activate Defender, follow these steps:

1. Click the Windows logo in the bottom-left corner of the screen. The Start menu will pop up.
2. Scroll down and click Windows Security to open the application.
3. On the Windows Security screen, if no antivirus program has been installed and running on your computer, the virus and protection icon will be unchecked.
4. Click on the Virus & Threat Protection icon.
5. Next, select Virus & Threat Protection Settings.
6. Flip the switch under Real-Time Protection.

> **NOTE** If you have another anti-malware product installed, you will see the screen shown in Figure 7.5 instead, which will offer you the option to scan with Defender as well.

FIGURE 7.5   Defender and another product

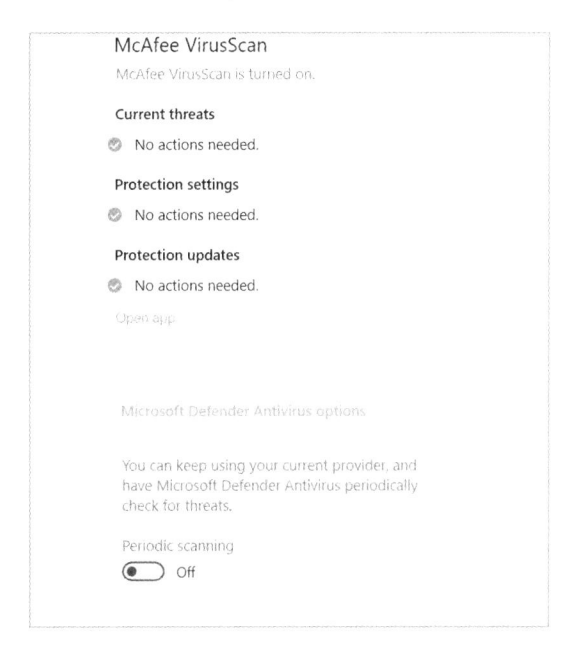

```
McAfee VirusScan
McAfee VirusScan is turned on.

Current threats
✓ No actions needed.

Protection settings
✓ No actions needed.

Protection updates
✓ No actions needed.

Open app

Microsoft Defender Antivirus options

You can keep using your current provider, and
have Microsoft Defender Antivirus periodically
check for threats.

Periodic scanning
⬤    Off
```

Updated definitions

If you are using Defender, you will want to keep the definitions updated. To do so, follow this procedure:

1. Select Windows Security and click/tap on the Virus & Threat Protection icon.
2. Click/tap on the Check for Updates link under Virus & Threat Protection Updates.
3. Click/tap on the Check for Updates button.
4. If a new security intelligence definition update is available, it will automatically download and install.

Firewall

You learned about Windows Firewall in Chapter 6, in the section named "Windows Defender Firewall." Please review that chapter.

Activate/deactivate

If your antivirus has a firewall, you can use that, but you can also use Windows Firewall. Go to Control Panel > All Control Panel Items > Security and Maintenance. Select the drop-down arrow next to Security to expand that section. Under Network Firewall, ensure that Windows Firewall is on.

Port security

One of the basic principles of security is to reduce the attack surface of all devices. This means shutting off all services and applications that are not required and closing all ports not being used. With respect to switches and hubs, it means disabling any ports that do not have devices connected to them. If this is not done, anyone could walk up to any unused wall jack and plug in a device, get an IP address through Dynamic Host Configuration Protocol (DHCP), and be on your network.

But sometimes you want to prevent someone from unplugging a legitimate device and plugging in one that is not legitimate. That's where port security comes in. By configuring port security on the port, you can prevent the transmission of data by any device other than the legitimate one. You can even shut the port down if this occurs.

Port security can also refer to the limitation of access that allows only well-known Transmission Control Protocol (TCP) and User Datagram Protocol (UDP) port numbers. Limiting access to allow only required ports reduces the attack surface.

Application security

While there are several ways to control the use of applications, you can control which applications can send data through the firewall as well. Filtering can be done on a port number or by simply identifying the application. When you are creating inbound and outbound rules, one of the steps is to identify the service or application. For example, to block Facebook, follow these steps:

1. Go to Outbound Rules and press New Rule in the column on the right.
2. In the New Outbound Rule Wizard, select Program (to block an application).
3. In the Program Path box, enter the path to the facebook.exe file (or browse to its location) and click Next.
4. Select the action to take. In this case, choose Block the Connection.
5. Select the network(s) where the rule applies (options are to the domain network, public networks, or trusted private networks).

Users and Groups

You learned about the Users and Groups tool in Chapter 6 in the section "Local Users and Groups (lusrmgr.msc)." Please review that section and chapter. In this section, you'll learn about various types of user accounts.

Local vs. Microsoft account

When you install Windows 10 or 11, you can choose to use either a local account or a Microsoft account. A local account will be good only for accessing the device. A Microsoft account will also give access to Microsoft services (such as Outlook), devices running on one of Microsoft's current operating systems (OSes), and Microsoft application software (including Visual Studio). While you can choose either during installation, Microsoft does not make it easy to find the option for local account, so I'll show you here (as Microsoft would prefer to keep you in their ecosystem).

1. Disconnect the computer from the network.
2. In the Sign in with Microsoft section, click the Next button without specifying an account name.
3. Click the Create Account option.
4. Click the Skip button.
5. Specify a name for your local account.
6. Click the Next button.
7. Create a password for the local account.
8. Click the Next button.
9. Confirm the password.
10. Click the Next button.
11. Select your first security question using the drop-down menu.
12. Confirm your first answer.
13. Click the Next button.
14. Repeat Steps 11, 12, and 13 two more times to complete setting up the local account security.
15. Continue with the on-screen directions.

Standard account/administrator

One of the security recommendations from Microsoft is to have administrative users log on with a standard user account and, when necessary, elevate the privileges of the account temporarily to perform a task and then remove that permission when the task is complete.

This is done by running the task, tool, or utility as an administrator. This can be done by right-clicking the tool and selecting Run as Administrator. Once the tool is closed, that security session ends, and the permissions are returned to those of a standard user. Having these highly privileged accounts logged in as infrequently as possible helps prevent hackers from gaining control of these accounts when they are live.

Guest user

You were introduced to the Guest account in Chapter 6, in the section "User Accounts." In Windows, the Guest account is automatically created with the intent that it is to be used when someone must access a system but lacks a user account on that system. Because it is so widely known to exist, I recommend that you not use this default account and instead create another one for the same purpose if you truly need one. The Guest account leaves a security risk at the workstation and should be disabled to prevent it from being accessed by those attempting to gain unauthorized access.

Power user

An account in the Power Users group is not as powerful as the Administrator account, but membership in this group gives read/write permission to the system, allowing members to install most software but keeping them from changing key OS files. This is a good group for those who need to test software (such as programmers) and junior administrators.

Login OS options

When users log into the system, they can authenticate in many ways besides using passwords. In this section, you'll learn more about authentication.

Username and password

While usernames and passwords are the most common authentication mechanisms used, they are probably the least secure because they are so easily stolen. If you are using these, follow the best practices you will learn later in this chapter, in the section "Password considerations."

Personal identification number (PIN)

A simpler option to the password/username option is a numeric PIN. While easier to remember, PINs may be easier to view and record from a distance because they are often simple four-character numbers. Moreover, because they are all numbers, there are fewer possible combinations, making them easier to crack.

Fingerprint

You learned about fingerprint locks for mobile devices in Chapter 1, in the section "Biometrics." This is a very secure option, as fingerprints (like all biometrics options) are difficult to copy. Review this technology in Chapter 1.

Facial recognition

You learned about facial recognition in Chapter 1, in the section "Biometrics." Please review that chapter for more information.

Single sign-on (SSO)

One of the bigger problems that larger systems must deal with is the need for users to access multiple systems or applications. This may require a user to remember multiple accounts and passwords. The purpose of an SSO is to give users access to all the applications and systems they need when they log on. This is becoming a reality in many environments, including Kerberos, Microsoft Active Directory, and some certificate model implementations.

> **NOTE** SSO is both a blessing and a curse. It's a blessing in that once users are authenticated, they can access all the resources on the network and browse multiple directories. It's a curse in that it removes the doors that otherwise exist between the user and various resources.

Passwordless/Windows Hello

Windows Hello is Microsoft's implementation of passwordless authentication. Passwordless authentication verifies a user's identity with something other than a password. The most common methods include verifying a secondary device in the user's possession, an account a user has, or a biometric trait that is unique to them, such as their face or fingerprint.

> **NOTE** Using Windows Hello requires one to be logged in with a Microsoft account.

To enable Windows Hello, follow these steps:

1. In the Settings app on your Windows device, select Accounts > Sign-In Options.
2. Under Additional Settings, turn on the following option: For improved security, only allow Windows Hello sign-in for Microsoft accounts on this device.

NTFS vs. share permissions

The New Technology File System (NTFS) was introduced with Windows NT to address security problems. Before Windows NT was released, it became apparent to Microsoft that a new file system was needed to handle growing disk sizes, security concerns, and the need for more stability than File Allocation Table 32 (FAT32) provided. NTFS was created to address those issues.

Although FAT was relatively stable if the systems that were controlling it kept running, it didn't do well when the power went out or the system crashed unexpectedly. One of the benefits of NTFS was a transaction tracking system, which made it possible for Windows NT to back out of any disk operations that were in progress when Windows NT crashed or lost power.

With NTFS, files, directories, and volumes can each have their own security. NTFS's security is flexible and built in. Not only does NTFS track security in ACLs, which can hold permissions for local users and groups, but each entry in the ACL can specify what type of access is given—such as read, write, modify, or full control. This allows a great deal of flexibility in setting up a network. In addition, special file-encryption programs were developed to encrypt data while it was stored on the hard disk.

Microsoft strongly recommends that all network shares be established using NTFS. Several current OSes from Microsoft support both FAT32 and NTFS. It's possible to convert from FAT32 to NTFS without losing data, but you can't do the operation in reverse (as you would need to reformat the drive and install the data again from a backup tape).

> If you're using FAT32 and want to change to NTFS, the `convert` utility will allow you to do so. For example, to change the E drive to NTFS, the command is `convert e: /FS:NTFS`.

Share permissions apply only when a user is accessing a file or folder through the network. Local permissions and attributes are used to protect the file when the user is local. With FAT and FAT32, you do not have the ability to assign "extended" or "extensible" permissions, and the user sitting at the console effectively is the owner of all resources on the system. As such, they can add, change, and delete any data or file that they want.

With NTFS as the filesystem, however, you are allowed to assign more comprehensive security to your computer system. NTFS permissions are able to protect you at the file level. Share permissions can be applied to the directory level only. NTFS permissions can affect users logged on locally or across the network to the system where the NTFS permissions are applied. Share permissions are in effect only when the user connects to the resource via the network.

> Share and NTFS permissions are not cumulative. Permission must be granted at both levels to allow access. Moreover, the effective permission that the user has will be the most restrictive of the combined NTFS permission and the combined share permissions.

Allow vs. deny

Within NTFS, permissions for objects fall into one of three categories: allow, not allow, and deny. When viewing the permissions for a file or folder, you can check the box for Allow, which effectively allows that group that action. You can also uncheck the box for Allow, which does not allow that group that action. Alternatively, you can check the box for Deny, which prevents that group from using that action. There is a difference between not allowing (a cleared checkbox) and denying (which specifically prohibits), and you tend not to see Deny used often. Deny, when used, trumps other permissions.

Permissions set at a folder are inherited down through subfolders, unless otherwise changed. Permissions are also cumulative: If a user is a member of a group that has read permission and a member of a group that has write permission, they effectively have both read and write permission.

Moving vs. copying folders and files

When you copy a file, you create a new entity. When you move a file, you simply relocate it and still have but one entity. This distinction is important for understanding permissions. A copy of a file will generally have the permissions assigned to it that are placed on newly created files in that folder—regardless of what permissions were on the original file.

A moved file, on the other hand, will attempt to keep the same permissions it had in the original location. Differences will occur if the same permissions cannot exist in the new location—for example, if you are moving a file from an NTFS volume to FAT32, the NTFS permissions will be lost. If, on the other hand, you are moving from a FAT32 volume to an NTFS volume, new permissions will be added that match those for newly created entities.

Folder copy and move operations follow similar guidelines to those with files.

File and folder attributes

Permissions can be allowed or denied individually on a per-folder basis. You can assign any combination of the values shown in Table 7.1.

Clicking the Advanced button allows you to configure auditing and ownership properties. You can also apply NTFS permissions to individual files. This is done from the Security tab for the file. Table 7.2 lists the NTFS file permissions.

TABLE 7.1 NTFS directory permissions

NTFS Permission	Meaning
Full Control	This gives the user all the other choices and the ability to change permission. The user also can take ownership of the directory or any of its contents.
Modify	This combines the Read & Execute permission with the Write permission and further allows the user to delete everything, including the folder.
Read & Execute	This combines the permissions of Read with those of List Folder Contents and adds the ability to run executables.
List Folder Contents	The List Folder Contents permission (known simply as List in previous versions) allows the user to view the contents of a directory and to navigate to its subdirectories. It does not grant the user access to the files in these directories unless that is specified in file permissions.
Read	This allows the user to navigate the entire directory structure, view the directory's contents, view the contents of any files in the directory, and see ownership and attributes.
Write	This allows the user to create new entities within the folder, as well as to change attributes.

TABLE 7.2 NTFS file permissions

NTFS permission	Meaning
Full Control	This gives the user all the other permissions, as well as permission to take ownership and change permission.
Modify	This combines the Read & Execute permission with the Write permission and further allows the user to delete the file.
Read	This allows the user to view the contents of the file and to see its ownership and attributes.
Read & Execute	This combines the Read permission with the ability to execute.
Write	This allows the user to overwrite the file, as well as to change attributes and see ownership and permissions.

By default, the determination of NTFS permissions is based on the *cumulative* NTFS permissions for a user. Rights can be assigned to users based on group membership and individually; the only time permissions do not accumulate is when the Deny permission is invoked.

Inheritance

Inheritance is the default throughout the permission structure unless a specific setting is created to override it. A user who has read and write permissions in one folder will have that in all the subfolders, unless a change has been made specifically to one of the subfolders.

Permission propagation

As mentioned earlier, permissions are cumulative. A user who is a member of two groups will effectively have the permissions of both groups combined. In cases where a user has a Deny permission from a group they are in, that overrules all other permissions they might have from other groups.

Shared files and folders

You can share folders and the files within them by right-clicking them and choosing Properties. In the Sharing tab, select Share and then select the users to share with, as shown in Figure 7.6.

Selecting Advanced Sharing settings will yield the interface shown in Figure 7.7.

2.2 Configure and apply basic Microsoft Window OS security settings

FIGURE 7.6 Sharing a folder

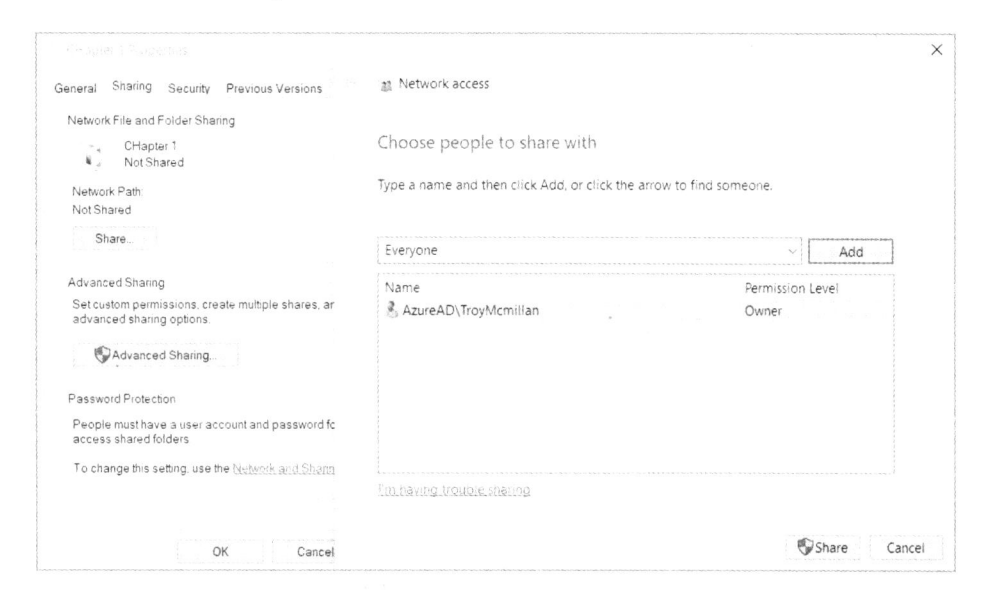

FIGURE 7.7 Advanced Sharing settings

Administrative shares vs. local shares

Administrative shares are created on servers running Windows on the network for administrative purposes. These shares can differ slightly based on which OS is running but always end with a dollar sign ($) to make them hidden. There is one share for each volume on a hard drive (e.g. c$, d$, etc.) as well as admin$ (i.e. the root folder, usually c:\windows) and print$ (i.e. where the print drivers are located). These shares are created for use by administrators and usually require administrator privileges to access.

Local shares, as the name implies, are those created locally on your workstation and are visible with the icon of a group of two individuals.

Run as administrator vs. standard user

One of the security recommendations from Microsoft is to have administrative users log on with a standard user account and, when necessary, elevate the privileges of the account temporarily to perform a task and then remove that permission when the task is complete.

This is done by running the task, tool, or utility as an administrator. This can be done by right-clicking the tool and selecting Run as Administrator. Once the tool is closed, that security session ends, and the permissions are returned to those of a standard user. Having these highly privileged accounts logged in as infrequently as possible helps prevent hackers from gaining control of these accounts when they are live.

User Account Control (UAC)

As you learned in Chapter 6, in the section "sfc," if you attempt to run System File Checker (SFC) or many other utilities from a standard command prompt, you will be told that you must be an administrator running a console session to continue. Rather than opening a standard command prompt, choose Start > All Programs > Accessories and then right-click Command Prompt and choose Run as Administrator.

The UAC will prompt you to continue, and then you can run SFC without a problem. When this function is enabled, which it is by default, you will always be challenged for the administrator password if you attempt any operation that requires that permission.

As you also learned in Chapter 6, on the Tool tab of System Configuration in the section "System Configuration (msconfig.exe)," you can enable and disable this function as well as many others. Once you highlight it and click Launch, you will see the box shown in Figure 7.8.

BitLocker

You were first introduced to BitLocker in Chapter 3, in the section "Trusted Platform Module (TPM) security features," when you learned how it can operate with a TPM chip. You also learned more about it in Chapter 6, in the section "BitLocker," where you learned its value in encrypting both startup files and data files.

FIGURE 7.8   UAC settings

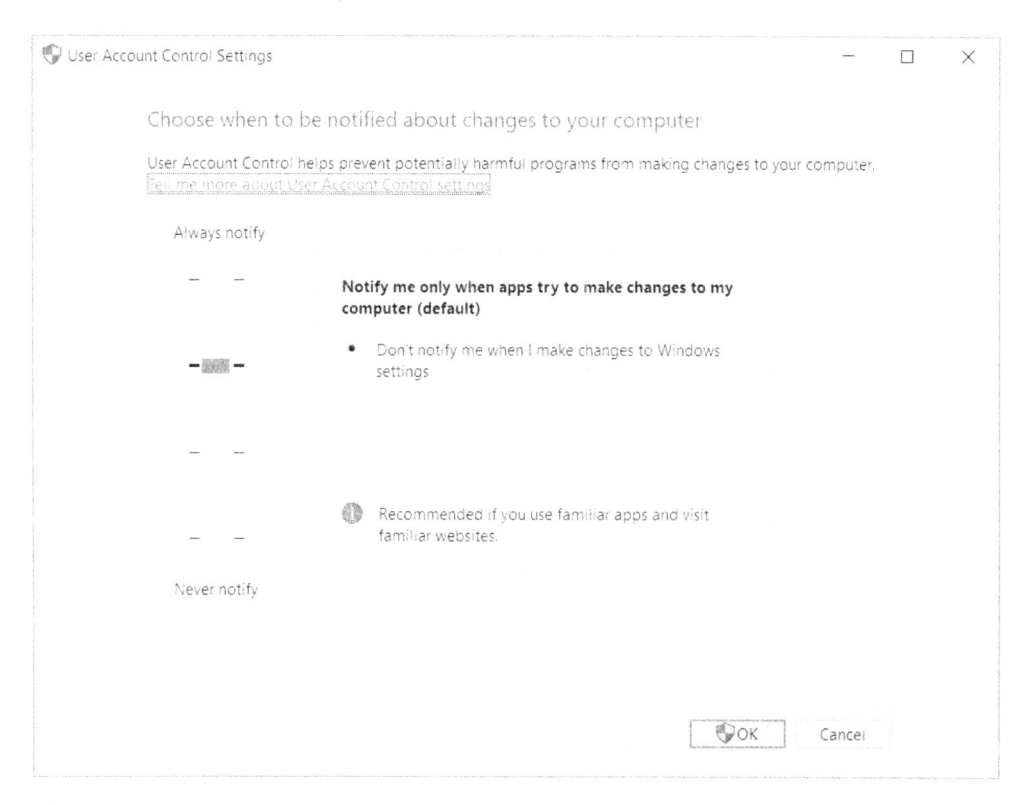

The BitLocker Drive Encryption Control Panel applet is used to turn on, suspend, or turn off BitLocker whole-drive encryption on your hard drives and flash drives, as shown in Figure 7.9.

BitLocker to Go

BitLocker to Go is simply the implementation of BitLocker encryption on portable or removable devices, such as USB flash drives or hard drives. However, it is restricted to Windows 10/11 Pro, Enterprise, or Education version.

Encrypting File System (EFS)

The Encrypting File System (EFS) is an encryption tool built into Windows. It allows a user to encrypt files that can be decrypted only by the user who encrypted the files. It can be used only on NTFS volumes and is simple to use.

FIGURE 7.9 BitLocker drive encryption

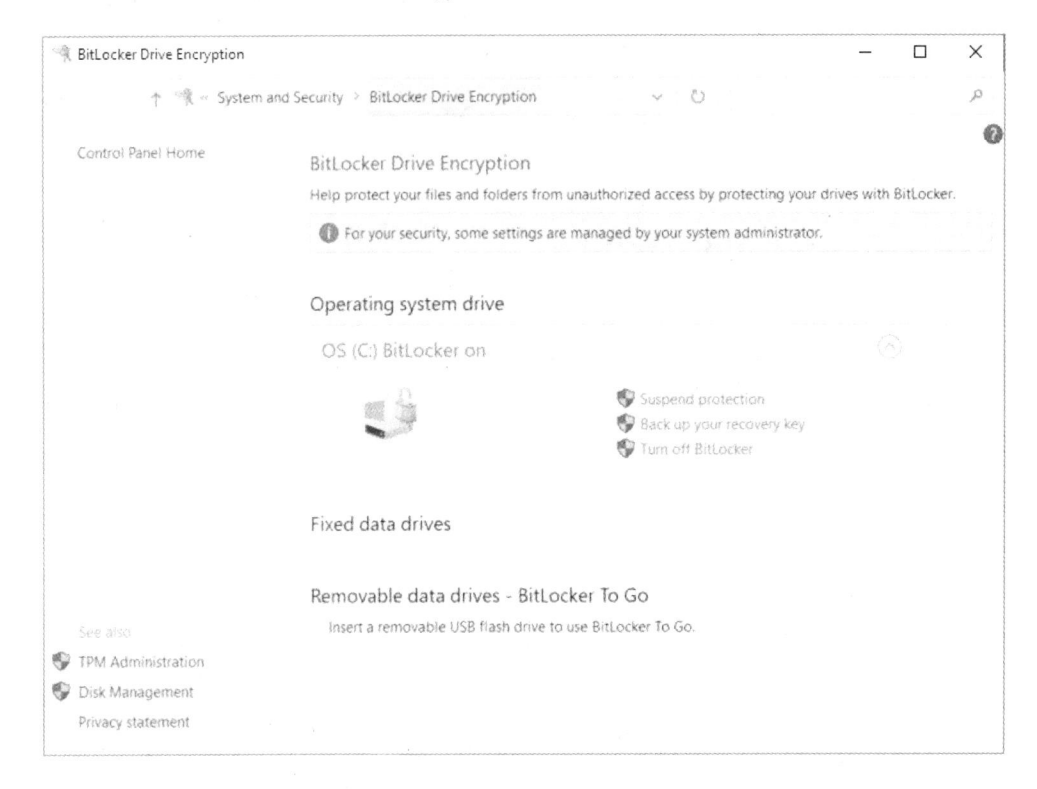

To encrypt a file, simply right-click the file, access the file properties, and on the General tab click the Advanced button. Doing so will open the Advanced Attributes dialog box, as shown in Figure 7.10. On this page, check the Encrypt Contents to Secure Data box.

Active Directory

Active Directory (AD) is the directory service used in Windows since Windows 2000. It is used to locate resources and is also the point of configuration for all things security in a Windows domain (a concept to be explained shortly). It has a hierarchical structure that can be leveraged when using one of the more powerful tools of AD called Group Policy. Let's survey some of the concepts of AD.

Joining domain

When a new AD structure is created, a new forest containing one domain is created. By default, all objects residing in a domain share the same security policies. Domains can be subdivided into organizational units (OUs), which can be used as targets for additional policies that you would like to confine to the OU. You learned how to join a system to a domain in Chapter 6, in the section "Domain setup." Please review that chapter.

FIGURE 7.10 Advanced attributes

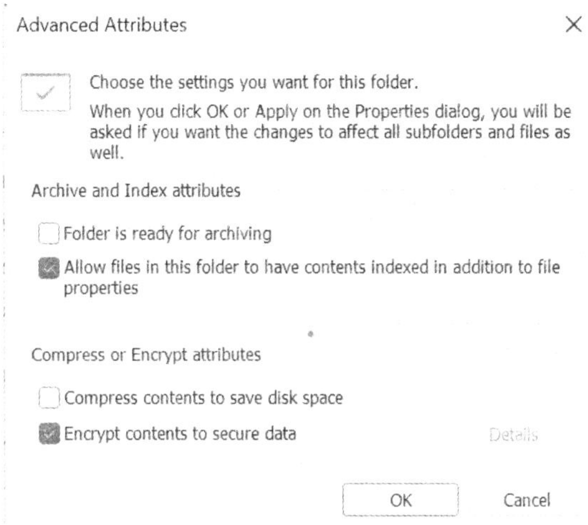

Assigning login script

While not required, login scripts assigned to a user run as soon as a user completes successful authentication. These scripts can automate a wide variety of operations, such as mapping drives for users and checking for updates.

To assign a login script to a user, you can follow these steps:

1. Open Computer Management.
2. In the console tree, expand Local Users and Groups and then click Users.
3. Double-click the user to which you want to assign a login script.
4. On the Profile tab, type the file name (and the relative path, if necessary) of the login script.

Moving objects within organizational units

As noted, domains can be subdivided into OUs, and OUs can also have child OUs. You can build whatever structure suits the efficient application of policies. While policy inheritance can be prevented, doing so complicates things, and a well-thought-out structure will result in allowing inheritance to operate. When you move objects from one container, such as an OU, into another one, security settings and group policies of the target container become effective. If security settings were applied directly to the object being moved, breaking inheritance, these settings would not be modified.

Assigning home folders

Home folders make it easier for an administrator to back up user files and manage user accounts by collecting the user's files in one location. If you assign a home folder to a user, you can store the user's data in a central location on a server and make backup and recovery of data easier and more reliable. If no home folder is assigned, the computer assigns the default local home folder to the user's account. The home folder can use the same location as the My Documents folder.

Applying Group Policy

When group policies are created, they can be applied to both computers and users and can be applied at either the domain or the OU level in the hierarchy.

When policies are added or updated, these changes are refreshed at certain intervals on the computers. Outside of these intervals, devices also check when rebooting and starting up. Finally, administrators can force an update at any time using the `gpudate` command.

Selecting security groups

There are a number of groups created on the OS by default. The following sections look at the main ones: Administrator, Power User, Guest, and Standard User.

Administrator

The Administrator account is the most powerful of all: It has the power to do everything from the smallest task all the way up to removing the OS. Because of the great power this account has and the fact that it is always created, many who try to do harm will target this account as the one they try to break into. To increase security, during the installation of the Windows OS in question, you are prompted for a name of a user who will be designated as the Administrator. The power then comes not from being truly called Administrator (in my case, it might now be tmcmillan, mcmillant, or something similar) but from being a member of the Administrators group (notice the plural for the group and singular for the user).

Because members of the Administrators group have such power, they can inadvertently do harm (such as accidentally deleting a file that a regular user could not). To protect against this, the practice of logging in with an Administrator account for daily interaction is strongly discouraged. Instead, system administrators should log in with a user account (lesser privileges) and change to the Administrators group account (elevated privileges) only when necessary for specific tasks.

Power User

As you learned earlier, the Power Users group is not as powerful as the Administrators group. Membership in this group gives read/write permission to the system, allowing members to install most software but keeping them from changing key OS files. This is a good group for those who need to test software (such as programmers) and junior administrators.

Guest

As you learned earlier, the Guest account is created by default (and should be disabled) and is a member of the Guests group. For the most part, members of the Guest account have the same rights as Users except they can't get to log files. The best reason to make users members of the Guests group is if they are accessing the system only for a limited time.

> As part of OS security, you should rename the default Administrator and Guest accounts that are created at installation.

Standard User

As you learned earlier in this chapter, this group is the default group to which regular users belong. Members of this group have read/write permission to their own profile. They cannot modify systemwide Registry settings or do much harm outside of their own account. Under the principle of least privilege, users should be made a member of the Users group only unless qualifying circumstances force them to have higher privileges.

Configuring folder redirection

Along with creating a home folder, folder redirection is an alternative method of automatically rerouting input/output (I/O) to/from standard folders (i.e. directories) to use storage elsewhere on a network.

Exam essentials

Identify the three built-in Windows groups. These are the Administrators, Power Users, and Guest users.

Describe the structure of Active Directory. When a new AD structure is created, a new forest containing one domain is created. Domains can be subdivided into organizational units (OUs), which can be used as targets for additional policies that you would like to confine to the OU.

2.3 Compare and contrast wireless security protocols and authentication methods

CompTIA wants administrators of small office/home office (SOHO) networks to be able to secure those networks in ways that protect the data stored on them. This objective looks at security protection that can be added to a wireless or wired SOHO network.

Protocols and encryption

More often, networks are using wireless as the medium of choice. It is much easier to implement, reconfigure, upgrade, and use than wired networks. Unfortunately, there can be downsides, and security is one of the largest.

The 802.11 standard applies to wireless networking, and there have been many versions of it released; the main ones are a, b, g, n, ac, and ax. Encryption has gone from very weak (Wired Equivalent Privacy [WEP]) to much stronger with increments along the way, including Wi-Fi Protected Access (WPA), Wi-Fi Protected Access 2 (WPA2), and implementations of Temporal Key Integrity Protocol (TKIP), and Advanced Encryption Standard (AES) encryption.

Wireless protocols were covered in detail in Chapter 2.

Wi-Fi Protected Access 2 (WPA2)

The WPA and WPA2 technologies were designed to address the core problems with WEP. These technologies implement the 802.11i standard. WPA implements most—but not all—of 802.11i to communicate with older wireless cards (which might still need an update through their firmware to be compliant), while WPA2 implements the full standard and is not compatible with older cards.

While WPA and WPA2 are primarily covered in Chapter 2, in the section "Explain wireless networking technologies," we need to say a few more words about these protocols. There are four variants, as described in Table 7.3.

> **WARNING**
> Never assume that a wireless connection is secure. The emissions from a wireless portal may be detectable through walls and for several blocks from the portal. Interception is easy to accomplish, given that radio frequency (RF) is the medium used for communication. Newer wireless devices offer data security, and you should use it. You can set up newer wireless access points (WAPs) and wireless routers to non-broadcast. This is also sometimes called *disabling the broadcast* of the service set identifier (SSID). Given the choice, you should choose to use WPA2, WPA, or WEP at its highest encryption level, in that order.

TABLE 7.3 WPA and WPA2

Protocol	Authentication	Encryption
WPA Personal	Passwords	TKIP
WPA Enterprise	RADIUS	TKIP
WPA2 Personal	Passwords	AES
WPA2 Enterprise	RADIUS	AES

Wi-Fi Protected Access 3 (WPA3)

Wi-Fi Protected Access 3 (WPA3) was announced in 2018 and makes the following enhancements to the protocol:

- Uses an equivalent 192-bit cryptographic strength in WPA3-Enterprise mode (AES-256 in GCM mode with SHA-384 as HMAC)
- Mandates the use of CCMP-128 (AES-128 in CCM mode) as the minimum encryption algorithm in WPA3-Personal mode
- Replaces the pre-shared key (PSK) exchange with the Simultaneous Authentication of Equals (SAE) exchange, resulting in a more secure initial key exchange in personal mode and forward secrecy
- Mitigates security issues posed by weak passwords and simplifies the process of setting up devices with no display interface
- Protects management frames as specified in the IEEE 802.11w amendment and also enforced by the WPA3 specifications

Temporal Key Integrity Protocol (TKIP)

WPA was able to increase security by using a TKIP to scramble encryption keys using a hashing algorithm. The keys are issued an integrity check to verify they have not been modified or tampered with during transit. While a good solution, it was far from perfect. Corporate security today favors WPA2 because it replaces TKIP with Counter Mode with Cipher Block Chaining Message Authentication Code Protocol (CCMP).

Advanced Encryption Standard (AES)

CCMP uses 128-bit AES with a 48-bit initialization vector, making it much more difficult to crack and minimize the risk of a replay attack. AES was also mentioned in Chapter 2, in the section "Explain wireless networking technologies."

Authentication

Authentication occurs when a user provides a username (identification) and then proper credentials (the authentication). In this section, we'll look at authentication, authorization, and accounting (AAA) services and the types of authentications.

Remote Authentication Dial-In User Service (RADIUS)/Terminal Access Controller Access-Control System Plus (TACACS+)

When users are making connections to the network through a variety of mechanisms, they should be authenticated first. These users could be accessing the network through any of the following:

- Dial-up remote access servers
- Virtual private network (VPN) access servers

- Wireless access points
- Security-enabled switches

At one time, each of these access devices would perform the authentication process locally on the device. The administrators would need to ensure that all remote access policies and settings were consistent across them all. When a password required changing, it had to be done on all devices.

To streamline this process, the Remote Authentication Dial-In User Service (RADIUS) and Terminal Access Controller Access-Control System Plus (TACACS+) networking protocols were developed to provide centralized authentication and authorization. These services can be run at a central location, and all the access devices, such as the access point (AP), remote access, VPN, and so on, can be made clients of the server. Whenever authentication occurs, the TACACS+ or RADIUS server performs the authentication and authorization. This provides one location to manage the remote access policies and passwords for the network.

Another advantage of using these systems is that the audit and access information (i.e. logs) are not kept on the access server.

TACACS and TACACS+ are Cisco proprietary services that operate in Cisco devices, whereas RADIUS is a standard defined in RFC 2138. Cisco has implemented several versions of TACACS over time. It went from TACACS to XTACACS to the latest version, TACACS+. The latest version provides authentication, authorization, and accounting, which is why it is sometimes referred to as an AAA service. TACACS+ employs tokens for two-factor, dynamic password authentication. It also allows users to change their passwords.

RADIUS is designed to provide a framework that includes three components. The *supplicant* is the device seeking authentication. The *authenticator* is the device to which they are attempting to connect (i.e. AP, switch, remote access server), and the *RADIUS server* is the authentication server. Note that the device seeking entry is not the RADIUS client. The authenticating server is the RADIUS server, and the authenticator (i.e. AP, switch, remote access server) is the RADIUS client.

In some cases, a RADIUS server can be the client of another RADIUS server. In that case, the RADIUS server acts as a proxy client for its RADIUS clients.

Kerberos

Kerberos is an authentication protocol that uses a client/server model developed by MIT's Project Athena. It is the default authentication model in the recent editions of Windows Server and is also used in Apple, Oracle, and Linux OSes.

Kerberos is an SSO system that uses symmetric key cryptography. Kerberos provides confidentiality and integrity. Kerberos assumes that messaging, cabling, and client computers are not secure and are easily accessible. In a Kerberos exchange involving a message with an authenticator, the authenticator contains the client ID and a timestamp. Because a Kerberos ticket is valid for a certain time, the timestamp ensures the validity of the request.

Multifactor

Multifactor authentication (MFA) was covered earlier in this chapter, in the section "Multifactor authentication." Please review that section.

Exam essentials

Understand wireless connectivity. Networks work in the same way whether there is a physical wire between the hosts or that wire has been replaced by a wireless signal. The same order of operations and steps are carried out regardless of the medium employed.

Describe the differences between the various implementations of WPA. They differ in their authentication methods and encryption provided. See both Table 7.3 and the section "Wi-Fi Protected Access 3 (WPA3)."

2.4 Summarize types of malware and tools/methods for detection, removal, and prevention

Over time, best practices have been developed through trial and error that help minimize the chances of getting viruses and reduce the effort involved in getting rid of malware. Some of these practices are discussed in this section.

Malware

Malware is a category of software that performs malicious activities on a device. It might wipe the hard drive or create a back door. In this section, we'll look at various types of malware and attacks.

Trojan

Trojan horses are programs that enter a system or network under the guise of another program. A Trojan horse may be included as an attachment or as part of an installation program. The Trojan horse can create a back door or replace a valid program during installation. It then accomplishes its mission under the guise of another program. Trojan horses can be used to compromise the security of your system, and they can exist on a system for years before they're detected.

The best preventive measure for Trojan horses is not to allow them entry into your system. Immediately before and after you install a new software program or OS, back it up!

If you suspect a Trojan horse, you can reinstall the original programs, which should delete the Trojan horse. A port scan may also reveal a Trojan horse on your system. If an application opens a TCP or IP port that isn't supported in your network, you can track it down and determine which port is being used.

Rootkit

Rootkits have become the software exploitation program du jour. They are software programs that have the ability to hide certain things from the OS. With a rootkit, there may be a number of processes running on a system that don't show up in Task Manager, or connections may be established/available that don't appear in a Netstat display—the rootkit masks the presence of these items. The rootkit does this by manipulating function calls to the OS and filtering out information that would normally appear.

Unfortunately, many rootkits are written to get around antivirus and antispyware programs that aren't kept up to date. The best defense you have is to monitor what your system is doing and catch the rootkit in the process of installation.

Virus

Viruses can be classified as polymorphic, stealth, retroviruses, multipartite, armored, companion, phage, and macro viruses. Each type of virus has a different attack strategy and different consequences.

> **Note:** Estimates for losses due to viruses are in billions of dollars. These losses include financial loss as well as lost productivity.

The following sections will introduce the symptoms of a virus infection, explain how a virus works, and describe the types of viruses you can expect to encounter and how they generally behave. How a virus is transmitted through a network will also be covered.

Symptoms of a virus/malware infection

Many viruses will announce that you're infected as soon as they gain access to your system. They may take control of your system and flash annoying messages on your screen or destroy your hard disk. When this occurs, you'll know that you're a victim. Other viruses will cause your system to slow down, cause files to disappear from your computer, or take over your disk space.

You should look for some of the following symptoms when determining whether a virus infection has occurred:

- The programs on your system start to load more slowly. This happens because the virus is spreading to other files in your system or is taking over system resources.

- Unusual files appear on your hard drive or files start to disappear from your system. Many viruses delete key files in your system to render it inoperable.

2.4 Summary of malware & tools/methods for detection, removal, & prevention 461

- Program sizes change from the installed versions. This occurs because the virus is attaching itself to these programs on your disk.
- Your browser, word-processing application, or other software begins to exhibit unusual operating characteristics. Screens or menus may change.
- The system mysteriously shuts itself down or starts itself up and does a great deal of unanticipated disk activity.
- You mysteriously lose access to a disk drive or other system resources. The virus has changed the settings on a device to make it unusable.
- Your system suddenly doesn't reboot or gives unexpected error messages during startup.

This list is by no means comprehensive. What is an absolute, however, is that you should immediately quarantine the infected system. It is imperative that you do all you can to contain the virus and keep it from spreading to other systems within your network or beyond.

How viruses work

A virus, in most cases, tries to accomplish one of two things: render your system inoperable or spread itself to other systems. Many viruses will spread to other systems given the chance and then render your system unusable. This is common with many newer viruses.

If your system is infected, the virus may try to attach itself to every file in your system and spread each time you send a file or document to other users. When you give removable media to another user or put it into another system, you then infect that system with the virus.

> **Note:** The best defense against a virus attack is to install and run antivirus software. The software should be on all workstations as well as the server.

Most viruses today are spread using email. The infected system attaches a file to any email that you send to another user. The recipient opens this file, thinking it's something you legitimately sent them. When they open the file, the virus infects the target system. The virus might then attach itself to all the emails the newly infected system sends, which in turn infects the recipients of the emails. Figure 7.11 shows how a virus can spread from a single user to thousands of users in a short time using email.

Types of viruses

Viruses take many different forms. The following briefly introduces these forms and explains how they work. These are the most common types, but this isn't a comprehensive list.

Armored virus   An *armored virus* is designed to make itself difficult to detect or analyze. Armored viruses cover themselves with protective code that stops debuggers or disassemblers from examining critical elements of the virus. The virus may be written in such a way that some aspects of the programming act as a decoy to distract analysis while the actual code hides in other areas in the program.

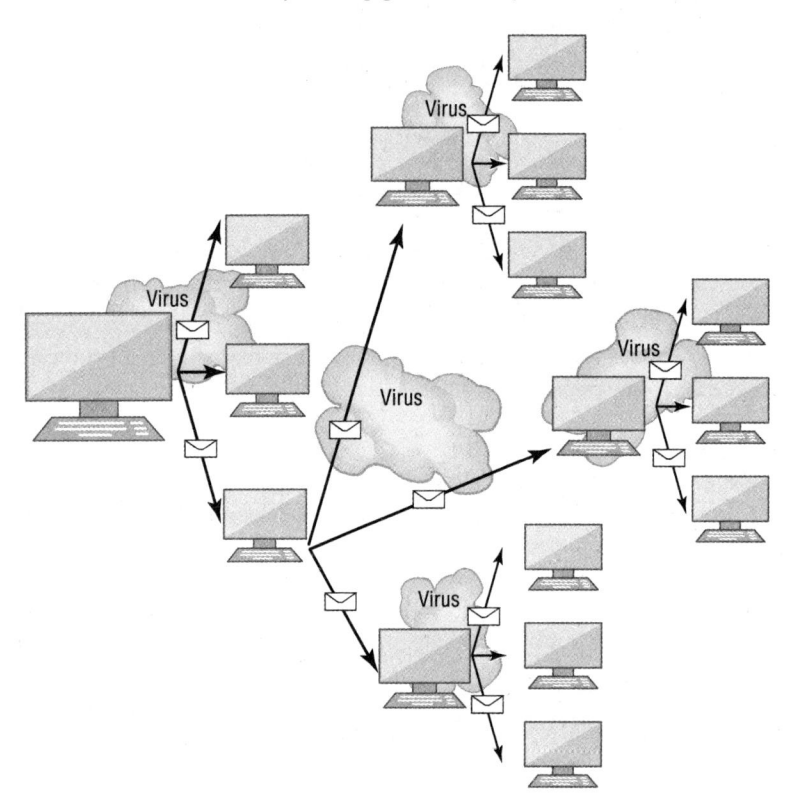

FIGURE 7.11 An email virus spreading geometrically to other users

From the perspective of the creator, the more time it takes to deconstruct the virus, the longer it can live. The longer it can live, the more time it has to replicate and spread to as many machines as possible. The key to stopping most viruses is to identify them quickly and educate administrators about them—the very things that the armor intensifies the difficulty of accomplishing.

Companion virus   A *companion virus* attaches itself to legitimate programs and then creates a program with a different extension. This file may reside in your system's temporary directory. When a user types the name of the legitimate program, the companion virus executes instead of the real program. This effectively hides the virus from the user. Many viruses that are used to attack Windows systems make changes to program pointers in the Registry so that they point to the infected program. The infected program may perform its dirty deed and then start the real program.

Macro virus   A *macro virus* exploits the enhancements made to many application programs. Programmers can expand the capability of applications such as Microsoft Word and Excel. Word, for example, supports a mini-BASIC programming language that allows files to

2.4 Summary of malware & tools/methods for detection, removal, & prevention

be manipulated automatically. These programs in the document are called *macros*. For example, a macro can tell your word processor to spell-check your document automatically when it opens. Macro viruses can infect all the documents on your system and spread to other systems via email or other methods.

Multipartite virus A *multipartite virus* attacks your system in multiple ways. It may attempt to infect your boot sector, infect all your executable files, and destroy your application files. The hope here is that you won't be able to correct all the problems and will allow the infestation to continue. The multipartite virus shown in Figure 7.12 attacks your boot sector, infects application files, and attacks your Word documents.

Phage virus A *phage virus* alters other programs and databases. The virus infects all these files. The only way to remove this virus is to reinstall the programs that are infected. If you miss even a single instance of this virus on the victim system, the process will start again and infect the system once more.

Polymorphic virus *Polymorphic viruses* change form in order to avoid detection. The virus will attempt to hide from your antivirus software. Frequently, the virus will encrypt parts of itself to avoid detection. When the virus does this, it's referred to as *mutation*. The mutation process makes it hard for antivirus software to detect common characteristics of the virus. Figure 7.13 shows a polymorphic virus changing its characteristics to avoid detection. In this example, the virus changes its signature to fool antivirus software.

> **NOTE** A *signature* is an algorithm or other element of a virus that uniquely identifies it. Because some viruses can alter their signature, it is crucial that you keep signature files current whether you choose to manually download them or configure the antivirus engine to do so automatically.

FIGURE 7.12 A multipartite virus commencing an attack on a system

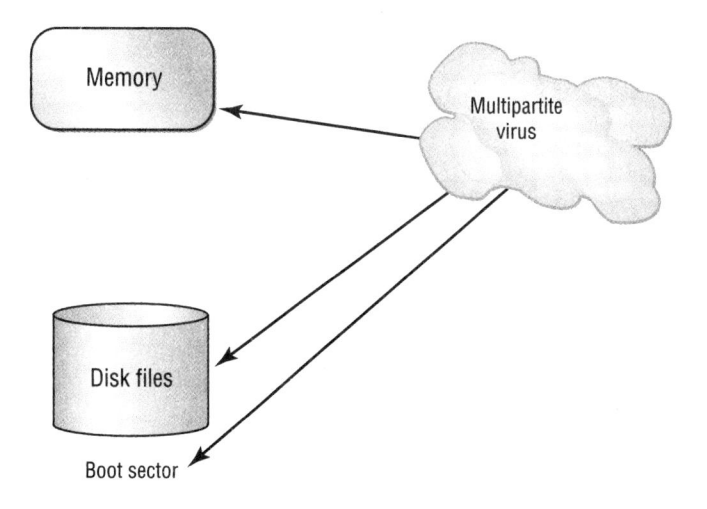

FIGURE 7.13 The polymorphic virus changing its characteristics

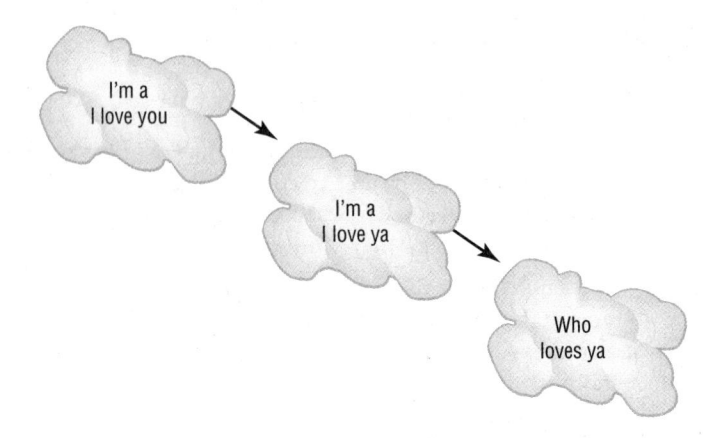

Retrovirus A *retrovirus* attacks or bypasses the antivirus software installed on a computer. You can consider a retrovirus to be an anti-antivirus. Retroviruses can directly attack your antivirus software and potentially destroy the virus definition database file. Destroying this information without your knowledge would leave you with a false sense of security. The virus may also directly attack an antivirus program to create bypasses for itself.

Stealth virus A *stealth virus* attempts to avoid detection by masking itself from applications. It may attach itself to the boot sector of the hard drive. When a system utility or program runs, the stealth virus redirects commands around itself to avoid detection. An infected file may report a file size different from what is actually present to avoid detection. Figure 7.14 shows a stealth virus attaching itself to the boot sector to avoid detection. Stealth viruses may also move themselves from file A to file B during a virus scan for the same reason.

Present virus activity

New viruses and threats are released on a regular basis to join the cadre of those already in existence. From an exam perspective, you need to be familiar with the world only as it existed at the time the questions were written. From an administrative standpoint, however, you need to know what is happening today.

To find this information, visit the CERT/CC Current Activity web page at `https://www.kb.cert.org/vuls/bypublic/desc/`. Here you'll find a detailed description of the most current viruses as well as links to pages on older threats.

FIGURE 7.14 A stealth virus hiding in a disk boot sector

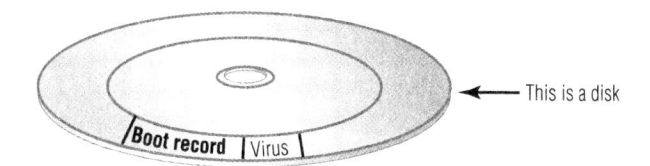

Spyware

Spyware differs from other malware in that it works—often actively—on behalf of a third party. Rather than self-replicating like viruses and worms, spyware is spread to machines by users who inadvertently ask for it. The users often don't know that they have asked for the spyware but have done so by downloading other programs, visiting infected sites, and so on.

Ransomware

Ransomware is a type of malware that usually encrypts the entire system or an entire drive with an encryption key that only the hacker possesses. Once they encrypt the machine, they can hold the data residing on the device hostage until a ransom is paid.

The latest version of this attack arrives as an attachment that appears to be a résumé. However, when the attachment is opened, the malware uses software called CryptoWall to encrypt the device. What usually follows is a demand for money to decrypt the device.

Keylogger

A keylogger records everything typed and sends a record of this to the attacker. It can be implemented as a malicious software package, maybe even as part of a rootkit, or it may be a hardware device inserted between the keyboard and the USB port.

Boot sector virus

Earlier in this section you learned that many viruses can infect the master boot record (MBR) of hard disks. (Some infect the boot sector of the hard disk instead of the MBR.) The infected code runs when the system is booted. If the virus cannot be removed due to encryption or excessive damage to existing code, the hard drive may need reformatting to eliminate the infection.

Cryptominers

Cryptominers are tools that generate new units of a cryptocurrency like Bitcoin. Cryptomining isn't itself malicious in nature. But bad actors are illegally accessing important business assets such as servers to use their processing power to solve the mathematical puzzles required to mine. This consumes CPU cycles and increases the power usage in the data center. The result will be slower performance, such as you might get from malware.

Stalkerware

Stalkerware is a category of malware that records every text, email, phone call, and online meeting while also maintaining constant awareness of the device's location using GPS. Its name comes from its use by those such as a former romantic partner or an abusively controlling current partner to "stalk" or pursue someone. Stalkers can also be individuals completely unknown to the target. These apps are easy to find and are often presented as a tool for parents to monitor a child's online activities and location.

Fileless

Fileless malware gets its name because, unlike many types of malware, it is not downloaded as a file. Rather, it works directly within a computer's memory instead of the hard drive. It can work in a couple of different ways:

- **Memory code injection.** Malicious code that powers fileless malware gets hidden inside the memory of otherwise innocent applications, often using vulnerabilities in programs like Flash and Java, as well as browsers.
- **Windows Registry manipulation.** Uses a malicious link or file that takes advantage of a trusted Windows process. After a user clicks on the link, the Windows process (using its security context and permissions) is then used to write and execute fileless code into the Registry.

Adware

Adware is a form of spyware that monitors the user's activity and responds by offering unsolicited pop-up advertisements and then gathers information about the user to pass on to marketers. Adware doesn't steal anything but tracks your Internet usage to tailor ads and junk email to your interests.

Potentially unwanted program (PUP)

Potentially unwanted programs (PUPs) are those that get onto your device without your knowledge. In that sense, every type of malware we have discussed fits the bill. In some cases, PUPs are bundled with free software, downloaded unintentionally, or distributed through deceptive advertising. They don't necessarily cause issues but do take up space on the device, and even harmless examples are sometime referred to as *bloatware* for their ability to slow the system.

Tools and methods

Whereas physical security focused on keeping individuals out, digital security focuses mostly on keeping harmful data/malware out. The areas of focus are antivirus software, anti-malware, Recovery Console, backup/restore, end-user education, software firewalls, and Domain Name System (DNS) configuration. Each of these is addressed in the sections that follow.

Recovery Console

The Recovery Console isn't installed on a Windows system by default. To install it, follow these steps:

1. Place the Windows disk (or a flash drive containing the installation files) in the system.
2. From a command prompt, change to the i386 directory of the installation files.
3. Type **winnt32 /cmdcons**.
4. A prompt appears, alerting you to the fact that 7 MB of hard drive space is required and asking whether you want to continue. Click Yes.

Upon successful completion of the installation, the Recovery Console is added as a menu choice at the bottom of the Startup menu. To access it, you must choose it from the list at startup. If more than one installation of Windows exists on the system, another boot menu will appear, asking which you want to boot into, and you must make a selection to continue.

To perform this task, you must give the administrator password. You'll then arrive at a command prompt. You can give a number of commands from this prompt, two of which are worth special attention: exit restarts the computer, and help lists the commands you can give. Table 7.4 explains some options.

Endpoint Detection and Response (EDR)

Endpoint Detection and Response (EDR) is a proactive endpoint security approach designed to supplement existing defenses. These products shift security from a reactive threat approach to one that can detect and prevent threats before they reach the organization. It focuses on three essential elements for effective threat prevention: automation, adaptability, and continuous monitoring.

TABLE 7.4 Recovery Console options

Option	Explanation
Startup Repair	Fixes missing or damaged system files, which might prevent Windows from starting correctly
System Restore	Restores your computer's system files to an earlier point in time without affecting your files, such as email, documents, or photos
System Image Recovery	Requires a system image, a personalized backup of the partition that contains Windows, and includes programs and user data, like documents, pictures, and music
Windows Memory Diagnostic Tool	Scans your computer's memory for errors

The advantage of EDR systems is that they provide continuous monitoring. The disadvantage is that the software's use of resources could impact performance of the device.

Managed Detection and Response (MDR)

Managed Detection and Response (MDR) is a cybersecurity service that, while much like EDR, goes a step further and performs threat hunting. It combines technology with human expertise to rapidly identify and limit the impact of threats by providing both monitoring and response. One of its biggest benefits is its ability to reduce time to detect (and therefore, time to respond) from many days to as little as a few minutes.

Extended Detection and Response (XDR)

Extended Detection and Response (XDR) is called extended because of its ability to "see" the entire attack. Rather than having to look in each system, XDR allows you to see the whole attack in one place, making it easier to spot and stop the threat. Because many security solutions operate in isolated silos, larger trends can't be recognized. XDR fixes this by giving you a complete view of all systems at once.

MDR vs. EDR vs. XDR: key differences

Table 7.5 compares the three forms of response tools described in this section: MDR, EDR, and XDR.

Antivirus/anti-malware

The primary method of preventing the propagation of malicious code involves the use of antivirus software. In Chapter 6, in the section "Antivirus," you learned the importance of keeping this software installed and updated. The primary method of preventing the propagation of malicious code involves the use of antivirus software, a type of application that is

TABLE 7.5 MDR vs. EDR vs. XDR

Criteria	EDR	MDR	XDR
Benefits	Detailed visibility and control	Hands-off protection	Full, unified view
Challenges	High-alert volume can overwhelm small teams	Can be costly, depending on the provider and organization size	Complex integration, especially for large or hybrid infrastructures
Cost	More cost-effective but resource-intensive for in-house teams	Higher cost due to human-led services but less need for internal resources	The most expensive solution

installed on a system to protect it and to scan for viruses as well as worms and Trojan horses. Most viruses have characteristics that are common to families of a virus or viruses. Antivirus software looks for these characteristics, or fingerprints, to identify and neutralize viruses before they impact you. Anti-malware software addresses malware types other than viruses, such as worms and trojans, although the function of the two tools overlaps to a certain degree.

Hundreds of thousands of known viruses, worms, bombs, and other malware have been defined. New ones are added all the time. Your antivirus software manufacturer will usually work hard to keep the definition database files current. The definition database file contains all the known viruses and countermeasures for a particular antivirus software product. If you keep the virus definition database files in your software up to date, you probably won't be overly vulnerable to attacks.

> The best method of protection is to use a layered approach. Antivirus software should be at the gateways, at the servers, and at the desktop. If you want to go one step further, you can use software at each location from different vendors to ensure that you're covered from all angles.

Email security gateway

In Chapter 2, you learned that a spam gateway is an appliance through which all email is examined, and all spam is removed or at least segregated from non-spam items. An email security gateway takes this concept a step further and identifies and blocks malicious emails before they reach inboxes. Secure email gateways (SEGs) work similarly to secure web gateways (SWGs) but focus on identifying threats in email traffic rather than a user's web browsing activity.

Software firewalls

You can add a second layer of defense by utilizing personal or software firewalls on devices. This can be in addition to your network firewall and can help prevent attacks locally on machines. The Windows Firewall is a good example of such a software firewall.

User education regarding common threats

In many cases, users are partly responsible for a virus infection. After an infection occurs is a great time to impress on users the principles of secure computing. They should be reminded that antivirus software and firewalls can go only so far in protecting them and that they should exercise safe browsing habits and refrain from opening any attachments in email from unknown sources, regardless of how tempting.

Anti-phishing training

In the next section, you will learn about social engineering attacks. *Phishing* is a form of social engineering in which you simply ask someone for a piece of information that you are missing by making it look as if it is a legitimate request. An email might look as if it is from a bank and contain some basic information, such as the user's name. In the email, it will often state that there is a problem with the person's account or access privileges. They will be told to click a link to correct the problem. After they click the link—which goes to a site other than the bank's—they are asked for their username, password, account information, and so on. The person instigating the phishing can then use the values entered there to access the legitimate account.

> **TIP** One of the best counters to phishing is to simply mouse over the Click Here link and read the URL. Almost every time it is pointing to an adaptation of the legitimate URL as opposed to a link to the real thing.

The only preventive measure in dealing with social engineering attacks is to educate your users and staff to never give out passwords and user IDs over the phone or via email or to anyone who isn't positively verified as being who they say they are.

OS reinstallation

In many cases, especially with some advanced malware, the only way to be assured that all of the infection and vulnerability created by the infection are removed is to format the hard drive and reinstall the OS.

Exam essentials

Differentiate antivirus and anti-malware software. Antivirus software addresses viruses, while anti-malware software addresses malware types other than viruses, such as worms and trojans, although the function of the two tools overlaps to a certain degree.

2.5 Compare and contrast common social engineering attacks, threats, and vulnerabilities

This objective explores security threats and vulnerabilities. A number of important topics are discussed in this section that fall into the realm of two broad categories: social engineering and malware. You'll look at malware and then several different types of attacks, as well as some of the reasons your network is vulnerable.

Social engineering

Social engineering is a process in which an attacker attempts to acquire information about your network and system by social means, such as by talking to people in your organization. A social engineering attack may occur over the phone, by email, or by a visit. The intent is to acquire access information, such as user IDs and passwords. When the attempt is made through email or instant messaging, it is known as *phishing* (discussed next) and often is made to look as if it is coming from sites where users are likely to have accounts (e.g. eBay and PayPal are popular).

These types of attacks are relatively low-tech and are more akin to con jobs. Take the following example. Your help desk gets a call at 4 A.M. from someone purporting to be the vice president of your company. She tells the help-desk personnel that she is out of town to attend a meeting, her computer just failed, and she is sitting in a hotel trying to get a file from her desktop computer back at the office. She can't seem to remember her password and user ID. She tells the help-desk representative that she needs access to the information right away or the company could lose millions of dollars. Your help-desk rep knows how important this meeting is and gives the vice president her user ID and password over the phone. This attack is known as *vishing*.

Another common approach is initiated by a phone call or email from your software vendor, telling you that they have a critical fix that must be installed on your computer system. If this patch isn't installed right away, your system will crash, and you'll lose all your data. For some reason, you've changed your maintenance account password, and they can't log on. Your system operator gives the password to the person. You've been hit again.

Phishing

You were introduced to phishing and the importance of training to prevent these attacks in the previous section of this chapter. You also learned about one variant, vishing. In this section, you'll learn about some other variants.

Vishing

You learned about vishing in the "Social engineering" section of this chapter. Please review that section.

Smishing

Smishing is a type of cybercrime that uses deceptive text messages to manipulate victims into divulging sensitive personal information, such as bank account details. The name is derived from a combination of "SMS" and "phishing."

QR code phishing

Quick response (QR) codes are two-dimensional barcodes that can be scanned easily with a camera or a code reader application. They operate like URLs in that they can lead to a website. QR phishing, sometimes also called *quishing*, is a type of phishing in which attackers create QR codes to redirect victims into visiting or downloading malicious content. So, in the same way a user might click on a URL link that appears to lead to a safe site while doing just the opposite, a user might scan a QR code that appears to lead to a safe site while doing just the opposite. Just as with malicious URLs, the goal is to harvest sensitive information, such as passwords, financial data, or personally identifiable information (PII).

Spear phishing/whaling

Two other forms of phishing to be aware of are *spear phishing* and *whaling*, which are similar in nature. With spear phishing, the attacker uses information that the target would be less likely to question because it appears to be coming from a trusted source. For example, instead of Wells Fargo sending you a message telling you to click here to fix a problem with your account, the message that is sent appears to be from your spouse and says to "click here to see a video of your children from last Christmas." Because it appears far more likely to be a legitimate message, it cuts through the user's standard defenses and has a higher likelihood of being clicked. Generating the attack requires much more work on the part of the miscreant and often involves using information from contact lists, friend lists from social media sites, and so on.

Whaling is nothing more than phishing, or spear phishing, for big users. Instead of sending out a "To Whom It May Concern" message to thousands of users, the whaler identifies one person from whom they can gain all the data they want—usually a manager or an owner—and targets the phishing campaign at them.

Shoulder surfing

Shoulder surfing involves nothing more than watching someone when they enter their sensitive data. They can see you entering a password, typing in a credit card number, or entering any other pertinent information. The best defense against this type of attack is simply to survey your environment before entering personal data. Privacy filters can be used that make the screen difficult to read unless you are directly in front of it.

Tailgating

Tailgating is the term used for someone being so close to you when you enter a building that they are able to enter right behind you without needing to use a key, a card, or any other security device. Many social engineering intruders who need physical access to a site will use this method of gaining entry. Educate users to beware of this and other social engineering ploys and prevent them from happening.

> Mantraps are a great way to stop tailgating. A *mantrap* is a series of two doors with a small room between them that helps prevent unauthorized people from entering a building. For more information, see the earlier section "Access control vestibule."

Impersonation

Impersonation occurs when an individual pretends to be an IT technician, heating and air conditioning (HVAC) repairman, or other personnel to get in the facility or to convince someone to disclose sensitive information.

Dumpster diving

It is amazing the information that can be gleaned from physical documents even in the age when there is such a push to go paperless. *Dumpster diving* is a common physical access method. Companies normally generate a huge amount of paper, most of which eventually winds up in dumpsters or recycle bins. Dumpsters may contain information that is highly sensitive in nature (such as passwords after a change and before the user has the new one memorized). In high-security and government environments, sensitive papers should be either shredded or burned. Most businesses don't do this. In addition, the advent of "green" companies has created an increase in the amount of recycled paper, which can often contain all kinds of juicy information about a company and its individual employees.

Threats

Social engineering attacks are not the only type with which we are confronted. There are many others of which to be aware. In this section, you'll learn about the major vulnerabilities and attacks you might face.

Denial of service (DoS)

A denial-of-service (DoS) attack is one in which the attacker's goal is to make the device unavailable to do its job. By sending hundreds or thousands of connection requests, the attack consumes all the resources of the device, leaving none for its regular work.

Distributed denial of service (DDoS)

A distributed denial-of-service (DDoS) attack is one in which the attacker recruits additional devices (called *zombies*) to assist in the DoS attack. This greatly magnifies the effect of the denial of service.

Evil twin

Rogue access points are access points (APs) that you do not control and manage. There are two types: those that are connected to wired infrastructure and those that are not. The ones that are connected to a wired network present a danger to both your wired and your wireless network. They may have been placed there by your own users without your knowledge, or they may have been purposefully put there by a hacker to gain access to the wired network.

FIGURE 7.15 Evil twin

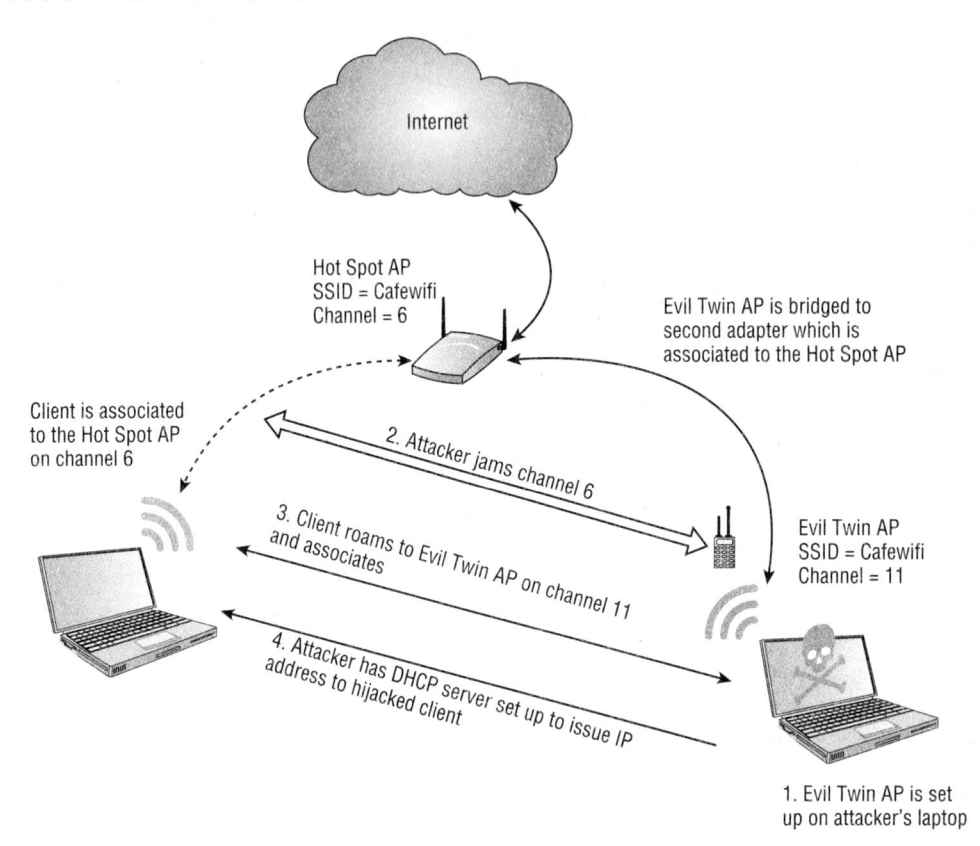

In either case, they allow access to your wired network. Wireless intrusion prevention system (WIPS) devices are usually used to locate rogue access points and alert administrators of their presence.

A special type of rogue AP, an *evil twin*, is one that has the same SSID as your legitimate AP, while residing on a different channel. The hacker jams the frequency (i.e. channel) where the legitimate AP is located, disconnecting all systems from that AP. At that point, all of the stations will associate and connect to the evil twin by SSID and not channel number. When the stations are connected to this evil twin, they are susceptible to peer-to-peer attacks from the hacker. This process is shown in Figure 7.15.

Zero-day attack

Vulnerabilities are often discovered in live environments before a fix or patch exists. Such vulnerabilities are referred to as *zero-day* vulnerabilities. A zero-day attack is one that occurs when a security vulnerability in an application is discovered on the same day that the application is released. Monitoring known hacking community websites can often provide an early alert because hackers often share zero-day exploit information.

New zero-day attacks are announced on a regular basis against a broad range of technology systems. You should create an inventory of applications and maintain a list of critical systems to manage the risks of these attack vectors.

Spoofing

Spoofing is the process of masquerading as another user or device. It is usually done to access a resource to which the hacker should not have access or to get through a security device like a firewall that may be filtering traffic based on a source IP address.

Spoofing can take various forms. A hacker may change their IP address to one that belongs to a trusted user or device to get through a firewall filtering at the IP layer. In other cases, they might spoof the media access control (MAC) address of a trusted device to defeat layer 2 security applied on a switch or wireless AP. It could also be the spoofing of a username and password to access a resource. Finally, it might be the spoofing of an email address to launch one of the email-based attacks.

On-path attack

An on-path attack, also called a man-in-the-middle (MITM) attack, is one in which the hacker uses one of several techniques to position themselves in the middle of a current communication session between two devices. One way they might do this is by polluting the ARP cache (mappings of IP addresses to MAC addresses) such that the users on either end of the session think they are sending data to one another when in reality they are sending it to the hacker. This allows the hacker to monitor the entire conversation.

Brute-force attack

A *brute-force attack* is a password, encryption key, or hash value attack that operates by attempting every possible combination of characters that could be in a password. These can be performed online or offline. Given enough time and processing power, any password can be cracked, so most enterprises use some sort of password policy that locks an account after a certain number of incorrect attempts. For this reason, online attacks are largely unsuccessful.

In contrast, the offline mode of the attack requires the attacker to steal the password file first but enables an unconstrained guessing of passwords, free of any application- or network-related rate limitations.

Dictionary attack

Dictionary attacks rely on the use of large files that contain words from the dictionary. These attacks are most often attempts to crack an encrypted password, by encrypting each word in the dictionary file using the same algorithm used to encrypt the users' passwords and then comparing this value to the encrypted password for a match. These attacks are performed offline to eliminate the disabling of the account through password policies.

Insider threat

Insider threats should be one of the biggest concerns for security personnel. Insiders have knowledge of and access to systems that outsiders do not have, giving insiders a much easier avenue for carrying out or participating in an attack. An organization should implement the appropriate event collection and log review policies to provide the means to detect insider threats as they occur. These threats fall into two categories: intentional and unintentional.

Intentional

Intentional insider threats are performed by insiders who have ill intent. These folks typically either are disgruntled over some perceived slight or are working for another organization to perform corporate espionage. They may share sensitive documents with others, or they may impart knowledge used to breach a network. This is one of the reasons that users' permissions and rights must not exceed those necessary to perform their jobs. This helps to limit the damage an insider might inflict.

Unintentional

Sometimes, internal users unknowingly increase the likelihood that security breaches will occur. Such unintentional insider threats do not have malicious intent; they simply do not understand how system changes can affect security.

Security awareness and training should include coverage of examples of misconfigurations that can result in security breaches occurring and/or not being detected. For example, a user may temporarily disable antivirus software to perform an administrative task. If the user fails to reenable the antivirus software, they unknowingly leave the system open to viruses. In such a case, an organization should consider implementing group policies or some other mechanism to periodically ensure that antivirus software is enabled and running. Another solution could be to configure antivirus software to automatically restart after a certain amount of time.

Recording and reviewing user actions via system, audit, and security logs can help security professionals identify misconfigurations so that the appropriate policies and controls can be implemented.

Structured Query Language (SQL) injection

A Structured Query Language (SQL) injection attack inserts, or "injects," a SQL query as the input data from the client to the application. This type of attack can result in the attacker being able to read sensitive data from the database, modify database data, execute administrative operations on the database, recover the content of a given file, and even issue commands to the OS.

Cross-site scripting (XSS)

Cross-site scripting (XSS) occurs when an attacker locates a website vulnerability and injects malicious code into the web application. Many websites allow and even incorporate user input into a web page to customize the web page. If a web application does not properly validate this input, one of two things could happen: The text may be rendered on the page, or a script may be executed when others visit the web page.

Business email compromise (BEC)

Business email compromise (BEC) is a form of social engineering in which a hacker sends email that appears to come from a company official, company department, or other trusted entity that attempts to trick someone into sending money or divulging confidential company info. This attack typically requires the hacker to compromise the email system of the person or organization to be impersonated, although it can also be done by altering the headers of the email such that it appears to come from a trusted entity.

Supply chain/pipeline attack

A supply chain/pipeline attack is one in which a malicious group or individual compromises a third-party vendor of an organization for the purpose of installing malware or back doors on the vendors' products or alternately using the access provided to the vendor to attack the network of the organization.

An example of the first scenario was the discovery of back doors installed in network routing equipment provided by a third-party vendor. These were used later to access a customer's network.

An example of the first scenario is the famous Target data breach. It was made possible using a privileged account assigned to the vendor for maintenance. The phishing attack that preceded the Target attack was used to obtain the password of the privileged account. Using this password, the hacker logged in and, under the security context of the privileged vendor, exfiltrated the data.

Vulnerabilities

Many attacks are made possible because our systems are not secured as well as they could be. When this is the situation, we say a vulnerability exists. In this section, you'll learn about some major vulnerabilities.

Noncompliant systems

Every organization should have a standard set of security requirements or standards. You should use some type of enterprise-grade malware management system that scans the network for noncompliant devices. Most of these systems can automate the entire process of locating, isolating, and remediating noncompliant devices.

Unpatched systems

When systems do not receive updates and patches, they will become susceptible to the issue that the patch was intended to resolve. When these are security updates, the situation becomes more serious. As you learned in the previous section, some type of enterprise-grade malware management system that scans the network for noncompliant devices will at least alert you to missing updates.

Unprotected systems (missing antivirus/missing firewall)

All systems should have antivirus software fully updated and a functional host-based firewall. This is in addition to the network firewalls you may have. When either of these utilities is *not* present, the system is vulnerable to all sorts of attacks.

End of life (EOL)

In Chapter 6, in the section "End of life (EOL)," you learned that systems that have reached EOL designation from the vendor need to be replaced. Please review that chapter.

Bring your own device (BYOD)

One of the decisions that must be made is whether to allow only company-owned mobile devices on the network or to allow personal devices as well. Many organizations have launched bring your own device (BYOD) initiatives. While this certainly makes the users happy, it brings with it new challenges in securing a wide range of user devices running on all sorts of platforms.

One of the ways enterprises have successfully implemented these initiatives without sacrificing the security of the network is by turning to enterprise mobility management systems. These systems can be used to control a wide variety of mobile devices and to manage the installation of updates, the tracking of devices, and the deployment of remote wipes and GPS location services when needed. Without one of these utilities, deploying BYOD can be a security nightmare.

Exam essentials

Know the various types of social engineering.   Social engineering variants include shoulder surfing (watching someone work) and phishing (tricking someone into believing they are communicating with a party other than the one they are communicating with). Variations on phishing include vishing and whaling as well as spear phishing.

Differentiate noncompliant and unpatched systems.   While noncompliant systems are those that do not confirm to the organizational security standard, unpatched systems are those that are missing antivirus or anti-malware software.

2.6 Given a scenario, implement procedures for basic small office/home office (SOHO) malware removal

Over time, best practices have been developed through trial and error that help minimize the chances of getting viruses and reduce the effort involved in getting rid of malware. Some of these practices are discussed in this section.

Investigate and verify malware symptoms

First, identify the symptoms the malware is producing as clearly as you can. In some cases, this will help identify the exact virus. In many scenarios, identifying the symptoms can help establish the severity of the infection, which is good to determine when IT resources are stretched thin and when battles must be chosen.

Quarantine infected systems

The infected system should be quarantined—removed from the network to prevent a spread of the infection to other systems. This is why it is a good practice to keep data on servers so that when user systems need to be quarantined, a new machine can be quickly imaged for the user to reduce the impact on productivity while the infected machine is cleaned.

Disable System Restore in Windows

System Restore is a useful tool in many cases, but when a virus infection occurs, it can be an ally of the virus. Virus scanners cannot clean infections from restore points, making reinfections possible. If a System Restore is performed after running an anti-spyware utility, viral objects may reappear. Disable System Restore before attempting to clean a system. When you do this, you will delete all restore points in the system, including any that may have an infection.

Remediate infected systems

Once the infected system has been quarantined, you must take steps to clean it. This three-step process is discussed in this section.

Update anti-malware software

Before scanning the system with anti-malware software, update the software and engine if necessary. Definition files can change daily, and the virus may be so new that it is not found in your current definitions file even if that file is only a week old.

Use wise scanning and removal techniques (e.g. safe mode, preinstallation environment)

Although you can run the scan and removal process from the graphical user interface (GUI), it is a best practice to do this either after booting to safe mode or from a preinstallation environment like Windows PE. Viruses that evade detection in the GUI cannot do so as easily in either of these environments.

Reimage/reinstall

In some cases, the infection cannot be safely removed, and the drive must be formatted (deleting everything, including the malware). If this is the case, the next step is to reinstall the operating system. This is a scenario in which using images of the operating system can speed recovery because the image can contain not only the operating system but also applications and settings.

Schedule scans and run updates

The antivirus software can be scheduled to perform a scan of the system. You should set this up to occur when the system is not in use, like at night. The scanning process will go faster then and will not affect users. Also, set the software to automatically check for and install any updates to the definition files and to the engine when available.

Enable System Restore and create a restore point in Windows

Although it is recommended that you disable System Restore before cleaning an infection, it is a good idea to create a restore point after an infection is cleaned. This gives you a clean restore point going forward in case the system becomes infected again at some point. For non-Windows systems, a backup should be performed at this time.

Educate the end user

In many cases, users are partly responsible for virus infection. After an infection occurs, it is a great time to impress on users the principles of secure computing. They should be reminded that antivirus software and firewalls can go only so far in protecting them and that they should exercise safe browsing habits and refrain from opening any attachments in email from unknown sources, regardless of how tempting.

Exam essentials

Identify the steps to remove malware.   According to best practices, the steps to address SOHO malware removal are as follows:

1. Identify malware symptoms.
2. Quarantine infected system.
3. Disable System Restore.
4. Remediate infected systems, including updating antivirus software.
5. Scan and remove the malware.
6. Enable System Restore and create a restore point.
7. Educate end users.

2.7 Given a scenario, apply workstation security options and hardening techniques

In the previous objectives, the importance of user education has been mentioned. The user represents the weakest link in the security chain, whether the harm comes to them in the form of malware, social engineering, or simply avoidable mistakes. The workstation represents the digital arm of the user and must be properly and adequately secured to keep the user—and the network—protected.

A number of best practices are involved with securing or *hardening* a workstation. While a checklist could take many pages depending on your environment, CompTIA has identified some that should appear on any roster, which are discussed in this section.

Data-at-rest encryption

Earlier in this chapter, in the section "Protocols and encryption," you learned about encryption protocols and algorithms. When we talk about data-at-rest, we are talking about data that is stored somewhere, as opposed to data that is in transit across a network. While data encryption is possible both on a drive level (BitLocker) and on an individual file level (EFS), always keep in mind the cost of encryption and save this tool for instances where you really need it. By cost, I mean that any encrypted file must be decrypted to be opened and encrypted again to be saved. It requires CPU cycles on the device. If you attempt to encrypt everything, the performance of the device may make it practically unusable. You must strike a balance between security and usability.

Password considerations

One of the strongest ways to keep a system safe is to employ strong passwords and educate your users in the best security practices. In this section, you'll explore various techniques that can enhance the security of your user passwords.

Complexity requirements

Passwords should be as long as possible. Most security experts believe a password of 10 characters is the minimum that should be used if security is a real concern. If you use only the lowercase letters of the alphabet, you have 26 characters with which to work. If you add the numeric values 0 through 9, you'll get another 10 characters. If you go one step further and add the uppercase letters, you'll then have an additional 26 characters, giving you a total of 62 characters with which to construct a password.

> **NOTE** Most vendors recommend that you use nonalphabetical characters, such as #, $, and %, in your passwords, and some go so far as to require it.

If you used a four-character password, this would be 62 × 62 × 62 × 62, equaling approximately 14 million password possibilities. If you used five characters in your password, this would give you 62^5, equaling approximately 920 million password possibilities. If you used a 10-character password, this would give you 62^{10}, or 8.4×10^{17}, equaling a very big number of possibilities. As you can see, these numbers increase exponentially with each character added to the password. The four-digit password could probably be broken in a fraction of a day, whereas the 10-digit password would take considerably longer and consume much more processing power.

If your password used only the 26 lowercase letters from the alphabet, the four-digit password would have 26^4, or 456,000 possible password combinations. A five-character password would have 26^5, or more than 11 million, and a 10-character password would have 26^{10}, or 1.4×10^{14}. This is still a big number, but it would take considerably less time to break it. National Institute of Standards and Technology (NIST) now considers password length more important than complexity.

Finally, passwords should be unique—that is, a user should *not* use the same password for two different purposes. Passwords should *not* be reused.

Expiration

The longer that a password is used, the more likely it is that it will be compromised in some way. It is for this reason that requiring users to change their passwords at certain intervals increases the security of their passwords. You should require users to set a new password every 30 days (more frequently for higher-security networks), and you must also prevent them from reusing old passwords. Most password management systems have the ability to track previously used passwords and to disallow users from recycling old passwords.

Basic Input/Output System (BIOS)/Unified Extensible Firmware Interface (UEFI) passwords

Passwords should be configured and required to access either the BIOS or UEFI settings on all devices. If this is not the case, it would be possible for someone to reboot a device, enter the settings, change the boot order, boot to an OS residing on a USB or optical drive, and use that OS as a platform to access data located on the other drives. While this is a worst-case scenario, there is also less significant mayhem a malicious person could cause in the BIOS and UEFI.

End-user best practices

While we do what we can as security professionals, ultimately we can't stand by and advise users on the safety of every action they take. In this section, you'll learn about some best practices to convey to your users in the hope they will follow them.

Use screensaver locks

A screensaver should automatically start after a short period of idle time and should require a password before the user can begin the session again. This method of locking the workstation adds one more level of security.

Log off when not in use

Users should be taught to log off when not using their accounts. This prevents access to rights and permissions attached to those accounts if someone compromises or steals their devices.

Secure/protect critical hardware (e.g. laptops)

Users should be taught to treat company devices as their own and protect them at all times. While you might not choose to have them bear the cost of replacing a damaged, stolen, or lost piece of hardware, you should impress upon them that they do bear responsibility for the safety of the hardware.

Secure personally identifiable information (PII) and passwords

While it may be obvious that passwords need to be protected, there are other types of information that if disclosed can cause severe damage and cost to the organization.

PII is any piece of information about a user that can be used alone or in combination with other pieces of information to identify an individual user. While it is the responsibility of all organizations to protect PII that they may possess, it is especially important in certain regulated industries, such as healthcare and finance.

The danger of leaking PII is that much of this information, such as addresses, Social Security numbers, and places of employment, can be used to perform identity theft, a growing concern worldwide.

Use password managers

Password managers are applications that make managing multiple passwords easier and safer, storing such passwords in an encrypted database. They typically require a user to generate and remember one "master" password to unlock and access the password file. Using password managers can help prevent users from using unsafe password practices.

Account management

While one account management technique has been discussed previously (i.e. preventing the reuse of passwords), there are a number of additional account management best practices that you should know and implement.

Restrict user permissions

When assigning user permissions, follow the principle of least privilege (discussed in the section "Principle of Least Privilege") by giving users only the bare minimum they need to do their job. Assign permissions to groups, rather than users, and make users members of groups (or remove them from groups) as they change roles or positions.

Restrict login times

Most users have a set work schedule, and it is only during these work hours that the user should access the network and its resources. Because an active account is an account vulnerable to misuse, any time you can disable an account while still allowing users to do their jobs enhances security, because a disabled account cannot be used for malicious purposes.

For this reason, many administrators allow users to log in only during certain hours. Typically, access is allowed from about an hour before their workday until about an hour after the day ends (to allow some flexibility). For certain users who tend to work throughout the day and night, this system may not work.

Disable guest account

To secure the system, disable all accounts that are not needed (especially the guest account). Next, rename the accounts if you can. (Microsoft won't allow you to rename an account to Administrator.) Finally, change the passwords from the defaults and add them to the cycle of passwords that routinely get changed.

Use failed attempts lockout

Earlier you learned that a brute-force attack is a password attack that attempts all character combinations until the password is discovered. You also learned that these attacks are typically performed offline and not in a live environment. Why is that? It's because almost all password systems are set up to allow only a set number of failed password attempts before the account is locked. While this policy may generate more password-reset calls than you would like, that effect can be mitigated by implementing a complementary policy that allows the account to be automatically reenabled after a set amount of time (say five minutes). When this policy is communicated to the users, they know just to wait for five minutes and try again.

Use timeout/screen lock

While the relative sensitivity of the data appearing on the screen of a user's computer can vary from time to time and from user to user, it is a good practice to protect that information when someone steps away from the device. Moreover, when the device is in an out-of-the-way location, it may even afford someone the chance to browse the device. For this reason, you should require a password-protected screensaver on all devices that kicks in after a short period of inactivity. On a Windows system, the Windows+L key will lock the screen.

Apply account expiration dates

Another account setting that is available to increase security is to apply an expiration date to a user's account. When the account expires, all the access tied to that account is gone until the account is reactivated. Many times, these expiration dates are used with temporary or guest employees. Setting the dates prevents human error from leaving the accounts active after temporary employees are gone.

Change default administrator's user account/password

All Windows devices and all infrastructure devices, such as routers, firewalls, switches, and wireless access points and controllers, come with default administrator accounts and default passwords. The names of these accounts and the default passwords are well known to malicious individuals. They can be looked up in five minutes on the Internet. Always change the default names and passwords for these accounts; otherwise, you might find someone else "owning" the device at some point in time.

Disable AutoRun

It is never a good idea to put any media in a workstation if you do not know where it came from or what it is. The reason is that the media (i.e. CDs, DVDs, and USBs) could contain malware. Compounding matters, that malware could be referenced in the `Autorun.inf` file, causing it to be summoned when the media is inserted in the machine and requiring no other action. `Autorun.inf` can be used to start an executable, access a website, or perform any of a large number of different tasks. The best way to prevent a user from falling victim to such a ploy is to disable the AutoRun feature on the workstation.

Microsoft has changed (by default, disabled) the AutoRun function on Windows 10 and 11. The reason Microsoft changed the default action can be summed up in a single word: security. That text-based `Autorun.inf` file not only can take your browser to a web page but also can call any executable file, pass along variable information about the user, or do just about anything else imaginable. Simply put, it is *never* a good idea to take any media whose source or contents you have no idea of and plug it into your system. Such an action opens up the user—and their network—to any number of possible tribulations. An entire business's data could be jeopardized by such a minuscule act if a harmful CD were to be placed in a computer at work by someone with elevated privileges.

Disable unused services

In Chapter 6, in the section "Application restrictions and exceptions," you learned that firewalls can block services. While the concern is often security, disabling unused services is also a performance issue. Every service that runs requires processing cycles and storage space. Therefore, disabling unused services frees up bits of both of these resources, leading to a better performing system.

Exam essentials

Understand the need for good passwords. Passwords are the first line of defense for protecting an account. A password should be required for every account, and strong passwords should be enforced. Users need to understand the basics of password security and work to keep their accounts protected by following company policies regarding passwords.

List some techniques that enhance account management. These techniques include but are not limited to disabling unused accounts, requiring frequent password changes, preventing the reuse of passwords, requiring complex passwords, and defining login hours for users.

2.8 Given a scenario, apply common methods for securing mobile devices

If laptops are easy to steal, smaller mobile devices are even more so. Because mobile devices are increasingly used to store valuable data and to perform functions once only in the domain of laptops and desktops, the need to secure these devices has grown. In this section, methods of securing mobile devices will be discussed.

Hardening techniques

Earlier in this chapter, in the section "Given a scenario, apply workstation security options and hardening techniques," you learned a number of best practices involved in securing or hardening a workstation. In this section, you'll learn about hardening techniques for mobile devices.

Device encryption

Full device encryption is available for smartphones and other mobile devices. Most companies choose to implement this through the use of an enterprise mobility management system, because it can also manage the installation of updates, the tracking of devices, and the deployment of remote wipes and GPS location services when needed. There are also third-party applications that can provide full device encryption.

Screen locks

One of the most basic (but not necessarily the most utilized) security measures you can take is to implement a screen lock on the device. This is akin to implementing the password that you use to log on to your desktop or laptop, but it's amazing how few people use this basic security measure. This can prevent someone from using the mobile device if it is stolen. There are several ways screen locks can be implemented, and in the following sections you'll examine each method.

Facial recognition

A face lock is one that uses a facial scan of the user to authenticate the user and, when successful authentication or facial recognition completes, unlocks the screen. It also is more secure than a passcode or swipe process.

PIN codes

Setting the password on an Android phone is done by navigating to Settings > Security and Privacy > Device Lock. On the Device Lock page, you can set the length of time the device remains idle until the screen locks, as well as choose a method from None, Swipe, Pattern, PIN, or Password. Select Password and then enter the desired password.

On an iOS-based device, navigate to Settings > Face ID and Passcode > Change Passcode to set the password and Settings > Display & Brightness > Auto-Lock to set the amount of time before the iPhone locks.

Fingerprint

Fingerprint locks are secured by a stored fingerprint scan that must be matched for access. You learned about fingerprint scanning earlier in this chapter, in the "Fingerprint" section on biometrics. Please review that section.

Pattern

Pattern locks eliminate the time taken while typing other passwords or numbers. You need to join the dots, and the phone is unlocked. An example of a pattern used to unlock a device is shown in Figure 7.16.

Swipe

Swipe locks use a gesture or series of gestures, sometimes involving the movement of an icon, to open the screen. In some cases, they require only knowledge of the mobile platform in use; they offer no security to the process because no authentication of the user is occurring.

FIGURE 7.16 Pattern code

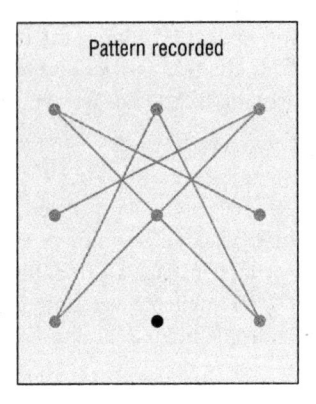

Pattern Code: 4 > 3 > 5 > 7 > 2 > 9 > 1 > 6

In other instances, like Android, they require a pattern between nine dots to be swiped to unlock the device.

Configuration profiles

Configuration profiles are collections of settings that can be applied to a mobile device. Apple devices use Extensible Markup Language (XML) files along with a tool called Apple Configurator. These profiles are not limited to Apple devices, however. Device management software, such as Microsoft Intune, can also automate the configuration of Android mobile devices as well as macOS and Windows systems by using configuration profiles.

Patch management

We've stressed continually the dangers of unpatched systems. Mobile devices also must be patched from time to time to address security and performance issues. In this section, we'll look at two critical components that must be patched as patches are released.

OS updates

Security patches and OS updates are available on an ongoing basis for both iOS and Android. For the iPhone, both OS updates and security patches are available at the Apple support site. Automatic updates can be enabled for the device in the App Store.

An auto-update feature is built into Android, and you can also manually check for patches and updates by navigating to Settings > About Phone > System Updates. Selecting these options will cause the phone to check for, download, and install patches or updates.

Application updates

Just as patches are released regularly for the applications that run on a desktop or laptop system, so are they also issued by vendors for the apps that run on mobile devices. While many vendors have created methods to alert you when patches are available, you should create a system for checking manually for these updates.

Endpoint security software

Earlier in this chapter, in the section "Endpoint Detection and Response (EDR)," you learned about EDR, a proactive endpoint security approach designed to supplement existing defense. Endpoint security software is any utility or tool that is used to secure individual systems, such as smartphones, laptops, desktops, printers, and even cameras. Let's look at some of the more important tools and settings that increase mobile device security.

Antivirus/anti-malware

Mobile devices can suffer from viruses and malware just like laptops and desktops can. Major antivirus vendors such as McAfee and Kaspersky make antivirus and anti-malware products for mobile devices that provide the same real-time protection that the products do for desktops. The same guidelines apply for these mobile devices: Keep them up to date by setting the device to check for updates whenever connected to the Internet.

Content filtering

Content filtering software examines all web connections, and in some cases emails, for objectionable content or sites that have been identified as off limits by the administrator. While this can be helpful in preventing the introduction of malware or in screening objectionable content, you should be aware that these filters are making educated guesses about what to deny and allow.

A filter will invariably deny content that should be allowed and allow content that should be denied. Try to be as specific as possible when defining keywords that are used to identify sites and content and set the expectation among users that the software is not perfect.

Locator applications

Locator applications like the Lost Android app for Android are available where apps are sold for Androids. These apps allow you to locate the device, to lock the device, and even to send a message to the device offering a reward for its return. Finally, you can remotely wipe the device. The iOS devices and the newer Android devices have this feature built in, and it performs all the same functions.

Remote wipes

Remote wipes are instructions sent remotely to a mobile device that erase all the data when the device is stolen. In the case of an iPhone, this feature is closely connected to the locator application (discussed in the previous section). To perform a remote wipe on an iPhone (which requires iOS 18.3), navigate to Settings > Apple Account. On this tab, ensure that Find My iPhone is enabled (i.e. set to On). Next, use the browser to go to iCloud.com and log in using the Apple ID you use on your phone.

Next, select the icon Find My iPhone. The phone's location will appear on a map. Click the phone. In the dialog box that opens, select Erase This Device. Then follow the onscreen instructions.

The Android phones do not come with an official remote wipe. You can, however, install an Android app that will do this. Once the app Lost Android is installed, it works in the same way the iPhone remote wipe does. In this case, you log into the Lost Android website using your Google login. From the app, you can locate and wipe the device.

Remote backup applications

Backing up your data with the iPhone can be done by connecting the device to iCloud. Go to Settings > [your name] > iCloud Backup. Turn on Backup this iPhone. iCloud automatically backs up your iPhone daily when the iPhone is connected to power, locked, and connected to Wi-Fi.

Android has always taken a cloud approach to backups. There are many Android apps now that can be used to back up data to locations such as Dropbox or Box.net.

Failed login attempts restrictions

Most of us have become accustomed to the lockout feature on a laptop or desktop that locks out an account after a certain number of failed login attempts. This feature is available on a mobile device and can even be set to perform a remote wipe of the device after repeated failed login attempts.

On iOS, the Erase Data function can be set to perform a remote wipe after 10 failed passcode attempts. After six failed attempts, the iPhone locks out users for a minute before another passcode can be entered. The device then increases the lockout time following each additional failed attempt.

Android does not have this feature built in but does provide application programming interfaces (APIs) that allow enterprise developers to create applications that will do this.

Policies and procedures

With the introduction of mobile devices to the network, changes and additions may be necessary in the organizational security policy. As procedures are derived from broader policies, these changes will also impact the procedures that users are required to follow.

In this section, you'll review issues that need to be considered with respect to policies and procedures.

Mobile device management (MDM)

You learned about MDM in the section "Mobile device management (MDM)" and in Chapter 1, in the section "Mobile device management (MDM)." Please review that section and Chapter 1.

Bring your own device (BYOD) vs. corporate owned

You learned the advantages and disadvantages to these two deployment options in Chapter 1, in the section "Device configurations." Please review that chapter.

Profile security requirements

The baseline or minimum security settings required on all mobile devices must be determined and standardized. This may require the creation of multiple security profiles based on different mobile device models and types, but the theory is the same. By defining a collection of security settings, implementing them on all devices, and constantly monitoring the settings for changes, you can ensure that these settings are maintained.

Exam essentials

Describe the options available to secure the data on a mobile device. These options include passcode locks, remote wipes, locator applications, failed login attempt restrictions, and remote backup applications.

List other security guidelines for mobile devices. Always keep antivirus definitions up to date and set the mobile device to automatically check for OS updates and patches.

2.9 Compare and contrast common data destruction and disposal methods

Think of all the sensitive data written to a hard drive. The drive can contain information about students, clients, users—anyone and anything. That hard drive can be in a desktop PC, a laptop, or even a printer. (Many laser printers above consumer grade offer the ability to add a hard drive to store print jobs.) If it falls into the wrong hands, you can lose valuable data and also risk a lawsuit for not properly protecting privacy. An appropriate data destruction/disposal plan should be implemented to avoid any potential problems.

Because data on media holds great value and liability, that media should never be simply tossed away for prying eyes to stumble upon. For the purposes of this objective, I'll talk about hard drives and the three key concepts to understand in regard to them: formatting, sanitation, and destruction. Formatting prepares the drive to hold new information (which can include copying over data already there). Sanitation involves wiping the data on the drive, whereas destruction renders the drive no longer usable.

> While this objective is focused on hard drives, data can also be stored on portable flash drives, backup tapes, CDs, or DVDs. In the interest of security, I recommend that you destroy any of them before disposing of them as well.

Physical destruction of hard drives

Physically destroying the drive involves rendering the component no longer usable. While the focus is on hard drives, you can also physically destroy other forms of media, such as flash drives and CD/DVDs.

Drilling/hammer

If you don't have the budget for a hard drive shredder, you can accomplish similar results in a much more time-consuming way with a power drill. The goal is to physically destroy the platters in the drive. Start the process by removing the cover from the drive—this is normally done with a Torx driver (while #8 does not work with all, it is a good one to try first). You can remove the arm with a slotted screwdriver and then the cover over the platters using a Torx driver. Don't worry about damaging or scratching anything because nothing is intended to be saved. Everything but the platters can be tossed away.

As an optional step, you can completely remove the tracks using a belt sander, grinder, or palm sander. The goal is to turn the shiny surface into fine powder. This adds one more layer of assurance that nothing usable remains. Always be careful to wear eye protection and not breathe in any fine particles that you generate during the grinding/destruction process.

Following this, use the power drill to create the smallest particles possible. A drill press works much better for this task than trying to hold the drive and drill it with a handheld model. Finally, you can use a hammer to destroy the platters as well; it provides a certain level of satisfaction if the drive died and you had to restore it from backup.

Please keep in mind that drilling a hole in the drive does not render it useless. Data restoration tools can recover everything remaining on the drive.

> Even with practice, you will find that manually destroying a hard drive is time-consuming. There are companies that specialize in this and can do it efficiently. One such company is Shred-it, which will pick it up from you and provide chain-of-custody assurance and a certificate of destruction upon completion.

Shredding

Many commercial paper shredders include the ability to destroy DVDs and CDs. Paper shredders, however, are not able to handle hard drives, and you need a shredder created for just such a purpose. Jackhammer makes a low-volume model that will destroy eight drives per minute and carries a suggested list price of just under $30,000. There are also many companies that specialize in data destruction, and they are located in almost every major city.

Degaussing

Degaussing involves applying a strong magnetic field to initialize the media (also referred to as *disk wiping*). This process helps ensure that information doesn't fall into the wrong hands.

Because degaussing uses a specifically designed electromagnet to eliminate all data on the drive, that destruction also includes the factory prerecorded servo tracks. You can find wand model degaussers priced at just over $500 or desktop units that sell for up to $30,000.

Incineration

A final option that exists for some forms of storage is to burn the media. Regardless of whether the media is a hard drive, CD, DVD, solid-state drive, or floppy disk, the media must be reduced to ash, or in the case of hard drive platters, the internal platters must be physically deformed using heat.

Recycling or repurposing best practices

Multiple levels of reformatting can be done to remove the contents of a drive. A standard format—accomplished using the OS's format utility (or similar)—can mark space occupied by files as available for new files without truly deleting what was there. Such erasing—if you want to call it that—doesn't guarantee that the information isn't still on the disk and recoverable.

Erasing/wiping

Overwriting the drive entails copying over the data with new data. A common practice is to replace the data with 0s. A number of applications allow you to recover what was there prior to the last write operation, and for that reason, most overwrite software will write the same sequence and save it multiple times.

Drive wipe

If it's possible to verify beyond a reasonable doubt that a piece of hardware that's no longer being used doesn't contain any data of a sensitive or proprietary nature, that hardware can be recycled (i.e. sold to employees, sold to a third party, donated to a school, etc.). That level of assurance can come from wiping a hard drive or using specialized utilities.

> **NOTE** Degaussing hard drives is difficult and may render the drive unusable.

If you can't be assured that the hardware in question doesn't contain important data, the hardware should be destroyed. You cannot, and should not, take a risk that the data your company depends on could fall into the wrong hands.

Low-level format vs. standard format

A low-level format (typically accomplished only in the factory) can be performed on the system, or a utility can be used to completely wipe the disk clean. This process helps ensure that information doesn't fall into the wrong hands.

Integrated development environment (IDE) hard drives are low-level formatted by the manufacturer. Low-level formatting must be performed even before a drive can be partitioned. In low-level formatting, the drive controller chip and the drive meet for the first time and learn to work together. Because IDE drives have their controllers integrated into the drive, low-level formatting is a factory process with these drives and does not depend on the OS.

> **WARNING**
> Never low-level format IDE or Small Computer System Interface (SCSI) drives! They're low-level formatted from the factory, and you might cause problems by using low-level utilities on these types of drives.

The main thing to remember for the exam is that most forms of formatting included with the OS do not actually completely erase the data. Formatting the drive and then disposing of it has caused many companies problems when the data has been retrieved by individuals who never should have seen it using applications that are commercially available.

Outsourcing concepts

Driven mainly by cost, many companies outsource some functions to a third party (e.g. outsourcing to cloud providers computing jobs that require a large number of processor cycles for a short duration). This situation allows a company to avoid a large investment in computing resources that will be used for only a short time. Assuming that the provisioned resources are dedicated to a single company, the main vulnerability associated with on-demand provisioning is traces of proprietary data that can remain on the virtual machine (VM) and may be exploited.

Third-party vendor

As part of prevention of privacy policy violations, any contracted third parties that have access to PII should be assessed to ensure that the appropriate controls are in place. In addition, third-party personnel should be familiarized with organizational policies and should sign nondisclosure agreements (NDAs).

Certification of destruction/recycling

Certificates of destruction are documents that attest to either the physical destruction of the media on which sensitive data was located or a scientifically approved method of removing the data from a drive. Earlier in this chapter, in the section "Physical destruction of hard drives," you were introduced to some methods of removal, both approved and unapproved.

These certificates are typically issued to the organization by a storage vendor or cloud provider to prove either that the data has been removed or that the media has been destroyed.

Regulatory and environmental requirements

There are also both regulatory and environmental considerations when disposing of equipment, and these considerations are still yours even if you engage a third party. From a regulatory standpoint, regulations specify you must protect health information and other examples of PII. This obligation continues until the privacy data is removed in the disposal process.

From an environmental standpoint, many computing systems contain dangerous metals that cannot be just dumped in the landfill. These items should be turned over to an electronic waste removal company.

Exam essentials

Understand the difference between standard and low-level formatting. Standard formatting uses OS tools and makes the drive available for holding data without truly removing what was on the drive (thus the data can be recovered). A low-level format is OS independent and destroys any data that was on the drive.

Understand how to physically destroy a drive. A hard drive can be destroyed by tossing it into a shredder designed for such a purpose, or it can be destroyed with an electromagnet in a process known as degaussing. You can also disassemble the drive and destroy the platters with a drill or other tool that renders the data irretrievable.

2.10 Given a scenario, apply security settings on SOHO wireless and wired networks

CompTIA wants administrators of SOHO networks to be able to secure those networks in ways that protect the data stored on them. This objective looks at security protection that can be added to a wireless or wired SOHO network. First, you'll look at issues specific to a wireless local area network (WLAN), and then you'll take a look at security considerations for wired and wireless networks.

Router settings

Today's SOHO networks will almost always contain a WLAN router to provide access to the local WLAN and beyond to the Internet. In this section, you'll learn about some of the key issues in setting up a home or SOHO WLAN router.

Change default passwords

Default accounts include not only those created with the OS installation but often also accounts associated with hardware. Wireless APs, routers, and similar devices often include accounts for interacting with, and administering, those devices. You should always change the passwords associated with those devices and, where possible, change the usernames.

If there are accounts that are not needed, disable them or delete them. Make certain you use strong password policies and protect the passwords with the same security that you do for any users or administrators. (In other words, don't write the router's password on an address label and stick it to the bottom of the router.)

In Windows, the Guest account is automatically created with the intent that it is to be used when someone must access a system but lacks a user account on that system. Because it is so widely known to exist, I recommend that you not use this default account and instead create another one for the same purpose if you truly need one. The Guest account leaves a security risk at the workstation and should be disabled to prevent it from being accessed by those attempting to gain unauthorized access.

> **TIP** Change *every* username and password that you can so they vary from their default settings.

IP filtering

IP address filtering is the selective admission of packets through the router that have been specified as allowed in the configuration. This technique is available on most WLAN routers and should be used to screen out unwanted IP addresses. You can also selectively deny certain types of traffic from *any* IP address by specifying the port number of the traffic type. The safest approach is to determine what needs to be allowed and disallow everything else. This follows the zero-trust model described earlier in this chapter, in the section "Zero-trust model."

Firmware updates

In the past, updating firmware on devices such as APs, routers, and switches was considered to be desirable but optional. More and more security attacks are based on attacking the firmware, and for this reason firmware updates should be part of whatever automated update system you might be using (not to mention the additional functionality and bug elimination you might experience). It may be that you can get on a mailing list for each vendor, so you can be notified when firmware updates are available. In any case, some systematic methods must be developed to ensure these updates are maintained.

Content filtering

You learned about content filtering earlier in this chapter, in the section "Router settings." Please review that section.

Physical placement secure locations

Just as you would not park your car in a public garage and leave its doors wide open with the key in the ignition, you should educate users not to leave a workstation that they are logged into when they attend meetings, go to lunch, and so forth. They should log out of the workstation or lock it. "Lock when you leave" should be a mantra with which they become familiar. Locking their workstation should require a password (usually the same as their user password) to resume working at the workstation.

Moreover, don't overlook the obvious need for physical security. Adding a cable to lock a laptop to a desk prevents someone from picking it up and walking away with a copy of your customer database. Laptop cases generally include a built-in security slot in which a cable lock can be added to prevent it from being carried away easily, like the one shown in Figure 7.17.

When it comes to desktop models, adding a lock to the back cover can prevent an intruder with physical access from opening the case and grabbing the hard drive or damaging the internal components. You should also physically secure network devices—routers, APs, and the like—by placing them in locked cabinets, if possible. If they are not physically

FIGURE 7.17 A cable in the security slot keeps the laptop from being carried away easily

secured, the opportunity exists for them to be stolen or manipulated in such a way to allow someone unauthorized to connect to the network.

Antenna and access point placement

Antenna placement can be crucial in allowing clients to reach the AP. There isn't any one universal solution to this issue, and it depends on the environment in which the AP is placed. As a general rule, the greater the distance the signal must travel, the more it will attenuate, but you can lose a signal quickly in a short space as well if the building materials reflect or absorb the signal. You should try to avoid placing APs near metal (including appliances) or near the ground. Placing them in the center of the area to be served and high enough to get around most obstacles is recommended.

On the other end of the spectrum, you have to contend with the problem of the signal traveling outside your intended network (known as *signal leakage*) and being picked up in public areas by outsiders. To lessen this problem, use RF-absorbent materials on external walls, essentially shielding the surroundings.

Radio power levels

On the chance that the signal is actually traveling too far, some APs include power-level controls that allow you to reduce the amount of output provided.

> **NOTE** You can find a great source for information on RF power values and antennas on the Cisco site at www.cisco.com/c/en/us/support/docs/wireless-mobility/wireless-lan-wlan/23231-powervalues-23231.html.

WPS

Wi-Fi protected setup (WPS) was a concept designed to make it easier for less knowledgeable users to add a new client to the WLAN without manually entering the security information on the client. One method involves pushing a button on the AP at the same time a client is attempting to join the network so that the settings are sent to the client. Other methods involve placing the client close to the AP, and near-field communication is used for the process.

Regardless of the details, as often happens when we try to make security simpler, we make it fail. It has been discovered that a hacker can identify the PIN used in a short period of time, and with it the network's WPA/WPA2 preshared key. For this reason, the Wi-Fi Alliance has recommended against using this feature.

Universal Plug and Play (UPnP)

Universal Plug and Play (UPnP) is a protocol that lets computers, printers, and other devices make themselves easily discoverable to a network router. Promoted by the UPnP Forum, a computer industry initiative, it is available on many wireless APs and routers. While it makes it easier to connect devices, it does have security issues.

Several studies has shown that more than 6,900 network-aware products from 1,500 companies at 81 million IP addresses responded to their discovery requests on the Internet. Depending on the security posture of the device, many of those devices can be accessed or manipulated. For this reason, many have called for disabling the UPnP feature on wireless routers or APs.

Screened subnet

Although the firewalls discussed thus far typically connect directly to an untrusted network (at least one interface does), a screened host is a firewall that is between the final router and the internal network. When traffic comes into the router and is forwarded to the firewall, it is inspected before going into the internal network.

A screened subnet takes this concept a step further. In this case, two firewalls are used, and traffic must be inspected at both firewalls to enter the internal network. It is called a screen subnet because there is a subnet between the two firewalls that can act as a demilitarized zone (DMZ) for resources from the outside world. A screened subnet is shown in Figure 7.18.

Configure secure management access

Finally, privileged access to the systems, especially the infrastructure devices such as the routers and switches that may be present, must be secured. Any default accounts (i.e. administrator, guest, etc.) should *not* be used, and specific accounts should be created for the management of these devices. Strong passwords should be created, and multifactor authentication should be configured if possible. Passwords should be changed as often as

FIGURE 7.18 Screened subnet

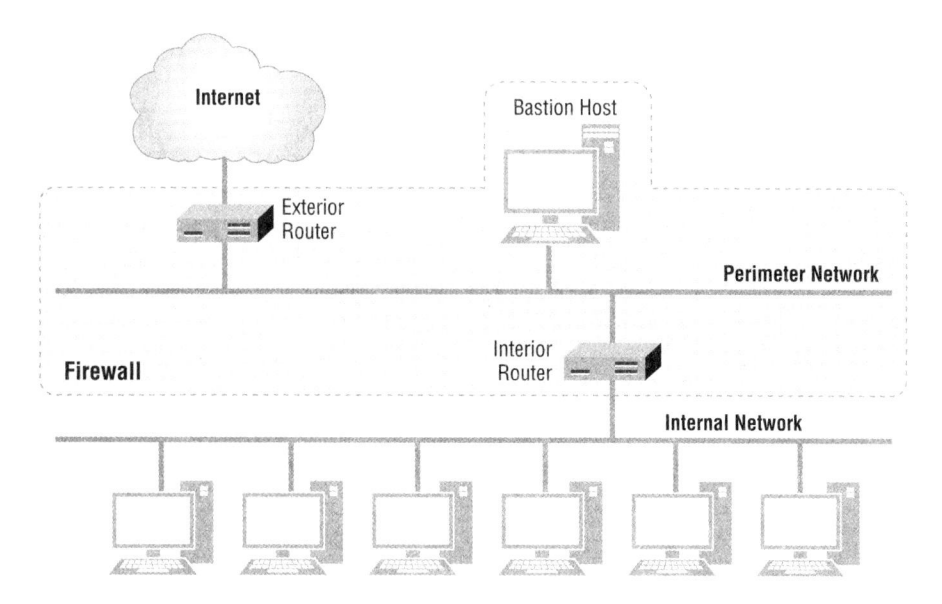

possible. Using a password manager application (covered earlier in this chapter) would be an even better solution.

Wireless specific

Wireless networks present a unique set of challenges that wired networks do not. The communication methods are somewhat different, as are the attack methods. In this section, security issues that are relevant only to a WLAN are discussed.

Changing the service set identifier (SSID)

Every wireless AP or wireless router on the market comes with a default SSID. These are published by the manufacturers, who make them available over the Internet. Cisco models use the name *tsunami*, for example. You should change these defaults and create a new SSID to represent your WLAN. Typically, when hackers see a default SSID, they make the reasonable assumption that if the SSID was left at the default, the administrator password was as well. So, if you also failed to change that, hackers can now log in, take over your AP, and lock you out.

Disabling SSID broadcast

One method of "protecting" the network that is often recommended is to turn off the SSID broadcast. The AP is still there and can be accessed by those who know about it, but it prevents those who are just scanning from finding it. This should be considered a weak form of security because there are still other ways, albeit a bit more complicated, to discover the presence of the AP besides the SSID broadcast.

Encryption settings

Earlier in this chapter, you learned about WLAN encryption and its value in the section "Protocols and encryption." Please review that section.

Configuring guest access

Many wireless routers allow you to create two networks: one network for your personal devices and a guest network for folks who are just visiting. While this may be beneficial, to increase security it is also possible to disable the guest network and guest access. As an example, the setting on a Motorola is shown in Figure 7.19.

Firewall settings

All devices, both wired and wireless, should have personal firewalls enabled and configured to protect each system. In Windows, you can simply leverage the personal firewall that comes on all Windows computers. For OSes that don't come with a personal firewall, third-party software should be implemented for this purpose. These firewalls help to prevent other devices from connecting to each station without the approval of the users.

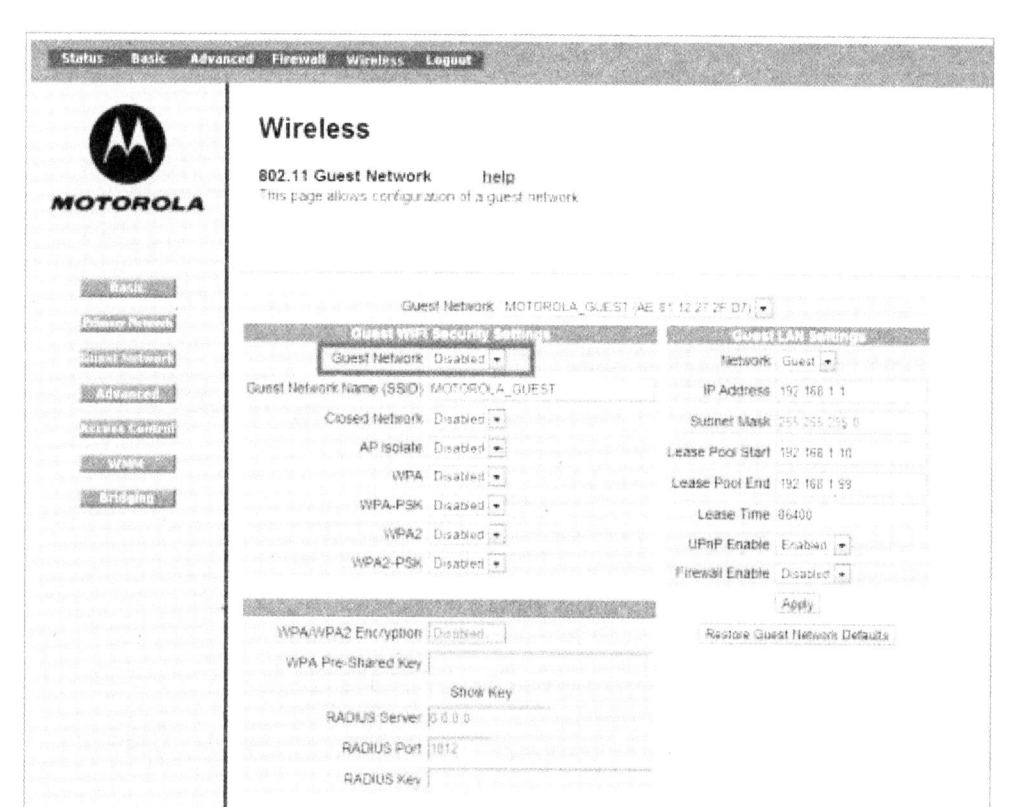

FIGURE 7.19 Disabling guest access

The presence of personal firewalls on all the devices does *not* mean you don't need a network firewall at the edge of the network and between sections of the network that may have varying security levels.

Disabling unused ports

Disable all unneeded protocols/ports. If you don't need them, remove them or prevent them from loading. Ports not in use present an open door for an attacker to enter. One easy way to do this is to disable them all, then turn on the ports you need.

> **TIP** Many of the newer SOHO router solutions (and some of the personal firewall solutions on end-user workstations) close down the Internet Control Message Protocol (ICMP) ports by default. Keep this in mind; it can drive you nuts when you are trying to see whether a new station, server, or router is up and running by using the `ping` command. This command depends on the use of ICMP.

Port forwarding/mapping

Another option to harden the network's entrance is to deploy port forwarding or mapping. *Port forwarding* is a function typically performed on the same device that may be performing network address translation (NAT). One port number is set aside on the gateway for the exclusive use of communicating with a service in the private network, located on a specific host. External hosts must know this port number and the address of the gateway to communicate with the internal service. The purpose of this is to hide the real IP address of the destination device or server to protect it from connections outside the LAN.

Exam essentials

Identify steps to harden a WLAN router. These steps include default password changes, IP filtering, firmware updates, and content filtering.

Describe mitigations specific to WLAN. These include changing the SSID, disabling SSID broadcast, setting encryption, disabling guest access, and changing channels.

2.11 Given a scenario, configure relevant security settings in a browser

Earlier in Chapter 6, you learned about settings involving the browser when we discussed Windows settings. In this final section of Chapter 7, we'll review some of those and dig deeper into some others.

Browser download/installation

In most cases, users will simply use the browser that comes with the OS. But in other cases, users will want to download and install a different browser. For example, a user may prefer the Google Chrome browser. Not all sources of these browser downloads are safe. In this section, you'll review some concepts we touched on earlier, way back in Chapter 1.

Trusted sources/untrusted sources

We spent some time in Chapter 1 discussing the difference between trusted and untrusted sources of any download. That applies to browsers as well. The best place to obtain browser downloads is the vendor website and not some third-party site that may be more interested in stealing your identity.

Hashing

Even when using a trusted site, you still can't be sure there isn't malware in the download. Hash functions are used to ensure integrity. Most providers also will provide what is called a *message digest* of the file you can also download.

Hash values, also referred to as *message digests*, are calculated using the original message. A hash function takes a message of variable length and produces a fixed-length hash value. If the receiver calculates a hash value that is the same, then the original message is intact. If the receiver calculates a hash value that is different, then the original message has been altered.

Browser patching

The browser is an application just like any other, and whether it is Windows Edge, Google Chrome, or Firefox, updates and security patches are released on a regular basis. You probably have even seen the little reminders in your browser that an update is available. While these updates may fix issues or increase performance, the most important reason to apply these updates is to keep the browser as secure as possible, because users are using it to navigate the most insecure network in the world, the Internet.

Extensions and plug-ins

Extensions and plugs-ins are extra components that you can install in the browser that may add features or enable the browser to interact more closely with a site. The problem is not all of these extensions are safe.

Trusted sources/untrusted sources

While it might be easy to tell you to only download extensions from vendors, many users, especially developers, will want to use plug-ins that were created by individual developers. If you plan to allow this, ensure that users:

- Investigate the developer's reputation.
- Read the explanation of the plug-in completely.
- Pay attention to the required permissions to operate. Are they too broad?
- Look for reviews.
- If it's open source, dig into the source code and verify its security.

Password managers

You learned about the value of password managers earlier in this chapter, in the section "Use password managers." Please review that section.

Secure connections/sites—valid certificates

Users must also be instilled with lot of skepticism regarding connecting to external sites—especially as it relates to insecure sites (i.e. HTTP). Later in Chapter 8, in the section "Certificate warnings," you'll learn more about certain types of certificate warning dialog boxes. Users should be instructed to regard all of these messages seriously, and *not* to dismiss them and continue connecting to the site.

Settings

In Chapter 6, in the section "Internet options," you learned about Internet settings that impact the browser. In this section, I'll refer you back to some security-related settings to review and discuss some other ones as well.

Pop-up blocker

Pop-up blocker was discussed in Chapter 6, in the section "Privacy." Please review that section. The setting is shown in Figure 7.20.

FIGURE 7.20   Pop-up blocker

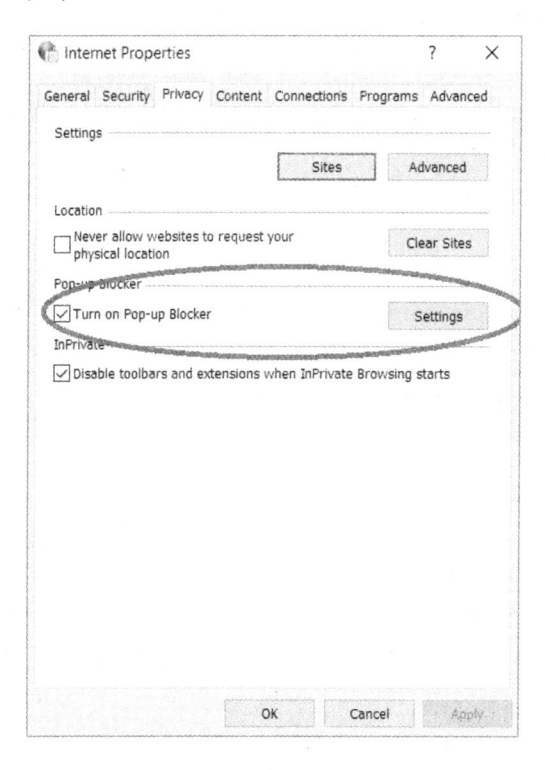

Clearing browser data/clearing cache

These two items are done in the same place. The clearing of browser data or history is done as shown in Figure 7.21. As you can see, you can select the exact data you would like to clear from these options:

- Browsing history
- Download history
- Cookies and other site data
- Cached images and files

Private-browsing mode

Most browsers today offer a private-browsing mode. So, what does this mean? Private browsers allow you to keep your Internet activity hidden from others who use the same computer or devices. This does not include:

- Your organization
- Your Internet service provider (ISP)

Cookies used during private-browsing sessions can provide information about your browsing behavior to third parties. This means your web activity can still be tracked.

The setting for opening an InPrivate window is shown in Figure 7.22.

FIGURE 7.21 Clear browsing data and cache

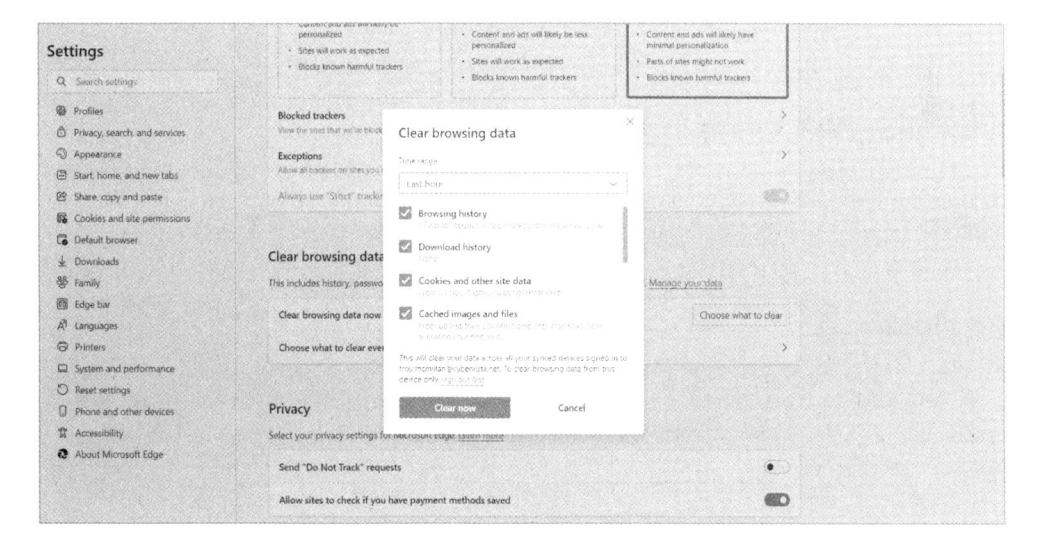

FIGURE 7.22 InPrivate browsing

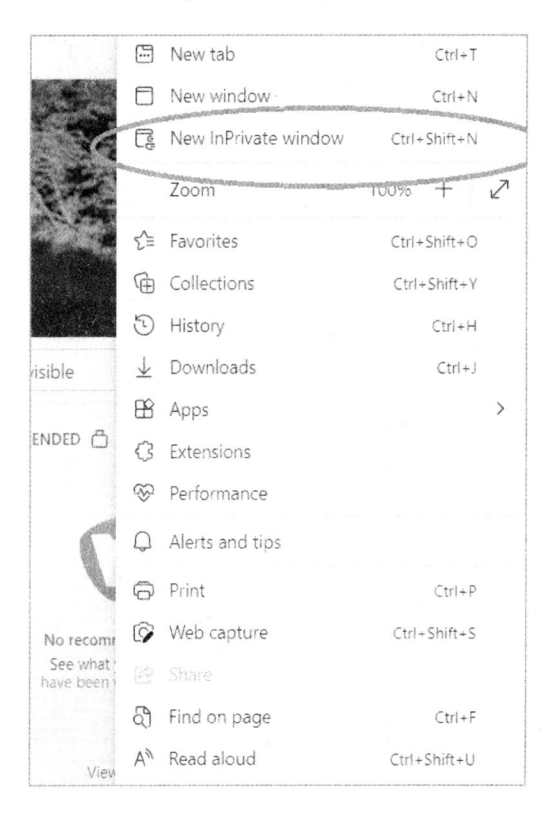

Sign-in/browser data synchronization

In Chapter 1, in the section "Mobile device synchronization," you learned about the synchronization of your sign-in and other browser data with a mobile device such as a smartphone or laptop. The settings are the same for desktop systems as well. Please review that chapter.

Ad blocker

Ad blockers are extensions that can be added to stop the constant stream of ads one encounters on the web. AdGuard AdBlocker is the easiest way to block ads in the Microsoft Edge browser. It effectively blocks all types of advertising on all web pages, even on Facebook, YouTube, and other sites.

Proxy

In Chapter 2, in the section "Proxy servers," you learned about proxy servers, and in Chapter 6, in the section "Proxy settings," you learned about configuring the proxy server address in Network and Internet Settings. Please review those chapters.

Secure DNS

DNS is a service that has been used maliciously both to obtain mapping records and to misdirect systems to malicious sites. Windows 11 offers a built-in feature called DNS over HTTPS (DoH) that encrypts your DNS queries, safeguarding your Internet activity from potential snoopers and cyber threats. By enabling DoH, you ensure that your DNS requests are encrypted, making your browsing experience more secure. To secure DNS on Windows, you can enable DoH. Here's how:

1. Go to Settings > Network & Internet > Select Your Connection> Hardware Properties and click the Edit button next to DNS Server Assignment button.
2. At Configure DNS Servers, select Set to Manual. In the window that pops up, use the drop-down menu to select Manual DNS settings.
3. At Enable IPv4, Flip the IPv4 switch to the On position. Enter the primary DNS server address (e.g. 8.8.8.8 for Google DNS) in the Preferred DNS box and the secondary DNS server address (e.g. 8.8.4.4) in the Alternate DNS box. Then set DNS Over HTTPs to the On position.

Browser feature management

Earlier in this section, you learned about browser extensions and plug-ins. Throughout this book, we have discussed Windows features. In this section, you'll learn how to enable and disable these components.

Enable/disable

Plug-ins and extensions are the same in general. Plug-ins are typically used to refer to software that adds functionality to a specific application. A plug-in for a web browser is often known as an *extension*. Plug-ins, extensions, and features can be disabled or enabled. Let's look at where you do this.

Plug-ins/extensions

In Microsoft Edge, extensions (i.e. plug-ins) are enabled by selecting the Extensions icon at the top-right of the page, next to the Bookmarks icon, as shown in Figure 7.23, where it is circled in red.

508 Chapter 7 ▪ Security

FIGURE 7.23   Extensions/plug-ins

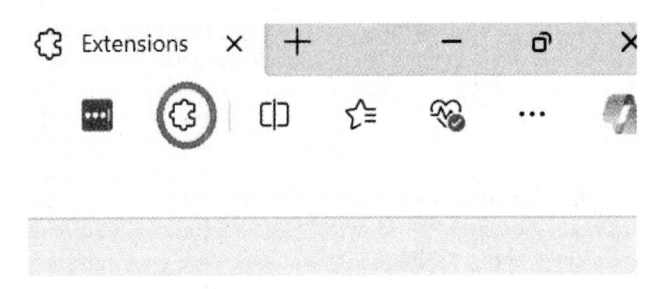

FIGURE 7.24   Manage extensions

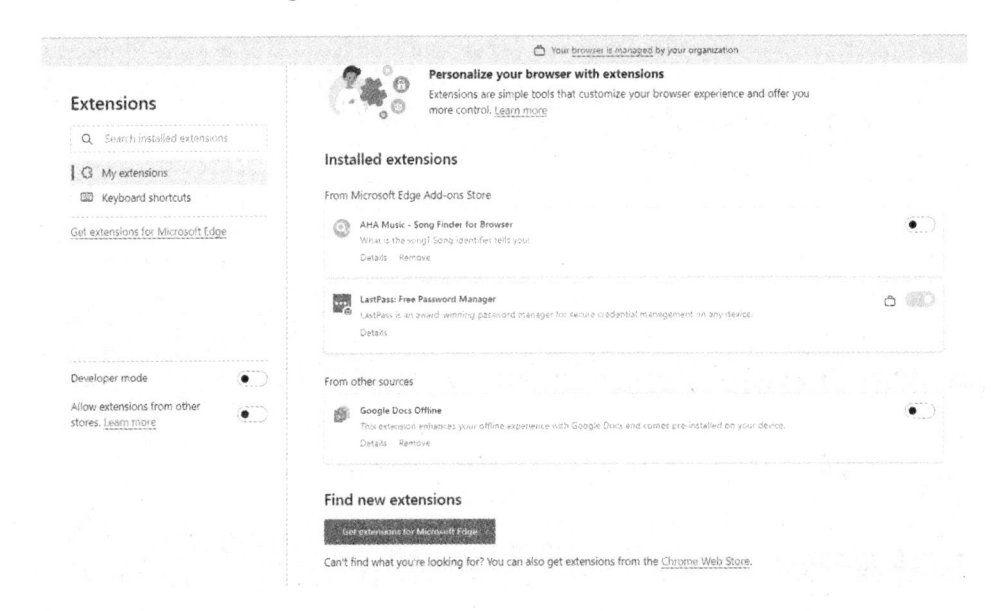

In the drop-down menu, select Manage Extensions. It yields the page shown in Figure 7.24. All extensions (i.e. plug-ins) will be listed, and you can enable or disable them. In Figure 7.24, you can see that the only extension currently enabled is LastPass: Free Password Manager.

Features

Features can be enabled or disabled by adding a command-line argument to the Properties page of the browser. The `--enable-features` and `--disable-features` options should be added to the desktop shortcut of the browser after its executable file name (i.e. msedge.exe or chrome.exe). This is shown in Figure 7.25. The command line `--disable-`

FIGURE 7.25 Disabling a feature

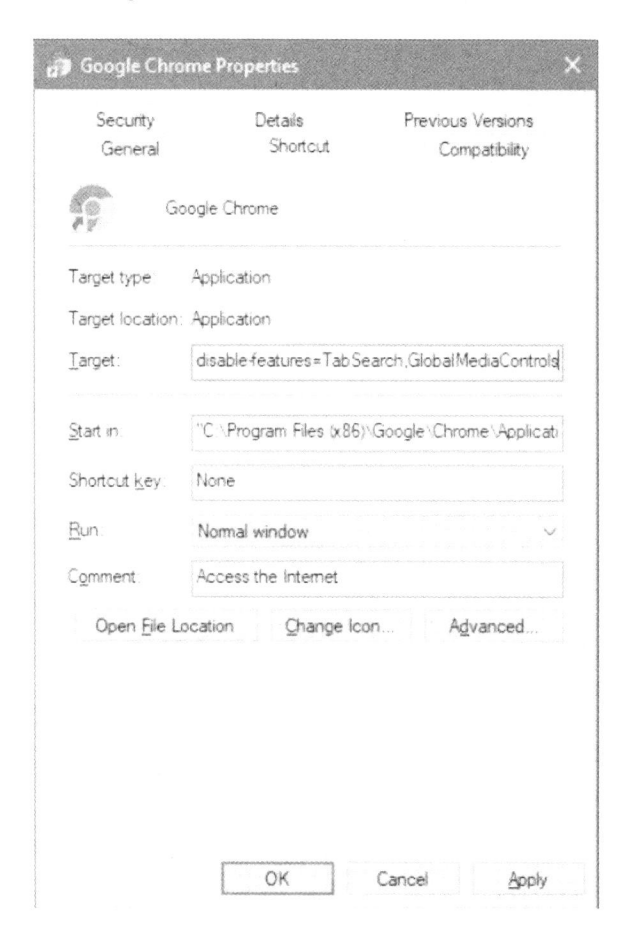

![Google Chrome Properties dialog showing the Shortcut tab with Target field containing "disable-features=TabSearch,GlobalMediaControls"]

`features=TabSearch,GlobalMediaControls` will disable the Tab Search and Global Media Controls features in the Chrome browser.

Exam essentials

Identify security settings related to the browser. These include using pop-up blocker, clearing browsing data, clearing cache, using private-browsing mode, synchronizing sign-in/browser data, and using ad blockers.

Review Questions

You can find the answers in the appendix.

1. Which of the following is a series of two doors with a small room between them?
   A. Mantrap
   B. Trapdoor
   C. Badgetrap
   D. Saferoom

2. Which of the following physical characteristics is used to identify the user?
   A. Hardware tokens
   B. Biometric locks
   C. Smart cards
   D. Badge readers

3. Which filtering type is done on a router or firewall?
   A. MAC address filtering
   B. Email filtering
   C. IP address filtering
   D. URL filtering

4. Which of the following is used to ensure integrity?
   A. Rainbow tables
   B. Encryption
   C. Hashing
   D. Serializing

5. Which of the following was created as a first stab at security for wireless devices?
   A. WPA
   B. WPA2
   C. TKIP
   D. WEP

6. Which of the following was used to increase security in WPA?
   A. TKIP
   B. AES
   C. IPSec
   D. SSL

7. Which type of virus covers itself with protective code that stops debuggers or disassemblers from examining critical elements of the virus?
   A. Companion
   B. Macro
   C. Armored
   D. Multipartite

8. What element of a virus uniquely identifies it?
   A. ID
   B. Signature
   C. Badge
   D. Marking

9. Which of the following is the term used for someone being so close to you when you enter a building that they are able to come in right behind you without needing to use a key, a card, or any other security device?
   A. Shadowing
   B. Spoofing
   C. Tailgating
   D. Keyriding

10. Which of the following is the process of masquerading as another user or device?
    A. Shadowing
    B. Spoofing
    C. Duplicating
    D. Masking

11. Which Windows group allows members to install most software but keeps them from changing key operating system files?
    A. Power Users
    B. Guests
    C. Administrators
    D. Users

12. Which NTFS permission is the least required to run a program?
    A. List Folder Contents
    B. Full Control
    C. Read
    D. Write

13. Which of the following passwords is the strongest?
    A. password
    B. pAssword
    C. Pa$$word
    D. P@ssw0rd

14. What principle should drive the granting of permissions?
    A. Separation of duties
    B. Least privilege
    C. Job rotation
    D. Open rights

15. Which type of screen lock uses gestures?
    A. Fingerprint
    B. Face
    C. Swipe
    D. Passcode

16. Which method deletes all content on a lost mobile device?
    A. Remote wipe
    B. Geofencing
    C. Screen lock
    D. Segmentation of data

17. Which of the following involves applying a strong magnetic field to wipe the media?
    A. Degaussing
    B. Incineration
    C. Hammer
    D. Deleting

18. Which method of destroying the data on a hard drive is most effective?
    A. Degaussing
    B. Incineration
    C. Clearing
    D. Deleting

19. Which of the following was a concept that was designed to make it easier for less knowledgeable users to add a new client to the WLAN without manually entering the security information on the client?

   A. SSID
   B. WPS
   C. WEP
   D. WPA

20. Which of the following should always be changed from the default?

   A. SSID
   B. WPS
   C. WEP
   D. WPA

Chapter 8

Software Troubleshooting

COMPTIA A+ 220-1202 EXAM OBJECTIVES COVERED IN THIS CHAPTER:

✓ **3.1 Given a scenario, troubleshoot common Windows OS issues**

- Blue Screen of Death (BSOD)
- Degraded performance
- Boot issues
  - Slow bootup
- Frequent shutdowns
- Services not starting
- Applications crashing
- Low memory warnings
- USB controller resource warnings
- System instability
- No OS found
- Slow profile load
- Time drift
- Common troubleshooting steps
  - Reboot
  - Restart services
  - Uninstall/reinstall/update applications
  - Add resources
  - Verify requirements
  - System file check
  - Repair/restore Windows
  - Reimage

- Roll back updates
- Rollback device drivers
- Rebuild Windows profiles

✓ **3.2 Given a scenario, troubleshoot common mobile OS and application issues**

- Application fails to launch
- Application fails to close/crashes
- Application fails to update
- Application fails to install
- Slow to respond
- OS fails to update
- Battery life issues
- Random reboots
- Connectivity issues
  - Bluetooth
  - Wi-Fi
  - Near-field communication (NFC)
- Screen does not autorotate

✓ **3.3 Given a scenario, troubleshoot common mobile OS and application security issues**

- Security concerns
  - Application source/unofficial application stores
  - Developer mode
  - Root access/jailbreak
  - Unauthorized/malicious application
    - Application spoofing
  - Common symptoms
    - High network traffic
    - Degraded response time
    - Data-usage limit notification
    - Limited Internet connectivity/no Internet connectivity

- High number of ads
- Fake security warnings
- Unexpected application behavior
- Leaked personal files/data

✓ **3.4 Given a scenario, troubleshoot common personal computer (PC) security issues**

- Common symptoms
  - Unable to access the network
  - Desktop alerts
  - False alerts regarding antivirus protection
  - Altered system or personal files/missing/renamed files/inability to access files
  - Unwanted notifications within the OS
  - OS updates failures
- Browser-related symptoms
  - Random/frequent pop-ups
  - Certificate warnings
  - Redirection
  - Degraded browser performance
    - Outdated browser
    - Too many tabs
    - Unused extensions
    - Cache and cookies
    - Slow Internet
    - Malware

This chapter focuses on the exam topics related to software troubleshooting. It follows the structure of the CompTIA A+ 220-1202 exam blueprint, Objective 3, and it explores the four subobjectives that you need to master before taking the exam.

3.1 Given a scenario, troubleshoot common Windows OS issues

Because it's software and there are so many places where things can go wrong, the operating system (OS) can be one of the most confusing components to troubleshoot. Sometimes, it seems a miracle that OSes even work at all, considering the hundreds of files that work together to make the system function. In this section, common OS issues and their solutions are covered.

Blue screen of death (BSOD)

Once a regular occurrence when working with Windows, blue screens (also known as the blue screen of death [BSOD]) have become less common. Occasionally, systems will lock up; you can usually examine the log files to discover what was happening when this occurred and take steps to correct it. Remember, when dealing with a blue screen, always ask yourself, "What did I just install or change?" In many cases, the change is involved in the BSOD. Also, keep in mind that, as the instructions on the blue screen will tell you, a simple reboot will often fix the problem. Retaining the contents of the BSOD can help you troubleshoot the issue. In most instances, you can find the BSOD error in Microsoft's knowledge base to help with troubleshooting.

The spinning pinwheel is displayed automatically by WindowServer when an application cannot handle all the events it receives. (WindowServer is the background process that runs the macOS graphical user interface.) To find out whether the central processing unit (CPU) is a bottleneck on performance, use Activity Monitor (/Applications/Utilities) to monitor the CPU's usage. The pinwheel (or beach ball) might also appear if you don't have enough random-access memory (RAM).

Software can also cause the pinwheel. Open Activity Monitor's CPU tab and sort by the % CPU column in descending order; the apps located at the top are the ones using the most CPU cycles. If an application is frozen, it will appear in red. If it is *not* a process with root listed as the user, quit it.

Degraded performance

Slow system performance can come from many issues. For the purposes of this discussion, I will focus on performance that deteriorates after being acceptable, as opposed to system performance that is poor from the outset (which could be a matter of insufficient resources, such as RAM). Here is a list of possibilities:

- The first thing to check for is the presence of a virus. If the system seems to have an overabundance of disk activity, scan it for viruses using a virus program that resides externally on a memory stick.
- Defragment the hard drive. The more fragmented it is, the slower the disk access will be.
- Check the space on the hard drive. When the partition or volume where the OS is located becomes full, performance will suffer. This is why it is a good idea to store data and applications on a different partition from that holding the OS files.
- Ensure that the latest updates are installed. In many cases, updates help to solve performance problems, so make sure they are current.
- Use Task Manager to determine whether a process is using too much memory or if the CPU is simply locked up (i.e. not responding), and if necessary, end the process.

Boot issues

Booting problems can occur with corruption of the boot files or missing components. Common error messages include an invalid boot disk, inaccessible boot drive, missing New Technology Loader (NTLDR) file, or missing BOOTMGR (which are discussed in more detail later in this section). Fortunately, during the OS installation, log files are created in `C:\Windows`. If you have a puzzling problem, look at these logs and see whether you can find error entries there.

You can configure system failure problems to write dump files (i.e. debugging information) for later analysis when they occur by clicking Start > Control Panel > System and then clicking the Advanced System Settings option. The Advanced tab of the System Properties dialog box should open. Then click the Settings button in the Startup and Recovery section. Here, in addition to choosing the default OS, you can configure whether events should be written to the system log, whether an alert should be sent to the administrator, and what type of memory dump should be written.

Slow bootup

Slow bootups can be caused by a number of issues. First, it could be that the system is struggling for resources. This might indicate a memory or hard drive issue. It also can slow down the startup if many programs are set to start at bootup.

In cases where the computer belongs to a domain, it could also be having trouble locating the domain controller and perhaps performing policy updates.

Finally, it could be that the device is set to access a distributed file system (DFS) share or another type of remote drive and locating the drive is the issue. (DFS is a system used to provide connections to shared folders without knowing their physical location.) The cause could also be the next issue on the list.

Frequent shutdowns

It doesn't get any more obvious that something is wrong than when the computer just shuts down on its own. In some cases, a blue screen on the display with a lot of text precedes this shutdown. If that occurs, the problem is related to the OS and might not involve a hardware issue. OS issues related to the BSOD were covered in the section "Blue screen of death (BSOD)" earlier in this chapter.

One common reason for shutdowns is overheating. Often when that is the case, however, the system reboots itself rather than just shutting down. Reboots are covered later in this section.

Always check the obvious, such as if the power cable is connected to the source of power. Check to see whether a breaker flipped in the power box as well. Checking these items is an example of starting the process at the physical layer. If the computer is plugged into a power strip or uninterruptible power supply (UPS) that has a fuse or breaker, check to see whether the fuse blew or the breaker flipped because of a power surge.

Services not starting

Sometimes when the system is started, you receive a message that tells you a service failed to start. When that occurs, use the event log to determine the service that failed. Then, to interact with the service, access the Administrative Tools section of Control Panel and choose Services to start the Services console. You can right-click any service and choose to start, stop, pause, resume, or restart it. You can also double-click the service to access its properties and configure things like the startup type, dependencies, and other variables.

If the service refuses to start, it could be that a service on which it depends will not start. To determine what services must be running for the problem service to start, select the Dependencies tab of the service's Properties dialog box, as shown in Figure 8.1.

In Figure 8.1 you can see that the Remote Desktop service depends on both the Remote Procedure Call (RPC) and Terminal Device Driver services to function. Try starting these services first. In some cases, you might need to trace the dependencies up several levels to get things going.

Applications crashing

Another possible symptom of a malware infection is the crashing of applications. While this will occur from time to time for other reasons, when it is occurring repeatedly, you should suspect malware. When the application that is crashing is your antivirus software, this is an

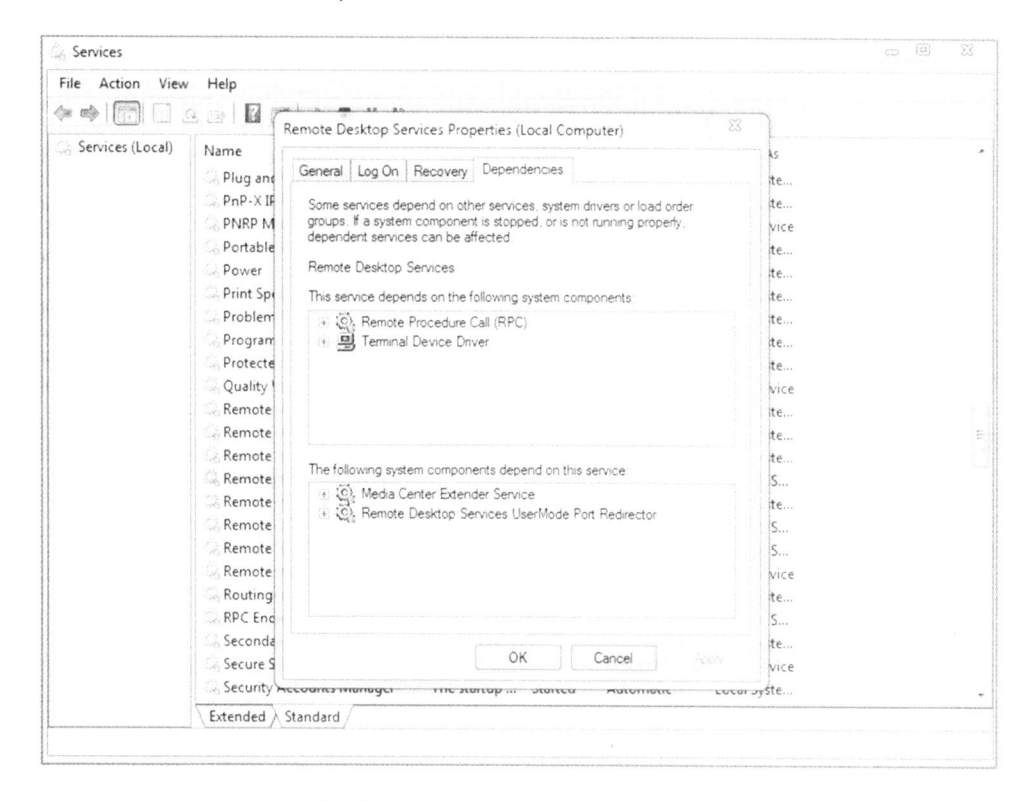

FIGURE 8.1   Service dependencies

even stronger indication of malware. Disabling or damaging your antivirus protection is the first thing that some types of malware attempt to do.

Low memory warnings

Another key indicator of a compromised host is increased memory consumption. Often, it is an indication that additional programs have been loaded into the RAM so they can be processed. Then, once they are loaded, they use RAM in the process of executing their tasks, whatever they may be. You can monitor memory consumption by using the same approach you use for CPU consumption. When checking Task Manager for memory issues, don't be surprised if you find that the culprit is your browser! If memory usage cannot be accounted, you should investigate it. (Review what you learned about buffer overflows, which are attacks that may display symptoms of increased memory consumption.)

USB controller resource warnings

Although it was mostly an issue with older Microsoft OSes, you might encounter the error message shown in Figure 8.2.

FIGURE 8.2 USB controller resource warnings

There are three major situations that can cause this:

- USB controller limit is exceeded—you've exceeded the available number of EndPoints. USB 3.0 controllers have a limit of 96 EndPoints per controller on Intel XHCI controllers, while AM4 controllers support 254 EndPoints.
- The USB port EndPoints usage exceeded the limit—most USB controllers are capped at 16 IN and 16 OUT EndPoints.
- Power being drawn from the USB devices exceeds the maximum capacity of the USB controller.

System instability

System instability can arise from issues with the OS or with applications. Specifically, these issues might be one of the following:

- Malware infection
- Damage due to shutdown during updates
- Damage to registry keys
- Unstable third-party applications
- Unstable hardware

No OS found

The "No operating system found" message can result from a number of issues. Among them are the following:

- Incorrect boot device order in the Basic Input/Output System (BIOS)
- Corrupted or missing boot sector
- Corrupted boot files

In short, the OS is not actually missing; the system is missing the file that can either locate it or load it.

In Windows 11, if using Startup Repair does not work, you might need to create a bootable disk to boot the device. The directions for this vary between the systems but can be found on the Microsoft site.

Slow profile load

Remote profiles are loaded from remote servers, and when network issues like the ones discussed in the previous section are present, this will hold up the startup process.

Time drift

When a system time keeps drifting, it is usually an issue with the complementary metal-oxide semiconductor (CMOS) battery.

The CMOS chip must have a constant source of power to keep its settings. To prevent data loss, motherboard manufacturers include a small battery to power the CMOS memory. On modern systems, this is a coin-style battery, about the diameter of a U.S. dime and about as thick. Figure 8.3 shows the location of the CMOS battery.

The CMOS clock is located on the computer's motherboard and keeps time when the computer is off. The OS gets its time from the BIOS clock at boot time. This clock can be set using the BIOS if it is not correct. Figure 8.4 shows the time setting.

FIGURE 8.3   CMOS battery

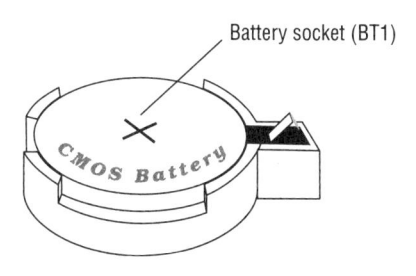

FIGURE 8.4   Setting the CMOS clock in the BIOS

Common troubleshooting steps

The following are some common approaches to addressing the issues described in the previous section.

Reboot

You would be surprised how many system issues can be solved by a simple reboot. Therefore, the first step in many guides is a reboot. Always try it first.

Restart services

In some cases, it may not be necessary to kill the service. It may be advisable to simply restart the service. See the earlier section of "Services not starting."

Uninstall/reinstall/update applications

To repair an application, consult the application vendor's website. Most applications allow for a repair function if you attempt to reinstall the application when it is already installed.

While updates sometimes cause issues, in most cases, they solve issues. When an issue involves possible driver problems, check to see whether any of the devices involved have new updates available. You can try this at Windows Update or by going to the vendor's website. Sometimes they have tools that can scan your entire system for potential driver updates.

Add resources

In some cases, there will be no escaping the fact that the system does not have the resources to handle the workload. Adding the following resources will address performance issues related to insufficient resources:

- Memory (more memory allows more data to be processed at a time)
- CPU (a faster CPU processes data faster)

Adding disk resources will be beneficial only when the partition where the OS is located is full. In that case, adding a disk and extending that partition to give it extra room will help.

Adding network interfaces will be beneficial only when a performance issue is due to slow in/out performance on the current interface(s).

Verify requirements

Some issues are related to not reading the instructions. All OSes and applications require computer resource minimums to function. In most cases, you will be alerted to the fact that you don't meet the minimums during the installation, but not always. If you have issues, always consider the possibility you need more resources. An even better approach would be to read the documentation prior to installation.

System file check

Some issues are caused by damaged or corrupted system files. In Chapter 6, in the section "OS management," you learned about the Windows tool System File Checker (SFC), which can be used to both verify system files and repair those that are damaged or corrupted.

Repair/restore Windows

In some cases, the easiest way to repair an issue is to completely reinstall the OS. This is one of the biggest reasons you should encourage users to store data on servers or cloud platforms rather than on the workstation. However, OS vendors are beginning to offer some options that have a less drastic effect on user data. They have also made it easier to perform various recovery types with no media.

For example, in Windows 10, there are several options presented when you choose to repair the computer. They are Refresh, Reset, and Restore. The effects of using the three options are as follows:

> **Refresh** This reinstalls Windows and keeps your personal files and settings. It also keeps the apps that came with your PC and the apps you installed from the Windows Store.
>
> **Reset** This reinstalls Windows but deletes your files, settings, and apps—except for the apps that came with your PC.
>
> **Restore** This is a way to undo recent system changes you've made by returning the system configuration to a previous point in time. It does not delete any files or applications, unless the application was installed after a restore point was taken.

To access these options, follow these steps:

1. Swipe in from the screen's right edge, tap Settings, and then tap Change PC Settings. (If you're using a mouse, point to the upper-right corner of the screen, move the mouse pointer down, click Settings, and then click Change PC Settings.)
2. Tap or click Update and Recovery and then tap or click Recovery.
3. You will now see the three options, as shown in Figure 8.5.

Reimage

In corporate environments that have a standard system image, especially in the case of a serious malware infection, it is simpler to just reimage the device and start over with a clean installation. For this reason, always encourage users to *not* save data on the local hard drive, as this will complicate the issue: Their data will be wiped out when the drive is reimaged! If they insist, at least convince them to perform their own data backups.

Roll back updates

Vendors test updates before rolling them out, but it is impossible for them to anticipate every scenario in which the update may be introduced. Because of this, an update might break

FIGURE 8.5 Recovery

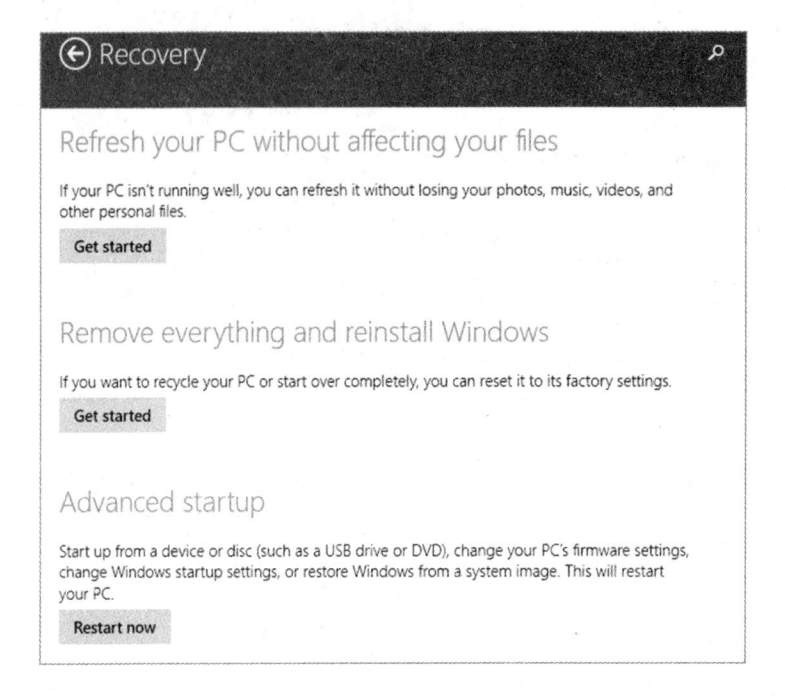

something. In that case, the issues should occur soon after the update. It's always worth the attempt to roll back the update, as it is simple to do. Just locate the update in the list of installed updates and select to remove the update.

Rollback device drivers

It's rare for a driver update to fail, but sometimes they do. If you install a new driver and there is an issue, you can use the Rollback Driver feature to revert to the old driver. The Rollback Driver button is found in Device Manager on the Driver tab of the device.

Rebuild Windows profiles

To fix a corrupted user profile on a Windows 10 computer, follow these steps:

1. Go to the Control Panel.
2. Go to User Accounts (or Accounts and Family Safety > User Accounts).
3. Click Manage Another Account.
4. Click Create a New Account (or Add a New User in PC settings in Windows 11) to create a new account on your computer.
5. Type a name and choose an account type.
6. Click Create Account.

7. Choose Account Type for New User.
8. Open File Explorer or My Computer.
9. Click Tools. If you don't see the Tools item at the top of the window, press the Alt key.
10. Click Folder Options.
11. Go to the View tab.
12. Check the Show Hidden Files and Folders option.
13. Uncheck the Hide Protected Operating System Files option.
14. Click Apply.
15. Click OK.
16. Go to `C:\Users\OLD_USERNAME`, where `C:\` is where your Windows is installed and `OLD_USERNAME` is the username that has the corrupted profile error.
17. From this folder (`OLD_USERNAME`), select all files except `Ntuser.data`, `Ntuser.data.log`, and `Ntuser.ini`.
18. Right-click these files (except the files mentioned in the previous step) and click Copy.
19. Go to `C:\User\NEW_USERNAME`, where `NEW_USERNAME` is the username you created as new.
20. Paste all the files in this folder, `NEW_USERNAME`.
21. Restart the computer and log in with the new username you've created.

Exam essentials

Identify the most common symptoms of OS and system boot problems. These include BSODs, boot failures, problems from improper shutdowns, spontaneous shutdowns/restarts, devices that fail to start, slow system performance, files that fail to open, missing items (e.g. NTLDR, `boot.ini`, OS, and GUI), and invalid boot disks.

Identify the most common solutions to OS issues. These include, but are not limited to, defragmenting the hard drive, rebooting, killing tasks, restarting services, updating network settings, reimaging/reloading the OS, rolling back updates, rolling back device drivers, and applying updates.

3.2 Given a scenario, troubleshoot common mobile OS and application issues

Mobile devices have their own unique sets of issues that might not be encountered with desktop computers. In this section, I'll discuss common issues and their solutions.

Application fails to launch

When applications will not launch, there are several possible explanations:

- Malware has infected the system and is using all the resources.
- Too many applications are open at the same time.
- Storage space is lacking to open the application file.
- Unstable Internet connection occurs when opening the app on a remote server.

Solutions within your control include:

- Scan for and remove malware.
- Close some applications.
- Add storage space.
- Move to a more stable Internet connection.

Application fails to close/crashes

Application crashes or lockups (i.e. where the application won't shut down) can also have a variety of causes, some of which also cause failures to launch. Causes can include the following:

- Inadequate testing before launch by developer
- Memory issues that are robbing the system of resources
- Malware infection
- Unstable network connection
- Corrupted cache files that have not been cleared in a long time

Solutions within your control include:

- Add memory or replace faulty memory.
- Scan for and remove malware.
- Move to a more stable Internet connection.
- Clear cache files.

Application fails to update

While vendors have attempted to make updates as trouble-free as possible, sometimes updates still fail. Some possible reasons for this include:

- **No room.** Updates must be downloaded before they can be executed. When there is a lack of space to hold the update, the process will fail.

3.2 Given a scenario, troubleshoot common mobile OS and application issues

- **Multiple updates in the queue in the wrong order.** Updates build on one another, and you might not be able to apply one until another has been applied. If the updates are out of order in the queue and you are attempting to apply one that has a prerequisite update that has not been run, the process will fail.
- **Drive conflicts.** Bad drivers and driver conflicts can cause all sorts of issues, among them failed updates.
- **Corrupted system files.** Updates may require the operation of a system file to complete. If system files are corrupted, it can cause an update to fail.
- **Update system failure.** Sometimes it's the fault of the application managing the updates. For example, there have been a number of occasions when the Windows Update system itself has caused updates to fail due to an issue with the Windows Update service.

Solutions within your control include:

- Add disk space.
- Apply updates in order.
- Update drivers.
- Scan the file system for errors and repair them.

Application fails to install

When you are attempting to install an app and you receive the message that the application has failed to install, there are a number of causes and possible solutions. Table 8.1 lists issues and possible solutions.

TABLE 8.1 Application installation issues and possible solutions

Issue	Possible solution(s)
Conflict with current version	Uninstall the conflicting app.
App signature mismatch	Ensure that you are installing an Android Package Kit (APK) signed with the same certificate as the existing one. If necessary, uninstall the existing version first.
Blocked application	Enable Unknown Sources: Android devices are typically set to block installations from unknown sources for security reasons.
Corrupt installation file	Redownload the installation file.
Insufficient storage space	Delete unnecessary files or apps.

Slow to respond

When malware is present and running in the background, it is using resources as well as running down your battery. That means when you are downloading or uploading data, the process is competing with the malware for resources. Therefore, slow data speeds or latency in the response might also be a sign of a malware infection. The solution? You guessed it, remove the malware.

OS fails to update

Malware may take certain measures to protect itself. One of these is to block you from accessing OS update sites like Windows Update. You never notice this because these updates can be set to run automatically. So when they fail, it might not be obvious that they did.

Another action the malware can take along the same lines is to disable your antivirus software. For this reason, any time your antivirus program notifies you that it is not functional or cannot update itself, you should consider this possibility and get it back up and running (if you can) as soon as possible.

Battery life issues

One of the biggest complaints that users lodge against their mobile devices is short battery life. When a battery is nearing the end-of-life (EOL) cycle, it will begin to fail to hold a charge; it could be that you need a new battery. However, there are a number of other things you can do to mitigate the problem:

- Change the location and brightness settings, because these components really eat power.
- Turn off Bluetooth and Wi-Fi when not needed. These also take power.
- Disable push notifications for nonessential apps.
- Close apps not in use.
- Prevent the device from overheating, which is bad for the battery.

Random reboots

As you learned in Chapter 3, in the section "Cooling," one of the biggest causes of random reboots is overheating of the system. A mobile device can overheat when you are doing too many things at once and also when you keep running the system when the battery is low. Reboots can also be caused by a malware infection and by failing updates that require reboots.

3.2 Given a scenario, troubleshoot common mobile OS and application issues

Solutions include:

- Shutting down some applications and letting the device cool
- Charging the battery
- Scanning for and remove malware

Connectivity issues

Some issues are related to the network connection of the device. In this section, you'll explore some variations on this theme.

Bluetooth

In Chapter 1, in the section "Bluetooth," you learned that unintended Bluetooth connections can be a serious issue. You also learned how to create a Bluetooth connection and about issues that can prevent a Bluetooth connection. Please review that chapter.

Wi-Fi

When there is no wireless connectivity, it is usually because of one of two things.

- The wireless capability is disabled (usually with a key combination or a function key); it is easy to disable inadvertently. There can also be a hardware switch on the side, front, or back of the case.
- The wireless antenna is bad, or the cable needs to be reseated.

Try the following steps when troubleshooting a lack of wireless connectivity:

1. Power cycle the access point (AP) or wireless router.
2. Power cycle the device.
3. On a laptop, check the hardware wireless button (if the laptop has one).
4. On a smartphone or tablet, check your wireless settings to ensure that Wi-Fi is turned on. Also ensure that Airplane mode is turned off.
5. Disconnect and reconnect the device.
6. Verify that the wireless device is using the correct password.

Near-field communication (NFC)

In Chapter 1, in the section "Near-field communications (NFC)," you learned about near-field communications. If NFC is not working on a mobile device, check the following:

- Ensure that it is NFC compatible—if so, there should be an NFC logo on the device.
- Remove the case or skin—in some cases, these might be blocking the transmission.

- When touching the NFC device or the mobile device to the top of the retail unit, check the connection status of the mobile device. The mobile device might not be recognized if you touch the wrong area of the unit or touch it too quickly.
- NFC sensitivity might not be strong enough to connect the unit.

Screen does not autorotate

Autorotate rotates the desktop to landscape or portrait mode automatically depending on the orientation of the screen. When the feature is not working, check the following:

- Check for updates.
- Try restarting.
- Disconnect the peripherals.
- Ensure rotation lock is turned off.
- If this is Windows, try running the Sensors troubleshooter.
- Update the motion sensor driver.
- On a Microsoft OS, as a last resort, edit the registry key. (The Windows Mobile Registry Editor is a powerful tool that allows you to edit the registry settings on your Windows mobile device.)

    Specifically, do the following:

    1. Navigate to `HKEY_LOCAL_MACHINE\SOFTWARE\Microsoft\Windows\CurrentVersion\AutoRotation`.
    2. Double-click the Enable DWORD and ensure that the value is set to 1. Click OK.
    3. Double-click the LastOrientation DWORD and ensure that the value is set to 0. Click OK.
    4. Double-click the SensorPresent DWORD and ensure that the value is set to 1. Click OK.
    5. Double-click the SlateEnable DWORD and ensure that the value is set to 1. Click OK.
    6. Save the Settings.

Exam essentials

Identify common mobile device issues. These include, but are not limited to, intermittent wireless, no wireless connectivity, no Bluetooth connectivity, random reboots, and battery issues.

3.3 Given a scenario, troubleshoot common mobile OS and application security issues

Mobile devices might use different OSes than desktop systems, and their applications might be packaged a bit differently, but they still can suffer from security issues. It logically follows that they must be secured as well. In this section of Chapter 8, I'll talk about the symptoms of security issues and describe some tools you can use in the struggle to protect these devices and their data.

Security concerns

Just as with desktop systems, mobile devices can suffer from security issues. In this section, you'll learn about some of the issues.

Application source/unofficial application stores

Android Package Kit (APK) is a file format that is used by Android OS. Android OS uses this file format for the distribution and installation of Android applications that can be mobile apps or mobile games. Proper APKs can access only a limited range of system resources.

Security issues can arise when APKs are obtained from questionable sources. Application signatures play an important role in device security and are used for permissions checks as well as software updates. Best practices with regard to developing applications to run on Android include the following:

- Review source code.
- Use automated testing.
- Sign system images.
- Sign applications.

While it is best for Apple devices to use the App Store as their source for applications, it is possible to obtain apps elsewhere. Always make sure it is from a source you trust.
To download and install, please do the following:

- Download the app.
- Locate the .pkg or .dmg file.
- Open and copy it to the Applications folder.

In some cases, the apps from other sources won't launch. If that occurs, try this:
- Open the Finder.
- Click the Applications folder in the sidebar. (You might need to unhide the sidebar if it is hidden.)
- Find the app and Control-click it.
- Click Open.

Developer mode

Developer mode in Windows 11 is a mode that can be used to test apps more easily, use the Ubuntu Bash shell environment, and change a variety of developer-focused settings. This setting is available in the Settings app. To access it, head to Settings > Update & Security > For Developers and select Developer mode.

The security issues arise from the fact that if you select Developer mode, you can install Universal Windows Platform (UWP) apps from outside of the Windows Store, even if they're not signed. For this reason, applications developed using this tool should undergo robust security assessment.

Root access/jailbreak

> **WARNING**
> The activities explained here may void your device's warranty. We do not recommend rooting or jailbreaking. This section describes the security issues associated with these activities.

While rooting or jailbreaking a device enables the user to remove some of the device's restrictions, it also presents security issues. Jailbreaking removes the security restrictions on your iPhone or iPad. This means apps are given access to the device's core functions, which normally requires the user's consent. It also allows the installation of apps not found in the App Store. One of the reasons those apps are not in the App Store is that they are either insecure or malware masquerading as a legitimate app. Finally, a rooted or jailbroken device receives no security updates, making it even more vulnerable.

Unauthorized/malicious application

Unsigned applications represent code that cannot be verified to be what it purports to be or to be free of malware. While many unsigned applications present absolutely no security issues, most enterprises wisely choose to forbid their installation. Mobile device management (MDM) software and security settings in the devices themselves can be used to prevent installation.

System apps are those that come preinstalled on the device. While these apps probably present no security issues, some of them run all the time, so it might be beneficial to remove them to save space and improve performance. The organization also might decide that removing some system apps is necessary to disable features in these apps, which can disclose information about the user or the device that could lead to a social engineering attack. By following the instructions found on the vendor's site, these apps can be removed.

Application spoofing

Mobile application spoofing is an attack where a malicious mobile app mimics the visual appearance of another one. A great example is when a social engineering attack leads the user to a fake website that looks just like a legitimate one (e.g. a bank site). While you can't stand over users and advise them at every turn, instilling users with a healthy dose of suspicion through security awareness training can certainly help.

Common symptoms

Just as with desktop systems, mobile devices will exhibit certain symptoms when security issues manifest themselves. This section surveys some of the more common symptoms of a security issue with a device.

High network traffic

Whenever the device appears to be utilizing CPU and memory at a rate that is not consistent with the user's activities, it is a sign that malware is possibly at work on the device. A good example of this is lots of network activity not initiated by the user. Malware will utilize resources in the process of performing whatever functions it has been designed to perform. When there is unexplained excessive resource usage, it is another indication that the device has been compromised. With respect to network traffic, the malware could be attempting to connect to the hacker.

Degraded response time

Whenever a device is sluggish, it means there is a struggle for resources in the system. While this could be due to attempting to do too many things at once (e.g. running too many apps), it can also be a sign of malware. Malware requires resources to operate, so again, when there is unexplained excessive resource usage, it is another indication that the device has been compromised.

Data-usage limit notification

When certain types of malware begin to operate on a mobile device, they may transmit data from the device to the hacker, or vice versa. Because this uses your data plan without your knowledge, you might suddenly find yourself over your data limit. You might not find this out until you receive your mobile device's bill for data and the amount due exceeds your mortgage payment. In cases such as this, the device should be immediately scanned for malware.

Limited Internet connectivity/no Internet connectivity

Whenever a device cannot access the Internet or can only access certain sites on the Internet, it is another sign of malware. Some malware creates entries in the Host file and prevents the system from using DNS to obtain the site's IP address. This results in being able to access only sites with Host file entries. In other cases, it simply prevents Internet access altogether.

High number of ads

When the system suddenly seems to be getting a lot of unsolicited ads, it is . . . you guessed it, a sign of malware; in this case, a type called adware. In Chapter 7, in the section "Malware," you learned about spyware that tracks your activity. Sometimes the spyware is not trying to steal data, but it's trying to learn your interests so it can target ads to those interests.

Fake security warnings

Users can be motivated to do things they shouldn't if they are alarmed or if they have been convinced that a situation is urgent. These two principles are what make social engineering attacks successful. When users receive warnings that their system has been compromised and that they need to install a software "solution," in a fit of fear they might disregard what you've taught them and install the software (thus, installing the malware). Users should be taught to never install these tools that are offered and to report any notices about a system compromise to the administrator.

Unexpected application behavior

Whenever applications exhibit odd behavior, it's a sign that an application is corrupted (at the least) and that malware is present (at the worst). If reinstalling the app does not solve the issue, it is time to suspect and look for malware.

Leaked personal files/data

Obviously, if personal files located on a mobile device suddenly are gone or suddenly are found to have been leaked, it is also a clue that the device has been compromised through either malware or social engineering.

Exam essentials

Describe common mobile device security issues. Some of the symptoms include high network traffic, low power, sluggish response, slow data speeds, high network traffic, and leaked personal files/data.

3.4 Given a scenario, troubleshoot common personal computer (PC) security issues

System issues in many cases have security breaches at the root of the cause. It has become almost a given that any problem that cannot be traced to any other cause should be attacked by first scanning for viruses and malware. This section discusses common symptoms of security-related failures and tools that can be used to mitigate the damage.

Common symptoms

Systems can display many symptoms when something is amiss. Not all are malware related, but crazy things start to happen when malware is introduced to a computer. This section discusses some of the strange behaviors of computers that are infected, as well as issues unrelated to malware.

Unable to access the network

When network connectivity is an issue, you should ensure the following about your configuration:

- Is the IP address in the same network as the default gateway address?
- Is the subnet mask correct?
- Is the default gateway address correct?
- If this is all correct, has the interface been enabled?
- If this is all correct, it's time to check the settings on the router.

Some malware will affect your Internet access. It may block you from accessing certain sites, or it may allow access to only a small number of sites. It has been reported that viral programs block access for certain programs and browsers while still allowing others to function. When access is denied, a message like the following is generated:

```
Unable to connect to HTTP Proxy. Your proxy may be misconfigured or
offline. -336
```

Moreover, this occurred even after the virus was supposedly cleaned from the system.

Desktop alerts

Sometimes you can tell by security warnings that the site you are on is attempting to attack your computer. This is true if you have a personal firewall, such as Windows Firewall. It can also occur when you have the phishing filter enabled in the browser. You will know when the system asks you whether you want to allow access to your machine from the site. Unless you initiated a download, don't allow it.

False alerts regarding antivirus protection

If you receive messages (again, usually at a suspect website) warning you that your system is infected, it will also usually offer to clean the system. At a minimum, they are trying to sell you anti-malware software through the bogus warning.

Worse, though, is that executing the "cleaning" sometimes results in the introduction of malware to the system—which was the whole point of the message to begin with. In general, pay no attention to these messages and try to close them and exit the website that generated them as quickly as possible.

Altered system or personal files/missing/renamed files/inability to access files

Many viruses will rename system files and adopt the name of the system file. This can help the virus escape detection when scanning occurs since most virus definitions identify the virus by the name of the file that introduced the virus. This renaming of the system file can cause big problems when the file is required and the virus file is incapable of providing the required functionality.

Another symptom of a viral infection is the deletion of files in the system. Many viruses delete key files in your system to render it inoperable. This could be one of the ways it renders any existing antivirus programs inoperable. It also can be part of disabling Internet access either completely or selectively.

Unwanted notifications within the OS

The operating system can generate a lot of messages called *notifications* that are designed to keep you informed about the health and security of the system. In some cases, you aren't really interested in all these messages. You can control the notifications that you review.

In System Settings as shown in Figure 8.6, you can allow or disallow any types of notifications. Before you go too crazy, keep in mind that you probably *want* to get some of the notifications.

OS update failures

Malware may take certain measures to protect itself. One of these is to block you from accessing operating system update sites like Windows Update. You never notice this because these updates can be set to run automatically, so when they fail, it might not be obvious that they did.

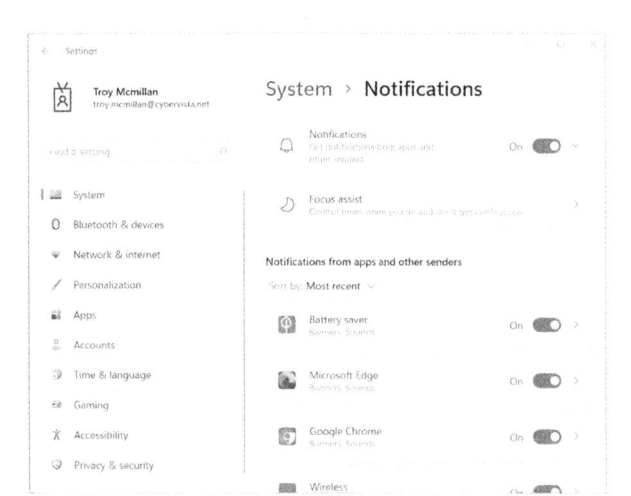

FIGURE 8.6   Notification settings

Another action the malware can take along the same lines is to disable your antivirus software. For this reason, any time your antivirus program notifies you that it is not functional or cannot update itself, you should consider this possibility and get it back up and running (if you can) as soon as possible.

Browser-related symptoms

Some issues are related to the browser. In this section you'll learn about browser-related problems.

Random/frequent pop-ups

Although relatively benign when compared with malware in general, pop-ups are annoying to users. They also use system resources as they open and in some cases can introduce additional malware when they open.

Fortunately, most browsers now contain pop-up blockers that can prevent unwanted pop-ups. In some cases, users want pop-ups to be allowed—in fact, some website functions fail when a pop-up blocker is enabled. For that reason, users can use the Pop-up Blocker Settings of Bing (or your browser of choice) to allow pop-ups for certain websites, as shown in Figure 8.7. Other browsers usually have a similar setting.

Certificate warnings

When you are bombarded with certificate error messages at every website you visit, it's another sign of malware. Some types of malware interface with the certificate authentication process.

FIGURE 8.7 The Pop-up Blocker Settings dialog

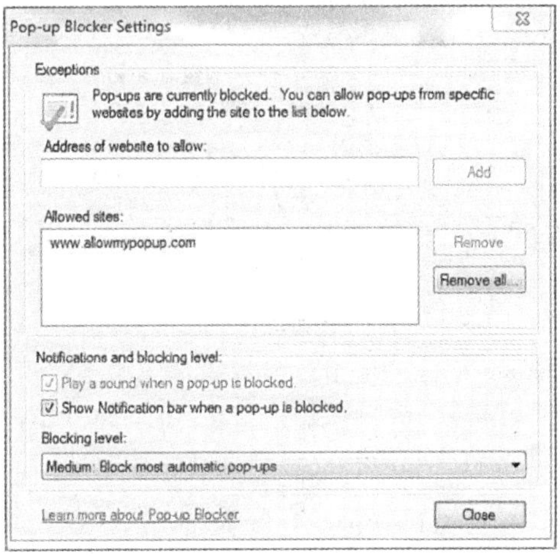

Redirection

A browser redirection is one of the most serious security problems. Browser hijacking software is external code that changes your browser settings. It may include changing your home page or adding or removing items from your favorites. Some sites will be added that point to dubious content. In most cases, the home page will revert to the unwanted destination even if you change it manually because the hijacker made Registry changes to your system. To prevent this from occurring, remember these tips:

- Avoid suspect sites.
- Use and update an antivirus program regularly.
- Tighten your browser security settings.

Once you are a victim, you may have to apply antivirus software from an external source.

Degraded browser performance

While some reasons for degraded browser performance are due to user behavior, most of the reasons are beyond the control of the user or are issues a user would normally never be aware of. Some possible reasons are covered in the following sections.

Outdated browser

When using an outdated browser, you can expect that performance will suffer and that security vulnerabilities may be present. This is due to performance and security issues that might have been addressed in updates or in a newer version of the browser.

Too many tabs open

Every tab that is open is consuming system resources. Train users to keep a minimum of tabs open to deliver the maximum of resources to the browser function.

Unused extensions

Browser extensions add functionality, but they consume resources. Review the installed extensions and remove any not used regularly.

Cache and cookies

Over time, the browser cache begins to fill with temporary Internet files and cookies. Maintaining this cache consumes resources. Regularly clear the browser's cache and cookies to remove temporary files that can accumulate over time.

Slow Internet connection

While not really a browser issue, a slow Internet connection might present itself as a slow browser issue. Since the browser uses the Internet connection to retrieve web content, performance will be affected if the connection is slow.

Malware

If you find that none of the other listed reasons are causing a slow browser, consider the possibility of malware. Malware will usually slow everything down, not just the browser.

Exam essentials

Identify the most common symptoms displayed from security issues. These include but are not limited to pop-ups, browser redirection, security alerts, slow performance, Internet connectivity issues, OS updates failures, rogue antivirus, and renamed system files.

Review Questions

You can find the answers in the appendix.

1. Which of the following is the first thing to check when system performance is sluggish?
   A. Malware
   B. Fragmentation
   C. Lack of space
   D. Missing update

2. When having issues accessing the network, what should you check last?
   A. IP address
   B. Subnet mask
   C. Default gateway
   D. Router settings

3. What is the third step in malware removal?
   A. Quarantine infected systems
   B. Remediate infected systems
   C. Disable System Restore in Windows
   D. Investigate and verify malware symptoms

4. The "No operating system found" message can result from a number of issues. Which of the following is *not* among them?
   A. Corrupted boot files
   B. Incorrect boot device order in the BIOS
   C. Missing boot sector
   D. Lack of permissions

5. Which of the following is the *least likely sign* of a malware infection?
   A. Slow performance
   B. High network traffic
   C. Data limit messages
   D. Overheating

6. What is external code that changes your browser settings?
   A. On-path attack
   B. Browser redirection
   C. SYN flood
   D. Fraggle

7. Which of the following is *not* a symptom of malware?
   A. Increase in performance
   B. Internet connectivity issues
   C. Browser redirection
   D. Pop-ups

8. Which of the following is the first step in malware removal?
   A. Remediate the infected systems
   B. Quarantine the infected systems
   C. Educate the end user
   D. Identify and research malware symptoms

9. What Windows service should be disabled before cleaning an infection?
   A. NAT
   B. System Restore
   C. Windows Firewall
   D. Antivirus

10. Which of the following does *not* negatively impact mobile battery life?
    A. Low brightness setting
    B. Location services
    C. Enabled Bluetooth
    D. Overheating device

11. Which of the following does not cause overheating of a mobile device?
    A. Excessive gaming
    B. Leaving the phone on
    C. Old battery
    D. Continuous online browsing

12. Which of the following is *not* an indication of a security issue with a mobile device?
    A. Power drain
    B. Weak signal
    C. Slow speeds
    D. Low resource utilization

13. Which of the following is an indication of a security issue with a mobile device?
    A. Low resource utilization
    B. Disabled microphone
    C. Enabled camera
    D. Authorized account access

Chapter 9

Operational Procedures

COMPTIA A+ 220-1202 EXAM OBJECTIVES COVERED IN THIS CHAPTER:

✓ **4.1 Given a scenario, implement best practices associated with documentation and support systems information management**

- Ticketing systems
  - User information
  - Device information
  - Description of problems
  - Categories
  - Severity
  - Escalation levels
  - Clear, concise written communication
    - Issue description
    - Progress notes
    - Issue resolution
- Asset management
  - Inventory lists
    - Make
    - Model
    - Serial number
  - Configuration management database (CMDB)
  - Asset tags and IDs
    - Barcodes
  - Procurement life cycle
  - Warranty and licensing
  - Assigned users

- Types of documents
  - Incident reports
  - Standard operating procedures (SOPs)
    - Software package custom installation procedure
  - New user/onboarding setup checklist
  - User off-boarding checklist
  - Service-level agreements (SLAs)
    - Internal
    - External/third-party
  - Knowledge base/articles

✔ **4.2 Given a scenario, apply change management procedures**
- Documented business processes
  - Rollback plan
  - Backup plan
  - Sandbox testing
  - Responsible staff members
- Change management
  - Request forms
  - Purpose of the change
  - Scope of the change
  - Change type
    - Standard change
    - Normal change
    - Emergency change
  - Date and time of change
    - Change freeze
    - Maintenance window
- Affected system/impact
- Risk Analysis
  - Risk level

- Change Board approvals
- Implementation
- Peer review
- End-user acceptance

✓ **4.3 Given a scenario, implement workstation backup and recovery methods**
- Backup
  - Full
  - Incremental
  - Differential
  - Synthetic full
- Recovery
  - In-place/overwrite
  - Alternative location
- Backup testing
  - Frequency
- Backup rotation schemes
  - On-site vs. off-site
    - On-site storage
    - Off-site storage
  - Grandfather/father/son (GFS)
  - 3-2-1 backup rule

✓ **4.4 Given a scenario, use common safety procedures**
- Electrostatic discharge (ESD) straps
- ESD mats
- Electrical safety
- Equipment grounding
- Proper power handling
- Proper component handling and storage
- Cable management
- Antistatic bags

- Compliance with government regulations
- Personal safety
  - Disconnect power before repairing PC
  - Lifting techniques
  - Fire safety
  - Safety goggles
  - Air filter mask

✔ **4.5 Summarize environmental impacts and local environment controls**

- Material Safety Data Sheet (MSDS) documentation for handling and disposal
  - Proper battery disposal
  - Proper toner disposal
  - Proper disposal of other devices and assets
    - Cell phones
    - Tablets
- Temperature, humidity-level awareness, and proper ventilation
  - Temperature
  - Humidity level
  - Ventilation
  - Location/equipment placement
  - Dust cleanup
  - Compressed air/vacuums
- Power surges, brownouts, and blackouts
  - Uninterruptible power supply (UPS)
  - Surge suppressor

✔ **4.6 Explain the importance of prohibited content/activity and privacy, licensing, and policy concepts**

- Incident response
  - Chain of custody
    - Tracking of evidence/documenting process
  - Inform management/law enforcement as necessary

- Report through proper channels
- Copy of drive (data integrity and preservation)
- Incident documentation
- Order of volatility
- Licensing/digital rights management (DRM)/end-user license agreement (EULA)
  - Valid licenses
  - Perpetual license agreement
  - Unexpired licenses
  - Personal-use license vs. corporate-use license
  - Open-source license
- Nondisclosure agreement (NDA)/mutual nondisclosure agreement (MNDA)
- Regulated data
  - Credit card payment information
  - Personal government-issued information
  - PII
  - Healthcare data
  - Data retention requirements
- Acceptable use policy (AUP)
- Regulatory and business compliance requirements
  - Splash screens

✔ 4.7 Given a scenario, use proper communication techniques and professionalism

- Professional appearance and attire
  - Match the required attire of the given environment
    - Formal
    - Business casual
- Use proper language and avoid jargon, acronyms, and slang, when applicable
- Maintain a positive attitude/project confidence
- Actively listen, take notes, and avoid interrupting the customer

- Be culturally sensitive
    - Use appropriate professional titles, when applicable
- Be on time (if late, contact the customer)
- Avoid distractions
    - Personal calls
    - Texting/social media sites
    - Personal interruptions
- Appropriately deal with difficult customers or situations
    - Do not argue with customer and/or be defensive
    - Avoid dismissing customers' problems
    - Avoid being judgmental
    - Clarify customer statements (i.e. ask open-ended questions to narrow the scope of the issue, restate the issue, or ask questions to verify understanding)
    - Use discretion and professionalism when discussing experiences/encounters
- Set and meet expectations/timeline and communicate status with the customer
    - Offer repair/replacement options, as needed
    - Provide proper documentation on the services provided
    - Follow up with customer/user at a later date to verify satisfaction
- Appropriately handle customers' confidential and private materials
    - Located on a computer, desktop, printer, etc.

✔ 4.8 Explain the basics of scripting

- Script file types
    - .bat
    - .ps1
    - .vbs
    - .sh
    - .py
    - .js

- Use cases for scripting
  - Basic automation
  - Restarting machines
  - Remapping network drives
  - Installing applications
  - Performing automated backups
  - Gathering information/data
  - Initiating updates
- Other considerations when using scripts
  - Unintentionally introducing malware
  - Inadvertently changing system settings
  - Browser or system crashes due to mishandling of resources

✔ 4.9 Given a scenario, use remote access technologies

- Methods/tools
  - RDP
  - VPN
  - Virtual network computer (VNC)
  - Secure Shell (SSH)
  - Remote monitoring and management (RMM)
  - Simple Protocol for Independent Computing Environments (SPICE)
  - Windows Remote Management (WinRM)
  - Third-party tools
    - Screen-sharing software
    - Videoconferencing software
    - File transfer software
    - Desktop management software
- Security considerations of each access method

✔ 4.10 Explain basic concepts related to artificial intelligence (AI)

- Application integration
- Policy

- Appropriate use
- Plagiarism
- Limitations
  - Bias
  - Hallucinations
  - Accuracy
- Private vs. public
  - Data security
  - Data source
  - Data privacy

This chapter focuses on exam topics related to operational procedures. It follows the structure of the CompTIA A+ 220-1202 exam blueprint, Objective 4, and it explores the 10 subobjectives that you need to master before taking the exam.

4.1 Given a scenario, implement best practices associated with documentation and support systems information management

If you ever heard the adage "the job isn't done till the paperwork is done," then you might grasp the importance of documentation. In this section, we'll talk about some of the documentation you should be generating and updating.

Ticketing systems

When network and security issues arise, organizations need some way to collect and store the details of each incident and a system to address each issue in a time frame that is appropriate for each incident, based on the incident's priority. In this section, you'll learn about the types of information that a ticketing system must collect to be able to accomplish this goal.

User information

A ticketing system must be capable of recording the user involved in the incident. This could be the person who reported the issue, but it might not. In some cases, one user might report an issue that impacts another user more directly, such as when one user discovers that a file owned by another user is suddenly gone. In other cases, a user might report an incident that could have been caused by another user. The system should be capable of collecting all user involvement.

Device information

All information about the devices involved should also be collected, including the device name, IP address, MAC address, subnet mask, and default gateway. If asset numbers are available, they should be included as well. In cases where device spoofing is involved, collecting all the data might make it possible to verify that someone is masquerading as a legitimate device.

Description of problems

A complete description of the incident should be generated. Keep in mind that as an investigation proceeds, the description might change as more information becomes available. Don't allow the team to get locked into the first impression of the event, which might cause a discounting of new evidence.

Categories

Not all incidents require the same sense of urgency. Categories should be created to prioritize incidents by their potential impact. For example, a data breach requires a greater sense of urgency than a password reset does.

Severity

Utilizing the assignment of incidents to severity categories, incidents should be dealt with not in the order they are received. Rather, they should be addressed by utilizing a system somewhat like triage in an emergency room, where treatment is based on the severity of the issue. As in an emergency room, a brand-new issue might require dropping efforts on other issues to address the new, more serious issue.

Escalation levels

Escalation procedures are created to prevent technicians from spending too much time on an issue that they don't completely understand. Creating levels or tiers of technicians with an increasing amount of knowledge and experience is a best practice. This offers two benefits. First, it encourages a faster solution by preventing issues from remaining unresolved due to a lack of skill by the responding technician. Second, it frees up more experienced technicians to deal with more serious issues. A hard time limit should be placed on the solution of issues before an escalation is required.

Clear, concise written communication

While technicians are not required to be professional writers, they do need to be able to create clear and concise written communications regarding an incident or issue. In this section, you'll learn what is included in a clear and concise issue statement.

Issue description

The issue description should describe the symptoms that caused the issue to be reported, which systems were affected, and which causes might have been initially suspected. Keep in mind, the problem description might change over time, as more data is collected. The documentation should reflect these changes to the description.

Progress notes

The progress notes should reflect every effort that has been made to resolve the issue and the results of each operation. These progress notes make a great reference as similar issues arise in the future. Placing them in a searchable database is a great idea.

Issue resolution

Once the issue is resolved, the solution must be recorded with great detail. This information should also be placed in a searchable database and used to generate a "lessons learned" document to initiate actions designed to prevent the same issue in the future.

Asset management

Asset or inventory management includes knowing what you have. You won't know that something is missing until you take an inventory, so this should be done on a regular basis. In this section, you'll learn about tools and methods used to maintain an inventory tracking system.

Inventory lists

The basis of any robust asset management system is the inventory list itself. If it's incorrect, then the whole system will fail. Inventory counts and recounts should be performed regularly to catch errors and identify thefts and other losses. What type of information is useful to record in these inventories? You might choose to record more, but the following three items should be included for sure.

Make

The manufacturer of each device should be recorded, along with the name they give the device.

Model

The exact model number should be recorded in full, leaving nothing out. Sometimes, those dangling letters at the end of the model number are there to indicate how this model differs from another or to indicate a feature, so be sure to record *all* of the model number.

Serial number

The serial number of the device should also be recorded. This number will be important to you with respect to the warranty and service support. You should be able to put your hands on this number quickly.

Configuration management database (CMDB)

Certainly, organizations could maintain proper inventory systems long before the advent of database systems, but database systems do have advantages. They can increase consistency and accuracy, which will help cut down on erroneous supply and stock records and lost items. They can also help create more dependable records for shipments and returns and better product relevancy. So, as you can see, these database systems can help with the entire asset procurement life cycle.

A configuration management database (CMDB) is one that provides a single source to track the complex arrangements of configuration items (CIs) and their dependencies, from the data center to the cloud and virtual environments. CIs comprise individual settings that have been made to the various infrastructure and endpoint devices. Configuration items and their associated product configuration information versions, in addition to their approved changes, form the basis of any current approved configuration audit.

Asset tags and IDs

If your organization places asset tags on devices, it probably means you have your own internal numbering or other identification system in place. Record that number and any other pertinent information that the organization deems important enough to place on the asset tag, such as region, building, and other critical information.

Barcodes

One popular method of tagging devices is with barcodes that can be read by scanners when performing an inventory. If the barcodes include radio frequency identification (RFID) tags, they can be read even from a short distance.

Procurement life cycle

Earlier in this chapter, in the section "Configuration management database (CMDB)," we mentioned the asset procurement life cycle. This life cycle comprises the steps in the process of obtaining, using, and disposing of an asset. It is important to track the asset throughout each stage in the life cycle. The major steps in this life cycle are:

- Acquisition
- Operations and maintenance
- Disposal and replacement

Warranty and licensing

Especially with respect to digital assets such as operating systems and applications, maintaining the proper number of licenses is critically important. Later in this chapter, you'll learn much more about licensing issues. For now, realize that tracking the proper number of licenses per software package is an important part of asset management because if you install the software on more systems than the number that have been licensed, you can be fined by the software vendor.

With respect to physical assets, such as devices, vehicles, and heating systems, the warranty information is also critical. This is why maintaining the serial number of each device is important, because serial numbers are how you will access your warranty services if needed. With some devices and systems, the warranty coverage might be so important to ensuring that you have a fault-tolerant environment that you might want to be alerted when devices are coming off warranty so you can replace them or extend the warranties.

Assigned users

Assets don't just sit in an asset safe somewhere. They are assigned to users for them to use. This creates two problems. First, they are out of your control. And making matters worse, the individual to whom you have turned the asset over might be careless, both from a physical security and from a logical security perspective. While we just have to accept these dangers and try to mitigate them with training as best we can, it *is* in our power to know who has been issued what assets. This becomes very important when a user leaves the organization and we need to get those assets back.

Types of documents

As you learned earlier in this chapter, "the job isn't done till the paperwork is done," so you likely grasp the importance of documentation. In this section, we'll talk about some documentation that you should be generating and updating.

Incident reports

Just as you should keep all technical articles that help to solve an issue, all incidents should be recorded in detail for future reference. Such documentation helps to identify recurring issues, for which the root cause has yet to be determined. With regard to security incidents, your incident-handling policy should support this effort.

Standard operating procedures (SOPs)

While policies are broad statements of intent, procedures are step-by-step instructions on how something is performed in an organization. They are especially relevant in scenarios where users might have performed an operation in a different manner in another organization. Called standard operating procedures (SOPs), they serve to maintain consistency of operations.

Software package custom installation procedure

When software packages are to be installed in a very specific manner, perhaps in an unusual manner, the exact procedures must be defined and communicated to all who might be installing such packages. This scenario is where a scripted installation might be advisable to ensure the installation is performed correctly.

New user/onboarding setup checklist

A new-user checklist is used to ensure that when a user is provisioned an account upon hiring, everything is supported. Examples of possible configuration items include:
- Username and password
- Group memberships

- Assignment of rights and permissions
- Signing of all new user documents (e.g. acceptable use policies (AUPs), nondisclosure agreements (NDAs), etc.)

User off-boarding checklist

A user off-boarding checklist is used to ensure that when a user leaves the company, certain tasks are completed. These include:

- The return of all devices
- The removal of all permissions
- The disabling or deletion of the user's account
- An exit interview

Service-level agreements (SLAs)

A service-level agreement (SLA) is a document indicating what is being paid and what the service includes. It should detail a schedule of service delivery, with incentives for beating or meeting deadlines and penalties for missing deadlines or failing to achieve prescribed metrics.

Internal

An internal SLA is one that is executed between divisions or departments in the same organization. For example, a sales department might have an SLA with the IT department to provide support services to them. In this case, payment will probably be in the form of an accounting charge between the departments, rather than a physical exchange of funds. Nevertheless, it should still contain financial incentives to encourage good performance and penalties to discourage poor performance.

External/third-party

An external SLA is one that is executed between the organization and a third party. In this case, the details of the agreement are even more important than with an internal agreement, because of the possibility of legal action becoming necessary in the case of extremely poor performance or non-delivery.

Knowledge base/articles

Often when troubleshooting an issue, you might find useful information in a knowledge base article. Vendors share these documents to assist technicians. You should keep these articles and tie them to the issues they solved to help solve future instances of the same issue. A knowledge base of issues that occur within your organization can also be helpful.

Exam essentials

Explain the importance of asset management and documentation. List what should be included when creating an asset inventory. Understand the importance of organizing and maintaining documentation. Describe some of the types of sensitive documents that require special treatment.

Identify information that should be tracked in an incident ticketing system. Tracked information should include user information, device information, description of issues, category of issue, and severity of incidents.

4.2 Given a scenario, apply change management procedures

There is an old saying that "too many cooks spoil the broth," and when it comes to managing networks, it certainly applies. When technicians make server changes that are not centrally managed and planned, chaos reigns. In such an environment, changes might be made that cause conflict. All organizations need a change management process whereby all changes go through a formal evaluation process before they are implemented.

This process ensures that all changes support the organization's goals and that the impact of each change is anticipated *before* the change is made. There should be a change management board (sometimes called a *change control board*) to which all changes are submitted for review. Only when the change has been approved should it be made.

Documented business processes

As organizations grow and develop, they generate business processes to follow. Sometimes these processes become almost ingrained in users, but over time the methods utilized may "drift" away from the original process. For this reason, all key business processes should be recorded and followed, and any change to such processes should undergo change management examination to ensure that it's beneficial to the entire organization and supports all of its goals.

Rollback plan

In Chapter 8, in the section "Common troubleshooting steps," you learned that you can roll back patch and driver updates as a troubleshooting step. When making a change that can potentially cause widespread issues, you should create a rollback plan that allows you to quickly reverse the change in case things go wrong. An additional step is to make the change in a test environment like a sandbox (discussed next) or on a small, low-impact section of the network. Please review Chapter 8.

Backup plan

Every organization should have a formal backup plan to protect critical data. Loss of proprietary data that imparts a business advantage to an organization can result in loss of revenue and even bankruptcy. Later in this chapter, in the section "9.3 Given a scenario, implement workstation backup and recovery methods," you will learn about various methods of backup that comprise the backup plan.

Sandbox testing

A sandbox is a virtual environment, disconnected from your physical and virtual production network. This isolation allows you to test changes to the IT environment without suffering the consequences of a bad outcome in the production network. This type of testing is becoming commonplace as more organizations embrace virtual networking.

Responsible staff members

Organizations find it beneficial to establish a process owner for each established business process. These individuals are responsible for establishing (through the change management process discussed in the next section), monitoring, and identifying necessary process changes. This ensures that outdated and inefficient processes are discontinued or altered to improve the process.

Change management

Changes to any process, including ones to the network environment, should be managed by a formal process called *change management*. In some instances, this process might feel as if it's impeding changes that need to be made quickly, and in some scenarios that might be the case. However, the benefit is that it avoids changes that cause other issues that weren't considered in the haste to implement the change. In this section, you'll learn about some considerations when referring alterations to the change management process.

Request forms

The process begins with a formal written request to make the change. This form is submitted to a change control board (covered later in this section) that will consider the change in light of many considerations in this section, such as its potential impact and what improvement it could bring. Finally, the potential risk of the change must be considered.

Purpose of the change

When any change is suggested, the proposed benefit derived from the change must be identified. Otherwise, there is no reason for the change. During the change management process, the relative costs and benefits to the overall organization will be weighed by a change management board or team.

Scope of the change

In some cases, a change might be beneficial for some users or groups but not others. So, we might limit the change (called *scoping*) to only those it will benefit. While scoping is not possible with some changes (i.e. cases where all must share any changes), it can be utilized in some specific cases where a change can be isolated to a certain group of users.

Change type

Not all change requests carry the same priority. It is critical that changes impacting service levels or performance be handled before those that do not, regardless of when the changes were requested. It might be useful to organize the changes into categories such as those described in this section.

Standard change

Standard changes are those with low impact that occur frequently and typically require no formal review or approval process. A request to change a password is a good example.

Normal change

Normal changes are those that carry more risk than a standard change but are still considered to be common. They typically require somewhat unique or novel approaches, unlike standard changes that can generally be accomplished through the use of step-by-step guides or some basic outlines. Such changes require review and approval from the change management board.

Emergency change

Emergency changes are those that need immediate attention, and as such carry high risk if not handled or handled incorrectly. Emergency changes are brought about as a response to unforeseen obstacles, such as security flaws and exploits.

Date and time of change

Once a change has been approved, the timing of it and its implementation must be carefully planned so as not to disrupt operations. Affected parties should be notified of the change and when it will occur. Any service disruptions must be announced ahead of time so users can plan for the disruption for the planned period of downtime.

Change freeze

Some days (or times during those days) should be off limits for making changes because of the disruptive impact that might occur. *Change freezes* are implemented during these times, which might be extremely busy times or times when mission-critical work is being done. In the case of emergency changes, a decision should be made if the change carries enough risk to require implementation during a change freeze.

Maintenance window

Maintenance windows are times during which normal maintenance is being performed on a system, when users might be instructed *not* to access the system. These windows should be announced ahead of time so that users can prepare for possible disruptions or for any major changes to the functioning of the service.

Affected system/impact

When changes are planned, each change should be documented, and the documentation should contain the following items:

- Date and time of change
- Affected system(s)
- Predicted impact on each system
- Duration

Risk analysis

Sometimes changes bring risks, which must be identified. All changes should undergo a risk analysis process to identify risks and any controls or countermeasures that can be implemented. The goal of such countermeasures may be to either reduce the organizational risk to a tolerable level or eliminate it entirely.

Risk level

While somewhat of an estimation at this point, a change should be assigned a risk level, which could be either descriptive (e.g. red, yellow, and green colors) or a numerical metric. It may be beneficial to bring in subject matter experts to help assign these values, which will be used by the less technical members of the change control board to assess the risk of each change.

Change board approvals

The change management or change control board should be composed of a cross-section of representatives from throughout the company. This way, each change can be assessed by each stakeholder group in the organization. The process should follow these steps:

1. All changes should be formally requested.
2. Each request should be analyzed to ensure that it supports all goals and polices.
3. Prior to formal approval, all costs and effects of the methods of implementation should be reviewed.

Implementation

Once approved, the change is scheduled and impacted users are notified of the change's time and date. In some cases of unusual or emergency changes, it might be necessary to create a step-by-step guide for making the change. When unusual risks exist or when the impact of the change might not be completely understood, withdrawal plans should be created to reverse said change.

Peer review

The change management process can be steadily improved by conducting peer reviews of the process. While those planning and making the changes should take part, it is even more important that the affected users take part, as they can describe impact to the work experience.

End-user acceptance

The change management board should include regular users so any proposed changes can be assessed for end-user acceptance. This can help to avoid widespread user dissatisfaction after the change.

Exam essentials

Identify what should be contained in a change request. These requests should contain the purpose of the change, the scope of the change, and the change type (i.e. standard, normal, or emergency).

Describe the steps in change management. These steps are as follows:

1. All changes should be formally requested.
2. Each request should be analyzed to ensure it supports all goals and polices.
3. Prior to formal approval, all costs and effects of the methods of implementation should be reviewed.
4. After changes are approved, the change steps should be developed.
5. During implementation, incremental testing should occur, relying on a predetermined fallback strategy if necessary.
6. Complete documentation should be produced and submitted with a formal report to management.

4.3 Given a scenario, implement workstation backup and recovery methods

Preventive maintenance is more than just manipulating hardware; it also encompasses backing up systems on a regular basis to prevent data loss. These procedures can include scheduled backups, backup testing, and backup media rotation schemes.

Backup

Backups are duplicate copies of key information, ideally stored in a location other than the one where the information is currently stored. Backups include both paper and computer records. Computer records are usually backed up using a backup program, backup systems, and backup procedures. In this section, you'll learn about different backup methods.

Full

A *full backup* is a complete, comprehensive backup of all files on a disk or server. The full backup is current only at the time it's performed. Once a full backup is made, you have a complete archive of the system at that point in time. A system shouldn't be in use while it undergoes a full backup, because some active files might not be included in the backup. Once the system returns to operation, the backup is no longer current. Making a full backup can be a time-consuming process on a large system due to the number of files it contains.

Incremental

An *incremental backup* is a partial backup that stores *only* the information that has been changed since the last full or incremental backup. For example, if a full backup were performed on a Sunday night, an incremental backup done on Monday night would contain only the information that had changed since Sunday night, a backup on Tuesday night would contain only information since Monday's incremental backup, and so forth. Such a backup is typically considerably smaller than a full backup. This backup system requires that each incremental backup be retained until a full backup can be performed. Incremental backups are usually the fastest backups to perform on most systems, and each incremental data set is relatively small, as you are only backing up data that has changed since the last incremental backup.

Differential

A *differential backup* is similar in function to an incremental backup, but it backs up any files that have been altered since the last full backup. If a full backup was performed on Sunday night, a differential backup performed on Monday night would capture the information that was changed only on Monday. A differential backup completed on Tuesday night would record the changes in any files from Monday and any changes in files on Tuesday. As you can see, during the week each differential backup would become larger; by Friday or Saturday night, it might be nearly as large as a full backup. This means the backups in the earliest part of the weekly cycle will be very fast, and each successive one will be slower.

Synthetic full

A *synthetic full backup* is a full backup performed by synthesizing (combining) the data from the previous full backup (either a regular full backup for the first backup or the previous synthetic full backup) and the periodic incremental backups. The incremental backups are the only files that need to be transferred during replication, greatly reducing the bandwidth needed for offsite replication.

Recovery

The primary starting point for disaster recovery involves keeping current backup copies of key data files, databases, applications, and paper records available for use. Your organization must develop a solid set of procedures to manage this process and to ensure that all key information is protected. A security professional can do several things in conjunction with systems administrators and business managers to protect this information. It's important to think of this problem as an issue that is larger than a single department.

In-place/overwrite

Sometimes, the recovery process is not simply a matter of recovering lost data. It might be the recovery of an operating system (OS) that is malfunctioning. While reimaging the system or reinstalling the OS is certainly an option, both are time-consuming. An in-place recovery is one in which system files (or other files) are replaced without changing anything else. In this case, the new file is written over the old file. This is known as an *overwrite recovery*.

Alternative location

While recovered files can be written back to the original location, you can also recover the file to an alternative location. Reasons for this can include the following:

- It allows you to restore previous versions of your files if they are lost, damaged, or accidentally modified.
- It provides a way to restore lost or corrupted files in the event of a disaster.

Keeping backup copies in a different physical location than the original data is recommended.

Backup testing

While many backup utilities offer a verification process, the *best* test is to attempt to restore the backup. While test restorations might not be appropriate after every backup, they should be completed often enough to ensure that you have not been creating corrupt backups for days on end.

Frequency

The frequency of backup testing should depend on the sensitivity and value of the data involved. For example, extremely mission-critical data might be tested after every backup, while the successful backup of less critical data might be verified only once every four backups.

Backup rotation schemes

When backups are performed, the data being backed up will be committed to some sort of media (e.g. tape, CD, DVD, remote hard drive in the cloud, etc.). The backup media can be reused but not forever, because there are limits as to how long the data is viable on it. Also, this media must be rotated so that wear on the tapes is even. In this section, you'll learn not only about backup media rotation schemes but also about storage location issues with the media.

On-site vs. off-site

The information you back up must be immediately available for use when needed. If a user loses a critical file, they won't want to wait several days while data files are sent from a remote storage facility. Two types of storage locations are available for data storage: on-site and off-site storage.

On-site storage

On-site storage usually refers to a location on the site of the computer center that is used to store information locally. On-site storage containers are available that allow tapes and other backup media to be stored in a reasonably protected environment in a building.

On-site storage containers are designed and rated for fire, moisture, and pressure resistance. These containers aren't *fireproof* in most situations, but they're *fire-rated*: A fireproof container should be guaranteed to withstand damage regardless of the type of fire or temperature. Fire ratings, however, specify that a container can protect the contents for a specific time period in a given situation.

If you choose to depend entirely on on-site storage, make sure the containers you acquire can withstand the worst-case environmental catastrophes that could happen at your location. Make sure as well that those containers are in locations where you can easily find and access them after a disaster (e.g. near exterior walls).

Off-site storage

Off-site storage refers to a location away from the computer center where paper copies and backup media are kept. Off-site storage can involve something as simple as keeping a copy of backup media at a remote office, or it can be as complicated as using a nuclear-hardened high-security storage facility. The storage facility should be bonded, insured, and inspected on a regular basis to ensure that all best-practice storage procedures are being followed.

Hardened data centers

Many data centers are located far underground. For example, Iron Mountains WPA-1 facility in western Pennsylvania is located 220 ft underground and uses a natural lake for cooling, optimizing energy efficiency while offering the highest levels of security and protection.

Determining which storage mechanism to use should be based on the needs of the organization, the availability of storage facilities, and the budget available. Most off-site storage facilities charge based on the amount of space your media requires and the frequency of access you need to the stored information.

Grandfather/father/son (GFS)

In the grandfather/father/son (GFS) scheme, three sets of backups are defined. Most often these three definitions are daily, weekly, and monthly. The daily backups are known as the sons, the weekly backups are the fathers, and the monthly backups are the grandfathers. Each week, one son advances to the father set. Each month, one father advances to the grandfather set.

Figure 9.1 displays a typical 5-day GFS rotation using 21 tapes. The daily tapes are usually differential or incremental backups. The weekly and monthly tapes must be a full backup.

FIGURE 9.1 GFS scheme

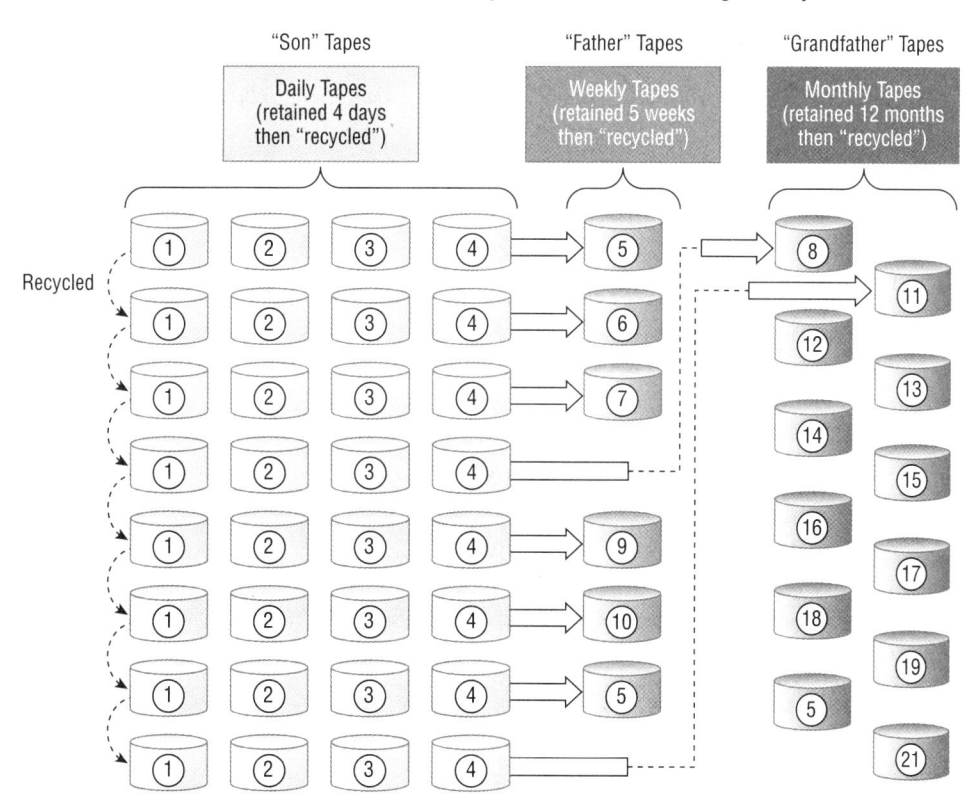

3-2-1 backup rule

The 3-2-1 rule is a best practice for backup and recovery. It is quite simple and means that when you build out your backup and recovery strategy, you should:

1. Keep at least three copies of your data.
2. Keep the backup data on two different storage types.
3. Keep at least one copy of the data off-site.

Exam essentials

List backup types. Three methods exist to back up information on most systems: full, differential, and incremental. A full backup backs up everything. An incremental backup is a partial backup that stores only the information that has changed since the last full or incremental backup. A differential backup is similar in function to an incremental backup, but it backs up any files that have been altered since the last full backup.

List characteristics of backup media rotation schemes. These include the method type, such as grandfather-father-son (GFS), the implementation type (i.e. on-site vs. off-site), and the media security method (such as utilizing the 3-2-1 rule).

4.4 Given a scenario, use common safety procedures

This objective deals with potential hazards, both to you and to the computer system. It focuses on protecting humans from harm due to electricity and on protecting computer components from harm due to electrostatic discharge (ESD).

> **NOTE**
>
> Electrostatic discharge (ESD) is the technical term for what happens whenever two objects of dissimilar charge come in contact—think of rubbing your feet on a carpet and then touching a light switch. The two objects exchange electrons to equalize the electrostatic charge between them. If the device receiving the charge happens to be an electronic component, there is a good chance it can be damaged.

FIGURE 9.2 Proper ESD strap connection

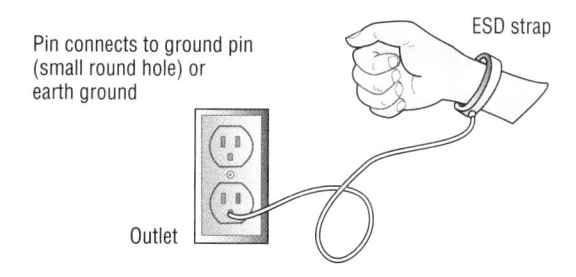

Electrostatic discharge (ESD) straps

Measures can be implemented to help contain ESD's effects. The easiest one you can implement is the *antistatic wrist strap*, also referred to as an *ESD strap*. You attach one end of the ESD strap to an earth ground (typically the ground pin on an extension cord) and then wrap the other end around your wrist. The strap grounds your body and keeps it at a zero charge (meaning any static electricity is discharged). Figure 9.2 shows the proper way to attach an antistatic strap.

If you do not have a grounded outlet available, you can achieve partial benefit simply by attaching the strap to the metal frame of the PC case and wrapping the other end around your wrist. Doing so keeps the charge equalized between your body and the case, so there is no electrostatic discharge when you touch components inside the case.

> **WARNING**
>
> An ESD strap is a specially designed device to bleed electrical charges away *safely*. It uses a 1 megaohm resistor to bleed the charge away slowly. A simple wire wrapped around your wrist will not work correctly and could electrocute you!
>
> Do *not* wear the ESD strap when you might potentially encounter a high-voltage capacitor, such as when working on the inside of a monitor or power supply. The strap could channel that voltage through your body!

ESD mats

It's possible to damage devices simply by laying them on top of a bench. For this reason, you should use an *ESD mat* (also known as an *antistatic mat*) in addition to your ESD strap. This mat drains excess charge away from any item coming in contact with it (see Figure 9.3). ESD mats are also sold as mouse/keyboard pads and prevent ESD charges from interfering with the operation of a computer.

FIGURE 9.3 Proper use of an ESD mat

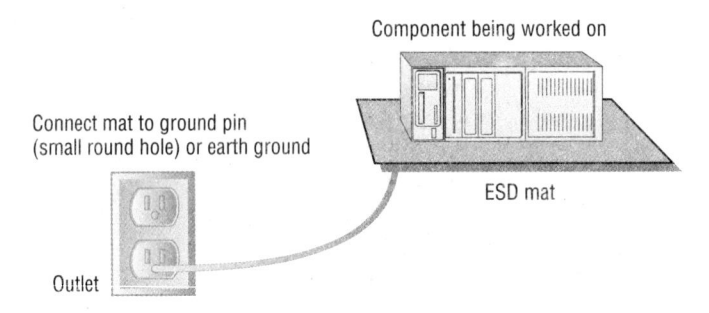

You can also purchase ESD floor mats for technicians to stand on while performing computer maintenance. These mats include a grounding cord, usually 6 to 10 ft in length.

Vendors have methods to protect components in transit from manufacture to installation. They can press the pins of integrated circuits (ICs) into antistatic foam to keep all the pins at the same energy potential. In addition, they ship circuit boards in antistatic bags (see upcoming section "Antistatic bags"). Unlike antistatic mats, these bags do not drain the charges away, however, and they should never be used in place of antistatic mats.

> **This ESD**
>
> The ESD that we are speaking about here does not have the capability to kill you since it doesn't have the amperage. What does represent a threat, though, is using a wrist strap of your own design that does not have the resistor protection built into it and accidentally touching something with high voltage while wearing said wrist strap. Without the resistor in place, the high voltage would be grounded through you!

Electrical safety

ESD is one of the most dangerous risks associated with working with computers. Not only does ESD have the potential to damage computer components, but it can also seriously injure you. Failing to understand the proper way to avoid it could cause you great harm.

Equipment grounding

The risk that a component could be damaged increases with the use of complementary metal-oxide semiconductor (CMOS) chips because these chips contain a thin metal-oxide layer that is hypersensitive to ESD. The previous generation's transistor–transistor logic (TTL) chips are more robust than the CMOS chips because they don't contain this metal-oxide layer. Most of today's ICs are CMOS chips, so ESD is more of a concern lately.

The lowest static voltage transfer that you can feel is around 3,000 V–it doesn't electrocute you because there is extremely little current. A static transfer that you can *see* is at least 10,000 V! Just by sitting in a chair, you can generate around 100 V of static electricity. Walking around wearing synthetic materials can generate around 1,000 V. You can easily generate around 20,000 V simply by dragging your smooth-soled shoes across a carpet in any room with very low humidity.

It would make sense that these thousands of volts would damage computer components. However, a component can be damaged with as little as 80 V. Meaning if your body has a small charge built up in it, you could damage a component without even realizing it.

Just as you can ground yourself by using the grounding strap we discussed previously, you can also ground the equipment upon which you're working. This is most often accomplished by using an ESD mat or a connection directly to a ground.

Proper power handling

You should never attempt to remove a case, open a case, or work on any element that is carrying electricity without first disconnecting it from the power source. If removing power from the device you are working on is more complicated than just unplugging it (i.e. requiring circuit breakers to be thrown, fuses to be removed, etc.), then you should use a voltmeter to ensure that the current is off at the device before proceeding.

Proper component handling and storage

When handling computer components (e.g. motherboards, network cards, etc.), it is easy to damage the delicate circuitry with the static electricity that builds up in your body in certain environments. In the next section, we'll talk about how you can protect these components and how you should store them when not in use.

Cable management

Proper cable management in the data center or server room makes the area safer for technicians (e.g. no more tripping over messy cables). It can also make troubleshooting easier by keeping things organized. Outages, downed systems, data transmission errors, and even overheating or fires can occur with power cables.

Better network cable management procedures include the following:

- Distinguish cables using color to enable quick identification.
- Use labels on cables, servers, and racks.
- Label both cable ends.
- Bundle cables to create space so air can circulate to cool cables.
- Separate different cable types.

- Use the correct cable length (i.e. get rid of excess cable).
- Wrap cables with fasteners and ties.
- Don't pull, stretch, bend, or twist cables.
- Document all cables and cable runs in the network.

Antistatic bags

When working with and storing components, it is a good idea to keep them in antistatic bags. Although you can buy these bags, replacement parts are usually packed in antistatic bags. If you keep these bags, you can reuse them later. These bags also can serve as a safe place to lay a component temporarily while working on a device.

Compliance with government regulations

It is your responsibility, as an administrator and a professional, to know (or learn) the regulations that exist for dealing with safety. You should know them from the local to the federal level and be familiar with the reporting procedures for incidents you face.

Personal safety

Nothing on a computer, server, router, and so on cannot be replaced or repaired. The same, however, is not true for you. It is imperative that you protect yourself from harm and follow all safety procedures when working with computers.

Disconnect power before repairing PCs

Earlier in this section, you learned that power should always be disconnected when working in a system. Please review the section "Proper power handling."

Lifting techniques

One easy way to get hurt is by moving equipment in an unsafe or improper way. Here are some safe lifting techniques for you to always keep in mind:

- Lift with your legs, not your back. When you have to pick something up, bend at the knees, not at the waist. You want to maintain the natural curve of the back and spine when lifting.
- Be careful not to twist when lifting. Keep the weight on your body's centerline.
- Keep objects as close to your body as possible and at waist level.
- Where possible, push instead of pull.

The goal in lifting should be to reduce the strain on lower back muscles as much as possible, because muscles in the lower back aren't nearly as strong as those in the legs or other parts of the body. Some people use a back belt or brace to help support and maintain the proper position while lifting.

Fire safety

Repairing a computer is not often the cause of an electrical fire. However, you should know how to extinguish such a fire properly. Three major classes of fire extinguishers are available, one for each type of flammable substance: A for wood and paper fires, B for flammable liquids, and C for electrical fires. The most popular type of fire extinguisher today is the multipurpose, or an ABC-rated, extinguisher. It contains a dry chemical powder that smothers and cools the fire at the same time. For electrical fires (which might be related to a shorted-out wire in a power supply), make sure the fire extinguisher will work for class C fires. If you don't have an extinguisher that is specifically rated for electrical fires (type C), you can use an ABC-rated extinguisher.

Safety goggles

In any environment where you might get dust or harmful materials in your eyes, you should wear safety goggles. For example, when working in a dusty shop area where a computer is located, this might be advisable. Another example might be when you are cleaning up toxic printer toner.

When spending long hours staring at a computer screen, you can wear safety glasses to reduce the eye strain stemming from this type of activity.

Air filtration mask

While safety goggles will protect your eyes from dust and other harmful particulates, they will do nothing to protect your lungs. Air filter masks should always be available, and technicians should be encouraged to wear them in any situation where safety goggles are called for, or in any scenario where they have reason to believe that the surrounding air might contain harmful compounds.

Exam essentials

Understand ESD. Electrostatic discharge (ESD) occurs when two objects of unequal electrical potential meet. One object transfers some charge to the other one, just as water can flow into an area with a lower water level.

Understand the antistatic wrist strap. An antistatic wrist strap is also referred to as an ESD strap. To use the ESD strap, you attach one end to an earth ground (typically the ground pin on an extension cord) and wrap the other end around your wrist. This strap grounds your body and keeps it at a zero charge, preventing discharges from damaging the PC components.

4.5 Summarize environmental impacts and local environment controls

Environmental harm can come from many sources. Not only should temperature and humidity elements be controlled, but administrators also should carefully monitor power, air, and particulates that can harm humans and computers. Not understanding environmental impacts and local controls can cause great harm by exposing the organization to fines and other legal penalties.

Material Safety Data Sheet (MSDS) documentation for handling and disposal

It is important that you know the potential safety hazards that exist when working with computer elements and how to address them. You must understand Material Safety Data Sheets (MSDSs) and know how to reference them when needed. Any type of chemical, equipment, or supply that has the potential to harm the environment or people must have an MSDS associated with it. Traditionally created by the manufacturer, you can obtain them from the manufacturer or from the Environmental Protection Agency (EPA) at www.epa.gov.

These sheets are not intended for consumer use but are aimed at emergency workers and employees who are exposed to the risks of the particular product. Among the information they include are items such as boiling, melting, and flash points and potential health risks. They also cover storage and disposal recommendations and the procedures to follow in case of spills or leaks.

Proper battery disposal

Batteries can contain a number of compounds and materials that should not make their way into landfills. The following are some examples:

- Rare earth metals
- Lead
- Cadmium
- Lithium
- Alkaline manganese
- Mercury

You should make battery recycling a standard procedure and follow local regulations for battery disposal when the time comes for disposal of batteries.

Proper toner disposal

Toner cartridges are another item that should not be thrown away. They should be recycled. Moreover, in any case where toner has been spilled, you should clean up with a special vacuum made for that purpose. If you use a regular vacuum, the metal toner will damage the vacuum.

Proper disposal of other devices and assets

Other devices and physical assets also require special handing when disposing of them. In this section, you'll learn about several examples.

Cell phones

Cell phones should not be thrown away, as they contain many of the same compounds found in laptops and desktops. Because the majority of the time the device is still perfectly functional (say, the user simply wanted a new phone), it should be sold or donated so that someone else can use it. Many cellular service providers will also accept trade-ins.

Tablets

Treat tablets in the same way you would cell phones and either sell, recycle, or donate them when disposing of them.

Temperature, humidity-level awareness, and proper ventilation

Three items closely related to an environmentally friendly computing environment are temperature, humidity, and ventilation. We will cover the most important elements with all three.

Temperature

Heat and computers don't mix well. Many computer systems require both temperature and humidity control for reliable service. Larger servers, communications equipment, and drive arrays generate considerable amounts of heat; this is especially true of mainframe and older minicomputers. An environmental system for this type of equipment is a significant expense beyond the cost of the actual computer system. Fortunately, newer systems operate in a wider temperature range. Most new systems are designed to operate in an office environment.

Humidity level

Another preventive measure you can take is to maintain the relative humidity at around 50%. Be careful not to increase the humidity too much to the point where moisture starts to condense on the equipment! It is a balancing act, keeping humidity at the right level, because low humidity causes ESD and high humidity causes moisture condensation. Both extremes are bad but have completely different effects.

Also, use antistatic spray, which is available commercially, to reduce static buildup on clothing and carpets. In a pinch, a solution of diluted fabric softener sprayed on these items will do the same thing, but don't spray it on equipment.

At the least, you can be mindful of the dangers of ESD and take steps to reduce its effects. Beyond that, you should educate yourself about the effects so you know when ESD is becoming a major problem.

Ventilation

Rounding out temperature and humidity is ventilation. It is important that air—clean air—circulate around computer equipment to keep it cool and functioning properly. Server rooms require much more attention to ventilation than office spaces but are the subject of other exams (e.g. Server+) and not test fodder for A+.

What *is* test fodder is the topic of ventilation within the computer itself—an inadequate flow of internal air within a computer is a common cause of overheating. To prevent it, know that all slot covers should remain in place and be replaced if a card is removed from the system. Know as well that internal fans should be periodically cleaned to ensure proper airflow. A missing slot cover or malfunctioning fan can lead to an inadequate flow of internal air.

Location/equipment placement

If the computer systems you're responsible for require special environmental considerations, you'll need to establish cooling and humidity control. Ideally, systems are located in the middle of the building, and they're ducted separately from the rest of the heating, ventilation, and air conditioning (HVAC) system. It's common for modern buildings to use a zone-based air conditioning environment, which allows the environmental plant to be turned off when a building isn't occupied. A computer room will typically require full-time environmental control.

Dust cleanup

One of the most harmful atmospheric hazards to a computer is dust. Dust, dirt, hair, and other airborne contaminants can be pulled into computers and build up inside. Because computer fans work by pulling air through the computer (i.e. usually sucking it in through the case vents and then pushing it out the power supply), it's easy for these contaminants to enter and become stuck. Every item in the computer builds up heat, and these contaminants are no exception. As they build up, they hinder the fan's ability to perform its function, and the components become hotter than they would otherwise. Figure 9.4 shows the inside of a system in use for only six months in an area with carpeting and other dusty surroundings.

Compressed air/vacuums

You can remove dust and debris from inside computers using compressed air blown in short bursts. The short bursts are useful in preventing the dust from flying too far out and entering another machine, as well as in preventing the can from releasing the air in liquid form. Compressed air cans should be held 2–3 inches from the system and always used upright, so the content is released as a gas. If the can becomes cold to the touch, discontinue using it until it heats back to room temperature.

4.5 Summarize environmental impacts and local environment controls

FIGURE 9.4 Dust built up inside the system

FIGURE 9.5 Dust collected in unused ports

WARNING It's possible to use an air compressor instead of compressed-air cans when you need a lot of air. If you take this approach, make sure you keep the pounds per square inch (PSI) at or below 40 and include measures on the air compressor to remove moisture.

Vacuums

Dust can build up not just within the computer but also in crevices on the outside. Figure 9.5 shows USB ports on the back of a system that have become a haven for small dust particles. These ports need to be blown out with compressed air or cleaned with an electronic vacuum before being used, or degradation of the device connected to them could occur.

Power surges, brownouts, and blackouts

A number of power-related threats can harm computers. An uninterruptible power supply (UPS) is a solution to a number of power-related threats that can harm computers. Among them are the following:

Blackout   This is a complete failure of the power supplied.

Brownout   This is a drop in voltage lasting more than a few minutes.

Sag   This is a short-term voltage drop.

Spike   The opposite of a sag, this is a short increase (typically less than one second) in voltage that can do irreparable damage to equipment.

Surge   This is a long spike (sometimes lasting many seconds). Though a surge is typically a less intense increase in power, it can also damage equipment.

The two solutions to know for the power issues on the exam are UPS systems and surge suppressors.

Uninterruptible power supply (UPS)

A battery backup, or uninterruptible power supply (UPS), keeps the system up and running for a short period of time when the normal power is removed (because of blackout, brownout, etc.). Even in installations that use generators to keep the systems running, battery backups are usually still used to keep the machines running while the generators come up to speed.

Most UPS units come with software that can be used to configure the actions to take when the battery backup is active. The software, for example, can be configured to shut down the connected devices when the battery begins to get low. Always ensure that the UPS provides the required voltage for all devices.

Surge suppressor

A surge suppressor keeps a spike from passing through it and onto the equipment that could be damaged. *Tripping* occurs when the breaker on a device, such as a power supply, surge protector, or UPS, turns off the device because it received a spike, such as from a nearby lightning strike. If the device is a UPS, when the tripping happens, the components plugged into the UPS should go to battery power instead of pulling power through the line. Under most circumstances, the breaker is reset, and operations continue as normal. Figure 9.6 shows a surge-protector power strip, with the trip button to reset at the top.

Nuisance tripping is the phrase used if tripping occurs often and isn't a result of a serious condition. If this continues, you should isolate the cause and correct it, even if it means replacing the device that continues to trip.

Surge suppressors (also known as *surge protectors*), either stand-alone or built into the UPS, can help reduce the number of nuisance trips. If your UPS doesn't have a surge protector, you should add one to the outlet before the UPS to keep the UPS from being damaged if it receives a strong surge. Figure 9.7 shows an example of a simple surge protector for a home computer.

FIGURE 9.6 The reset button on the top of a surge-protector power strip

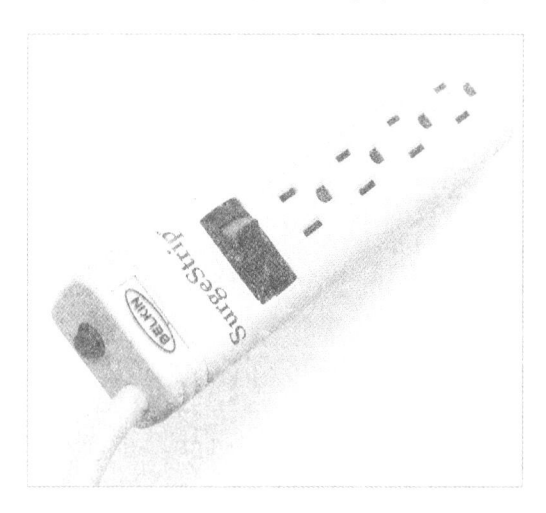

FIGURE 9.7 A simple surge protector

All units are rated by UL Solutions for performance. One thing you should never do is plug a UPS or any computer equipment into a ground fault circuit interrupter (GFCI) receptacle. These receptacles are intended for use in wet areas, and they trip easily.

WARNING Don't confuse a GFCI receptacle with an isolated ground receptacle. Isolated ground receptacles are identifiable by orange outlets and should be used for computer equipment to avoid their picking up a surge passed to the ground by any other device.

Exam essentials

Know that you might need to report incidents. When incidents happen, you must always document them, and every attempt should be made to do so both fully and truthfully. Depending on the type of incident, you might also need to report it to other authorities, such as the EPA.

Know what components are not suitable for a landfill. Batteries, cathode ray tubes (CRTs), and circuit boards are all examples of items that should not be thrown away normally because of the elements used in them. Batteries contain metals such as lead and nickel, circuit boards contain lead solder, and CRTs contain phosphors. They should be recycled.

Know the safety procedures to follow when working with computers. Be careful when moving computers or working around any electrical components. Know that liquids and computers don't mix and keep the systems as clean and dust-free as possible to ensure optimal operation.

4.6 Explain the importance of prohibited content/activity and privacy, licensing, and policy concepts

Working in the IT profession, it is entirely possible that you will encounter a situation where you find proof of a user or a number of users engaging in activities that are prohibited. Those activities can include any number of things, and the prohibition may range from a company policy (e.g. you cannot use social media during working hours), all the way up to a federal law (e.g. you cannot traffic in child pornography). You have an obligation to respond appropriately and accordingly.

Incident response

Regardless of whether you agree with a prohibition, when you encounter instances where users are taking part in activities in violation of it, you must respond in a professional and legal manner.

The extent to which a security event causes harm to your network largely depends on the speed and quality of your response to the incident. By following a structured incident response policy, you greatly enhance the chances of minimizing the damage and being able to bring parties to justice in the case of illegal activity. The following sections cover some important guidelines regarding the incident response process.

Chain of custody

An important concept to keep in mind when working with incidents is the chain of custody. You must follow the correct documentation process and ensure the proper collection of evidence.

Tracking of evidence/documenting process

When you begin to collect evidence, you must keep track of that evidence at all times and show who has it, who has seen it, and where it has been, which is known as the *chain of custody*. This evidence must always be within your custody, or you're open to disputes about whether it has been tampered with. Follow the proper chain of custody and documentation policies to ensure you're acting above board during incident responses.

Inform management/law enforcement as necessary

Part of identifying the problem involves identifying what policy or law prohibits such an action. Prohibited content generally falls within the following categories. Note, this list should not be considered as all-encompassing and representing everything prohibited, because many companies have numerous other policies:

- Exploiting people (in any way, such as sexually, violently, etc.)
- Promoting harassment of any person or group
- Containing or promoting anything illegal or unauthorized
- Promoting racism, hatred, bigotry, or physical harm
- Containing adult content involving nudity or sexual acts
- Violating privacy rights, copyrights, contract rights, or defamation rights
- Spreading viruses or malware of any sort
- Impersonating someone
- Soliciting information from anyone younger than 18
- Promoting pyramid schemes, junk mail, chain letters, spam, and so on

Report through proper channels

Once you have identified prohibited content or activity, you must report it through the proper channels. If the violation is one only of company policy, then usually the company's human resources (HR) department is the proper channel. If the violation is of a law, then often you must contact legal authorities—notifying the appropriate internal resources as well. If a federal law is violated and you tell only an internal resource (e.g. an HR manager), it does not absolve you of responsibility if that person does not continue to report it up the appropriate chain.

> Law enforcement personnel are governed by the rules of evidence, and their response to an incident will be largely out of your control. You need to carefully consider involving law enforcement *before* you do so. There is no such thing as dropping charges. Once they begin, law enforcement professionals are required to pursue an investigation.

Copy of drive (data integrity and preservation)

You also have an obligation to preserve any content found until it is turned over to the appropriate authority. Doing so might require commandeering anything from a flash drive up to a network server. Until someone in a position of authority relieves you of the responsibility, you must preserve the data or device in the state in which you discovered it. If you are ever unsure of how to proceed, you should immediately contact your supervisor.

Knowing what to do when something is discovered might not come naturally. It is a good idea to include the procedures you'll generally follow in an incident response plan (IRP). An IRP outlines what steps are needed and who is responsible for deciding how to handle a situation.

> Your company policies should clearly outline who needs to be informed, what they must be told, and how you (and the company) should respond to the situation.

Incident documentation

During the entire process, you must document the steps you take to identify, detect, and report the problem. This information is valuable and will often be used should the problem escalate to a court of law. Many help-desk software systems provide detailed methods you can use to record procedures and steps.

Order of volatility

Before collecting any evidence, an organization should consider the order of volatility, which ensures that investigators collect evidence from the components that are most volatile first. The order of volatility, according to Request For Comment (RFC) 3227, "Guidelines for Evidence Collection and Archiving," is the collection of items as follows:

1. CPU, cache, and register content
2. Routing table, Address Resolution Protocol (ARP) cache, process table, and kernel statistics
3. Memory
4. Temporary file system/swap space
5. Data on hard disk
6. Remotely logged data
7. Data contained on archival media

Licensing/digital rights management (DRM)/end-user license agreement (EULA)

While many in the IT community would like to think that software, music files, and movie files should be free, that is not the case. Using any of these items without paying for them is illegal. Operating systems (OSes), application software, and many third-party utilities require a license to legally use them. When you make a purchase, you are buying a license to use the software. You are not buying the software itself. It also requires that you accept an end-user license agreement (EULA), whereby you agree to use the software as described in that agreement.

Music and movie files, on the other hand, are protected by digital rights management (DRM). This management system maintains control over these files and ensures that they are installed only on devices that belong to the person who purchased the file, with the end goal being to prevent users from sharing and giving these files away without paying for them.

Not all software requires a license. In the next sections, we'll talk about software that doesn't require a license and discuss the differences between personal and enterprise licenses.

Valid licenses

Software licenses must be purchased for each instance of the software you plan to deploy. Software piracy is the unauthorized reproduction or distribution of copyrighted software. Although software piracy is a worldwide issue, it is much more prevalent in Asia, Europe, Latin America, Africa, and the Middle East. Part of the problem with software piracy stems from the cross-jurisdictional issues that arise. Obtaining the cooperation of foreign law enforcement agencies and government is often difficult or impossible. Combine this with the availability of the hardware needed to create pirated software and the speed with which it can be made, and you have a large problem that will only increase in size over the coming years.

Security professionals and the organizations they work with must ensure that the organization takes measures to ensure that employees understand the implications of installing pirated software. In addition, large organizations might need to use an enterprise software inventory application that will provide administrators with a report on the software that is installed.

Perpetual license agreement

A perpetual license is one sold on a one-time-only basis, and the licensee can then use a copy of the software forever. The licensee, also known as a license holder, has indefinite access to a specific version of a software program by paying for it only once.

Unexpired licenses

Pay attention to how long a license lasts. A perpetual license doesn't expire. Once you purchase it, you have rights to use the software for as long as you like. A term license expires after a specified period of time (often one year) and must be periodically renewed. Having an expired license is just as bad as having no license at all.

Personal-use license vs. corporate-use license

While an individual software license entitles a single user to install and use a piece of commercial software, an enterprise license purchase is based on a number of seats or devices on which the software can be legally installed. Also, while each individual license comes with installation media, the purchase of an enterprise license comes with a single version of the installation media, which can be installed on the number of devices specified in the license agreement.

Open-source license

Open-source software is free and available to all. Commercial software, on the other hand, requires the purchase of a license to legally use the software. While there is an obvious monetary advantage to using open-source software, the organization or user must typically have a deeper understanding of the software than may be required to use commercial software successfully. Another advantage of commercial software is the ongoing support the vendor can provide in using the software, while a user of open-source software is pretty much on their own when issues arise. The good news is that open-source software has large active user communities, though their information might not be as authoritative as manufacturer support.

Nondisclosure agreement (NDA)/mutual nondisclosure agreement (MNDA)

A nondisclosure agreement (NDA) is an agreement between two parties that defines what information is considered confidential and cannot be shared outside the two parties. An organization may implement NDAs with personnel regarding the intellectual property of the organization. NDAs can also be used when two organizations work together to develop a new product. Because certain information must be shared to make the partnership successful, NDAs are signed to ensure that each partner's data is protected. A mutual nondisclosure agreement (MNDA) is an agreement between two parties that commits *both* parties to the agreement.

Regulated data

Some data types require special attention because they are regulated, meaning their proper handling is specified by regulation. In this section, we'll look at some of these types of data.

Credit card payment information

Credit card data is some of the most sensitive data there is; users and customers depend on organizations to protect it. The Payment Card Industry Data Security Standard PCI DSS v4.0, an information security standard used to handle credit cards from major card brands, was released in Quarter 1 (Q1) of 2022. It encourages and enhances cardholder data security and facilitates the broad adoption of consistent data security measures globally.

Personal government-issued information

Information such as driver's license numbers, Social Security numbers, and other government-issued identifiers must be kept confidential, because when used together, these pieces of information can be used to steal an identity. These values are also considered personally identifiable information (PII), covered in Chapter 7.

PII

Personally identifiable information was covered in Chapter 7. Please review that chapter.

Healthcare data

Protected health information (PHI), also referred to as *electronic protected health information* (EPHI or ePHI), is any individually identifiable health information. The National Institute of Standards and Technology (NIST) Special Publication (SP) 800-66 provides guidelines for implementing the Health Insurance Portability and Accountability Act (HIPAA) Security Rule in the United States.

Data retention requirements

Once data has reached the end of its life cycle, you should either properly dispose of it or ensure that it is securely stored. Some organizations must maintain data records for a certain number of years per local, state, or federal laws or regulations. This type of data should be archived for the required period. In addition, any data that is part of litigation should be retained as requested by the court of law, and organizations should follow appropriate chain of custody and evidence documentation processes. Data archival and destruction procedures should be clearly defined by the organization.

All organizations need procedures set in place for the retention and destruction of data. Data retention and destruction must follow all local, state, and government regulations and laws. Documenting proper procedures ensures that information is maintained for the required time to prevent financial fines and possible incarceration of high-level organizational officers. These procedures must include both retention period and destruction process.

Acceptable use policy (AUP)

The most effective method of preventing viruses, spyware, and harm to data is education. Teach your users not to open suspicious files and to open only files that they're reasonably sure are virus-free. They need to scan every disk, email, and document they receive before they open it. You should also have all workstations scheduled to be automatically scanned on a regular basis.

While education is important, in most cases you must also attempt to control what users do. An AUP is a document that specifies what users can and cannot do, and it should be signed by all during the hiring process. This creates a contract that can be used later to form the basis for disciplinary measures. These measures or consequences for noncompliance should be spelled out ahead of time. The AUP should be reviewed at least annually, and if changes are made, personnel should have to sign the agreement again.

Regulatory and business compliance requirements

It is your responsibility, as an administrator and a professional, to know (or learn) the regulations that exist for dealing with safety. You should know them from the local to the federal level and be familiar with the reporting procedures for incidents with which you are faced.

If employees are injured, for example, you might need to contact the Occupational Safety and Health Administration (OSHA). On its website (www.osha.gov), you can find links to information about issues of compliance, laws and regulation, and enforcement.

The EPA offers basic information here: www.epa.gov/osw/conserve/materials/ecycling/index.htm

Splash screens

A splash screen, also known as a launch screen, is the first screen that a user sees when opening your app, and it stays visible while the app is loading. Password-protected lock screens, a related concept, can be used to prevent access to the desktop when a user steps away from the system. Many regulations, such as NIST, PCI DSS, and ISO 27001, require that organizations implement some sort of screen lock timer to promote security. If you are required to comply with one of these standards and a lock screen is not implemented, you will be considered out of compliance.

Exam essentials

Report prohibited content and activities.   You have an obligation to report prohibited activities and content to the appropriate authorities when you uncover them. You must ascertain which authority is prohibiting the actions and notify them.

Document and preserve the evidence.   It is imperative that the evidence be documented and preserved until turned over to the appropriate authority. In some cases, this can include commandeering a removable drive, a computer, or even a server. Failure to do so can leave you facing fines and other punishments.

4.7 Given a scenario, use proper communication techniques and professionalism

It's possible that you chose computers as your vocation instead of public speaking because you want to interact with people on a one-on-one basis. As unlikely as that possibility might be, it still exists.

Some have marveled at the fact that CompTIA includes questions about customer service on the A+ exam. A better wonder, however, is that there are those in the business who need to know these items and don't. Possessing a great deal of technology skill does not immediately endow one with great people skills. A bit more on appropriate behavior as it relates to the IT field follows.

Professional appearance and attire

You cannot change first impressions, and if you make a bad first impression, it can be difficult to recover and gain a customer's trust. In this section, I will discuss appearance and how you present yourself to your customers.

Match the required attire of the given environment

When deciding the right appearance to present to a customer, it is useful to consider the environment in which you will meet the customer and perform the work. There are two basic approaches to this: formal and business casual.

Formal

If you're going into an environment where the prevailing custom regarding proper dress is formal or is unknown, you should assume that you need to wear formal business attire (i.e. shirt, tie, dress pants, and jacket). This will ensure the best possible first impression.

Business casual

Never assume this is the case, but if you can identify the prevailing custom regarding work attire to be business casual, then by all means go that route. However, what is considered business casual? Business casual options differ from company to company. For example, it can mean any of these things:

- Business dress pants/skirt, khakis, dark jeans without holes
- Button-down shirts, sweaters, or dress shirts
- Closed-toed shoes, such as loafers or oxfords

- Optional belt that matches your shoes
- Optional cardigan or sport coat, especially for added warmth during colder months

Whenever in doubt, always overdress for the job.

Use proper language and avoid jargon, acronyms, and slang, when applicable

Avoid using jargon, abbreviations, slang, and acronyms. Every field has its own language that can make those from outside the field feel lost and as if you are projecting an air of superiority. Place yourself in the position of someone not in the field and explain what is going on using words they can understand.

Be honest and fair with the customer, whoever that is, and try to establish a personal rapport. Tell them what the problem is, what you believe is the cause, and what can be done in the future to prevent it from recurring.

Alert your supervisor if there is a communication barrier with the customer (e.g. the customer is deaf or does not speak the same language as you do). This is particularly important if the barrier will affect the problem resolution or the amount of time it will take.

If you're providing phone support, do the following:

- Always answer the telephone in a professional manner, announcing the name of the company and your name.
- Make a concentrated effort to ascertain the customer's technical level and then communicate at that level, not above or below it.

Maintain a positive attitude/project confidence

Maintain a positive attitude. Your approach to the problem and the customer can be mirrored back. Moreover, project confidence in dealing with the issue because that engenders more cooperation and patience from the customer, both of which directly impact the success of your troubleshooting efforts.

Actively listen, take notes, and avoid interrupting the customer

Good communication includes listening to what the user, manager, or developer is telling you and making certain that you understand completely what they are trying to say. Just because a user or customer doesn't understand the terminology, syntax, or concepts that you do doesn't mean they don't have a real problem that needs addressing. You must, therefore, be skilled not only at listening but also at translating. Professional conduct encompasses politeness, guidance, punctuality, and accountability. Always treat the customer with the same respect and empathy you would expect if the situation were reversed. Likewise, guide the customer through the problem and explanation. Tell them what has caused the problem they're currently experiencing and offer the best solution to prevent it from recurring.

Listen intently to what your customer is saying. Make it obvious to them that you're listening and respecting what they're telling you. If you have a problem understanding them, go to whatever lengths you need to remedy the situation. Look for verbal and nonverbal cues that can help you isolate the problem. Avoid interrupting the customer, because that telegraphs that what they have to say is not important enough for you to listen.

Be culturally sensitive

It is important as well to be culturally sensitive—not everyone enjoys the same humor. Moreover, be mindful of the difference in the way business is conducted in different cultures and be flexible in your approach based on this. For example, different cultures may have issues with physical contact, even with what you might see as normal, such as shaking hands. When you sense that the customer prefers a more formal relationship with you, try to reflect that in your approach.

Use appropriate professional titles, when applicable

While many folks are not put off at all when you address them by their first name, in many cultures it is considered rude to do so. In addition, you should address the customer using the appropriate title when applicable. Not all cultures are as informal as what you might have become accustomed to. Again, sensitivity to the customer's approach to you can be a valuable clue to how the customer would prefer to interact with you.

Be on time (if late, contact the customer)

Punctuality is important and should be part of your planning process before you arrive at the site. If you tell the customer you'll be there at 10:30, you need to make every attempt to be there at that time. If you arrive late, you have given them false hope that the problem would be solved by a set time. That false hope can lead to anger when you arrive late and appear to not be taking their problem as seriously as they are. Punctuality continues to be important throughout the service call and doesn't end with your arrival. If you need to leave to get parts, tell the customer why and when you'll be back, and then be there at that time. If for some reason you can't return at the expected time, alert the customer and inform them of your new return time.

In conjunction with time and punctuality, if a user asks how much longer the server will be down and you respond that it will be up in five minutes, only to have it remain down for five more hours, you're creating an opportunity for resentment and possibly anger. When estimating downtime, always allow for more time than you think you'll need, just in case other problems occur. If you greatly underestimate the time, always inform the affected parties and give them a new time estimate. Here's an analogy that will put it in perspective: If you take your car to get the oil changed and the counter clerk tells you it will be finished in "about 15 minutes," the last thing you want is to be doing is still sitting there 4 hours later.

Avoid distractions

It is important that you avoid distractions while working on a customer's or user's problem. Those distractions can come in the form of personal calls, discussions with co-workers, or other personal interruptions.

If you arrive at the site to troubleshoot a problem and there are distractions there of the customer's making (e.g. children present, TV blaring, etc.), you should politely ask the customer to remove the distractions if possible. If the area you will be working in is cluttered with personal items (e.g. mementos, stuffed animals, etc.), ask the customer to relocate the items as needed or ask them if it is OK to do so before you relocate the items.

Personal calls

Taking personal calls while working with a customer can make the customer feel as if their problem is being minimized. Spend time solving the problem and interacting with the customer and then attend to any personal calls after you leave. In fact, it's not a bad idea to silence the ringer on your phone when you're on-site.

If you are anticipating an important call that cannot be avoided, let the customer know beforehand so they will understand that this interruption is coming.

Texting/social media sites

Keep in mind that when you are supporting a customer, you are working on their time and not your own. You are also using their equipment, not your own. Consequently, avoid any use of the customer's equipment or time for personal texts or visits to social media sites. It is allowable, however, to use the time and the equipment for legitimate research or other activities that are directly related to solving the customer's issues.

Personal interruptions

The broad category of personal interruptions includes anything that takes you away from focusing on the customer and is not job-related. Spend your time dealing with the customer first and solving their problems before attending to personal issues.

Appropriately deal with difficult customers or situations

Handle complaints as professionally as possible. Accept responsibility for errors that might have occurred on your part and never try to pass the blame. Remember, the goal is to keep them as a customer, not to win an argument.

Do not argue with customers and/or be defensive

Avoid arguing with a customer, because doing so serves no purpose; resolve their anger with as little conflict as possible. Moreover, don't be defensive when the customer questions your approach and thought process. While they might be uninformed about troubleshooting, they deserve to understand why you are doing what you are doing.

Avoid dismissing customers' problems

Just as personal calls and interruptions can make it seem as if you are not taking the customer seriously enough, so, too, can dismissing their problems as less important than they believe they are. It is important to put yourself in their shoes and see the issue from their perspective. What might seem trivial to you might be a vital issue for them.

Avoid being judgmental

It is important not to minimize their problem or appear judgmental. While you might think it should be intuitive that changes made to files must be saved to be persistent, the user might be new to computing and won't appreciate a condescending attitude.

Clarify customer statements (i.e. ask open-ended questions to narrow the scope of the issue, restate the issue, or ask questions to verify understanding)

The most important skill you can have is your ability to listen. You have to rely on the customer to tell you the problem and describe it accurately. They can't do that if you're second-guessing them, jumping to conclusions, or interrupting them before the whole story is told. Ask questions that are broad and open-ended at first and then narrow them down to help isolate the problem. This is particularly necessary when you are trying to solve the problem remotely. For example, start by asking your customers questions like these:

- What were you doing *before* the problem occurred?
- What application were you using when the problem occurred?

It's also your job to help guide the user's description of the problem. Here are some example questions:

- Is the printer plugged in?
- Is your printer online?
- Are any lights flashing on it?

Restate the issue to the customer to ensure that you correctly understand what they are telling you (e.g. "There is only one green light lit, correct?"). Ask questions as needed that verify your understanding of the problem. The questions you ask should help guide you toward isolating the problem and identifying possible solutions.

Use discretion and professionalism when discussing experiences/encounters

Although it might make you feel better about a particularly trying experience with a customer to vent about it on social media, don't do that. Not only is it entirely possible that the post might somehow find its way to the attention of the customer, it reflects poorly on you as someone who shares their business dealings with the world.

Set and meet expectations/timeline and communicate status with the customer

Customer satisfaction goes a long way toward generating repeat business. If you can *meet* the customer's expectations, you'll almost assuredly hear from them again when another problem arises. If you can *exceed* the customer's expectations, you can almost guarantee that they will call you the next time a problem arises.

Customer satisfaction is important in all communication media—whether you're on-site, providing phone support, or communicating through email or other correspondence.

Share the customer's sense of urgency. What might seem like a small problem to you can appear to the customer as if the whole world is collapsing around them.

Offer repair/replacement options, as needed

If there are multiple solutions to the problem that the customer is encountering, offer options to them. Those options often include repairing what they already have or replacing it. If the repair could lead to a recurrence of the situation but the replacement will not, then that should be explained to them clearly.

The ramifications of each choice should be clearly explained along with costs (estimates, if necessary), so they can make the decision they deem in their best interest. If you are unable to resolve the issue, explain to the customer what to do and make sure to follow up properly to forward the issue to appropriate personnel.

Provide proper documentation on the services provided

Document the services you provided so there is no misunderstanding on the part of the customer. Supply them with the documentation and keep a copy handy to refer to should any questions arise. Clearly explain the cause of the problem and how to avoid it in the future.

It is important that the documentation be complete, so that if you do not refer to it for quite some time (years), you will still be able to understand and explain what was done.

Follow up with customer/user at a later date to verify satisfaction

When you finish a job, notify the user that the job has been completed. Make every attempt to find the user and inform them of the resolution. If it's difficult to find them, leave a note for them to find when they return, explaining the resolution. You should also leave a means by which they can contact you, should they have a question about the resolution or a related problem. In most cases, the number you leave should be that of your business during working hours and your cell phone, where applicable, after hours.

If you do not hear back from the customer, follow up with them at a later date to verify that the problem is resolved and they are satisfied with the outcome. One of the best ways to retain customers is to let them know that you care about their success and satisfaction.

Appropriately handle customers' confidential and private materials

The goal of confidentiality is to prevent or minimize unauthorized access to files and folders and disclosure of data and information. In many instances, laws and regulations require specific information confidentiality. For example, Social Security numbers, payroll and employee files, medical records, and corporate information are high-value assets. This information could create liability issues or embarrassment if it fell into the wrong hands. Over the last few years, there have been several cases in which bank account and credit card numbers were published on the Internet. The costs of these types of breaches of confidentiality far exceed the actual losses from the misuse of this information.

> **TIP** Confidentiality entails ensuring that data expected to remain private is seen only by those who should see it. Confidentiality is implemented through authentication and access controls.

Just as confidentiality issues are addressed early in a project's design phase, you as a computer professional are expected to uphold a high level of confidentiality. Should a user approach you with a sensitive issue—telling you their password, asking for assistance obtaining access to medical forms, and so on—it's your obligation as part of your job to make certain that information passes no further.

Located on a computer, desktop, printer, etc.

Technicians might come into contact with confidential information in the course of performing their job duties. That information could come in the form of data stored on a computer, desktop information, data (in any form) on a printer, or confidential information in many other locations. When that possibility exists, ask users to remove such confidential information or close the application that displays it (saving their work before they close).

If the area where you will be working is cluttered with personal information (e.g. printed customer lists), ask the customer to relocate the items if possible. No confidential information should ever be disclosed to outside parties.

Exam essentials

Use good communication skills. Listen to the customer. Let them tell you what they understand the problem to be and then interpret the problem and see whether you can get them to agree to what you're hearing them say. Treat the customer, whether an end user or a colleague, with respect and take their issues and problems seriously.

Deal appropriately with confidential data. You—as a computer professional—are expected to uphold a high level of confidentiality. No confidential information should ever be disclosed to outside parties.

4.8 Explain the basics of scripting

Scripts are used to automate anything that can be accomplished at the command line. It prevents having to manually type in the commands and allows you to schedule a script file to run at a certain time. This section discusses the basics you should know.

Script file types

Script files can come in various file types. In this section, we'll look at these file types.

.bat

Batch file or files with a `.bat` extension are used to automate a command or set of commands each time you execute the batch file.

.ps1

Files with the `.ps1` extension are used to script tasks in PowerShell, a powerful scripting language used by Microsoft.

.vbs

The `.vbs` files are Visual Basic script files. The VBScript scripting language contains code that can be executed within Windows or Internet Explorer via the Windows-based script host.

.sh

Files that contain the `.sh` file extension are self-extracting files. The file contains selected files and a shell script, along with instructions on how to extract the contents of the `.sh` file archive.

.py

A `.py` file is one written in the Python language. Python runs on Windows, macOS and Linux/UNIX.

.js

A `.js` file is a text file containing JavaScript code that is used to execute JavaScript instructions in web pages.

Use cases for scripting

Scripting makes the scheduling and automation of any function possible. In this section, you'll learn about some of the use cases for creating and scheduling scripts to run.

Basic automation

Any task can be automated by creating a script that performs the function and then scheduling it to run at the proper time. For example, you can use the at command to schedule a command, script, or program to run at a specified date and time.

Restarting machines

Many systems benefit from a restart from time to time. Rather than placing this task on a checklist and dedicating a technician's time to walking over to the machine and manually restarting the system, you can schedule the process to occur on a regular basis.

Remapping network drives

Users need easy access to network systems and network locations where they can safely save data. Mapping network drives makes this much easier for users. This can be done from the command line so it can be automated. Using the at command, you can schedule this command that maps a network drive:

    net use DRIVE: PATH

Installing applications

Applications use special file types to install the application. A good example is a Microsoft .msi file. Regardless of the installation file types (.exe, .bat, etc.), the installation can be scheduled by using the at command. This is especially useful when installing on multiple systems. You can do this with a single command if you reference the systems correctly.

Performing automated backups

Many backup tools and utilities allow for the scheduling of backups. So, why would you use a script? Customization. Scripts offer much more granular control over how the backup is performed than using the scheduling in backup software. For example, if you need to pull information from your backup software and put it into a spreadsheet to generate a special report, you can only do this with a script.

Gathering information/data

Sometimes, you need to gather information on a system, such as the software currently installed or the CPU types in use. To do this on a large scale manually can be overwhelming, but scripts can be created to interrogate the system and return an answer for each.

Initiating updates

Many organizations automate the installation of updates through tools such as Windows Update, but sometimes you have an update that you do *not* want widely installed. Maybe you want it installed only on certain systems. In that case, you could use a script to install it on the system that requires it.

Other considerations when using scripts

While scripting is an amazing tool, you need to be mindful of some issues. In this section, you'll learn about some of these issues.

Unintentionally introducing malware

One of the ways you can introduce malware when scripting is when you reference a file to execute that *is* malware. This can happen if you haven't verified the integrity of the file you are referencing. Any time you download an installation file of anything, always check its integrity by verifying its hash value. If a hash value is not provided, that is a red flag indicating that you need to go elsewhere for that file.

Inadvertently changing system settings

When constructing your script, be very careful that the script does *only* what you want and does not make other unwanted changes. This can happen when copying scripts from websites that you don't fully understand.

Browser or system crashes due to mishandling of resources

Sometimes poorly written scripts can cause resource issues that can lead to a browser crash or even a complete system crash. Say a script is written in such a way that you're specifying you want only one byte to be read from the universal asynchronous receiver-transmitter (USART) hardware buffer. If there isn't a byte to be read by the script, it can cause a wait for data that might never come, causing your program to "freeze."

Exam essentials

Identify script file types. These include .bat, .ps1, .vbs, .sh, .pyc, and .js.

4.9 Given a scenario, use remote access technologies

As an A+ technician, there will be times when you need to make a remote connection to another device for the purpose of managing the device. In this section, we'll review some of the options for this and the security issues with each.

Methods/tools

Let's begin by looking at some available options for remote access, and in the following section, you'll learn about the security considerations of each.

RDP

You learned about Remote Desktop Protocol (RDP) in Chapter 4. Please review that chapter.

VPN

You learned about virtual private networks (VPNs) in Chapter 2. Please review that chapter.

Virtual Network Computing (VNC)

Virtual Network Computing (VNC) operates much like RDP but uses Remote Frame Buffer (RFB) protocol. Unlike RDP, VNC is platform independent. For example, it could be used to transmit between a Linux server and a macOS laptop. The VNC system contains the following components:

- The VNC server is the program on the machine that shares its screen.
- The VNC client (or viewer) is the program that watches, controls, and interacts with the server.
- The VNC protocol (i.e. RFB) is used to communicate between the VNC server and client.

Secure Shell (SSH)

You learned about Secure Shell in Chapter 2. Please review that chapter.

Remote monitoring and management (RMM)

Remote monitoring and management (RMM) is not a product but rather a process that can be performed by many different tools. It is the process of supervising and controlling IT systems with locally installed agents that can be accessed by a management service provider. Some example products include:

- Atera RMM
- SuperOps RMM
- NinjaRMM by NinjaOne
- N-able RMM

Simple Protocol for Independent Computing Environments (SPICE)

The Simple Protocol for Independent Computing Environments (SPICE) is a remote-access system built for virtual environments, which can view the "desktop" not only on the server, but also from anywhere on the Internet—using a wide variety of machine architectures.

The client connection to the SPICE remote desktop server consists of multiple data channels, each of which is run over a separate socket connection. The data channel can be operated in clear text or in Transport Layer Security (TLS) (i.e. encrypted) mode, allowing the administrator to choose between security and performance.

In SPICE, a manager process runs on the management workstation that requests information about the devices on the network, while an agent process runs on each of the managed devices and transfers the collected information to the manager. The information is in the form of key-value pairs called object identifiers (OIDs).

Windows Remote Management (WinRM)

WS-Management (Web Services-Management) is a Distributed Management Task Force (DMTF) open standard defining a Simple Object Access Protocol (SOAP)–based protocol for the management of servers, devices, applications, and various web services. It provides a common way for systems to access and exchange management information across the IT infrastructure.

The Microsoft implementation of WS-Management is called Windows Remote Management (WinRM). A command-line tool, WinRM is built into Windows OSes and allows scripts and commands to be invoked on Windows-based machines or a large set of remote machines without using RDP or logging into the remote machine. It is based on .NET and PowerShell, making the execution of PowerShell 2.0 scripts and cmdlets on remote systems possible.

Third-party tools

There are also third-party tools that sometimes include screen- and file-sharing features. Let's briefly discuss these capabilities.

Screen-sharing software

Many of the collaboration or meeting software packages, such GoTo Meeting, Webex, and Adobe Connect, offer a screen-sharing option. These are also possible in third-party remote access software, such as GoToMyPC, LogMeIn, and RemotePC.

Videoconferencing software

With the increase in remote work, videoconferencing and virtual meetings have become very commonplace. Tools such as Zoom and Google Chat allow groups of users meet, share screens, work on common documents, and continue to get work done as if in office.

File transfer software

Many of the collaboration or meeting software packages, such as GoTo Meeting, Webex, and Adobe Connect, also offer a file-sharing option. In many collaboration solutions, multiple users can even edit a document at the same time. These functions are also possible in third-party remote access software, such as GoToMyPC, LogMeIn, and RemotePC.

Desktop management software

Desktop management software is designed to allow for control of what is available to users on their desktops as well as other settings. It allows IT departments to find, manage, and control endpoints, such as desktop computers or mobile devices, on local and remote sites without the need for physical access to these devices. Also called endpoint management software, it has many of the same features as Windows Group Policy but is vendor neutral. Examples include the following:

- Tivoli Endpoint Manager
- ManageEngine Desktop Central
- Symantec Client Management Suite

Security considerations of each access method

Except for Telnet, which is completely insecure, RDP and third-party methods are generally secure and encrypted. However, you should ensure the following about the solution you select:

RDP   Ensure that all passwords are complex and that rights are restricted to the minimum to do the job.

VPN   Ensure that the most secure protocols (such as IPsec) are in use and that all passwords are complex.

SSH   Ensure that all passwords are complex and that rights are restricted to the minimum to do the job.

RMM   Select the most secure tool available. Ensure that all passwords are complex and that rights are restricted to the minimum to do the job.

MSRA   Strictly control the process of soliciting help and ensure that the helpers do not take advantage of users while they have control of the users' systems.

Third-party methods   Ensure that you understand the security capabilities and the shortcomings of the specific method under consideration.

Exam essentials

Describe common remote access tools.   These include Telnet, RDP, SSH, and third-party screen- and file-sharing tools such as LogMeIn and GoToMyPC.

Describe security considerations of each remote access method.   This includes the following:

- **RDP:** Ensure that all passwords are complex and that rights are restricted to the minimum to do the job.

- **VPN:** Ensure that the most secure protocols (such as IPsec) are in use and that all passwords are complex.
- **SSH:** Ensure that all passwords are complex and that rights are restricted to the minimum to do the job.
- **RMM:** Select the most secure tool available. Ensure that all passwords are complex and that rights are restricted to the minimum to do the job.
- **MSRA:** Strictly control the process of soliciting help and ensure that the helpers do not take advantage of users while they have control of the users' systems.
- **Third-party methods:** Ensure that you understand the security capabilities and shortcomings of the specific method under consideration.

4.10 Explain basic concepts related to artificial intelligence (AI)

Several editions of this book ago, the big buzzword was "cloud." Now it seems the new buzzword is artificial intelligence (AI). AI dominates technical conversations these days. While some fear it will take the jobs of humans, others say AI will not take jobs but will create new different jobs. In this final section of the chapter, you will learn some of the basics of AI.

Application integration

Most people are familiar with ChatGPT. An example of generative AI, this tool can be used to gather and organize data and even create summaries of what it finds. While standalone AI is powerful, to be truly useful AI must be integrated into an organization's applications. In fact, organizations do this not to get ahead of the competition but to keep up with the competition. Application integration connects AI applications with other software. It enables them to swap data and boost the product's capabilities. However, regardless of whether one is dealing with standalone AI or embedded AI, humans are required to check and verify AI content, as it cannot be trusted (at least at this point in development) to be correct all the time.

Policy

If an organization is going to take advantage of AI, it should create an AI policy to guide its use. AI can mislead, misinform, and manipulate information. It can leak sensitive information. It can also cause privacy or competition concerns. You still need to follow existing laws related to intellectual property or suffer lawsuits that could damage the business.

So, what should be in this policy? What kinds of issues are of concern? Two critical issues stand out: appropriate use and plagiarism.

Appropriate use

The company should define appropriate uses for AI. Some examples deployed so far include:

- Manufacturing robots
- Self-driving cars
- Smart assistants
- Healthcare management
- Automated financial investing
- Virtual travel agent
- Social media monitoring
- Marketing chatbots

Rather than just allowing users to use AI in any way they want, the organization must define as a company how AI is used. You should define those uses as well as how it should *not* be used. Later in this chapter, you will learn about the limitations of AI, and in the next section, some of the more serious errors it can make. Because of these dangers and limitations, the policy needs to clearly address proper use of AI.

Plagiarism

One of the biggest issues that has emerged with the use of AI is the abuse of intellectual property. While AI can generate content that does *not* plagiarize, it quite often copies content created and owned by others. When using AI to create content, the resulting content must be checked by a human to ensure this is not happening and that AI is not creating content that is incorrect. You will learn more about this phenomenon in the next section.

Limitations

We've made passing references to some of the limitations of AI. In this section, we'll look at three limitations in detail: bias, hallucinations, and accuracy.

Bias

When we say that content created by AI has bias, we mean that it is the type of slanted content one might expect from a human who has an agenda or an axe to grind. So, how does AI become biased? This primarily arises due to low quantity and quality of data during the training process. While it is possible to remove bias by altering the training procedure of AI systems, the source of bias is generally understood to originate in the training data itself. An old computing adage might apply here: garbage in, garbage out. The training data must be free of bias.

Hallucinations

Occasionally (some say more than occasionally), AI will return an answer to a question that is flat-out *wrong*. This behavior has come to be known as a hallucination. Issues like hallucinations make enterprises reluctant to deploy generative AI applications. What causes hallucinations and how can they be prevented?

While in some cases, a lack of context provided by the user causes this error (i.e. user error), most of the problems are derived from—you guessed it—the training data. Issues include data that is:

- Outdated or low quality
- Incorrectly classified or labeled
- Rife with factual errors, inconsistencies, or biases

Other causes include:

- Insufficient programming to interpret information correctly
- Confusion caused by colloquialisms, slang expressions, or sarcasm

The solution is:

- Better training data
- Better programming
- Avoidance of colloquialisms, slang expressions, or sarcasm

Accuracy

Even when not hallucinating, AI can provide inaccurate or misleading information, which has reduced confidence in AI results and slowed its adoption. Examples of inaccurate output include:

- Incorrect or misleading information
- Content choices that unfairly favor or disfavor a particular group
- Misunderstanding or misrepresentation of the data

Increasing accuracy can be achieved by:

- Improving the training data
- Improving the AI algorithm itself

Private vs. public

AI can be implemented into two main categories: public and private. Table 9.1 compares the two implementations:

TABLE 9.1 Private vs. public AI

Implementation	Population served	Access type
Public AI	Global	Open
Private AI	Specific organization	Restricted

The implementation chosen impacts AI in several ways. Let's examine how these impacts are felt.

Data security

As you can see in Table 9.1, public AI is open to all, and as such, one of the biggest concerns is their handling of data and maintaining its privacy. These systems collect large amounts of user data to improve the AI algorithm, but the data might be misused by the organizations that own and operate the service. Laws and regulations for protecting user data and privacy are limited at this stage of AI development.

Private AI is attractive because organizations can control and secure their data, minimizing the risk of data breaches and unauthorized access. Data used to fine-tune a private AI implementation is curated by a team of hired engineers, data scientists, and software developers to design and train the model.

Data source

As stated previously, the source of public AI data is the Internet, while private AI uses only data specified and curated by the organization.

Data privacy

At this point, you should understand that private AI provides more privacy while public AI provides less privacy.

Exam essentials

Understand the possible issues with AI accuracy. Examples of inaccurate output include:

- Incorrect or misleading information
- Content choices that unfairly favor or disfavor a particular group
- Misunderstanding or misrepresentation of the data

Review Questions

You can find the answers in the appendix.

1. Which of the following is the least important piece of information to record about each device for proper asset inventory?
   A. Make
   B. Model
   C. Serial number
   D. Operating system

2. Which of the following is false with respect to change management?
   A. All changes should be formally requested.
   B. Each request should be analyzed to ensure it supports all goals and polices.
   C. After formal approval, all costs and effects of the implementation methods should be reviewed.
   D. After changes are approved, the change steps should be developed.

3. What is the process called that ensures all configuration changes are beneficial?
   A. Change management
   B. Acceptable use
   C. Separation of duties
   D. Risk analysis

4. Which of the following are created to prevent technicians from spending too much time on an issue they don't completely understand?
   A. Escalation levels
   B. Phased deployments
   C. Scenario triage
   D. Runbooks

5. If you use incremental backups every day except Monday, when you do a full backup, how many backup tapes will be required if there is a drive failure on Wednesday after the backup has been made?
   A. 4
   B. 3
   C. 2
   D. 1

6. If you use differential backups every day except Monday, when you do a full backup, how many backup tapes will be required if there is a drive failure on Wednesday after the backup has been made?

A. 4
B. 3
C. 2
D. 1

7. Which of the following is *not* a safe lifting technique to keep in mind?
   A. Lift with your back, not your legs.
   B. Be careful not to twist when lifting.
   C. Keep objects as close to your body as possible.
   D. Where possible, push instead of pull.

8. What class of fire extinguisher is used for paper fires?
   A. A
   B. B
   C. C
   D. D

9. Any type of chemical, equipment, or supply that has the potential to harm the environment or people must have what document associated with it?
   A. SOW
   B. MSDS
   C. SLA
   D. MOU

10. What humidity level should be maintained for computing equipment?
    A. 50%
    B. 40%
    C. 60%
    D. 30%

11. Which of the following is *not* part of the first response to an incident?
    A. Shut down the affected system.
    B. Identify the incident.
    C. Report the incident though proper channels.
    D. Preserve the data/device.

12. Which of the following is a secure substitute for Telnet?
    A. RDP
    B. SSH
    C. SSL
    D. VPN

13. Which of the following is false regarding dealing with customers?
    A. Always answer the telephone in a professional manner, announcing the name of the company and your name.
    B. Make a concentrated effort to ascertain the customer's technical level and communicate above it.
    C. Use proper language (i.e. avoid jargon, acronyms, and slang when applicable).
    D. Maintain a positive attitude/project confidence.

14. Which of the following should the IT professional do when dealing with customers?
    A. Use appropriate professional titles, when applicable.
    B. Take personal calls.
    C. Use the customer's equipment for personal messages.
    D. Talk to coworkers while interacting with customers.

15. Which of the following is written in Python?
    A. .psi
    B. .vbs
    C. .sh
    D. .py

16. How is the warranty status of a device determined?
    A. By model number
    B. By serial number
    C. By date of deployment
    D. By device name

17. Which of the following is a command-line tool?
    A. RDP
    B. Screen sharing
    C. File sharing
    D. SSH

18. Which of the following is the least secure remote access technology?
    A. RDP
    B. Screen sharing
    C. Telnet
    D. SSH

Appendix

Answers to the Review Questions

Chapter 1: Mobile Devices

1. B. Yahoo recommends using IMAP as an email client.

2. B. Many laptop manufacturers will consider a warranty void if an unauthorized person opens a laptop's case and attempts to repair it.

3. B. Many laptop manufacturers will consider a warranty void if an unauthorized person opens a laptop's case and attempts to repair it. Some models of notebook PCs require a special T8 Torx screwdriver. Most PC toolkits come with a T8 bit for a screwdriver with interchangeable bits.

4. B. As you can imagine, setting up iCloud email on an iOS device is simple because the applications all reside in the Apple ecosystem. First, set up an iCloud email account. If you have an email address that ends with @mac.com or @me.com, you already have an equivalent address that's the same, except it ends with @icloud.com.

5. C. When removing the connector attached to the old drive's signal pins and attaching it to the new drive, make sure it's right side up and do not force it. Damaging the signal pins may render the drive useless.

6. A. The 1.8 inch hard drive is the smallest. It was originally used in subnotebooks and audio players.

7. A. The advantage of solid-state drives is that they are not as susceptible to damage if the device is dropped, and they are generally faster because no moving parts are involved. They are, however, more expensive, and when they fail they don't typically display any advanced warning symptoms like a magnetic drive will do.

8. C. Authenticator applications, such as Google Authenticator, make it possible for a mobile device to use a time-based one-time password (TOTP) algorithm with a site or system that requires such authentication.

9. D. While adding other options may or may not help performance, adding memory always helps.

10. B. You will need the following information to complete this setup:
    - The FQDN of your POP3 server or IMAP server (this server receives the emails sent to you, so it's sometimes called incoming)
    - The FQDN of your SMTP server (this server sends your email to the recipient's email server, so it's sometimes called outgoing)
    - The port numbers used for both server types
    - The security type used (if any)

11. C. Laptops can support plug and play at three levels, depending on how dynamically they're able to adapt to changes.

    Cold docking: The laptop must be turned off and back on for the change to be recognized.

    Warm docking: The laptop must be put in and out of suspended mode for the change to be recognized.

    Hot docking: The change can be made and is recognized while running normal operations

12. A. Subscriber identity module (SIM) cards are an integrated circuit (IC) intended to securely store an international mobile subscriber identity (IMSI) number and its related key.

13. A. A Global Positioning System (GPS) uses satellite information to plot the global location of an object and use that information to plot the route to a second location.

14. A. Mobile device management (MDM) policies can be created in Active Directory (AD), or they can be implemented through MDM software. This software allows you to exert control over the mobile devices, even those you do not own if they have the software installed.

15. A. Many external devices will ask for a PIN when you select the external device from the list of discovered devices. In many cases, the PIN is 0000, but you should check the manual of the external device.

16. C. POP3 uses port 110 by default.

17. C. Hybrid storage products have a magnetic disk and some solid-state memory. These drives monitor the data being read from the hard drive, and they cache the most frequently accessed bits to the high-speed flash memory.

18. D. Most mobile devices now offer the option to incorporate biometrics as an authentication mechanism. The two most common implementations of this use fingerprint or facial scans or facial recognition technology.

Chapter 2: Networking

1. D. POP3 uses port 110. SSH uses port 22, FTP uses ports 20 and 21, and Telnet uses port 23.

2. A. FTP uses ports 20 and 21. POP3 uses port 110, SSH uses port 22, and Telnet uses port 23.

3. B. SSH uses port 22, POP3 uses port 110, FTP uses ports 20 and 21, and Telnet uses port 23.

4. B. Switches operate at layer 2. Routers operate at layer 3. Repeaters and hubs operate at layer 1.

5. D. Hubs operate at layer 1. Switches and bridges operate at layer 2. Routers operate at layer 3.

6. B. Switches operate at layer 2. Routers operate at layer 3. Hubs and repeaters operate at layer 1.

7. B. The class B range is 172.16.0.0–172.31.255.255. The other ranges are private address ranges.

8. A. Symmetric DSL (SDSL) offers an upload speed equal to the download speed. The other versions all have slower upload speeds than download speeds.

9. B. Industrial control system (ICS) is a general term that encompasses several types of control systems used in industrial production. The most widespread is supervisory control and data acquisition (SCADA). SCADA is a system operating with coded signals over communication channels so as to provide control of remote equipment.

10. A. 802.11a operates in the 5.0 GHz range. The other standards all operate in the 2.4 GHz range.

11. D. 802.11a and 802.11g have a maximum rate of 54 Mbps. 802.11b has a maximum of 11 Mbps, and 802.11 has a maximum of 2 Mbps.

12. D. 802.11g has a distance that is the cell size of 125 ft. The others have a distance of 115 ft.

13. B. DNS servers resolve IP addresses to hostnames. HTTP servers are web servers. DHCP servers provide automatic IP configurations. SQL is a database server.

14. C. DHCP servers provide automatic IP configurations. DNS servers resolve IP addresses to hostnames. HTTP servers are web servers. SQL is a database server.

15. D. Syslog servers are used to store the log files that contain system messages and errors. DNS servers resolve IP addresses to hostnames. HTTP servers are web servers. DHCP servers provide automatic IP configurations.

16. C. The Class B range is 128–191. The Class A range is 1–126. The Class C range is 192–223.

17. B. The Class A range is 1–126. The Class B range is 128–191. The Class C range is 192–223.

18. A. The Class C range is 192–223. The Class A range is 1–126. The Class B range is 128–191. The 224 range is for multicasting.

19. C. A personal area network (PAN) is a LAN created by personal devices. A wide area network (WAN) is a collection of two or more LANs, typically connected by routers and dedicated leased lines. Occasionally, a WAN will be referenced as a metropolitan area network (MAN) when it is confined to a certain geographic area, such as a university campus or city. Wireless mesh networks (WMN) are a form of an ad hoc WLAN that often consist of mesh clients, mesh routers, and gateways.

20. B. Metropolitan area network (MAN) is the term occasionally used for a WAN that is confined to a certain geographic area, such as a university campus or city. A personal area network (PAN) is a LAN created by personal devices. A wide area network (WAN) is a collection of two or more LANs, typically connected by routers and dedicated leased lines. Wireless mesh networks (WMNs) are a form of an ad hoc WLAN that often consist of mesh clients, mesh routers, and gateways.

21. A. A wide area network (WAN) is a collection of two or more LANs, typically connected by routers and dedicated leased lines.

22. A. Wire crimpers look like pliers but are used to attach media connectors to the ends of cables. A cable stripper is used to remove the cable's outer covering to get to the wire pairs within. A PoE injector is a device that can be used to provide PoE to a device when the switch does not support PoE. It plugs into the wall, then a line providing data and PoE is run to the device, and another cable runs to the switch. A toner probe has two parts: the tone generator (called the toner) and the tone locator (called the probe). The toner sends the tone, and at the other end of the cable, the probe receives the toner's signal. This tool makes it easier to find the beginning and end of a cable.

23. B. A cable stripper is used to remove the cable's outer covering to get to the wire pairs within. A PoE injector is a device that can be used to provide PoE to a device when the switch does not support PoE. It plugs into the wall, then a line providing data and PoE is run to the device, and another cable runs to the switch. Wire crimpers look like pliers but are used to attach media connectors to the ends of cables. A toner probe has two parts: the tone generator (called the toner) and the tone locator (called the probe). The toner sends the tone, and at the other end of the cable, the probe receives the toner's signal. This tool makes it easier to find the beginning and end of a cable.

24. D. A toner probe has two parts: the tone generator (called the toner) and the tone locator (called the probe). The toner sends the tone, and at the other end of the cable, the probe receives the toner's signal. This tool makes it easier to find the beginning and end of a cable. Wire crimpers look like pliers but are used to attach media connectors to the ends of cables. A cable stripper is used to remove the cable's outer covering to get to the wire pairs within. A PoE injector is a device that can be used to provide PoE to a device when the switch does not support PoE. It plugs into the wall, then a line providing data and PoE is run to the device, and another cable runs to the switch.

Chapter 3: Hardware

1. C. Twisted pair (TP) is commonly used in office settings to connect workstations to hubs or switches. It comes in two varieties: unshielded (UTP) and shielded (STP). Fiber optic, serial, and coaxial do not come in shielded and unshielded versions.

2. B. Cat 5 transmits data at speeds up to 100 Mbps and was used with Fast Ethernet (operating at 100 Mbps) with a transmission range of 100 meters. It contains four twisted pairs of copper wire to give the most protection. Although it had its share of popularity (it's used primarily for 10/100 Ethernet networking), it is now an outdated standard. Newer implementations use the 5e standard. Cat 4 transmits at 16 Mbps, and Cat 6 transmits at 1 Gbps.

3. A. Fiber-optic cabling is the most expensive type of those discussed for this exam. Although it's an excellent medium, it's often not used because of the cost of implementing it. It has a glass core within a rubber outer coating and uses beams of light rather than electrical signals to relay data. None of the other options uses glass in its construction.

4. A. An RJ-11 is a standard connector for a telephone line and is used to connect to a DSL modem and landline phones. It looks much like an RJ-45 but is noticeably smaller. The RJ-45 is used for networking. RS-232 is a serial connector. BNC is a coaxial connector.

5. A. An RJ-11 is a standard connector for a telephone landline and is used to connect to a DSL modem. It looks much like an RJ-45 but is noticeably smaller. The RJ-45 is used for networking. BNC is a coaxial connector. The RS-232 standard has been commonly used in computer serial ports. A serial cable (and port) uses only one wire to carry data in each direction; all the rest are wires for signaling and traffic control.

6. B. The RJ-45 is used for networking. Bayonet Neill-Concelman (BNC) connectors are sometimes used in place of RCA connectors for video electronics, so you might encounter these connectors, especially when video equipment connects to a PC. In many cases, you might be required to purchase an adapter to convert this to another form of connection because it is rare to find one on a PC. An RJ-11 is a standard connector for a telephone landline and is used to connect to a DSL modem. It looks much like an RJ-45 but is noticeably smaller. RS-232 is a serial connector.

7. B. Small outline DIMM (SoDIMM) RAM is used in portable computers (i.e. laptops, notebooks, and subnotebooks), which require smaller sticks of RAM because of their smaller size. SoDIMM can have 72, 144, or 200 pins. Dual inline memory module (DIMM) is a full-size RAM type. Rambus is a type of RAM but not used in laptops, and Bayonet Neill-Concelman (BNC) is a connector for coaxial cabling.

8. D. Double data rate synchronous dynamic random-access memory (DDR SDRAM) is double data rate 2 (DDR2). This allows for two memory accesses for each rising and falling clock and effectively doubles the speed of DDR. DDR2-667 chips work with speeds at 667 MHz and are also referred to as PC2-5300 modules. DDR3 is the higher-speed successor to DDR and DDR2. Portable computers (i.e. notebooks and subnotebooks) require smaller sticks of RAM because of their smaller size. One of the two types is small outline DIMM (SoDIMM), which can have 72, 144, or 200 pins.

9. B. DDR4 SDRAM is an abbreviation for double data rate fourth-generation synchronous dynamic random-access memory. DDR4 is not compatible with any earlier type of RAM. The DDR4 standard allows for dual inline memory modules (DIMMs) of up to 64 GB in capacity, compared to DDR3's maximum of 16 GB per DIMM. DDR3 and DDR2 are backward-compatible, and there is no DDR5.

10. B. Compact Disc-ReWritable (CD-RW) media is a rewritable optical disc. A CD-RW drive requires more sensitive laser optics. It can write data to the disc but also has the ability to erase that data and write more data to the disc. CD, DVD, and CD-ROM are all read-only.

11. A. M.2, formerly known as the Next Generation Form Factor (NGFF), is a specification for internally mounted computer expansion cards and associated connectors. It replaces the mSATA standard. M.2 modules are rectangular, with an edge connector on one side and a semicircular mounting hole at the center of the opposite edge. Non-Volatile Express (NVMe) is an open logical device interface specification for accessing nonvolatile storage media attached via a PCI Express (PCIe) bus. Serial ATA and Serial ATA 2.5 are computer bus interfaces that connect host bus adapters to mass storage devices, such as hard disk drives, optical drives, and solid-state drives.

12. **C.** At 10,000 rpm, the latency will decrease to about 3 ms. Data transfer rates also generally go up with a higher rotational speed but are influenced by the density of the disk (i.e. the number of tracks and sectors present in a given area). Latency at 5,400 rpm will be 5.56 ms. At 7,200, it will be 4.17, and at 15,000 it will drop to 2.

13. **A.** Laptops and other portable devices utilize an expansion card called a mini PCI. It has the same functionality as the PCI but has a much smaller form factor. PCI and PCIe are used in desktops. Serial Advanced Technology Attachment (SATA) is a drive connector.

14. **A.** Unified Extensible Firmware Interface (UEFI) is a standard firmware interface for PCs, designed to replace Basic Input/Output System (BIOS). Non-volatile random-access memory (NVRAM) is RAM that retains its data during a reboot. Complementary metal-oxide semiconductor (CMOS) is a battery type found on motherboards, and cylinders/heads/sectors (CHS) is a drive geometry concept.

15. **A.** The pins in the printhead are wrapped with coils of wire to create a solenoid and are held in the rest position by a combination of a small magnet and a spring. To trigger a particular pin, the printer controller sends a signal to the printhead, which energizes the wires around the appropriate print wire. This turns the print wire into an electromagnet, which repels the print pin, forcing it against the ink ribbon and making a dot on the paper.

16. **B.** The heating element for a thermal printer is what generates the heat and does the actual printing. It is often the most expensive component.

17. **C.** Calibration ensures proper alignment. When a printer gets out of calibration, the print quality will decline. When a new cartridge is loaded, the printer will usually perform a calibration, but you might need to do this manually from time to time, especially on printers that are not used often enough to require a cartridge change as often as a calibration may be required.

18. **D.** There can be damage to the drum or charging roller, and if there is, replacing the cartridge will help with the problem.

19. **C.** In 2004, the ATX 12V 2.0 (now 2.03) standard was passed, changing the main connector from 20 pins to 24. The additional pins provide +3.3V, +5V, and +12V (the fourth pin is a ground) for use by PCIe cards. When a 24-pin connector is used, there is no need for the optional 4- or 6-pin auxiliary power connectors.

20. **D.** Testing the power supply is *not* part of regular maintenance. Replacing the toner, applying the maintenance kit, cleaning, and calibrating are all part of maintenance.

21. **C.** The SATA power connector consists of 15 pins, with 3 pins designated for 3.3V, 5V, and 12V, and with each pin carrying 1.5 amps. This results in a total draw of 4.95 watts + 7.5 watts + 18 watts, or about 30 watts.

22. **A.** First, verify that there is toner in the cartridge. If it's an old cartridge, you can often shake it slightly to free up toner once before replacing it.

23. A. RAID 0 is also known as *disk striping*. This is technically not RAID because it doesn't provide fault tolerance. Data is written across multiple drives, so one drive can be reading or writing while the next drive's read/write head is moving. This makes for faster data access.

24. B. This applies a uniform positive charge (about +600V) to the paper. When the paper rotates past the drum, the toner is pulled off the drum and onto the paper. Then the paper passes through a static eliminator that removes the positive charge from it. Some printers use a transfer corona wire, while others use a transfer corona roller.

25. B. Print jobs can also be submitted through the SMB protocol. The SMB printing function is used to print data by directly specifying this machine on the computer.

26. C. In some cases, you are printing a document that is so secure that random users visiting the printer to pick up their finished print jobs cannot see it. Many printers have the ability to hold the print job until you enter a PIN that releases the job to be printed while you physically monitor the process. These are called secure prints.

27. C. When printing with a Bluetooth-enabled device (such as mobile phone) and a Bluetooth-enabled printer, all you need to do is get within range of the device (i.e. move closer), select the print driver from the device, and choose Print.

28. A. When you install a printer driver for the printer you are using, it allows the computer to print to that printer correctly, assuming you have the correct interface configured between the computer and printer. Also, keep in mind that drivers are OS-specific, so you need to select the one that is for both the correct printer and the correct OS.

29. B. An optional component that can be added to printers (usually laser but also inkjet) is a duplexer. This can be an optional assembly added to the printer or built into it, but the sole purpose of duplexing is to turn the printed sheet over so it can be run back through the printer and allow printing on both sides.

30. C. The orientation of a document refers to how the printed matter is laid out on the page. In landscape orientation, the printing is written across the paper turned on its long side, while in portrait the paper is turned up vertically and printed on from top to bottom. The driver is the software that communicates between the printer and the OS. Duplexing makes it possible to print on both sides. To collate is to create multiple copies with all sets in correct page order.

31. A. Continuous-feed paper feeds through the printer using a system of sprockets and tractors. Sheet-fed printers accept plain paper in a paper tray. Impact is a printer type, not a paper type. Thermal printers are continuously fed through a roll but do not use a system of sprockets and tractors.

32. B. In a laser printer, never reuse paper that has been through the printer once. Although it might look blank, you're repeating the charging and fusing process on a piece of paper that most likely has something already on it.

33. A. The printer controller is a large circuit board that acts as the motherboard for the printer. It contains the processor and RAM to convert data coming in from the computer into a picture of a page to be printed. The imaging drum is the drum where the toner is placed on the correctly charged area. The toner cartridge is the container holding the toner. The maintenance kit contains items that should be changed periodically.

Chapter 4: Virtualization and Cloud Computing

1. **B.** Software as a Service (SaaS) involves the vendor providing the entire solution. This includes the operating system, the infrastructure software, and the application. Infrastructure as a Service (IaaS) provides only the hardware platform to the customer. Platform as a Service (PaaS) provides a development environment. Security Information and Event Management (SIEM) is a system that aggregates all log files and analyzes them in real time for attacks.

2. **A.** When a company pays another company to host and manage a cloud environment, it is called a public cloud solution. If the company hosts this environment itself, it is a private cloud solution. A hybrid cloud solution is one in which both public and private clouds are part of the solution. A community cloud is one in which multiple entities use the cloud.

3. **B.** One of the advantages of a cloud environment is the ability to add resources as needed on the fly and release those resources when they are no longer required. This makes for more efficient use of resources, placing them where needed at any particular point in time. These include CPU and memory resources. This is called rapid elasticity because it occurs automatically according to the rules for resource sharing that have been deployed. On-demand refers to the ability of the customer to add resources as needed. Virtual sharing and stretched resources are not terms used when discussing the cloud.

4. **A.** There are three models for implementing VDI:

   Centralized model: All desktop instances are stored in a single server, requiring significant processing power on the server.

   Hosted model: Desktops are maintained by a service provider. This model eliminates capital cost and is instead subject to operation cost.

   Remote virtual desktops model: An image is copied to the local machine, making a constant network connection unnecessary.

   There is no local model.

5. **C.** Platform as a Service (PaaS) involves the vendor providing the hardware platform and the software running on the platform. This includes the operating system and infrastructure software. The company is still involved in managing the system. Software as a Service (SaaS) involves the vendor providing the entire solution. This includes the operating system, the infrastructure software, and the application. Infrastructure as a Service (IaaS) provides only the hardware platform to the customer. Data as a service (DaaS) is a business model where data is made available on demand and regardless of the consumer's location or infrastructure.

6. A. Some of the virtualization products, however (e.g. Microsoft's Hyper-V, Windows 7 Virtual PC, and Windows 8 Client Hyper-V), require that the motherboard support hardware-assisted virtualization. The benefit derived from using hardware-assisted virtualization is it reduces overhead and improves performance. It does not improve security, lower power consumption, or ease troubleshooting.

7. B. The hypervisor is the software that allows the VMs to exist. Dual in-line memory module (DIMM) is a type of memory. There is no software called Azureware, and NAT is a service that translates private IP addresses to public ones.

8. A. Infrastructure as a Service (IaaS) provides only the hardware platform to the customer. Software as a Service (SaaS) involves the vendor providing the entire solution. This includes the operating system, the infrastructure software, and the application. Platform as a Service (PaaS) provides a development environment. Security Information and Event Management (SIEM) is a system that aggregates all log files and analyzes them in real time for attacks.

9. A. Virtual desktop infrastructures (VDIs) host desktop operating systems within a virtual environment in a centralized server. Users access the desktops and run them from the server.

10. D. Hypervisors (Type 1) interact directly with the hardware. While VMware vSphere is a Type 1, the other options are Type 2.

Chapter 5: Hardware and Network Troubleshooting

1. B. The steps are as follows:
    1. Identify the problem.
    2. Establish a theory of probable cause (question the obvious).
    3. Test the theory to determine cause.
    4. Establish a plan of action to resolve the problem and implement the solution.
    5. Verify full system functionality and, if applicable, implement preventive measures.
    6. Document findings, actions, and outcomes.
2. D. The steps are as follows:
    1. Identify the problem.
    2. Establish a theory of probable cause (question the obvious).
    3. Test the theory to determine cause.
    4. Establish a plan of action to resolve the problem and implement the solution.
    5. Verify full system functionality and, if applicable, implement preventive measures.
    6. Document findings, actions, and outcomes.

Chapter 5: Hardware and Network Troubleshooting 617

3. A. One common reason for shutdowns is overheating. Often when that is the case, however, the system reboots itself rather than just shutting down.

4. D. A bad network interface card (NIC) driver would cause the NIC not to work but would not cause a system lockup.

5. B. Once a regular occurrence when working with Windows, blue screens (also known as the blue screen of death [BSOD]) have become much less frequent.

6. A. While Microsoft users have the blue screen of death (BSOD) to deal with, Apple users have also come to have the same negative feelings about the pinwheel of death. This is a multicolored pinwheel mouse pointer that appears when a crash has occurred.

7. A. Pixels are the small dots on the screen that are filled with a color; as a group, they present the image you see on the screen.

8. C. While an incorrect subnet mask will make networking impossible, it does not cause sluggish system performance. Sluggish performance can be caused by many different issues, including the following:

- Malware consumes resources and may cause it.
- A full system drive can cause slow performance.
- Drive fragmentation will slow performance.
- Insufficient RAM can cause slow performance.
- Overheating is occurring.
- Outdated drivers and software need to be updated.
- Pirated software is being used.

9. A. The backlight is the light in the device that powers the LCD screen. It can go bad over time and need to be replaced, and it can also be held captive by the inverter. The inverter takes the DC power the laptop is providing and boosts it up to AC to run the backlight. If the inverter goes bad, you can replace it on most models. (It's cheaper than the backlight.)

10. B. Touch flow, or TouchFLO, is a user interface feature designed by HTC. It is used by dragging your finger up and down or left and right to access common tasks on the screen. This movement is akin to scrolling the screen up and down or scrolling the screen left and right.

11. B. With laser printers, streaks usually indicate that the fuser is not fusing the toner properly on the paper. It could also be that the incorrect paper is being used. In laser printers, you can sometimes tell the printer that you are using a heavier paper. For a dot-matrix printer, you can adjust the platen for thicker paper.

12. C. In laser printers, faded output usually indicates that the toner cartridge is just about empty. You can usually remove it, shake it, and replace it, and then get a bit more life out of it before it is completely empty. It is a signal, however, that you are near the end.

13. B. You might be able to ping the entire network using IP addresses, but most access is done by name, not by IP address. If you can't ping resources by name, the Domain Name Server

(DNS) is not functional, meaning either the DNS server is down or the local machine is not configured with the correct IP address of the DNS server.

14. C. If the computer cannot connect to the default gateway, it will be confined to communicating with devices on the local network. This IP address should be that of the router interface connecting to the local network.

Chapter 6: Operating Systems

1. D. Windows 10 Home is the only system listed that cannot be a member of a domain.

2. A. The md command is the shorthand version of the mkdir command and is used to create a new folder. Its syntax is md [<drive>:]<path>.

3. B. This tool lets you shut down nonresponsive applications selectively in all Windows versions. In current versions of Windows, it can do much more easily. Task Manager allows you to see which processes and applications are using the most system resources, view network usage, see connected users, and so on.

4. C. As the name implies, from this tab you can configure connections for an Internet connection, a dial-up or VPN connection, and LAN settings.

5. D. The Recovery section of Update and Security contains settings to reset the PC and to boot to advanced options when there are boot issues.

6. A. In Windows 10 when you make a new connection, you are asked to identify whether it is a private or public network. If you choose the private, network discovery is on by default, allowing you to see other computers and other computers to see you. If you choose Public, network discovery is turned off.

7. B The dir command is simply used to view a listing of the files and folders that exist within a directory, subdirectory, or folder.

8. C. The change directory (cd) command is used to move to another folder or directory. It is used in both Linux and Windows.

9. A. Device Manager shows a list of all installed hardware and lets you add and remove items, update drivers, and more.

10. B. Every program and process theoretically could have its own logging utility, but Microsoft has come up with a rather slick utility, Event Viewer, that tracks all events on a particular Windows computer through log files.

11. D. Force Quit can be used on a Mac to stop an unresponsive application. To use this function, follow these steps:
    1. Choose Force Quit from the Apple menu or press Command+Option+Esc.

    2. Select the unresponsive app in the Force Quit Applications window and then click Force Quit.

12. B. Differences between 64-bit and 32-bit systems include their hardware requirements and the types of applications you can run on them. You can run a 32-bit application on either a 64-bit or a 32-bit operating system, but you can run 64-bit applications only on a 64-bit system.

13. A. The minimum of RAM required should be viewed as just that, a minimum. Make sure you have more than required for satisfactory performance.

14. C. Outside of a large corporate enterprise, most installations occur by using the CD that came with the software or by placing these same files on a USB stick and accessing them from the USB drive.

15. C. Many proprietary operating systems that reside on devices such as access points, switches, routers, and firewalls are Linux-based. Linux systems also predominate in the software development area.

16. A. `net use` can also be used to connect to a shared printer: `net use lpt1: \printername`.

17. A. In Linux, a `shell` is a command-line interface.

18. B. In Apple, Mission Control provides a quick way to see everything that's currently open on your Mac

Chapter 7: Security

1. A. A mantrap is a series of two doors with a small room between them. The user is authenticated at the first door and then allowed into the room. At that point, additional verification will occur (such as a guard visually identifying the person), and then the person is allowed through the second door. A trapdoor is a doorway that is usually hidden. A saferoom is a room that is impenetrable from outside, and badgetrap is not a term used when discussing doorway systems.

2. B. Biometric devices use physical characteristics to identify the user. Such devices are becoming more common in the business environment. Biometric systems include hand scanners, retinal scanners, and, possibly soon, DNA scanners. Hardware tokens are devices that contain security credentials. Smart cards are cards that contain a chip and credentials. Badge readers are devices that read the information on a card and allow or disallow entry.

3. C. IP address filtering is the type of filtering done on a router or firewall, based on IP addresses. As physical addresses are MAC addresses, MAC address filtering is the not the correct answer. Email filtering is the filtering of email addresses from which one is allowed to receive mail. URL filtering restricts the URLs that can be reached with the browser.

4. C. Hash values, also referred to as message digests, are calculated using the original message. A hash function takes a message of variable length and produces a fixed-length hash value. If the receiver calculates a hash value that is the same, then the original message is intact. If the receiver calculates a hash value that is different, then the original message has been altered.

5. D. Wired Equivalent Privacy (WEP) is a standard that was created as a first stab at security for wireless devices. Using WEP-encrypted data to provide data security has always been under scrutiny for not being as secure as initially intended. Wi-Fi Protected Access (WPA) and WPA2 are later methods that came after WEP. Temporal Key Integrity Protocol is the encryption method used in WPA.

6. A. WPA was able to increase security by using a Temporal Key Integrity Protocol (TKIP) to scramble encryption keys using a hashing algorithm. TKIP is the encryption method used in Wi-Fi Protected Access (WPA). Advanced Encryption Standard (AES) is the encryption used in WPA2. Internet Protocol Security (IPSec) is an industry-standard encryption method, and Secure Sockets Layer (SSL) is an encryption method used in many VPNs.

7. C. An armored virus is designed to make itself difficult to detect or analyze. Armored viruses cover themselves with protective code that stops debuggers or disassemblers from examining critical elements of the virus. A companion virus is one that attaches to a file or adopts the name of a file. A macro virus is one that hides in macros, and a multipartite virus is one that has multiple propagation methods.

8. B. A signature is an algorithm or other element of a virus that uniquely identifies it. Because some viruses have the ability to alter their signature, it is crucial that you keep signature files current, whether you choose to manually download them or configure the antivirus engine to do so automatically. An ID is any type of identifying badge or marker. A badge is something worn to provide identification. Marking is not a word typically used when discussing algorithms or attacks.

9. C. Tailgating is the term used for someone being so close to you when you enter a building that they are able to come in right behind you without needing to use a key, a card, or any other security device. Many social-engineering intruders needing physical access to a site will use this method of gaining entry. Shadowing is when one user monitors another for training. Spoofing is the adoption of another's email address, IP address, or MAC address. Keyriding is not a word typically used when discussing social engineering.

10. B. Spoofing is the process of masquerading as another user or device. It is usually done for the purpose of accessing a resource to which the hacker should not have access, or to get through a security device such as a firewall that may be filtering traffic based on source IP address. Shadowing is when one user monitors another for training. Duplication is the creation of a matching object. Masking is not a term used when discussing impersonation.

11. A. The Power Users group is not as powerful as the Administrators group. Membership in this group gives read/write permission to the system, allowing members to install most software but keeping them from changing key operating system files. This is a good group for those who need to test software (such as programmers) and junior administrators. The Guests group is used to allow restricted access to the device. The Administrators group allows full access to the device. The rights held by the Users group are a compromise between Admin and Guest.

12. B. Full Control allows everything.

13. D. Although length is now considered the most important password security factor, complexity is also a factor, and these examples are all the same length. The password P@ssw0rd contains four character types, the most of any of the options, which increases the strength of the password. Password and pAssword contains only two types of characters. Pa$$word contains three types.

14. B. When assigning user permissions, follow the principle of least privilege by giving users only the bare minimum they need to do their job. Separation of duties prescribes that any operation prone to fraud should be broken up into two operations with different users performing each. Job rotation has the same goal but accomplishes it by requiring users to move around from job to job. Open rights is not a term used when discussing permission and rights.

15. C. Swipe locks use a gesture or series of gestures, sometimes involving the movement of an icon to open the screen. In some cases, they require only knowledge of the mobile platform in use; they offer no security to the process because no authentication of the user is occurring. Fingerprint locks open when the correct fingerprint is presented. Facial locks require a matching face scan to open. Passcode locks require the configured passcode to unlock.

16. A. Remote wipe gives you the ability to delete all content when a device is stolen or lost. Geofencing allows you to restrict use of the device to a geographic area. Screen locks prevent access to the home screen on the device. Segmentation of data is the separation of personal data from enterprise data on a device.

17. A. Degaussing involves applying a strong magnetic field to wipe the media (also referred to as disk wiping). This process helps ensure that information doesn't fall into the wrong hands. Incineration is the burning of the storage device. Hammers can be used to destroy the device. Deleting is the least effective way of removing information.

18. B. Physically destroying the drive involves rendering the component no longer usable.

19. B. Wi-Fi protected setup (WPS) was a concept that was designed to make it easier for less knowledgeable users to add a new client to the WLAN without manually entering the security information on the client. One method involves pushing a button on the access point (AP) at the same time a client is attempting to join the network, so that the settings are sent to the client. Other methods involve placing the client close to the AP, and near-field communication is used for the process. Service set identifier (SSID) is the name of the WLAN. Wired Equivalent Privacy (WEP) and Wi-Fi Protected Access (WPA) are wireless security protocols.

20. A. Every wireless access point (AP) or wireless router on the market comes with a default service set identifier (SSID). Cisco models use the name tsunami, for example. You should change these defaults and create a new SSID to represent your WLAN. Wi-Fi protected setup (WPS) was a concept that was designed to make it easier for less knowledgeable users to add a new client to the WLAN, without manually entering the security information on the client. One method involves pushing a button on the AP at the same time a client is attempting to join the network, so that the settings are sent to the client. Other methods involve placing the client close to the AP, and near-field communication is used for the process. Wired Equivalent Privacy (WEP) and Wi-Fi Protected Access (WPA) are wireless security protocols.

Chapter 8: Software Troubleshooting

1. A. Although all of these can cause sluggish performance, the first thing to check for is the presence of a virus. If the system seems to have an overabundance of disk activity, scan it for viruses using a virus program that resides externally on a memory stick.

2. D. When network connectivity is an issue, you should answer the following about your configuration:
   - Is the IP address in the same network as the default gateway address?
   - Is the subnet mask correct?
   - Is the default gateway address correct?
   - If this is all correct, has the interface been enabled?
   - If this is all correct, is it time to check the settings on the router?

3. C. The steps are:
   1. Investigate and verify malware symptoms.
   2. Quarantine infected systems.
   3. Disable System Restore in Windows.
   4. Remediate infected systems.
   5. Schedule scans and run updates.
   6. Enable System Restore and create a restore point in Windows.
   7. Educate the end user.

4. D. Lack of permissions will not generate this error. The following issues can:
   - Incorrect boot device order in the BIOS
   - Corrupted or missing boot sector
   - Corrupted boot files

5. D. Overheating is usually a hardware issue rather than a malware issue. However, malware causing runaway central processing usage might cause overheating.

6. B. Browser redirection is one of the most serious security problems. Browser hijacking software is external code that changes your browser settings. It may include changing your home page or adding or removing items from your favorites. An on-path attack is when the malicious individual positions themself between two communicating systems, receiving all

data. A SYN flood is a form of a denial-of-service (DoS) attack. Fraggle is an attack using User Datagram Protocol (UDP) packets.

7. A. Malware never increases performance.

8. D. The steps are as follows:
   1. Identify and research malware symptoms.
   2. Quarantine the infected systems.
   3. Disable System Restore (in Windows).
   4. Remediate the infected systems.
   5. Schedule scans and run updates.
   6. Enable System Restore and create a restore point (in Windows).
   7. Educate the end user.

9. B. Although it is recommended that you disable System Restore before cleaning an infection, it is a good idea to create a restore point after an infection is cleaned. This gives you a clean restore point going forward in case the system becomes infected again at some point. Network address translation (NAT), the Windows Firewall, and your antivirus should not be disabled.

10. A. A low brightness setting does not negatively impact battery life. A high setting, however, does. Location services, Bluetooth, and overheating do not negatively affect battery life.

11. B. While leaving the phone on will run down the battery, it alone will not cause the phone to overheat. Excessive gaming, using an old battery, and continuous online browsing will cause overheating.

12. D. On the contrary, evidence of malware or other issues is usually accompanied by very high resource utilization. Unusual loss of power, slow speeds, and a weak signal are all signs of security issues.

13. C. When cameras have been enabled when they weren't previously, it is an indication of compromise. Low resource utilization, a disabled microphone, and authorized use of the device are not symptoms of a security issue.

Chapter 9: Operational Procedures

1. D. While the operating system (OS) might be important, for warranty issues, these other pieces are more important. The make, model, and serial number are all important.

2. C. All costs and effects of the implementation methods should be reviewed prior to formal approval. The other statements are true.

3. A. During the change management process, the relative costs and benefits to the overall organization will be weighed by a change management board or team. Acceptable use is a policy that defines what users can and cannot do. Separation of duties is a concept where any operation prone to fraud should be broken into two jobs and assigned to two people. Risk analysis is a process that identifies risk and mitigations.

4. A. Creating levels or tiers of technicians with an increasing amount of knowledge and experience is a best practice. This offers two benefits. It encourages a faster solution by preventing issues from remaining unresolved due to a lack of skill by the responding technician, and it frees up more experienced technicians to deal with more serious issues.

5. B. Because an incremental backup backs up everything that has changed since the last backup of any type, each day's tape is unique, so you will need the Monday full backup and the incremental tapes from Tuesday and Wednesday.

6. C. Because a differential backup backs up everything that has changed since the last full backup, each day's incremental tape contains what was on the previous day's tape. So, you need only the last differential and the last full backup.

7. A. Lift with your legs, not your back. When you have to pick something up, bend at the knees, not at the waist. The other options are all safety recommendations.

8. A. A is for wood and paper fires, B is for flammable liquids, C is for electrical fires, and D is for metal fires.

9. B. Any type of chemical, equipment, or supply that has the potential to harm the environment or people must have a material safety data sheet (MSDS) associated with it. These are traditionally created by the manufacturer, and you can obtain them from the manufacturer or from the Environmental Protection Agency (EPA). A statement of work (SOW) is a document that indicates the work to be performed. A service-level agreement (SLA) is a document that indicates what is being paid and what the service is. A memorandum of understanding (MOU) is a document that indicates the intent of two parties to do something together.

10. A. Maintain the relative humidity at around 50%. Be careful not to increase the humidity too far—to the point where moisture starts to condense on the equipment!

11. A. You should *not* shut down the system until evidence such as memory contents is gathered.

12. B. Secure Shell (SSH) is an encrypted alternative when connecting to a device from the command line.

13. B. If you're providing phone support, make a concentrated effort to ascertain the customer's technical level and communicate at that level, not above or below it.

14. A. You should use appropriate professional titles, when applicable, and never take personal calls, use the customer's equipment for personal messages, or talk to coworkers while interacting with customers.

15. D. A .py file is one written in the Python language. Python runs on Windows, macOS, and Linux/UNIX. A .vbs file is a Visual Basic file. An .sh file is a script programmed for Bash, a type of UNIX shell.

16. B. This is why maintaining the serial number of each device is important—because that is how you will access your warranty services when needed.

17. D. If you don't need access to the graphical interface and you just want to operate at the command line, you have two options: Telnet and SSH. While Telnet works just fine, it transmits all the data in clear text, which obviously would be security issue. Remote Desktop and screen sharing are graphical concepts, while file sharing is not a command-line utility.

18. C. While Telnet works just fine, it transmits all the data in clear text, which obviously would be a security issue. Remote Desktop and screen sharing are graphical concepts that can be secured, while Secure Shell (SSH) is an encrypted technology.

Index

Please note that page numbers referring to Figures are followed by the letter '*f*', while references to Tables are followed by the letter '*t*'.

A

AAA (authentication, authorization, and accounting), 62, 65, 438, 457, 458
AC (alternating current), 105, 162
access control vestibule (mantrap), 427, 428*f*
access token, 321
accessories, mobile devices, 18–29
    docking station, 18, 27, 28, 29
    headsets, 23
    installation, 25
    port replicator, 27, 28
    replacement, 25–6
    speakers, 23–4, 25*f*, 26
    stylus, 23
    use of, 29
    volume settings, 24
    webcam, 16, 27
account expiration dates, 485
account management, 484–5
accounting, 62, 175, 458, 558
ACLs (access control lists), 69, 436, 445
acoustical detection systems, 430
Active Directory Recycle Bin, 301
active heat sink, 159
AD (Active Directory)
    directory services, 439
    domain, 297, 323, 366, 375
    function, 452
    Lightweight Extensible Authentication Protocol, 52
    policy enforcement, 34
    security settings, configuring/applying, 452–5
    SSO, 444
ad blockers, 506
adapters, 117–18
    AC adapter, 105, 162
    DVI to HDMI, 118
    DVI to VGA, 118
    USB to Ethernet, 118, 119*f*
address A *see* IP4 address (A)
address AAAA *see* IP6 address (AAAA)
ADF (automatic document feeder)/flatbed scanner, 168
administrative drives, default, 367
administrative privileges, 325
administrative shares, 366–7
    vs. local shares, 450
Administrative Tools, 342, 344–6*t*
Administrators group, 272, 281, 282, 454
Advanced Network Settings, 12, 14*f*
adware, 466
AES (Advanced Encryption Standard), 55, 456, 457
AGP (Accelerated Graphics Port), 133, 157, 157*f*
AI (artificial intelligence)
    accuracy, 602
    application integration, 600
    appropriate use, 601
    bias, 601
    data security, 603
    hallucinations, 602
    limitations of, 601–2
    plagiarism, avoiding, 601
    policy, 600–1
    private vs. public, 602–3
air filtration mask, 573
Airplane mode, 220, 362, 531

Index

alarm systems/motion sensors, 530
alkaline batteries, 574
AMD (Advanced Micro Devices), 149–50t
Android devices, 26, 30, 31, 34, 36–9,
    221, 487–90
  Chrome OS *see* Google Chrome
  Google, Android OS from, 256
  Lost Android app, 489, 490
  operating system, 221, 256
  pairing, finding device for, 31–2
  patch management, OS updates, 488–9
antennae, 16, 21, 498
  disconnecting, in wireless card, 12–13
anti-malware software, updating, 480
antistatic bags, 570, 572
antistatic mats, 569, 570, 570f
antistatic wrist strap, 569, 573
antivirus, 478, 538
  malware prevention, 468–9
  updates, 378, 489
  see also malware
APFS (Apple File System), 258
APIPA (Automatic Private IP
    Addressing), 82, 227
APIs (application programming
    interfaces), 256
APK (Android Package Kit), 533
Apple, 20
  App Store, 34, 259, 376, 488
  Apple CarPlay, 36
  Apple Configurator, 33
  Apple File System *see* APFS (Apple
    File System)
applications 408, 490, 600
  crashes, 208, 520–1
  distribution methods
    downloadable package, 406
    image deployment, 406–7
    ISO-mountable, 406, 407f
    local, 406
    network-based, 406
    physical media vs. mountable
      ISO file, 406
  impact considerations for new apps, 407–8
  installing according to requirements, 595
    32.bit vs. 64-bit, 404, 405
    CPU, 405
    dedicated vs. integrated graph-
      ics card, 404
    distribution methods, 406–7
    OS compatibility, 405
    RAM, 405
    system requirements, 404–5
    VRAM, 405
  troubleshooting
    failing to close/crashing, 528
    failing to install, 529
    failing to update, 528–9
    failure to launch, 528
  virtualization *see* virtualization
App-V (Application Virtualization),
    Microsoft, 186
APs (access points), 56, 62, 72, 227
  evil twin, 473, 474
  and LAN network, 86, 87
  Linux-based, 256, 390
  rogue, 473, 474
  wireless access points, 456, 458, 485
APT (Advanced Package Tool), 396
AR (augmented reality), 23
archives, 284, 585
  backups, 378, 564
ARM (Advanced RISC Machine), 155
ARP (Address Resolution Protocol),
    76, 475, 582
asset management
  asset tags and IDs, 556
  assigned users, 557
  barcodes, 556
  centralized software, 413
  importance, 559
  inventory lists, 555
  procurement life cycle, 556
  warranty and licensing, 556–7
asset tags and IDs, barcodes, 556

ATA (Advanced Technology Attachment) drives, 116, 117, 138
attributes
    advanced, 452, 453f
    biometrics, 433
    displays, 105–6
    file and folder, 447–8
ATX (Advanced Technology Extended), 142
audio issues, 218
audit logs, 167
AUP (acceptable use policy), 585–6
authentication, 14, 15, 34, 39, 52, 68, 167, 228, 230
    fingerprint, 14, 15–16
    multifactor, 39, 436–8
    protocols, 70, 71
    RADIUS/TACACS+, 457–8
    single-factor, 436
    three-factor, 437
    two-factor, 436–7, 458
    wireless networking protocols, 457–9
authentication server, 434, 458
authorization, 457, 458
    see also AAA (authentication, authorization, and accounting)
AutoRun, disabling, 485–6
Azure Virtual Desktop, 272

B

backlight, 103, 104, 218
backups, 490, 564–7
    archives, 378, 564
    off-site storage, 566–7
    rotation schemes, 565–8
    3-2-1 rule, 568
    Time Machine tool, 378
    upgrade considerations, 268
badge reader, 429
badging, 167
barcodes, 471, 556
bare-metal hypervisors, 189

baseband LAN, 86
batteries, 6, 207, 220, 574
    battery life issues, 220, 530
    complementary metal-oxide semiconductor, 153, 210, 214, 523, 523f
    monitoring and maintaining, 5–7
    nickel cadmium (NiCd), 222
    simulated, 222
    swollen, 220
BD-RE (Blu-ray Disc Recordable Erasable), 140
BEC (business email compromise), 477
beep codes, 201, 202
best practices
    end-user, 483–4
    macOS/desktop OS 378, 379, 379f
    recycling/repurposing, 493–4
    updates, 378
bezel, display, 16
bias, 601, 602
biometrics, 14–16
    fingerprint scanner, 433–4
BIOS/UEFI settings, 8, 151, 201, 210, 213, 217
    boot options, 152–4
    passwords, 153, 483
    TPM security features, 152
    UEFI replacing BIOS, 275
    USB permissions, 152
BitLocker
    data-at-rest encryption, 481
    encryption, 273, 451
    FileVault, 388
    security settings, configuring/ applying, 450–1
    Trusted Platform Module, 152, 154, 273, 450
    Windows 10 Home edition, 270
BitLocker Drive Encryption Control Panel, 451, 452f
BitLocker to Go, 451
blackout, 578
blank display, 226

Index

blank paper, 173, 234
blank screen, 206–7, 210
blue screen of death *see* BSOD (blue screen of death)
Bluetooth, 12, 21, 36, 57
    connection methods, mobile devices, 22–3
    connectivity issues, 164, 531
    disabling/enabling, 31, 223
    finding device for pairing, 31–2
    iOS devices, 31, 32, 40
    mobile device network connectivity and application support, 31–2
    poor connectivity, 223
    speeds, 22*t*
Blu-ray
    BD-R and BD-RE formats, 141
    Bonus View, 140
    optical drives, 139
BNC (Bayonet Neill–Concelman) connectors, 88, 107, 109*f*
bollards, 427, 428*f*
booting the system
    boot methods, 260–1
    boot sector virus, 465
    bootable device not found message, 212
    external/hot-swappable drive, 261
    internal hard drive (partition), 261
    Internet-based methods, 260–1
    multiboot system, 261
    NetBoot, 260
    Preboot Execution Environment, 260
    random reboots, 530–1
    safe mode, 222
    slow bootup, 519–20
    solid-state/flash drives, 260
    troubleshooting of issues, 519–20
    universal serial bus, 260
BOOTP (Bootstrap Protocol), 68
bricking of device, 153
broadband, 13, 30, 85, 86, 110
broken screen, 221–2
brownout, 578

browser feature management, 507–9, 509*f*
browser-related symptoms, 539–41
    random/frequent pop-ups, 539, 540*f*
    redirection, 540, 541
browsers, clearing, 505
browsers, configuring security settings, 502–9
    browser feature management, 507–9
    description of settings, 504–7
    downloads and installations, 502–3
    trusted vs. untrusted sources, 502–3
brute-force attack, 475
BSOD (blue screen of death), 204, 210, 527
    error code, 202, 203*f*, 518
    error messages
        Data_Bus_Error, 203
        irq1_not_less_or_equal, 204
        Page_Fault_in_nonpaged_area, 203
        Unexpected_Kernel_Mode_Trap, 203
    frequent shutdowns, 520
    proprietary crash screens, 202–4
    troubleshooting, 518–19
bubble jet printers *see* inkjet printers
burn-in, 217
burning smell, 208
burnt-out bulb, 216
business apps, 37–40
    mail, 37–9
BYOD (bring your own device), 33, 264, 478
    vs. corporate owned, 491

C

cable lock, 431, 497
cable stripper, 88, 89*f*
cable tester, 90
cables
    cable/DSL, 86
    connections, 7, 146, 227, 232
    DB9, 123, 124*f*
    hard drive, 116–17
    incorrect cabling, 228
    managing of, 571–2

microphone, 17
modem, 74, 75, 120
network *see* network cables
peripheral, 111
physical cabling issues, 216
plenum-rated, 110
safety procedures, 571–2
television, 107
types, 106–18
unshielded twisted pair, 88
video, 113
see also connector types; USB (universal serial bus)
cache, clearing, 505
CAD (computer-aided design), 404
CAD/CAM (computer-aided design/computer-aided manufacturing), 157
Calendar app, 36
calibration
cursor drift/touch, 224–5
inkjet printers, 172
laser printers, 169, 170
cameras, 16, 23, 27, 65
canonical name (CNAME), 66
capacitance detectors, 430
capacitor swelling, 208–10
capture cards, 157
CD-ROM (CD-Read-Only Memory), 140, 285
CD-RW (CD-ReWritable), 140
CDs (compact discs), 263, 264, 284, 376, 406, 486, 492, 493, 565
bootable, 260, 262
drives, 260, 261
see also DVDs (digital versatile discs)
cell phones, /tablets, 22, 29, 575, 592
see also iPhone; smartphones
cellular location services, 32–3
CentOS 8, 397
centralized processing, 33, 189, 413, 458
CERT (Computer Emergency Response Team) organization, 464
Certificate Manager, 293, 295f

certificate warnings/certificates of destruction, 495, 504
CF (CompactFlash) cards, 138
chain-of-custody documents, 432, 581–2
change management procedures, 559–63
date and time, 561–2
documented business processes, 559–61
maintenance window, 561–2
process, 560–3
channels
configurations, 128–9
frequencies, 57–8t
selection, 56–7
widths, 57
charging port, 224
ChatGPT, 600
chip creep, 207
Chrome OS, 256
CIDR (Classless Inter-Domain Routing), 82, 84
CIFS (Common Internet File System), 53
Citrix Independent Computing Architecture, 186
Citrix Presentation Server, 186
Class A address, 78, 84
Class B address, 78, 84
Class C address, 78, 84
classful subnetting, 83
classless subnetting, 83
clean install, 261–3, 273, 274–5
unattended/attended, 262–3
cleaning cycle, printheads, 172, 231
clicking sounds (click of death), 212
client-server network, 366, 367f
synchronization, 34
cloud services
Cisco Meraki, 33
hardware, 168
Software as a Service, 192
storage, 40, 193
cloud storage, 409, 410f, 410t
business apps, 37, 40
file synchronization, 193

cloud-based productivity tools
    collaboration, 411–12
    email systems, 409
    installing and configuring, 409–13
    sync/folder settings (storage), 409, 410*f*, 410*t*
cloud-computing concepts, 191–3
    virtualization 186, 187, 189
clutch actuator, 234
CMDB (configuration management database), 555–6
CMOS (complementary metal-oxide semiconductor)
    battery, 153, 210, 214, 523, 523*f*
    chips, 523, 570
    clock, 523, 523*f*
    memory, 523
    Setup programs, 153
coaxial cable, 107, 109
cold docking, 27
collaboration tools, 411–12
command-line tools, OSes, 305–27
    disk management, 315–18
    file management, 318–19
    informational, 319–23
    navigation, 305–6
    network, 306–15
    OS management, 323–6
communication skills, 554–5
    avoiding jargon and slang, 588
    clarifying customer statements, 591
    issue description, 554
    issue resolution, 555
    progress notes, 555
communications interfaces, 132–4
    form factors, 133
    M.2, 134, 146
    mini PCIe, 13, 133, 157
    Non-Volatile Memory Express, 133–4
    Serial Advanced Technology Attachment, 133
    Small Computer System Interface/SAS, 133

compatibility considerations
    application and driver support/backward compatibility, 268
    applications and OS compatibility, 405
    hardware, 268–9
    motherboards, 147–51
    operating systems, 259, 268–9
    upgrade path and OS compatibility, 268
concentric circles of protection, 431*f*
configuration profiles, 488
configuration settings, 166–7
connection methods, mobile devices, 18–23
    Bluetooth, 22–3
    connector types, 19
    Lightning connector, 20, 21*f*
    speeds, 22*t*
connectionless protocols, 53–4
connection-oriented protocols, 54
connectivity/connectivity issues, 222–3, 236
    Bluetooth, 223, 531
    device, 164
    slow Internet connection, 541
    Wi-FI, 531
connector types
    external SATA, 146
    F-type (RG-59), 120
    headers, 146
    Lucent connector, 120, 121*f*
    M.2, 134, 146
    motherboards, 143–6, 147*f*
    Peripheral Component Interconnect, 143–4
    power connector, 145
    punchdown block, 121
    RJ-11, 119, 120*f*
    RJ-45, 107, 119, 120*f*
    Serial Advanced Technology Attachment
        20-pin, 162
        24-pin, 160, 162
    storage area network, 146, 147*f*
    straight tip, 107, 120
    subscriber connector, 120
    see also under USB (universal serial bus)
containerization, 189, 190*f*

Index 633

content filtering software, 489, 497
continuous lighting, 434
cooling of CPU, 158–9
copper cables, 107–8
    Cat 5, 107
    Cat 5e, 107
    Cat 6, 107
    Cat 6a, 108
    Cat 7, 108
    Cat 7a, 108
corona assembly, 233
corona wires, cleaning, 231
corporate email configuration, two-factor authentication, 437, 458
CP/M (Control Program/Monitor), 305
CPU (central processing units)
    Advanced RISC Machine, 155
    architecture, 148, 155, 404, 405
    circuit board, 148–9
    cooling of CPU, 158–9
    expansion card, 156–8
    single-core processors, 151
    32-bit/64-bit, 155, 404
    troubleshooting, 201–10
    x86/x64, 155
CPU sockets, 147–51
    multisocket, 151
    Pentium II, 147
    types, 149–50t
credit card payment information, 584–5
crimper, 88
critical components, accessing, 18
CRT (cathode ray tube), 217
cryptominers, 465
cursor drift/touch calibration, 224–5
cylinders, 130, 131f

D

daisy-chaining, 20
data
    corrupted, 212

data-at-rest encryption, 481
data-usage limit notification, 535
destruction and disposal methods *see* data destruction and disposal methods
double data rate (RAM), 126
integrity and preservation, 582
leaking of, 536
privacy, 603
regulated *see* regulated data
retention requirements (archives), 585
security, 603
source, 603
wireless/cellular data network (enable/disable), 29
data caps, recognizing, 36
data destruction and disposal methods
    degaussing, 493
    drive wipe, 493–4
    erasing/wiping, 493–4
    incineration, 493
    low-level vs. standard format, 494
    outsourcing concepts, 494–5
    physical destruction of hard drives, 492–3
    power drills, 492
    recycling/repurposing best practices, 493–4
    regulatory and environmental requirements, 495
    shredding, 493
data lOSes prevention *see* DLP (data lOSes prevention)
database servers, 62
date/time, inaccurate system, 210
DB9 cable, 123, 124f
DBC (direct burial cabling), 110
DC (direct current), 105, 222, 224
DDoS (distributed denial of service) attack, 473
DDR (double data rate) RAM
    DDR SDRAM (double data rate 2), 126
    DDR3 (double data rate version 3), 126
    DDR4 (double data rate version 4), 126, 127t
    DDR5 (double data rate version 5), 126

Defender Antivirus, 440–1
defragmenting, 214
    Disk Defragmenter, 301–2, 303f
degaussing, 493
DEP (Data Execution Prevention), 337
desktop computers
    built-in microphone, lack of, 17
    corporate device configuration, 33
    hosted desktops, 189
    liquid crystal display, 218
    remote virtual desktops, 189
    synchronizing to, 35
    see also installation and uninstallation of applications, macOS/desktop OS; macOS/desktop OS
desktop management software, 599
desktop virtualization, 189
device connectivity, 164
Device Diagnostics tool in Android, 221, 222
device encryption, 487
Device Manager, 293, 294f, 342, 343f
DFS (distributed file system), 520
DHCP (Dynamic Host Configuration Protocol), 51, 53, 68–9, 83
    Automatic Private IP Addressing, 82
    connectionless protocols, 53
    exclusions, 69
    intermittent Internet connectivity, 230
    intermittent wireless connectivity, 227
    leases, 68–9
    NetBoot, 260
    networked hosts, services provided by, 61
    port security, 442
    reservations, 69
    scope, 69
dictionary attack, 475–6
digital assistants, 26
digital security, 459–70
    adware, 466
    malware see malware
    potentially unwanted program, 466
    tools and methods, 466–70

digitizer, 105, 223–4
dim images, 218
DIMMs (dual inline memory modules), 125, 126
directory services, 439
Disk Cleanup, 301, 303f
Disk Defragmenter, 301–2, 303f
disk imaging, 264
Disk Management, 9, 10f, 11, 284–93
    adding arrays, 291
    adding drives, 289
    assigning/changing drive letters, 289, 290f
    directories, 286
    drive status, 286, 286f
    extending partitions, 288
    folders, 286
    Initialize Disk option, 288f
    Initialize Disk pop-up, 288f
    initializing, 287–8
    mounting, 286
    shrinking partitions, 289, 290f
    splitting partitions, 288
    storage spaces, 291, 292f, 293
    Task Scheduler, 293
    volume size, setting, 289, 290f
disk management commands, 315–18
    CHKDSK, 316
    DISPART, 317
    FORMAT, 316, 317T
disk mirroring (RAID 1), 134–5
disk striping (RAID 0), 134
Disk Utility
    disk maintenance utilities, 387–8t
    FileVault, 388
    Force Quit, 388, 389f
    macOS, 387, 388
    pinwheel of death, 205
    terminals, 388, 389f
disk wiping, 493
display components, 103–6
    inverters, 105
    liquid crystal display, 103–4

Index   635

Mini-LED, 103, 104
organic light-emitting diode, 103, 104
touch screen/digitizer, 105
DisplayPort, 113–15, 218
displays, 106
   attributes/characteristics, 105–6
   burn-in, 217
   color gamut, 106
   components *see* display components
   pixel quality, 105
   refresh rates, 105
distorted image, 219
distribution methods, apps *see under* applications
DKIM (DomainKeys Identified Mail), 68
DLP (data lOSes prevention), 439
DMA (direct memory access), 298
DMARC (Domain-based Message Authentication, Reporting, and Conformance), 68
.dmg, macOS/desktop OS, 375–6, 387, 533
DMTF (Distributed Management Task Force), 598
DMZ (demilitarized zone), 499
DNS (Domain Name System), 51, 67, 228, 312, 466, 507
   Domain-based Message Authentication, Reporting, and Conformance, 68
   DomainKeys Identified Mail, 68
   intermittent Internet or wireless connectivity, 227, 230
   IPv4 address (A), 66, 67, 77, 79
   IPv6 address (AAAA), 66, 78, 81
   network configuration concepts, 66–8
   record types, 66, 67t
   server, 60, 67, 312
docking station, 18, 27, 28, 29
documentation and support systems information management, 553–9
   asset management, 555–7
   document types, 557–8
   incident reports, 557
   knowledge base/articles, 558

   new user/onboarding setup checklist, 557–8
   service-level agreements, 558
   software package custom installation procedure, 557
   standard operating procedures, 557
   ticketing systems, 553–5
   tracking of evidence/documenting process, 581
DoH (DNS over HTTPS), 507
domains, 366, 367f, 452
   domain setup, 366, 367f
door locks, 65, 430–1
DoS (denial-of-service), 473
dot-matrix printers *see* impact printers (dox-matrix printers)
drawing pad, 28
drive conflicts, 529
drive imaging, 264
drivers
   appropriate, for a given operating system, 163
   cellular cards, 13
   drive configurations, 134–6
   fixing of problems, 202, 264
   OS-specific, 163
   preinstalled, 16
   purpose of, 164
   third-party, 266
   translation of software commands into understandable commands, 164, 231
   updating, 207, 219
DRM (digital rights management), 583
DSL (digital subscriber line)/modem, 75, 86, 88, 107, 119
DSSS (direct-sequence spread spectrum), 58
dual-channel memory, 128
dumpster diving, 473
duplexing assembly, 166
DVD-ROM (digital versatile disc read-only memory), 140
DVDs (digital versatile discs), 217, 485, 492, 493
   see also CDs (compact discs)

DVI (Digital Visual Interface) connectors, 113, 114–15
   DVI-A, 115
   DVI-D, 115
   DVI-I, 115
DVI to-HDMI adapter, 118
DVI-to-VGA adapter, 118, 119f
dye sublimation, thermal printers, 173

E

ECC (error correction code), vs. non-ECC RAM, 127
EDR (Endpoint Detection and Response), 467–8, 489
EFS (Encrypting File System), 451–2
elasticity, 193
electrical safety, 570
electromechanical alarm systems, 430
electrophotographic printer *see* laser printers
email
   business email compromise, 477
   cloud-based productivity tools, 409
   multifactor authentication, 437
   network scan services, 168
   protocols, 37–9
   security gateway, 469
   viruses, 461, 462f
emergency lighting, 434
EMI (electromagnetic interference), 16, 230
emulators, 187, 388
enabling, 31, 222, 370, 507
encryption
   Advanced Encryption Standard, 55, 456, 457
   BitLocker, 273, 451
   BitLocker Drive Encryption Control Panel, 452f
   data-at-rest, 481
   device, 487
   FileVault, 388
   and protocols, 456
   settings, 500
   Trusted Platform Module, 154–5
endpoint security software, 489
energy efficiency, 162
environmental impacts and local environment controls, 574–80
   battery disposal, 574
   cell phones and tablets, disposal of, 575
   compressed air/vacuums, 576
   dust cleanup, 576, 577f
   humidity level, 575–6
   location/equipment placement, 576
   Material Safety Data Sheet documentation, 574–5
   power surges, 578
   surge suppressor, 578–9
   temperature, 575
   toner disposal, 575
   uninterruptible power supply, 578
   vacuums, 577
   ventilation, 576
EOL (end of life), 478, 259, 269
   batteries, 220, 530
EP (electrophotographic) printers *see* laser printers
EP (enterprise portal), cartridge/drum, 231, 233, 234
EPA (Environmental Protection Agency), 574
equipment grounding, 570–1
equipment locks, 431
erasure lamps, poor quality, 234
error messages
   beeps, 201–2
   blue screen of death
      Data_Bus_Error, 203
      irq1_not_less_or_equal, 204
      Page_Fault_in_nonpaged_area, 203
      Unexpected_Kernel_Mode_Trap, 203
   bootable device not found, 212
   OS not found, 212
   see also troubleshooting
eSATA (external SATA), 116, 117, 146
ESD (electrostatic discharge), 568, 569f, 575

electrical safety, 570
equipment grounding, 570–1
mats, 569–70
straps, 569
eSIM (embedded SIM), 31
Ethernet, 79, 86, 164
cabling, 107, 108
Fast, 107
network/networking, 71, 75, 107
network interface card, 158
Power over Ethernet, 73, 74
RJ-45 connector, 119
USB to Ethernet converters, 118, 124
EULA (end-user license agreement), 583
Event Viewer, 282, 283f, 284
evil twin, 473, 474f
exFAT (Extensible File Allocation Table), 258
exit roller, 232
expansion cards, 156–8
expansion slot, 208
ext4 (fourth extended file system), 258
Extended File System *see* XFS (Extended File System)
extended read/write times, 214
extension and plug-ins, 503
external SATA (eSATA) *see* eSATA (external SATA)
external/hot-swappable drive, 261
eXtreme Digital cards *see* xD (eXtreme digital) cards

F

FaceTime, 385
facial recognition technology, 14, 487
factory reset, 222
failed attempts lockout, 484–5, 490
failed login attempts restrictions, 490
false acceptance rate (FAR), 433
false rejection rate (FRR), 433
fans, 153, 158, 208

FAT (File Allocation Table), 257
FAT32 (File Allocation Table 32), 266, 285, 445, 446
feature updates, 269
feeders
inkjet printers, 171
thermal printers, 173
see also ADF (automatic document feeder)/flatbed scanner
fencing, 431–2
FHSS (frequency-hopping spread spectrum), 58
fiber-optic cabling, 110
multi-mode or single-mode, 111
FIFO (first in, first out) order, MMC, 284
File Explorer Options
General tab, 347, 348f
Hide extensions, 347
View Options, 347f, 348–9
View tab, 346–7, 347f
file management commands
md, 318, 319t
rmdir, 318, 319t
robocopy, 319, 320t
file synchronization, 193
file transfer software, 598
fileless malware, 466
fileshare, 61
FileVault, 388
FileZilla (FTP app), 51
fingerprint lock, 14, 15–16, 487
fingerprint scanner, 433–4
Fios (fiber optic service), 85, 110
fire safety, 573
Firefox browser, 503
firewalls
description, 72
Linux-based, 256
local area network, 86
local OS firewall settings, 369–71
missing, 478
network firewalling, 63
OS security settings, 441–2

firewalls (*continued*)
   settings, 500–1
   software, 469
   syslog, 61
   Windows Defender Firewall *see* Windows Defender Firewall
   wireless and wired networks, applying security settings, 500–1
firmware
   language, 164, 231
   multifunction devices/printers and settings, 163–4
   updates, 496–7, 502
flash drives, 136–7
flat namespace, 52
fluorescent lighting, 104, 434
folder redirection, configuring, 455
form factors
   communications interfaces, 133
   hard drives, 131–2
   motherboards, 141–3
   random-access memory, 125–6
   solid-state drives, 133
formatting, 266
FQDN (fully qualified domain name), 38
frequencies
   channels, 57–8*t*
   wireless networking technologies, 55–6
frozen print queue, 236
FRT (facial recognition technology), 434
FRU (field replaceable unit), 224
FTP (File Transfer Protocol), 50, 51, 53, 370
FTTH (Fiber to the Home), 85, 110
F-type (RG-59) connector, 120
fuzzy image, 216–17

G

generalization, 263
GFCI (ground fault circuit interrupter), 579
GFS (grandfather/father/son) backup scheme, 567

ghosting, 234
goggles, 573
Google Chat, 598
Google Chrome, 8, 502, 503
Google Play, 34
Google/inbox (Gmail), 38
gpedit.msc tool, 273
GPS (Global Positioning System), 32
GPT (GUID Partition Table), 267
GPU (graphics processing unit), 404
group policy, applying, 454
Group Policy Editor, 273, 295, 297*f*
GRUB (bootloader program), Linus, 403
guess access, configuring, 500, 501*f*
guest account, disabling, 484
GUI (graphical user interface), 480
GUID (globally unique identifier), 267, 286

H

hacking, 407, 475
hard drive cables, Serial Advanced Technology Attachment, 116–17
hard drives/HDDs (hard disk drives), 9–11, 210–15
   1.8 inch vs. 2.5 inch, 11
   2.5 inch, 132
   3.5 inch, 132
   backup of old, 9
   form factors, 131–2
   Initialize Disk, 11, 12*f*
   LED status indicators, 211
   magnetic, 11–12
   migration, 11, 12*f*
   Performance tab, 8, 9*f*
   physical destruction, 492–3
   problems with
      audible alarms, 215
      bootable device not found, 212
      clicking sounds, 212
      data lOSes/corruption, 212
      extended read/write times, 214

Index

grinding noises, 211
input/output operations per second, 214
missing array, 214
missing drives in OS, 214
slow access, 214
troubleshooting of issues, 210–15
replacement, 9–10
spindle speeds, 131
storage, 130–2
hardening techniques, 481, 486–8
hardware, 95–182
adapters, 117–18
attributes, 105–6
BIOS/UEFI *see* BIOS/UEFI settings
cable types, 106–18
Central Processing Unit, 155–9
compatibility, upgrade considerations, 268–9
connector types, 119–23, 124*f*
CPU architecture *see* CPU (central processing units)
critical components, accessing, 18
encryption, 154–5
monitoring *see* maintenance and monitoring of mobile device hardware
motherboards, 141–51
multifunction devices/printers and settings, 162–8
power supply, 160–2
printer maintenance, 169–76
RAM characteristics, 125–9
review questions, 177–82
securing and protecting critical hardware, 483
storage devices, 130–41
Windows requirements, 275
hardware tokens, 437
hashing, 503
HDD (hard disk drive) *see* hard drives/HDDs (hard disk drives)
HDMI (High-Definition Multimedia Interface), 113, 218
adaptors/connectors, 113*f*, 118
HDSL (high bit-rate DSL), 75
headers, 146
headsets, 23, 24, 32
Health Insurance Portability and Accountability Act (HIPAA) Security Rule, US, 585
heat sinks, 158–9
HFS (Hierarchical File System), 258
hole punch jams, 235
home folders, assigning, 453–4
hosted desktops, 189
hot docking, 27
hotspots, 18, 23
mobile, 30, 362
HPC (high-performance computing), 11, 104, 105
HSM (hardware security module), encryption, 155
HTTP (Hypertext Transfer Protocol), 50, 52, 54, 62, 370
HTTPS (Hypertext Transfer Protocol over Secure Sockets Layer), 53, 54, 507
hubs
Ethernet cable connected to, 372
multiport, 19
and network cables, 107
and patch panels, 72
port security, 442
rack-mounted, 121*f*
and switches, 71
USB, 19, 20
and wired connections, 372
humidity level, 575–6
HVAC (heating, ventilation and air conditioning) system, 576
hybrid drives, 10–11
Hyper-V, 187
hypervisors, 154, 187
Type 1, 189, **195**
Type 2, 190
types, 190*f*

I

IaaS (Infrastructure as a Service), 192, **194**
IAM (identity and access management), 439
IANA (Internet Assigned Numbers Authority), 79
ICA (Independent Computing Architecture), 186
iCloud, 37–8, 385
ICMP (Internet Control Message Protocol), 308, 370
IDC (insulation displacement connector), 90
IDE (integrated development environment), 494
IDE (Integrated Drive Electronics), 117, 138
identity synchronization, 412
IDF (intermediate distribution frame), 121
image creation, 263–4
image deployment, 264, 406–7
IMAP (Internet Message Access Protocol), 37, 38, 50, 51, 340
    IMAP4, 52
iMessage, 385
impact printers (dox-matrix printers)
    faded prints, 233
    maintenance, 175–6
    multipart paper, 175
    replacement of paper or parts, 176
impersonation, 473
improper charging, 222
incident response, 580–2
incineration, 493
incorrect color display, 217–18
Indexing Options, 342, 344f
infected systems
    how viruses work, 461
    quarantining, 479
    remediating, 479–80
informational commands, 319–23
    `hostname`, 319–20
    `netuser`, 320, 321t
    `whoami`, 321, 322t
    `winver`, 321, 322f

Infrastructure as a Service *see* IaaS (Infrastructure as a Service)
Initialize Disk, 11, 12f
injectors, Power over Ethernet, 73
ink cartridges, inkjet printers, 171, 172, 233
    see also toner; toner cartridges
inkjet printers
    calibration, 172
    cleaning of printheads, 172
    clearing of jams, 172–3
    components, duplexing assembly, 166
    feeder, 171
    ink cartridges, 171, 172
    maintenance, 171–3
    piezoelectric, 170
    printheads, 171, 172
    replacement of cartridges, 172
    thermal *see* thermal printers
    vertical black lines on the page, 231
in-place upgrade, 273–4
insider threat, 476
installation and uninstallation of applications, macOS/desktop OS
    App Store, 534
    file types
        .app, 375
        .dmg, 375–6, 387, 533
        .pkg, 375, 376, 533
    uninstallation process, 376
installations, operating system, 259–69
    boot methods, 260–1
    clean install, 261–3, 273, 274–5
        unattended/attended, 262–3
    creating an image, 263–4
    image creation, 263–4
    image deployment, 264
    installation types, 261–3
    remote network installation, 264
    repair installation, 265
    third-party drivers, 266
    upgrades, 263
    zero-touch deployment, 264–5

instant messaging, 412
integrated print server, 61
Intel/Intel Corporation, 151, 154
    audible alarms, 215
    XHCI controllers, 522
intentional insider threat, 476
interference
    electromagnetic, 16
    external, 230
    intermittent wireless connectivity, 227
internal hard drive (partition), 261
Internet appliances, 63
Internet connection types, 85–6
inventory lists, 555
inverters, 103, 105, 106
I/O (input/output), 455
IOPS (input/output operations per second), 214
iOS devices
    Apple Configurator and BYOD, 33
    Apple File System, 258
    Apple iOS, 256
    Bluetooth, enabling, 31, 32, 40
    compared with Android systems, 259
    continuity, 386
    Drive (iCloud Drive), 385
    Erase Data function, 490
    FaceTime, 385
    iCloud email, setting up, 38–9
    iPadOS variant, 256
    locator apps, 489
    mobile OSes, 256
    OS updates, 488
    PIN codes, 487
    remote apps, 490
IoT (Internet of Things), 63–4
IP (Internet Protocol), 50, 260
IP addresses, 77–81
    Automatic Private IP Addressing, 82, 227
    Class A address, 78, 84
    Class B address, 78, 84
    Class C address, 78, 84
    connectivity issues, 236
    gateway, 84
    IPv4, 66, 67, 77, 79
    NIC configuration, 79
        static vs. dynamic, 83
        subnet mask, 83–4
        wired, 80
        wireless, 81
    private or public, 78, 79
iPadOS, 256
iPhone
    Calendar app, 36
    contacts, 36–7
    data caps, recognizing, 36
    iPadOS, 256
    networks, 29
    Wi-FI, 30
IPS (in-plane switching), liquid crystal display, 103, 104
IPv4 address (A), 66, 67, 77, 79
    compared with IPv6, 82t
IPv6 address (AAAA), 66, 78, 81
    compared with IPv4, 82t
IRQs (share interrupt requests), 144, 298
ISO (International Standards Organization)
    CD-ROM/CD-RW, 140
    ISO-mountable file, 406, 407f, 408
    least privilege principle, 436
    NFC standard, 21
    splash screens, 586
ISP (Internet service provider), 230
ITX (Information Technology eXtended), 143

J

jailbreaking, 534
Java, 256
JavaScript, 349, 594
JIT (just-in-time) access, 438
jitter, 228–9
joining domain, 452

K

Kerberos, 458
key fobs, 432
keyboard cadence, 433
keyboard/keys, 7, 432
keychain drives *see* flash drives
keylogger, 465
keystone effect, 219
knowledge base/articles, 202, 558

L

LAN (local area network), 86–7, 88, 107
    `ping` command, 309
    settings, 327, 373
laptops, 6, 7, 16, 17, 24, 27, 112, 224
    documentation/instruction manual, 8, 12, 13
    HDD/SDD replacement, 9–10
    installation issues, 225
    overheating, 223
laser printers
    calibration, 169, 170
    cleaning, 169, 170
    device connectivity, 164
    double/echo images on print, 234
    duplexing assembly, 166
    faded prints, 233
    maintenance, 169–70
    maintenance kit, applying, 169, 170
    storing of toner, 170
    toner replacement, 169
    vertical black lines on the page, 231
latency
    network issues, 229–30
    spindle speeds, 131
Layer 3 (network layer) routing, 50
LC (Lucent connector), 107, 120, 121*f*
LCD (liquid crystal display), 103–4
    dim images, 218
    inverters, 105
    in-plane switching, 103, 104
    touch screens, 105
    twisted nematic, 103
    vertical alignment, 103, 104
LDAP (Lightweight Directory Access Protocol), 52–3
least privilege principle, 435–6
LEDs (light-emitting diodes), status indicators, 211
legacy software/OS, 187
legacy system, 187
LGA (land grid array), 148
licensing
    assignment, 412–13
    open-source license, 584
    perpetual license agreement, 583
    personal-use vs. corporate-use license, 584
    unexpired licenses, 583
    valid licences, 583
lifting techniques, 572–3
light switches, 65
lighting, 434–5
Lightning connector, 20, 21*f*, 123, 124*f*
limited connectivity, authentication issues, 228
Linux client/desktop OS, 255, 256
    access points, 256, 390
    administrative commands, 395–6
    command-line tools, 305–6*t*, 308
    common commands
        `apt`, 396
        `cat`, 399–400
        `chmod`, 392–3
        `chown`, 393
        `cp`, 392
        `curl`, 398
        `df`, 401
        `dig`, 397, 398–9
        `dnf`, 397
        `du`, 400–1
        `find`, 394

Index

`fsck`, 394–5
`grep`, 394
`ip`, 397–8
`ls`, 390
`man`, 399
`mount`, 395
`mv`, 391
`network`, 397–9
`ping`, 397, 398
`ps`, 400
`pwd` vs. `passwd`, 390–1, 391*t*
`rm`, 392
`su/sudo`, 395–6
`top`, 400
`traceroute`, 314, 397, 399
`yum`, 396–7
common configuration files, 402
components, OS
    bootloader, 403
    kernal, 403
    systemd, 402, 403*t*
`/etc/fstab file`, 402
`/etc/hosts file`, 402
`/etc/passwd file`, 402
`/etc/shadow file`, 402
file management commands, 390–4
filesystem management commands, 394–5
firewall, 256
fourth extended file system (ex4), 258
informational commands, 399–401
nano (text editor), 401
package management commands, 396–7
Red Hat version, 185, 258
root account, 403
routers, 256, 390
switches, 256
text editors, 401
liquid cooling, 159
liquid damage, 222, 223
load balancers, 63
local OS firewall settings, 369, 370
Local Users and Groups, 293, 296*f*
location services, 32–3, 163

locator apps, 489
logging off when not in use, 483
logical security, 435–9
login script, assigning, 453
login times, restricting, 484
logon ID, 321
loopback plug, 90
LQ (letter quality), impact printers, 174

M

M.2 (previously NGFF), 134, 146
MAC address, 72, 76, 87, 228, 475
    device information, 553
    malfunctioning NIC, 228
    spoofing, 475
macOS/desktop OS, 255, 256, 308, 375–89
    /Applications, 377
    /Library, 377
    /System, 377
    /Users, 377
    /Users/Library, 377
    Apple ID and corporate restrictions, 378–9
    best practices
        antivirus, 378
        backups, 378
        Rapid Security Response, 379
        updates/patches, 378, 379*f*
    Disk Utility, 387–8, 389*f*
    installation and uninstallation of applications *see* installation and uninstallation of applications, macOS/desktop OS
    printers and scanners, 381, 382*f*
    system folders, 377
    system preferences *see* system preferences, macOS
magnetic storage, 11–12
    see also hard drives/HDDs (hard disk drives)
magnetometers, 435
Mail, 340, 341*f*

mail server, 52, 61
mainboards *see* motherboards
maintenance and monitoring of mobile device hardware, 5–18
   batteries, 5–7
   hard disk drive/solid-state drive, 8–11
   hybrid drives, 10–11
   keyboard/keys, 7
   random-access memory, 7–8
   wireless cards, 12, 13*f*, 14*f*, 15*f*
   see also printer maintenance
malware, 459–66
   antivirus updates, 378, 489
   browser-related symptoms, 541
   comparison of response tools, 468
   education of end user, 480
   fileless, 466
   memory code injection, 466
   mobile devices, troubleshooting, 224
   removal, in SOHO networks, 479–81
      disabling System Restore in Windows, 479
      enabling System Restore, 480
      investigating and verifying malware symptoms, 479
      quarantining infected systems, 479
      remediating infected systems, 479–80
   rootkits, 460
   sandboxing, 185
   Trojan horses, 459–60
   trusted vs. untrusted sources, 34
   unintentionally introducing, 596
   updating anti-malware software, 480
   Windows Registry manipulation, 466
   zero-day, 185
   see also viruses
MAN (metropolitan area network), 87
mantrap *see* access control vestibule; access control vestibule (mantrap)
master computer, 263
MBR (master boot record), 267, 268, 465
MDIX (auto-medium-dependent interface crossover), 158
MDM (mobile device management), 33–4, 438–9, 491
   Bring Your Own Device, 33
   corporate applications, 34
   corporate device configuration, 33
   device configurations, 33
   disallowing apps from unknown sources, 34, 35*f*
   policy enforcement, 34
   time-based one-time password, 34
   trusted vs. untrusted sources, 34, 35*f*
MDR (Managed Detection and Response), 468
memory cards, 137–9
   CompactFlash, 138
   microSD, 138, 139*f*
   miniSD, 138, 139*f*
   SD card, 137–8
   xD, 138–9
mercury vapor lamp, 435
metered utilization, 192–3
   ingress/egress, 193
MFA (multifactor authentication), 459
Micro-ATX motherboard, 142, 143*f*
microchips, with antennas, 21
microphone, 16–17, 23
microSD cards, 138, 139*f*
Microsoft Drive Optimizer *see* Disk Defragmenter
micro-USB, 18–19
migration, 11, 12*f*
MIMO (multiple in/multiple out), 59
Mini-LED (mini light-emitting device), 103, 104
miniSD cards, 138, 139*f*
mini-USB, 18–19
minutiae matching, 433–4
MITM (man-in-the-middle) attack, 475
MMC (Microsoft Management Console), 273, 277
   Disk Management, 284–93
   Event Viewer, 282, 283*f*, 284
   FIFO, 284

illustration, 283f
log files, 284
Log Properties dialog box, 284, 285f
snap-in, 282–97
MMS (multimedia), 386
MNDA (mutual nondisclosure agreement), 584
mobile device network connectivity and application support, 29–34
    Bluetooth, 31–2
    hotspot, 30
    3G, 4G and 5G mobile technology/platforms, 29–30
    Wi-Fi, 30
    wireless/cellular data network (enable/disable), 29
mobile device synchronization, 24–40
    ActiveSync, 410f
    synchronization methods, 35–6
    synchronize to an automobile, 36
    synchronize to cloud, 35
    synchronize to desktop, 35
mobile devices
    BYOD vs. corporate owned, 33
    configurations, 33
    mobile device management, 33–4
    monitoring, maintaining and replacing, 5–18
    replacement, 5–18
    review questions, 41–3
    updates to OS, 219
mobile devices, securing, 486–91
    endpoint security software, 489
    failed login attempts restrictions, 490
    hardening techniques, 481, 486–8
    locator apps, 489
    patch management, 488–9
    policies and procedures, 490–1
    remote backup apps, 490
mobile devices, troubleshooting, 219–26
    Android, 533
    broken screen, 221–2
    cursor drift/touch calibration, 224–5
    degraded performance, 226
    digitizer issues, 223–4
    improper charging, 222
    liquid damage, 223
    malware, 224
    overheating, 223
    physically damaged ports, 224
    poor battery health, 220
    poor connectivity, 222–3
    stylus failing to work, 226
    swollen battery, 220
    unable to install new applications, 225
mobile digital keys, 433
mobile hotspot, 23, 30
mobile OSes, 256
modem, 74, 75, 120
modular power supply, 161
Molex connectors, 122, 123f
motherboards, 141–51
    Advanced Technology Extended, 142
    application crashes, 208
    capacitor swelling, 208–9
    compatibility, 147–51
    connector types, 143–6, 147f
    CPU sockets, 147–51
    form factors, 141–3
    Information Technology eXtended, 143
    Micro-AXT, 142, 143f
    sizes, 143, 144f
    troubleshooting *see* troubleshooting
    wattage needs, 161
mouse, 27, 28, 105, 142, 224, 470
    and accessibility issues, 381
    external, 224
    pads, 569
    pinwheel pointer, 204
movable lighting, 434
MPEG (Moving Picture Experts Group), 157
mSATA (Mini-Serial Advanced Technology Attachment), 134
MS-DOS (Microsoft Disk Operation System), 305
MSDS (Material Safety Data Sheet), 574

MSRA, 599, 600
multiboot system, 261
multifactor authentication, 436–8
multifunction devices/printers and settings, 162–8
   appropriate drivers for a given operating system, 163
   automatic document feeder)/flatbed scanner, 168
   badging, 167
   configuration settings, 166–7
   device connectivity, 164
   firmware, 163–4
   network scan services, 167–8
   Printer Control Language, 163
   public/shared devices, 165–6
   security, 167
   unboxing of device and considering set-up location, 163
   user authentication, 167
multipart paper, 175
multiple-barrier systems, 430
multisocket, 151
multitenancy, 193
MX (mail engager), 67

N

NAT (network address translation), 188, 372–3, 502
National Institute of Standards and Technology (NIST), 585
navigation commands
   change directory (cd), 305–6*t*
   dir, 305–6*t*, 307*t*
NDAs (nondisclosure agreements), 494, 584
NDS (Novell Directory Services), 52
near-field scanner, 16
NetBIOS/NetBT (NetBIOS over TCP/IP), 52
NetBoot, 260
network cables, 106–11
   cable tester, 90

coaxial cable, 107, 109
copper, 107–8
   Cat 5, 107
   Cat 5e, 107
   Cat 6, 107
   Cat 6a, 108
   Cat 7, 108
   Cat 7a, 108
direct burial, 110
intermittent wireless connectivity, 227
multi-mode fiber, 111
optical, 110–11
plenum-rated, 110–11
shielded twisted pair, 110
single-mode fiber, 111
T568A/T568B standards, 107, 108
unshielded twisted pair, 110
network commands
   `ipconfig`, 306, 308, 309*f*
   mapped drives, 313*f*, 314*f*
   `net use`, 313, 314*f*
   `netstat`, 310, 311*f*, 311*t*
   `nslookup`, 312–13
   `pathping`, 314, 316*f*
   `ping`, 308–10
   `tracert`, 314, 315*f*, 315*t*
network configuration concepts, 66–71
   Domain Name System, 66–8
   Dynamic Host Configuration Protocol, 68–9
   virtual local area networks, 69, 71
   virtual private network, 69–70, 71
network installation, 264
network issues
   cables, 227
   DHCP issues, 227
   DNS problems, 227
   high latency, 229–30
   interference, 227
   intermittent wireless connectivity, 227
   jitter, 228–9
   limited connectivity, 228
   network interface cards, 227

Index 647

poor VoIP quality, 229
port flapping, 229
slow speeds, 228
network scan services, 167–8
network tap, 90
network types, 86–8
   local area network, 86–7
   metropolitan area network, 87
   personal area network, 87
   storage area network, 87
   wide area network, 87
   wireless local area network, 88
networked hosts, services provided by, 60–5
   Internet appliances, 63, 64
   legacy/embedded systems, 64–6
   server roles, 60–2
      web servers, 62, 63
networking, 45–94
   client network configuration, 371
   common devices, 71–6
   domain joined vs. workgroup, 366–9
      domain setup, 366, 367f
      file servers, 368
      mapped drives, 368–9
      printers, 368
      shared resources, 366–7
   establishing connections, 371–2
   features, configuring on client/desktop, 365–75
   File Explorer navigation, 373
   local OS firewall settings, 369–71
   metered connections and limitations, 375
   network configuration concepts, 66–71
   network types, 85–6
   networked hosts, services provided by, 60–5
   networking tools, 88–90
   ports and protocols, 50–4
   proxy settings, 372–3
   public vs. private network, 373, 374f
   review questions, 91–4
   small office/home office network, 76–84
   virtual private network, 372
   wired, 372
   wireless, 372
   wireless networking protocols, 55–60
networking hardware
   access points *see* APs (access points)
   cable modem, 74
   digital subscriber line, 75
   firewall, 72
   media access control address, 76
   network interface cards, 75
   optical network terminal, 75
   patch panel, 72
   Power over Ethernet, 73–4
   routers, 71
   switches, 71–2
networking tools, 88–90
   cable stripper, 88, 89f
   cable tester, 90
   crimper, 88
   loopback plug, 90
   network tap, 90
   punchdown tool, 90
   toner probe, 89
   Wi-FI analyzer, 89
NFC (near-field communications), 21–2, 59, 531–2
NGFF (Next Generation Form Factor) *see* M.2 (previously NGFF)
NIC (Network Information Center), 79
NIC (network interface card), 223, 227, 228
NiCd (nickel cadmium) batteries, 222
NICs (network interface cards), 75, 79, 158
NLQ (near letter-quality) printer, 174
   see also impact printers (dox-matrix printers)
NM (twisted nematic), liquid crystal display, 103, 104
noises, 174, 430
   clicking, 212, 215
   grinding, 208, 211, 234
   loud, 210
   unusual, 208
noncompliant systems, 477

notebooks, 5, 12, 27
    subnotebooks, 11, 125
NS (name server), 67
NTFS (New Technology File System), 257, 285
    permissions, 446
        administrative shares vs. local shares, 450
        directory, 447t
        file, 448t
        file and folder attributes, 446
        NTFS vs. share permissions *see* NTFS vs. share permissions
NTFS vs. share permissions, 445–50
    administrative shares vs. local shares, 450
    allow vs. deny, 446
    cumulative NTFS permissions, 448
    file and folder attributes, 447, 448t
    inheritance, 448
    moving vs. copying folders and files, 447
    NTFS directory permissions, 447t
    NTFS file permissions, 448t
    permission propagation, 448
    shared files and folders, 448, 449f
NTP (Network Time Protocol), 61, 62
nuisance tripping, 578
NVMe (Non-Volatile Memory Express), 132–4
NVMHCIS (Non-Volatile Memory Host Controller Interface Specification), 132–4

O

OEM (original equipment manufacturer), 265
    Windows 95 Service Release 2, 257
OFDM (orthogonal frequency-division multiplexing), 58, 59
OLED (organic light-emitting diode), 103, 104, 217
on-path attack, 475
ONTs (optical network terminals), 75
operating systems (OSes), 8, 26, 163, 212, 214, 243–416, 470
    applications, installing, 404–8
    appropriate command-line tools, using, 305–27
    cloud-based productivity tools, 409–13
    common types/purpose, 255–9
    compatibility concerns, 259, 268–9
    disk management, 315–18
    file system types, 257–8
    installations and upgrades, 259–66
    Linux *see* Linux client/desktop OS
    local firewall settings, 369–71
    macOS/desktop OS *see* macOS/desktop OS
    no OS found, 522–3
    partitioning, 266–9
    print commands, translation by driver to firmware language, 164, 231
    review questions, 414–16
    security settings, configuring/applying, 450–5
    troubleshooting common issues, 518–27
    updates, 219, 259, 266, 269, 488
    vendor life-cycle limitations, 258–9
    workstation systems, 255–6
    see also Windows 10; Windows 11; Windows Defender Firewall; Windows OSes; Windows settings, configuring
operational procedures, 545–606
    acceptable use policy, 585–6
    artificial intelligence, 600–3
    change management, 559–63
    communication techniques/professionalism, 587–93
    documentation and support systems information management, 553–9
    environmental impacts and local environment controls, 574–80
    incident response, 580–2
    licensing *see* licensing
    mutual nondisclosure agreement, 584
    nondisclosure agreement, 584
    regulated data, 584–5
    regulatory and business compliance requirements, 586
    remote access technology, 596–9

review questions, 604–6
safety, 568–73
scripting, 594–6
workstation backup and recovery methods, 563–8
optical cables, 110–11
optical drives, 139
optical trackpad, 28
orientation, 166, 235
OS (operating system) *see* operating systems (OSes)
OS management commands
    `gpresult`, 323–4, 325*t*
    `gpupdate`, 323, 324*t*
    System File Checker (SFC), 324–6, 326*t*
OSes (workstation systems), 255–6
OSHA (Occupational Safety and Health Administration), 586
OSI (Open Systems Interconnection) model, 51, 228
OUI (organizationally unique identifier), 76
OUs (organizational units), 452, 453
Outlook for Android, 38–9
outsourcing concepts, 494–5
overheating, 207–8, 223

P

PaaS (Platform as a Service), 192
package management (Linux) commands
    `apt`, 396
    `dnf`, 397
    `yum`, 396–7
page printers *see* laser printers
pairing
    Bluetooth with headsets, 23
    enabling, 31
    finding Android device for, 31–2
    NFC not requiring, 21
    PIN codes, 32
palm print scanner, 434
PAM (privileged access management), 438

PAN (personal area network), 21, 87, 88
paper pickup roller, 232
paper tray, settings, 166
partitioning, 266–9
    basic, 267
    dynamic partitions, 266
    extended, 267, 288
    GUID Partition Table (GPT), 267
    logical, 267
    primary, 267
    shrinking partitions, 289, 290*f*
    splitting, 288
    striped partitions, 266
passive heat sink, 158–9
passwords
    Basic Input/Output System, 153
    BIOS/UEFI settings, 483
    boot password, 153
    complexity requirements, 482
    of default administrator, changing, 485
    expiration, 482
    password manager, 483, 500
    password policy, 475
    Telnet, 51
    username and password, 444
    see also Windows Hello
patch cable, 158
patch management, 488–9
patch panel, 72, 73*f*
pattern locks, 487, 488*f*
Payment Card Industry Data Security Standard PCI DSS, 584–5
PCI (Peripheral Component Interconnect), 133, 157
    bus connectors, 145*f*
    motherboards, 143–4
    slots, 144, 145*f*
PCIe (mini PCI Express), 13, 133, 144, 157
PCL (Printer Control Language), 163, 231
PCs *see* personal computer (PC) considerations
PCMCIA (Personal Computer Memory Card International Association), 138
PDA (personal digital assistant), 87

PDL (page description languages), 231
Peltier components, CPUs, 158
Performance Monitor, 295, 296f
perimeter, 430
peripheral cables, 111
permissions
    administrative shares vs. local shares, 450
    file and folder attributes, 446
    inheritance, 448
    NTFS directory, 447t
    propagation, 448
    restricting user permissions, 484
    USB, 152
    see also NTFS vs. share permissions
personal computer (PC) considerations
    altered system or personal files/missing/renamed files/inability to access files, 538
    desktop alerts, 538
    disconnecting power before repair, 572
    false alerts regarding antivirus protection, 538
    OS update failures, 538–9
    unable to access the network, 537
    unwanted notifications within the OS, 538
PGA (pin grid array), 147, 148f
phishing, 469–70, 471
photoelectric alarm systems, 430
physical access security, 432–5
physical barriers, 430
physical media access control address *see* MAC address
physical privacy and security, 427, 429
    biometrics, 14–16
physical replacement secure locations, 497–8
physical security, 427–32
pickup roller, 232
piezoelectric printers, 162
    see also inkjet printers
PII (personally identifiable information), 483, 494, 585
PIN (personal identification number), 14, 32, 107, 155, 444, 487
PIR (passive infrared systems), 430
pixels
    dead, 217, 219
    defining function of, 105
    pixel quality, 105
    screen resolution, 106
    stuck, 217
.pkg, macOS/desktop OS, 375, 376, 533
PLCs (programmable logic controllers), 64
plenum-rated cable, 110
PoE (Power over Ethernet) *see under* Ethernet
pointer drift, 224
policy enforcement, 34
POP3 (Post Office Protocol 3), 37, 50, 52, 61, 370
pop-up blocker, 504
pop-up windows, 24, 34
port number, 50
port replicator, 27, 28
ports
    disabling, 152
    flapping of, 229
    forwarding and mapping, 502
    open, 72
    physically damaged, 224
    port numbers, 50
    port security, 442
    and protocols *see* ports and protocols
    Thunderbolt, 112
    unused, disabling, 501
    USB connectors, 19
ports and protocols
    connectionless protocols, 53–4
    connection-oriented protocols, 54
    Domain Name System, 51
    Dynamic Host Configuration Protocol, 51
    File Transfer Protocol, 51
    Hypertext Transfer Protocol, 52, 53, 54
    Hypertext Transfer Protocol over Secure Sockets Layer, 53, 54
    Internet Message Access Protocol, 37, 38, 52
    Lightweight Directory Access Protocol, 52

NetBIOS over TCP/IP, 52
Open Systems Interconnection, 51
Post Office Protocol 3, 52
Remote Desktop Protocol, 53
Secure Shell protocol, 51, 54
Server Message Block/Common Internet File System, 53
Simple Mail Transfer Protocol, 51
Simple Network Management Protocol, 52
Telnet, 51, 54
POST (Power-on Self-test)
    beeps, 201–2, 210
    boot password, 153
    incorrect color display, 217–18
PostScript, 163
Power Options, 349–52
    choosing what closing the lid does, 351
    Ease of Access, 352
    Fast Startup, turning on, 351
    Hibernate, 350
    Power Plans, 350
    Sleep/Suspend, 350
    Standby, 351
    USB Selective Suspend, 352
power supply
    disconnecting power before repair, 572
    electrical safety, 570
    energy efficiency, 162
    handling power, 571
    input 110–120 VAC vs. 220–240 VAC, 160
    lack of, 207
    modular, 161
    output 3.3V vs. 5V vs. 12V, 160
    redundant, 160–1
    20-pin to 24-pin motherboard adapter, 160
    wattage rating, 161–2
presentation tools, 411
principle of least privilege, 435–6
print quality, 167
print servers, 61, 166
printer issues, 230–6
    connectivity issues, 236

double/echo images on print, 234
    faded prints, 233
    finishing, 235
    frozen print queue, 236
    garbled print, 231–2
    grinding noise *see* noises
    incorrect page orientation, 235
    lines on printed pages, 230
    multipage misfeed, 233
    multiple prints pending in queue, 233
    paper jams, 172–3, 232–3
    paper not feeding, 233
    speckling on printed pages, 234
    staple jams, 235
    tray not recognized, 235–6
    vertical black or white lines on the page, 231
    see also trays, printer
printer maintenance
    impact printers, 174–6
    inkjet printer, 171–3
    laser printers, 169–70
    thermal printer, 173–4
printers
    adding IP address, 369*f*
    domain joined vs. workgroup, 368
    maintaining *see* printer maintenance
    printheads *see* printheads
    rollers, 170, 171, 232, 234
    troubleshooting *see* printer issues
    Windows settings, configuring, 334, 335*f*
    see also impact printers (dox-matrix printers); inkjet printers; laser printers; thermal printers
printheads, 171, 172, 176, 231
privacy settings, 330, 359, 381, 382*f*
private addresses, 78
private-browsing mode, 505, 506*f*
professionalism
    appearance, 587–8
    avoiding distractions, 590
    confidential material, handling, 593

professionalism (*continued*)
   cultural sensitivity, 589
   customer, avoiding interrupting, 588–9
   difficult customers/situations, dealing with, 590–1
   expectations, meeting, 592
   follow-up, 592
   language, 588
   non-judgmental attitude, 591
   personal calls, minimizing, 590
   personal interruptions, avoiding, 590
   positive attitude, 588
   professional titles, respect for, 589
   proper documentation, 592
   punctuality, 589
   repair/replacement options, offering, 592
   see also communication skills
profile security requirements, 491
projectors
   adjusting, in case of distorted image, 219
   burnt-out bulb, 216
   conference-room, 113
   fuzzy images, 216–17
   incorrect input source, 216
   intermittent shutdown, 218
   video-related problems, 215
   see also video, projector, and display issues (troubleshooting)
proprietary crash screens, 202–4
      error messages, 203–4
      pinwheel of death, 204–6
proxies
   clients, 458
   firewall, 72
   servers, 64, 78, 82, 362, 507
   settings, 372–3, 507
PS (PostScript), 163
PSTN (public switched telephone network), 229
public addresses, 79
public shared devices, 165–6
punchdown block, 121
punchdown tool, 90

PUP (potentially unwanted program), 466
PWOD (pinwheel of death), 204
PXE (Preboot Execution Environment), 260
PXE ROM (Preboot Execution Environment Read-Only Memory), 264

Q

QoS (quality of service), 229
QR (quick response) codes, 471–2
quad-channel memory, 128–9
quartz lamp, 435

R

radio power levels, 498
RADIUS (Remote Authentication Dial-In User Service), 457–8
RADSL (rate-adaptive DSL), 75
RAID (Redundant Array of Independent Disks), 61, 134–6
   built-in controller, 213
   ceasing to work, 213
   degraded array, 215
   failure, 212–13, 215
   Intel Controller audible alarm, 215
   missing array, 214
   NTFS, support for, 257
   RAID 0, 134, 291
   RAID 1, 134–5, 213
   RAID 5, 135, 136*f*, 213, 291
   RAID 6, 135, 136*f*
   RAID 10, 136, 137*f*
RAM (random-access memory), 7–8
   applications, installing according to requirements, 405
   characteristics, 125–9
   double data rate, 126
   dual inline memory module, 126
   error correction code vs. non-ECC RAM, 127

Index

form factors, 125–6
memory chips, 125
non-parity and parity, 127
small outline dual-inline memory module, 125
support limitations, 273
troubleshooting *see* troubleshooting
upgrading, 8
random shutdown, 208
ransomware, 465
rapid elasticity, 193
RBAC (role-based access control), 272
RDP (Remote Desktop Protocol), 53, 186, 272–3, 597, 599
reading tags, 21
realms, 366
Recovery Console, 467
recovery partition, 265
Red Hat Enterprise Linux 7, 185, 258
reference computer, 263
refresh rates, 105
ReFS (Resilient File System), 257
Registry Editor, 304
regulated data
   credit card payment information, 584–5
   data retention requirements, 585
   healthcare, 585
   personal government-issued information, 585
   personally identifiable information, 585
reimaging, 480
reinstallation, 480
remote access technology, 596–9
   methods and tools, 597–9
   security considerations of each method, 599
   third-party tools, 598–9
remote problems, 228
remote virtual desktops, 189
remote wipes, 490
removable storage, 136–9
   flash drives, 136–7
   memory cards, 137–9

optical drives
   Blu-ray, 139, 140–1
   CD-ROM/CD-RW, 140
   DVD-ROM/DVD-RW/DVD-RW DL, 140
repair installation, 265
replacement of mobile device hardware, 5–18
   accessories, 25–6
   batteries, 6
   HDD/SDD, 9–10
   hybrid drives, 10–11
   keyboards/keys, 7
   microphone, 17
   speakers, 26
   wireless cards, 12, 13*f*, 14*f*, 15*f*
   see also maintenance and monitoring of mobile device hardware; mobile devices
reservations, DHCP, 69
resolution
   adjusting, 217, 219
   changing settings, 219
   of customer problems, 588, 592
   High-Definition Multimedia Interface, 113
   higher-resolution monitors, 105
   issue, 555
   mismatch between settings and refresh rate, 217
   name, 66, 67, 79, 227, 313, 402
   and performance, **416**
   print quality, 167
   screen, 105, 106
   system preferences, 379
   techniques, 219
   Video Graphics Array, 115
   see also ARP (Address Resolution Protocol); screen resolution
Resource Monitor, 298, 299*f*
resources
   dedicated, 192
   mishandling, 596
   shared, 192, 366–7
   troubleshooting, 524
restarting machines, 595

retina scanner, 433
review questions
    hardware, 177–82
    mobile devices, 41–3
    networking, 91–4
    operating systems, 414–16
    operational procedures, 604–6
    security, 510–13
    troubleshooting, 237–9
    virtualization and cloud computing, 194–5
RF (radio frequency), 21
RFB (Remote Frame Buffer), 597
RFC (Request for Comment), 582
RFI (radio frequency interference), 230
RFID (radio frequency identification), 21, 22, 59–60, 429
RG-59 connector (F-type), 120
RGB (red, green and blue), 105
RIS (Remote Installation Services), 264
RJ-11 (registered jack 11) connector, 75, 107, 119, 120*f*
RJ-45 (registered jack 45), 107, 119, 120*f*
RMM (remote monitoring and management), 597, 599
rollers, printer, 170, 171, 232, 234
root account, 534
rootkits, 460
router settings, 496–500
    changing default passwords, 496
    firmware updates, 496–7
    IP filtering, 496
routers
    channels, 56
    copper, 107
    default administrator's user account/password, 485
    firmware updates, 496
    function of, 71
    legacy/embedded systems, 64
    Linux, 256, 390
    local area networks, 86
    misconfiguration, 228
    networking hardware, 71
    physical placement secure locations, 497
    secure management access, 499
    settings, 496–500
    syslog, 61
    T568A/T568B standards, 108
    Universal Plug and Play, 498, 499
    VPN, 70
    wide area networks, 87
    wireless, 456, 496, 500
RPC (Remote Procedure Call), 520
RPS (redundant power supply), 160–1
RSR (Rapid Security Response), 379
RTUs (Remote Terminal Units), 64
Run as Administrator, 443, 450

S

SaaS (Software as a Service), 192, 438
safety procedures, 568–73
    air filtration mask, 573
    antistatic bags, 570, 572
    cable management, 571–2
    compliance with government regulations, 572
    component handling and storage, 571
    disconnecting power before repairing PCs, 572
    electrical safety, 570
    electrostatic discharge *see* ESD (electrostatic discharge)
    equipment grounding, 570–1
    fire safety, 573
    goggles, 573
    lifting techniques, 572–3
    personal safety, 572–3
    power handling, 571
SAML (Security Assertion Markup Language), 438
SAN (storage area network), 87, 88
    motherboards, 146, 147*f*
sandbox, 185, 560

SATA (Serial Advanced Technology
        Attachment)
    cables, 116–17
    communications interfaces, 133
    IOPS values, 214
    motherboards, 145
    SATA 3/SATA 6, 133
satellite, 32, 85, 88
SC (subscriber connector), 107, 120
SCADA (supervisory control and data
        acquisition), 64
scaling, adjusting, 219
scanners
    automatic document feeder)/flatbed
        scanner, 168
    fingerprint, 433–4
    macOS/desktop OS, 381, 382f
    near-field scanner, 16
    palm print scanner, 434
    retina, 433
    scheduling scans, 480
    wise scanning and removal techniques, 480
screen
    blank, 206–7, 210
    broken, 221–2
    failure to autorotate, 532
    flashing, 217
    locks, 487–8
    proprietary crash screens, 204–6
    resolution, 106
    splash, 586
    touch screen *see* touch screen
screened subnet, 499
screensaver locks, 483
screen-sharing software, 598
screwdrivers, 7, 492
script file types
    .bat, 594
    .js, 594, 596
    .ps1, 594, 596
    .py, 594
    .sh, 594, 596
    .vbs, 594, 596

scripting
    automation, 595
    information gathering, 595
    initiating updates, 595–6
    installing applications, 595
    restarting machines, 595
    using cases for, 594
    see also script file types
SCSI (Small Computer System
        Interface), 87
    Serial Attached SCSI (SAS), 133
SD (Secure Digital) cards, 137
SDHC (Secure Digital High Capacity)
        cards, 137
SDK (software development kit), 256
SDR SDRAM (single data rate SDRAM), 126
SDRAM (synchronous dynamic random-access
        memory), 126
SDSL (symmetric DSL), 75
SDXC (Secure Digital Extra Capacity)
        cards, 137, 258
SECC (Single Edge Contact
        Cartridge), 147, 148f
secure connections/sites, 504
secure management access, 499–500
secured prints, 167
security, 65, 167, 489, 599, 603
    application source/unofficial application
        stores, 533–4
    authentication, 167, 457–9
    badging, 167
    browsers, configuring settings, 502–9
    data destruction and disposal
        methods, 491–5
    logical, 435–9
    malware removal *see* digital secu-
        rity; malware
    measures and purposes, 427–39
    mobile devices, securing, 486–91
    personal computer issues, 537–41
    physical, 427–32
    physical access, 432–5
    review questions, 510–13

security (continued)
    settings, configuring and applying *see* security settings, configuring/applying
    SOHO wireless and wired networks, applying settings, 495–502
    threats and vulnerabilities, tackling, 473–8
    Trusted Platform Module, 152
    virtualization, 187–9
    wireless security protocols, 456–7
    workstation security options and hardening, 481–6
    see also authentication
security groups, selecting
    Administrator, 454
    Guests, 454–5
    Power Users, 454
    standard users, 455
security guards, 431
security settings, configuring/applying, 440–55
    Active Directory, 452–5
    BitLocker *see* BitLocker
    BitLocker to Go, 451
    Defender Antivirus, 440–1
    Encrypting File System, 451–2
    Firewall, 441–2
    Login OS options, 444–5
    NTFS vs. share permissions, 445–50
    User Account Control, 301, 450
    Users and Groups, 442–4
sensors, 64
server locks, 431
server roles, AAA, 62
server-based application virtualization (terminal services), 186
SFC (System File Checker), 450
share permissions, 446, 450
shoulder surfing, 472
S-HTTP (secure HTTP), 54
shutdowns
    blue screen of death, 520
    frequent, 520
    projector, 218
    random, 208
    updates, during, 522

SID (security identifiers), 321
sign-in/browser data synchronization, 506
SIM (subscriber identity module) OS, 30–1
SIMMs (single inline memory modules), 125
SIP (Session Initiation Protocol), 229
SIPS (Super-IPS), 104
64-bit OS, Windows, system requirements for, 415
SLAs (service-level agreements), internal/external or third-party, 558
sluggish performance, 207
S.M.A.R.T. (Self-Monitoring, Analysis, and Reporting Technology), 213
smart cards, 432
smartphones
    broken screen, 221
    cameras, 23
    charging port, 224
    installation issues, 225
    mobile OSes, 256
    and NFC cards, 21
    operating systems, 255, 256
    see also iPhone
SMB (Server Message Block), 168
SMF (single-mode fiber), 111
smishing, 471
SMS (send and receive text), 386
SMS (Short Message Service), 437
SMTP (Simple Mail Transfer Protocol), 38, 51
SNMP (Simple Network Management Protocol), 52
SoA (Start of Authority), 67
SOAP (Simple Object Access Protocol), 598
social engineering, 469, 470, 471–3
SoDIMMs (small outline dual-inline memory modules), 125
sodium vapor lamp, 435
software tokens, 437
SOHO (small office/home office) network, 63, 76–84, 455
    IP addresses, 77–81
    malware removal *see under* malware
    wireless and wired networks, applying security settings, 495–502

SOPs (standard operating procedures), 557
Sound applet, 340, 341f
sound card, 156
sound icon in system tray, 23, 24f
Sound Panel, 16, 17f
sound volume control, 23, 24f
spam gateways, 63
spam management, 67
speakers, 23–4
    installation, 25
    internal, 26
    no sound from, 26
    voice-enabled smart speaker/digital assistant, 26
SPF (Sender Policy Framework), 68
SPICE (Simple Protocol for Independent Computing Environments), 597–8
spindle speeds (5,400; 7,200; 10,000; and 15,000 rpm), 131
spoofing, 475, 535
spreadsheets, 411
spyware, 465
SQL (Structured Query Language), 476
SS7 (Signaling System 7) protocol, 229
SSD (solid-state drive), 10–11, 42, 130
    boot methods, 260
    form factors, 133–4
    improved performance, 11
    IOPS values, 214
    migration, 11, 12f
    Performance tab, 8, 9f
    pros and cons, 11
    replacement, 9–10
    storage devices, 132
    see also hard drives/HDDs (hard disk drives); hybrid drives
SSH (Secure Shell) protocol, 51, 54, 597, 599
SSID (service set identifier), 65, 456, 474
    changing, 500
    disabling broadcast, 500
    voice-enabled smart speaker/digital assistant, 26
    Wi-FI connections, 30
SSL (Secure Sockets Layer), 51

SSL/TLS (Secure Sockets Layer/Transport Layer Security) protocol, 54
SSO (single sign-on), 438, 444–5, 458
ST (straight tip) connector, 107, 120
stalkerware, 466
standby lighting, 434
static eliminator strip, 233
storage devices
    communications interfaces, 132–4
    comparing/contrasting, 130–41
    drive configurations, 134–6
    hard drives, 130–2
    My Cloud Mirror, 211
    Redundant Array of Independent Disks, 134–6
    removable storage, 136–9
    solid-state drive, 132
storage spaces, 291, 292f, 293
    see also Disk Management
STP (shielded twisted pair), 110
striping with parity (RAID 5), 135, 136f
stylus, 23, 226t
subnet mask, 83–4
subnetting, 83
supply chain/pipeline attack), 477
surges, power, 578
swipe locks, 487–8
switches
    common network devices, 71–2
    FORMAT, 317T
    and hubs, 71
    light switches, 65
    managed, 72
    misconfiguration, 228
    netstat, 311t
    nslookup, 312t
    ping, 310t
    Power over Ethernet, 74
    SFC, 326t
    tracert, 315t
    unmanaged, 72
synchronization, 193, 412
    mobile device, 24–40
syslog, 61

Sysprep, 263–4
system boards *see* motherboards
System Configuration, 298–301
    Boot tab, 299, 300*f*
    General tab, 299, 300*f*
    Services tab, 299, 301*f*
    Startup tab, 301, 302*f*
    Tools tab, 301
system instability, 522
system preferences, macOS, 379–86, 380*f*
    accessibility, 381, 383*f*
    continuity, 386
    Display, 379, 380*f*
    Dock, 386
    Drive (iCloud Drive), 385
    FaceTime, 385
    features, 384
    Finder, 385, 386*f*
    iCloud, 385
    iMessage, 385
    keychain drives, 384
    multiple desktops, 384
    Network, 379, 381*f*
    printers and scanners, 381, 382*f*
    privacy settings, 330, 381, 382*f*
    Spotlight, 385
    Time Machine tool, 383
System Restore, disabling and enabling, 479–80
system settings, inadvertently changing, 596
Systems Manager (Cisco), 33

T

T568A/T568B standards, 107, 108
tablets, 5, 19, 122
    broken screen, 221
    cursor drift/touch calibration, 224
    disposal, 575
    mobile OSes, 256
    operating systems, 255, 256
TACACS+ (Terminal Access Controller Access-Control System Plus), 457–8

tailgating, 472
Task Manager, 7, 8*f*, 12, 276–82, 460
    App History tab, 282
    Details tab, 281
    illustration, 277*f*
    Performance tab, 277, 279*f*, 280
    Processes tab, 280–1
    Services tab, 277, 278*f*
    Startup tab, 277, 278*f*
    Users tab, 281, 282*f*
    Windows 10, 276
    Windows 11, 276
    see also operating systems (OSes); Windows 10; Windows 11; Windows OSes
Task Scheduler, 293, 294*f*
TCP (Transmission Control Protocol), 50, 51, 53–4
    compared with UDP, 50–1
    poor VoIP quality, 229
    port security, 442
TCP/IP (Transmission Control Protocol/Internet Protocol), 50–5, 76, 81*f*
    printer, adding, 368*f*
    subnet mask, 83, 84
technology, point-to-multipoint, 85
telemetry, 64
Telnet, 51, 54
temperature, 575
Terminal Device Driver, 520
test development, 186
tethering, 23
text editors, Linux, 401
TFTP (Trivial File Transfer Protocol)
    connectionless protocols, 53–4
    NetBoot, 260
thermal compound, 159
thermal pads, 159
thermal paper, 174
thermal paste, 159
thermal printers
    cleaning heating element, 174
    debris, removing, 174
    dye sublimation, 173

feed assembly, 173–4
heating element, 174
maintenance, 173–4
paper, 174
replacement of paper, 174
thermal transfer, 173
thermal wax-transfer, 173
see also inkjet printers
thermostat, 65
third-party drivers, 266, 494
third-party tools, 598–9
32-bit OS, Windows, 415
threats, 473–7
    user education, 469–70
thumb drives *see* flash drives
Thunderbolt, 112, 113f
ticketing systems, 553–5
    categories, 554
    clear, concise written
        communication, 554–5
    description of problems, 554
    device information, 553–4
    escalation levels, 554
    severity, 554
    user information, 553
time drift, 523
Time Machine tool, 378, 383
timeout/screen lock, 485
TKIP (Temporal Key Integrity Protocol),
    55, 456, 457
TLS (Transport Layer Security), 598
TN (twisted nematic), 103, 104
toner
    cleaning up, 573
    disposal, 575
    fused, 236
    particles, special cleaner for, 170
    replacing, 169, 170
    specks, 234
    spills, 575
    transferring from EP cartridge, 233
    vertical black or white lines on
        the page, 231
toner cartridges, 163, 231, 233, 234

toner probe, 88, 89
TOTP (time-based one-time password), 34, 437
touch screen, 23, 105, 222, 225
TouchFLO, 221
TPM (Trusted Platform Module)
    BitLocker, 152, 154, 273, 450
    chips, 273
    encryption, 154–5
    security features, 152
`traceroute`, 314, 397, 399
track points, 18, 28, 29
trackpad, 18, 28, 29, 224, 225, 384
tractor feed, 175
trays, printer
    checking, 172
    and feeders, 171
    multipage misfeed, 233
    not recognized, 235–6
    paper jams, 232
    settings, 166, 236
triple-channel memory, 128
tripping, 578
Trojan horses, 459–60
troubleshooting
    blue screen of death, 518–19
    booting issues, 519–20
    common mobile OS and application
        issues, 527–32
        application failing to close/crashes, 208,
            520–1, 528
        application failing to launch, 528
        application fails to update, 528–9
        battery life issues, 530
        connectivity issues, 531–2
        failure to update, 530
        near-field communication, 531–2
        random reboots, 530–1
        security, 533–6
        slow to respond, 530
    common steps
        add resources, 524
        reboot, 524
        rebuilding Windows profiles, 526–7
        reimage, 525

Index

troubleshooting (*continued*)
   repair/restore Windows, 525
   restart, 524
   rollback device drivers, 526
   roll back updates, 525–6
   system file check, 525
   uninstall/reinstall/update applications, 524
   verify requirements, 524
  common symptoms
   drive and RAID issues, 210–15
   mobile device issues, 219–26
   motherboards, RAM, CPUs and power, 201–10
   network issues, 227–30
   video, projector, and display issues, 215–19
  data-usage limit notification, 535
  degraded performance/response time, 519, 535
  Developer mode, 534
  drive and RAID issues, 210–15
   audible alarms, 215
   bootable device not found, 212
   clicking sounds, 212
   data lOSes/corruption, 212
   extended read/write times, 214
   grinding noises, 211
   input/output operations per second, 214
   LED status indicators, 211
   missing array, 214
   missing drives in OS, 214
   RAID ceasing to work, 213
   RAID failure, 212–13
   S.M.A.R.T. failure, 213
  fake security warnings, 536
  frequent shutdowns, 520
  high network traffic, 535
  high number of ads, 536
  leaked personal files/data, 536
  limited Internet connectivity/no Internet connectivity, 536
  low memory warnings, 521
  microphone and speakers, 16, 17*f*
  mobile devices, 220–6
  motherboards, RAM, CPU and power, 201–10
   application crashes, 208
   blank screen, 206–7
   burning smell, 208
   capacitor swelling, 208–10
   inaccurate system date/time, 210
   no power, 207
   overheating, 207–8
   Power-On Self-Test beeps, 201–2
   proprietary crash screens, 202–6
   random shutdown, 208
   sluggish performance, 207
   unusual noise, 208
  network issues *see* network issues
  OS issues, common, 518–27
  printer issues, 230–6
  review questions, 237–9
  services not starting, 520
  slow profile load, 523
  system instability, 522
  time drift, 523
  unauthorized/malicious application, 534–5
  unexpected application behavior, 536
  video, projector, and display issues *see* video, projector, and display issues (troubleshooting)
  see also mobile devices, troubleshooting
TSP (Touch Screen Panel)
  Dot Mode, 222
  Grid Mode, 222
TTL (transistor-transistor logic) chaps, 570
20-pin motherboard adapter, 162
24-pin motherboard adapter, 160, 162
two-factor authentication (2FA), 437, 458
TXT (text), 67
Type 1 hypervisor, 189, **195**
Type 2 hypervisor, 190

U

UAC (User Account Control), 301, 450, 451f
UDP (User Datagram Protocol), 50, 51
   compared with TCP, 53–4
   poor VoIP quality, 229
   port security, 442
UEFI (Unified Extensible Firmware Interface), 267, 275
UE-V (User Experience Virtualization), Windows 10, 272
UNC (Universal Naming Convention), 368
unintentional insider threat, 476
unprotected systems, 478
updates
   antivirus/malware, 378, 489
   Apple, 379
   application, 489
   automatic, 413
   best practices, 378
   browser patching, 503
   damage due to shutdown during, 522
   definitions, 441
   degraded performance if not done, 519
   device encryption, 487
   failure to update, 528–9, 530
   feature, 269
   firmware, 496–7, 502
   licensing assignment, 412
   limitations, 259
   login scripts, 453
   macOS/desktop OS, 378, 379f
   missing, 478
   multiple in the queue, in wrong order, 529
   multitouch, 222
   new system, 351
   operating systems, 219, 259, 266, 269, 488, 491
   optional, 269
   policy, 520
   rolling back, 525–6
   routers, 496
   scheduling, 480
   scripting, 595–6
   security, 188, 354, 478
   software, 295
   system failure, 529
   test development, 186
   third-party drivers, 266
   unavailable, 259, 269
   uninstalling/reinstalling or updating applications, 524
   unpatched systems, 478
   Windows 11 editions, 270
upgrade considerations, operating systems, 268–9
   application and driver support/backward compatibility, 268
   backup files, 268
   hardware compatibility, 268–9
   OS compatibility/upgrade path, 268, 273–5
   in-place upgrade, 273–4
   user preferences, 268
   see also installations, operating system
UPnP (Universal Plug and Play), 498–9
UPS (uninterruptible power supply), 207, 520, 578, 579
URL (uniform resource locator), 261, 472
USART (universal asynchronous receiver-transmitter) hardware buffer, 596
USB (universal serial bus), 18–19
   advantages of, 18–19
   boot methods, 260
   connector types and cables, 18–19, 27
      DB9, 123, 124f
      Lightning, 123, 124f
      Mini and Micro versions, 19, 122
      Molex, 122, 124f
      Type A, 19
      Type B, 19, 20f
      Type C, 19, 122
      USB 1.1, 19
      USB 2.0, 19, 111
      USB 3.0, 19, 20f, 111, 352
      USB-C, 18, 20f, 116, 122

USB (universal serial bus), (*continued*)
   controller resource warnings, 521–2
   device connectivity, 164
   disabling ports, 152
   permissions, 152
   ports, 19, 20
   serial connector, 111, 112*f*
   USB to Ethernet adapters, 118, 119*f*
   webcam peripheral, 16
   see also connector types
User Accounts, 342, 343*f*
user authentication, 167
user preferences, upgrade considerations, 268
username and password, 444
Users and Groups
   guest user, 443–4
   local vs. Microsoft account, 442–3
   power user, 444
   standard account/administrator, 443
UTM (unified threat management), 63
UTP (unshielded twisted pair), cables, 88, 110
UWP (Universal Windows Platform), 534

V

VA (vertical alignment), liquid crystal display, 103, 104
VDI (virtual desktop infrastructure), 189
vendor life-cycle limitations, 258–9
ventilation, 576
VESA (Video Electronics Standards Association), 113
VFAT (Virtual File Allocation Table), 257
VGA (Video Graphics Array), 115
   DVI to VGA adapters, 118, 119*f*
VHDSL (very high bit-rate DSL), 75
video, projector, and display issues (troubleshooting), 215–19
   audio issues, 218
   burnt-out bulb, 216
   dead pixels, 217
   dim images, 218
   display burn-in, 217
   distorted image, 219
   flashing screen, 217
   fuzzy image, 216–17
   incorrect color display, 217–18
   incorrect input source, 216
   intermittent projector shutdown, 218
   physical cabling issues, 216
   sizing issues, 219
video cables, 113
video card, 156–7
video surveillance, 429
videoconferencing, 27, 411, 598
virtualization
   applications, 186, 187
   and cloud computing, 183–95
   concepts, 185–91
   hardware, 154
   requirements/security, 187–9
   storage, 188–9
   User Experience Virtualization, Windows 10, 272
viruses
   armored, 461
   companion, 462
   email, 461, 462*f*
   macro, 462–3
   mobile devices, troubleshooting, 224
   multipartite, 463
   phage, 463
   polymorphic, 463, 464*f*
   present activity, 464
   purpose of, 461
   retrovirus, 464
   stealth, 464, 465*f*
   symptoms of a virus/malware infection, 460–1
   types, 461–4
vishing, 471
VLANs (virtual local area networks), 69
VM (virtual machine), 494
VMDK (virtual machine disk), 188–9
VMs (virtual machines)

cross-platform virtualization, 187
legacy software/OS, 187
network, 188
purpose, 185–7
security, 187, 188
storage, 188–9
VNC (Virtual Network Computing), 597
vNICs (virtual network interface cards), 188
voice calls, 437
VoIP (Voice over Internet Protocol), 64, 229
volume settings, 24
VPN (virtual private network), 69–70, 71, 327, 597, 599
establishing network connections, 372
remote-access VPNs, 70
routers, 70
site-to-site VPNs, 70
VR (virtual reality), 23
VRAM (video random-access memory), 405
VRT (voice recognition technology), 434
vulnerabilities, 477–8

W

WAN (wide area network), 87, 88, 111, 309
WAP (wireless access point), 456, 458, 485
warm docking, 27
warranties, 7, 556
water damage, 222
wattage rating, power supply, 161–2
wave motion detectors, 430
WDS (Windows Deployment Services), 264
web caching, 64
web servers, 62, 63
webcam, 16, 27
WEP (Wired Equivalent Privacy), 55, 456
Wi-Fi, 16, 29, 30, 531
Wi-Fi Properties Screen, 12, 15*f*
Wi-Fi tab, 12, 13*f*
Wi-FI analyzer, 89
Windows 10, 255
additional tools, 297

BitLocker, 270
corrupted user profile, 526
cursor drift/touch calibration, 224
default sound playback device, changing, 218
editions, 269–70
Enterprise Edition, 270, 273
feature across editions, 271*t*
Home Edition, 270
local vs. Microsoft account, 442
Mail, 340
minimum requirements, 273, 274*t*
network connections, 371
Pro Edition, 270, 273
Pro for Workstations edition, 270
public/shared devices, 165
Remote Desktop Client, 272
repair installation, 265
Server Message Block supporting, 53
settings, configuring
Accounts, 364, 365*f*
Apps, 356, 358*f*
Control Panel, 340
Devices and Printers applet, 334*f*
Gaming, 363
Network and Internet, 362
Personalization, 356, 357*f*
Power Options, 350*f*
Privacy and Security, 359
Privacy tab, 330, 331*f*
Programs tab, 332, 332*f*, 333*f*
System, 360
Time and Language, 352, 353*f*
Task Manager, 276, 279*f*
TPM security features, 152
upgrading to, 274
User Experience Virtualization, 272
video cards, 156
zero-touch deployment, 264
Windows 11, 255
additional tools, 297
blue screen of death, 202
Client Hyper-V, 187

Index

Windows (*continued*)
    Control Panel, 340
    dedicated vs. integrated graphics card, 404
    default sound playback device, changing, 218
    Enterprise Edition, 271
    feature across editions, 272*t*
    fingerprint authentication, 15–16
    Home Edition, 270
    Installation Assistant, 274
    local vs. Microsoft account, 442
    Mail, 340
    NIC configuration, 79, 80, 80*f*
    no OS found, 523
    Pro Edition, 271
    public networks, 374*f*
    settings, configuring
        Accounts, 364, 365*f*
        Apps, 356, 358*f*
        Devices and Printers applet, 335*f*
        Gaming, 363
        Network and Internet, 362
        Personalization, 356, 357*f*
        Privacy and Security, 355*f*
        Privacy tab, 330, 331*f*
        Programs tab, 332, 333*f*
        Remote tab, 338, 339*f*
        System, 360
        Time and Language, 352, 353*f*
        Windows Update, 356*f*
    Task Manager, 276, 279*f*
    upgrading to, 274
    User Accounts, 342, 343*f*
    virtual machines, purpose, 185
    zero-touch deployment, 264
Windows 2000, 452
Windows application installation and configuration concepts, 415
Windows Autopilot, 264, 265
Windows Defender Firewall, 338–9, 340*f*, 442
    activate/deactivate, 441
    enable/disable, 370
Windows Edge browser, 503

Windows Hello, 14, 15, 445
    see also PIN (personal identification number)
Windows OSes
    BitLocker, 273
    client/desktop, configuring networking features on, 365–75
    command-line tools, 305–27
    desktop styles/user interfaces, 272
    domain vs. workgroup, 272
    features and tools
        comparing/contrasting basic features, 269–75
        feature differences, 271–3
        using, 276–304
    `gpedit.msc`, 273
    hardware requirements, 275
    Media Player, 271
    N versions, 271
    RAM support limitations, 273
    Remote Desktop Protocol, availability of, 272–3
    settings, configuring, 327–65
    upgrade paths, 273–5
    Windows Virtual Desktop User Rights, 272
    see also Windows 10; Windows 11
Windows Server 2022, 185
Windows settings, configuring, 327–65
    Accounts, 364, 365*f*
    Administrative Tools, 342, 344–6*t*
    Advanced tab, 332, 333*f*, 334, 337*f*
    Apps, 356, 358*f*
    Connections tab, 327, 328*f*
    Content tab, 327
    Device Manager, 342, 343*f*
    devices and printers, 334, 335*f*, 361
    File Explorer Options, 346–9
    gaming, 363
    General tab, 328, 329*f*, 330*f*
    Indexing Options, 342, 344*f*
    Mail, 340, 341*f*
    Network and Internet, 361–2
    network and sharing center applet, 336

performance, 337
Personalization, 356, 357f
Power Options, 349–52
Privacy and Security, 359
Privacy tab, 330, 331f
programs and features, 334, 335f
Programs tab, 332, 333f
Remote tab, 338, 339f
Security tab, 328, 329f
Sound applet, 340, 341f
system/system protection, 336, 338
   System Protection tab, 338, 339f
Time and Language, 352, 353f
Update and Security, 354–5t
User Accounts, 342, 343f
Windows Defender Firewall, 338–9, 340f
WinRM (Windows Remote Management), 598
WIPS (wireless intrusion prevention system), 474
wired and wireless networks, intermittent wireless connectivity, 90, 227
wired networking connections, 55, 83, 163, 164, 372, 500
   external interference, 230
   limitations of, 456, 473, 474
   Network and Sharing Center, 336
wireless and wired networks, applying security settings
   firewall settings, 500–1
   router settings, 496–500
   small office/home office network, 495–502
   wireless specific, 500
wireless cards, 12–13
   Advanced Network Settings, 12, 14f
   Bluetooth, 12
   cellular card, 13
   mini PCIe, 13
   in notebooks, 12
   Wi-Fi Properties Screen, 12, 15f
   Wi-Fi tab, 12, 13f
wireless local area network *see* WLAN (wireless local area network)
wireless networking protocols, 55–60

802.11, 12, 13, 23, 29, 30, 56, 57, 372
   comparison of standards, 55t
   standards, 55, 55t, 58–60, 86, 88, 158, 456
802.11a, 56, 58, 164
802.11ac (Wi-Fi 5), 56, 59, 164
802.11ax (Wi-Fi 6), 56, 59, 164
802.11b, 58, 164
802.11g, 58, 164
802.11n, 56, 58, 59
channels, 56, 57–8t
frequencies, 55–6
wireless security protocols, 455–9
   authentication, 457–9
WISPs (wireless Internet service providers), 86
WLAN (wireless local area network), 56, 72, 88, 223, 227, 500
word processing tools, 411
workstation backup and recovery methods, 563–8
   alternative location, 565
   backup testing, frequency, 565
   backups, 564
   in-place/overwrite, 565
   recovery, 565
workstation security options, 481–6
   account management, 484–5
   BIOS/UEFI passwords, 483
   changing default administrator's user account and password, 485
   data-at-rest encryption, 481
   disable AutoRun, 485–6
   end-user best practices, 483–4
   hardening techniques, 481, 486–8
   unused services, disabling, 486
WPA (Wi-Fi Protected Access), 55, 456
WPA2 (Wi-Fi Protected Access 2), 456
WPA3 (Wi-Fi Protected Access 3), 457
WPAN (wireless personal area network), 87
WPS (Wi-Fi protected setup), 498
wrap plugs *see* loopback plug
WWAN (wireless wide area network)/cellular network, 372

X

xBaseT networks, 107
xD cards, 138–9
XDR (Extended Detection and Response), 468
XFS (Extended File System), 258
XML files, 262
XSS (cross-site scripting), 477

Y

Yahoo, 29

Z

zero-day attack, 474–5
zero-touch deployment, 264–5
zero-trust model, 436
zombies, 473
Zoom, 598

Online Test Bank

Register to gain one year of FREE access after activation to the online interactive test bank to help you study for your CompTIA A+ certification exams—included with your purchase of this book!

To access our learning environment, simply visit www.wiley.com/go/sybextestprep, follow the instructions to register your book, and instantly gain one year of FREE access after activation to all of the chapter questions and the practice tests in this book, so you can practice in a timed and graded setting.